I0814565

"Dr. Burer's commentary on Galatians performs a wonderful service for students of Paul and this letter. It stays very focused on the text and clearly presents the options at all key points that one faces in reading it. It also makes clear the reason for the choices he has made. The letter is covered thoroughly but the reader is not lost in endless detail about interpretive options, which would risk distracting from the text itself by debating about it. As such, it is a judicious treatment of the epistle that allows the teaching and the theology of the letters to shine forth. This makes the commentary an exceedingly useful companion to have as one studies this key epistle of Paul."

—Darrell L. Bock, senior research professor of New Testament studies, Dallas Theological Seminary; executive director for cultural engagement, Howard G. Hendricks Center for Christian Leadership and Cultural Engagement

"Dr. Michael Burer has done a wonderful service to the church and its servants in this volume on Galatians. It is thorough, accessible, and useful for those in the trenches of ministry. It is carefully written, not losing the forest for the trees, while bringing clarity to the towering oaks that get our attention."

—Travis Chappell, pastor, Fellowship Bible Church, Greenville, TX

"Burer's volume on Galatians is a wealth of exegetical wisdom: an abundance of text-critical, grammatical, and interpretive insights, valuable theological reflection, and helpful pastoral guidance. A real treasure!"

—J. Scott Duvall, professor of New Testament, Ouachita Baptist University

"Preachers require commentaries that deliver what they promise, and Dr. Michael Burer's Evangelical Exegetical Commentary on Galatians checks every box. Dr. Burer approaches Galatians with strong evangelical convictions and meticulously executes the exegetical process, analyzing grammar and word meanings, hunting down fuzzy antecedents, and untangling theological ambiguities until clarity emerges; he then concludes each section with applicable insights that are robust, pastoral, and—as his pastor can attest—authentic. Since the gospel matters, then gospel clarity matters, and this work contributes to that end."

—Brad L. Henderson, senior pastor, Trinity Bible Church

"Michael H. Burer is a burgeoning scholar who has provided us with a top-notch commentary on Galatians for the Evangelical Exegetical Commentary series. Burer does not skirt vexing introductory or exegetical problems, yet he avoids pedanticism and skillfully guides readers to the central issues and unpacks the riches of the core themes of this gem of Paul's writings. Burer blends his earlier linguistic and historical Jesus studies with his more recent Pauline studies to provide an extensive analysis of the crucial historical and theological features of Galatians, as is evident in his treatment of the situation with Peter in Galatians 2:11–14, and current interpretative issues with regard to Judaism and the Law and the New Perspective on Paul in 2:15–21. He carefully interacts with the most recent scholarship on Galatians while drawing on ancient Christian commentaries to produce a solid, informed reading of this crucial letter. I highly recommend this insightful commentary by a careful exegete, diligent professor, and faithful pastor."

—MICHAEL J. WILKINS, distinguished professor emeritus of New Testament language and literature, Talbot School of Theology, Biola University

GALATIANS

EVANGELICAL EXEGETICAL COMMENTARY

GALATIANS

Michael H. Burer

Galatians
Evangelical Exegetical Commentary

Copyright 2024 Michael H. Burer

Lexham Academic, an imprint of Lexham Press
1313 Commercial St., Bellingham, WA 98225
LexhamPress.com

You may use brief quotations from this resource in presentations, articles, and books.
For all other uses, please write Lexham Press for permission.
Email us at permissions@lexhampress.com.

Unless otherwise noted, Scripture quotations are the author's own translation.

Print ISBN 9781683597506
Digital ISBN 9781683597513
Library of Congress Control Number 2023948049

Series Editors: Tremper Longman III, Andreas J. Köstenberger, Benjamin L. Gladd
Lexham Editorial: Derek R. Brown, John Barach, Erin Magnum
Cover Design: Brittany Schrock, Fanny Palacios
Typesetting: ProjectLuz.com

23 24 25 26 27 28 29 / IN / 12 11 10 9 8 7 6 5 4 3 2 1

To my wife, Melony, and my children, Michael, Madeline, and Max.
Thank you for your constant love and support!

Contents

Commentary Editors

General Editor
Tremper Longman III

Senior Old Testament Editor
David T. Lamb

Assistant Old Testament Editor
JoAnna M. Hoyt

Senior New Testament Editor
Andreas J. Köstenberger

Assistant New Testament Editor
Benjamin L. Gladd

Previous Commentary Editors

General Editor (2009–2022)
H. Wayne House

Old Testament Editor (2009–2022)
William D. Barrick

New Testament Editor (2009–2020)
W. Hall Harris

Assistant New Testament Editor (2011–2020)
Andrew W. Pitts

Acknowledgments

I wish to thank the following people for their gracious support throughout this project:

- the administration of Dallas Theological Seminary for sabbatical leaves during 2010–2011 and 2019–2020, which enabled substantial time for research and writing;
- my colleagues in the New Testament Department at DTS for their encouragement;
- my interns at DTS during the writing of this commentary who supplied research help and sharpened my thinking: Raymond Baclit, Greg Barnhill, Peter Battaglia, Sarah Cramer Cho, Marjorie Cooper, Chris Frost, Josh Kocher, Aaron Massey, Daniel Pfeifer, Stephen Prabhakar, Bradley Smith, Robin Thompson, Daniel Walter, and Jeff Wipplinger.

To our Lord Jesus Christ be all the glory!

Michael H. Burer
October, 2023
Forney, Texas

Editors' Preface

The Bible is true in everything it intends to teach. At the same time, it is not always clear—which means it is not always obvious what it intends to teach, thus the need for commentary. The Evangelical Exegetical Commentary intends to help scholars, pastors, and laypeople understand Scripture in order to inform their understanding of God, motivate them to faithful action, and encourage their faith. We have recruited some of the best evangelical scholars to explore the meaning and application of the various books of the Old and New Testaments. Experts in the best sense of the word, they are doing their scholarship in the service of the church. They share a high regard for the Bible as God's Word, having honed their skills in biblical scholarship over decades of study.

The present commentary series is, first of all, *evangelical.* As the title of the series suggests, our contributors write from an evangelical perspective. While evangelicalism can be defined and exemplified in more than one way, evangelicals are united in recognizing the primary authority of Scripture for our knowledge of God and as a guide to faithful living.

The Evangelical Exegetical Commentary is also *exegetical.* The emphasis is on the original meaning of the text, starting with a close reading of the original languages in their original context. The biblical books, after all, were not written directly to us today, but to the faithful who were contemporary with the authors. Still, the fact that the church recognizes these books as canonical means that though they may not have been written *to* us, they were written *for* us.

Our hope and prayer, as editors and as contributors, is that these commentaries will help you so understand Scripture to inform your minds but also to stimulate your imaginations, to fire your emotions with faith, and to cultivate faithful obedience of God.

Tremper Longman III, General Editor

David T. Lamb, Senior Old Testament Editor

JoAnna M. Hoyt, Assistant Old Testament Editor

Andreas J. Köstenberger, Senior New Testament Editor

Benjamin L. Gladd, Assistant New Testament Editor

Abbreviations

1	first person
1 Cor	1 Corinthians
1 En.	1 Enoch
1 Esd	1 Esdras
1 Macc	1 Maccabees
1Qs	Rule of the Community
2	second person
2 Bar.	2 Baruch
2 Cor	2 Corinthians
2 En.	2 Enoch
2 Esd	2 Esdras
2 Kgdms	2 Kingdoms
2 Macc	2 Maccabees
2 Tim	2 Timothy
3	third person
3 Kgdms	3 Kingdoms
3 Macc	3 Maccabees
4 Kgdm	4 Kingdoms
4 Macc	4 Maccabees
AB	Anchor Bible
ABD	Freedman, D. N., ed. *Anchor Bible Dictionary*. 6 vols. New York: Doubleday, 1992.
Abraham	Philo, *On the Life of Abraham*
abs.	absolute
acc.	accusative
ACCSNT	Ancient Christian Commentary on Scripture: New Testament
AcT	*Acta Theologica*
act.	active
adj.	adjective/adjectival
adv.	adverb/adverbial
Ag. Ap.	Josephus, *Against Apion*
Anab.	Xenophon, *Anabasis*
Ant.	Josephus, *Antiquities of the Jews*
ANTC	Abingdon New Testament Commentaries
aor.	aorist
Apoc. Mos.	Apocalypse of Moses
Art.	Plutarch, *Artaxerxes*
As. Mos.	Assumption of Moses

AUSS	*Andrews University Seminary Studies*
b.	Babylonian Talmud
BAR	*Biblical Archaeology Review*
BBR	*Bulletin for Biblical Research*
BBRSup	Bulletin for Biblical Research Supplement Series
BDAG	Danker, F. W., W. Bauer, W. F. Arndt, and F. W. Gingrich. *Greek-English Lexicon of the New Testament and Other Early Christian Literature*. 3rd ed. Chicago: University of Chicago Press, 2000.
BDB	Brown, F., S. R. Driver, and C. A. Briggs. *A Hebrew and English Lexicon of the Old Testament*. Clarendon: Oxford, 1907.
BDF	Blass, F., A. Debrunner, and R. W. Funk. *A Greek Grammar of the New Testament and Other Early Christian Literature*. Chicago: University of Chicago Press, 1961.
BECNT	Baker Exegetical Commentary on the New Testament
Ber.	Berakot
Bib	*Biblica*
BibInt	*Biblical Interpretation*
BNTC	Black's New Testament Commentaries
BR	*Biblical Research*
BSac	*Bibliotheca Sacra*
BT	*The Bible Translator*
BTB	*Biblical Theology Bulletin*
ca.	circa
CBQ	*Catholic Biblical Quarterly*
CEV	Contemporary English Version
Comm. Gal.	Jerome, *Commentariorum in Epistulam ad Galatas libri III*
Confusion	Philo, *On the Confusion of Tongues*
conj.	conjunction
Creation	Philo, *On the Creation of the World*
CTJ	*Calvin Theological Journal*
CTM	*Concordia Theological Monthly*
CTQ	*Concordia Theological Quarterly*
CTR	*Criswell Theological Review*
CurBR	*Currents in Biblical Research*
Cyr.	Xenophon, *Cyropaedia*
dat.	dative
Did.	Didache
dir.	direct
EDNT	Balz, H., and G. Schneider, eds. *Exegetical Dictionary of the New Testament*. 3 vols. Grand Rapids: Eerdmans, 1990–1993.
Esth	Esther
ESV	English Standard Version
Eth. nic.	*Ethica nicomachea*
ETL	*Ephemerides theologicae lovanienses*

EvQ	*Evangelical Quarterly*
Exp. Gal.	*Expositio in epistulam ad Galatas*
ExpTim	*Expository Times*
fclBZNW	*Beihefte zur Zeitschrift für die neutestamentliche Wissenschaft*
fem.	feminine
fut.	future
Gal	Galatians
gen.	genitive
Gen. Rab.	*Genesis Rabbah*
Geog.	Strabo, *Geography*
GTJ	*Grace Theological Journal*
HALOT	*The Hebrew and Aramaic Lexicon of the Old Testament.* Edited by Ludwig Köhler, Walter Baumgartner, M. E. J. Richardson, and Johann Jakob Stamm. Leiden: Brill, 1994.
HBT	*Horizons in Biblical Theology*
Herm. Mand.	Shepherd of Hermas, Mandate(s)
Hist. eccl.	Eusebius, *Historia ecclesiastica*
Hom. Gal.	John Chrysostom, *Homiliae in epistulam ad Galatas commentarius*
HTR	*Harvard Theological Review*
HvTSt	*Hervormde teologiese studies*
ICC	International Critical Commentary
Imm	*Immanuel*
impf(s).	imperfect(s)
impv(s).	imperative(s), imperatival
indic.	indicative
indir.	indirect
inf.	infinitive
IVPNTC	IVP New Testament Commentary
Jas	James
JBL	*Journal of Biblical Literature*
Jdt	Judith
JETS	*Journal of the Evangelical Theological Society*
JGRChJ	*Journal of Greco-Roman Christianity and Judaism*
Jos. Asen.	Joseph and Aseneth
JSNT	*Journal for the Study of the New Testament*
JSNTSup	Journal for the Study of the New Testament Supplement Series
JTS	*Journal of Theological Studies*
Jub.	Jubilees
Judg	Judges
L&N	Louw, J. P., and E. A. Nida, eds. *Greek-English Lexicon of the New Testament: Based on Semantic Domains*. 2nd ed. New York: United Bible Societies, 1989.
LCL	Loeb Classical Library

LEH	Lust, J., E. Eynikel, and H. Hauspie, eds. *A Greek-English Lexicon of the Septuagint*. 2 vols. Stuttgart: Deutsche Bibelgesellschaft, 1992–1996.
Life	Josephus, *The Life*
LNTS	Library of New Testament Studies
LSJ	Liddell, H. G., R. Scott, and H. S. Jones. *A Greek-English Lexicon*. 9th ed. with revised supplement. Oxford: Clarendon, 1996.
LXX	Septuagint
m.	Mishnah
Magn.	Ignatius, *To the Magnesians*
masc.	masculine
Meg.	Megillah
Mek. Exod.	*Mekilta Exodus*
MGS	Montanari, F. *The Brill Dictionary of Ancient Greek*. Edited by M. Goh and C. Schroeder. Leiden: Brill, 2015.
MHT	Moulton, J. H., W. F. Howard, and N. Turner. *A Grammar of New Testament Greek*. 4 vols. Edinburgh: T&T Clark, 1908–1976.
midd.	middle
Moses	Philo, *On the Life of Moses*
MSJ	*The Master's Seminary Journal*
MT	Masoretic Text
NA[27]	*Novum Testamentum Graece*, Nestle-Aland, 27th ed.
NA[28]	*Novum Testamentum Graece*, Nestle-Aland, 28th ed.
NAB	New American Bible
NAC	New American Commentary
Names	Philo, *On the Change of Names*
NASB	New American Standard Bible
Naus.	Demosthenes, *Contra Nausimachum et Xenopeithea*
NCBC	New Century Bible Commentary
Neot	*Neotestamentica*
NET	New English Translation
neut.	neuter
NIBC	New International Biblical Commentary
NICNT	New International Commentary on the New Testament
NIDNTTE	Silva, M. *New International Dictionary of New Testament Theology and Exegesis*. 5 vols. Grand Rapids: Zondervan, 2014.
NIDOTTE	VanGemeren, W. A. *New International Dictionary of Old Testament Theology and Exegesis*. 5 vols. Grand Rapids: Zondervan, 1997.
NIGTC	New International Greek Testament Commentary
NIV	New International Version
NIVAC	NIV Application Commentary
NKJV	New King James Version
NLT	New Living Translation

nom.	nominative
NovT	*Novum Testamentum*
NRSV	New Revised Standard Version
NT	New Testament
NTL	New Testament Library
NTS	*New Testament Studies*
obj.	object/objective
OCD	Hornblower, S., and A. Spawforth, eds. *Oxford Classical Dictionary*. 4th ed. Ox-ford: Oxford University Press, 2012
OT	Old Testament.
OTM	Oxford Theological Monographs
P. Tebt.	Tebtunis Papyri
p(p).	page(s)
pass.	passive
pf.	perfect
Phld.	Ignatius, *To the Philadelphians*
pl.	plural
plupf.	pluperfect
PNTC	Pillar New Testament Commentary
Pol. *Phil.*	Polycarp, *To the Philippians*
poss.	possessive
Posterity	Philo, *On the Posterity of Cain*
POxy	Oxyrhynchus Papyri
Pr. Man.	*Prayer of Manasseh*
prep(s).	preposition(s)
pres.	present
Pss. Sol.	Psalms of Solomon
ptc.	participle
Qidd.	Qiddušin
RB	Revue biblique
RestQ	*Restoration Quarterly*
RevExp	*Review and Expositor*
RivB	*Rivista biblica italiana*
Rom	Romans
RSV	Revised Standard Version
Šabb.	Šabbat
Sanh.	Sanhedrin
SBG	Studies in Biblical Greek
SBLDS	Society of Biblical Literature Dissertation Series
SEÅ	*Svensk exegetisk arsbok*
sg.	singular
SHBC	Smyth & Helwys Bible Commentary
SIG	Dittenberger, W., ed. *Sylloge Inscriptionum Graecarum*. 4 vols. 3rd ed. Leipzig: Hirzel, 1915–1924.
Sir	Sirach
SNTSMS	Society for New Testament Studies Monograph Series

SNTW	Studies of the New Testament and Its World
Sol.	Plutarch, *Solon*
SP	Sacra Pagina
Spec. Laws	Philo, *On the Special Laws*
ST	*Studia Theologica*
Str-B	Strack, H. L., and P. Billerbeck. *Kommentar zum Neuen Testament aus Talmud und Midrasch*. 6 vols. Munich: Beck, 1922–1961.
subj.	subjective
subst.	substantival
SwJT	*Southwestern Journal of Theology*
T. Jud.	Testament of Judah
T. Levi	Testament of Levi
T. Sol.	Testament of Solomon
TDNT	Kittel, G., and G. Friedrich, eds. *Theological Dictionary of the New Testament*. Translated by G. W. Bromiley. 10 vols. Grand Rapids: Eerdmans, 1964–1976.
Them	Themelios
Thesm.	Aristophanes, *Thesmophoriazusae*
TJ	*Trinity Journal*
TLG	Thesaurus Linguae Graecae
TLNT	Spicq, C. *Theological Lexicon of the New Testament*. Trans. and ed. J. D. Ernest. 3 vols. Peabody, MA: Hendrickson, 1994.
TLOT	Jenni, E., ed. *Theological Lexicon of the Old Testament*. With assistance from C. Westermann. Translated by M. E. Biddle. 3 vols. Peabody, MA: Hendrickson, 1997.
Tob	Tobit
TWOT	Harris, R. L., G. L. Archer Jr., and B. K. Waltke, eds. *Theological Wordbook of the Old Testament*. 2 vols. Chicago: Moody Press, 1980.
TynBul	*Tyndale Bulletin*
UBS	*The Greek New Testament*, United Bible Societies
v(v).	verse(s)
voc.	vocative
WBC	Word Biblical Commentary
Wis	Wisdom of Solomon
WTJ	*Westminster Theological Journal*
WUNT	Wissenschaftliche Untersuchungen zum Neuen Testament
y.	Jerusalem Talmud
YJS	Yale Judaica Series
ZAW	*Zeitschrift für die alttestamentliche Wissenschaft*
ZECNT	Zondervan Exegetical Commentary on the New Testament
ZNW	*Zeitschrift für die neutestamentliche Wissenschaft*

Introduction

Introductions to commentaries are interesting things. Given the point of a commentary—to explain the meaning of the biblical book under consideration—introductions should serve to provide information about a book to aid in exegesis and interpretation. Traditionally the information provided has been historical and linguistic, but recent trends have seen the addition of theological and social scientific tools to the toolbox. Even so, the goal remains to explain the text in light of these differing contexts.

My aim in this introduction is not to sort out all the historical issues of the book within the context of the early church in the first century, but to focus on what can be stated positively about the historical context of the book within the traditional categories of introduction with the goal of setting the stage for the interpretation so the reader can be well prepared to dive into the exegesis.

Author

There is no serious doubt that Paul is the author of Galatians. This has been continually accepted by virtually all readers of the book throughout its history of interpretation, even during the modern period.[1] However, a positive defense of his authorship is helpful to affirm several key elements of the book and to set the stage for exegesis. This is accomplished with three lines of investigation: internal evidence, which includes attributed authorship, the book's style and content, and internal connections to Romans (another undisputed book); external evidence, which includes the early and consistent attribution of Galatians to Paul through citations and considerations of canonicity; and

1. Even as skeptical as F. C. Baur was on the authorship of the Pauline corpus, Galatians was one of his central Pauline books. See F. C. Baur, *Paulus, der Apostel Jesu Christi. Sein Leben und Wirken, seine Briefe und seine Lehre. Ein Beitrag zu einer kritischen Geschichte des Urchristenthums* (Stuttgart: Becher & Müller, 1845), 248. For English translation, see F. C. Baur, *Paul the Apostle of Jesus Christ, His Life and Works, His Epistles and Teachings: A Contribution to a Critical History of Primitive Christianity*, 2nd ed., trans. E. Zeller, vol 1 (London: Williams and Norgate, 1873), 246. For a thoroughly tongue-in-cheek argument against Pauline authorship, see H. W. Hoehner, "Did Paul Write Galatians?," in *History and Exegesis: New Testament Essays in Honor of Dr. E. Earle Ellis for His 80th Birthday*, ed. Sang-won Son (London: T&T Clark, 2006), 150–69. Hoehner accepted Pauline authorship of Galatians. Here, as an indictment of inconsistent skeptical method, he shows how scholarly arguments against Ephesians (e.g., based on vocabulary) can readily be used against Galatians, too.

a review of the history of discussion, which will show that no substantive argument against Pauline authorship of Galatians has ever been made.

Internal evidence. The fact that Paul's name is included as the author of the book of Galatians is an important part of the internal evidence and should not be simply brushed aside. In Gal 1:1 he is named as the author, and his well-known role as an apostle is highlighted. His authorship is reaffirmed as he mentions himself again in Gal 5:2 in an emotionally wrought portion of the letter. There is no textual uncertainty surrounding these readings, so internal Pauline attribution is sure in this regard.[2]

The style and content of the book of Galatians are generally agreed to be a sign of authenticity for Pauline authorship. What we see written therein strikes the reader as intensely personal and true to form based on what we know of Paul as a person and author. The grammar and syntax of the book are striking in places. Paul's language appears to wrestle with the Galatian difficulties in the moment of writing, right before our eyes, rather than showing the mark of a pseudonymous author who would polish carefully before publication. Paul mentions many things that ring true as intensely personal. Among other things, he expresses doubt about the outcome of his ministry (Gal 2:2; 4:11). He reports intense disagreement he had with Peter, arguably Jesus's lead apostle (Gal 2:11–14). He relates a time of intense personal sickness (Gal 4:13). He expresses anger and exasperation at his opponents in a crude way (Gal 5:12). He writes personally to affirm the words of the book as his apostolic communication (Gal 6:11). The content impresses almost every reader as from Paul himself, rather than from an ardent imitator.

Romans is another generally undisputed book within the Pauline corpus,[3] and connections between Galatians and Romans affirm Paul as the author. They each center around a similar theme, that of righteousness as indicated by the δικ- word group. Paul consistently emphasizes this word group in each: seventy-six times in Romans, fourteen times in Galatians. In terms of simple word counts, Romans and Galatians have the most occurrences of this word group among all the Pauline epistles. In addition, Paul uses these words in key places in each book. In Rom 1:16–17 where Paul sets out the theme of the book, he uses the noun δικαιοσύνη ("righteousness") and the adjective δίκαιος ("just"). In Rom 3:21–26 where Paul sets out the key argument, he uses the noun δικαιοσύνη four times, the verb δικαιόω ("justify") twice, and the adjective δίκαιος ("just") once. In Gal 2:15–21 where Paul sets out the theme of this book, he uses the verb δικαιόω four times and the noun δικαιοσύνη once. In Gal 3:6–14, a central theological argument of the book, Paul uses

2. One might be tempted to argue that the repetitions of Paul's name within the book are a sign of authenticity. For example, Galatians has two occurrences of Paul's name, 1 Corinthians has seven, Philemon has 3, etc. Unfortunately for this argument, other generally undisputed books (e.g., Romans and Philippians) have only one mention of Paul's name.

3. For a concise, helpful statement on this issue, see C. E. B. Cranfield, *The Epistle to the Romans*, ICC, 2 vols. (Edinburgh: T&T Clark, 1975–1979), 1:1–2.

the noun δικαιοσύνη once, the verb δικαιόω twice, and the adjective δίκαιος once. In addition to the use of similar words and concepts, in each book Paul uses the OT in similar ways to reinforce and support his arguments. He cites Hab 2:4 in both Rom 1:17 and Gal 3:11. The person of Abraham forms an important theological argument in both Rom 4 and Gal 3; in both places he is used as a prototype of the person justified by faith alone. Even though the situation of each letter is different, they are similar enough that one can readily regard them as springing from the same theologically creative mind.

External evidence. The book of Galatians was cited as Scripture by early church fathers such that it had the status of Scripture in the early church from the very beginning. Two church fathers, Polycarp and Irenaeus, prove this point. Born ca. AD 70 and martyred ca. AD 156, Polycarp wrote an epistle to the Philippian church sometime around the martyrdom of Ignatius AD 108–15.[4] In this letter he cites Gal 6:7:

> Gal 6:7 Μὴ πλανᾶσθε, θεὸς οὐ μυκτηρίζεται. (Do not be deceived. **God is not mocked**.)
>
> Polycarp 5:1 Εἰδότες οὖν ὅτι θεὸς οὐ μυκτηρίζεται, ὀφείλομεν ἀξίως τῆς ἐντολῆς αὐτοῦ καὶ δόξης περιπατεῖν.[5] (Therefore, because we know that **God is not mocked**, we ought to walk worthy of his commandment and glory.)

The phrase εἰδότες ὅτι which introduces the common wording strengthens the likelihood that this is an intentional citation. He also cites Gal 4:26:

> Gal 4:26 ἡ δὲ ἄνω Ἰερουσαλὴμ ἐλευθέρα ἐστίν, ἥτις ἐστὶν μήτηρ ἡμῶν· (Now the Jerusalem above is free, which is our mother.)
>
> Polycarp 3:2–3 ὃς καὶ ἀπὼν ὑμῖν ἔγραψεν ἐπιστολάς· εἰς ἃς ἐὰν ἐγκύπτητε, δυνηθήσεσθε οἰκοδομεῖσθαι εἰς τὴν δοθεῖσαν ὑμῖν πίστιν, ἥτις ἐστὶν μήτηρ πάντων ἡμῶν (who also when he was absent wrote letters to you, which if you examine carefully, you will be able to build yourselves up in the faith which was given to you, [the faith] which is the mother of us all.)

This citation is intriguing because in context Polycarp encourages the church regarding Paul's teaching among them in person and in his epistles, all of which will build them up in the faith. So Polycarp uses Paul's own words to encourage fidelity to Paul's own teaching. Polycarp continues in the same passage with a possible citation of Gal 5:14:

> Gal 5:14 ὁ γὰρ πᾶς νόμος ἐν ἑνὶ λόγῳ πεπλήρωται, ἐν τῷ· Ἀγαπήσεις τὸν πλησίον σου ὡς σεαυτόν. (For the whole Law has been fulfilled in the one saying: "Love your neighbor as yourself.")

4. W. R. Schoedel, "Polycarp, Epistle of," *ABD*, 5:390.

5. Greek text of this citation and those following is taken from M. W. Holmes, ed., *The Apostolic Fathers: Greek Texts and English Translations* (Grand Rapids: Baker, 2007).

> Polycarp 3:3 ἥτις ἐστὶν μήτηρ πάντων ἡμῶν, ἐπακολουθούσης τῆς ἐλπίδος, προαγούσης τῆς ἀγάπης τῆς εἰς θεὸν καὶ Χριστὸν καὶ εἰς τὸν πλησίον. ἐὰν γάρ τις τούτων ἐντὸς ᾖ, πεπλήρωκεν ἐντολὴν δικαιοσύνης· ὁ γὰρ ἔχων ἀγάπην μακράν ἐστιν πάσης ἁμαρτίας. ([the faith] which is the mother of us all, with hope following and love for God and Christ and for neighbor going before. For if anyone is in their company, he has fulfilled the righteous commandment, for the one who has love is far from all sin.)

There are similar ideas expressed as well in Rom 13:8, which could also be a source of this citation.[6] However, the Galatians passage should be preferred on the grounds that in the near context Paul discusses hope and love (see Gal 5:6), important concepts to Polycarp's argument. What is clear in any case is that soon after the end of the first century Galatians was cited by Polycarp. He does not specifically designate his citations as Scripture, but they have weight as such in his arguments.

Irenaeus followed soon thereafter and consistently cited Galatians as Scripture. He lived ca. AD 140 to ca. AD 200 and ministered as the bishop of Lyon in Gaul. In his writings he clearly and explicitly cites Galatians ten times to support his arguments. Similar to Polycarp, he does not call Galatians "Scripture," but it certainly has that status within his writings.[7] This means that Galatians, along with the twenty-some-odd other books Irenaeus cited in similar fashion, were regarded as canonical around AD 180 in southern France.[8] Seen together, Polycarp and Irenaeus provide proof that Galatians was regarded as Scripture consistently throughout the second century.

Flowing from the early regard of Galatians as Scripture, it was consistently regarded as canonical during the early centuries. The earliest canonical list, that of Marcion published approximately AD 140, includes Galatians. Marcion's significance on this matter is largely because of the reaction he provoked: By his heretical views and by his exclusion of many books the church already regarded as canonical, he forced the church to wrestle very carefully with which books were considered canonical and why. However, the fact that he did include some NT books, even with alterations and excisions, affirms their early canonical status. Clearly he was working from an accepted starting point from which he could retract texts as his theology desired.[9] From approximately

---

6. Rom 13:8 is preferred by Oxford Society of Historical Theology, *The New Testament in the Apostolic Fathers* (Oxford: Clarendon, 1905), 90, because it is a more developed discussion of the concept.

7. See, for example, *Against Heresies* 4.21.1 where he cites the entirety of Gal 3:5–9 to support the argument that the present faith of believers was prefigured in Abraham.

8. B. M. Metzger, *The Canon of the New Testament: Its Origin, Development, and Significance* (Oxford: Oxford University Press, 1987), 155.

9. See Metzger, *Canon*, 90–99, for a full discussion of Marcion's influence on the development of the canon.

the same time period as Irenaeus, the Muratorian Canon also lists Galatians. We can add to this the evidence of $\mathfrak{P}^{46}$, the earliest manuscript of the Pauline epistles. Dating to the early part of the third century AD, it contains the entire text of Galatians. Although not a canonical list as such, it is still helpful evidence that Galatians was considered both Pauline and canonical. From the earliest times, then, there was never any doubt as to Galatians' place in the canon, arguably due to the certainty that Paul was the author.

History of discussion. At no point during the history of discussion about Galatians was Pauline authorship ever seriously doubted. Irenaeus consistently identifies Paul as the author of Galatians. For example, see *Against Heresies* 3.22.1 where he cites Gal 4:4: "The Apostle Paul, moreover, in the Epistle to the Galatians, declares plainly, 'God sent His Son, made of a woman.' "[10] He never registers any doubt that Paul was the author. The same can be said of Chrysostom (ca. 347–407), Jerome (ca. 347–420), Augustine (354–430), and other church fathers.[11] This confidence in Paul as the author of Galatians is consistent throughout even the modern period. No one doubted it until the nineteenth century, and no serious attention has been paid to these minority viewpoints.[12] Burton, lxxi, summarizes the situation quite well: "Modern criticism as represented by scholars of all schools of thought ... ratifies the tradition of centuries that the letter to the Galatians was written, as it claims to have been, by Paul, the Christian apostle of the first century."

Recipients, Date, and Relationship to Acts

When Paul identifies the recipients of this letter, he uses a phrase that is easily translated but whose referent is difficult to pin down: ταῖς ἐκκλησίαις τῆς Γαλατίας, "to the churches of Galatia" (Gal 1:2). The noun Γαλατία is a place name, so minimally Paul simply identifies the recipients as the churches within a geographic region identified as Galatia. Later in the book he identifies the believers to whom he writes with the related noun Γαλάτης used for inhabitants of that region: Ὦ ἀνόητοι Γαλάται, "O foolish Galatians!" (Gal 3:1).

The key issue is what region Paul intended when he referred to Galatia. The two possible referents have come to be known as North Galatia and South Galatia. The North Galatia theory argues that the place name refers to the region in central Asia Minor controlled by Celtic immigrants,

---

10. *The Writings of Irenaeus*, ed. Alexander Roberts and W. H. Rambaut (Edinburgh: T&T Clark, 1883), 1:359.

11. See, e.g., Chrysostom, *Hom. Gal.* 1.1–3, where he discusses why Paul includes others with him as sending the letter; Jerome, *Comm. Gal.* 1.1.1, where he discusses why Paul defined his apostleship as he did; Augustine, *Exp. Gal.* 7, where he discusses Paul's persecution of the church.

12. See Burton, lxix–lxxi, for a review of the few scholars who have doubted Galatians' authenticity as a Pauline work.

commonly known as Galatians, who settled in the region during the third century BC. The South Galatia theory argues that the place name refers to the Roman province of Galatia established by Augustus in 25 BC, which included not only that original Galatian region but also territory further south, extending all the way to the Mediterranean Sea. When Paul wrote, the northern area was rural, with only a few cities, while the southern area was largely urbanized; the northern area retained cultural and tribal ties to the older Galatian kingdoms, while the southern area was culturally Greek.[13] To summarize perhaps too succinctly, in the North Galatia theory the name Galatia is ethnic, while in the South Galatia theory the name is political.

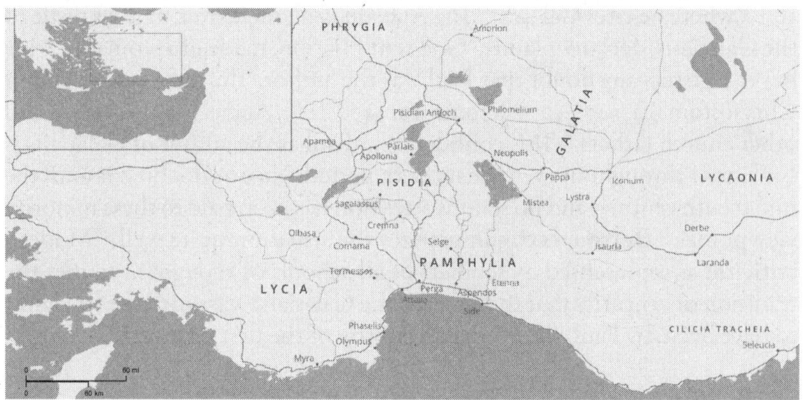

The South Galatia theory allows for an earlier date for the writing of the letter because that theory argues that the churches to which Paul wrote were established in cities of southern Asia Minor during his first missionary journey detailed in Acts 13–14. During that journey he visited Pisidian Antioch (Acts 13:13–52), Iconium (Acts 14:1–7), Lystra (Acts 14:8–18), and then Derbe (Acts 14:19–20). On the way back to Jerusalem he visited each city in turn (Acts 14:21), encouraging each church and establishing elders (Acts 14:22–23). In contrast, the North Galatian theory allows for a later date for the writing of the letter because that theory argues that the churches to which Paul wrote were established in cities of central Asia Minor, most likely during his second missionary journey (Acts 15:36–18:22) when he went through the region of Phrygia and Galatia (Acts 16:6). Paul visited that region again during his third missionary journey (Acts 18:23–21:14, see esp. 18:23), but since Acts says he was "strengthening all the disciples," it does not sound as if he was planting churches during that visit.

Another issue related to this problem is how Galatians relates to the book of Acts. Was Paul's visit to Jerusalem in Gal 2:1–10 the same as the Acts 15 visit? If so, then one of the authors has erred, because in Galatians Paul identifies this as his second visit to Jerusalem while in Acts Luke describes this as his third visit. This is a question of some consequence. On the one

13. J. D. Grainger, *The Galatians: Celtic Invaders of Greece and Asia Minor* (Yorkshire: Pen & Sword History, 2020), 216–19.

hand, Paul emphasizes his complete honesty in all that he is saying to the Galatians (see Gal 1:20). Any hint of dishonesty or confusion on Paul's part could cause him to lose the Galatians to the opponents. On the other hand, if these passages refer to different visits, then Luke's testimony in Acts is called into question, as there Paul's second visit to Jerusalem is undertaken for famine relief with no hint of theological strife or discussion regarding the place of Gentiles in the nascent church (Acts 11:27–30).

Was Paul's visit to Jerusalem recounted in Acts 15 the same visit that he recounts in Gal 2? If so, then the difficulties that arose in the Galatian churches could be placed later in time, after he visited northern Asia Minor. If they are not the same visit, then the likely candidate for the Gal 2 visit is the Acts 11 visit, which allows for the problems in the Galatian church to arise early, after his initial visit to southern Galatia but before the Jerusalem Council. Answering this question requires us to reconstruct Paul's visits to Jerusalem based on the information given in Acts and Galatians with reference to date and location. Galatians mentions two visits to Jerusalem, and since Paul is reporting on his own travels, many treat his report as a historically sound starting point for the discussion:

> Gal 1:18 — first postconversion visit
> Gal 2:1–10 — a conference visit

Acts, on the other hand, mentions five visits to Jerusalem:

> Acts 9:26–30 — first postconversion visit
> Acts 11:27–30 — famine relief visit
> Acts 15:1–30 — conference visit
> Acts 18:22 — quick visit
> Acts 21:15–17 — arrest visit

Solving this disparity in the number and order of visits centers on what Luke has done in the book of Acts. Reconstructions that accept the historicity of Acts allow two possible points of connection:

> The visit which Paul reports in Gal 2:1–10 is that which Luke reports in Acts 15:1–30.
>
> Alternatively, the visit which Paul reports in Gal 2:1–10 is that which Luke reports in Acts 11:27–30.

Reconstructions that question the historicity of Acts follow these lines:

> In reality, the visits described in Gal 2:1–10 and Acts 15:1–30 are the same visit, but Luke has mistakenly recorded two visits by misunderstanding two parallel reports of the visit as referring to two separate events.
>
> In reality, the visits described in Gal 2:1–10 and Acts 15:1–30 are the same visit, which Luke properly relates. The problem comes with Acts 11:27–30. Luke misplaces a report of the collection visit (Rom 15:25–33; 1 Cor 16:1–4; 2 Cor 1:16; Acts 21:15–17), by placing it earlier in his account for some reason.

> In reality, the visits described in Gal 2:1–10 and Acts 15:1–30 are the same visit, which Luke properly relates. However, Luke presents two problems: The Jerusalem Council detailed in Acts 15 actually took place later during the visit of Acts 18:22, and Luke has mistakenly fabricated the visit described in Acts 11:27–30.

I accept the historicity of Acts both on theological and evidentiary grounds,[14] so my choice is between the first two options. These can also be favored on the grounds that they are the simplest reconstructions of the data available from the two books.

The evidence for the view that Gal 2:1–10 = Acts 15 relies upon the strong similarities between the accounts. Both conference accounts reference the same issue, participants, and decision. But arguments against this view are strong: Gal 2:1–10 includes no references to the decrees of the Jerusalem conference (Acts 15:20, 29). It would be eminently logical for Paul to mention them, almost mandatory given the situation he is in with the Galatian churches. This reconstruction makes Peter and Barnabas's withdrawal from table fellowship (Gal 2:11–14) very difficult to explain since it would show continued conflict after the Jerusalem Council. But the major argument of Galatians does not require mentioning the decrees of the Jerusalem Council. The Council decrees did not negate Paul's argument that circumcision was not necessary. The Galatians were apparently eager to follow decrees from the Jerusalem church, so Paul saw no need to mention them and thereby confuse the issue. The issue of Peter and Barnabas's withdrawal was not difficult because of an association of Gal 2:1–10 and Acts 15, but because their actions in Gal 2:1–10 were problematic in and of themselves, contrary to the gospel.

The view that Gal 2:1–10 = Acts 11:27–30 has a good deal of evidence on its side. The conflict in Antioch (Gal 2:11–14) was similar to the conflict in Jerusalem before the conference (Acts 15:1–2). Both involved conflict over the application of Jewish Law to Gentile converts and in both a delegation of some type wrestled with the issue. The situation surrounding the famine relief visit matches Gal 2:1–10, even though the events are written from a different perspective. Barnabas went to Antioch because of Gentile conversions (Acts 11:19–26). It is likely that he discussed the Gentile mission with Jerusalem leaders upon his return, even if the trip was concerned primarily with famine relief. The Council decrees are not mentioned in Galatians because they have not yet been issued. The actions of Peter and Barnabas in Gal 2:11–14, then, occur before the Jerusalem Council, at a time when there were no guidelines regarding table fellowship between Jewish and Gentile believers.

But there is no record of any type of conference in Acts 11:27–30 and no indication that Paul and Barnabas met with any apostles. This view requires accepting that there were two conferences in Jerusalem within the span of a

---

14. For a very reasonable assessment on this matter, see chapter 3 of I. H. Marshall, *Luke: Historian & Theologian*, New Testament Profiles (Downers Grove, IL: InterVarsity, 1988).

few years, but it is unlikely that there were two conferences where the same people debated the same issue with the same outcome. In addition, this view has some chronological problems. The "three years" (Gal 1:18) and the "fourteen years" (Gal 2:1) have to be concurrent, not consecutive, in order to account for the chronological framework established by the crucifixion in AD 33 and Paul's Corinthian ministry, dated by Gallio's proconsulship (Acts 18:12), as AD 51/52. It also compresses the second missionary journey, since it has to occur between the Jerusalem Council (probably in AD 48 or 49) and Paul's meeting with Gallio in Corinth (AD 51/52) after being there for eighteen months.

Considering all the evidence, I accept the view that Gal 2:1–10 = Acts 11:27–30. This reconstruction allows the Gal 2 visit to function as an event that helps set in motion tensions that culminate in the Jerusalem Council. There are hints in what Paul wrote that the issue was not settled at that first visit, especially with regard to the "false brothers" who crashed the discussion. In addition, I do not think the chronological problems posed by this view are insurmountable. I would accept the South Galatia theory and date Galatians as written on the eve of the Jerusalem Council, probably in AD 49.

What does this mean, then, with regard to the recipients, the date Paul wrote, and the framework for understanding the book? The people to whom Paul wrote were believers in churches he established during his first missionary journey to cities in southern Asia Minor, namely, Pisidian Antioch, Iconium, Lystra, and Derbe. Paul wrote this letter as pressures more broadly relating to Jew/Gentile relationships in the early church were coming to a head, soon to be addressed in the forthcoming Jerusalem Council of Acts 15, but also as specific events were occurring (the discord in Antioch, the arrival of the opponents among the Galatian churches) that made the issue immediate and pressing for Paul and these churches he loved.

The resultant framework that explains the book is the immediate, pressing, unresolved tension over how Jews and Gentiles should relate in the church and what requirements would be placed upon Gentiles for their full inclusion in the people of God. The first issue is the practical outworking of the second, and the second is the essential, theological question Paul seeks to answer in the book. Paul has already preached to the Galatians a gospel that exalts Christ's death on the cross as entirely sufficient to bring all into relationship with God. The bubbling tension surrounding Gentiles' full inclusion in the people of God on no basis other than faith forces Paul to write to these churches to clarify what he had preached to them before and its outworking in their relationships.

Occasion and Opponents

Addressing the occasion for the book of Galatians requires that one identify Paul's opponents who had influenced the Galatians to turn away from Paul's gospel. This in turn, however, forces a recognition similar to one undertaken in the prior section: This is a longstanding problem within the history of interpretation of Galatians, intimately related to other issues such as the recipients and date of the letter, and we provide the most reasonable context for exegesis by acknowledging that a perfect answer on this question is elusive but not required for understanding the letter sufficiently. The limited overview that I give here serves to provide a minimal framework for understanding the book. In short, I will argue that after Paul had completed his first missionary journey and left the churches of South Galatia, Jewish Christian missionaries entered the very same churches he had just established to "correct" his assertion that Gentiles need only to exercise faith to join with believing Jews in the people of God. Instead, they proclaimed that in order to have a full and complete relationship with God, Gentiles needed to be circumcised as a sign of obedience to the Law. This act would make them party to the covenant with Abraham, finalizing their faith in the Messiah Jesus and making it permanently effective. This assertion and requirement on the part of the opponents was fundamentally contrary to the gospel Paul preached to the Galatians, which had elevated Christ's death and a response of faith as the only necessary means for entering and sustaining a relationship with God. Paul wrote Galatians to overcome the influence of these opponents by convincing the Galatians to return to their original acceptance of his gospel.

Determining the identity of the opponents in Galatians is challenging because there are only hints of who they are and what they preach scattered throughout the book. Paul does not identify them directly by name, which he was not afraid to do to his opponents on occasion (see, e.g., his derogatory mention of Demas and Alexander the coppersmith in 2 Tim 4:10, 14). He does not systematically present their teaching or respond to it point by point. What Paul does, however, is create an argument in response to the situation they created, and so we can sufficiently reconstruct in summary form what they did and said.

Paul's first mention of his opponents is in the introduction to the letter in Gal 1:6–10. He focuses on them in v. 7 when he identifies them somewhat obliquely: οἱ ταράσσοντες ὑμᾶς καὶ θέλοντες μεταστρέψαι τὸ εὐαγγέλιον τοῦ Χριστοῦ, "those who disturb you and want to alter the gospel of Christ." This phrasing identifies them by their negative effect on the Galatians and their destructive stance toward the gospel. This provides the context for Paul's strong curse in Gal 1:8–9 upon those who preach a different gospel: Paul spoke generally enough to refer to anyone who proclaims a different gospel, but the target in his sights was the opponents who were doing that specifically among the Galatians.

The next mention Paul makes that needs to be discussed relative to the opponents is Gal 2:4–5:

> διὰ δὲ τοὺς παρεισάκτους ψευδαδέλφους, οἵτινες παρεισῆλθον κατασκοπῆσαι τὴν ἐλευθερίαν ἡμῶν ἣν ἔχομεν ἐν Χριστῷ Ἰησοῦ, ἵνα ἡμᾶς καταδουλώσουσιν—οἷς οὐδὲ πρὸς ὥραν εἴξαμεν τῇ ὑποταγῇ, ἵνα ἡ ἀλήθεια τοῦ εὐαγγελίου διαμείνῃ πρὸς ὑμᾶς

> because of the sneaky false brothers who slipped in to spy on our freedom that we have in Christ in order that they might enslave us, to whom not even for a moment did I yield in submission so that the truth of the gospel would remain with you.

I should state clearly from the outset that this passage does not discuss Paul's opponents in Galatia but rather his opponents in Jerusalem who inserted themselves into the Jerusalem meeting. Even so, this passage is important to discuss because it illustrates the kind of people Paul was up against as he worked through this issue in his churches. One cannot say for certain that the same people who crashed the meeting in Jerusalem were the same people causing trouble among the Galatians, but they certainly held the same beliefs and were willing to cause trouble to proclaim their gospel. Paul describes their opposition in terms that imply warfare, and the issue at stake is nothing other than freedom versus slavery. The opponents were eager to promote obedience to the Law, which in Paul's eyes amounted to slavery, not the freedom in Christ that he preached.

The next mention of opponents is as oblique as the previous. In Gal 2:11–12 Paul discusses these people relative to Peter's behavior in Antioch:

> Ὅτε δὲ ἦλθεν Κηφᾶς εἰς Ἀντιόχειαν, κατὰ πρόσωπον αὐτῷ ἀντέστην, ὅτι κατεγνωσμένος ἦν. πρὸ τοῦ γὰρ ἐλθεῖν τινας ἀπὸ Ἰακώβου μετὰ τῶν ἐθνῶν συνήσθιεν· ὅτε δὲ ἦλθον, ὑπέστελλεν καὶ ἀφώριζεν ἑαυτόν, φοβούμενος τοὺς ἐκ περιτομῆς.
>
> But when Cephas came to Antioch, I personally took a stand against him because he had condemned himself. For before certain people from James arrived, he would regularly eat with the Gentiles. But when they arrived, he consistently withdrew and separated himself because he was afraid of those who were circumcised.

As in the passage just mentioned, I do not claim that these people are the same with whom Paul contends in Galatia, but they certainly embody the same ideals. The people Paul mentions here are closely associated with James, the leader of the church in Jerusalem, and they were circumcised. One can also assume from their influence upon Peter that they were actively pro-circumcision, which led to conflict between the Jews and Gentiles in Antioch. Peter would not have been persuaded against common table fellowship with Gentiles simply by the presence of more Jews, who were already present in Antioch apparently without contention. The difficulty must have come from some type of pressure they applied to the situation, which created an environment in which Peter felt it necessary to withdraw from that common table fellowship. This pro-circumcision, influential group is the exact same kind of opponent that had influenced the Galatians, against whom Paul had to work after they had disturbed them.

Paul's next mention of the opponents begins the central section of the book. In Gal 3:1 he says, Ὦ ἀνόητοι Γαλάται, τίς ὑμᾶς ἐβάσκανεν, "You foolish

Galatians! Who cast a spell on you for envy?" He asks the Galatians about the identity of the opponents only for rhetorical purposes, as they certainly would have known who they were. Paul's point is to cast the persuasion they exercised as entirely negative. Magic serves as a metaphor, describing how quickly and wrongly the Galatians have been persuaded away from Paul's gospel. This persuasion is featured again in the next mention of the opponents when Paul discusses their desire for the Galatians in Gal 4:17:

> ζηλοῦσιν ὑμᾶς οὐ καλῶς, ἀλλὰ ἐκκλεῖσαι ὑμᾶς θέλουσιν, ἵνα αὐτοὺς ζηλοῦτε
>
> They are not devoted to you in the right way. Rather, they want to exclude you so that you will in turn be devoted to them!

The point of this description is to show that the eager devotion the opponents have for the Galatians amounts to psychological manipulation as it is designed to put the Galatians on the "outside" of the people of God so that they would become devoted to the teaching of the opponents so they could get back on the "inside."

In Gal 5:1–2 Paul admonishes the Galatians against accepting circumcision, which provides a direct look at what the opponents were teaching:

> Τῇ ἐλευθερίᾳ ἡμᾶς Χριστὸς ἠλευθέρωσεν· στήκετε οὖν καὶ μὴ πάλιν ζυγῷ δουλείας ἐνέχεσθε. Ἴδε ἐγὼ Παῦλος λέγω ὑμῖν ὅτι ἐὰν περιτέμνησθε, Χριστὸς ὑμᾶς οὐδὲν ὠφελήσει.
>
> Christ truly set us free! So stand firm and do not be subject again to a yoke of slavery. Look—I, Paul, say to you that if you submit yourself to circumcision, Christ will not help you in any way.

The opponents had been pushing the Galatians to accept circumcision to ensure their place within the people of God, and Paul describes this as "a yoke of slavery." It would amount to taking on the entirety of the Law, which was not a burden God intended them to bear. It would amount to being enslaved again, instead of being free as Christ had intended and accomplished.

In Gal 5:7 Paul again asks the Galatians about the opponents, referencing them with regard to their effect on the Galatians:

> Ἐτρέχετε καλῶς· τίς ὑμᾶς ἐνέκοψεν τῇ ἀληθείᾳ μὴ πείθεσθαι;
>
> You were running so well! Who hindered you such that you do not obey the truth?

Paul uses the metaphor of a race to describe the Galatians' relationship to God in Christ. They began the race well and were making progress along the course of his gospel. Someone cut in on them (τίς ὑμᾶς ἐνέκοψεν), resulting in them no longer obeying the truth of what Paul preached to them. Paul then speaks of the certainty of the judgment the opponents will bear in v. 10:

> ὁ δὲ ταράσσων ὑμᾶς βαστάσει τὸ κρίμα, ὅστις ἐὰν ᾖ.
>
> the one who confuses you, whoever that may be, will bear his judgment.

This statement hearkens back to the judgment Paul proclaimed in Gal 1:8–9 upon those who preach another gospel. The one who confuses the Galatians by preaching a different gospel will certainly bear judgment. The final clause of the paragraph shows very clearly what Paul thinks of the opponents, and it clarifies exactly what they were demanding of the Galatians:

> ὄφελον καὶ ἀποκόψονται οἱ ἀναστατοῦντες ὑμᾶς.
>
> I wish those who trouble you would even mutilate themselves!

In a fit of frustration Paul expresses a desire for those who trouble the Galatians to cut off the member in question in the act of circumcision. They were asking the Galatians to accept circumcision, but doing this to enter the people of God was nothing more than self-mutilation.

In the conclusion to the letter in Gal 6:11–18, Paul makes several statements about his opponents that flesh out the picture painted in miniature so far. His central thesis about them is found in vv. 12–13:

> ὅσοι θέλουσιν εὐπροσωπῆσαι ἐν σαρκί, οὗτοι ἀναγκάζουσιν ὑμᾶς περιτέμνεσθαι, μόνον ἵνα τῷ σταυρῷ τοῦ Χριστοῦ μὴ διώκωνται. οὐδὲ γὰρ οἱ περιτεμνόμενοι αὐτοὶ νόμον φυλάσσουσιν, ἀλλὰ θέλουσιν ὑμᾶς περιτέμνεσθαι ἵνα ἐν τῇ ὑμετέρᾳ σαρκὶ καυχήσωνται.
>
> Those who want to make a good showing in the flesh, these compel you to be circumcised only so that they will not be persecuted with regard to the cross of Christ. For these who are circumcised do not themselves obey the Law, but they want you to be circumcised so that they might boast in your flesh.

This deep dive into the opponents' motives and actions shows clearly what Paul thinks of them: They are hypocritical charlatans whose focus on the body is antithetical to the cross of Christ. Their motives are entirely self-serving. They desire to make a change to the bodies of the Galatians so they might look good before others (v. 12a), not before God who is Paul's only concern (see Gal 1:10). Their goal is to avoid persecution that has come to them because of the cross (v. 12b); this means they are Christian in one sense because they are connected to the cross, but they have perverted that dedication into self-defense. Paul's proper understanding of the place of the Law in this new era of faith in Christ allows him to judge these opponents as hypocrites: They do not obey the Law as a whole (v. 13a). The only reason they push the Galatians to be circumcised is so that they might boast about their accomplishment (v. 13b). Their dedication to the Law, even though it may appear devout on the surface, is actually minimal and self-serving.

From these elements we can paint a picture of the opponents and their involvement in the churches of Galatia so that we have a good foundation on which to base the exegesis. In prior scholarship these opponents have often been described as "Judaizers," that is, Jews who were seeking simply to draw Gentile Christians away from Christ back to Judaism. This simplistic picture, however, does not match the portrait Paul paints of his opponents. Instead, these individuals were solidly within the social circles of Jewish Christians. I will not go so far to state that they were believers as such, given the harsh words Paul says about them, for example, calling them "false brothers" in Gal 2:4. The status of their spiritual life before God has to remain an open question. But these individuals were so thoroughly inside the community of Jewish Christians that they found a way to crash a private meeting between Paul and the leaders in Jerusalem. They were identified with James so closely that their presence was able to cause Peter to change his behavior radically vis-à-vis Gentiles in Antioch. To restate what I said before, I do not claim that the particular people involved in the events of Gal 2:1–10 and 2:11–14 were the same people who preached to the Galatian churches. But they were of a piece with them in their theology and action as they influenced Gentiles in the early church. So they were within the early church, most likely Jews who had accepted Jesus as Messiah, but radically different from Paul in their opinion of the basis for integration of Gentiles into the nascent church.

The identity of these opponents in terms of their social grouping (e.g., Jews vs. Jewish Christians) is not nearly as important for Paul, however, as their actions within the circles of the Galatian churches. Paul regards these people as opponents for two primary reasons: their teaching that Gentiles needed to accept circumcision to be fully accepted by God, and the destabilizing effect they were having on the Galatian congregations, the latter clearly the result of the former. Paul intended the entirety of the book of Galatians to negate the effect the opponents were having on the Galatian churches by showing definitively that the teaching of the opponents was not to be accepted through an assertion of his apostolic authority, the divine origin of his gospel, and the theological foundation for both. Central to Paul's argument against the opponents is his major theological argument that Gentile Christians are indeed related to Abraham, but not through circumcision or any obedience to the Torah. Rather, they are related to Abraham because they are in Christ by faith, and as such there is no other requirement to be laid on them. Discussions about the opponents are often long and involved, but the central fact is clear: These individuals were laying an additional requirement beyond simple faith in Christ upon the Gentiles in the Galatian churches. Paul roundly rejected that and wrote to bring the Galatians back to a pure acceptance of his gospel and his gospel alone.

Galatians and Romans

There is no doubt by any casual reader of Galatians and Romans that these two books cover much the same ground. They have similar language and theological themes, the latter often appearing as a more mature expression of the former. Their differences are certainly pronounced: Most notably, in Galatians Paul has to address a specific problem among churches he established and knew well, while in Romans Paul presents his gospel more generally to churches he has not yet met. Even so, it is clear that they spring from the same mind, and scholarship has always recognized Paul as the author of both.

What I wish to outline here is the relationship between the two and how I have handled that in regard to the exegesis. By almost every reconstruction of the chronological data, Paul wrote Galatians before he wrote Romans. Accepting this, the question then becomes how the exegete allows Romans to impact his understanding of Galatians. Although complete objectivity on this issue is not required nor possible, as a rule I hold to a rather strict chronological limitation in this regard that affects how I have worked through the exegesis of the book. When wrestling with the thoughts of an author who has a corpus of more than one work, I interpret the later works in the light of the former, not vice versa. I operate this way because of a simple but convincing argument: A later book cannot provide an interpretive context for an earlier book on the grounds that it was not written yet and the thoughts of the author it represents were not yet formulated. Put more as a principle, earlier works provide a context for later works, not vice versa. To be clear, there are instances in which this principle can be overridden in practice, especially if an author shows consistency of thought over time. If that consistency can be proven or is already well known, a later work can be profitably tapped for exegetical help in an earlier one. The question we must ask in this instance is, how consistent was Paul between the two books? Arguably he was very consistent in some ways but not so in others. For example, Abraham is a key person who provides theological grounding for his argument in each book, but in Romans Paul also refers to the person of Adam to make his theological arguments.[15] The Holy Spirit is a key part of Paul's argument in each book, but the nuances of the Spirit's role in the life of the believer are greatly expanded in Romans. Suffice it to say that there are clear theological connections between Paul's thoughts as expressed in each book, but there are some differences of nuance that require elaboration and explanation. For that reason, in my exegesis of Galatians I have as much as possible bracketed my understanding of Romans so that my exegesis of Galatians can be based on the evidence for that book. My goal is to explain Galatians in its fullness so that it can be appreciated on its own merits, not as a Cliff Notes version of the (perhaps) more beloved later book.

Exegetical and Theological Overview

The book of Galatians provides the reader a great deal to process concerning exegetical and theological themes. There are classic *topoi* to consider, such as justification by faith and Paul's handling of the Torah, and there are more recent considerations, such as the New Perspective on Paul. Each of these will be handled in depth in the course of the exegesis as warranted by the

15. Paul's earliest references to Adam are in 1 Cor 15:22, 45.

particular paragraphs. My purpose for this section of the introduction is to provide an overview of broad exegetical and theological considerations that have guided my exegesis and that will help the reader understand the commentary while at the same time giving an overview of the message and argument of the book.

What has impressed me throughout the writing of the commentary is the intensely *pastoral* nature of Paul's interaction with the Galatian congregations. By pastoral I mean the outworking of Paul's love for the congregation manifested in his intense concern that they follow and fulfill what God desires for them. In this instance, what God desires for them is the full inclusion of Gentiles into the churches on the basis of faith in Christ alone without any consideration for obedience to the Torah, and the manifestation of Paul's love and concern ranges from gentle guidance to angry admonition to exasperated frustration. Paul had a pastoral crisis on his hands: These churches were turning from what he had preached to them to another message that would destroy them. He had to rely upon every tool in his toolbox to bring them back into his fold: encouragement and challenge, exegetical and theological reasoning, gentle persuasion and passionate argumentation, scriptural admonitions and cultural analogies. The exegetical and theological point is that everything Paul says and everything he does with what he says in the book is designed to accomplish that singular pastoral goal: bringing the Galatians back into the fold of his Christ-centered, Torah-free gospel.

In tandem with the pastoral nature of Paul's writing in the book of Galatians is its *personal* nature. Paul never hesitated to display his own thoughts or emotions when it helped accomplish his purposes, and that is certainly the case here. On a macro-level this helps explain paragraphs in the text that appear to be somewhat disconnected from the context (e.g., Gal 4:12–20, which appears to interrupt the flow of Paul's exegetical and theological argument). In places like this Paul jumps to an intensely personal place; it is as if he is writing and is suddenly overcome with emotion for the Galatians, spurred on by his argument as a whole and his pastoral goal. This means that the flow of the book is not necessarily guided by a logical argument throughout, but it can still be understood as unified, consistent, and complete as the personal guides the implementation of the pastoral.

The book of Galatians is also extremely *practical*. By this I do not mean practical for you and me, the modern readers, in that there are ready commands to obey within our contexts, although Paul certainly includes those (e.g., Gal 6:1–10). Rather, I mean practical for the original readers, the churches of Galatia, in that there were very important real-world effects Paul desired to set in motion with his writing. The opponents had arrived on the scene in these churches and begun teaching in such a way that negative real-world effects were set in motion. Unity within the congregations was harmed as the opponents encouraged Gentiles to commit to the Law. Events similar to Peter's withdrawal from table fellowship were likely occurring regularly as the presuppositional inclinations of Jewish Christians were stoked to preserve their cultural and religious heritage. Gentiles may have even been pushed so far as to be circumcised, permanently altering their bodies in the hope of pleasing God. All of this was counter to the gospel Paul had preached to the Galatian churches, and everything he wrote was designed to reverse these real-world effects. Paul wanted to see the church unified as a single community in Christ, dedicated to the gospel, led by the Holy Spirit. In this he was eminently practical in that he sought change among the churches in keeping with the gospel he proclaimed.

All of this has ramifications for the exegesis of the text and the theology drawn from it. Galatians is in no way a dispassionate discourse on disconnected theological issues that interested the churches in Galatia and on which Paul had thought well, such that he could expound on them. Rather, it is a pastoral, personal, and practical letter that seeks to accomplish a very serious and urgent goal: returning the Galatian churches to a proper understanding and practice of his gospel so that they would welcome Gentiles into fellowship with open arms with no requirement other than faith in Jesus Christ. Everything I have written about the text is guided by this framework. Certainly some sections advance part of Paul's goal over others. For example, chapter 3 addresses the theological connection those of faith have to Abraham through Jesus; that is a theological aspect of understanding Paul's gospel. But that material is included to accomplish Paul's pastoral, personal, practical goal of bringing the Galatian churches back to proper practice, and the exegesis and theology are advanced when the reader recognizes that the shape they take are due to Paul's multifaceted, real-world goal.

Within that framework, the reader can understand the following overview of the message and argument of Galatians. Paul begins his letter to the churches in Galatia with a salutation infused with theology. As he greets them, he emphasizes the divine source of his apostleship and the eschatological rescue Jesus accomplished in his self-sacrifice on the cross. This framing enables the readers to understand just what is at stake in the following letter.

The body of the letter begins with a personal defense of Paul's gospel as the first means to call the Galatians back to fidelity. Paul first expresses frustration at the current situation in Galatia, which finds the churches pulled away from the gospel Paul proclaimed to a false imitation. Paul responds to this situation with a condemnation of those who preach the other gospel and a reaffirmation of his apostolic and personal desire to please God only.

Paul then moves into a detailed testimony of his apostolic calling. He explains his movements and contacts in and around the early church to show that his apostolic ministry is not self-serving or manipulative in any way. Rather, it represents God's divine calling upon his life. Following this, Paul then explains how his gospel gained agreement among the Jerusalem apostles, which enables the Galatians to see how the opponents have misrepresented those individuals in some way, and how further conflict with Peter proved the proper understanding of Paul's gospel. Reading this, the Galatians would surely be able to apply Paul's response to Peter to their very own situation.

To close his personal defense of his gospel, Paul explains the theological points highlighted by the practical concerns on which he and Peter disagreed. Advancing the argument, Paul explains how justification before God is based only on faith in Christ, of which the Law has no part or parcel. Paul's own experience of this justification apart from the Law enabled his participation with Christ, which is both proof of and paradigm for his gospel. This section, having broached several important theological themes, serves as a bridge to the central section of the letter body.

The body of the letter continues with an exegetical, theological defense of Paul's gospel as a foundation for his call for fidelity to his gospel. To start this section, Paul points to the clear role of the Spirit in their midst when they responded to Paul's gospel with faith in Christ. This implicitly proves the verity of Paul's gospel vis-à-vis that of the opponents.

Paul then explains how justification based on faith in Christ alone is the proper understanding of the gospel from the Scriptures. The example of Abraham, who received justification only through his faith in God, serves as the paradigm for mankind's response to God. This is supported by a proper understanding of the Law drawn from the Hebrew Scriptures. The Law curses any who do not obey it completely, but Christ has redeemed believers from that curse through his death so that they can receive the blessing God promised to him. Paul further explains that the promise God made has primacy over the Law; the latter has reached its end, but the former continues and is applied to those who have faith in Jesus, which makes them heirs of the promise God made. Paul then interrupts his exegetical, theological explanation with a personal appeal for the Galatians to return to his gospel. To close the exegetical, theological defense of his gospel, Paul appeals to an analogy from Scripture based on the two sons of Abraham, Ishmael and Isaac. Believers are associated with Isaac because of his connection to promise, not Ishmael, who was connected to slavery. This further reinforces Paul's entire argument of how the Scriptures support his gospel.

The body of the letter then closes with an exposition of the proper outworking of Paul's gospel in community. Paul hits the central theme first with a clear focus on freedom, which leads to a warning against returning to the Law, which would be tantamount to returning to slavery. Paul then explains the way that this freedom found in Christ, not the Law, works out in the community. Central to the outworking of this freedom is the working of the Spirit. Only through the Spirit can the power of the flesh be overcome, so the believer must constantly live under the control of the Spirit, which leads to practical, pastoral care of believers in the congregation as each cares for others in their midst and even those outside the congregation. This beautiful picture, this ecclesiastical vision, implicitly supports Paul's call to fidelity as it can be achieved only through faith in Christ, which enables the Spirit's work in the congregation.

The closing of the letter allows Paul to reiterate the teaching of the letter body, clarifying his central concerns. The opponents fall squarely within

Paul's sights here. He exposes their hypocrisy toward the Law by showing their true motives in seeking to have Gentiles adhere to it. Paul contrasts their self-serving attitude with his own, which seeks only to exalt Christ's self-sacrifice on the cross that enables the believer to live differently vis-à-vis the world. With this final admonition to be faithful to his gospel, Paul pronounces the closing benediction upon his readers.

Outline

- I. Introduction (1:1–5)
- II. A personal defense of Paul's gospel (1:6–2:21)
  - A. The exclusivity of his gospel (1:6–10)
  - B. Paul's personal testimony of his apostolic calling (1:11–24)
  - C. Agreement then conflict over his gospel (2:1–14)
    - 1. Agreement in Jerusalem (2:1–10)
    - 2. Conflict with Peter (2:11–14)
  - D. Paul's gospel as justification through faith in Christ alone (2:15–21)
- III. An exegetical, theological defense of Paul's gospel (3:1–4:31)
  - A. The Holy Spirit as proof of his gospel (3:1–5)
  - B. Justification through faith alone as central to the Scriptures (3:6–4:7)
    - 1. The example of Abraham (3:6–9)
    - 2. Faith, not the Law, for connection to Abraham (3:10–4:7)
  - C. Encouragement to return to his gospel (4:8–20)
  - D. Analogy from Abraham's sons (4:21–31)
- IV. The proper outworking of Paul's gospel in community (5:1–6:10)
  - A. Freedom as central (5:1)
  - B. Warning against returning to slavery under the Law (5:2–12)
  - C. The multifaceted outworking of the gospel in community (5:13–6:10)
    - 1. Freedom in community (5:13–15)
    - 2. Guided by the Holy Spirit (5:16–25)
    - 3. Practical concern for others (6:1–10)
- V. Benediction (6:11–18)

Selected Bibliography

Baur, F. C. *Paul the Apostle of Jesus Christ: His Life and Works, His Epistles and Teachings: A Contribution to a Critical History of Primitive Christianity*. 2 vols. Trans. E. Zeller. London: Williams and Norgate, 1873.

———. *Paulus, der Apostel Jesu Christi: Sein Leben und Wirken, seine Briefe und seine Lehre: Een Beitrag zu einer kritischen Geschichte des Urchristenthums*. Stuttgart: Becher & Müller, 1845.

Carson, D. A., and D. J. Moo. *An Introduction to the New Testament*. 2nd ed. Grand Rapid: Zondervan, 2005.
Cranfield, C. E. B. *The Epistle to the Romans*. 2 vols. ICC. Edinburgh: T&T Clark, 1975–1979.
Grainger, J. D. *The Galatians: Celtic Invaders of Greece and Asia Minor*. Yorkshire: Pen & Sword History, 2020.
Gundry, R. H., and R. W. Howell. "The Sense and Syntax of John 3:14–17 with Special Reference to the Use of οὕτως ... ὥστε in John 3:16." *NovT* 41 (1999): 24–39.
Guthrie, D. *New Testament Introduction*. 4th ed. Downers Grove, IL: InterVarsity, 1990.
Hoehner, H. W. "Did Paul Write Galatians?" In *History and Exegesis: New Testament Essays in Honor of Dr. E. Earle Ellis for His 80th Birthday*, ed. S. Son, 150–69. London: T&T Clark, 2006.
Holmes, M. W., ed. *The Apostolic Fathers: Greek Texts and English Translations*. Grand Rapids: Baker, 2007.
Irenaeus. *The Writings of Irenaeus*. Edited by A. Roberts and W. H. Rambaut. Edinburgh: T&T Clark, 1883.
Marshall, I. H. *Luke: Historian & Theologian*. New Testament Profiles. Downers Grove, IL: InterVarsity, 1988.
Metzger, B. M. *The Canon of the New Testament: Its Origin, Development, and Significance*. Oxford: Oxford University Press, 1987.
Oxford Society of Historical Theology. *The New Testament in the Apostolic Fathers*. Oxford: Clarendon, 1905.
Schoedel, W. R. "Polycarp, Epistle of." *ABD* 5:390.

Commentary Bibliography

Betz, H. D. *Galatians*. Hermeneia. Philadelphia: Fortress, 1979.
Bruce, F. F. *The Epistle to the Galatians*. NIGTC. Grand Rapids: Eerdmans, 1982.
Burton, E. de W. *A Critical and Exegetical Commentary on the Epistle to the Galatians*. ICC. Edinburgh: T&T Clark, 1920.
Calvin, J. *Commentaries on the Epistles of Paul to the Galatians and Ephesians*. Trans. W. Pringle. Grand Rapids: Eerdmans, 1948.
Cousar, C. B. *Reading Galatians, Philippians, and 1 Thessalonians: A Literary and Theological Commentary*. Macon, GA: Smyth & Helwys, 2001.
de Boer, M. C. *Galatians: A Commentary*. NTL. Louisville, KY: Westminster John Knox, 2011.
deSilva, D. A. *The Letter to the Galatians*. NICNT. Grand Rapids: Eerdmans, 2018.
Dunn, J. D. G. *The Epistle to the Galatians*. BNTC. Grand Rapids: Baker, 1993.
Fee, G. D. *Galatians*. Pentecostal Commentary Series. Blandford Forum, Dorset, UK: Deo, 2007.
Fung, R. Y. K. *The Epistle to the Galatians*. NICNT. Grand Rapids: Eerdmans, 1988.

Garlington, D. *An Exposition of Galatians: A New Perspective/Reformational Reading*. 2nd ed. Eugene, OR: Wipf and Stock, 2004.

———. *An Exposition of Galatians: A Reading from the New Perspective*. Eugene, OR: Wipf and Stock, 2007.

George, T. *Galatians*. NAC. Nashville: Broadman and Holman, 1994.

Guthrie, D. *Galatians*. NCBC. Grand Rapids: Eerdmans, 1973.

Hansen, G. W. *Galatians*. IVPNTC. Downers Grove, IL: InterVarsity, 1994.

Harmon, M. S. *Galatians*. EBTC. Bellingham, WA: Lexham Academic, 2021.

Hays, R. B. "Galatians." In *The New Interpreter's Bible*. Edited by L. E. Keck, vol. 11, 181–348. Nashville: Abingdon, 2000.

Jervis, L. A. *Galatians*. NIBC. Peabody, MA: Hendrickson, 1999.

Keener, C. S. *Galatians*. Grand Rapids: Baker, 2019.

Lenski, R. C. H. *St. Paul's Epistles to the Galatians, to the Ephesians, and to the Philippians*. Minneapolis: Augsburg, 1937.

Lightfoot, J. B. *St. Paul's Epistle to the Galatians*. 1865. Repr. Peabody, MA: Hendrickson, 1999.

Longenecker, R. N. *Galatians*. WBC. Dallas: Word, 1990.

Lührmann, D. *Galatians*. Translated by O. C. Dean Jr. Continental Commentary. Minneapolis: Fortress, 1992.

Luther, M. *Galatians*. Crossway Classic Commentaries. Wheaton: Crossway, 1998.

Martyn, J. L. *Galatians*. AB. New York: Doubleday, 1997.

Matera, F. J. *Galatians*. SP. Collegeville, MN: Liturgical, 1992.

McKnight, S. *Galatians*. NIVAC. Grand Rapids: Zondervan, 1995.

Moo, D. J. *Galatians*. BECNT. Grand Rapids: Baker, 2013.

Morris, L. *Galatians: Paul's Charter of Christian Freedom*. Downers Grove: InterVarsity, 1996.

Oakes, P. *Galatians*. Paideia. Grand Rapids: Baker, 2015.

Ramsay, W. M. *A Historical Commentary on St. Paul's Epistle to the Galatians*. 1900. Repr. Grand Rapids: Baker, 1965.

Rapa, R. K. "Galatians." In *The Expositor's Bible Commentary, rev. ed., ed.* T. Longman III and D. E. Garland, vol. 11, 547–640. Grand Rapids: Zondervan, 2008.

Ridderbos, H. N. *The Epistle of Paul to the Churches of Galatia*. NICNT. Grand Rapids: Eerdmans, 1953.

Schreiner, T. R. *Galatians*. ZECNT. Grand Rapids: Zondervan, 2010.

Soards, M. L., and D. J. Pursiful. *Galatians*. SHBC. Macon, GA: Smyth & Helwys, 2015.

Stott, J. R. W. *The Message of Galatians: Only One Way*. The Bible Speaks Today. Downers Grove: InterVarsity, 1968.

Williams, S. K. *Galatians*. ANTC. Nashville: Abingdon, 1997.

Witherington, B. III. *Grace in Galatia: A Commentary on St. Paul's Letter to the Galatians*. Grand Rapids: Eerdmans, 1998.

Grace and Peace from God and Christ (1:1–5)

Textual Notes

1:3 The pronoun ἡμῶν moves within the manuscript tradition but without significantly changing the meaning. In most manuscripts and several versions the pronoun modifies κυρίου (so 𝔓46.51vid B D 1739 𝔐 vg sy sa bomss et al.), but this appears to be an alteration of Paul's more common formula in which the pronoun modifies πατρός (so ℵ A 33 et al.). Most of Paul's other greetings that mention both God and Jesus Christ show no such variation with the pronoun that modifies πατρός (Rom 1:7; 1 Cor 1:3; 2 Cor 1:2; Eph 1:2; Phil 1:2; Phlm 3). Other greetings do show some variation: Some manuscripts lack ἡμῶν in the greeting of 2 Thess 1:2, and in 1 Tim 1:2 because of the placement of ἡμῶν at the end of the greeting, some scribes introduced it there following πατρός. When all the evidence is considered, likely the reading ἀπὸ θεοῦ πατρὸς καὶ κυρίου ἡμῶν Ἰησοῦ Χριστοῦ was an early variant originally made for pious reasons[1] which then became widely adopted. With this particular textual problem, Paul's usage elsewhere is the best guide for determining the more likely original word order here.

1:4 Here NA^{28} accepts the reading ὑπέρ. The preps. περί and ὑπέρ overlap in meaning and sound in Koine Greek,[2] which accounts for frequent variation between the two in the manuscript tradition. Both can indicate for whom an action was done, but ὑπέρ provides more specific semantic content than περί by focusing on the personal interest of the obj.[3] In this textual problem the change would be intentional on the part of scribes, as this single word variation does affect the sense. The only other place Paul uses either περί or ὑπέρ with ἁμαρτία is 1 Cor 15:3. The significance of ὑπέρ there as part of a key Christian confession could have swayed scribes to replace περί with ὑπέρ in Gal 1:4, but equally significant uses of περί with ἁμαρτία elsewhere

1. B. M. Metzger, *A Textual Commentary on the Greek New Testament* (New York: United Bible Societies, 1994), 520.

2. A. T. Robertson, *A Grammar of the Greek New Testament in the Light of Historical Research* (Nashville: Broadman, 1934), 629.

3. See BDAG, 1030–31.

in the NT (John 8:46; 15:22; 16:8, 9; 1 John 2:2; 4:10; Rom 8:3; Heb 5:3; 10:6, 8, 18, 26; 13:11; 1 Pet 3:18) might have created change in the opposite direction. In addition, if the wording of 1 Cor 15:3 is pre-Pauline, which is frequently argued for that material,[4] then it would not have as much weight in assessing Pauline style here. Paul does use ὑπέρ elsewhere in Galatians in a soteriological context (2:20; 3:13), not περί, but the obj. of the prep. in those places is personal and thus not exactly parallel to this passage. When external evidence is considered, on all counts περί is favored. It has stronger manuscripts on its side, wider geographical distribution, and genealogical solidarity in the Alexandrian and Byzantine text types. The prep. ὑπέρ is not weakly represented, especially with its support from several strong Alexandrian manuscripts, but it has less support on other counts. Based upon 1 Cor 15:3 and the other occurrences in Galatians, ὑπέρ would be favored here, but no scribe seeing ὑπέρ would have replaced it with the slightly weaker περί. The reading that best explains the rise of the other then is περί, so it is more likely original here.[5]

1:4 The reading ἐκ τοῦ αἰῶνος τοῦ ἐνεστῶτος πονηροῦ should be regarded as original because of much stronger support from key Alexandrian mss (𝔓[46.51vid] ℵ* A B 33 1739 et al.). The variant ἐκ τοῦ ἐνεστῶτος αἰῶνος πονηροῦ could have arisen from homoioteleuton, but more likely it arose as a conscious change on the part of scribes to create a smoother reading that distributed the two attributives.[6]

4. See the brief argument in R. E. Ciampa and B. S. Rosner, *The First Letter to the Corinthians*, PNTC (Grand Rapids: Eerdmans, 2010), 745–46, and the more extensive argument in A. C. Thiselton, *The First Epistle to the Corinthians*, NIGTC (Grand Rapids: Eerdmans, 2000), 1186–89.

5. This reading is also accepted by Lightfoot, 73, in contrast with almost all other commentators.

6. For discussion of this grammatical tendency, see BDF, §269(1); MHT, 3:186.

Translation

1 From Paul,[7] an apostle not from men nor through[8] any man[9] but through
Jesus Christ and God the Father who raised him from the dead, **2** and from[10]
all the brothers with me.

To the churches of Galatia.[11]

3 Grace and peace to you from God our Father and the Lord Jesus Christ,
4 who gave himself for our sins to rescue us from this present evil age in
keeping with the will of our God and Father, **5** to whom be glory forever
and ever. Amen!

Commentary

The opening of an ancient Greek letter served the very practical yet pedestrian purpose of identification. With a few words, the author would identify himself and the recipients while passing along a simple greeting, usually the stereotypical Greek word χαίρειν. This simple formula of author-recipients-greeting occurs with great regularity in ancient Greek letters, although often with expected variation.[12] Biblical Greek reflects this wider trend to a certain extent,[13] but notable variation and development comes in the letters of Paul, who did not hesitate to alter the normal formula to suit his own purposes. Paul developed the letter opening for theological assertion and literary function; consequently in Pauline letters his first words take on rhetorical

---

7. The addition of the word "From" in the translation to indicate the sender of the letter has become common in various Bible translations (see, e.g., NET, CEV). It is functionally equivalent to the simple use of the name in the nom. case in Greek letter openings. Compare this simple one-word addition to the more expansive "This letter is from Paul" in the NLT.

8. Compare "by human agency" (NET), "through the agency of man" (NASB), which explicitly bring out the force of διά plus the gen.

9. This is an appropriate translation to bring out the generic force of ἀνθρώπου.

10. I have repeated the addition of "from" here to emphasize the support Paul received from his associates in the sending of the letter.

11. I have set this line apart to show that it has a different function than the surrounding material.

12. See F. X. J. Exler, *The Form of the Ancient Greek Letter of the Epistolary Papyri (3rd c. B.C. - 3rd c. A.D.): A Study in Greek Epistolography* (Chicago: Ares, 1976), 23, 61.

13. For examples in the LXX see, among others, 1 Esd 8:9; Esth 8:12b; 1 Macc 10:18; 3 Macc 3:12. Interesting variation occurs in 1 Esd 6:8 (which lacks an identification of the author) and 2 Macc 1:1 (which has the unusual order recipients-greeting-authors-greeting). In the NT see Acts 23:26 for the simplest example. Acts 15:23 and Jas 1:1 are not as detailed as Pauline letter openings, but they show some expansion relative to the simpler greeting form common in the wider world.

and functional importance beyond that found in the letters of the wider world. They assert theological truth that foreshadows the development of the letter's argument, and they prepare the recipients to respond properly to the contents.

1:1 Παῦλος. The name which begins the letter denotes the author: It is Paul,[14] the missionary apostle who had evangelized the Galatians in the past and now challenges them in writing. In keeping with literary convention, Paul begins every single one of his letters with his name, so much so that it appears routine.[15] The connotation that his name brings to each individual letter, however, should not be overlooked. Just as we respond emotionally when receiving a letter from a close friend or relative, the Galatians would have had a collective, emotional response when Paul's letter arrived. Paul and the Galatians had a prior relationship marked by deep bonds between them.[16] He writes to them now not simply to convey information but to exercise pastoral care as a practical function of those bonds. Paul expected that the Galatians would respond to him positively, even in the midst of the current crisis, and he surely hoped the mention of his name would invoke in the Galatians strong feelings of association, respect, and love. Paul's name had rhetorical power because of the past history he and the Galatians shared, and it takes on even more power as the strong, unexpected tone of the letter becomes evident through the beginning of the letter body.

ἀπόστολος. Paul regularly added titles to his name in the opening of his letters.[17] The word δοῦλος was one such designation (Romans; Philippians;

---

14. Paul's name presents an interesting conundrum. Paul never referred to himself with the Jewish name Saul; the book of Acts shows that he bore that name in addition to the Roman name Paul. Coming from a Torah-observant Jewish family (an inference from the phrase Ἑβραῖος ἐξ Ἑβραίων in Phil 3:5), Paul was likely given the Hebrew name Saul at birth. Later, similarly to many diaspora Jews, Paul adopted a Roman name with a similar sound to his given name (Martyn, 82). The name Παῦλος was likely a cognomen, not a family name (*nomen*) or personal name (*praenomen*); see Witherington, 69–70; deSilva, 113.

15. The inverse where the recipient is listed first does occur in the wider world; see Exler, *Ancient Greek Letter*, 40–49, for examples. This inverted order normally occurs in petitions, complaints, and applications (so Exler, *Ancient Greek Letter*, 23). This would involve a lower-ranking individual writing to a higher-ranking individual, so the inversion may be an attempt to persuade the recipient through honoring him; see S. A. Adams, "Paul's Letter Opening and Greek Epistolography: A Matter of Relationship," in *Paul and the Ancient Letter Form,* ed. S. E. Porter and S. A. Adams, Pauline Studies 6 (Leiden: Brill, 2010), 40n21. Nothing should be inferred from Paul's use of the normal word order. In listing himself first Paul is simply following convention, as he pulls rank over the recipients in other ways when needed.

16. This is conveyed, for example, by both the tone and content of Gal 4:12–20.

17. The exceptions are 1 and 2 Thess.

Titus), *ἀπόστολος* another (Romans; 1 Corinthians; 2 Corinthians; Galatians; Ephesians; Colossians; 1 Timothy; 2 Timothy; Titus). The insertion of titles in ancient Greek letters was not all that common. Letters that do have inserted titles for the sender are almost all from people in a position of authority.[18] This implies that Paul seeks to increase his influence in the letter with a more commanding literary presence.[19] Given the crisis Paul faced, this strategy would have been perfectly understandable.

The meaning of the word *ἀπόστολος* cannot be underestimated in terms of its importance. In describing himself with this word, Paul focuses upon both his role as sent from God to convey the gospel message and his authoritative role to interpret and apply that message.[20] This is brought out in the dynamic translation "Paul, an apostle—that is to say a person who has been sent on a mission" (Martyn, 81).

οὐκ ἀπ' ἀνθρώπων οὐδὲ δι' ἀνθρώπου. After identifying himself as an *ἀπόστολος*, Paul describes more fully what kind of *ἀπόστολος* he was through three prepositional phrases. Drawing upon the basic idea that an *ἀπόστολος* was commissioned, authorized, and sent, Paul clarifies the source of his apostolic commission. The phrase *οὐκ ἀπ' ἀνθρώπων* denies that any person commissioned Paul. The phrase *δι' ἀνθρώπου* focuses on personal agency.[21] Paul precludes any person as an agent, enabler, or helper in his apostolic commission. It is not clear that Paul has a particular referent in mind for the two forms of *ἄνθρωπος*. He might be referring to distinct entities such as the Jerusalem or Antioch church with the pl. and Peter or Barnabas with the sg. (see Fung, 36–37; Longenecker, 4; Dunn, 26; Martyn, 84),[22] but this is not certain, nor is it necessary to identify the referents to understand Paul's meaning. With these two phrases Paul simply removes any human source or agency for his authoritative role as an apostle. Nowhere else does Paul qualify his apostolic status in this way; thus he provides an important insight into his central concern, the ultimate source of his authority and gospel (Williams, 34).

---

18. An example interesting for its ostentatiousness, although certainly not unique, is P. Lond. 6.1912 (accessed at http://papyri.info/ddbdp/p.lond;6;1912). Here the greeting reads Τιβέριος Κλαύδιος Καῖσαρ Σεβαστὸς Γερμανικὸς Αὐτοκράτωρ ἀρχιερεὺς μέγειστος δημαρχικῆς ἐξουσίας ὕπατος ἀποδεδιγμένος Ἀλεξανδρέων τῇ πόλει χαίρειν, "Tiberius Claudius Caesar Augustus Germanicus, Emperor, Great High Priest, Holder of the Tribunician Power, Consul Designate: To the City of the Alexandrians, greetings." I suppose the supreme ruler of the Western world could be forgiven for such display.

19. Adams, "Paul's Letter Opening," 50.

20. For further discussion, see the excursus.

21. See BDAG, 225.

22. See also M. Silva, *Interpreting Galatians: Explorations in Exegetical Method* (Grand Rapids: Baker, 2001), 54.

ἀλλὰ διὰ Ἰησοῦ Χριστοῦ καὶ θεοῦ πατρός. With this phrase Paul turns to the true source of his apostleship: Jesus Christ and God the Father. The conj. ἀλλά reinforces the negations of the prior prepositional phrases; in this instance Paul presents truly an either/or distinction. As with the occurrence in the prior prepositional phrase, the prep. δία denotes personal agency, but the distinction between source and agency, that is, between ἀπό and δία in this context, should not be drawn too hard.[23] Paul intends the second occurrence of δία to be broad enough to cover any assertion that would also be covered by ἀπό. The clear point is that Paul's status and role as an apostle originates with the Lord, not man. The single use of the prep. governing both substantives points to a singularity of purpose and action between God and Christ in Paul's apostolic call (see Burton, 5).

In discussing who is in fact the source of his apostleship, Paul first mentions Jesus Christ, then God the Father. This is likely due to the imprint of his conversion experience, when Paul saw the risen Christ (Acts 9:1–19).[24] But grammatically θεοῦ πατρός is tied to the same occurrence of δία, so there is no practical or theological division between them. Paul views both Christ and God as equally the source and ultimate agent of his apostolic call. With this connection Paul identifies Jesus as on par with the Father, thus showing important theological development in one of the earliest Christian writings (de Boer, 24).[25]

In referring to God as Father, Paul takes up a theological concept with prior expression in the OT. This metaphor for describing God's relationship to his people was well developed within Judaism, finding frequent expression in the OT and Second Temple literature.[26] Jesus developed this concept further by applying it to himself in a particular way: He viewed God as his own Father, understanding his existence and ministry in light of this relationship.[27] In the context of the opening to Galatians, because of the qualifying phrase τοῦ ἐγείραντος αὐτὸν ἐκ νεκρῶν which follows θεοῦ πατρός, this specific relationship between Jesus and God is in view with Paul's identification of

23. Silva, *Interpreting Galatians*, 53–54.

24. So also Fee, 14–15. Compare Acts 22:1–21; 26:12–20, where Paul, not the narrator of Acts, describes his conversion experience. For an analysis of Lukan redaction in and among these three accounts, see C. W. Hedrick, "Paul's Conversion/Call: A Comparative Analysis of the Three Reports in Acts," *JBL* 100 (1981): 415–32.

25. Theodoret, *Epistle to the Galatians* 1.1, argues on the basis of the single prep. governing the two nouns that Paul teaches no difference in nature between Jesus and God. See M. J. Edwards, ed., *Galatians, Ephesians, Philippians*, ACCSNT 8 (Downers Grove, IL: InterVarsity, 2005), 2.

26. See, among others, Exod 4:22; Deut 32:6; Ps 2; Isa 63:16; Hos 11:1; Tob 13:4; Sir 23:1, 4; 3 Macc 5:7.

27. For a short defense of the historicity of this aspect of Jesus's self-conception, see M. H. Burer, *Divine Sabbath Work*, BBRSup 5 (Winona Lake, IN: Eisenbrauns, 2012), 130–32.

God as Father, not the more normal corporate relationship emphasized by Paul elsewhere (for example, twice later in the letter opening). Thus Paul's intention here is to firmly ground his apostolic status in the work of Jesus Christ that was done through the will of Christ's own Father, the great God of Israel.[28]

τοῦ ἐγείραντος αὐτὸν ἐκ νεκρῶν. With πατρός Paul identifies who God is, and with τοῦ ἐγείραντος αὐτὸν ἐκ νεκρῶν he describes what God has done. God acted tangibly and powerfully in the resurrection of Jesus and in that act demonstrated his paternal relationship to Jesus.[29] This is a key facet of the gospel that Paul proclaims (see Rom 7:4; 10:9; 1 Cor 6:14; 15:15; Col 2:12). Since his gospel proclaimed to the Galatians has come under fire, Paul highlights from the outset that God has acted definitively in the resurrection of Jesus. Any modification of Paul's message about that event is an assault both upon the historical fact of the resurrection and the theological truth that God was at work in it (see similarly Calvin, 24–25).

1:2 καὶ οἱ σὺν ἐμοὶ πάντες ἀδελφοί. With this interesting phrase Paul identifies the co-senders of the letter. These brothers in the faith are unnamed, but his identification of them is somewhat emphatic. Both modifiers (σὺν ἐμοί and πάντες) are in first attributive position, which heightens their force; the former emphasizes proximity to Paul, and the latter emphasizes extent and unanimity. Paul mentions co-senders in his letter openings more often than not.[30] Although not very common in ancient Greek letters, identifying a co-sender served to provide legal confirmation of the letter and its message.[31] With the identification of this group of unnamed Christian associates,[32] Paul affirms himself as the authoritative source of the letter, yet at the same time provides confirmation that his message is not idiosyncratic (so also deSilva, 116).[33] In addition to the weight of Paul's personality in this correspondence,

---

28. The translation "through Jesus Christ and God his Father" would bring out this point with clarity, although it suffers from slight awkwardness.

29. The mention of resurrection evokes an eschatological context (Dunn, 29), and this is reiterated in 1:4 with more explicit content.

30. Paul does not mention co-senders in Romans, Ephesians, or the Pastoral Epistles.

31. See Adams, "Paul's Letter Opening," 40–44; M. L. Stirewalt Jr., *Paul, the Letter Writer* (Grand Rapids: Eerdmans, 2003), 37–42.

32. Similar wording in Phil 4:21, where "perhaps even Paul's ministerial coworkers" are intended (Witherington, 74), argues that these people would be more important rather than less. Longenecker, 5, argues the letter was written at Syrian Antioch, so these people would be the leaders of that church.

33. P. L. Tite, "How to Begin, and Why? Diverse Functions of the Pauline Prescript with a Greco-Roman Context," in Porter and Adams, *Paul and the Ancient Letter Form,* 87; *contra* Lightfoot, 73.

the Galatians must also feel the force of the broader Christian fellowship in concert with Paul's message.[34]

ταῖς ἐκκλησίαις τῆς Γαλατίας. Paul identifies the recipients of the letter crisply and directly. As with many of Paul's letters, Galatians is written to a group, not an individual. This book has the distinction of being written to a group of groups. This is in contrast to singular churches identified explicitly in 1 Cor 1:2; 2 Cor 1:1; 1 Thess 1:1; 2 Thess 1:2; and implicitly in Eph 1:1;[35] Phil 1:1; Col 1:2. Galatians was written as a circular letter that would eventually make its way to each congregation in turn. Because Paul does not differentiate among the different churches, they were likely equally affected by the problem against which he writes (Martyn, 86). Paul does not define or explain his use of the term ἐκκλησία. In secular Greek the term simply meant an "assembly" or "gathering."[36] In the LXX the term was applied to the nation of Israel (see Deut 31:30 for a clear example). From an early time this term was naturally applied to gatherings of Christ followers and eventually came to refer to the collective group of individuals who were connected spiritually to Christ.[37]

1:3 χάρις ὑμῖν καὶ εἰρήνη ἀπὸ θεοῦ πατρὸς ἡμῶν καὶ κυρίου Ἰησοῦ Χριστοῦ. The wording of this initial greeting in Galatians is found verbatim in several other Pauline letters (Rom 1:7; 1 Cor 1:3; 2 Cor 1:2; Eph 1:2; Phil 1:2; 2 Thess 1:2; Phlm 3). In contrast to the short greeting χαίρειν which marked most ancient Greek letters, Paul's expansion of the formula appears striking and novel. The consistency of this wording in many of Paul's epistles points to his bedrock theological convictions that undergird it.

χάρις ὑμῖν. The word order of the greeting is significant, but most translations obscure it. The dat. pronoun ὑμῖν is connected to χάρις; thus a more literal translation of "grace to you and peace" has warrant (e.g., ESV, CSB)

---

34. Marius Victorinus, *Epistle to the Galatians* 1.1.1, argues that Paul intends to shame the Galatians because they are thinking differently than everyone else. See "Edwards, *Galatians, Ephesians, Philippians*, 3. That may have been a result of Paul's statement, but I do not think that was his intention.

35. Despite much argumentation in support of the view that Ephesians was a cyclical letter, I cannot affirm that hypothesis as the best explanation for the evidence on the question. For discussion see H. W. Hoehner, *Ephesians: An Exegetical Commentary* (Grand Rapids: Baker, 2002), 78–79.

36. LSJ, 509; MGS, 632.

37. Even though the word was used in political contexts in secular Greek that implied a particular type of rhetoric or discourse among the assembly, I see no warrant for those connotations here (*contra* Witherington, 75). In my mind the historical situation is too different between those contexts to make that connection. One difference between the NT and LXX usage of the term worthy of note is that the LXX usage focused upon the entire body of Israel while the early NT usage focused upon local gatherings (Dunn, 30–31).

instead of the more idiomatic "grace and peace to you" (NET). Here Paul implies a distinction between the grace given to humanity and the peace that results from that grace. The first word compactly expresses the entirety of God's disposition toward believers; the latter expresses the entirety of the benefits received (see Longenecker, 7; Fee, 17). Simply stated, " 'Grace' is fundamental, 'peace' is its result" (Lenski, 27).

The key term χάρις was the theological air that Paul breathed: the unmerited favor of the Lord that he had personally experienced.[38] This concept frames the broad context for the specific argument of Galatians that follows. The meaning of χάρις is broad and capable of a variety of nuances, from the concrete to the abstract, from the objective to the subjective. The classical period exhibited a wide range of meanings, covering all different combinations of nuance; these remain active through the Koine period reaching into the specific corpus of the NT. Among others, we can identify an objective sense ("beauty"), a subjective sense ("favor"), a subjective sense on the part of the actor ("kindness, goodwill"), a subjective sense on the part of the receiver ("thankfulness, gratitude"), and a concrete sense ("favor, boon").[39] Within the LXX a more specific subset of meanings occurs, the most important of which is grace in a subjective sense on the part of the actor, referring specifically to "the Lord's kindness received gratuitously."[40] A text that illustrates this sense well is Gen 6:8: Νωε δὲ εὗρεν χάριν ἐναντίον κυρίου τοῦ θεοῦ, "And Noah found grace before the Lord God." Here the underlying Hebrew term for χάριν is חֵן, a term that has a similar range of meaning as χάρις does relative to the subjective and objective aspects.[41] Grace is the entire scriptural testimony of who God is and how he acts toward mankind. By using this term Paul invokes the entire biblical witness as the Galatians begin to read his letter. In Gal 1:3 χάρις at a minimum means the subjective aspect of the divine attitude toward the believer, that is, God's gracious disposition toward the Galatians stemming from his very character, but it is not limited simply to divine favor in attitude. Given the contextual expansion in vv. 4–5, the meaning of χάρις moves into beneficent action, that is, concrete manifestations of God's kindness toward those whom he loves. Thus the pronoun ὑμῖν does not simply reidentify the recipients of the letter. Instead, it freshly identifies the Galatians as direct recipients of God's grace.

καὶ εἰρήνη. The meaning of the word εἰρήνη overlaps a great deal with the English word "peace." It refers to the absence of discord, or stated more positively, the presence of accord or harmony between two parties, whether individual or collective, public or private. In the LXX εἰρήνη is practically the

---

38. For a study that sees the political and social background of patronage and benefaction behind this concept, see J. R. Harrison, *Paul's Language of Grace in Its Graeco-Roman Context*, WUNT 2.172 (Tübingen: Mohr Siebeck, 2003).

39. See LSJ, 1978–79; MGS, 2341–42.

40. LEH, 2:513.

41. *HALOT*, 332; L. Freedman, "חֵן et al.," *TWOT*, 5:26–28.

default translation for the Hebrew term שָׁלוֹם, which broadly means "peace, welfare, prosperity."[42] This Hebrew word was often used as a synonym for divine deliverance,[43] and this connotation becomes critical for the NT usage of the Greek word εἰρήνη.[44] Here the word εἰρήνη hovers between both the general and specific nuances of שָׁלוֹם. The traditional, general concepts of welfare and prosperity are in view, but they have specific, focused content: Similar to the force of χάρις in this greeting, this state of well-being is sourced in God and his activity on behalf of the believer. The state of well-being is both existential and eschatological, given the future-looking focus of Paul's statement in v. 4.

ἀπὸ θεοῦ πατρὸς ἡμῶν καὶ κυρίου Ἰησοῦ Χριστοῦ. Within the context of the greeting specifically and Paul's theological thought more broadly, this prepositional phrase identifies the source of the grace and peace that the Galatian believers experience. In contrast to Paul's statement of his apostleship in v. 1, where he mentioned Jesus Christ first, here Paul mentions God the Father first. Very likely this is due to his bedrock theological conviction that salvation begins ultimately in the mind and action of God. Christ is then mentioned second as the primary agent of that salvation, who acts completely in concert with the divine will, as Paul expresses in the next verse. When Paul first mentioned θεοῦ πατρός in v. 1 he used no qualifying pronouns. Here that is not the case; θεοῦ πατρός is modified by the gen. pronoun ἡμῶν to indicate the fatherly relationship of God to believers and then by extension the believers' familial connection to one another. As part of Paul's strategy to motivate the Galatian believers with this letter, the pronoun is powerful. As an "inclusive we,"[45] this pronoun links Paul and the co-senders of the letter on one side to the Galatian believers on the other in a positive way. Although the tenor of the letter will soon become difficult, even adversarial, Paul begins with a collective, unifying tone to motivate the Galatians emotionally to accept his message.

Here Paul adds the word κυρίου as an appellation for Jesus Christ. "Lord" very early became a common title for Jesus. The fact that Paul uses the term with no explanation or clarification is a sign that this function of the word antedates his usage.[46] The simple meaning of the term pointed to one with

---

42. See *HALOT*, 1506–7, for bibliography and further analysis.

43. See *HALOT*, 1509–10, for further analysis.

44. BDAG, 288, states, "Since, acc. to the prophets, peace will be an essential characteristic of the messianic kgdm. (εἰ. as summum bonum: Seneca, Ep. 66, 5), Christian thought also freq. regards εἰ. as nearly synonymous w. messianic salvation εὐαγγελίζεσθαι εἰ. *proclaim peace*, i.e. messianic salvation."

45. For discussion and explanation, see D. B. Wallace, *Greek Grammar Beyond the Basics: An Exegetical Syntax of the New Testament* (Grand Rapids: Zondervan, 1996), 397–99.

46. L. W. Hurtado, "Lord," in *Dictionary of Paul and His Letters,* ed. G. F. Hawthorne, R. P. Martin, and D. G. Reid (Downers Grove, IL: InterVarsity, 1993), 562.

authority and power,[47] but the connotation of the term within the wider cultural context of early Christianity was perhaps more important than the word's denotation. Within Judaism, the noun κύριος frequently referred to God himself and was used to translate various forms of the divine name in the LXX.[48] Within wider Greco-Roman culture, various deities as well as the emperor were routinely referred to as κύριος. Thus the use of κύριος as an appellation for Jesus was both a critical step in theological reflection about his identity and nature and an implicit claim that someone other than a deity or the emperor was in charge (so also Martyn, 88). Applying this word to Jesus claimed for him both deity and worldly authority. These concepts do not become a central part of Paul's exposition in Galatians as they do elsewhere,[49] but they do form the background of his theological thought about Jesus's identity.

1:4 τοῦ δόντος ἑαυτὸν περὶ[50] τῶν ἁμαρτιῶν ἡμῶν. This phrase describes in a very compact way Jesus's willingness to sacrifice himself on the cross.[51] The prepositional phrase with περί indicates the object to which Jesus's act of self-sacrifice relates. The nature of that relation is not explicit (as it would be with ὑπέρ), so from this short phrase one cannot argue for a full-orbed concept like substitutionary atonement. However, Paul clearly intends to show that the positive action of Christ giving himself was done to offset the negative realities associated with sins, whatever those may be.[52] In light of the immediately following material, one could readily construe that his emphasis is not on substitution from the penalty of sin but rescue from its controlling power (so Martyn, 90–91; *contra* Burton, 12).[53] By focusing on Christ's self-directed death, Paul conveys concisely the entire situation of the Galatian churches and their relation to the Law: "No other satisfactions can lawfully be brought into comparison with that sacrifice of himself which Christ offered to the Father; that in Christ, therefore, and in him alone, atonement for sin, and perfect righteousness, must be sought" (Calvin, 26). When Christ's death is properly in view, nothing else can crowd the picture.

---

47. Often this usage was weakened to a simple sign of deference or respect, like the English honorific "sir."

48. The divine name יהוה is translated by the noun κύριος in the LXX 6,126 out of 6,828 times that it occurs.

49. See, e.g., Col 2:15.

50. For rationale on preferring περί over ὑπέρ as the original reading here, see the Textual Notes.

51. See 1 Tim 2:6 and Titus 2:14 for similar expressions.

52. Some Jewish texts saw martyrdom and self-sacrifice as spiritually efficacious; see, e.g., 2 Macc 7:37–38; 4 Macc 6:28–29; 17:21–22.

53. See also V. P. Furnish, " 'He Gave Himself [Was Given] Up ...': Paul's Use of a Christological Assertion," in *The Future of Christology: Essays in Honor of Leander E. Keck*, ed. A. J. Malherbe and W. A. Meeks (Minneapolis: Fortress, 1993), 109–10, 113.

The word ἁμαρτία can refer generally to failure, fault, or error without any spiritual connotation,[54] but the meaning of guilt or sin with regard to divine standards is quite common in the NT.[55] Both meanings are attested frequently in extrabiblical and biblical Greek. With this term in Gal 1:4 Paul refers to the acts of humankind that violate God's standards of holiness and behavior. The context provides no clarification for what sins might be in view. Likely Paul has nothing specific in mind, but one cannot help but suggest that the Galatians' defection from the gospel that Paul preached is a possible referent. For the second time in the letter opening, Paul uses the gen. pronoun ἡμῶν to indicate possession. As before, this is an "inclusive we," designed to create an emotional connection between Paul and the Galatians. They have each benefitted from Christ's selfless giving of himself on the cross, and consequently the Galatians should carefully hear Paul's message to them.

ὅπως ἐξέληται ἡμᾶς. After mentioning Jesus's crucifixion for sin, Paul now expresses the purpose of this self-giving act. Paul has already stated that Christ gave himself on the cross "for our sins," but Christ also had an eschatological purpose that this clause elucidates. The verb ἐξαιρέω (here in the aor. subjunctive form ἐξέληται) has a variety of meanings that amount to logical variations depending upon the voice. In the classical period the varied meanings of "take out," "remove," "get rid of," "destroy," and "deliver" were all common; they are found as well in the LXX and Koine period.[56] The use of ἐξαιρέω in Gal 1:4 is the only Pauline use. Some of the other NT uses have the meaning of "take out" or "remove." Matthew uses the word to refer to the graphic, literal removal of an important body part as part of a hyperbolic argument.[57] Other NT uses focus upon the connotation of rescue: Acts 7:10, 34; 12:11; 23:37; 26:17 are similar to Gal 1:4 in that they all refer to deliverance from real peril in some concrete way. That sense of urgency and peril is certainly present here. Humanity is in danger in this present evil age, but Christ's death for sin was accomplished so that we might be rescued out of it.

ἐκ τοῦ αἰῶνος τοῦ ἐνεστῶτος πονηροῦ. Paul here identifies that from which people are separated in the act of rescue: "the present evil age," or "the evil age [currently] present."[58] This brings into focus Paul's eschatology, which provides important structure to his theology. Like many Jews, Paul regarded history as divided into two grand epochs: the present age and the age to

---

54. LSJ, 77; MGS, 103.

55. BDAG, 50–51.

56. LSJ, 581; MGS, 710; LEH, 1:156.

57. Matt 5:29; 18:9.

58. Elsewhere in the NT, when two modifiers occur and both appear to be in second attributive position, usually the second is predicate; see John 5:30; 8:16; 1 Tim 5:25; Rev 4:7. Rev 14:10 appears to be a true grammatical parallel, but that text is difficult for other reasons, not the least of which is untangling how the nine genitives in a row should be grouped.

come.[59] The present age is marred by evil in every facet of existence. In the age to come God will rule completely, and his righteousness and holiness will be the norm. The cataclysmic event that divides the two ages is understood variously within Jewish sources, but within Pauline thought this event is clearly the death and resurrection of Jesus. The past historical fact of the passion coupled with the future, full arrival of the age to come creates an overlapping, intermediate time often characterized with the paradoxical phrase "already/not yet." Through Christ's death and resurrection some of the eschatological blessings are already experienced by believers presently in their relationship to God and within the church, but the full and final consummation of these blessings still remains in the future.[60] Paul's mention of believers' rescue from this present evil age reflects this dynamic. The death of Christ for sin is the basis for all blessings that the believer receives; some of these blessings are active now, while others will be active in the future.

κατὰ τὸ θέλημα τοῦ θεοῦ καὶ πατρὸς ἡμῶν. The prep. *κατά* often indicates the norm or standard by which an action is done, but here the idea is deeper than that, extending as well into cause.[61] God's will was not just the standard by which Christ acted; it was also the motivating cause. God's will governed Christ's own intentions; they shared a unity of purpose. The repetition of the pronoun *ἡμῶν* with *πατρός* reemphasizes the familial tone that Paul struck in v. 3 within the greeting proper. This phrase denotes at the same time God's gracious concern for humanity as shown in his will and Christ's complete obedience and unity to that will in his attitude.

1:5 *ᾧ ἡ δόξα εἰς τοὺς αἰῶνας τῶν αἰώνων, ἀμήν*. Paul regularly includes doxologies in his letters (see Rom 11:36; 16:27; Eph 3:21; Phil 4:20; 1 Tim 1:17; 2 Tim 4:18), but rarely in the openings. His inclusion of one here is a natural, emotional response to the truth that he just finished describing, namely, that the gracious will of God motivated Christ's rescue of believers. It also provides a solemn note akin to a liturgical pause. Given the strong tone of the letter that is about to commence, Paul seeks to strike an appropriate note to close the opening and move to the body of the letter. God is the ultimate recipient of all glory from those whom Christ redeems. The glorification of God is certainly meant to be a present reality, but the eschatological note struck here is noticeable and profound: God receives praise now and forever! The final word of the doxology is *ἀμήν*, a word of strong affirmation. It is simply a transliteration of the Hebrew word אָמֵן, which is used with the

---

59. See H. Sasse, "*αἰών*," *TDNT*, 1:206–7, for discussion on the use of this term in Jewish apocalyptic literature.
60. For a helpful overview of this topic, see L. J. Kreitzer, "Eschatology," in Hawthorne, Martin, and Reid, *Dictionary of Paul and His Letters*, 253–69.
61. See BDAG, 512–13.

exact same force.[62] By ending the letter opening with this doxology, Paul invites the Galatians to affirm with him the efficacy and centrality of Christ's redemptive work. Thus he lays the groundwork for a proper response to the body of the letter.

When thinking about the letter to the Galatians as a whole, one may regard the introduction as out of place because it does not mention the central concerns of Paul's argument. He does not mention his opponents. He does not discuss the Law. He does not mention the implication of his gospel for Gentiles. He instead focuses on the self-sacrifice of Jesus Christ on the cross for sins and the eschatological redemption of believers. Far from being out of place, however, these realities ground Paul's theology and his practical, pastoral concerns. Christ has died to rescue all believers. This is what Paul has proclaimed in his gospel and the truth to which he desires the Galatians to return.

Theological Comments

Although the letter opening usually serves the simple, practical purpose of identifying the sender and recipient, Paul develops it to make bold theological assertions about God, Jesus Christ his Son, and his own role in God's divine plan. At the very beginning of the opening, Paul identifies himself as an apostle (1:1), which implies that his ministry, which the Galatians had experienced before in person and now in literary presence, was not of his own initiative. Paul makes this explicit by describing his ministry as sourced in and enabled by both Christ and God. Thus we should understand Paul's ministry not simply as apostleship, but more exactly as sent, commissioned, ordained apostleship under the authority of God and Christ.

Paul quickly moves beyond his own role as an apostle to the contours of God's divine plan, according to which Paul had the privilege of announcing the gospel. By being the apostle to the Gentiles, Paul helps bring God's plan to fruition. In a concise way Paul describes God's action in Christ with its spiritual, eschatological effects: Jesus gave himself on the cross as a sacrifice for sin so that he could rescue believers out of the present evil age in preparation for the eschatological renewal promised in the OT. Christ's was "an unfolding drama decisive for human destiny" (Williams, 36), "an apocalyptic rescue operation" (Hays, 202). All this was done in keeping with God's will, for which God deserves to be praised forever.[63]

It is important to note that Paul avoids an anthropocentric starting point for his epistle. Rather, he starts with a Christocentric focus. Certainly humanity is affected by what Christ has done—objectively in that Christ rescues believers from the old age, subjectively in that believers are no longer

62. Cf. BDAG, 53. See, for example, its frequent use in Deut 27:15–26.

63. See the similar review of theological themes by deSilva, 112.

under the power of the present evil age but freed to live in a new manner of life (Fung, 41–42). But nothing about humanity answers the problem that occasioned the epistle. Paul finds his answer to the Galatian problem solely in Christ and the redemptive work God accomplished through him.

Application and Devotional Implications

Applying Paul's letter openings challenge us for a number of reasons. Normally at this point Paul does not include any explicit exhortation as he does at later points in his letters, so there are no commands that could naturally form a foundation for application. Also, in the letter openings Paul does not present his ideas fully fleshed out. They are usually in seminal form, which makes an explicit application difficult. Add to this that many of his letter openings are similar, and the process of application becomes muddled and indistinct.

Applying the particular letter opening of Gal 1:1–5 is challenging as well because of a central assertion Paul makes at the very beginning: He is an apostle with direct, divine ordination and calling (1:1). This was a particular role that he and only a few others had within the early church.[64] It would be natural for the present-day reader to make an analogy for application between Paul's role as apostle and the modern role of pastors, elders, deacons, and other leaders and offices within the contemporary church, but this fails because the authority present church leaders exercise is both an order of magnitude less than that which Paul exercised and entirely derivative, valid only when it works in concert with and submission to the authoritative revelation of the biblical text. Indeed, asserting that present pastoral authority is absolute, on the same level as Paul's authority, generally leads to abuse and problems in the local church.

The way forward is found in the function of the letter opening form. Paul sought to connect with his readers in such a way that they were predisposed to hear his message and respond positively. He accomplished this through an explanation of his apostolic role and God's grand plan, of which he was a part. His expansion upon the normal greeting form amounted to a call to worship (Martyn, 87). Thus Paul desired to prepare for the reception of his message through explanation of key theological truths and an invitation to worship God together in community, albeit a geographically distanced one. As contemporary readers of his letter, we are in the same position as the Galatians were originally. The application of this letter opening resonates with the same notes of understanding and preparedness. What is our understanding of Paul's role in the early church? We must acknowledge the divine

64. As a Protestant I do not see apostolic succession as present within the church today. This is in obvious contrast to the Roman Catholic Church, which sees apostolic succession as current and ultimately expressed in the office of the Pope. See §§77, 857 of the Catechism of the Catholic Church.

origin of his apostleship and the authority he exercised in writing Galatians. Are we open to the message he proclaimed and willing to change our beliefs, attitudes, and actions as directed? Just as the Galatians needed to be ready for correction in beliefs and behaviors, we need the same readiness, especially as it relates to the centrality of Christ's redemptive work.[65] Do we see Paul's proclamation of the gospel to the Galatians as part of God's divine plan for the ages? Often we look through lenses that allow us to see only our small slice of history; in response to this letter opening, we need to realize that God is at work in this present age through the proclamation of the gospel to bring the age to come. Do words of worship come to our lips as easily as they did for Paul? When we understand what God is doing on a grand scale, we should quickly respond with worship and praise.

Additional Exegetical Comments

1:1 Because of the strong words and tone Paul uses to highlight the nature of his apostleship, many commentators argue that Paul's purpose in writing Galatians was to defend his apostleship against attackers (so, e.g., Hays, 202, but compare his discussion on Paul's reasons for writing on pp. 184–87). This is a possible way to construe Paul's purpose, but it overemphasizes the letter beginning at the expense of the clear focus upon the gospel in the letter body. Paul's emphasis upon his apostolic *role* here serves to prefigure his emphasis upon his apostolic *message*: "He proclaims the divine origin of his apostleship in order to establish the divine origin of the Torah-free gospel that he preaches among the Gentiles. … In other words, the emphasis upon Paul's apostleship has the rhetorical function of grounding the Torah-free gospel in God and Jesus rather than of defending Paul from the attacks of opponents" (Matera, 41). This is not to deny that attacks upon Paul were present or that here Paul does compose a rebuttal against those who would minimize his apostleship. Rather, it simply argues that Paul focuses his attention elsewhere in the main argument of the letter.

Selected Bibliography

Adams, S. A. "Paul's Letter Opening and Greek Epistolography: A Matter of Relationship." In *Paul and the Ancient Letter Form*, ed. S. E. Porter and S. A. Adams, 33–55. Leiden: Brill, 2010.

65. An important aspect of this application is Paul's focus upon the congregations in Galatia. It was not a question of the security of their individual salvation, but rather one of their state as a church and their collective advocacy of the true gospel. "None of God's elect will ever utterly or finally fall away, and the gates of hell certainly will never prevail against the church of Jesus Christ. But there is no such thing as 'eternal security' for a local congregation that has lost its first love" (George, 84). As a church turns away from the true gospel, it will as a body lose the health that the gospel provides.

Burer, M. H. *Divine Sabbath Work*. BBRSup 5. Winona Lake, IN: Eisenbrauns, 2012.

Ciampa, R. E., and B. S. Rosner. *The First Letter to the Corinthians*. PNTC. Grand Rapids: Eerdmans, 2010.

Edwards, M. J., ed. *Galatians, Ephesians, Philippians*. ACCSNT 8. Downers Grove, IL: InterVarsity, 2005.

Exler, F. X. J. *The Form of the Ancient Greek Letter of the Epistolary Papyri (3rd c. B.C.–3rd c. A.D.): Study in Greek Epistolography*. 1923. Repr. Chicago: Ares, 1976.

Harrison, J. R. *Paul's Language of Grace in Its Graeco-Roman Context*. WUNT 2.172. Tübingen: Mohr Siebeck, 2003.

Hedrick, C. W. "Paul's Conversion/Call: A Comparative Analysis of the Three Reports in Acts." *JBL* 100 (1981): 415–32.

Hoehner, H. W. *Ephesians: An Exegetical Commentary*. Grand Rapids: Baker, 2002.

Hurtado, L. W. "Lord." In *Dictionary of Paul and His Letters*, ed. G. F. Hawthorne, R. P. Martin, and D. G. Reed, 560–69. Downers Grove, IL: InterVarsity, 1993.

Kreitzer, L. J. "Eschatology." In *Dictionary of Paul and His Letters*, ed. G. F. Hawthorne, R. P. Martin, and D. G. Reed, 253–69. Downers Grove, IL: InterVarsity, 1993.

Stirewalt, M. L. Jr. *Paul, the Letter Writer*. Grand Rapids: Eerdmans, 2003.

Thiselton, A. C. *The First Epistle to the Corinthians*. NIGTC. Grand Rapids: Eerdmans, 2000.

Tite, P. L. "How to Begin, and Why? Diverse Functions of the Pauline Prescript with a Greco-Roman Context." In *Paul and the Ancient Letter Form*, ed. Stanley E. Porter and Sean A. Adams, 57–99. Leiden: Brill, 2010.

Excursus: The Meaning of ἀπόστολος

During the classical period, ἀπόστολος did not normally carry the meaning that is common in the NT; it was primarily used in naval or commercial contexts to refer to ships sent out for different purposes.[66] The meaning of "envoy" or "messenger" was not unheard of; it simply was rare.[67] In the LXX the only occurrence of ἀπόστολος is in 3 Kgdms 14:6 in the text of Codex Alexandrinus. Here Ahijah speaks as a divine messenger to the wife of Jeroboam when she inquires about the fate of her son: ἐγώ εἰμι ἀπόστολος πρός σε σκληρός. Here ἀπόστολος is a messenger from God in a very strict sense,

66. In this instance the word was accented as ἀποστόλος; see LSJ, 220.

67. A clear example of this meaning is found in Herodotus 1.21: ὁ μὲν δὴ ἀπόστολος ἐς τὴν Μίλητον ἦν, "So the envoy went to Miletus." For text and translation, see Herodotus, *The Persian Wars*, vol.1, *Books 1–2*, trans. A. D. Godley, LCL 117 (Cambridge, MA: Harvard University Press, 1920), 22–25.

which is a subset of the use found in the NT.[68] Even so, the usage prior to the NT lacks the full sense that *ἀπόστολος* developed.

Within the NT the term carries both the denotation of messenger, that is, one sent out for a particular task, and the connotation of status and authority granted to the messenger by the sender. The latter is sometimes completely eclipsed (John 13:16) or muted (Luke 11:49; Acts 14:4), but very often it is in full force. The notion of status would be paramount in the uses of *ἀπόστολος* in the Gospels (Matt 10:2//Mark 3:14//Luke 6:13) and Acts 1–2, as well as in all the occurrences within the Pauline writings. This sense of authority and status does not come from Greek usage of the term, but rather from the Hebrew concept of שָׁלִיחַ that undergirds it. The שָׁלִיחַ was a legal proxy, authorized to perform a binding action on behalf of another. As Rengstorf describes, this authority was absolute:

> The Rabbis summed up this basis of the שָׁלִיחַ in the frequently quoted statement: שְׁלוּחוֹ שֶׁל אָדָם כְּמוֹתוֹ, "the one sent by a man is as the man himself" (Bet., 5, 5), i.e., the שָׁלִיחַ is as good as the שֹׁלֵחַ in all that he says and does in execution of his commission. Thus one may become betrothed through a שָׁלִיחַ (Kid., 2, 1; T. Kid., 4, 2; T. Yeb., 4, 4). In such a case the one commissioned validly performs all the ceremonies in place of the bridegroom concerned. Similarly there may be a valid execution of the ceremonial of divorce through a commissioned representative; the powers of the latter are so extensive that the divorce accomplished or initiated by him cannot be reversed by the husband (Git., 4, 1). Mutatis mutandis the same is true of any legal transaction (e.g., a purchase, T. Yeb., 4, 4, or the killing of the Passover lamb by a slave, Pes., 8, 2 etc.).[69]

It is this sense of legal authorization that most strongly influences the Pauline usage of the term. When calling himself an *ἀπόστολος*, Paul certainly does intend to convey the fact that he was entrusted with a message for delivery to the universal church (Burton, 2). More than this, though, with the term he refers to himself as one granted authority to act on behalf of the one who sent him. This sense of authorization is especially important in the context of Galatians as a whole, which exhibits an intense struggle between Paul and the opponents concerning his status as an apostle and the nature of the gospel he proclaimed. This legal background does not explain the entire semantic range of the term or the whole reality of the permanent role Paul and others had as apostles (Longenecker, 3), but it elucidates an important nuance of Paul's apostolic commission sometimes overlooked.[70]

---

68. For further discussion of this text, see K. H. Rengstorf, "ἀπόστολος," *TDNT*, 1:413–14.

69. Rengstorf, "ἀπόστολος," *TDNT*, 1:415.

70. Martyn, 93, argues that the development of the Jewish concept was later than the development of the Christian concept but they may share common roots in the servants sent by kings of Israel to accomplish specific tasks.

Excursus: The Pre-Pauline Formula of Galatians 1:4

In Galatians 1:4 there is evidence that Paul cites preexisting material, more specifically, a theological formula that originated in the Jewish Christian community that explained the theological import of Christ's death. The exact extent of the preexisting material is not entirely clear, but most scholars agree that Paul is using something in Gal 1:4 not original to himself.

The clearest evidence for pre-Pauline material is in Gal 1:4a. In describing Christ's death, Paul writes τοῦ δόντος ἑαυτόν ("who gave himself"). More commonly Paul uses some form of παραδίδωμι with the reflexive pronoun (see Rom 4:25; 8:32; 1 Cor 11:23; Gal 2:20; Eph 5:2), although δίδωμι plus the reflexive pronoun is not unheard of (see 1 Tim 2:6; Titus 2:14). Paul also writes that Christ gave himself περὶ τῶν ἁμαρτιῶν ("for sins").[71] This phrasing is out of character with Paul's other writing in two ways: Paul prefers to speak of "sin" in the sg. (using the pl. twelve times but the sg. fifty-two times), and he more often uses a personal pronoun to describe the beneficiaries of Christ's death (see, e.g., Rom 5:8). Add to this the parallel with 1 Cor 15:3 ("Christ died for our sins according to the Scriptures"), which Paul himself states is received tradition, and there is a good case that when Paul writes "who gave himself for our sins" he is using preexisting material. There are other arguments for seeing even more of this verse as preexisting material, but these points are the strongest.[72] In addition to these linguistic factors, there is a strong conceptual connection to Jesus's own statement about the value of his death in Mark 10:45 and the further connection of that Jesus saying to the fourth Servant Song in Isaiah 53. Very likely these connections were made prior to Paul, as there is considerable evidence that the early church saw Jesus's ministry in light of Isaiah 53.[73] Paul simply used an expression here in his writing of Galatians that showcased those prior connections.

---

71. I accept the reading περί instead of ὑπέρ; see Textual Notes for discussion.

72. A key work that discusses this passage at length is F. Bovon, "Une formule prépaulinienne dans l'Épître aux Galates (Ga 1:4–5)," in *Mélanges offerts à Marcel Simon: Paganisme, Judaïsme, Christianisme: Influences et affrontements dans le monde antique,* ed. A. Benoit, M. Philonenko, and C. Vogel (Paris: Éditions E. de Boccard, 1978), 91–107. Bovon argues that the entirety of Galatians 1:4–5 is pre-Pauline. I am not convinced except for Galatians 1:4a, but Bovon's arguments are weighty and worth considering. Other commentators also see preexisting material beyond 1:4a, including Longenecker, 7; Cousar, 23; Bruce, 75.

73. There is some debate about how these connections were made. Many, such as Betz, 42, argue that Jewish martyrdom theology enabled the early church to make the connection. A better argument in my view is the one made by R. E. Ciampa, *The Presence and Function of Scripture in Galatians 1 and 2*, WUNT 2.102 (Tübingen: Mohr Siebeck, 1998), 57–59. He argues that Jewish martyrdom theology and early Christian theological reflection on the death of Christ were parallel hermeneutical streams that both drew from Isa 53. For a recent treatment of this topic, see D. L.

It is one thing to state that Paul used a theological formula here. It is quite another to flesh out the import of this linguistic, conceptual, historical analysis. There are three important conclusions worth considering in this context. On the basis that Paul wrote Galatians as one of the earliest of his epistles, this pre-Pauline formula would be evidence that the Christian community from the earliest times saw Christ's death as atoning for sin in some capacity. Jesus died in AD 33. Within fifteen or so years after his death, Christians were preaching and teaching the self-directed, sacrificial death of Jesus. It would be difficult to defend a full statement of the doctrine of substitutionary atonement from this one passage, but what this passage proclaims is certainly a constituent part of that doctrine. In other words, the death of Christ as atonement for sin was part of the earliest doctrine of the Christian church.

The presence of pre-Pauline material here and elsewhere in his epistles shows that Paul was not a maverick. On the contrary, he was in touch with and in continuity with other Christians, passing along the central teachings he had learned. This strengthens his arguments and shows that it is his opponents who were on the fringe, not him, when it came to understanding the Christian faith.[74]

This pre-Pauline formula is critical given the depth of conflict Paul describes in Galatians. This conflict was justified because his opponents were in some aspect turning away from this central teaching about the sacrificial nature of Christ's death. Paul cites this formula here to force his opponents to acknowledge that their disagreement was not over peripheral matters. Rather, it was a central disagreement over the value and effect of Christ's death, and Paul had the earliest Christian theological reflection on his side. Indeed, Paul's interpretation of this tradition in the balance of v. 4 as rescue from sin's power in this present evil age mirrors his later argument that to fall back under the power of the law is tantamount to going back into slavery.[75]

Bock and M. Glaser, eds., *The Gospel According to Isaiah 53: Encountering the Suffering Servant in Jewish and Christian Theology* (Grand Rapids: Kregel, 2012).

74. This is true even if the pre-Pauline material is found only in 1:4a, as I would argue. The fact that Paul immediately reinterprets Christ's death as eschatological causes some to argue that the formula was foreign to Paul (so Martyn, 90), but this is an overstatement. Paul's construction advances the understanding of Christ's death but should not be understood as a rejection of its fundamental assertion that his death was also expiatory (so Hays, 203).

75. Furnish, " 'He Gave Himself,' " 113.

The Problem of a Different Gospel (1:6–10)

Textual Notes

1:6 The reading ἐν χάριτι Χριστοῦ ("by the grace of Christ") shows multiplied variation in the manuscripts. The presence of Χριστοῦ alone following ἐν χάριτι is the best candidate for the original reading, but the variants are theologically interesting. Two readings appear to be expansions of shorter readings and as such can be readily dismissed based on preference for the shorter reading. The reading ἐν χάριτι Ἰησοῦ Χριστοῦ occurs in D 326 1241^{s} *pc* sy^{h**}; this variant is minimally attested and very likely a scribal expansion of the shorter reading ἐν χάριτι Χριστοῦ. In addition, the reading θεοῦ in 327 *pc* and Theodoret of Cyrrhus is also minimally attested and would appear to be a scribal expansion of the shorter reading ἐν χάριτι, likely in harmony with Paul's numerous statements elsewhere that connect grace to God. One variant that has a decent chance of being original is the shortest reading: the simple reading ἐν χάριτι in 𝔓^{46vid} F* G H^{vid} ar b and some church fathers. This reading is exegetically equivalent to the reading ἐν χάριτι θεοῦ; if no name were present, most likely θεοῦ would be implied. This reading fails, though, on the weakness of its external evidence, supported by only part of the Western text.[1] The reading of NA^{28} has strong support from Alexandrian and Byzantine manuscripts. It is also the harder reading, not conforming to Pauline style. Thus ἐν χάριτι Χριστοῦ should be judged as original on both internal and external evidence.

1:9 The reading εὐαγγελίζηται ὑμῖν of the NA^{28} text, which I accept as original, reflects two text-critical problems. The first is the spelling of the verb; the second is the presence of the pronoun. The verb is alternately spelled εὐαγγελίσηται, supported by א A 81 104 326 1241^{s} b d g; εὐαγγελίζεται, supported by K P 0278 365 614 1505 1881 and roughly half of the Byzantine text; and εὐαγγελίζηται, supported by 𝔓^{51vid} B D F G H L Ψ 6 33 630 945 1175 1739^{*vid} 2464 vg ar and roughly half of the Byzantine text. Based on external evidence, εὐαγγελίζηται should be preferred because of the wider geographic

1. See B. M. Metzger, *A Textual Commentary on the Greek New Testament* (New York: United Bible Societies, 1994), 520.

distribution of the reading. The reading εὐαγγελίζεται is the hardest reading, but it borders on being too hard, given that the third class condition most normally takes the subjunctive. There is not much difference in meaning between the other two options; one might expect the aor. subjunctive here, given the gravity of the utterance, but on that reasoning then the pres. subjunctive could be preferred as the harder reading. Given all considerations, the reading εὐαγγελίζηται is preferred.

The problem of the pronoun is difficult because its position in the clause varies. It is omitted only by ℵ* F G Ψ b g ar; this evidence is not weighty enough to give the omission much consideration as original. The pronoun precedes the verb in 𝔓[51vid] B H 630 1179 1739[*vid]; as with the omission, this evidence is too slim to give this reading much credence. Thus external evidence favors the inclusion of the pronoun after the verb. Internally the pronoun is favored on the grounds that Paul would have preferred a particular statement here instead of a general one; scribes might have been motivated to remove the pronoun to make the statement more universal. Although not without its problems, the presence of the pronoun after the verb is the reading more likely to be original, so the reading of the NA[28] text should be accepted. The brackets in NA[28] indicate that solving this problem is quite difficult.

Translation

6 I am astounded because[2] you are so quickly deserting[3] the one who called
you by the grace of Christ to a different gospel **7** (which is not really another),
if there were not those who disturb you and want to alter the gospel of
Christ.[4] **8** But even if we or an angel from heaven should preach to you
differently from what we preached to you,[5] that one must be condemned
to destruction![6] **9** As we have said before, even now I say again: If anyone

2. Most translations take the ὅτι clause as content, while I take it as causal. Compare, e.g., "I am astonished that you are so quickly deserting ..." (NET).
3. I chose this word to bring out the negative nuance of μετατίθημι. Compare the less nuanced phrase "turning away" (CSB, NKJV, NLT).
4. This translation brings out the rhetorical function of the εἰ clause to highlight the presence of the opponents and thus cast blame upon them, the position I adopt in the commentary.
5. The force of the relative clauses in vv. 8 and 9, each of which acts as a noun clause, is difficult to bring out in English. Another valid translation option would be "something other than what we preached to you." Most translations specify the referent by adding the word "gospel," e.g., "But even if we ... should preach a gospel contrary to the one we preached to you" (NET).
6. The phrase ἀνάθεμα ἔστω is translated variously: "let him be condemned to hell!" (NET); "a curse be on him!" (CSB; similarly ESV, NRSV, NKJV); "let them be under God's curse!" (NIV, similarly NLT).

preaches differently from what you received, that one must be condemned to destruction! **10** Now do I try to persuade people or God? Or do I seek to please people? If I were still pleasing people, I would not be Christ's slave.

Commentary

To those familiar with the Pauline correspondence as a whole, Gal 1:6–10 shocks with its abrupt and harsh tone. Readers are much more accustomed to prayer and thanksgiving at this point in Paul's letters. This paragraph—an anti-thanksgiving of sorts—indicates that something is very wrong between Paul and the Galatians. A valid observation on its face, this inference is mitigated by two factors, one related to the letter form generally and one related to Paul specifically.

Concerning the introductory thanksgiving in the letter form, current scholarship does not regard this to be as fixed as once thought. As Arzt-Grabner explains,

> A thanksgiving is a well-known convention of ancient Greek epistolography, but it was not used as a mere formula that could be expressed every time independently from the actual situation of the letter writer and the recipient. It is used often when a letter writer has received good news about the well-being of her or his recipient.[7]

In light of the fact that Paul had not received good news about the Galatians—indeed, he had received quite the opposite—a thanksgiving in this epistle would have been entirely out of place. Another approach relative to the epistolary form views Paul's thanksgivings as a variation of the very common health wish, the lack of which here would in fact be notable.[8] One important consideration is that Galatians was likely the first of Paul's letters; if so, then he would not have developed his thanksgiving form, so to speak.[9] As far as we know, the Galatians had no prior correspondence with Paul that would

---

7. P. Arzt-Grabner, "Paul's Letter Thanksgiving," in *Paul and the Ancient Letter Form,* ed. S. E. Porter and S. A. Adams, Pauline Studies 6 (Leiden: Brill, 2010), 157. Arzt-Grabner's general assertion is further affirmed by R. E. Van Voorst, "Why Is There No Thanksgiving Period in Galatians? An Assessment of an Exegetical Commonplace," *JBL* 129 (2010): 153–72.

8. D. W. Pao, "Gospel Within the Constraints of an Epistolary Form: Pauline Introductory Thanksgivings and Paul's Theology of Thanksgiving," in Porter and Adams, *Paul and the Ancient Letter Form,* 115.

9. E. R. Richards, *Paul and First-Century Letter Writing: Secretaries, Composition, and Collection* (Downers Grove: InterVarsity, 2004), 132; Pao, "Epistolary Form," 115. *Contra* Dunn, 39, who argues that Paul set his pattern with his first letter, 1 Thessalonians. Either way, Galatians was written early, so speaking of any pattern set by this point should be taken with a grain of salt.

have included a thanksgiving.[10] Regardless of the epistolary convention that frames Paul's thoughts here, the content is enough to shock the reader into stunned attention as Paul begins his letter body by getting to the point of the matter. In this way, even though this is not a thanksgiving, this section serves a similar function as the Pauline thanksgiving by signaling the major theme of the letter (Matera, 107), and it does so with a tone that indicates urgency and gravity.[11] The Galatians have turned away from the gospel that they believed, which Paul had preached to them. With this rebuke Paul defends his gospel, chastising the Galatians with the intention of renewing their commitment to what they had originally received, and he highlights in bold relief the false gospel that was tempting them away (Martyn, 107).

1:6 Discerning exactly what Paul means to communicate in vv. 6–7 is a difficult task as the language is ambiguous and the interpretive theories numerous. I have been convinced by the work of Troy W. Martin,[12] who has ably elucidated and strengthened the earlier arguments of Heinrich A. Schott and Cornelius Lapide,[13] that here Paul is using the idiom of θαυμάζω with εἰ μή to shift the blame from the Galatians to his opponents. Contrary to most commentators, the essential force of εἰ μή is not that of an exception to the preceding relative clause. Rather, each particle functions normally, the εἰ introducing the protasis of a condition and the μή negating the protasis. Thus Paul expressed surprise at the Galatians if there were no opponents preaching differently than he did. Clearly there are opponents present, so the apodosis remains unfulfilled. The function of the clause works rhetorically to shift blame, which was a common tactic within judicial rhetoric. Paul condemns what the Galatians have done but at the same time places the blame squarely on the shoulders of his opponents.[14] Paul will resume this blame explicitly in 6:11–18.

Θαυμάζω ὅτι. Paul begins the letter body with a statement of amazement. Ancient letter writers drew from well-known, stereotyped expressions to make their arguments; this is just such an expression.[15] The verb θαυμάζω could indicate positive or negative feelings depending upon the context.[16] Here Paul expresses feelings that would be decidedly negative in light of

---

10. Van Voorst, "Why Is There No Thanksgiving," 161.

11. Richards, *Paul and First-Century Letter Writing*, 132–33.

12. T. W. Martin, "The Syntax of Surprise, Irony, or Shifting of Blame in Gal 1:6–7," *BR* 54 (2009): 79–98.

13. H. A. Schott, *Epistolae Pauli ad Thessalonicenses et Galatas* (Leipzig: Joannis Ambrosii Barthii, 1834); C. A. Lapide, *In Epistolas Divi Pauli*, Commentaria in Scripturam Sacram 18 (Paris: L. Vivès, 1876).

14. Luther, 46, 50, essentially argues for this sense in his exposition.

15. See E. R. Richards, *The Secretary in the Letters of Paul*, WUNT 2.42 (Tübingen: Mohr Siebeck, 1991), 204–5, for one such list of expressions.

16. BDAG, 444.

what follows. This is an aggressive beginning to the letter body, meant to get the readers' attention and begin the process of motivating their repentance and renewal. The ὅτι clause does not express the content that amazed Paul, but rather the reason he is astonished. Given the stylized nature of the θαυμάζω expression in ancient Greek letters, with which the Galatians likely would have been familiar in some way, the rebuke here is likely not expressing intense surprise as much as it expresses "disappointment and reproach" with a goal of changing the behavior of the recipients (Williams, 38).

οὕτως ταχέως. There are two possible meanings for this phrase: It either refers to the speed with which an action itself is done, without reference to any other action, or to the brief interval after which one action takes place with reference to another.[17] If Paul intends the former, he is amazed because the Galatians so rapidly and speedily turned from the gospel once they began that action; it was not a long, slow, arduous, pained defection. If Paul intends the latter, he is amazed because in such a short time after they accepted his gospel, they turned away from it. The language is vague enough that a decision on this matter is quite difficult. I am persuaded by a parallel in Diodorus Siculus that the quickness of the action is in view, not the brevity of the interval. In the aftermath of the Syracusan War, Syracuse had taken many Athenians captive and then held a debate to determine their fate. The citizens initially called for death to the generals and slavery for the others, but a man named Nicolaus gave a speech and persuaded the crowd to more moderate action. Then a man named Gylippus gave a second speech. He proposed severe action against the captives and ultimately carried the day. He began his speech thusly:

> θαυμάζω μεγάλως, ἄνδρες Συρακόσιοι, θεωρῶν ὑμᾶς οὕτως ταχέως, περὶ ὧν ἔργῳ κακῶς πεπόνθατε, περὶ τούτων τῷ λόγῳ μεταδιδασκομένους
>
> I am greatly surprised, men of Syracuse, to see that you so quickly, on a matter in which you have suffered grievously by deeds, are moved to change your minds by words.[18]

In this context the rapidity of the change in emotional state of the assembly is in view. Gylippus remarks about what has occurred in front of him, and the ptc. μεταδιδασκομένους emphasizes the citizens' change of mind. This is a strong linguistic and rhetorical parallel to Paul's statement, which lends credence to the view that οὕτως ταχέως refers to the speed of the action, not the brevity

---

17. The English phrase "so quickly," common in many translations (e.g., NET, NIV, NASB, ESV, NRSV), can similarly be understood in either sense.

18. *Bibliotheca historica* 13.28. Greek text and translation are from Diodorus Siculus, *Library of History*, vol. 5, *Books 12.41–13*, trans. C. H. Oldfather, LCL 384 (Cambridge, MA: Harvard University Press, 1950), 196–97.

of the interval.[19] Paul's amazement then would be due both to the fact that the Galatians turned from the gospel and the speed with which they turned.[20]

μετατίθεσθε. In Gal 1:6 Paul uses a word with highly negative connotations to describe the present action of the Galatian believers. The verb μετατίθημι can be neutral, simply meaning "to change, alter," either with reference to location (e.g., Gen 5:24; Deut 27:17; Acts 7:16; Heb 11:5) or something more intrinsic to the thing itself (e.g., Heb 7:12;[21] Jude 4). The midd. voice of this verb takes on a particular nuance of "change one's mind," and in a political or religious context the word's connotation can become negative.[22] Polybius relates the time Callicrates addressed the Roman senate to encourage action against those in Achaea who would not follow Rome's dictates:

> ἐὰν μὲν οὖν ὑπὸ τῆς συγκλήτου γίνηταί τις ἐπισημασία, ταχέως καὶ τοὺς πολιτευομένους μεταθέσθαι πρὸς τὴν Ῥωμαίων αἵρεσιν, καὶ τοὺς πολλοὺς τούτοις ἐπακολουθήσειν διὰ τὸν φόβον
>
> If the senate now gave some token of their disapproval the political leaders would soon go over to the side of Rome, and the populace would follow them out of fear.[23]

The context of political allegiance colors the use of μετατίθημι here and implies disloyalty to the home state and subservience to Rome. A philosophical context gives an even stronger connotation. See Diogenes Laertius, who discusses Dionysius's change of philosophical stance:

> Διονύσιος ὁ μεταθέμενος εἰς τὴν ἡδονήν: διὰ γὰρ σφοδρὰν ὀφθαλμίαν ὤκνησεν ἔτι λέγειν τὸν πόνον ἀδιάφορον
>
> Dionysius, who became a renegade to the doctrine of pleasure, for owing to the severity of his ophthalmia he had no longer the nerve to call pain a thing indifferent.[24]

---

19. Even so, I certainly appreciate the statement of Bruce, 80: "This expression does not afford any precise indication of the interval between the Galatians' conversion and Paul's reception of the disquieting news about them; he is emphasizing his astonishment, but the shorter the interval, the more pointed would his 'so soon' be."

20. The impf. verb ἐτρέχετε in 5:7 also supports this interpretation because it implies some duration to their prior, proper attitude toward Paul's gospel. A quick defection would be in contrast to that lengthier acceptance.

21. Note that the noun form μετάθεσις occurs in this passage as well as the verb.

22. A negative nuance is not required, however. Josephus, *Ant.* 20.38, uses the verb to describe the conversion of Izates to Judaism.

23. *Histories* 24.9.6. Greek text and translation are taken from Polybius, *The Histories*, vol. 5, *Books 16–27*, trans. W. R. Paton, LCL 160 (Cambridge, MA: Harvard University Press, 2012), 510–11.

24. *Lives of Eminent Philosophers* 7.37. Greek text and translation are taken from Diogenes Laertius, *Lives of Eminent Philosophers*, vol. 3, *Books 6–10*, trans. R. D. Hicks, LCL 185 (Cambridge, MA: Harvard University Press, 1925), 148–49.

In this context Dionysius has rejected his former stance of indifference to pain in light of the discomfort that his disease brought. A third example from 2 Macc 7:24 shows the negative sense that this verb takes on in a religious context. Here Antiochus Epiphanes is torturing seven Jewish brothers, encouraging them to reject their faith by eating pork. He takes a particular tack with the youngest:

> ἀλλὰ καὶ δι᾽ ὅρκων ἐπίστου ἅμα πλουτιεῖν καὶ μακαριστὸν ποιήσειν μεταθέμενον ἀπὸ τῶν πατρίων
>
> but [Antiochus] promised with oaths that he would make him rich and enviable if he would turn from the ways of his ancestors (NRSV)

In this context the verb could even be translated "apostatize," as Antiochus wanted the son to reject everything about Judaism; the verb μετατίθημι portrays that total rejection. Given this background, Paul's use of the verb in Gal 1:6 is striking in its severity. It is not as if the Galatians are simply making a different choice than Paul did, or that they are expressing their faith in a different yet equally legitimate way. Paul interprets their acceptance of the opponents' viewpoint as desertion from God, a change of allegiance, a rejection of what they had received. This word carries a strong condemnation, showing clearly that Paul in no way approves of their change of mind.

ἀπὸ τοῦ καλέσαντος ὑμᾶς ἐν χάριτι Χριστοῦ εἰς ἕτερον εὐαγγέλιον. Paul explains in theological terms what the Galatians' new allegiance means. The prepositions ἀπό and εἰς show respectively from whom and to what the Galatians are defecting. In a sense the latter defines the former, that is, desertion to a different gospel embodies a desertion from God who redeemed the Galatians in Christ. Paul uses the subst. ptc. τοῦ καλέσαντος to identify God, focusing on his action toward believers.[25] Paul often uses the verb καλέω and the related noun κλῆσις as technical terms to describe God's sovereign call for salvation.[26] Sometimes the words refer holistically to the entirety of the salvation experience, as here, but sometimes they refer to one aspect of it.[27] The words emphasize the unilateral nature of salvation: God calls, and

---

25. Because I accept the reading of the NA[28] text here with Χριστοῦ as the gen. modifier of χάριτι, the possibility that τοῦ καλέσαντος ὑμᾶς refers to Christ is rejected out of hand (*contra* Lenski, 34–35). It is possible to take the phrase τοῦ καλέσαντος ὑμᾶς ἐν χάριτι Χριστοῦ as "from Christ who called you in grace," but Paul's general use of καλέω for God in soteriological contexts is evidence against this view (Burton, 20). On the same grounds, Paul as the referent for this phrase can be excluded as well. See 1:15 for a near example where καλέω applies to God.

26. K. L. Schmidt, "καλέω," *TDNT*, 3:489; J. Eckert, "καλέω et al.," *EDNT*, 2:242.

27. This is evidenced within Galatians itself, as the four uses of καλέω each have a different nuance. In 1:6 the focus is on calling to salvation through the preaching of the gospel. In 1:15 Paul uses the word to describe his own calling to apostolic ministry. In 5:8 the pres. tense ptc. implies a present calling for the Galatians to turn back

humanity answers. God invites, and humanity responds. It speaks of God's initiative, power, and grace compared to humanity's inability and weakness. Paul uses the pronoun ὑμᾶς very particularly here to refer to the Galatians as the object of God's calling in this context. This is what makes their defection so astounding. Through Paul's prior preaching God had called the Galatians to himself, and now they were turning away from him in what amounted to a personal affront. After accepting the invitation for salvation, they were now refusing it.

The phrase ἐν χάριτι Χριστοῦ has two possible meanings. It could refer to the means by which God issued his divine call ("the one who called you by the grace of Christ"), or it could be the goal or intended result of the calling ("the one who called you to the grace of Christ").[28] The essential question is what force καλέω with ἐν has in this context. Elsewhere in the NT each meaning is clearly attested.[29] Because of the emphasis in the letter opening on the self-sacrifice of Christ in accordance with God's will, means is a better fit here. This phrase both explains the nature of God's calling—it was done by means of the gracious action of Christ's self-sacrifice[30]—and clarifies the dangerous situation in which the Galatians find themselves. The Galatians have not only turned away from God; they have also turned away from Christ, the only means of salvation.[31]

The phrase εἰς ἕτερον εὐαγγέλιον explains to what the Galatians have turned. The phrase itself is not difficult to understand. The word εὐαγγέλιον simply means "good news," and in the NT it refers to the good news about Jesus Christ, that is, the announcement that he has brought salvation

---

from their flirtation with the Law, that is, it is a call to repent. In 5:13 the emphasis is on the ethical, spiritual life as the goal of the calling.

28. J. Eckert, "καλέω et al.," *EDNT*, 2:243.

29. For goal see 1 Cor 7:15; Eph 4:4; Col 3:15; 1 Thess 4:7. For means see Matt 22:43; Rom 9:7; Heb 11:18; 1 Pet 5:10. Although the prep. immediately follows this verb in Matt 5:19, the prepositional phrase does not modify the verb in that passage. Fee, 23–24, argues for locative on the basis that Paul tends to use the simple dat. χάριτι to indicate means and that in the immediately following context Paul expresses agency with διά (καλέσας διὰ τῆς χάριτος αὐτοῦ in 1:15); thus ἐν χάριτι must be distinct in meaning here.

30. The absence of the article before χάριτι could make this word qualitative in force (so Burton, 21). The specific mention of Christ's self-sacrifice in the prior context argues against that view, as does the corollary to Apollonius' Canon developed by D.W. Hedges, "Apollonius' Canon and Anarthrous Constructions in Pauline Literature: An Hypothesis" (M.Div. Thesis, Grace Theological Seminary, 1983).

31. Paul elsewhere argues that Israel's election was in grace and extended to Gentiles by that same grace (Dunn, 41; see Rom 9:7–11, 24–26; 11:5–6). Thus this emphasis on grace subtly undercuts the theological arguments of Paul's opponents.

to humanity through his death and resurrection.[32] The adj. ἕτερος basically means "different," thus the Galatians have turned to "a different gospel," a different proclamation about Christ from that which Paul had preached and they had believed. The difficulty with this phrase is not its meaning, but rather its referent. Paul and his opponents shared some common ground: They both proclaimed Christ as the Messiah, the one who acted on God's behalf, who was the locus of Christian worship, and with whom believers had a living, active relationship. But Paul's opponents taught that the benefits of Christ must be accrued through proper obedience to the Law, while Paul's gospel proclaimed that the blessings of salvation were available through faith in Christ alone. On this key element Paul and his opponents differed, and Paul saw this as truly a "different gospel."

1:7 ὃ οὐκ ἔστιν ἄλλο. This short little phrase, meant by Paul to clarify in some sense his prior statement about the Galatians defecting "to a different gospel," does not readily yield its sense. There are essentially two issues in play: the lexical difference (if any) between ἕτερος and ἄλλος, and the actual difference in content between the gospels Paul and his opponents proclaimed.

As far as the meaning of the words is concerned, it is commonly argued that in classical Greek ἕτερος meant "another of a different kind" and ἄλλος meant "another of the same kind."[33] If this difference in meaning holds here, Paul would be essentially making a tautologous argument: "You are turning to a different gospel, which is not of the same kind." This distinction in meaning can be overstated even on the basis of classical usage, as ἕτερος regularly was used to identify other members of a group, or the second member of two things, which would naturally share a similar characteristic.[34] Even if this distinction is appropriate for the classical period, there is no guarantee that it held up during the Koine period, which saw many of the subtleties of classical Greek disappear.[35] It is entirely possible that here Paul intends no distinction between the meaning of ἕτερος and ἄλλος,[36] perhaps using both for stylistic variation while intending the more general meaning "another, different" for both. One helpful argument for sorting this out is the implication of how many entities are being compared with the terms. Paul appears to use ἕτερος with a dual meaning in that he compares two things together, while

32. Dunn, 41–42, argues that Paul's use of the term εὐαγγέλιον here means that his opponents in Galatia were Christian missionaries. For further discussion of the meaning of εὐαγγέλιον in the cultural context, see George, 93–94; Hays, 205; Garlington 2004, 67; Schreiner, 86.

33. See Schreiner, 86, for some helpful, compact information on this score.

34. See LSJ, 702; MGS, 833–34.

35. See D. B. Wallace, *Greek Grammar Beyond the Basics: An Exegetical Syntax of the New Testament* (Grand Rapids: Zondervan, 1996), 19–20, for a short list of syntactical differences between classical and Koine Greek.

36. See BDAG, 399.

ἄλλος has no such connotation and could refer to any number of entities in comparison (Moo, 86–87). "The difference in v. 6 and 7 is not 'different in kind' versus 'another of the same kind,' but 'a gospel in contrast to the true gospel' or 'a competing gospel' versus 'simply another' " (Moo, 87). On this basis the meaning of ἕτερος and ἄλλος would not be distinct in this passage. In the first phrase Paul would be making a clear distinction between his true gospel and the false gospel of his opponents based on their differences; in the second he would be emphasizing that the opponents' so-called gospel is not one among the possible iterations of the gospel based on its nature. This construal is attractive given the different expressions of the gospel Paul himself acknowledges are within apostolic bounds.[37] The central emphasis of Paul's statements here is that the opponents have crossed over that boundary into something that is distinct from, and indeed contrary to, his apostolic gospel. No matter the specific nuances of these terms, Paul's conclusion about the preaching of his opponents is clear: "It is clear from the sequel (vv. 8f) that in Paul's judgment any 'gospel' that differs fundamentally from the one which he preached to the Galatians is no gospel at all, and this verdict he immediately passes on the new doctrine which was claiming the allegiance of his Galatian converts" (Fung, 45).

εἰ μή τινές εἰσιν οἱ ταράσσοντες ὑμᾶς. The syntactical connection of this phrase to the preceding context is difficult to sort out. Usually this clause is understood to modify the relative clause which immediately precedes. The discourse function of the negation with exception is to empty totally a defined set with the negation, then with the exception to place back in the set the one item that fits, thus emphasizing it.[38] In Paul's discussion he has in mind a set of one unique entity, that is, the gospel. An individual's preaching is either in that set or out of it, either in accord with the gospel or not. Paul effectively points to an area of similarity with the negative statement but then discounts that with the exceptive clause. However, following Martin this would not be an exceptive clause but the protasis of a conditional clause.[39] Paul sets up the condition that would actualize his expressed surprise in v. 6. If Paul's opponents were not presently preaching to the Galatians, he would in fact be surprised at them. The opponents are indeed exercising present influence over the Galatians, however, so Paul is not surprised. "The θαυμάζω εἰ μή expression permits Paul to communicate his surprise at the Galatians' actions were it not for the presence of the agitators. This expression allows Paul to articulate his disapproval of the Galatians' actions while at the same time shifting the blame to the agitators and away from the Galatians."[40] Thus

37. See the subsequent discussion in 2:1–10 about his gospel to the Gentiles and Peter's to the circumcised.

38. S. E. Runge, *Discourse Grammar of the Greek New Testament: A Practical Introduction for Teaching and Exegesis* (Peabody, MA: Hendrickson, 2010), 83–84.

39. See again Martin, "Syntax of Surprise," 83–84.

40. Martin, "Syntax of Surprise," 89.

Paul is rhetorically and pastorally sensitive, seeking to bring the Galatians back into the fold while at the same time condemning those who have drawn them away by highlighting the dissimilarity of their preaching.

The content of the conditional clause focuses on the present action of the opponents that has a negative effect on the Galatians. His simple statement *τινές εἰσιν* on the face of it identifies these people as present in the midst of the Galatians,[41] which effectively acknowledges that the crisis is acute and Paul's task is difficult. The opponents are there and he is not, except in literary presence, and thus he must work carefully in his letter to mitigate their influence. Paul defines his opponents' gospel as negative because of the effect they have upon the Galatians. The verb *ταράσσω* means "to shake, stir"; applied to individuals it takes on the figurative meaning of "stir up, disturb, unsettle."[42] Paul's opponents were in the process of doing this action to the Galatians. The joyous confirmation in Christ the Galatians had experienced by believing in Paul's gospel had been unsettled by these opponents. This was enough to mark their gospel as heterodox. Lukan parallels to the use of this term (Luke 1:12; 24:37–38; Acts 15:24) show the severity of this emotional disturbance. "Paul is not identifying the Teachers as persons who confuse the Galatians. He is saying that they are frightening the Galatians out of their wits, intimidating them with the threat of damnation if they do not follow the path prescribed in the Teachers' message!" (Martyn, 112; see also de Boer, 42–43).[43]

καὶ θέλοντες μεταστρέψαι τὸ εὐαγγέλιον τοῦ Χριστοῦ. This second phrase completes the protasis of the conditional clause, offering the second description of Paul's opponents that shows how their gospel is heterodox because of what they desire to accomplish with it. The transitive uses of the word *μεταστέφω* all orbit around the idea of "turning around." The figurative meaning of the term is "to change, alter" something, often into the opposite,[44] which fits well the other occurrence of the term in the NT.[45] Paul intends a negative connotation, such as "distort, pervert, turn into the opposite." The presence of the article with *εὐαγγέλιον* is anaphoric, referring back to the prior

41. The use of this vague phrase could be a way to minimize the importance of these individuals (Williams, 39; Fung, 45), but it is more likely that Paul simply did not know them personally (see de Boer, 42, for discussion).

42. BDAG, 990–91.

43. Interestingly we will see that Paul turns the tables on this threat.

44. BDAG, 641.

45. In Acts 2:20, which quotes Joel 2:31, heavenly bodies will be altered: *ὁ ἥλιος μεταστραφήσεται εἰς σκότος καὶ ἡ σελήνη εἰς αἷμα*, "the sun will be changed into darkness and the moon into blood." In this instance the meaning is neutral, reflecting phenomenological language.

anarthrous mention of εὐαγγέλιον in v. 6.[46] Paul first states that the Galatians are turning to a "different gospel," then he decries those who desire to alter "the gospel of Christ." The anaphoric article ties these two occurrences of "gospel" together. Any alteration of the gospel of Christ is a different gospel.

Paul claims here that the individuals in view are in fact preaching a different gospel. They are disturbing the Galatians, provoking them to move from the sure foundation Paul laid for them in his proclamation. They desire to alter the gospel the Galatians had received. Paul seeks not to alienate the Galatians but instead to call them to account and bring them back to his proclamation while at the same time condemning those who now preach to them.

1:8 *ἀλλὰ καὶ ἐὰν ἡμεῖς ἢ ἄγγελος ἐξ οὐρανοῦ εὐαγγελίζηται ὑμῖν.* In this verse and the next Paul severely condemns anyone who preaches differently than he did. His tone is strong and unyielding; he brooks no dissent. The key grammatical structure in this verse is the third class condition marked by *ἐάν* with the subjunctive, which is strengthened by the ascensive *καί*: "But even if we or an angel from heaven should preach to you ..." The protasis of this condition is entirely hypothetical and unlikely of fulfillment,[47] but that in fact strengthens the severity of its condemnation: If these hypothetical preachers are condemned, then the real ones causing trouble in Galatia are most certainly condemned.

Paul identifies himself and *οἱ σὺν ἐμοὶ πάντες ἀδελφοί* (Gal 1:2) as the first set of hypothetical preachers with the pronoun *ἡμεῖς*. It is possible that the pronoun here is an example of the "editorial we," but that is unlikely given that Paul identifies his associates in the letter opening.[48] Here they join him in the condemnation, amplifying its force. Paul then mentions another hypothetical preacher, *ἄγγελος ἐξ οὐρανοῦ*, "an angel from heaven." Angels were common figures in Jewish apocalyptic who offered authoritative interpretation of divine revelation.[49] Paul mentions angels later in his argument (3:19; 4:14) with the same connotation of their interpretive function as mediators of revelation from God.[50] Paul wants this hypothetical protasis to border on the impossible: There is no way he would change the gospel that he preached to the Galatians, nor would an angel from heaven sent from God himself preach in conflict with Paul's divinely sanctioned message. But

---

46. For discussion on the anaphoric use of the article, see Wallace, *Greek Grammar*, 217–20; A. T. Robertson, *A Grammar of the Greek New Testament in the Light of Historical Research* (Nashville: Broadman, 1934), 762.

47. See Wallace, *Greek Grammar*, 696–97, for the range of meanings for the third class condition.

48. *Contra* Wallace, *Greek Grammar*, 396.

49. J. J. Collins, "Introduction: Toward the Morphology of a Genre," in *Semeia 14: Apocalypse: The Morphology of a Genre* (Missoula, MT: SBL, 1979), 6.

50. Paul uses this connotation in 2 Cor 11:14 for entirely negative effect.

even though this would never happen, if these individuals did in fact preach differently, despite their past history or divine nature and function, they would be condemned.[51]

παρ' ὃ εὐηγγελισάμεθα ὑμῖν. Paul's concern is not that someone would preach again to the Galatians. Rather, his concern is the veracity of their content. This clause highlights the differences from what the Galatians had previously heard through Paul's own preaching. The prep. παρά carries the meaning of "that which does not correspond to what is expected."[52] The translation "different from" or "other than" (so NIV) brings out this nuance. Many English translations use the word "contrary to" for this idea (so NET, CSB, ESV, NRSV, and others), but this is too strong a wording that actually ends up diluting Paul's idea. The danger in what the opponents were preaching was not in its bold contrast from what Paul preached but in its subtle difference. By emphasizing any difference at all, no matter how small, Paul actually speaks more emphatically. The content of Paul's past preaching in Galatia is the plumb line. Anyone who deviates from that in any way falls under this condemnation.

ἀνάθεμα ἔστω. The word ἀνάθεμα and its cognate ἀνάθημα are noun forms of ἀνατίθημι, which can mean "to set up as a votive gift, dedicate."[53] These two nouns generally refer to something that has been devoted to a deity. This dedication can be positive, like a gift or offering, or negative, in that the object is cursed, given over to the deity, and destined for judgment. The use of these words in the NT is greatly informed by their use in the LXX. The form ἀνάθημα occurs five times in the LXX, three times with the positive meaning of "votive offering, gift" (Jdt 16:19; 2 Macc 9:16; 3 Macc 3:17) and twice with the negative meaning "thing devoted to destruction, accursed" (both in Deut 7:26). The cognate ἀνάθεμα occurs twenty-one times in the LXX; most of these uses are negative, referring to something dedicated to God for judgment. In every instance where there is an underlying Hebrew text extant the words ἀνάθεμα and ἀνάθημα translate the Hebrew term חֵרֶם which is practically identical in meaning to the Greek term.[54] The Hebrew word refers to the "ban," when an object or person was dedicated to God for destruction and thus banned from normal use or contact by the people of

51. D. F. Tolmie, "Angels as Arguments? The Rhetorical Function of References to Angels in the Main Letters of Paul," *HTS Teologiese Studies/Theological Studies* 67 (2011): 2, argues that the reference to an angel here has two additional functions: With it Paul emphasizes how sure he is about the correctness of his views, and in a subtle way he affirms himself by putting himself in good company: "He thereby implies that he himself and such an angel would act in a similar way, thus suggesting that, like the angel, he is obedient to God."

52. BDAG, 758.

53. LSJ, 123; MGS, 157.

54. See C. Brekelmans, "חֵרֶם," *TLOT*, 474–77, for a helpful overview of the Hebrew term.

Israel. For example, in Deut 7:16–26 the Israelites are commanded to utterly destroy the people resident in the land, as well as every vestige of idolatry. The concluding verse drives home the consecration of these items to divine wrath by using this Hebrew term. Similarly Joshua 6–7 capitalizes on this negative nuance with the destruction of Jericho and the subsequent sin of Achan.

The meaning of *ἀνάθεμα* in Gal 1:8–9 is very similar to that found in the LXX: Paul is dedicating to God those who preach another gospel for the purpose of destruction. The NET brings this nuance out well: "let him be condemned to hell!" (so also God's Word Translation, Good News Translation).[55] The NET translator's note offers a helpful explanation: "The translation gives the outcome which is implied by this dreadful curse." In this context the word is not ecclesiological but rather soteriological and eschatological, referring to juridicial destruction.[56] That Paul curses with a concept straight from the Law, which his opponents purport to espouse, is a rhetorically powerful move on his part; it effectively turns the tables on his opponents, using their own adherence to the Law against them. If the Galatians did not understand the OT context of the curse, the opponents would have been forced to explain it to them (de Boer, 46–47).[57]

1:9 *ὡς προειρήκαμεν, καὶ ἄρτι πάλιν λέγω.* With this clause Paul focuses attention on what he is about to say because of the differences between vv. 8 and 9. As argued above, the third class condition in v. 8 is entirely hypothetical because of the nature of the specified actors. In contrast, the first class

---

55. C. Jordan, *The Cotton Patch Version of Paul's Epistles* (New York: Association, 1968), 94, has a particularly colorful paraphrase of this passage: "Now get this straight: Even if we or an angel fresh out of heaven preaches to you any other message than the one we preached to you—to hell with him!"

56. *Contra* Betz, 54. See J. Behm, "*ἀνάθεμα* et al.," *TDNT*, 1:354. Lenski, 40–41, says, "The later ecclesiastical 'anathema' found in the Decrees of the Council of Trent is the continuation of 'accursed.' It is not known whether anathema was used in excommunication from the synagogue. Any late ecclesiastical use of this word sheds no light on our passage. Paul is not acting as a human court nor is he calling on the Galatian churches to act as a court by pronouncing an anathema. An angel would not be subject to a human court. The view that Paul is exercising the right of excommunication is not substantiated but answered by 1 Cor. 5:3–5. Paul had no such right, did not pretend to have it." Williams, 40–41, does not use the term excommunication, but he makes an argument that sounds similar: The function of the curse was to place the Galatians in the place of ancient Israel relative to those who were cursed. Just as Israel was responsible to remove from their midst those things and people that were under the ban, the Galatians were now responsible to remove from their midst those preachers whom Paul had placed under this curse.

57. For an extremely helpful analysis that recognizes the full power of Paul's curse, see K. A. Morland, *The Rhetoric of Curse in Galatians: Paul Confronts Another Gospel*, Emory Studies in Early Christianity (Atlanta: Scholars, 1995).

condition in v. 9 is immediately applicable to the Galatians. The phrase ὡς προειρήκαμεν points back to what Paul just said in v. 8 (so also Bruce, 84). The phrase καὶ ἄρτι πάλιν λέγω looks forward to what Paul is about to say in v. 9. Paul does not want his readers to miss what he is about to say, so he sets it up with a weighty introduction.

εἴ τις ὑμᾶς εὐαγγελίζεται παρ' ὃ παρελάβετε, ἀνάθεμα ἔστω. In this restatement of his curse, Paul uses a first class condition instead of another third class condition. The first class condition generally means "assumed true for the sake of argument" but often takes on a more particular force depending upon the context.[58] Paul knows that certain individuals are in fact preaching something other than what the Galatians received from him. This condition then, even though formally first class, takes on a stronger nuance than "assumed true." It serves as sure juridicial condemnation upon these preachers while guiding the Galatians through an emotional process designed to return them to Paul's side. The condition here on the one hand condemns Paul's opponents, and on the other subtly enjoins repentance from the Galatians.

Two details of the protasis combine to make this statement generally true but also presently applicable to the Galatians' situation. Instead of "we" or "an angel from heaven" Paul uses the indefinite pronoun τις and the pres. indic. εὐαγγελίζεται. Anyone at that moment preaching to the Galatians, encouraging them to turn away from Paul's gospel, falls under this condemnation. The noun clause παρ' ὃ παρελάβετε is structurally similar to the noun clause in v. 8. The verb παραλαμβάνω evokes the connotation of passing on received tradition that is foundational to the life of the church.[59] This verb brings an air of solemnity to Paul's statement and invokes his own role as an apostle in the passing along of received teaching.

It is a truism in literature studies that repetition denotes importance, and that is certainly the case here. There can be no doubt Paul intends his repeated curse in vv. 8–9 to be taken with utmost seriousness. With this curse Paul warns the Galatians about the danger of following those who preach differently than he did, but he also condemns his opponents, who may have even been present in the congregation when the letter was read. It would be hard to imagine a more effective opening salvo in the battle with the opponents Paul now undertakes.

1:10 Ἄρτι γὰρ ἀνθρώπους πείθω ἢ τὸν θεόν; Here Paul offers a rhetorical question to explain the severity of his curse. The condemnation Paul has just handed down is so harsh, and the influence among the Galatians of those whom Paul has condemned so strong, that Paul seeks immediately to justify himself to protect against any pushback on the part of the Galatians. So the persuasion and pleasing to which Paul refers in this verse are his immediately prior statements in vv. 6–9. The heart of the question comes with the

58. Wallace, *Greek Grammar*, 690–94.

59. BDAG, 768. See also the well-known use in 1 Cor 15:3.

wording ἀνθρώπους πείθω ἢ τὸν θεόν, and the implied answer is not as clear as one might think. The force of this, the first of two questions, hinges on the meaning of the verb πείθω and whether Paul intends his two rhetorical questions to be parallel. The verb πείθω in context could mean either "persuade" or "please."[60] The former meaning would make the two questions different because it accords well with the dir. obj. ἀνθρώπους but not the dir. obj. τὸν θεόν. The latter meaning would make the two rhetorical questions parallel because it makes good sense with both dir. objs. The key exegetical conundrum is the meaning of πείθω with τὸν θεόν as a dir. obj. This construction does not occur elsewhere in the NT or the LXX,[61] but it does occur twice in Josephus, passages that shed some good light on what Paul says here. In the first passage, Josephus, *Ant.* 4.123, relates part of what Balaam said to Balak when he tried to curse the Israelites. He describes why he will set up altars and make sacrifices:

> εἰ πεῖσαι τὸν θεὸν δυνηθείην ἐπιτρέψαι μοι τοὺς ἀνθρώπους ἀραῖς ἐνδῆσαι
>
> if perchance I may persuade God to suffer me to bind these people under a curse.[62]

In this context the meaning "persuade" is quite appropriate. To Balaam it is an open question whether God will respond to his request, so he seeks to persuade him with sacrifices. In the second passage, Josephus, *Ant.* 8.255, relates the siege of Jerusalem by Shishak. Rehoboam and the people sought God's help to no avail:

> καὶ τὸν θεὸν ἱκετευόντων δοῦναι νίκην καὶ σωτηρίαν, ἀλλ' οὐκ ἔπεισαν τὸν θεὸν ταχθῆναι μετ' αὐτῶν
>
> Although [they] entreated God to grant them victory and deliverance, they did not prevail upon God to side with them.[63]

As with the prior passage, "persuade" is perfectly appropriate here; that meaning fits the context of what the inhabitants of Jerusalem were trying

60. BDAG, 791. For the latter BDAG also gives the gloss "win over," but this strikes me as essentially the same as "persuade."

61. Matthew 27:43 reads πέποιθεν ἐπὶ τὸν θεόν, which has the pf. tense, not the pres., and the prep. ἐπί, not the simple acc. case. This wording is different enough structurally that I do not consider it parallel. The LXX occurrences (2 Chr 16:7; Isa 10:20) are similar to the Matthew passage, using the pf. tense plus prep.

62. Greek text and translation taken from Josephus, *Jewish Antiquities*, vol. 2, *Books 4–6*, trans. H. S. J. Thackeray and R. Marcus, LCL 490 (Cambridge, MA: Harvard University Press, 1930), 60–61.

63. Greek text and translation taken from Josephus, *Jewish Antiquities*, vol. 3, *Books 7–8*, trans. R. Marcus, LCL 281 (Cambridge, MA: Harvard University Press, 1934), 354–55.

to do. These parallels inform the meaning of πείθω in Gal 1:10. Paul likely intends the meaning "persuade": "Now am I trying to persuade people or God?" The answer to the choice he poses is the former option; Paul is trying to persuade people, very specifically the Galatians. Paul would have no need to persuade God, as he is already on Paul's side in this issue. This is contrary to an implied charge of Paul's opponents,[64] who likely argued that they were more in keeping with God's revelation than Paul was. Thus the two rhetorical questions are not parallel. They each emphasize a different aspect of Paul's stance and respond to different implied questions. With this first question, Paul focuses upon his act of persuasion and the intended result.

ἢ ζητῶ ἀνθρώποις ἀρέσκειν; With this question Paul moves to a different topic, from his actions to his motivations. The verb *ζητῶ* is progressive in force, referencing again what Paul had just said, and it makes the whole statement conative. The verb *ἀρέσκω* roughly means "to please," and depending upon the context this could be positive or negative.[65] Paul uses the term both ways, even with people as the obj. For example, Paul admonishes believers in Rom 15:2, using this verb in a positive sense: *ἕκαστος ἡμῶν τῷ πλησίον ἀρεσκέτω εἰς τὸ ἀγαθὸν πρὸς οἰκοδομήν*, "Let each of us please his neighbor for his good to build him up." But then in 1 Thess 2:4 Paul argues that he undertakes his ministry of the gospel to please God, not men: *ἀλλὰ καθὼς δεδοκιμάσμεθα ὑπὸ τοῦ θεοῦ πιστευθῆναι τὸ εὐαγγέλιον, οὕτως λαλοῦμεν, οὐχ ὡς ἀνθρώποις ἀρέσκοντες, ἀλλὰ θεῷ τῷ δοκιμάζοντι τὰς καρδίας ἡμῶν*, "but just as we have been approved by God to be entrusted with the gospel, so we declare it, not to please people but God, who examines our hearts." This latter verse is a close conceptual parallel to Gal 1:10, as it shows the same attitude which Paul adopts relative to his ministry as an apostle. The answer to this rhetorical question then is clearly "No!" Paul seeks to please God, not humanity, and whenever the two are in conflict, God wins out in Paul's affections and intentions.

εἰ ἔτι ἀνθρώποις ἤρεσκον, Χριστοῦ δοῦλος οὐκ ἂν ἤμην. With this second class condition Paul offers the logical proof for the implied answer to the previous rhetorical question, namely, that he does not seek to please people. As a contrary-to-fact condition, it remains entirely unfulfilled. Even so, it draws a logical conclusion important to the argument, ultimately affirming the negation of the protasis. The subtext of Paul's argument runs thusly:

> If I were seeking to please people,
> I would not be a servant of Christ.

---

64. R. Bultmann, "πείθω," *TDNT*, 6:2. See also A. Feuillet, "Chercher à persuader Dieu (Ga 1:10a): Le début de l'Épitre aux Galates et la scène matthéenne de Césarée de Philippe," *NovT* 12 (1970): 350–60, who argues that Paul uses πείθω to mean "persuade" here but with the intention of being absurd.

65. BDAG, 129–30.

[Obviously I am a servant of Christ,
so you can conclude that I am not seeking to please people.][66]

Paul uses the phrase Χριστοῦ δοῦλος as the conceptual equivalent of ἀπόστολος. Paul refers to his apostolic call, already affirmed at the beginning of the epistle, as proof that he seeks to please God and not people.[67] Thus there is an *inclusio* between v. 1 and v. 10 to close the opening of the letter body, joining it tightly to the letter opening itself.

With this paragraph Paul quickly and sharply highlights the central issue of the letter. The Galatians are turning from the gospel that Paul had preached to them. He desires to renew their fidelity to the gospel he preached because it manifested the grace of Christ to the Galatians. The other gospel preached by his opponents is proven false because of its bad effects upon the Galatians and the desire of those preachers to pervert what Paul proclaimed. The curse Paul pronounces upon anyone who preaches differently than he did comes down squarely upon the opponents who were presently preaching to the Galatians. Paul defends these strong statements with an analysis of his own actions and motives, that is, he should be trusted because he seeks to persuade the Galatians to return to the gospel he preached and to please God alone as an apostle of Jesus Christ.

Theological Comments

The central theological point of this paragraph is the reality and singularity of the gospel that Paul preached. His perplexity that the Galatians had turned from it was not born simply out of their capriciousness, as if he were surprised that they had gone from one vehement opinion to its opposite with a rapid about-face. Instead, his amazement arose from the reality that they were leaving behind. Their original response of faith to Paul's gospel had brought them into contact with the Creator God who had called the Galatians to himself. They had truly benefited from Christ's grace because they had been proleptically rescued from this present evil age (1:4). In their defection they were turning away from the only salvation available to them, back to the evil age from which Christ had saved them (Matera, 49). The Galatians were leaving behind something real—the revelation of God and Christ in the gospel—and turning instead to something patently false, hence Paul's rebuke and warning to them. In tandem with his concern for the Galatians is his approach to his opponents. Paul did not suffer any competitors to his

66. M. Winger, "Unreal Conditions in the Letters of Paul," *JBL* 105 (1986): 110–12, argues that the full form of the second class condition here—secondary tenses of the indic. plus ἄν in the apodosis—is actually unusual in Paul and a sign of intense emotion.

67. Betz, 54–56, argues that the statements in this verse refer to negative connotations of rhetorical persuasion, which Paul rejects.

gospel. He did not allow any alternate views about the sufficiency of Christ's self-sacrifice. His approach to the gospel was exclusive to the extreme, and preachers who proclaimed any measure of difference were condemned. Thus the exclusivity of the gospel is front and center, as well as Paul's pastoral care and fierce protection with respect to it.

A theological sub-point is also important to note here. Paul's attitude in this paragraph is intensely personal. He does not condemn false preaching *per se*, but rather those people who preach a false gospel.[68] This strikes contemporary readers as very harsh, but condemnations of this sort have biblical roots. Note well Jesus's preaching in Matt 7:15–16a: "Watch out for false prophets, who come to you in sheep's clothing but inwardly are voracious wolves. You will recognize them by their fruit." Paul strikes with clarity a similar note in Gal 1:7, when he focuses upon the distress among the Galatians caused by his opponents. Instead of confirming the Galatians in their relationship with the one who called them, as Paul's preaching did, these preachers were disturbing them and shaking their foundations. On that basis alone, these individuals should be condemned.

To speak in contemporary theological categories, Paul's emphasis here is soteriology, not Christology. He does not argue with the Galatians or his opponents based upon their understanding of the nature of Christ. Likely they all proclaimed that Christ was the Messiah! The problem arose when they added to the gospel by insisting that observing the Law was necessary to be saved (Schreiner, 90; so also George, 95). Paul's theological conclusion was clear: Even if the nature of Christ is proclaimed correctly, any addition of works or personal achievement to his self-sacrifice on the cross renders that message a non-gospel, and those who add such things are subject to a curse.

Application and Devotional Implications

In Titus 1:9 Paul writes about qualifications for an elder in the church: "He must hold firmly to the faithful message as it has been taught, so that he will be able to give exhortation in such healthy teaching and correct those who speak against it." This verse expresses in the abstract exactly what Paul was seeking to accomplish concretely in his epistle to the Galatians. The "faithful message" of Titus 1:9 is the gospel that Paul had proclaimed to the Galatians. The Galatians were not holding to it firmly, and thus with his stern rebuke Paul sought to bring them back to fidelity. His opponents had erred in their understanding of the gospel and were tangibly altering it, and thus with his curse against those who preach differently Paul sought to correct them. At the center of this emotional exchange was Paul's commitment to the gospel,

68. This of course does not mean that doctrinal fidelity is not important. It simply emphasizes that believers must not only correct false teaching on an academic level, but they also must personally rebuke those who espouse it.

the good news about the self-sacrifice of Christ that frees humanity from the dominion of sin and rescues us from this present evil age.

Three entailments to this ardent devotion to the gospel present themselves for consideration. First, devotion to the gospel creates doctrinal fidelity. Paul differed with his opponents on the nature of the gospel and its requirements upon the Galatians. He preached the sufficiency of Christ, while they preached Christ applied through adherence to the Law. This difference was doctrinal, and Paul refused to admit any variance in the gospel that he proclaimed. In the same way we need to adhere faithfully to the preached word of Christ crucified, the only sufficient means for salvation. Second, devotion to the gospel fosters pastoral care. Paul's pain was not just that the Galatians had turned from the gospel but what that lack of fidelity led to with regard to their spiritual state. He cared deeply for these believers and wanted them to experience fully the joy of their salvation. When they turned away from the gospel and experienced distress, Paul felt it. Thus he was motivated to care for them as a pastor, to bring them back to the fold with all the means available to him. Third, devotion to the gospel also requires a public defense. Paul was not afraid to take on his opponents. In fact, he had to do so in order to remain true to his own convictions and calling. Our contemporary society does not appreciate principled believers; it regularly seeks to vacate their influence under the mantra of tolerance. But when it came to the gospel Paul was not tolerant, nor was he afraid to create conflict over it. Neither should believers be tolerant or afraid when the gospel is at stake. "The message of Galatians is that there is only one gospel—and that we as God's people are responsible both to proclaim and live out the ethical implications of that gospel as a clarion call to a lost world that remains subject to the wrath of God" (Rapa, 567).[69]

In addition, we must carefully evaluate ourselves to ensure that we are on the right side of Paul's gospel. After our initial acceptance of God's gracious gift of salvation in Christ, it is undeniably easy to creep over to the side of Paul's opponents by adding behavioral requirements to gospel acceptance. It is alarmingly easy to look down on other believers who do not behave as we do, forgetting that we are all saved by grace. But we would be remiss if we did not take to heart the reality that we are all subject to error in this regard:

> This kind of reflection more likely puts us as readers on the less presumptuous side of things in this passage. ... Here is the place to learn the humility that will keep me from standing on the wrong side of vv. 6–9; here is the constant reminder that I am a sinner, saved by the grace of him who gave himself for our sins, which

69. Luther, 47, with characteristic color, states it this way: "Similarly, parents, when their child is bitten by a dog, will chase the dog but sympathize with and comfort the child."

means not only forgiveness in the present, but the final rescue of us from this present evil age. (Fee, 28)

Additional Exegetical Comments

1:7 It is possible that with the verb *ταράσσω* Paul intends to refer to 1 Chr 2:7 where Achan[70] is called "the troubler of Israel" (so Longenecker, 16). On the one hand the possibility of the allusion is strengthened by the reference in 1 Chr 2:7 to the חֵרֶם. This would fit the conceptual framework of the curses that Paul utters in the following context. On the other hand the linguistic connection is not strong, as the Hebrew verb עכר used in 1 Chr 2:7 is nowhere translated in the LXX by *ταράσσω*. If this is an allusion, it is entirely conceptual, not linguistic.

1:8 Neyrey argues on the basis of social-scientific research that Gal 1:8 constitutes a "witchcraft allegation" and that the "angel from heaven" here "should be unmasked as a deceiving 'angel of light,' i.e., as Satan in disguise."[71] His discussion of the social-scientific research is illuminating, but his attempts to apply it to Galatians appear overdrawn. His specific argument about 1:8 simply does not fit the context: Paul joins himself to the "angel from heaven," and the hypothetical nature of the condition is entirely lost if this angel is in fact Satanic.

1:8–9 Witherington, 79–80, arguing on the basis of the rhetorical classification of this paragraph as an *exordium*, points to the curses as one of Paul's strategies to establish his authority before his audience: "he is a figure of power, one who can pronounce an anathema." Regardless of the rhetorical classification, the basic assertion of this as a function of the curses is likely correct, although not at the expense of the central doctrinal issues in play. De Boer, 45, takes a different tack, arguing that the curses are meant to undermine the authority of Paul's opponents.

1:10 Feuillet argues for several points of correspondence between Gal 1–2 and the Matthean version of Peter's confession of Christ at Caesarea Philippi (Matt 16:13–23).[72] With these allusions, Paul would be implicitly contrasting himself with Peter, who in following his own convictions was wrong then and now: "When Paul declaired that he did not seek to please men, he implicitly

---

70. The MT here has the spelling Achar (עָכָר) instead of Achan (עָכָן), but this is likely an intentional change to create assonance with the verb עוֹכֵר that follows. The reading עָכָן does have support in a few manuscripts.

71. J. H. Neyrey, "Bewitched in Galatia: Paul and Cultural Anthropology," *CBQ* 50 (1988): 72–100. He makes a similar categorization of "witchcraft accusation" in Gal 3:1, which is more plausible there than here.

72. Feuillet, "Chercher à persuader Dieu," 350–60.

opposed Peter, who, at Antioch, acted against his own convictions so that he would not displease Jewish Christians."[73]

1:10 Hunn argues that v. 10 is paradigmatic for understanding Paul's subsequent argument.[74] Paul seeks not to defend his gospel or his apostolate but rather his singular desire to please God instead of people. Hers is a convincing argument that makes good sense of the flow of Gal 1–2, but I believe the clearer evidence is for a dual purpose of defending both gospel and apostleship, the latter in service to the former.

Selected Bibliography

Arzt-Grabner, P. "Paul's Letter Thanksgiving." In *Paul and the Ancient Letter Form*, ed. S. E. Porter and S. A. Adams, 129–58. Pauline Studies 6. Leiden: Brill, 2010.

Collins, J. J. "Introduction: Towards the Morphology of a Genre." In *Semeia 14: Apocalypse: The Morphology of a Genre*, 1–20. Missoula, MT: SBL, 1979.

Diodorus Siculus. *Library of History. Vol. 5, Books 12.41–13*. Trans. C. H. Oldfather. LCL 384. Cambridge, MA: Harvard University Press, 1950.

Diogenes Laertius. *Lives of Eminent Philosophers. Vol. 2, Books 6–10*. Trans. R. D. Hicks. LCL 185. Cambridge, MA: Harvard University Press, 1925.

Feuillet, A. "Chercher à persuader Dieu (Ga 1:10a): Le début de l'Épitre aux Galates et la scène matthéenne de Césarée de Philippe." *NovT* 12 (1970): 350–60.

Hedges, D. W. "Apollonius' Canon and Anarthrous Constructions in Pauline Literature: An Hypothesis." M.Div. Thesis, Grace Theological Seminary, 1983.

Hunn, D. "Pleasing God or Pleasing People? Defending the Gospel in Galatians 1–2." *Bib* 91 (2010): 24–49.

Jordan, C. *The Cotton Patch Version of Paul's Epistles*. New York: Association, 1968.

Josephus. *Jewish Antiquities. Vol. 2, Books 4–6*. Trans. H. St. J. Thackeray, and R. Marcus. LCL 490. Cambridge, MA: Harvard University Press, 1930.

———. *Jewish Antiquities. Vol. 3, Books 7–8*. Trans. R. Marcus. LCL 281. Cambridge, MA: Harvard University Press, 1934.

Lapide, C. A. *In Epistolas Divi Pauli*. Commentaria in Scripturam Sacram 18. Paris: L. Vivès, 1876.

---

73. "quand Paul déclare ne pas chercher à plaire aux hommes, il s'oppose implicitement à Pierre, qui, à Antioche, était allé dans sa conduite à l'encontre de ses propres convictions, afin de ne pas déplaire aux judéo-chrétiens." Feuillet, "Chercher à persuader Dieu," 360.

74. D. Hunn, "Pleasing God or Pleasing People? Defending the Gospel in Galatians 1–2," *Bib* 91 (2010): 24–49.

Martin, T. W. "The Syntax of Surprise, Irony, or Shifting of Blame in Gal 1:6–7." *BR* 54 (2009): 79–98.

Morland, K. A. *The Rhetoric of Curse in Galatians: Paul Confronts Another Gospel.* Emory Studies in Early Christianity Atlanta: Scholars, 1995.

Pao, D. W. "Gospel Within the Constraints of an Epistolary Form: Pauline Introductory Thanksgivings and Paul's Theology of Thanksgiving." In *Paul and the Ancient Letter Form*, ed. S. E. Porter and S. A. Adams, 101–27. Leiden: Brill, 2010.

Polybius. *The Histories. Vol. 5, Books 16–27.* Trans. W. R. Paton. LCL 160. Cambridge, MA: Harvard University Press, 2012.

Richards, E. R. *Paul and First-Century Letter Writing: Secretaries, Composition, and Collection*. Downers Grove: InterVarsity, 2004.

———. *The Secretary in the Letters of Paul.* WUNT 2.42. Tübingen: Mohr Siebeck, 1991.

Schott, H. A. *Epistolae Pauli ad Thessalonicenses et Galatas*. Leipzig: Joannis Ambrosii Barthii, 1834.

Tolmie, D. F. "Angels as Arguments? The Rhetorical Function of References to Angels in the Main Letters of Paul." *HTS Teologiese Studies/Theological Studies* 67 (2011).

Van Voorst, R. E. "Why Is There No Thanksgiving Period in Galatians? An Assessment of an Exegetical Commonplace." *JBL* 129 (2010): 153–72.

Excursus: The Connection of Galatians 1:10 to its Context

The first major structural issue in the book of Galatians concerns the placement of 1:10. It could be connected to what precedes, creating a paragraph out of 1:6–10 (so among others NET, Schreiner, Longenecker), or it could be connected with what follows, creating a paragraph out of 1:6–9 (so among others NA[28], ESV). This ambiguity arises because of lexemes and logic. In the NA[28] text both 1:10 and 1:11 have γάρ as the conj., which can indicate a variety of logical connections. Consequently the reader cannot easily tell on the face of it how Paul intends this passage to be divided.

The textual variant concerning the coordinating conj. in 1:11 bears testimony to the ambiguous sense of the logical flow of the passage. NA[28] accepts γάρ as original, while οὖν and δέ are listed as variant readings. I follow the reading of NA[28] here, but it is not hard to see why the other conjunctions entered the manuscript tradition, as they both clarify the logical connections more than γάρ does. Hand in hand with the ambiguity of γάρ is the content of v. 10 itself, which does not decisively connect with what precedes or what follows. In vv. 8–9 Paul has just pronounced a withering curse upon any who would preach a different gospel than the one he preached. Paul's argument in v. 10 shows that his desire is to please God, proven by his present ministry as an apostle. This assessment of who Paul seeks to please could very naturally follow from this condemnation, offering a clarification of Paul's intent underlying the curse, namely, to please God by preserving the content and character of the gospel. But this assessment in v. 10 could also very naturally lead into what follows in v. 11, where Paul begins a discussion of the divine nature of the gospel he received: Paul preaches this divine gospel because his most central desire is to please God through his ministry as an apostle. Thus the logic of the argument in v. 10 fits very well either as a conclusion to what came before or as an introduction to what follows.

On the basis of text criticism and logic it appears there is an impasse, but there are three additional pieces of evidence that sway me to place v. 10 with what precedes instead of what follows. First, in v. 10 Paul describes himself as a "servant of Christ." Given the preceding context, this is functionally equivalent to calling himself an apostle. Thus between v. 1 and v. 10 there is an *inclusio*: Paul begins and ends this introductory section with reference to his role as an apostle. Second, in v. 11 Paul begins the verse with a strongly transitional statement: "For I want you to know ..." Other places where Paul uses this formula exhibit the force of a transition, although not disconnected from the prior context (see, e.g., 1 Cor 12:3; 15:1; 2 Cor 8:1). This is also a sterotyped formula used often in Greco-Roman letters when the author wanted to give his readers a new piece of information. Third, the *exordium* of the ancient letter established rapport with the audience by identifying the situation that gave rise to the letter and establishing the author's credibility. If the section of Galatians beginning at 1:6 is in fact an *exordium*, then v. 10 very naturally fits within that (Rapa, 564, 566). Thus on this evidence I regard v. 10 as a conclusion to the opening salvo of the letter, which then naturally leads into the discussion of Paul's gospel in the balance of the chapter. Regardless of the structural conclusion one makes here, Paul has linked his ideas very closely together here in this section of the letter. They naturally flow one into the other, so any division should be seen as transitional, not disjunctive.[75]

75. Betz, 46, argues that this smooth connection is due to the nature of 1:10–11 as the *transitus* or *transgressio*: "The purpose of this *transitus* is to provide an end to the *exordium*, which is distinguishable but in harmony with the beginning of the *narratio*. ... Verses 10–11 meet these requirements very well."

Paul Defends his Gospel (1:11–24)

Textual Notes

1:11 The reading γάρ is most likely original, but the variation here presents some interesting problems. The reading οὖν, supported by the Alexandrian uncial 0278, cannot be considered original because of the paucity of its external support, but it does offer evidence for the nature of the problem. If οὖν were present at this point in the text, it would offer a strong transition to a new topic, thus creating a new paragraph at 1:11; verse 10 on this construal would join what precedes. If a scribe saw οὖν in the text in v. 11, it is highly unlikely he would replace it with δέ or γάρ. We can thus regard οὖν as a scribal clarification of the ambiguous connections δέ or γάρ would make in these verses. Trying to decide between δέ and γάρ, however, is more challenging. The external evidence is fairly evenly divided. Both conjunctions have excellent witnesses for support, but those for δέ are slightly better in terms of date and character. The conj. δέ has geographical distribution in the Alexandrian and Byzantine text types, while γάρ is found in the Alexandrian and Western text types. The former can claim genealogical solidarity within the Alexandrian and Byzantine text types, while the latter can claim only that for the Western text type. Based on external evidence, δέ is to be preferred slightly. Internal evidence leads in a different direction, however. If the variant reading of δέ is accepted as original (so NET), then the division between the verses becomes clearer: γάρ in v. 10 offers a causal conclusion to 1:6–9, and the δέ of 1:11 serves to mark the transition to a new paragraph. For this reason γάρ is more ambiguous than δέ and should be considered the harder reading. A scribe would more likely have replaced γάρ with δέ than vice versa.[1] So on this basis γάρ is the reading more likely to give rise to the others and should be preferred as original.

1:15 The presence or absence of ὁ θεός in this verse is a difficult problem to solve. NA[28] includes the text in brackets as a sign of the difficulty of the problem. The UBS[4] committee was divided, with the majority arguing that

1. See also M. Zerwick, *Biblical Greek: Illustrated By Examples*, trans. J. Smith, Scripta Pontificii Instituti Biblici 114 (Rome: Pontifical Biblical Institute, 1963), 159.

the words were original. There is excellent external evidence on both sides. The inclusion is supported by strong Alexandrian manuscripts (א A 0278 33 1739), and it has geographic distribution across all text types. The omission is also supported by excellent Alexandrian witnesses (𝔓[46] B) and some of the Western tradition. The presence of Latin witnesses that support the shorter reading tips the scale in its favor, as the omission of *deus* cannot be explained as an error of sight as in the Greek texts. The internal evidence is difficult to evaluate. A scribe could have easily omitted ὁ θεός through an error of sight given the spelling of ὁ ἀφορίσας which immediately follows (the possibility of which increases for 𝔓[46] given its omission of the phrase *καὶ καλέσας διὰ τῆς χάριτος αὐτοῦ* later in the verse), but an intentional addition of the words for clarity is equally if not more possible, especially given Paul's shift in person here from first to third. Thus the reading that best explains the rise of the other is the omission, so here the canon of the shorter reading prevails. Paul's meaning is not affected, as God is clearly the referent of the ptc. even if it stands alone.

1:18 The reading Κηφᾶν is replaced by Πέτρον in the vast majority of manuscripts, but this change is surely secondary. Peter's Aramaic name has impeccable support from Alexandrian witnesses (𝔓[46.51] א* A B 33 1739*) at this point in the text, and quite simply it is the harder reading. Scribes would very naturally have changed the Aramaic name Κηφᾶν to Peter's more widely used Greek name Πέτρος, as evidenced by the correction in א and the marginal reading in 1739. For similar textual problems, see 2:9, 11, 14.

Translation

11 For I would have you know,[2] brothers and sisters,[3] the gospel that was preached by me—it is not human in nature![4] **12** For I did not receive it from any man, nor was I taught it, but I received it[5] through a revelation about Jesus Christ. **13** For you heard previously about my life in Judaism:[6]

---

2. In my opinion the more traditional translation of *γνωρίζω* as "I make known to you" (NKJV) is not clear, idiomatic English. The wording I have used here is found in ESV, NASB. Other translations use "I want you to know" (NET, CSB, NRSV, NIV).

3. Here I follow recent scholarship that sees the pl. ἀδελφοί as referring to all members of the group regardless of sex; see BDAG, 18.

4. See BDAG, 513, for suggestions on how to translate the use of *κατά* here. I have retained some of the awkwardness of the Greek word order for rhetorical effect.

5. The phrase "I received it" is only implied in the Greek text.

6. The ὅτι here is epexegetical, offering further explanation of Paul's former life. In English the colon is appropriate to make that connection (so also CSB).

I intensely persecuted the church of God and was working to destroy it,[7]
14 and I advanced in Judaism far beyond many contemporaries of my people
because I was such a strong zealot for my ancestral traditions. **15** But when the
one who appointed me at birth and called me through his grace determined[8]
16 to reveal his Son to me so that I would preach him to the Gentiles, I did
not immediately consult with flesh and blood,[9] **17** nor did I go to Jerusalem
to those who were appointed to be apostles before me,[10] but I went to Arabia
and again returned to Damascus. **18** Then after three years I went to Jerusalem
to get acquainted with Peter,[11] and I stayed with him fifteen days. **19** But I
did not see any other of the apostles except James, the Lord's brother. **20**
(Concerning the things I am writing to you, look, before God I swear that I
am not lying!)[12] **21** Then I went to the regions of Syria and Cilicia. **22** Now
I was personally unknown to the churches of Judea in Christ, **23** but they
simply kept hearing, "The one who persecuted us before now proclaims the
faith that he previously tried to destroy!" **24** And they consistently glorified
God in light of my circumstances.[13]

Commentary

On the heels of Paul's strident condemnation of those who preach another gospel is his intensely personal yet theologically profound argument for the divine origin of his gospel. Paul explains the grounds for his call for fidelity to his gospel to the exclusion of all others. The passage opens with the central thesis that governs the balance of chapter 1 and most of chapter 2, namely,

---

7. The impf. tenses here are difficult to convey in idiomatic English. Paul intends to portray activities that were ongoing in duration.

8. For "determined" see BDAG, 404.

9. I have retained this metaphor (so also NASB, NKJV) because it is clear in English. Compare "any human being" (NET, NRSV, NIV, NLT); "with anyone" (CSB, ESV).

10. The Greek text here lacks a verbal idea: πρὸς τοὺς πρὸ ἐμοῦ ἀποστόλους. I included the word "appointed" as an implication of the temporal idea Paul states explicitly.

11. Other translations emphasize different nuances of the verb ἱστορῆσαι, some less explicit than others: "to visit Cephas and get information from him" (NET); "to get to know Cephas" (CSB, similarly NLT); "to visit Cephas" (ESV, NRSV); "to see Peter" (NKJV).

12. I have retained some of the awkwardness of the Greek word order for rhetorical effect.

13. The phrase ἐν ἐμοί here refers not to Paul as an individual, but the circumstances pertaining to him.

that Paul's gospel has a divine, not human, origin.[14] Then Paul proceeds to substantiate that claim through a rehearsal of his life relative to his conversion. He begins with the general activity of his preconversion life, then he proceeds to explain the divine origin of his conversion as a historical turning point. He then explains his activity following his conversion as proof of this thesis. His personal history acts as a testimony to the divine nature of the gospel he preached. His focus on God's choice of himself as apostle to the Gentiles pairs naturally with this argument. Even the geography of his travels adds to the discussion because it shows an appropriate independence from Jerusalem. The Archimedean point of all this history, though, is his own conversion on the Damascus road. In that event God revealed Christ to Paul and changed him from a persecutor of the church to its most ardent supporter, even an apostle to the Gentiles. Although not certain beyond doubt, it is feasible that the general shape of Paul's argument in this largely autobiographical section derives from the tactics of his opponents: They may have claimed that Paul received his gospel from Jerusalem and then distorted it, so Paul counterclaims that his gospel was received independently of Jerusalem and then later ratified by the key apostles (Schreiner, 118).

1:11 Γνωρίζω γὰρ ὑμῖν, ἀδελφοί. Paul begins this section with a common epistolary formula: "For I make known to you ... " As such, this marks a transition to a new topic, but it should not be regarded as disjunctive from the prior paragraph. All this material, from 1:6 to the end of chapter 2, serves the same purpose, namely, to defend Paul's gospel. Paul now provides particular details in support of the primary assertions already made. As a metacomment this phrase attracts extra attention to the following proposition. Burton, 35, notes this well: "The assertion that follows is in effect the proposition to the proving of which the whole argument of 1:13–2:21 is directed." This means that vv. 11–12 serve an important thematic purpose in the flow of the argument.[15] They are the central thesis that Paul seeks to defend. Paul ultimately seeks

14. In one sense the division between chapters 1 and 2 of Galatians is artificial, since the greater part of chapter 2 serves also to substantiate Paul's central thesis in 1:11–12. However, in the latter chapter Paul speaks more carefully about his relation to the Jerusalem apostles, so it is helpful to separate that material and consider it a different section. Even so, one should recognize the paradigmatic force of 1:11–12 as binding chapters 1 and 2 together ultimately in Paul's thought.

15. Betz, 44, regards v. 11 as the final verse of the *exordium*. Verse 12 then is the *propositio* that begins the *narratio*. The information in the *narratio* serves essentially to support the *propositio* (p. 61). Although he divides the material differently, functionally the force is the same.

to defend his gospel, although his apostolic authority must be addressed as part of that debate.[16]

τὸ εὐαγγέλιον τὸ εὐαγγελισθὲν ὑπ' ἐμοῦ. The way Paul describes his gospel is a bit unusual, but it serves his purposes well. There are two important observations to make here about this phrase. First, Paul describes his gospel with an aor. adj. ptc., but his central assertion that follows (οὐκ ἔστιν κατὰ ἄνθρωπον) uses the pres. tense when one might have expected him to use the impf., referencing the past time of his preaching. With this switch from aor. to pres., Paul juxtaposes what he proclaimed in the past with the present state of that proclamation. Neither at the time he preached to the Galatians before nor in the present could his gospel be described as human in nature. Then and now his gospel has retained its divine character. Second, the fact that Paul uses the pass. ptc. plus ὑπ' ἐμοῦ is unusual. Compare this to 1 Cor 15:1: Γνωρίζω δὲ ὑμῖν, ἀδελφοί, τὸ εὐαγγέλιον ὃ εὐηγγελισάμην ὑμῖν, which is a much more natural phrasing. The difference in voice can be attributed to the different occasions between the two statements. In 1 Cor 15 Paul discusses the common confession he and the Corinthian church share, part of which they were in danger of rejecting, namely, the resurrection. Thus in Corinth Paul emphasizes the commonality of the gospel that he preached and that they believed as received from trustworthy sources. Not so in Galatia. Because the point of contention was over the implications of the gospel, particular implications that Paul made central in his ministry to the Gentiles, and not the commonly known facts of the gospel as such, he needed to focus on its divine origin (Hansen, 41–42). His use of the pass. ptc. plus ὑπ' ἐμοῦ enables him to move the focus off himself ever so slightly. Yes, he was the one who proclaimed it, but he was not its ultimate source or origin.[17] This also focuses attention on what was distinctive about Paul's proclamation. Clearly he, the leaders of the Jerusalem church, the Twelve, and even his opponents shared a conviction that Christ was the Messiah promised by God, crucified then raised on the third day. The difference of understanding was in the present role of the Law in light of the crucified Messiah. "It was, therefore, not his preaching of 'Christ crucified' that was being called into question by the Judaizers in Galatia, but the implications which Paul drew from that regarding God's acceptance of Gentile believers apart from their conformity to the Mosaic law" (Longenecker, 23). Paul did not require any

---

16. This is not an unimportant question: Paul's central concern was the message he proclaimed, and the status of his apostolic office was only important as it related to that message. This becomes an important question of application, which will be discussed below in the section Application and Devotional Implications.

17. See W. R. Baird, "What is the Kerygma: A Study of 1 Corinthians 15:3–8 and Galatians 1:11–17," *JBL* 76 (1957): 181–91, for a short but helpful study on the differences in the kerygma in 1 Cor 15:3–8 and Gal 1:11–17 in light of the stances of C. H. Dodd and R. Bultmann. For a Bultmannian analysis of Gal 1, see M. Winger, "Tradition, Revelation and Gospel: A Study in Galatians," *JSNT* 53 (1994): 65–86.

acceptance, acquiescence, or obedience to the Mosaic Law from those whom he evangelized. Therein lies the distinctiveness of his gospel.

ὅτι οὐκ ἔστιν κατὰ ἄνθρωπον. The latter half of this sentence explains the preceding noun phrase *τὸ εὐαγγέλιον τὸ εὐαγγελισθὲν ὑπ' ἐμοῦ*, "the gospel that was preached by me." Paul's gospel is not according to man. This assertion is similar to that which he made about his apostleship. In 1:1 Paul stated that he was an apostle *οὐκ ἀπ' ἀνθρώπων οὐδὲ δι' ἀνθρώπου ἀλλὰ διὰ Ἰησοῦ Χριστοῦ καὶ θεοῦ πατρὸς τοῦ ἐγείραντος αὐτὸν ἐκ νεκρῶν*, "not from men nor through any man but through Jesus Christ and God the Father who raised him from the dead." Paul uses *κατά* here rather than *ἀπό* or *διά*, but his sentiment is entirely the same. The prep. *κατά* in the phrase *κατὰ ἄνθρωπον* focuses upon a standard or norm,[18] and the noun takes on a generic force. Thus Paul casts his net widely: He denies that his preached message was in any way associated with, sourced in, created by, or controlled by any mortal man. Paul intends *κατά* to cover a wide range of meanings, and the negation he uses emphasizes the divine origin of his gospel as complete and total.

1:12 *οὐδὲ γὰρ ἐγὼ παρὰ ἀνθρώπου παρέλαβον αὐτό, οὔτε ἐδιδάχθην*. With these statements Paul explains further how his gospel was not according to man. His initial phrasing concerns his reception of the gospel. The verb *παραλαμβάνω* carries an important religious sense of the reception of tradition,[19] sometimes paired with a form of *παραδίδωμι* to describe the act of passing along the tradition. Elsewhere Paul uses these terms to describe his own role in the transmission of teaching about Christ (see, e.g., 1 Cor 11:23, where both terms occur relative to the Lord's Supper, and 1 Cor 15:3 where they occur relative to Paul's reception and transmission of the gospel). He even used the word *παρελάβετε* earlier in 1:9 to describe the Galatians' reception of the gospel. Paul thus affirms that transmission did take place between him and the Galatians, but denies that transmission took place from anyone else to him. He was the first to proclaim the gospel he preaches.[20] He then declares simply *οὔτε ἐδιδάχθην*, "neither was I taught." This verb expands upon the idea of receiving tradition, clarifying the means by which the tradition would have been received.[21] Paul's emphasis on the divine nature of the gospel is

---

18. BDAG, 512.

19. So A. Kretzer, "*παραλαμβάνω*," *EDNT*, 3:30.

20. At first blush this might appear to be in conflict with 1 Cor 15:3, but the resolution is found in the context. There Paul emphasizes the common confession that all Christians share, regardless of ethnicity, about the facts of Christ's death and resurrection. Here Paul wrestles with the specific implications of Christ's death for Gentiles; it is that gospel for the Gentiles that he proclaims, as chapter 2 will make very clear.

21. D. C. Arichea Jr. and E. A. Nida, *Galatians: A Translator's Handbook on Paul's Letter to the Galatians* (New York: United Bible Societies, 1976), 17, says, "*I did not*

maintained as this would imply that he did not sit under a teacher to learn his gospel (Moo, 93).

ἀλλὰ δι' ἀποκαλύψεως Ἰησοῦ Χριστοῦ. Paul now describes the theological crux of his argument, his line in the sand that demarcates those who preach a different gospel versus those who are faithful to his own. It is Paul's rhetorical, theological linchpin and deserves careful attention. Paul begins the phrase with the conj. ἀλλά. This marks the following phrase as a counterpoint to the negative points he had just made about how he did not receive his gospel. The prepositional phrase that follows, δι' ἀποκαλύψεως Ἰησοῦ Χριστοῦ, is a positive, theologically powerful assertion about how Paul did in fact receive his gospel. The Greek word ἀποκάλυψις bears the most weight in the phrase. It commonly meant "revelation, disclosure."[22] Its connotation, however, is strongly eschatological: "To describe this event as an 'apocalypse' not only underlined its heavenly authority but also implied that it had eschatological significance, that is, as the key which unlocked the mystery of God's purpose for his creation, the keystone of the whole arch of human history" (Dunn, 53). The gen. Ἰησοῦ Χριστοῦ that follows is either a subj. gen. ("the revelation that Jesus Christ made [of himself]") or an obj. gen. ("the revelation about Jesus Christ"). The prep. διά plus the gen. here indicates means, but this would accommodate either an objective or subjective idea, and within the limited information given so far either would be acceptable to the sense. The key for most interpreters is the subsequent context: As 1:15–16 will show, God was at work communicating to Paul through this revelation of Christ, and thus it would be slightly awkward for Ἰησοῦ Χριστοῦ to be a subj. gen. Two other data are helpful here: When Paul uses the cognate verb ἀποκαλύπτω in the act. voice, expressing a subject as the agent of the verb, it is God explicitly twice (1 Cor 2:10; Phil 3:15) and implicitly once (Gal 1:16).[23] He also uses the phrase ἀποκάλυψις κυρίου ['Ἰησοῦ] twice (1 Cor 1:7; 2 Thess 1:7), and each time it has to be an obj. gen.[24] Thus the phrase δι' ἀποκαλύψεως Ἰησοῦ Χριστοῦ most likely means "by means of a disclosure [from God] about Jesus Christ." The referent of this revelation is the appearance of Christ to Paul at his conversion, which fundamentally changed both his understanding about who Jesus was and his attitude toward him. So at the same time Paul refers to the tangible, objective revelation of Christ to him on the road to Damascus but also to the internal, subjective revelation of new understanding about him that came from that appearance. More importantly for the function of this section, we should understand the salient point: God had revealed Jesus Christ to Paul, and

---

receive it from any man refers to the initial reception of the gospel, while *nor did anyone teach it to me* refers to his growing understanding of its contents."

22. BDAG, 112.

23. This argument builds on that presented in M. Silva, *Interpreting Galatians: Explorations in Exegetical Method* (Grand Rapids: Baker, 2001), 68.

24. Silva, *Interpreting Galatians*, 68.

thus God is powerfully at work in Paul's present proclamation of the gospel just as he was the origin of its transmission to him.

Paul emphasizes in 1:11–12 his independence from any other person vis-à-vis his reception of the gospel, but this independence should not be construed as absolute, as the following context indicates. Paul's assertion of independence does not mean that he did not learn anything about Jesus from other people. Surely he learned of Christ and the church from others before his conversion. Otherwise, he would not have known enough about the Jewish believers to consider them a threat to Judaism. Surely when he did have contact with other believers after his conversion he learned particulars about the life and ministry of Jesus and grew in his knowledge of the meaning of the gospel. But this subsequent contact was not the root or source of his knowledge of the risen Christ and how the gospel was now available to the Gentiles. This knowledge came from God himself through Christ.

> Paul's point in Galatians is not that he was opposed to or ignorant of this developing Christian tradition, but simply that he was not dependent upon it for his knowledge of Christ. The Jesus traditions which he later learned, incorporated into his letters, and passed on to his churches only served to confirm what he already knew by direct revelation to be true. (George, 110)

1:13 *Ἠκούσατε γὰρ τὴν ἐμὴν ἀναστροφήν ποτε ἐν τῷ Ἰουδαϊσμῷ*. Paul now turns to discuss his personal history as proof for the divine origin of his gospel. "Paul's radical change of allegiance and behavior is the effect that demonstrates the cause, namely, God's direct intervention in his life, which became the source of the gospel he proclaimed" (deSilva, 140). Interestingly, he does not start by simply stating the facts of his preconversion life in Judaism, but rather he indirectly calls the Galatians to serve as witnesses to them. He states Ἠκούσατε ... ποτε, "you heard ... previously." This brings up a question of where they had heard it. Did Paul tell them? This is plausible, as Paul could have readily used his personal testimony as an initial means of proclaiming the gospel to the Galatians (Lightfoot, 81). It is also possible that the Galatians had heard about Paul's preconversion life from his opponents, likely in an attempt to discredit his current minimization of the Law as compensation for over-zealous persecution of the church (so also Dunn, 55). Either way, Paul's present emphasis is on what the Galatians had heard about him and how that contrasts with his present behavior.

Paul begins by stating the fact of his preconversion life and then describing it further with an appositional ὅτι clause. The noun ἀναστροφή which Paul uses here has a rather general meaning of "conduct, way of life."[25] He then

25. Dunn, 56, makes much of a few places where the verb ἀναστρέφω translates a Hebrew *Vorlage* of הלך within a context of Jewish principles and practices (see, e.g., Prov 20:7), but these are too few to have a notable effect upon the connotation of

modifies this noun with the prepositional phrase ἐν τῷ Ἰουδαϊσμῷ: "[my way of life] in Judaism." With this phrase Paul positions himself as an authentic Jew (Dunn, 56), even more so than his opponents (cf. also Phil 3:4). The word Ἰουδαϊσμός is a rare term in Greek. It shows up initially in the LXX five times (2 Macc 2:21; 8:1; 14:38 [twice]; 4 Macc 4:26), then in the NT twice (Gal 1:13, 14), and then subsequently in the Apostolic Fathers (among others see Ign. *Magn.* 8:1; 10:3; *Phld.* 6:1; the latter two passages contrast this with Χριστιανισμός). These uses show that the word focuses not upon Jewishness as an ethnicity or race, but upon Jewishness as a faith, belief, or way of life.[26] For example, 4 Macc 4:26 describes how Antiochus tried to make Jews renounce their Judaism:

> αὐτὸς διὰ βασάνων ἕνα ἕκαστον τοῦ ἔθνους ἠνάγκαζεν μιαρῶν ἀπογευομένους τροφῶν ἐξόμνυσθαι τὸν Ιουδαϊσμόν
>
> he himself through torture compelled each one of the nation to renounce Judaism by means of tasting defiled food.[27]

In the debate concerning whether Paul considered himself converted or completed, this word is an important datum. By using it Paul focuses not on his ethnicity as a Jew but upon his Jewish system of belief. The flow of the argument through the rest of the paragraph and indeed into the next chapter shows the same (especially so in light of 2:15). Thus this word strengthens the argument that the experience Paul had upon the Damascus road can properly be considered a conversion in that he exchanged one belief system for another.

ὅτι καθ' ὑπερβολὴν ἐδίωκον τὴν ἐκκλησίαν τοῦ θεοῦ καὶ ἐπόρθουν αὐτήν. The lengthy ὅτι clause that follows at this point in the text extends to the end of v. 14. Paul uses it to further explain what his way of life in Judaism was like. The wording here in the first part of the description is terse and compact, and with good reason: Surely from his present vantage point as an apostle it pains Paul to discuss how he acted previously. This self-description brings to mind other passages in which Paul describes his former behavior with regret (see 1 Cor 15:8–10; Phil 3:6; 1 Tim 1:12–15). It serves the purpose, though, of defending his gospel by casting his conversion in bold relief, so Paul does not hesitate to discuss it. He begins by noting his well-known persecution of the church. The verb διώκω regularly means "persecute" and in this context refers to Paul's particular acts of persecution, while the verb πορθέω means

---

this noun. The same effect is achieved by the prepositional phrase ἐν τῷ Ἰουδαϊσμῷ which modifies the noun ἀναστροφήν.

26. For a helpful study on this term, see Y. Amir, "The Term Ἰουδαϊσμός (IOUDAISMOS), A Study in Jewish-Hellenistic Self-Identification," *Imm* 14 (1982): 34–41.

27. Translation taken from R. Brannan, K. M. Penner, I. Loken, M. Aubrey, and I. Hoogendyk, eds., *The Lexham English Septuagint* (Bellingham: Logos Bible Software, 2012).

"destroy, annihilate" and points to his ultimate goal.[28] Paul uses the impf. tense to portray the open-ended nature of these actions. Indeed, he was in the very process of carrying out these actions at the time of his conversion.[29] The prepositional phrase καθ' ὑπερβολήν is used adverbially to describe the intensity and extent of Paul's persecution. It could be translated literally as "according to excess," but in English adverbs that have a denotation of intensity communicate the concept more clearly (cf. ESV, NLT "violently"; NET "savagely"). Paul routinely describes the church with the gen. modifier τοῦ θεοῦ which indicates possession.[30] Because ἐκκλησίαν is sg., this phrase shows Paul's seminal thinking about what is normally called the universal church. His actions were ultimately not against particular congregations but against the whole entity; this makes his actions all the more egregious. This gen. adjunct focuses Paul's persecution on its ultimate object. Paul was not simply persecuting the church; he was also fighting against God.[31] This makes God's grace to him in his conversion all the more powerful.

One may wonder why Paul undertook such intense, violent action against the early church. Part of the answer lies in the ethnicity of the early believers. At the time of Paul's conversion the church was still essentially Jewish. Simply thinking that Paul persecuted believers *per se* skews the picture; one must instead recognize that Paul was persecuting *Jewish* Christians. As a devout Jew, Paul would have seen his actions against Jewish believers as a means of purifying Israel to hasten the eschatological age with important biblical and historical precedents (see Longenecker, 28–29 for helpful discussion and passages). He was not simply angry at them for leaving Judaism; he was zealous for Israel as a whole and saw their persecution and punishment at his hands as a divinely sanctioned means of restoration. While Paul himself does not make any ethnic distinctions when he discusses persecuting the church (Bruce, 90), the testimony of Acts 8:1 shows that Paul approved of

---

28. BDAG, 853.

29. Note that in Acts 9:3 the use of the temporal inf. phrase ἐν τῷ πορεύεσθαι to connect the plans for persecution and the event of conversion. This open-ended portrayal is why many classify the impf. verb ἐπόρθουν as a conative impf: Paul intended to destroy the church but was not able to carry out the action (see Wallace, *Greek Grammar*, 550–52, for discussion of this grammatical category). This analysis is true enough, but it does not take into account the lexical mismatch between πορθέω in Greek and "destroy" in English. The latter is notably consummative, while the former is not.

30. See 1 Cor 1:2; 10:32; 11:16, 22; 15:9; 2 Cor 1:1; 1 Thess 2:14; 2 Thess 1:4.

31. This finds theological parallel in Acts 9:4–5, where in appearing to Paul the risen Christ identifies himself as the object of Paul's persecution.

Stephen's execution. So at least he persecuted Hellenistic Jews, which may have been because of a more relaxed stance toward the Torah.[32]

1:14 καὶ προέκοπτον ἐν τῷ Ἰουδαϊσμῷ. Paul now turns his attention from the persecution he undertook to the religious aspects of his life in Judaism. Paul again uses an impf. tense verb, here προέκοπτον, to describe his past situation. The verb προκόπτω means to "advance" or "progress," and in secular Greek philosophy it was used to describe "moral and intellectual progress."[33] The impf. tense action should be construed as customary, marking out the general contours of Paul's life. Paul describes himself as continually progressing in his Jewish belief and practice.

ὑπὲρ πολλοὺς συνηλικιώτας ἐν τῷ γένει μου. Just as Paul was intense in his persecution of the church, he was intense in his practice of Judaism. Paul positions himself as more advanced in Judaism than his contemporaries. Even though ὑπὲρ πολλοὺς συνηλικιώτας is not totally exclusive as it uses a form of πολύς instead of πᾶς, Paul clearly intends to set himself above and beyond any other Jew of his age in terms of his devotion to Judaism. He then qualifies this statement about his contemporaries further in an intriguing way with the prepositional phrase ἐν τῷ γένει μου. The noun γένος refers to a group connected by some common bond. It can mean a very large group, like "nation, people" or a small group, like "family"; it can also mean "class, kind," with focus on common traits as opposed to politics or blood.[34] By mentioning συνηλικιώτας together with ἐν τῷ γένει μου, Paul implies that he had his own distinct group of contemporaries within Judaism. In other words, Paul was not just better than the average Jew. He was better than even his select group of contemporaries who were zealous for Judaism. He was better than the best.

περισσοτέρως ζηλωτὴς ὑπάρχων τῶν πατρικῶν μου παραδόσεων. The closing clause of v. 14 explains the basis for Paul's progress within Judaism, using language that conveys intensity. The verb of the clause is ὑπάρχων, which is used simply as a synonym for the more common equative verb εἰμί. The word ζηλωτής acts as the predicate nom., describing Paul himself, and the adv. περισσοτέρως explains to what extreme extent Paul lived as a zealot. The word ζηλωτής can have political denotations, but Paul intends a general meaning here, along the lines of "ardent supporter, enthusiast."[35] Even so, the term is

32. See the "Additional Note" on 1:23 in Moo, 117: "Many argue that the 'church' that Paul was trying to 'destroy' was specifically the Greek-speaking Jewish Christian church that began to play fast and loose with the torah." He helpfully references here M. Hengel and A. M. Schwemer, *Paul Between Damascus and Antioch: The Unknown Years* (London: SCM, 1997), 36–37; C. M. Pate, *The Reverse of the Curse: Paul, Wisdom, and the Law*, WUNT 114 (Tübingen: Mohr Siebeck, 2000), 154–57.

33. LSJ, 1487; MGS, 1773.

34. BDAG, 194–95.

35. See BDAG, 427.

not without important background to explain Paul's intentions. The concept of zeal connects Paul to key people in Israel's history who boldly protected Israel against spiritual apostasy, such as Phinehas and the Maccabees.[36] Before his conversion Paul saw himself as rightly following in their footsteps against a Jewish sect that was subverting Israel's fidelity to God (see George, 115–16; deSilva, 143). The phrase τῶν πατρικῶν μου παραδόσεων shows that for which Paul was a ζηλωτής. Paul does not repeat the word Ἰουδαϊσμός to identify Jewish faith and practice, nor does he use the word νόμος, either of which one would reasonably expect given the immediately preceding context on the one hand and Paul's argument in the book on the other.[37] Instead, Paul describes himself as a zealot for "my ancestral traditions." The term παράδοσις regularly refers to teaching passed along within a religious tradition;[38] the adj. πατρικός identifies these traditions as related to Paul's ancestors (somewhat akin to the English adj. *paternal*, although with referent beyond immediate parentage).[39] Within Judaism, however, there was a very specific referent to "the traditions of the fathers."[40] Josephus in two texts connects this idea clearly with the oral traditions that had developed within the context of Pharisaism. In *Ant.* 13.297–98, he describes how the Sadducees and Pharisees differ concerning "the tradition of the fathers," a passage worth citing in full:

> νῦν δὲ δηλῶσαι βούλομαι ὅτι νόμιμά τινα παρέδοσαν τῷ δήμῳ οἱ Φαρισαῖοι ἐκ πατέρων διαδοχῆς, ἅπερ οὐκ ἀναγέγραπται ἐν τοῖς Μωυσέος νόμοις, καὶ διὰ τοῦτο ταῦτα τὸ τῶν Σαδδουκαίων γένος ἐκβάλλει, λέγον ἐκεῖνα δεῖν ἡγεῖσθαι νόμιμα τὰ γεγραμμένα, τὰ δ᾽ ἐκ παραδόσεως τῶν πατέρων μὴ τηρεῖν.
>
> For the present I wish merely to explain that the Pharisees had passed on to the people certain regulations handed down by former generations and not recorded in the Laws of Moses, for which reason they are rejected by the Sadducaean group, who hold that only those regulations should be considered valid which

36. See Num 25:11 (LXX); Josephus, *Ant.* 12.271.

37. Paul does not use the latter word until Gal 2:16, the key theological statement of the book.

38. BDAG, 763.

39. BDAG, 788. "The adjective makes the impression that this Pharisaism was a trait of long standing in the family. Its proudest and most militant member was Saul" (Lenski, 53).

40. There is some variation concerning what word is used as the adjunct. Compare τὴν παράδοσιν τῶν πρεσβυτέρων (Matt 15:2 // Mark 7:3) to the wording of the following texts from Josephus.

> were written down (in Scripture), and that those which had been handed down by former generations need not be observed.[41]

In *Ant.* 13.408, Josephus references the reforms made after the death of Alexander by Alexandra, during whose reign the Pharisees gained great prominence:

> Ἡ δὲ ἀρχιερέα μὲν ἀποδείκνυσιν Ὑρκανὸν διὰ τὴν ἡλικίαν, πολὺ μέντοι πλέον διὰ τὸ ἄπραγμον αὐτοῦ, καὶ πάντα τοῖς Φαρισαίοις ἐπιτρέπει ποιεῖν, οἷς καὶ τὸ πλῆθος ἐκέλευσε πειθαρχεῖν, καὶ εἴ τι δὲ καὶ τῶν νομίμων Ὑρκανὸς ὁ πενθερὸς αὐτῆς κατέλυσεν ὧν εἰσήνεγκαν οἱ Φαρισαῖοι κατὰ τὴν πατρῴαν παράδοσιν, τοῦτο πάλιν ἀποκατέστησεν. τὸ μὲν οὖν ὄνομα τῆς βασιλείας εἶχεν αὐτή, τὴν δὲ δύναμιν οἱ Φαρισαῖοι.
>
> Alexandra then appointed Hyrcanus as high priest because of his greater age but more especially because of his lack of energy; and she permitted the Pharisees to do as they liked in all matters, and also commanded the people to obey them; and whatever regulations, introduced by the Pharisees in accordance with the tradition of their fathers, had been abolished by her father-in-law Hyrcanus, these she again restored. And so, while she had the title of sovereign, the Pharisees had the power.[42]

Thus with the phrase τῶν πατρικῶν μου παραδόσεων Paul identifies the specific traditions that he followed, those of the Pharisees. But more than this, he acknowledges that his allegiance was less to the Law as such and more to the traditions that had grown up around it.[43] Thus Paul sets the stage for a continued close reading of the Law as an appropriate part of his Christian faith while rejecting the extra tradition associated with the Law by certain parts of Judaism.

Paul's personal testimony serves as an argument against the direction the Galatians were taking (Hansen, 44). Paul's devotion to the principles and practices of Judaism led only to violence against the church of God, not to a fulfillment of God's will in Christ. Surely his personal example would warn them off the path toward these same principles and practices they were taking.

---

41. Greek text and translation taken from Josephus, *Jewish Antiquities*, vol. 5, *Books 12–13*, trans. R. Marcus, LCL 365 (Cambridge, MA: Harvard University Press, 1943), 376–77.

42. Greek text and translation taken from Josephus, *Jewish Antiquities*, vol. 5, *Books 12–13*, 432–33.

43. Moo, 102, argues that Paul and other Jews like him likely did not separate the OT law and their interpretation of it, much as contemporary advocates of theological positions do not distinguish between Scripture and their interpretive elaborations.

1:15 Ὅτε δὲ εὐδόκησεν ὁ ἀφορίσας με ἐκ κοιλίας μητρός μου. Paul now describes his conversion, which changed his mind about the Judaism to which he had been so completely devoted, showing that God was the one who changed him. Conceptually this clause is the linchpin on which the proof of his life turns. At the start of the temporal adv. clause is the verb εὐδόκησεν. This verb reflects a mental attitude of approval or pleasure and by extension can denote, as it does here, a specific determination or action that arises from that attitude.[44] Paul uses this verb with God as the subject on a few other occasions, each of which has important theological weight (1 Cor 1:21; 10:5; Col 1:19). Also on occasion he uses the noun form εὐδοκία with a similar effect (Eph 1:5, 9; Phil 2:13). With this verb Paul claims insight into the will of God, and even more particularly that which brought God pleasure and satisfaction. His description of God consists of two subst. ptcs. governed by the same article, ὁ ἀφορίσας ... καὶ καλέσας,[45] and it clearly fits Granville Sharp's rule in terms of structure and semantics.[46] The first subst. ptc. is from the verb ἀφορίζω, which means "to separate, set apart, appoint."[47] Paul identifies himself as its dir. obj. and then modifies the verb with the prepositional phrase ἐκ κοιλίας μητρός μου. This prepositional phrase is routinely used in the LXX and the NT to mean "from birth,"[48] so there is an emphasis on length of time, but the collocation with ὁ ἀφορίσας creates an emphasis upon the selection by God of a particular individual for his purposes.

καὶ καλέσας διὰ τῆς χάριτος αὐτοῦ. Paul continues his description of his conversion by identifying God with the second subst. ptc. καλέσας. This is modified by the prepositional phrase διὰ τῆς χάριτος αὐτοῦ and is strikingly similar to the phrasing in 1:6, τοῦ καλέσαντος ὑμᾶς ἐν χάριτι Χριστοῦ. In that passage the word καλέω referred to the entirety of the salvation experience, and the prepositional phrase identified Christ's grace as the means by which the call was accomplished. The emphasis in the present passage is on Paul's particular call to ministry; the collocation with the prior ptc. phrase limits

44. LSJ, 710; MGS, 842; BDAG, 404.

45. I do not regard the longer reading with ὁ θεός as original. See Textual Notes and the NET text critical note in Gal 1:15 on the word "one."

46. Granville Sharp's Rule in technical contexts is referred to as a TSKS construction; this stands for "The"-Substantive-*Kai*-Substantive. (I have always been befuddled at the mix of English and Greek in this standard abbreviation. I guess naming it the ASKS construction, for Article-Substantive-*Kai*-Substantive, would produce too many questions.) This well-documented rule of Greek grammar states that when two substantives are governed by the same article, joined by καί, and the substantives are personal, sg., and common, both substantives will refer to the same entity. See Wallace, *Greek Grammar*, 270–90, for a detailed discussion of this rule and its application to numerous texts in the NT. For a complete treatment, see D. B. Wallace, *Granville Sharp's Canon and Its Kin*, SBG (New York: Peter Lang, 2009).

47. BDAG, 158.

48. So BDAG, 550.

the application of the calling to Paul's apostleship, not more generally his salvation as such.[49] The prepositional phrase here also indicates the means by which the call was accomplished. It is possible that αὐτοῦ also refers to Christ in this context, but that is less likely than a reference back to God by way of the previous subst. ptc. ὁ ἀφορίσας. Paul thus emphasizes his call as founded in God's grace which set him apart for ministry.

In describing his own divine call, Paul alludes to Isa 49, evoking God's call upon his special servant in that text. Paul was called from his mother's womb like that servant (see Isa 49:1). God chose to reveal his Son in Paul just as God chose to reveal himself in the servant (see Isa 49:3). Paul will share the gospel with the nations, just as God will use his servant to bring salvation to the ends of the earth (see Isa 49:6). "Paul saw his life and ministry as the fulfillment of God's promise to raise up a servant through whom eschatological salvation would reach to the ends of the earth and incorporate the gentiles within the people of God" (Harmon, 66).[50]

1:16 ἀποκαλύψαι τὸν υἱὸν αὐτοῦ ἐν ἐμοί. The complementary inf. ἀποκαλύψαι completes the idea of the verb εὐδόκησεν from the prior verse; this action is the one that God was pleased to do. The verb ἀποκαλύπτω occurs here (and in 3:23), but it is not intended to be understood separately from the mentions of ἀποκάλυψις in 1:12 (and 2:2). There is an extremely close semantic overlap between the cognate noun and verb, so the inf. phrase ἀποκαλύψαι τὸν υἱὸν αὐτοῦ should be understood to have the same meaning as the noun phrase ἀποκαλύψεως Ἰησοῦ Χριστοῦ in 1:12. Here as there Paul refers to the objective revelation of Jesus Christ to him by God at the point of his conversion.

The sense of the prepositional phrase ἐν ἐμοί is difficult to pin down. It could variously mean "in me" with a locative idea, in the sense of "within my person/spirit"; "with reference to me" as a point of reference, in the sense of "within my experience"; or "to me" in the sense of "to me as a recipient." Often ἐν with the dat. stands in for the ordinary dat. when used as an indir. obj.[51] This would fit the idiom of ἀποκαλύψαι, which uses the acc. to show the thing revealed and the dat. to show the person who receives the revelation. It also fits the following clause where Paul speaks of proclaiming Christ to others, which follows logically if Christ had been revealed to him as a recipient. Paul here thus identifies the Son as the one revealed and himself as the recipient of that revelation for further proclamation.

ἵνα εὐαγγελίζωμαι αὐτὸν ἐν τοῖς ἔθνεσιν. This ἵνα clause identifies God's purpose in revealing Jesus to Paul: so that Paul might proclaim him among

---

49. "It is true enough that the same grace called him to be an apostle, and even that both calls were united in one grand act; yet here Paul distinguishes and lets the infinitive say how he was made an apostle" (Lenski, 56).

50. See also M. S. Harmon, *She Must and Shall Go Free: Paul's Isaianic Gospel in Galatians*, BZNW 168 (Berlin: De Gruyter, 2010), 75–89.

51. BDAG, 329.

the Gentiles. One grammatical point worth noting because of its theological significance is that this clause does not modify ἀποκαλύψαι alone. Rather, it modifies the main verb εὐδόκησεν in conjunction with the related complementary inf. Thus the grammatical connection is not solely to the revelation but to God's good pleasure to reveal. To be more precise, Paul does not intend to convey that the purpose of the revelation was so he could proclaim Christ. Rather, the purpose of God's will in revealing Christ to Paul was for him to proclaim Christ. This grammatical point means Paul dives deeper into the divine purposes than what one might understand initially. The stress is on God's actions as determined by his will, not his actions alone. This is certainly subtle, but it reinforces Paul's argument that his gospel, and more specifically his commission to share that gospel with the Gentiles, has a divine origin deep in the mind of God.

Paul describes his actions with the verb εὐαγγελίζομαι, which he used previously in his condemnation of those who preach differently in 1:8–9 and in the description of his preaching in 1:11. The prior uses of the verb focused upon the act or content of Paul's preaching; here with the prepositional phrase ἐν τοῖς ἔθνεσιν Paul focuses upon the recipients. The personal pronoun αὐτόν as the dir. obj. of the verb here is significant as it equates the person of Jesus Christ with the gospel (Betz, 72). The prep. ἐν when used with a pl. personal obj. can define the group among which an activity takes place,[52] but the verb εὐαγγελίζω uses the dat. to show the person(s) who receives a message.[53] This idea could be translated as "among," but the more natural English idiom is "to the Gentiles" (see similar Pauline uses in Rom 2:24; 1 Cor 5:1; Col 1:27). This identification of the Gentiles as recipients of the gospel in conjunction with his conversion focuses attention further on the unique nature of Paul's ministry and what he proclaimed.

At this point in the text it is easy to move forward into Paul's description of his travels, glossing over what Paul has just said. However, in order to fully appreciate his argument, a central observation about the temporal dependent clause in vv. 15–16a needs to be stated. With this clause Paul furthers his argument that his gospel does not originate with men, as his conversion was not due to any human activity, but this is not all he states. Paul here argues that his conversion and his gospel originated in a revelation that changed his view of Christ, but there is still more. The central observation one must note in order to feel the full weight of Paul's statement is that God himself was pleased to act to bring about Paul's conversion and his gospel. God had set Paul apart. God had called Paul by his grace. God had revealed Christ to Paul. God had intended for Paul to proclaim Christ among the Gentiles. Paul moves past any occasional, historical circumstance regarding the origins of his proclamation and makes a foundational, theological assertion about how his gospel came about. If we say anything about the origin of Paul's gospel and

52. BDAG, 326–27.
53. BDAG, 402.

want to be Pauline about it, we must state that God was the ultimate source and origin of his ministry and gospel. In a very real sense, all else is tangential.

εὐθέως οὐ προσανεθέμην σαρκὶ καὶ αἵματι. Paul now moves from the historical moment of his conversion to a discussion of his travels after that point, which helps prove what he just proclaimed. To show that his conversion was divinely instigated, he recounts that he did not seek human assistance afterwards. Paul begins by stating what he did not do and where he did not go. It is possible that the adv. ἐυθέως modifies the verb ἀπῆλθον in v. 17b, such that the sense is "I did not consult with flesh and blood ... but I immediately went to Arabia," but the distance between the adv. and the that second indic. is against this view. In addition, Paul does describe in 2:1–10 an eventual consultation with the Jerusalem apostles, so likely he would not want to make an absolute statement here that would need qualification later. The better sense is to take the adv. as modifying the phrase that immediately follows with an emphasis upon the timing: "I did not immediately consult with flesh and blood [but I did later, as I will soon describe]."[54] The verb προσανατίθημι in this context means simply "to consult with someone" or "take counsel with someone."[55] Paul did not seek out any information or clarification on what had happened to him. The phrase σὰρξ καὶ αἷμα is relatively common in the NT and simply means "mortal" or "human" in contradistinction to the divine.[56]

1:17 οὐδὲ ἀνῆλθον εἰς Ἱεροσόλυμα. While the prior statement is general—Paul did not consult with any human regarding his gospel after his conversion—this statement is particular and appropriate to the nature of the issue with which Paul was wrestling with the Galatian churches. Movement and geography are critical to Paul's argument. This verse is the first instance of multiple references to travel and locations that reflect important events relative both to Paul's activities and his theological arguments. These function not only in terms of his personal narrative but also hermeneutically; note, for example, the important use of places in the well-known analogy of chapter 4. Paul here states that after his conversion he did not go up to Jerusalem. The verb

54. The influence of the adv. εὐθέως is so significant that Martyn, 181, takes it as determinative for issues of chronology later marked with ἔπειτα: The first adv. marks the anchor point for all later chronological demarcations, such that 1:18 and 2:1 should each be measured from this point of Paul's calling.

55. See LSJ, 1501; MGS, 1792; BDAG, 876. J. D. G. Dunn, *The Theology of Paul's Letter to the Galatians*, New Testament Theology (Cambridge: Cambridge University Press, 1993), 67, argues that the word means "consult in order to be given a skilled or authoritative interpretation," with support from Diodorus Siculus 17.116.4. The meaning of the verb there, however, is highly contextualized (note the collocation with περὶ τοῦ σημείου) and not universally applicable.

56. BDAG, 915. See Matt 16:17 and Eph 6:12 for representative examples. See John 1:13 for an intriguing theological expansion of this idea.

ἀνέρχομαι, which means "to go up, ascend,"[57] is not used for any reason other than Jerusalem's location. Because of its setting on hills, surrounded by valleys, one could speak of "going up to" Jerusalem or "coming down from" it.[58] The most important point about this negative assertion is the significance of the city. Jerusalem was the theological, cultural, and social center of the early church for many years following the ministry of Jesus. The early chapters of the book of Acts show the importance of the city as both the place where the church existed and also the place from which its apostles and leaders guided it. It is not without importance that the Jerusalem Council of Acts 15 took place there as opposed to other developing Christian centers. Paul even testifies to the centrality of Jerusalem when he describes it as a starting point for his ministry in Rom 15:19. In Gal 2 Jerusalem takes on a negative role as a foil to his gospel, against which he must defend his ministry. So by asserting that he did not go to Jerusalem after his conversion, Paul clearly marks his gospel as separate from the early Christian traditions and authority associated with that city. At the time of his conversion, Paul was near the city of Damascus (Acts 9:3) and then spent some time in that city (Acts 9:8–9, 19–23). Paul's statement here emphasizes that when he left Damascus he did not first return to Jerusalem.[59]

πρὸς τοὺς πρὸ ἐμοῦ ἀποστόλους. Paul clarifies his negative statement further by describing not just where he did not visit, but whom he did not visit. He did not go to Jerusalem "to those who were [appointed to be] apostles before me." With this statement Paul identifies a group of people as important to the early church as the city of Jerusalem itself. Paul's language emphasizes unity with this group but also difference. He identifies these individuals as ἀπόστολοι, having the same function and calling from God as he did. But he goes further to qualify this group with a temporal modifier. The prepositional phrase πρὸ ἐμοῦ refers to chronological order. Coupled with the emphasis Paul places on the source and origin of his apostolic role, he identifies these individuals as apostles who received their commission earlier in time than he did. The import of the modifier is not simply to acknowledge their chronological priority but also to recognize their leadership because of their chronological priority.[60] But Paul's recognition of this fact makes his point:

---

57. BDAG, 77.

58. The verbs ἀναβαίνω and καταβαίνω are used much more commonly in this idiom than compounds of ἔρχομαι like ἀνέρχομαι and κατέρχομαι, but even so this idiom was not the most common way to speak of travel to and from this city. Most occurrences of language that reference travel to and from Jerusalem simply have verbs that describe motion generally, not necessarily motion up or down a gradient.

59. Paul's description of his movements here creates tension with the description in Acts 9, which places Paul's return to Jerusalem after his escape from Damascus.

60. Note how this is shown in the latter two categories of meaning for the word πρό in BDAG, 864.

He did not deem it necessary to see the recognized leaders of the church in Jerusalem after his conversion.

The identity of these prior apostles is an important question. Clearly Paul regards them as people of importance; otherwise, he would not mention that he did not go to see them. Determining exactly who they are is not as easy as one might think. The simplest solution is that Paul here refers to the Twelve, the original group whom Jesus called and whose ministry began the early church. This would be an understandable way to construe the use of the noun ἀπόστολος given its use elsewhere in the NT, especially in the Gospels (see, e.g., Matt 10:2; Mark 3:14; Luke 6:13). However, there is little to no evidence that the twelve apostles as a group continued to minister in Jerusalem for any length of time after the resurrection, and there are indications in the biblical text that other individuals were also considered to be apostles.[61] For example, James appears to be part of the apostolic band given what Paul says in v. 19. So most likely restricting this group to the Twelve is not what Paul had in mind. At the other extreme, given the description of conflict Paul relates in Gal 2 plus the depiction of the Jerusalem Council in Acts 15, it is possible that Paul has in mind James and his fellow leaders separate from any of the original Twelve, even excluding Peter. The difficulty here is that the noun ἀπόστολος did carry some association with the original disciples; Peter was associated with Jerusalem as Paul himself indicates later in this chapter. The best solution takes into account both the meaning of the term and the historical fact of James as the leader of the Jerusalem church. Paul refers to Peter and James specifically, but also others of the Twelve who may have been associated with the Jerusalem church.

ἀλλ' ἀπῆλθον εἰς Ἀραβίαν. Paul now begins to describe in a positive way his movements after his conversion. The simple statement ἀπῆλθον εἰς Ἀραβίαν is as enigmatic as it is short. It is rather simple to understand: Paul went to Arabia. The difficulty comes in determining exactly where this place was and why Paul traveled there. The contemporary geopolitical entity of Saudi Arabia does cover much of the same area as the ancient term, but when applied to the ancient Near East the term could refer to territories further north and west. In Roman terminology Arabia extended further north than present-day Saudi Arabia, comprising parts of Transjordan, the Negev, southern Syria, and the northwestern portion of the Arabian peninsula.[62] Within this general geographic region kingdoms independent from Rome, like that of the Nabateans south of Damascus, could also be referred to by this name.[63] But the name could also refer to territories to the west, such as the Sinai Peninsula, evidenced by Paul's usage in Gal 4. So the question here is, did

61. The strongest evidence for this is the distinction between the Twelve and the apostles implied in 1 Cor 15:5, 7.

62. R. H. Smith, "Arabia (Place)," *ABD*, 1:325; U. Borse, "Ἀραβία," *EDNT*, 1:149. See also Josephus, *Ant.* 14.15.

63. BDAG, 127–28.

Paul stay in the general region of Damascus after his conversion, or did he undertake a longer trip to the Sinai Peninsula? Given that he mentions a return to Damascus as the next stop on his postconversion journey, the most reasonable assumption is that he meant the desert area south of Damascus in the kingdom of the Nabateans (so also Keener, 91). Travel within the general area of Damascus—instead of an arduous trek of hundreds of miles to the Sinai Peninsula—makes much more sense of what we do know of Paul's travels.

The purpose for the journey is even more difficult to ascertain. Paul gives no rationale for the travel other than the general argument of this paragraph, that is, as proof that the gospel he preached was not received from any human source. Instead of making a trip to Jerusalem to visit key Christian leaders, which would have been eminently logical and appropriate, Paul instead makes a trip to the desert. Paul makes no positive statement of the trip's value. It is reasonable to assume that it gave Paul time for reflection and communion with God, important given the radical nature of his conversion. This is argued suggestively by Lightfoot, 89–90, given the implication from Paul's statement that he did not confer with "flesh and blood." But it is also possible that Paul went there as a nascent missionary given the clear nature of his call. This is argued by Bruce, 96, primarily in light of Paul's hasty retreat from the area detailed in 2 Cor 11:32–33. A quiet spiritual retreat would not have precipitated a kidnapping attempt. A missionary journey is argued more convincingly by Bauckham on the basis of close kinship between Jews and Nabateans on the one hand and in fulfillment of Isaianic prophecy on the other.[64] Either judgment has to be tentative, however, because Paul simply does not say why he took this trip or what he did while he was there.

καὶ πάλιν ὑπέστρεψα εἰς Δαμασκόν. After his time in the Syrian desert south of Damascus, Paul returned to that city. As with his time in Arabia, there is no discussion of what Paul did here or why he considered this return necessary.[65] The mention serves his argument simply because Damascus is a place where the important Christian leaders were not. In Acts 9 Luke shows Damascus to be an important location for Paul after his conversion. Although Acts 9 does not indicate any travel to the desert area south of Damascus on Paul's part, the mentions of time in that narrative are general enough that a sojourn outside the city of some duration is not outside the realm of possibility.[66] Paul himself mentions his presence in Damascus in

---

64. R. Bauckham, *The Jewish World Around the New Testament*, WUNT 233 (Tübingen: Mohr Siebeck, 2008), 260–62.

65. BDF, §484, considers πάλιν ὑπέστρεψα a pleonasm presumably because the idea of "again" is present in the verb ὑποστρέφω.

66. Acts 9:9 specifically mentions ἡμέρας τρεῖς, but this was the period of time before Ananias visited and restored Paul's sight. Acts 9:19 mentions ἡμέρας τινάς as the time Paul spent in Damascus with the disciples, during which he began preaching the gospel. Acts 9:22 would imply some duration of time in the area, and the clause Ὡς

only one other text, 2 Cor 11:32–33, where he relates the plot on his life and confirms the details of Acts 9:23–25.

1:18 Ἔπειτα μετὰ ἔτη τρία. This is the first of three chronological markers Paul uses to organize the description of his travels after his conversion (the others occur in 1:21; 2:1). The adv. ἔπειτα is a generic word that indicates chronological progression without reference to duration. Here it is used without any specific sequential markers, but the prior context indicates a time separate from and later than Paul's time in Damascus. The difficulty with this phrase is less with the adv. and more with the phrase μετὰ ἔτη τρία. The prep. μετά with the acc. case indicates a following time frame, "after three years" in this instance. The reference point to start the time frame is unclear, as Paul does not specifically indicate that in this context. The two best options are his conversion (referenced in 1:15–16) and his return to Damascus (referenced in 1:17). Because there is not a great time difference between these two events, there is little impact upon interpretation. Paul uses the phrase ἔπειτα μετὰ ἔτη τρία to indicate that it was three years after his conversion and the following activity centered around the city of Damascus that he visited Jerusalem and the apostles there. So if Paul was converted within a year or two after Christ's death and resurrection in AD 33,[67] then this would be sometime in Ad 37–38.[68]

ἀνῆλθον εἰς Ἱεροσόλυμα ἱστορῆσαι Κηφᾶν. Paul now describes his first journey to Jerusalem after his conversion. This is an important journey for him to make, but he mentions it to support his current argument: The fact that it occurred a significant period of time after his conversion emphasizes his distance from the Jerusalem apostles and thus the independence and divine authority of his gospel. He states as a simple matter of fact that he went up to Jerusalem, adding the aor. inf. ἱστορῆασι and its dir. obj. Κηφᾶν to explain the purpose for his visit. Only after significant time had passed did he go to Jerusalem to visit with Peter. Paul's retelling of his personal history balances his independence from and connection to the Jerusalem apostles.

The inf. ἱστορῆσαι expresses why Paul went to Jerusalem and what he did during his time with Peter. Within Paul's personal narrative in Galatians, this is the first contact with the Jerusalem apostles. He has gone to great lengths to proclaim his independence from them, so here he chooses his words very carefully so as not to undermine his total message. The verb ἱστορέω means

---

δὲ ἐπληροῦντο ἡμέραι ἱκαναί in v. 23 certainly allows enough time for a visit outside the city.

67. For Christ's crucifixion, death, and resurrection in AD 33, see H. W. Hoehner, *Chronological Aspects of the Life of Christ*, Contemporary Evangelical Perspectives (Grand Rapids: Zondervan, 1977), 95–114.

68. Moo, 108, argues for a reference point of conversion because of Paul's rhetorical point in this section: He is not focused upon his nascent Christian ministry but rather on his contact with the Jerusalem apostles.

to visit for the purpose of learning something,[69] but some nuances associated with this word demand closer attention. At issue is what Paul sought to learn. Did he visit Peter to learn more details about Christ whom he was already proclaiming? Or did he visit Peter to learn more about Peter himself, that is, to become acquainted with him? Both situations are possible here and indeed could both be true, given the length of time Paul spent with Peter. LSJ argues the first situation applies on the grounds that the personal acc. is the person consulted with reference to some other information.[70] The drawback with LSJ's argument is that Paul does not list any information sought; the personal noun Κηφᾶν is the only obj. of the inf. In addition, there are many other texts that use ἱστορέω with the idea of becoming acquainted with someone.[71] So the better fit in the context is that Paul went to Jerusalem to get acquainted with Peter, not to learn about Christ. This would not deny that Peter may have informed Paul more particularly about Jesus, especially his earthly life and ministry, since Peter was an eyewitness to so much. It simply shows that was not Paul's purpose in going because he did not need that information to establish his gospel. His terse description implies the visit was informal and short, which belies any sense of formal dependence by Paul upon Peter. "To learn about the details of Jesus's earthly life from Peter and to be subordinate to or dependent on Peter for his apostleship and Gentile mission are clearly quite different matters. Paul is willing to acknowledge the former, but he is adamant in his rejection of the latter" (Longenecker, 38). Paul deftly balances himself between two extremes: He did not immediately go to the Jerusalem apostles after his conversion, thus strengthening his argument that his gospel was divinely received, but he did not stay away permanently, thus showing he is not a renegade and that there is continuity between his message and theirs.

Paul identifies the person whom he visited as Κηφᾶν, the acc. form of the name Κηφᾶς. This is the Aramaic surname given to Simon, the *de facto* leader of Jesus's twelve disciples. He was also given the name Πέτρος as a Greek equivalent to Κηφᾶς.[72] Paul was aware of both Κηφᾶς and Πέτρος as surnames for Simon, as he uses both in his letters.[73] In 1 Corinthians he uses only the name Κηφᾶς, in reference to a particular faction of the Corinthian church that had identified specifically and exclusively with Peter (1 Cor 1:12; 3:22) and simply as his name (1 Cor 9:5; 15:5). The only other book in which Paul mentions Simon is Galatians, and Paul uses both names (Κηφᾶς in Gal 1:18; 2:9, 11, 14; Πέτρος in 2:7, 8). The question is whether Paul means something particular by using a particular name. Given the Aramaic origin of Κηφᾶς, Paul may have used that name to emphasize Simon's Jewishness vis-à-vis his own ministry among the Gentiles, but that fails on the basis of Gal 2:8 where

69. BDAG, 483.

70. LSJ, 842.

71. See references in G. Schneider, "ἱστορέω," *EDNT*, 2:207.

72. See Matt 16:18; Mark 3:16; Luke 6:14; John 1:42.

73. Nowhere does Paul use the name Σίμων or the Semitic form Συμεών.

Paul mentions Simon's ministry to the Jews but uses the name Πέτρος. The most natural explanation is that Paul knew both names and simply used one or the other for stylistic variation.

καὶ ἐπέμεινα πρὸς αὐτὸν ἡμέρας δεκαπέντε. Paul describes his visit with Peter with a statement about the duration: "I stayed with him fifteen days." This reaffirms the purpose of Paul's visit to Jerusalem to get acquainted with Peter and implies that he was successful in developing a relationship. The length of time implies a great deal of personal time together; a fifteen-day visit would include two full Sabbaths as well as multiple opportunities for meals. Given the nature of the conflict discussed later in Gal 2, this is not an unimportant detail. Even so, Paul does not make any of this explicit and simply states the time as an attendant detail to the visit itself.

1:19 ἕτερον δὲ τῶν ἀποστόλων οὐκ εἶδον. In defending his gospel Paul walks a fine line between independence on the one hand and continuity on the other. He wants to show himself as independent from the Jerusalem apostles to prove that his gospel was divinely received, but he also wants to show continuity with them. In the prior verse he had focused on his connection to Peter through a personal visit, but now he turns again to his independence. This statement qualifies his visit to Jerusalem, limiting it considerably. The main verb of this clause is εἶδον, used here literally to emphasize Paul's limited contact with Peter. The dir. obj. of the verb is brought forward in the clause to emphasize it. Paul did visit with Peter while in Jerusalem, but he did not even see any other of the apostles, except as qualified in the following phrase.

εἰ μὴ Ἰάκωβον τὸν ἀδελφὸν τοῦ κυρίου. With this phrase Paul qualifies his prior statement, which on the face of it would deny contact with any apostles other than Peter. The phrase εἰ μή indicates an exception to the prior negated clause.[74] In addition to Simon, Paul also saw James. Paul describes James as τὸν ἀδελφὸν τοῦ κυρίου. This additional phrase served at a minimum to disambiguate this James from other individuals with the same name, but it also functioned as an honorific. This James was the brother of Jesus and the leader of the church in Jerusalem. He was in every sense a leader in the early church. He wrote the NT book that bears his name. The narrative of the Jerusalem Council in Acts 15 shows his important role as an arbiter in that debate. In Gal 2 Paul relates how his influence was clearly felt far beyond the city of Jerusalem. He was for all intents and purposes equal to the Twelve in influence and authority. Paul used the noun ἀπόστολος previously in the book to refer to one who has been specially commissioned by the Lord for the proclamation of the gospel. Here ἀπόστολος would retain a technical sense of one who saw and was commissioned by the risen Lord, but this

---

74. BDAG, 278.

would be distinct from membership in the Twelve.[75] This is supported by Paul's argument in 1 Cor 15:5, 7, which implies different groups that could properly be called apostles: the Twelve of whom Peter was the head and a larger group of leaders who had seen and been commissioned by the risen Lord of whom James was the head.[76] On this basis, the place of James as a leader in the early church cannot be denied, and Paul's mention of meeting him makes sense given the purpose of his visit to get acquainted with Peter as a leader of the church.

It is worthwhile to think briefly about why Paul did not speak about Peter and James in reverse order, that is, why he did not say that he went to get acquainted with James and also saw Peter. Peter has primacy in Paul's argument for the simple reason that Peter was a more prominent leader than James. Peter was more important objectively than James because James was not a disciple of Jesus during his earthly ministry as Peter was. Peter was also more important subjectively to Paul: Emphasizing his connection to Peter implicitly emphasizes his connection to Jesus rather than the Jerusalem church. This fits into Paul's overarching argument that his gospel had a divine origin rather than a human one mediated through human leaders, whether of the church in Jerusalem or somewhere else.

1:20 *ἃ δὲ γράφω ὑμῖν, ἰδοὺ ἐνώπιον τοῦ θεοῦ ὅτι οὐ ψεύδομαι.* This strong assertion of honesty on the part of Paul has two parts. The first is the relative clause, "regarding what I write to you."[77] The balance of the sentence is where Paul asserts his truthfulness. The particle ἰδού garners attention for what follows. It is a somewhat rare word in Paul, occurring only nine times; this occurrence is the only one in Galatians.[78] Each time the emotional and rhetorical force of the word is in full view. Paul means to get his readers' attention and drive home an important point to them. The actual content of Paul's assertion elides a key term; likely ὀμνύω is implied before ἐνώπιον τοῦ θεοῦ. Paul thus makes a solemn oath.[79] The content of the oath is then indicated by the ὅτι clause, namely, that Paul is not lying in what he has said.

The function of the oath means more than Paul simply asserting his truthfulness. In the ancient Near East the taking of oaths was a recognized

75. For discussion regarding the grammar here, see L. P. Trudinger, "'ΕΤΕΡΟΝ ΔΕ ΤΩΝ ΑΠΟΣΤΟΛΩΝ ΟΥΚ ΕΙΔΟΝ, ΕΙ ΜΗ ΙΑΚΩΒΟΝ: A Note on Galatians 1:19," *NovT* 17 (1975): 200–202; G. Howard, "Was James an Apostle? A Reflection on a New Proposal for Gal. i 19," *NovT* 19 (1977): 63–64.

76. P. W. Barnett, "Apostle," in *Dictionary of Paul and His Letters,* ed. G. F. Hawthorne and R. P. Martin (Downers Grove, IL: InterVarsity, 1993), 48.

77. See Wallace, *Greek Grammar*, 203–4, for a discussion of the "accusative of respect or (general) reference."

78. For other occurrences see Rom 9:33; 1 Cor 15:51; 2 Cor 5:17; 6:2 (2x), 9; 7:11; 12:14.

79. See BDF, §397.3, and A. T. Robertson, *A Grammar of the Greek New Testament in the Light of Historical Research* (Nashville: Broadman, 1934), 1034.

practice, but Judaism put specific limits upon it because of the underlying covenant relationship with God. Israelites were to take oaths only using God's name as a sign of fidelity to him rather than to the idols of the surrounding peoples (Deut 6:13; 10:20).[80] Swearing falsely in God's name was forbidden because that would result in profaning his name (Lev 19:12). Paul could be invoking that religious context with the implied judgment for contradicting the oath. By using a metaphor of presence (ἐνώπιον τοῦ θεοῦ), Paul implies that he stands before God and will be subject to his judgment if his words are false.[81] The Roman context could also come into play here: Paul might be offering a voluntary oath, which in Roman law asserted truthfulness and showed a willingness to go to court to resolve a matter.[82] It is doubtful that Paul actually expected to go to court; likely he invokes the oath as a way to show his willingness to stand before God on the matter. No matter the background, given Paul's arguments previously in the chapter concerning his role as an apostle called by God, his acting with authority, and his willingness to call down God's curse upon those who preach a different gospel (see 1:8–9), this oath should not be taken lightly. It is not simply an asseveration that his words are true; it is a functional proof that Paul speaks the truth about whom he saw during the time he describes.

1:21 *Ἔπειτα ἦλθον εἰς τὰ κλίματα τῆς Συρίας καὶ τῆς Κιλικίας.* After his short, fifteen-day visit to Jerusalem, during which Paul visited with Peter and saw James, he then went to the districts of Syria and Cilicia. He did not linger in Jerusalem or even Judea such that he might have been further influenced by the Jerusalem church. This second occurrence of the word ἔπειτα simply indicates chronological sequence without regard to any duration just as the first one does. The word κλίμα is rare in the NT; it occurs three times, only in Paul (here; Rom 15:23; 2 Cor 11:10). It functions along with a number of other words to indicate geopolitical entities, none of the words having strong distinctions between them.[83] Syria at this time was roughly contiguous with modern-day Syria, extending north from the city of Damascus; the city of Antioch was its capital. The region of Cilicia was Syria's neighbor to the west, further along the southeastern coast of Asia Minor; Tarsus was its capital.

---

80. Note how this practice was portrayed already in the Pentateuch; see Gen 21:23; 24:3; 31:53. See as well the interesting passage in Gen 22:16, where God swears by his own name.

81. In contemporary English one often punctuates an utterance with "I swear to God!" to drive home the fact of what is said. This originally had a similar import as oaths within Judaism (witness the swearing of oaths in legal contexts with the phrase "so help me God"), but in current usage that context of judgment is practically nonexistent. The idea now simply indicates emphasis.

82. J. P. Sampley, " 'Before God, I Do Not Lie' (Gal. I:20): Paul's Self-Defence in the Light of Roman Legal Praxis," *NTS* 23 (1977): 477–82.

83. See L&N, §1.79.

Paul thus speaks of a journey into regions a fair distance from Jerusalem. Given the traditional connection of Paul with Tarsus (see Acts 9:11; 21:39; 22:3) and his going there after a plot on his life while in Jerusalem (Acts 9:30), it may be that Paul returned there to use it as a base of operations. The implication from Gal 2:1 that he was gone quite a while from Jerusalem and Judea also supports this notion. The reason he went is revealed only through an inference from v. 22: If the Judean churches heard that he was preaching the gospel during this time, it is reasonable to conclude that Paul was involved in evangelism in those areas.[84] For the purpose of his present argument, though, the fact that he went is all that he asserts here. These travels, along with the time they took, strengthen his claim of independence from the Jerusalem church and its leaders.

1:22 ἤμην δὲ ἀγνοούμενος τῷ προσώπῳ. Paul distances himself even further from the Jerusalem church by denying contact and direct acquaintance with the larger circle of churches in Judea that would have been directly influenced by it. The verb ἀγνοέω in this context means "to not know, to be ignorant."[85] The phrase ἤμην ἀγνοούμενος could be construed as an impf. periphrastic construction, but given the dat. phrases that follow it is better to understand this as a predicate adj. ptc. (so Burton, 167) describing Paul vis-à-vis the Judean churches. An acceptable translation would be "I was unknown." Many translations treat the phrase τῷ προσώπῳ in an idiomatic fashion, referencing personal knowledge and contact (e.g., "But I was personally unknown to the churches of Judea"). This is certainly true and idiomatic English, but as an assertion of independence, its strength is in its literalness. For rhetorical effect it can be taken at face value: The churches in Judea had not seen Paul's face, that is, he was "unknown by face." This is especially pointed in light of the next verse, which shows that Paul was known to them only by reputation.

ταῖς ἐκκλησίαις τῆς Ἰουδαίας ταῖς ἐν Χριστῷ. These words identify the frame of reference for the prior statement. Paul was personally unknown not to everyone in the area but specifically to the churches. Which churches are in view is specified by the following words. The gen. τῆς Ἰουδαίας indicates a place, that is, Judea, and the second attributive ταῖς ἐν Χριστῷ describes the spiritual state of these churches. Judea was well known as the land where the Jewish people lived. It could refer to the smaller district around Jerusalem to the west of the Dead Sea, as opposed to other regions in the area like Galilee, Samaria, Perea, and Idumea. More likely, though, Paul intends a broader reference to the Roman province of Judea, which would include these areas

84. See Longenecker, 40: "What Paul did between his first postconversion visit to Jerusalem (1:18–20) and his second postconversion visit (2:1–10) can be inferred from the verb εὐαγγελίζεται ('he is preaching') of v 23. So it may be concluded that this was a period of evangelization, though probably not a full-blown Gentile mission as he later took up."

85. BDAG, 12.

as well (Longenecker, 41). What strikes the contemporary reader is the apparent redundancy: It comes across as odd to refer to Christian churches as being "in Christ." This further description makes sense, though, because the word ἐκκλησία was a more general term than the English term "church." As discussed concerning the use of the term in 1:2, the term more generally meant an "assembly" or "gathering."[86] Since this section details Paul's personal history, which involved persecution of the church as an ardent Jewish zealot, Paul felt the need to clarify that it was "assemblies *in Christ*" that did not know him as opposed to Jewish assemblies or synagogues in Judea that likely did know him. This explanation would be strengthened if Galatians were the first of Paul's letters. But Paul in other places references churches and even saints in this way, reflecting his fundamental belief about what a church or saint actually is. There is a close parallel in 1 Thess 2:14, τῶν ἐκκλησιῶν τοῦ θεοῦ τῶν οὐσῶν ἐν τῇ Ἰουδαίᾳ ἐν Χριστῷ Ἰησοῦ, which mirrors the current passage by using second attributive position and all three relevant nouns. There are also looser examples in 1 Cor 1:2; 1 Thess 1:1; 2 Thess 1:1. References to saints in Christ occur in Eph 1:1; Phil 1:1; 4:21; Col 1:2. So this language prevents any confusion of referent, and it reflects Paul's fundamental conviction about the nature of the church.

1:23 μόνον δὲ ἀκούοντες ἦσαν. The Judean churches knew about Paul through word of mouth. They had heard about his dramatic conversion and subsequent evangelism. The word μόνον has an adv. use,[87] appropriate in light of the prior limitation Paul mentioned in the previous verse. The Judean churches did not know Paul personally; they were only hearing about him. The verb phrase ἀκούοντες ἦσαν is an impf. periphrastic construction, stressing the ongoing nature of what Paul describes; this emphasizes as well the length of time Paul was gone from Jerusalem.[88] Although not the major emphasis of Paul's argument here, this amplifies the point that he did not associate with these churches personally or directly.

ὅτι Ὁ διώκων ἡμᾶς ποτε νῦν εὐαγγελίζεται τὴν πίστιν ἥν ποτε ἐπόρθει. The content of what the Judean churches did hear crisply combines Paul's pre- and postconversion lives. The ptc. phrase ὁ διώκων ἡμᾶς ποτε is roughly equivalent to an impf. (Burton, 58)[89] and marks who Paul was before: "the one who was persecuting us previously." The main verb εὐαγγελίζεται indicates present, ongoing action, marking who Paul is now, that is, one who "proclaims the faith." This is the first occurrence of πίστις or any of its cognates in the book. This word could essentially be a metonymy for the gospel about Jesus Christ,

86. LSJ, 509; MGS, 632.

87. BDAG, 659.

88. Note BDF, §134, when discussing *constructio ad sensum*: "Feminine or neuter personal collectives standing in the plural may be continued by a masculine plural: G 1: 23 μόνον δὲ ἀκούοντες ἦσαν refers to ταῖς ἐκκλησίαις v. 22."

89. See also Robertson, *Grammar*, 892.

faith being the human response to this good news, or it could be a broader circumlocution for the entire Christian confession and belief.[90] The latter would be somewhat unexpected in Paul's early writings, plus that definition does not appear to fit the other uses of πίστις within Galatians. But given what Paul described about his own personal history, which involved intense persecution of Christian assemblies, the former could be too limited. What sways me here is Paul's use of the noun in the rest of Galatians, which certainly favor the first option. The churches of Judea recognized that Paul as a persecutor had set himself against the good news of Jesus Christ, the gospel itself.[91] Paul was in the process of destroying the church but never brought that action to fruition. Now he proclaims that very same gospel. Important to note is the implicit connection now seen between the gospel of the Jerusalem church and the one Paul was proclaiming (Lenski, 65). There is not a hint of difference; Paul's testimony is that the Judean churches saw him as now acting in concert with what they believed. This is further evidence and argument against Paul's opponents.

1:24 *καὶ ἐδόξαζον ἐν ἐμοὶ τὸν θεόν*. This short verse functions as an encouraging coda. The meaning is not difficult to discern: The Judean churches were praising God because of Paul's conversion and subsequent ministry of evangelism. The impf. form ἐδόξαζον indicates ongoing action similarly to the impfs. in the immediately prior verses. The phrase ἐν ἐμοί is more logically causal,[92] but BDAG places this verse under the meaning "marker denoting the object to which someth. happens or in which someth. shows itself, or by which someth. is recognized, to, by, in connection with." The idea of reference would be appropriate to explain the use here. Although tangential to the argument that Paul was independent of the churches in Judea, this short phrase in a roundabout way confirms Paul's status as an apostle and guardian of the true gospel of Jesus Christ in contrast to his opponents. Even though he formerly was a persecutor of the church, congregations in the region he had attacked gave him their implicit approbation through praise to God with reference to his activities. This tacit approval without personal contact further proves that Paul is in the right and his opponents are in the wrong.[93]

---

90. This difficulty is reflected in how BDAG lists this verse under two definitions; see BDAG, 820.

91. "It is a striking proof of the large space occupied by 'faith' in the mind of the infant Church, that it should so soon have passed into a synonym for the Gospel" (Lightfoot, 86).

92. See BDAG, 329.

93. So also Hansen, 51: "Paul really turns the tables on those troublemakers. They had apparently appealed to the practice of the Jerusalem church and the Judean churches to persuade the Galatian churches to adopt the Jewish way of life. But now Paul appeals to the example of the same churches."

Paul's defense of his gospel in this paragraph covers a lot of ground. His personal history proves the action of God himself in his conversion. His travels after his conversion show that he was not beholden to the Jerusalem apostles but instead learned about them in appropriate ways. His reputation among the churches of Judea demonstrates his effective ministry without any input from contemporary Christian leaders. These data affirm the thesis of this section, that Paul's gospel has a divine origin in the revelation he received about Jesus Christ (1:12–13). Upon this foundation Paul will next describe the subsequent contact he did have with the church leaders in Jerusalem.

Theological Comments

Within this section of the book of Galatians, Paul tells his own personal history vis-à-vis the gospel he proclaimed. Paul recounts in essence his testimony: his life before he believed the gospel, his moment of conversion, and his changed life afterwards. The space Paul allots to this history does not mean, though, that he considers himself the locus of attention or the canon of measurement. Instead, at the center of this story stands the gospel he proclaimed and the God who revealed it to him.

The theological linchpin of this story is the action of God in history to reveal Christ to Paul (Gal 1:15–16). Paul consistently emphasizes that the gospel he proclaimed did not originate with himself or any other person. God's desire to reveal Christ (εὐδόκησεν ... ἀποκαλύψαι) forms the theological and historical center of Paul's personal history and his understanding of the gospel. The gospel received and proclaimed by Paul began in the very mind of God and thus cannot ever be marginalized, minimized, or modified.

This leads to Paul's conviction about the centrality of his gospel. The entire narrative arc of Paul's personal story focuses upon the gospel: his opposition to it, his confrontation with it, his submission to it, his proclamation of it. The testimony he proclaims shows the power of this gospel: Paul begins as its most vehement persecutor and then ends as its most ardent supporter, bearing witness to the gospel's reality and centrality.

An important discussion here about the testimony Paul relates is whether he describes a conversion—that is, a moment in which his convictions about the identity of Jesus and the gospel about him were changed from denial to belief and acceptance—or whether he describes a call—that is, a moment in which his personal path and actions were decisively changed from a persecutor of the church to the apostle of the Gentiles. The best stance is to recognize the connection between conversion and call in Paul's life and history. Paul came to a moment when he changed his mind about Christ and became a believer and follower through the powerful intervention of God in the revelation of the risen Christ. At this same moment, his role as apostle to the Gentiles was clearly revealed to him (see the ἵνα clause in 1:16 and the corroborating texts of Acts 9:15; 22:15, 21; 26:17, 18). The revelation of

Christ to Paul changed not only his stance toward Christ but also his stance toward the gospel itself. For Paul conversion and call cannot be separated.[94]

Application and Devotional Implications

In this intensely personal section of the book of Galatians, Paul relates his personal experience with the gospel. He describes his life both before and after his conversion, thus providing proof for his affirmation that his gospel is from God and grounds for his call to remain faithful to it. Application of Paul's history to the contemporary reader cannot be direct, though, because his conversion also involved a unique call to be an apostle to the Gentiles. Proper understanding of Paul's uniqueness prevents us from reliving his history as our own, but it does provide the key for proper application of what he has written. To properly apply this passage, the contemporary reader should recognize not that we are apostles in the position of Paul, but rather that we are members of the church in the position of the Galatians. Just as Paul called upon them to maintain fidelity to his gospel, through his writing he calls us to do the same. To that end, we must accept what Paul has asserted about himself just as he expected the Galatians to do. Do we recognize Paul's authority as an apostle in what he wrote and what he commands? Oftentimes Christians favor particular sections of the Bible over others; Jesus and his loving red letters might receive preference over Paul's plain typeface and more strident tone. But the same God who sent Christ to earth also revealed him to Paul and commissioned him to proclaim the gospel. We cannot invite Jesus in to dine but leave Paul outside the door begging. Do we recognize the divine origin of the gospel as Paul did? The gospel that evangelicals proclaim is not a human invention, although it certainly has been explained and passed down through human means. It finds its source in the mind of God, and as such it demands full and total allegiance and obedience. Do we believe in the gospel's transforming power as evidenced in Paul's life? Paul presented himself as an example of one who was changed by his contact with

---

94. This separation seems to be implied by Lightfoot, 82, who when discussing the "three separate stages in the history of the Apostle's consecration to his ministry" mentions "the conversion and call to the Apostleship" as the second one. See also Moo, 98–99, who argues that referring to this as a call "drastically underplays Paul's own claim about the dramatic change that his conversion involved" and that conversion is an appropriate term because the change in Paul was "thoroughgoing." DeSilva, 146, rightly cautions us not to view conversion simply as a "personal decision for Christ" but also as Paul's recognition of God's destiny upon him. See also R. G. Hoerber, "Paul's Conversion/call," *Concordia Journal* 22 (1996): 186–88. This interpretation is *contra* Dunn, 63–64, who rejects "conversion" in very strong terms, and Betz, 64, who is more moderate in his rejection of "conversion" but uses the term to discuss the meaning of v. 15 (p. 69).

it, becoming a proclaimer instead of a persecutor. Paul's testimony convinces us of the gospel's power, further affirming its divine origin.

At the center of Paul's autobiography is a divine moment of confrontation. In one decisive moment God revealed Christ to Paul. He was confronted with the divine identity and reality of the risen Christ and could no longer assent to anything contrary. The mode of this confrontation was unique to Paul. We recognize that in the current time Christ normally reveals himself through the preaching of the gospel and the ministry of the church. But the experience of confrontation is common to all who follow Jesus. In the proclamation of the gospel, just as God was pleased to reveal Christ to Paul, he is pleased to reveal Christ to all. The gospel is not solely about facts, persuading people concerning Jesus, his divinity, and his atonement for sin. It is also about a moment of confrontation with the risen Lord. In the gospel God apprehends the individual with divine reality as revealed in Christ; when people truly see that reality, they consent and follow him. We should live in expectation of that revelation as we proclaim the gospel. Our God acts to confront all mankind, and we should expectantly look for him to do so.

When God confronts, lives are transformed. The point of Paul's testimony must not be overlooked: He was violently opposed to the gospel and the church it created, but when faced with the revelation of Christ, Paul could not help but believe and change his convictions. This conversion affected every part of his life, even his most deeply held theological beliefs:

> Paul was utterly extreme. On the one hand, he raged for the traditions and went far beyond the Mosaic law; on the other hand, he now stood for complete liberty even from the Mosaic law and was the very apostle of this liberty. Once the supreme protagonist of the traditions, now the very apostle of Christian liberty! Let the Galatians visualize the gulf that lay between these extremes. How was it possible that such a fanatic traditionalist should now be the apostle of perfect Christian liberty? If he was converted at all he should have been a Judaizer like those referred to in Acts 15:5. But we already have the full answer: "Jesus Christ's revelation," v. 12. (Lenski, 54)

As believers who relate to the same God and receive revelation about the same Christ, we should similarly believe in the transforming power of the gospel and pray for its power to be fully actualized in our own lives.

Additional Exegetical Comments

1:11–17 There is some evidence that Paul designed this section to mirror prophetic call narratives of the OT; see the arguments made by Baird, supported by reference to Habel.[95] There certainly is credence for this connection, but even so it exists to serve the primary function of this section, namely, that Paul's gospel is divine in origin. The emphasis upon the nations in two important prophetic call narratives (Jer 1:5; Isa 49:1–6) coupled with Paul's own ministry to the Gentiles strengthens Paul's argument here (Cousar, 32).

1:15 Both Bercovitz and Knox argue that this verse, along with other data, supports the argument that Paul was already a believer when the risen Christ appeared to him on the Damascus road.[96] Despite the obvious conflict with the account of Paul's conversion in the book of Acts this view creates, it also struggles to properly explain Paul's use of the verb καλέω. Bercovitz (whom Knox supports) argues that this verb is "a technical term which means the effectual call to belief,"[97] that is, it only refers to the precise moment when a person believes in Christ as Messiah and Savior and then becomes part of the church. This tight definition fails upon broader examination of word usage. Sometimes it does refer to the particular moment of conversion for an individual (e.g., 1 Cor 7:18), but other uses cannot be explained in this way. Some uses only make sense if καλέω is understood as the sovereign call of God exercised by the divine will in eternity past to be actualized in particular times and places (e.g., Rom 8:30). So even though Knox tempers Bercovitz's conclusion by arguing that there may be no tangible, measurable difference in time between the call and conversion, the central thesis should be rejected.

1:17 Wright argues that by going to Arabia, Paul is invoking the pattern of Elijah.[98] There is much to commend Wright's hypothesis on the grounds of the intertextuality he discusses, but the primary problem is his assumption that Arabia must mean the more restricted region of the Sinai peninsula, when this is not certain. Even so, he presents some intriguing parallels for consideration that inform Paul's conception of his calling and vocation.

1:17 In the LXX, as in the NT, there are two spellings for the name Jerusalem. Ἰερουσαλήμ is the much more common one, occurring hundreds of times, while Ἱεροσόλυμα is much rarer, occurring only dozens of times. Longenecker, 33–34, states that the former has sacred connotations and the latter profane, but the relatively even distribution of the terms within the NT would argue against that thesis. Murphy-O'Connor makes a more feasible argument that

---

95. W. Baird, "Visions, Revelation, and Ministry: Reflections on 2 Cor 12:1–5 and Gal 1:11–17," *JBL* 104 (1985): 651–62; N. C. Habel, "Form and Significance of the Call Narratives," *ZAW* 77 (1965): 297–323.
96. J. P. Bercovitz, "Kalein ('to call') in Gal 1:15: Evidence that Paul Was Already a Believer When Christ Appeared to Him?" *Proceedings* 5 (1985): 28–38; J. Knox, "On the Meaning of Galatians 1:15," *JBL* 106 (1987): 301–4.
97. Bercovitz, "Kalein," 30.
98. N. T. Wright, "Paul, Arabia, and Elijah (Galatians 1:17)," *JBL* 115 (1996): 683–92.

Paul's normal usage was the Semitic Ἰερουσαλήμ. He shifted to the Greek Ἱεροσόλυμα when countering his opponents' use of that term, which they used with the Galatians as the more comprehensible spelling for Greek speakers.[99] This is a helpful explanation, but it changes nothing with regard to reference or nuance. Nothing should be made of the fact that Paul uses one spelling here and another in 4:25–26.

Selected Bibliography

Amir, Y. "The Term Ἰουδαϊσμός (IOUDAISMOS), A Study in Jewish-Hellenistic Self-Identification." *Imm* 14 (1982): 34–41.

Arichea, D. C. Jr., and E. A. Nida. *Galatians: A Translator's Handbook on Paul's Letter to the Galatians*. New York: United Bible Societies, 1976.

Baird, W. "Visions, Revelation, and Ministry: Reflections on 2 Cor 12:1–5 and Gal 1:11–17." *JBL* 104 (1985): 651–62.

———. "What is the Kerygma: A Study of 1 Corinthians 15:3–8 and Galatians 1:11–17." *JBL* 76 (1957): 181–91.

Barnett, P. W. "Apostle." In *Dictionary of Paul and His Letters*, ed. G. F. Hawthorne and R. P. Martin, 45–50. Downers Grove, IL: InterVarsity, 1993.

Bauckham, R. *The Jewish World Around the New Testament*. WUNT 233. Tübingen: Mohr Siebeck, 2008.

Bercovitz, J. P. "Kalein ('to call') in Gal 1:15: Evidence that Paul Was Already a Believer When Christ Appeared to Him?" *Proceedings* 5 (1985): 28–38.

Dunn, J. D. G. *The Theology of Paul's Letter to the Galatians*. New Testament Theology. Cambridge: Cambridge University Press, 1993.

Habel, N. C. "Form and Significance of the Call Narratives." *ZAW* 77 (1965): 297–323.

Harmon, M. *She Must and Shall Go Free: Paul's Isaianic Gospel in Galatians*. BZNW 168. Berlin: De Gruyter, 2010.

Hengel, M., and A. M. Schwemer. *Paul Between Damascus and Antioch: The Unknown Years*. London: SCM, 1997.

Hoehner, H. W. *Chronological Aspects of the Life of Christ*. Contemporary Evangelical Perspectives. Grand Rapids: Zondervan, 1977.

Hoerber, R. G. "Paul's Conversion/call." *Concordia Journal* 22 (1996): 186–88.

Howard, G. "Was James an Apostle? A Reflection on a New Proposal for Gal. i 19." *NovT* 19 (1977): 63–64.

Josephus. *Jewish Antiquities*. Vol. 5, *Books 12–13*. Trans. R. Marcus. LCL 365. Cambridge, MA: Harvard University Press, 1943.

Knox, J. "On the Meaning of Galatians 1:15." *JBL* 106 (1987): 301–4.

Murphy-O'Connor, J. "Paul in Arabia." *CBQ* 55 (1993): 732–37.

99. J. Murphy-O'Connor, "ΙΕΡΟΣΟΛΥΜΑ/ΙΕΡΟΥΣΑΛΗΜ in Galatians," *ZNW* 90 (1999): 280–81.

Pate, C. M. *The Reverse of the Curse: Paul, Wisdom, and the Law*. WUNT 114. Tübingen: Mohr Siebeck, 2000.

Sampley, J. P. "'Before God, I Do Not Lie' (Gal. 1:20): Paul's Self-Defence in the Light of Roman Legal Praxis." *NTS* 23 (1977): 477–82.

Trudinger, L. P. "'ΕΤΕΡΟΝ ΔΕ ΤΩΝ ΑΠΟΣΤΟΛΩΝ ΟΥΚ ΕΙΔΟΝ, ΕΙ ΜΗ ΙΑΚΩΒΟΝ: A Note on Galatians 1:19." *NovT* 17 (1975): 200–202.

Wallace, D. B. *Granville Sharp's Canon and Its Kin*. SBG New York: Lang, 2009.

Winger, M. "Tradition, Revelation and Gospel: A Study in Galatians." *JSNT* 53 (1994): 65–86.

Wright, N. T. "Paul, Arabia, and Elijah (Galatians 1:17)." *JBL* 115 (1996): 683–92.

Paul's Interaction with the Jerusalem Apostles (2:1–10)

Textual Notes

2:5 In order to ameliorate the anacoluthon that marks vv. 4–5, D* b and a few church fathers omit the words *οἷς οὐδέ*. This makes the verb *εἴξαμεν* the main verb of vv. 4–5 but without negation. The prepositional phrase *διὰ τοὺς παρεισάκτους ψευδαδέλφους* that begins v. 4 would then modify *εἴξαμεν*. The sentence then could logically imply that Titus was indeed circumcised but willingly, not under compulsion. In this instance the canons of the shorter reading and the harder reading conflict. The shorter reading should be rejected on the paucity of the witnesses that support it and on the grounds that it is clearly a motivated reading to make the text more intelligible.[1]

2:6 In the majority of manuscripts the article ὁ is lacking before the noun θεός. The external evidence is fairly evenly divided. The shorter reading is supported by B C D 1739 1881 2464 𝔐 et al., while the longer reading is supported by 𝔓[46] ℵ A 33 81 104 1175 and a few other manuscripts. The shorter reading has better geographical distribution, occurring in all text types, but the longer reading has the support of older, stronger manuscripts. Internal evidence is also closely matched. A scribe would be much more likely to add the article if it were lacking rather than omit it if present, but Paul much more commonly uses the article with the nom. θεός when it is the subject of the clause.[2] On balance it is best to prefer the longer reading here on the basis of Pauline style and the exceptional witnesses that support it.

---

1. B. W. Bacon, "The Reading of οἷς οὐδέ in Gal. 2:5," *JBL* 42 (1923): 69–80, makes a noble attempt to defend the Western reading, which would imply that because of the false brothers Paul submitted to the Jerusalem apostles for a time, that is, he did not consistently maintain his stance as an apostle independent from them. In my opinion his argument is ultimately unsuccessful.

2. There are seven places where Paul uses an anarthrous θεός. Five of these can reasonably be construed as predicate nominatives (Rom 8:33; 1 Cor 8:4, 6; Phil 2:13; 1 Tim 2:5). Only two are truly anarthrous subjects (2 Cor 5:19; 1 Thess 2:5).

2:9 There is an interesting amount of variation at this point in the text. The reading of NA[28] is Ἰάκωβος καὶ Κηφᾶς καὶ Ἰωάννης, supported by א B C I[vid] Ψ 0278 33 1739 1881 2464 𝔐 and the Vulgate, Syriac, and Coptic. The majuscule A stands alone in its reading Ἰάκωβος καὶ Ἰωάννης. 𝔓[46] and the Latin manuscript r read Ἰάκωβος καὶ Πέτρος καὶ Ἰωάννης. The interesting variant Πέτρος καὶ Ἰάκωβος καὶ Ἰωάννης is read by D F G 629 ar b vg[mss] Tertullian Ambrosiaster Pelagius. Both external and internal evidence point to the reading adopted by the NA[28] text as most likely original. The external evidence supporting this reading has the best witnesses and geographical distribution. In addition, there is genealogical solidarity in both the Alexandrian and Western text types. The singular reading of A probably arose through homoioteleuton. As far as internal evidence is concerned, the reading Ἰάκωβος καὶ Κηφᾶς καὶ Ἰωάννης best explains the rise of the others. Scribes would have likely exchanged the less common name Κηφᾶς for the more common Πέτρος. The variation Πέτρος καὶ Ἰάκωβος καὶ Ἰωάννης probably arose through harmonization to the more common order of those names in the Gospels (even though James the apostle is not in view here in Galatians). It could also have arisen to maintain the priority of Peter (Lightfoot, 109). There is no reason to doubt the text of NA[28] as the best reading.[3]

Translation

1 Then after fourteen years I again went up to Jerusalem with Barnabas, taking along Titus as well. **2** I went up because of the revelation,[4] and I presented to them for consideration the gospel that I am preaching to the Gentiles, but privately to those who are highly regarded in case I was running or had run in vain. **3** But not even Titus who was with me, even though he was Greek, was compelled to be circumcised. **4** This issue came up[5] because of the sneaky false brothers who slipped in to spy on our freedom that we have in Christ

---

3. Lightfoot, 109, also supports the reading Ἰάκωβος καὶ Κηφᾶς καὶ Ἰωάννης for two reasons that also tangentially support his view that Gal 2 refers to the Jerusalem Council of Acts 15. First, because James the son of Zebedee had died between Paul's two Jerusalem visits, there was no need to specify which James as Paul did in 1:19. Second, James is mentioned first in accordance with his primary role at the Jerusalem Council.

4. Contrary to other English translations, I treat this "revelation" as definite in that it refers to the revelation of Christ Paul mentioned previously in 1:15–16. Compare "I went there because of *a revelation*" (NET, emphasis added) and most other English translations.

5. The phrase "This issue came up" is not in the text. I have supplied it to smooth out Paul's rough syntax here.

in order that they might enslave us,[6] **5** to whom not even for a moment did we yield in submission so that the truth of the gospel would remain with you. **6** And from those who are regarded as something[7] (whoever they were matters nothing to me; God does not play favorites![8])—for those who are highly regarded did not submit anything for my consideration,[9] **7** but on the contrary when they saw that I had been entrusted with the gospel for the uncircumcised just as Peter was for the circumcised **8** (for the one who worked on Peter's behalf for his apostleship to the circumcised worked also on my behalf to the Gentiles) **9** and when they recognized the grace that was given to me, James and Cephas and John, the ones highly regarded to be pillars, extended to me and Barnabas the right hand of fellowship, clarifying that we would preach to the Gentiles and they to the circumcised. **10** We only had to remember the poor, the very thing I was intent on doing.

Commentary

Having discussed his personal history surrounding his conversion and call in Gal 1:11–24 in such a way to highlight his independence from the Jerusalem apostles, Paul now turns his attention to the contact he did have with them as part of the argument for the divine origin of his gospel (so also Dunn, 87; George, 135; Oakes, 66). Those whom he deliberately avoided after the risen Lord interrupted his zealous plans to persecute the church now enter his narrative as strong supporters of his ministry to the Gentiles. But support from these leaders does not come without its tensions. Paul expresses at the same time his fear that they would not sanction his ministry and his ultimate dependence upon God with an attendant disregard for human approbation. This tension explains some of the grammatical difficulties in this section: Beset by anacoluthon, the reader sometimes struggles to makes sense of the flow of Paul's argument. Even so, the final point is clear: The last proof of the divine nature of Paul's gospel comes through its ratification by the Jerusalem leaders on the basis of God's activity in Paul himself.

6. The NLT makes the referent here very clear: "They wanted to enslave us and force us to follow their Jewish regulations."

7. Translations here vary widely: "those who were influential" (NET, similarly ESV); "those recognized as important" (CSB); "those who were supposed to be acknowledged leaders" (NRSV); "those who were of high reputation" (NASB); "those who were held in high esteem" (NIV); "the leaders of the church" (NLT).

8. This phrase is a functional translation. A more formal one would be "God does not receive the face of man."

9. After the parenthetical statement, Paul does not pick up where he left off with the first part of the sentence. In the translation I have retained the breaks in Paul's syntax.

It is apparent in this passage that Paul now treads very carefully regarding the defense of his gospel. He wants to show deference to the Jerusalem apostles without undue veneration, and he wants to assert his independence from them while receiving their approbation. It is without doubt "a delicate rhetorical and political balancing act" (Hays, 221). Paul had previously shown that he did not learn his gospel from the Jerusalem apostles; now he shows that they did not add anything to it either (Moo, 118). This proof is emphasized through the two halves of the paragraph. Verses 1–5 emphasize that Titus was not forced to be circumcised, and vv. 6–10 emphasize that the Jerusalem leaders added nothing to Paul's gospel or his ministry (Schreiner, 118).

Paul applies this prior meeting with the Jerusalem apostles to the contemporary problem in Galatia. The general situation is the same: Various opponents of Paul are doing all they can to force Gentile converts to be circumcised. The conflict Paul experienced in Jerusalem prefigures the conflict now occurring in Galatia, and Paul's retelling of the prior event is shaped by what the Galatians now experience (Hays, 221). Paul desires that the Galatians handle the opponents in their midst with the same resistance he mustered against the opponents in Jerusalem (Longenecker, 61; Witherington, 127; de Boer, 111). The argument against circumcision in Galatia from Paul's previous experience is two-fold: The Jerusalem church acknowledged Paul's gospel even though he did not require circumcision, and Paul himself refused to compromise his gospel. The Galatians should then do the same and not submit to circumcision (Matera, 78).

2:1 Ἔπειτα διὰ δεκατεσσάρων ἐτῶν πάλιν ἀνέβην εἰς Ἱεροσόλυμα. The kernel of Paul's sentence is the simple assertion πάλιν ἀνέβην εἰς Ἱεροσόλυμα, "I again went up to Jerusalem." The chronological markers require some attention for proper understanding. The first, the adv. ἔπειτα, is easy to understand, while the second, the prepositional phrase διὰ δεκατεσσάρων ἐτῶν, has engendered much debate. This third occurrence of the adv. ἔπειτα (see 1:18, 21 for the other two) fits Paul's goal of this section: It assures his readers that his narrative is complete with no gaps (Longenecker, 44). It implies that Paul omits no visit to Jerusalem or any contact with the church there or its leaders (Bruce, 106; Fung, 85). This is important given his desire to prove that he was appropriately independent from the Jerusalem apostles. If he had left out a visit, he would have been open to the charge of deception. The chronological sequence and logical flow of the argument highlighted by the adv. help prove that he was independent of the Jerusalem apostles (Burton, 68; Soards and Pursiful, 55).

The more difficult issue surrounding ἔπειτα relates to the specific chronology for Paul's travels that it implies vis-à-vis the phrase διὰ δεκατεσσάρων ἐτῶν. The basic problem is that the adv. is ambiguous relative to the starting point for the length of time expressed: Whether the time span of fourteen years indicated here should be measured from Paul's conversion and the immediate, subsequent visit to Arabia (1:15–17) or from his first visit to

Jerusalem (1:18) is unclear. Added to this is the ambiguity of time measurement in the ancient world. Recounted periods of time were not necessarily exact from a modern viewpoint; they could be understood to be inclusive, with parts of a time period being counted as a whole.[10] Given these two points of ambiguity, Paul could be dating this second visit to Jerusalem anywhere from about 12 years to more than 17 years after his conversion (Moo, 121). From the standpoint of exegesis, uncertainty on this issue cannot be removed, and any solution has to factor in broader issues of Pauline chronology and the relationship of Acts to Galatians (see Burton, 68; Longenecker, 45; Dunn, 87; Hays, 222; Schreiner, 119; Moo, 121). There are weighty arguments on both sides. My present preference is to see the three years and fourteen years as overlapping, both measured from Paul's conversion, because Paul regarded his conversion as a definitive, personal, apocalyptic moment. It would make sense for his conversion to become a point of measurement for everything else.[11] Others, though, have argued that the central point is the length of time Paul was out of contact with Jerusalem; consequently a consecutive ordering of events would make the best sense.[12] Suffice it to say that the issue is more important for Pauline chronology than for interpretation of the passage (de Boer, 107n158). Simply put, whatever the chronological outcome, Paul has described a chain of events that proves appropriate independence from the Jerusalem apostles and more broadly the divine nature of his gospel. Whether this visit was 12 or 17 years after his conversion makes little difference to the overall force of his argument or the exegesis of the passage.

μετὰ Βαρναβᾶ. With this short prepositional phrase Paul identifies an important traveling companion on this Jerusalem visit. Even though Paul mentions him only three times in Galatians (here; 2:9, 13), the figure of Barnabas looms large in the text.[13] This same Barnabas was a key figure in the early expansion of the gospel to the Gentiles as detailed in Acts; that role clearly comes into play in Paul's current argument. Barnabas was a Jew, initially mentioned in Acts as an example of generous giving in the Jerusalem

---

10. The classic example of this is the length of time Jesus's body was in the tomb. In terms of exact number of hours, his body was in the tomb less than two days if a day is strictly defined as a contiguous 24-hour period: Assuming burial by 6 p.m. on Friday and resurrection by 6 a.m. on Sunday, Jesus would have been in the tomb only 36 hours. In terms of an inclusive reckoning, however, Jesus was in the tomb three days: part of Friday, all day Saturday, and part of Sunday.

11. Similarly Calvin, 48; Bruce, 109; Longenecker, 45; George, 136; Rapa, 575–76.

12. See Burton, 66; Betz, 83; Soards and Pursiful, 56. Some point to the use of πάλιν in 2:1 as support for the consecutive view; see Lightfoot, 102; Matera, 71; Witherington, 126.

13. The Pauline texts outside Galatians that mention Barnabas are similarly sparse. Paul mentions him in 1 Cor 9:6 as continuing in a trade while engaging in missionary work just as Paul did. Then he mentions him in passing in Col 4:10 simply to identify which Mark he means, that is, the cousin of Barnabas.

church (Acts 4:36–37) but mentioned later as an early advocate for Paul among the apostles (Acts 9:26–27) and a pioneer in the Gentile mission both to and from Antioch (Acts 11:19–26; 13:1–3). He was with Paul in the events leading up to the Jerusalem Council and stood with him in defense of the Gentile mission (Acts 15:1–35). He is important to Paul's argument in Galatians because he experienced, promoted, and defended the spread of the gospel to the Gentiles. At this point in the Galatians text he serves as a confirming witness to Paul's defense of the divine nature of his gospel and its implications of freedom from the Law for the Gentiles before the Jerusalem leaders. The language here implies that Barnabas and Paul traveled as equals, especially in contrast to the verb *συμπαραλαμβάνω* used to describe Titus's role in the phrase that follows.[14]

It is a legitimate question whether the Galatians knew Barnabas personally, but this is a question that cannot be answered directly from the text. Other factors must be considered, such as the relationship of Galatians to Acts, the audience of the book, and Pauline chronology. Since Paul offers no explanation of who Barnabas is, the implication is that the Galatians knew him. This offers some support for the South Galatia theory as Barnabas was with Paul when these cities were evangelized (Dunn, 90; Schreiner, 120). On the North Galatia theory, Paul would have traveled to Galatia without Barnabas. They parted ways in Acts 15:39, and Paul's first visit to Galatia would have been in Acts 16:6. Given the status Barnabas held among the early believers, however, the Galatians could have known him by reputation, perhaps even from Paul himself. I accept that Paul wrote to the churches in South Galatia (see the Introduction for discussion), so Paul identifies Barnabas by name only because he is known personally to the Galatians, having been among them with Paul during his first missionary journey. This explains as well why Paul would even mention him at all: If he were known to the Galatians, the opponents may have used his subsequent actions in Antioch as an argument against Paul (Moo, 122). It also makes the opponents' actions more striking, as they would be demanding that the Galatians turn not just from Paul but from Barnabas as well, both of whom founded their

---

14. There is often discussion in the commentary literature about the relationship of Paul to Barnabas. If Gal 2 is taken to be Paul's recounting of the visit to Jerusalem in Acts 11:27–30, there seems to be a mismatch regarding which one was considered the senior apostle. In Acts Barnabas appears to be the senior apostle, while Galatians seems to present Paul as the leader. See, e.g., Burton, 69; Bruce, 107; Longenecker, 46, who regard Barnabas as the senior leader on this visit; *contra* Fung, 85, who states that the wording in each case cannot be used as a claim to priority. Albeit an interesting question, answering it does not add anything practically to the exegesis of the passage, given that Paul's primary point is to discuss his apostleship and gospel vis-à-vis the Jerusalem apostles, not Barnabas.

churches (Lenski, 69). Paul mentions him in the context of support for his gospel to undercut their use of him in opposition to it.[15]

συμπαραλαβὼν καὶ Τίτον. The word *συμπαραλαμβάνω* means "to take along as an assistant, take to help."[16] In the NT the word is used only with reference to Paul's traveling companions (here; Acts 12:25; 15:37, 38). The implication is that Titus served as an assistant of some kind to Paul, which makes good sense given what we know about him. Titus was a Gentile believer, converted to Christ through Paul's ministry (Titus 1:4). Evidently from Antioch (Bruce, 107), he was sent by Paul as his representative to the Corinthian church (see 2 Cor 8:23 and other places in that epistle) and tasked with appointing elders in Crete (Titus 1:5). He played an important role in extending Paul's ministry, and in this instance he served to support Paul personally in his travel. Similarly to Barnabas, it is possible that the Galatians knew Titus by reputation, perhaps even from their knowledge of this exact event (Dunn, 90), but given that Paul describes Titus's ethnicity in v. 3, it is not entirely clear that would have been the case.

One wonders whether Paul brought Titus along for some reason other than personal assistance. Paul may have intentionally included Titus in his travels as a test case for his gospel,[17] sort of an apostolic "poke in the eye" to the Jerusalem leaders. On the other hand, Titus may have unintentionally become just such a test case through the actions of others who advocated for his circumcision.[18] Given that Paul took this journey for the specific purpose of defending his gospel preached among the Gentiles, it would make perfect sense for him to bring Titus as an example. Titus was part of the fruit of Paul's gospel (Martyn, 190), so Paul took the initiative to bring him along as a representative of Gentile Christians (Fung, 86). Even if Titus did not start the journey as a test case for Paul's gospel, in retrospect he had become one (Bruce, 111). So Paul's mention of Titus here is not simply historical but also rhetorical, as in hindsight "the very composition of the delegation bore witness to the gospel" (Hays, 223).

The introduction of Barnabas and Titus at this point in the text as fellow participants in the visit serves to corroborate Paul's statements that follow. The Galatians do not have only Paul's words to go on. Two important Christian leaders were also present at the meeting he is about to describe; indeed, each had an important role to play in the Gentile mission. Similarly to the brothers with Paul mentioned in the introduction (Gal 1:2), the

---

15. R. Bauckham, "Barnabas in Galatians," *JSNT* 2 (1979): 61–70, has an insightful investigation into the mentions and non-mentions of Barnabas in Galatians. Essentially Barnabas' actions played into the claims of the opponents, so Paul had to judiciously minimize his role as a defender of the gospel.

16. LSJ, 1680; MGS, 2005.

17. So Burton, 69; Lenski, 75; Betz, 85, 88; Fung, 91; Matera, 72; George, 142; Witherington, 128; Hays, 222; Garlington 2007, 103–4.

18. So Bruce, 111.

presence of Barnabas and Titus in the narrative strengthens Paul's position against that of his opponents.

2:2 ἀνέβην δὲ κατὰ ἀποκάλυψιν. With this phrase Paul describes the motivation or basis for this trip to Jerusalem. The prep. κατά has a different meaning here than in in Gal 1:11; here Paul's focus is on cause.[19] The revelation is the same one Paul mentioned in 1:12, namely, the revelation of Jesus Christ that led to Paul's conversion.[20] Paul's point is that the revelation of Christ he received ultimately caused him to go to Jerusalem to confer with the leaders there. It is not as if the revelation specifically drove him to go. Rather, it set in motion his ministry to the Gentiles, which ultimately led to this conference.

There are other reasonable options for the referent of the revelation worthy of mention here. If Gal 2 retells the same visit to Jerusalem as that in Acts 11:27–30, then the revelation to which Paul refers could be Agabus's prophecy (Rapa, 576; Moo, 123).[21] Against this is the fact that Paul himself received many different revelations (Lenski, 70; Betz, 85; Longenecker, 47). If the connection to Acts 11 is primary, there is not enough information to differentiate between Agabus or Paul as the recipient (Schreiner, 121). The revelation may have been directed to Paul outside of any connection to Acts 11; he could have simply received it within the context of the worshiping assembly (Matera, 72; Hays, 223). All things considered, the repetition of the key term ἀποκάλυψις here and in 1:12 creates an important connection between the accounts. Paul marks this journey to Jerusalem as a necessary outcome of the revelation of Christ he received initially, again supporting his argument that his gospel has a divine origin. He did not go to Jerusalem under the influence of any individual or church, or even because of his own initiative (Lenski, 69; Fung, 87). His journey to Jerusalem, despite possible appearances, actually shows Paul to be independent of the Jerusalem apostles and subservient to Christ. It makes Paul's gospel and his ministry an issue of God's activity (Martyn, 190). The pattern of Paul's original revelation that created his call and commission is characteristic of his continuing ministry (Betz, 85; Oakes, 68; Soards and Pursiful, 59). This reference to that

---

19. See BDAG, 513: "Instead of 'in accordance w.' κ. can mean simply *because of, as a result of, on the basis of.*"

20. The anarthrous noun could rule out an anaphoric reference back to 1:12 (Dunn, 91; Witherington, 131; similarly Fung, 86). If this noun were articular it would certainly be anaphoric. Nouns in prepositional phrases can lack the article and still be definite; see D. B. Wallace, *Greek Grammar Beyond the Basics: An Exegetical Syntax of the New Testament* (Grand Rapids: Zondervan, 1996), 247. So ultimately this noun can still have anaphoric force even though anarthrous because Paul would be referring to the one and only revelation in context, that of Christ to him on the Damascus road.

21. Witherington, 131, argues favorably for this on the grounds that the revelation could have been a prophecy directed toward Paul.

revelation forces the Galatians to consider that God was at work in Paul in all aspects of his ministry, and it raises the stakes of their potential rejection of his gospel.

καὶ ἀνεθέμην αὐτοῖς. The verb *ἀνατίθημι* occurs only twice in the NT (see also Acts 25:14), and in each case it implies the presentation of something for consideration with the connotation of seeking another's opinion.[22] In the present passage Paul presents his gospel to the church in Jerusalem for understanding and consideration. This becomes vivid in light of the indirect question in the latter part of the verse that shows that Paul thought he might have undertaken his ministry to the Gentiles in vain. The meaning of this verb is not so strong, however, to mean "submit for approval" with reference to his gospel. Paul had already explained his bedrock conviction that his gospel was received from God; the balance of the paragraph explains in a number of ways that Paul did not need the approval of the Jerusalem apostles. But practically the time had come for Paul to present his ministry to the Jerusalem church, and he honestly recognizes the interpersonal dynamics in play:

> Paul has chosen a verb which would give no ground whatsoever to those who might have argued that Paul went up to Jerusalem in order to refer his gospel to the Jerusalem leadership and to ask them for an authoritative ruling on it. The language implies that Paul counted their opinion on the matter referred as something he valued (were they not the first to receive the gospel?), but not as something which determined the truth or otherwise of his gospel. (Dunn, 92)[23]

At this point in the text the antecedent of the pronoun *αὐτοῖς* is unclear, and the number of meetings Paul had is also unclear. The phrase *κατ' ἰδίαν δὲ τοῖς δοκοῦσιν* that follows definitely references a private meeting with the church leaders, but it is not clear if that should be taken as a clarification of the vague personal pronoun (so Schreiner, 121; Moo, 123–24) or as a description of an entirely different meeting (so Burton, 70–71).[24] If *Ἱεροσόλυμα* in 2:1 is a metonymy for the church, then the pl. pronoun would refer to the church as a whole (so Martyn, 191), it being the closest antecedent. Paul usually repeats the word to which an epexegetical addition with *δέ* applies, so the phrase about the private meeting could be taken as a new concept (Burton, 70–71). Considering the wider context, however, a single, smaller meeting could be favored. When Paul first went to Jerusalem he met with church leaders only (Witherington, 133), and his repeated emphasis is on the Jerusalem apostles, not the Jerusalem Christians as a whole (Fung, 88).

22. BDAG, 74.

23. Similarly Lenski, 72; Bruce, 109.

24. The use of the vague pl. pronoun to refer only to the Jerusalem apostles is considered *constructio ad sensum* by BDF, §282.1.

Paul would thus intend the discourse that follows, where he mentions Peter, James, and John, to govern this pronoun. On the whole, the evidence favors two meetings as the preferred understanding, that is, first Paul had a meeting with the larger church and then a private meeting with the Jerusalem apostles. When Paul first visited Jerusalem (1:18), his nascent ministry had not garnered much attention. In the interim his reputation had become much more widely known (1:22–24). It makes a great deal of sense to think that his appearance in Jerusalem at this point, with Barnabas and Titus as his companions, would have been of interest to the entire church. The matter under discussion would have then been referred by the church to a smaller, private meeting for final resolution (Longenecker, 47; Dunn, 93).[25]

τὸ εὐαγγέλιον ὃ κηρύσσω ἐν τοῖς ἔθνεσιν. This phrase is what Paul presented to the Jerusalem leaders for their consideration, "the gospel that I proclaim to the Gentiles." In Gal 1:11 when Paul mentions the gospel, his focus is upon his own role in the proclamation. Here his focus is upon the Gentiles as the recipients of his message. The pres. tense of κηρύσσω in the relative clause is significant, as the impf. would be expected since Paul is recounting what he had been preaching at the time of this Jerusalem journey. With the pres. tense Paul emphasizes the message he currently preaches; his gospel has not changed (Lightfoot, 103; Soards and Pursiful, 60). This strikes a note of constancy with the message he still proclaims, previewing the affirmation he ultimately received from the Jerusalem leaders.

κατ' ἰδίαν δὲ τοῖς δοκοῦσιν. This short phrase identifies a second meeting Paul had while in Jerusalem. After a public meeting with the church, Paul then met privately with the leaders. Since Paul identifies Peter, James, and John later as "pillars," it is possible that the influential people mentioned here includes more from the Jerusalem church than just the apostles (Matera, 73). Even if this is correct, the final emphasis in the paragraph falls upon the apostles because those are the key people with the authority to consider Paul's message. The phrase κατ' ἰδίαν occurs regularly in the NT with the meaning "privately."[26] The ptc. δοκοῦσιν, from the verb δοκέω, carries the sense "to have a reputation, to be someone of repute."[27] Although this meaning for the verb is somewhat rare in the NT (occurring here in Gal 2 with each occurrence of δοκέω and Mark 10:42), the meaning is clear and attested elsewhere, Plato, *Gorgias* 472a, being a clear example. Some conclude that Paul uses the term ironically (so Longenecker, 48), that is, he uses the term but does not agree

25. Dunn, 93, goes on to argue that "the 'sneaking in' to which Paul refers in 2:4 was actually the more traditionalist faction of the Jerusalem church 'gate-crashing' the private meeting to ensure that concerns and fears roused at the larger gathering were properly safeguarded." See as well Longenecker, 48: "So 'those reputed to be important' should probably be understood as the first of a series of descriptions amplifying αὐτοῖς, 'them.' "

26. BDAG, 467.

27. BDAG, 255.

with the truth that a literal reading would convey. A better argument is that the irony comes from Paul's repeated use of it (de Boer, 107): Repeating the term draws attention to it, but it is clear from Paul's overarching point that the status of these individuals is not his central concern.[28] More importantly for understanding Paul's meaning is why he used this term and not something else, like τοῖς ἀποστόλοις, to identify the Christian leaders in Jerusalem as he did in 1:19. If this group of leaders was larger than the apostles, then using a different term would make sense, but if Peter, James, and John alone are in view, Paul's language has to be explained. The answer lies in the delicate balance Paul strikes here between the authority of the Jerusalem apostles and his own certain conviction about being in the right. Because this term focuses on reputation, on how the individual is viewed from a human standpoint, Paul used it to acknowledge openly the position of authority these individuals possessed, while at the same time subtly emphasizing that God has the ultimate say in whether his gospel is approved. He would have hesitated to use the term ἀπόστολος for them in this context since that was the key term he used to cement his own authority with the Galatians. With this phrasing, Paul can defer to their leadership and at the same time maintain his own, recognizing that each must submit to God in these matters. Paul respects these leaders but does not overestimate their authority (Lightfoot, 103; Betz, 87; Longenecker, 48; de Boer, 107; Schreiner, 121).

μή πως εἰς κενὸν τρέχω ἢ ἔδραμον. Despite the somewhat obtuse nature of this phrase, it is quite moving because it conveys the very human emotions Paul felt in light of the struggle he was facing. On the surface it offers an explanation of why Paul met with the Jerusalem church, but underneath it shows Paul expressing a real concern that he hoped this Jerusalem meeting would resolve. In essence, Paul expresses fear that his ministry would come to nothing. The verb τρέχω, used here twice, is a common metaphor for exertion or effort.[29] Paul uses it elsewhere as a metaphor for ministry (1 Cor 9:24, 26; Phil 2:16), and here specifically for his efforts in Gentile evangelism. Paul expresses a real fear that at the moment of the meeting his current ministry would have been counted as null and void and his future ministry halted.[30] The prepositional phrase εἰς κενὸν expresses the goal or result of the running, which in this instance comes to naught; the word κενός in this context means "without result."[31] Paul's fear is not about whether he was right about the gospel. There is absolutely no way Paul's understanding of the gospel was in

---

28. It is also quite feasible that Paul's repetition of this language for the Jerusalem leaders derived from his opponents' use of this argument in their attacks on him (Lenski, 71; Witherington, 134).

29. BDAG, 1015. The form τρέχω could be an indic., but the conceptual parallel in 1 Thess 3:5, where Paul expresses fear "that our labor would be in vain" (εἰς κενὸν γένηται ὁ κόπος ἡμῶν), affirms the subjunctive here (Lightfoot, 103).

30. See BDF, §361: "Μήπως ἔδραμον G 2:2 is not unreal, s. §370(2)."

31. BDAG, 539.

doubt. The entire force of the letter would be undercut if that were the sense here. Rather, in Paul's mind his fear concerned the practical validity of the ministry he had undertaken on behalf of the Gentiles (Burton, 66, 73; Bruce, 111; Matera, 73; Witherington, 134; Schreiner, 122). A negative outcome in Jerusalem would create a divide in the one church of God between Jew and Gentile (Lightfoot, 103–104; Dunn, 94; George, 140; Hays, 223). "The good news has power only as it fulfills the single plan of the biblical God" (Moo, 125). So Paul did not enter Jerusalem full of bluster. Rather, he met with the Jerusalem church to make a final determination about the value of his ministry to the Gentiles. This was an important, pregnant moment. Paul was not certain of the outcome, nor did he approach this meeting lightly.

2:3 *ἀλλ' οὐδὲ Τίτος ὁ σὺν ἐμοί, Ἕλλην ὤν*. Titus was a Greek and would not have been circumcised as a child, so his presence at the meeting would have forced the issue regardless of Paul's intentions in bringing him.[32] Did Gentiles need to be circumcised in order to fully participate in the communal life of the church? With this parenthetical statement, Paul prefigures the outcome of the meeting he had gone to Jerusalem to pursue. Titus was not compelled to be circumcised, and that would be the model for all Gentiles.[33] Titus represented in a sense the whole of Paul's ministry as apostle to the Gentiles (so Burton, 75; Longenecker, 50; Matera, 80; Witherington, 135; Garlington 2007, 107; de Boer, 111). If Gentiles were to be circumcised, this would have been the time to make that call, but "not even" (*οὐδέ*) Titus was required to be circumcised. The phrase *Τίτος ὁ σὺν ἐμοί* indicates that Titus was likely present with Paul at this private meeting with the Jerusalem leaders. The ptc. phrase *Ἕλλην ὤν* is concessive; it asserts something as true despite the truth of the main statement. Paul uses the term *Ἕλλην* not in a strict sense of nationality but in a broader sense of culture and affinity.[34] Greek in contrast to Jew was a common way to categorize the world from a Jewish perspective

32. See discussion under 2:1 for whether Paul deliberately brought Titus along as a test case.

33. A comparison is often made to Timothy's circumcision (Acts 16:3), but that is a different situation because their cases are entirely different: Timothy had a Jewish mother and was therefore Jewish, while Titus was a Gentile. See Lightfoot, 105; Lenski, 75; Betz, 89; George, 146–47; Schreiner, 124. Paul allowed circumcision as a sign of Jewish identity, but not as a gospel requirement (George, 144–45). I think Luther ably dissects Paul's point on this matter: Circumcision in itself is not wrong, so Jews may continue to be circumcised as they wish, but there can simply be no requirement placed upon Gentiles to receive circumcision. "It is neither sin nor righteousness to be circumcised or uncircumcised, just as it is neither sin nor righteousness to eat or drink (1 Corinthians 8:8). People who say anything different are both foolish and wicked" (Luther, 71).

34. BDAG, 318.

(Dunn, 95). Titus was not compelled to be circumcised even though he was among ardent Jewish Christians.

ἠναγκάσθη περιτμηθῆναι. The verb ἠναγκάσθη carries the sense of compulsion, force, or strong requirement.[35] It is aor. pass., but the agent is not expressed. Context would certainly point to the leaders in Jerusalem with whom Paul was meeting as the ones who might have compelled Titus to be circumcised (Dunn, 96), but the next verse indicates there was a third party involved. Based on what Paul says there, it is very likely that those vociferous individuals were the ones who attempted to compel circumcision. The verb ἀνακάζω occurs two other times in Galatians (2:14; 6:12), the latter of which is also connected to circumcision. Perhaps under the same influence as that which created the text critical problem in v. 5, some argue that Titus was indeed circumcised, but willingly, not through compulsion.[36] This should be rejected out of hand because "οὐδὲ ἠναγκάσθη denies not the attempt to compel but the success of the attempt" (Burton, 76) and it goes against the entire argument of the book (Schreiner, 126).[37]

The verb περιτμηθῆναι refers to circumcision, the practice that Jews regarded as a sign for those who were party to the Abrahamic covenant (Gen 17). This was not the only aspect of Jewish practice with which Paul had to wrestle relative to the Galatians. Later in Gal 2 the issue of food requirements creates conflict between him and Peter, and Paul mentions issues of the calendar in 4:10. Circumcision was the central practice of Jewish piety, however, and as such it had become an issue among the Galatian congregations. Even though Judaism was not unanimous on whether converts had to be circumcised (Betz, 89), the vast majority of Jews required it for full incorporation into Judaism (Schreiner, 123). The Maccabean crisis in the second century BC had recently reinforced its importance on the Jewish psyche, essentially making non-circumcision a nonstarter for devout Jews (Dunn, 96). Consequently circumcision was most often a necessary requirement for Gentile conversion (Oakes, 64–65).[38] In the theological context in which Paul found himself, it represented obedience to the Law more generally (Moo, 120) and had become an issue because the mission of Paul and Barnabas among the Gentiles had become so successful (de Boer, 115n169). But the Jewish emphasis on circumcision was problematic for Paul because of soteriology, eschatology, and anthropology (Oakes, 69). There was no way that requiring circumcision of Gentiles could fulfill what God was

---

35. BDAG, 60.

36. See F. C. Burkitt, *Christian Beginnings: Three Lectures* (London: University of London Press, 1924), 118. He colorfully states, "Who can doubt that it was the knife which really did circumcise Titus that has cut the syntax of Gal. ii 3–5 to pieces?"

37. See de Boer, 111n164, for good contextual arguments why in the end Titus was not circumcised at all versus being circumcised willingly.

38. See Exod 12:48; Esth 8:17 (LXX); Jdt 14:10; Josephus, *Ant.* 13.257–58.

accomplishing with the gospel, and for that reason Paul opposed it for Gentiles.[39]

2:4 δὶα δὲ τοὺς παρεισάκτους ψευδαδέλφους. At this point in the text Paul's syntax and grammar become much more difficult to follow. A textbook example of anacoluthon, this verse begins with no apparent connection to what precedes, and the sentence that follows does not express a grammatically complete thought. Anacoluthon often occurs because of emotion as an author writes, which could certainly be the case here (so George, 141). Paul on the one hand has just expressed a deep fear about his meeting with the Jerusalem leaders in the latter part of 2:2, and then on the other hand mentioned Titus's lack of circumcision, which prefigured the meeting's positive outcome.[40] With this anacoluthon, the reader is left holding the bag: Paul states this as a cause, a normal meaning for the prep. διά, but for what it is a cause is uncertain. William Walker revisits an older argument to make sense of this construction.[41] Instead of considering vv. 4–5 to be a parenthesis, anacoluthon, or the like, he argues that the prepositional phrases κατὰ ἀποκάλυψιν in v. 2 and διὰ τοὺς παρεισάκτους ψευδαδέλφους in v. 4 are parallel, both modifying the verb ἀνέβην at the beginning of v. 2 and offering the primary reasons why Paul went to Jerusalem. Each would then be followed by brief parenthetical material that expands upon them. This view works best if Gal 2:1–10 is regarded as detailing Paul's Jerusalem Council visit, as it would align nicely the preaching of Paul's opponents in Acts 15:1 and Gal 2:4. But even if one does not equate those two passages as the same visit, this view has some merit because it makes good sense of the larger structure of the passage. It is not a perfect interpretation, however, as it requires the reader to mentally connect the prepositional phrase in v. 4 to a verb that is quite far away at the beginning of v. 2. There is enough grammatical water under the semantic bridge by this point that the connection would be very hard to make.[42] Given that Paul felt free to repeat ἀνέβην in close context already in v. 1 and 2, it seems reasonable that he would repeat that here as well for

39. "In the person of Titus the whole gospel as it was preached by Paul, by Peter (Acts 11:1–18; 15:7–11), and by all the apostles came to be embodied. That gospel would have crumbled and fallen if this man would have been circumcised at the demand of the Judaizers. That is why he was not circumcised, not even for minor, secondary, innocent reasons. Once the Judaizers made their demand regarding Titus, they destroyed all reasons for his ever being circumcised" (Lenski, 76).

40. Both Lightfoot, 104, 106, and Dunn, 97, have extremely colorful statements about what caused Paul's convoluted syntax here.

41. W. O. Walker Jr., "Why Paul Went to Jerusalem: The Interpretation of Galatians 2:1–5," *CBQ* 54 (1992): 503–10.

42. Walker, "Why Paul Went," 509–10, discusses this as the most difficult objection against his view, citing Burton, 80–81, who does not accept this interpretation on those very grounds.

clarity if he intended διὰ τοὺς παρεισάκτους ψευδαδέλφους to apply strictly to the visit under discussion.[43] The answer is best found in the immediate context: At the meeting Paul had with the Jerusalem leaders, some people had attempted to compel Titus to be circumcised. It was this issue of compulsory circumcision that was raised by the false brothers (so Burton, 81; de Boer, 112; Moo, 127).[44] With this prepositional phrase Paul identifies a secondary problem that arose during the meeting with the leaders in Jerusalem about the primary issue of Paul's ministry among the Gentiles.

Paul identifies his opponents here as τοὺς παρεισάκτους ψευδαδέλφους, "the devious, false brothers." This short phrase presents three interrelated interpretive problems. First, who exactly were the individuals whom Paul identified as "false brothers"? Second, where had these false brothers been causing trouble? Third, did Paul intend his language to be understood as metaphorical or literal? Regarding their identification as "false brothers," the lexical force of the term ψευδάδελφος is transparent: The prefix ψευδ- means "false," so its connection with ἀδελφός means "false brother, one who is not truly a brother."[45] It is fair to acknowledge at the outset that Paul's language here is polemical: This reflects his deeply negative assessment of those who favored circumcision for Gentiles (Betz, 90; Schreiner, 125; Moo, 127). Very likely neither the Jerusalem apostles nor the wider church there would agree with Paul's assessment; they probably regarded these individuals as Christian brothers (Burton, 78; Bruce, 112; Dunn, 97).[46] "They were orthodox and conscientious Jewish Christians, who were concerned both for the purity of the Christian message amongst Gentiles and for the welfare of Jewish believers amidst the rising tide of Jewish nationalism" (Longenecker, 51). To put a point on it, they "simply understood the nature of their Christian existence in different terms" (Betz, 90). Their emphasis upon their Judaism pointed the church down the path of Torah observance, with circumcision for Gentiles who wished to join the community as the most notable result. This emphasis, however, ran counter to Paul's gospel because it meant that Gentiles could not be accepted as Gentiles, and thus these "false brothers" implicitly denied the universality of the gospel (Longenecker, 51). They had not truly grasped the basic point of the gospel, that is, justification apart

---

43. This view should be contrasted with the construal that sees an ellipsis between v. 3 and 4, in which a reference to the present situation should be supplied. See B. Orchard, "Ellipsis Between Galatians 2:3 and 2:4," *Bib* 54 (1973): 469–81; B. Orchard, "Once Again the Ellipsis Between Gal 2:3 and 2:4," *Bib* 57 (1976): 254–55.

44. Betz, 89–90, argues that it was the whole, entire affair, that is, the dispute and subsequent visit to Jerusalem. Rapa, 576, argues that the matter in view is Gentile/Jewish association: "Their concern appears to have centered at least in part in the freedom of Jewish and Gentile Christians to associate (cf. 2:11–15) and the question of ritual implications for Jewish and Gentile Christians inherent in such association."

45. BDAG, 1096.

46. This would be true regardless of where these individuals had been active.

from works of the Law (Fung, 94). Paul's language about them, even though polemical, reveals a fundamental reality in play: The good news about Jesus creates a new community, and membership in that community is now open to all by faith alone. Those who act or teach differently show themselves to be not fully within that community, despite any appearances to the contrary.

Regarding where these opponents had been active, their location is unclear due to the anacoluthon of this sentence. Given the fact that Paul in vv. 1–3 describes his return to Jerusalem and the outcome regarding Titus related to his meeting there, Jerusalem is a very likely candidate for the location of the "false brothers" (so Moo, 128). These individuals would have been active in the same social spheres at the same time that Paul was present for his consultation with the Jerusalem leaders. This is not the only option, however. In the following paragraph Paul describes difficulties after the Jerusalem meeting caused by people advocating for Torah observance in Antioch; that latter city could be where these individuals were located (so Bruce, 116–17; Fung, 91).[47] Galatia itself is even possible, given the occasion of the letter that caused Paul to write in the first place. Of the three locations, Jerusalem is the best option for two primary reasons: First, the prior mention in the context makes it the most likely frame of reference for Paul's statements in vv. 4–5. Second, the language Paul uses makes the best sense if something happened in Jerusalem that should not have happened, that is, certain people gained access to the private meeting who should have been excluded (Witherington, 136).

Regarding Paul's language, the adj. παρείσακτος describes entering secretly or furtively.[48] It is related to the verb παρεισάγω, which means to enter privately or perhaps surreptitiously.[49] A negative connotation is very common with this word and fits the context here.[50] The use of the verb κατασκοπέω later in the verse connotes war-time activity, metaphorical in this context, so likely the use of παρείσακτος is metaphorical as well. Paul was describing these individuals with a metaphor that evoked the danger of a military battle (Betz, 89, 90; Dunn, 99; George, 147; Hays, 225). These false brothers sneaked like an enemy into a place where they should not have been. The next question is to what exactly the metaphor refers. Could Paul simply refer to the efforts

---

47. Fung, 92, clarifies helpfully regarding the way vv. 3–5 hang together in this view: "On the understanding, then, that v. 3 belongs to the time of the private conference but vv. 4f. to a later occasion, the three verses together mean that the issue of compulsory circumcision did not even arise on the earlier occasion, though Titus, a Greek of Gentile origin, was present; and that it was brought up only at a later period as a result of the machinations of certain pseudo-Christians." This is *contra* Matera, 74, and Hays, 225, who see the infiltration as occurring in Antioch but prior to the Jerusalem meeting.

48. LSJ, 1333; MGS, 1576; BDAG, 774.

49. LSJ, 1333; MGS, 1576; BDAG, 774.

50. W. Michaelis, "παρεισάγω, παρείσακτος," *TDNT*, 5:824.

of the false brothers to push Torah observance generally as being "sneaky"? Or did they actually sneak in somehow into a meeting to which they were not invited and should not have attended? Although certainty cannot be claimed, given Jerusalem as the location where these individuals were active and the occurrence of two meetings when Paul was there, it would make sense that these individuals made their way somehow into the second, more private meeting Paul had with the Jerusalem leaders.

οἵτινες παρεισῆλθον κατασκοπῆσαι. Paul continues his description of these interlopers with a relative clause to describe their actions. The relative pronoun οἵτινες is used here "to emphasize a characteristic quality, by which a preceding statement is to be confirmed."[51] These actions on their part confirm Paul's assertion that they are indeed sneaky false brothers. The verb παρεισέρχομαι means "to slip in, sneak in"[52] and echoes the use of παρείσακτος earlier in the verse. The inf. κατασκοπῆσαι indicates the purpose for which these false brothers entered the community. The verb κατασκοπέω has two different shades of meaning. On the one hand it can mean simply "to inspect, to look at closely," but on the other hand it can take on a more technical nuance of "to spy on, to reconnoiter."[53] It is very often used in a context of military warfare, and that metaphorical nuance is present at this point in the text. Paul describes his opponents as engaging in warfare against him and the freedom that comes from his preaching. When they slipped into this meeting, their goal was to reconnoiter exactly what Paul's preaching was about so they might halt his advance. The negative connotations have an important rhetorical function: They help the Galatians evaluate properly the motives of Paul's opponents in Jerusalem, which in turn helps them evaluate similarly the motives of those who trouble them in Galatia.

τὴν ἐλευθερίαν ἡμῶν ἣν ἔχομεν ἐν Χριστῷ Ἰησοῦ. Grammatically this phrase is the dir. obj. of the inf. κατασκοπῆσαι; this is what Paul's opponents intended to spy on. This phrase defines the central issue surrounding Paul's gospel that created conflict with his opponents. The question for Paul was one of ἐλευθερία, "freedom," of which the implied opposite is slavery to the Torah.[54] In Paul's thought the freedom is from circumcision and by extension from the Law (Burton, 82; Matera, 74–75; de Boer, 113–14). It entailed free association of Jew and Gentile in the new community without restriction or requirement (Bruce, 112; Matera, 82; Hays, 225). The gospel Paul preached did not require circumcision or obedience to any other Torah requirement on the part of the Gentiles. These requirements were no longer appropriate in light of freedom in Christ. That Paul would emphasize this makes good

51. BDAG, 729.

52. BDAG, 774.

53. LSJ, 912; MGS, 1080. For the former see Xenophon, *Cyr.* 7.1.39; for the latter see Plutarch, *Sol.* 9.

54. Paul will develop this idea more carefully in the central section of the book. The concept of freedom also becomes important to his ethical imperatives (see 5:1, 13).

sense, as within Jewish thought there was a connection between the Law and freedom, the essential argument being that obedience to the Torah makes the individual truly free. Paul's opponents had likely emphasized this connection to the Galatians,[55] causing Paul to emphasize it here. Each of the modifiers to ἐλευθερίαν is theologically significant. The pl. pronoun ἡμῶν implies Paul conceives of this as a larger question that affects Jews and Gentiles alike (Burton, 82). The pres. tense of the verb ἔχομεν indicates that the freedom is indeed experienced in the present time; it is a theological reality that the opponents cannot truly take away. The prepositional phrase ἐν Χριστῷ Ἰησοῦ indicates the sphere in which the freedom is attained.[56] Those who are in Christ enjoy this freedom due to their new location in Christ.

ἵνα ἡμᾶς καταδουλώσουσιν. This ἵνα clause indicates the purpose for which Paul's opponents were spying on the freedom he preached. They intended to reduce Paul and the Galatians to slavery. As with other concepts in this section, this language is metaphorical. Paul equates any mandate to obey the Torah as slavery since he had preached freedom from Torah in Christ to the Gentiles. Since his opponents in this incident advocated circumcision for Gentiles generally and Titus in particular, Paul appropriately describes their actions with the word καταδουλόω. The verb is fut. here but equivalent to the subjunctive.[57] Robertson and Wallace both argue that this verb is causative, an important distinction.[58] Paul does not argue that these interlopers wished to enslave others to themselves but rather to the Law; this same thinking shows up later in Gal 4:8–12. This short phrase emphasizes a dynamic of the Jerusalem meeting that is often overlooked: The private meeting was not dyadic but triadic, as there were three parties involved (Burton, 77; Witherington, 127; Hays, 221). There are some important nuances to note as a result. Paul's polemical stance here is against the false brothers, who entered the meeting in some fashion inappropriately; Paul does not take this stance against the Jerusalem leaders or apostles. The false brothers on their part did not put pressure on Paul directly but on the Jerusalem apostles to take a hard stance against Gentile non-circumcision (de Boer, 115). In turn, likely

---

55. See Martyn, 219, who cites *m. ʿAbot* 6:2; Sir 6:23–29; Philo, *Good Person* 45; Jas 1:25. Cf. also Soards and Pursiful, 64; Garlington 2007, 114. J. Neusner, *The Mishnah: A New Translation* (New Haven: Yale University Press, 1988), does not include chapter 6 in his translation of *ʿAbot*, presumably because it is a later addition; see as well H. Danby, *The Mishnah* (London: Oxford University Press, 1933), 458n12, who argues that it was likely added after the eleventh century AD. The general assertion is true, however, even if *m. ʿAbot* 6:2 is excluded on the basis of a late date.

56. Longenecker, 52, argues that ἐν indicates both instrumentality and sphere. Burton, 83, sees this as causal ground or basis.

57. Wallace, *Greek Grammar*, 571.

58. A. T. Robertson, *A Grammar of the Greek New Testament in the Light of Historical Research* (Nashville: Broadman, 1934), 801–802; Wallace, *Greek Grammar*, 412.

the apostles recommended to Paul that he yield on the matter "as a charitable concession to the prejudices of the Jewish converts" (Lightfoot, 105).

2:5 οἷς οὐδὲ πρὸς ὥραν εἴξαμεν τῇ ὑποταγῇ. As with v. 4, this verse begins in such a way that the connection between it and what precedes is difficult to determine. The relative pronoun οἷς has τοὺς ψευδαδέλφους as its antecedent, and that is enough to make the conceptual connection clear. Paul relates his refusal to submit to the demands of those who opposed his gospel at the Jerusalem meeting. The verb εἴκω can mean "to yield, give way," sometimes within a military context to mean "retreat."[59] The phrase πρὸς ὥραν indicates a short moment of time.[60] The translation "not even for a moment" (compare, e.g., ESV, NET) captures the sense nicely. The phrase τῇ ὑποταγῇ is a dat. of manner; the word means "a state of submissiveness."[61] Paul's dealings with the interlopers and the Jerusalem leaders in no way involved any submission on his part. He stood his ground and refused to yield in any way to those who would require Torah obedience on the part of the Gentiles. Paul's statement can be understood as rhetorical motivation to the Galatians to also stand their ground.

ἵνα ἡ ἀλήθεια τοῦ εὐαγγελίου διαμείνῃ πρὸς ὑμᾶς. This ἵνα clause explains either Paul's purpose in not yielding to the opponents or the result of him not yielding to the false brothers. Given the insecurity Paul expressed earlier in v. 2, result is possible, but given Paul's goal for these meetings and the fact that the verb διαμείνῃ is aor. tense instead of pres.—the latter would fit result better—purpose is the better choice. Paul resisted any attempts to force Gentiles into Torah obedience so that the truth of the gospel he preached would remain effective and viable. The phrase ἡ ἀλήθεια τοῦ εὐαγγελίου is unusual; one would more likely expect here the simple τὸ εὐαγγέλιον. It is not a common phrase in the NT, as it occurs only twice in the NT, both times in Galatians (here; 2:14).[62] The force of the gen. noun is ambiguous. The gen. could be apposition ("the truth that is the gospel"), attributed ("the true gospel"), or source ("the truth from the gospel"). In Galatians Paul describes the gospel quite carefully relative to his ministry (see 1:11 and 2:2), and in the context of the meeting with the Jerusalem leaders, Paul likely uses this phrase to focus on his particular preaching of the gospel. This then would be a gen. of source ("the truth from the gospel") and ἀλήθεια would be less the doctrinal, theological truth about the gospel and more the practical implications for Gentiles that flow from it (similarly Longenecker, 53; de Boer, 115). But this reality for the Gentiles reflects back on the gospel itself:

---

59. LSJ, 485; BDAG, 281. See MGS, 601, which makes the latter nuance clear.

60. BDAG, 1102.

61. BDAG, 1041.

62. There is some similar phrasing in Eph 1:13 and Col 1:5, but neither is exactly parallel.

> The particular aspect of the "truth of the gospel" in view here is its power both to bring Gentiles into relationship with God and to maintain them in that relationship right up through the judgment day. Titus, the test case before the council, is a Gentile who has believed the gospel, and he need not add circumcision (or by derivation, obedience to the law of Moses) to that step of faith. By extension, then, the "truth of the gospel" refers to the inherent power of the gospel, by God's grace, to justify and vindicate at the last judgment any human being. Grace is the critical matter. (Moo, 130)

The verb *διαμείνῃ* expresses the verbal action that Paul had as his purpose. Coupled with the prepositional phrase *πρὸς ὑμᾶς* it means simply that Paul intended the message of the gospel as he preached it to remain with the Galatians. The Galatians in this instance represent all Gentiles (Burton, 86; Dunn, 101; Longenecker, 53; Hays, 225).[63] Paul saw this conflict as affecting not simply the Galatians but all Gentiles, the focus of his ministry. His concern was the larger issue of God's plan and work in the world.

2:6 *ἀπὸ δὲ τῶν δοκούντων εἶναί τι*. In this verse Paul turns away from the interlopers to his interactions with the Jerusalem apostles, but even though the topic is more pleasant, this verse is still marked by grammatical breaks. In any case, the import of the verse is clear: Paul's message was not altered in any way by the Jerusalem leaders. The focus of this prepositional phrase falls upon the Jerusalem leaders, here identified with the ptc. *τῶν δοκούντων* in a manner similar to that in v. 2. The difference is that here Paul expresses more fully the idea of human reputation with the addition of *εἶναί τι*. Taken as a whole the phrase *τῶν δοκούντων εἶναί τι* means "those who are regarded to be something." Paul does two things at the same time: He acknowledges the reputable position of the Jerusalem leaders, but he also minimizes them by focusing on their human reputation vis-à-vis God's final approval. This is brought into focus much more clearly with the parenthetical statement that follows. This description of the Jerusalem leaders creates an implicit contrast with the false brothers. If anyone could challenge his gospel, it would be someone of repute, not the false brothers who were seeking to overturn the freedom he proclaimed.

ὁποῖοί ποτε ἦσαν οὐδέν μοι διαφέρει. This is the first clause of a parenthetical statement that Paul inserts in the middle of his argument to offset the reputation of the Jerusalem leaders. The leading phrase *ὁποῖοί ποτε ἦσαν* is an indirect question: "whoever they were." The balance of the clause expresses Paul's disregard for human status and position: "matters nothing to me." The

---

63. *Contra* Lenski, 79, who argues that Paul had only the Galatians in mind: If the apostles ruled against him, he and Barnabas would have had to return to Galatia and essentially undo their ministry there. Similarly George, 151.

force of the impf. verb ἦσαν is not easy to ascertain.[64] At issue is the particular time frame in view. Three options present themselves: First, the apostles may have died, so Paul naturally refers to them with a past tense. Second, Paul no longer regards them in the same way in his writing as he did at the meeting. Third, Paul doesn't care about their past, whether positive or negative. In light of Paul's implicit claim to equality with the twelve apostles, the third option should be preferred (Moo, 132).[65] Paul did not share their history, but he was equally an apostle. Betz, 94, interprets this passage in light of the Stoic doctrine of *adiaphora*, "matters of indifference." This principle allows Paul to relativize the authority of the apostles. This fits with Paul's strategy in this argument: Paul did not reject the authority of the apostles, only "an obsequious veneration of them" (Schreiner, 126). Thus he can at the same time acknowledge their place but minimize their influence.

πρόσωπον ὁ θεὸς ἀνθρώπου οὐ λαμβάνει. The second clause of Paul's parenthetical statement is marked by asyndeton like the first, but the logical connection is still clear. This clause gives the grounds for Paul's measured disregard for human position.[66] This statement is a gnomic truth cast in metaphorical language. A literal translation could be "God does not receive the face of man." The metaphor means that God does not show partiality between individuals; he treats all equally and does not "receive one man's face" over another. Even though humanity favors certain individuals over others, as was certainly the case in how the false brothers favored the Jerusalem apostles over Paul, God does not act that way. The appropriate answer to the conflict at hand can be given only by God himself, which he already did through his revelation to Paul and the commission of him as an apostle. The concept of God's impartiality toward humanity is fundamental to Jewish thought (Betz, 95; Dunn, 103; George, 156), but it also has Stoic roots (Longenecker, 54).[67] This statement reflects as well upon Paul and his apostleship. Paul had encountered the risen Lord, and through that encounter God made him an apostle without regard to who he was or his prior history (Burton, 87; Lenski, 83; Fung, 96). The implicit consequence is that Paul's testimony about the gospel has an equal claim to validity.

ἐμοὶ γὰρ οἱ δοκοῦντες οὐδὲν προσανέθεντο. Here Paul describes how the leaders in Jerusalem did not change his message in any way. The conj. γάρ marks the true connection between vv. 5 and 6, that is, Paul did not yield to his opponents because the leaders responded favorably to his message. Paul used the verb προσανατίθημι previously in 1:16 to describe what he did not

64. See BDF, §330, for discussion on how the tense can assimilate within the indirect question.

65. See also Lightfoot, 107, 108; Burton, 87; Fung, 95; Longenecker, 54; Dunn, 102; Schreiner, 127. Calvin, 54, argues that Paul has priority in time specifically in mind.

66. For a similar statement directed toward Jesus, see Luke 20:21.

67. Dunn, 103, cites Deut 10:17; 2 Chr 19:7; Sir 35:12–13; Jub. 5:16; Pss. Sol. 2:18; 1 En. 63:8; and Rom 2:11 in support.

do after his conversion—that is, he did not consult with anyone about his revelation—and he used the cognate verb ἀνατίθημι to describe what he did do in the context of this Jerusalem meeting—that is, he presented his gospel for consideration to the Jerusalem leaders. The meaning of προσανατίθημι as "to add, contribute" best fits the context given that the question was whether additional requirements from the Torah should be placed upon Gentiles who were now followers of Christ.[68] Thus Paul sums up succinctly the result of the meeting: The Jerusalem leaders added nothing to Paul's preaching. It remained exactly the same as before. The import of this conclusion really cannot be understated:

> We should not underestimate how astonishing a decision was here made: that Jews, leaders of a movement focused on Messiah Jesus, should agree in considered and formal terms that circumcision need no longer be required of Gentiles wishing to be counted full members of what was still a sect of second-Temple Judaism—and that, despite the plainest possible teaching of scripture (Gen. 17:9–14)! (Dunn, 104)

In short, Paul's ministry as the apostle to the Gentiles and his preaching that declared no Torah obligation upon them was as complete and perfect as the apostles' own ministry among the Jews (Lightfoot, 108; Lenski, 82; Bruce, 117; Fung, 95). This undercuts the arguments of the false brothers and exalts Paul's status as equal to the Jerusalem apostles.

2:7 ἀλλὰ τοὐναντίον. The beginning of v. 7 sets up a strong contrast with the final statement of v. 6. Instead of degenerating into a battle royal, the meeting in Jerusalem became an expression of unity between Paul and the Jerusalem leaders. The conj. ἀλλά introduces a positive counterpart to the final phrase of v. 6, and τοὐναντίον, an adv. construction meaning "on the contrary, on the other hand,"[69] provides additional strong contrast. Paul emphatically sets up a positive outcome to the meeting he describes.

ἰδόντες ὅτι πεπίστευμαι. This phrase gives the grounds for the positive outcome to the meeting, which Paul will describe at the end of v. 9. The ptc. ἰδόντες is most naturally temporal, but even so the ὅτι clause (here indicating the content of what was seen) serves as a basis for the positive outcome. The temporal nuance is not an unimportant point of exegesis: Paul implies that at some point the leaders did not see this point. The meeting on Paul's part was an attempt to make sure that they did indeed see and recognize Paul's ministry on equal footing with Peter's. The verb πεπίστευμαι is somewhat unexpected in this context. Paul uses the verb πιστεύω fifty-four times, and only four of those are pf. (1 Cor 9:17; here; 2 Tim 1:12; Titus 3:8). The pf. focuses the present results of a past completed action, and in this context

---

68. So BDAG, 876; *EDNT*, 3:162, but under the spelling προσανατίθεμαι.

69. LSJ, 555; MGS, 2134; BDAG, 330.

Paul uses this pf. pass. verb to refer his conversion and call as apostle to the Gentiles. The pf. tense is important because its emphasis on the continued results of a past action implies that Paul has a "permanent commission" (Lightfoot, 109). The meaning of the verb πιστεύω in this context is "entrust."[70] The agency of this pass. verb is not expressed, but the larger context of the book identifies God as the ultimate agent. The only other place Paul uses this verb in this exact same form is in 1 Cor 9:17, and there the context is also about Paul's ministry from God. In English one would not expect a pf. here but a past pf. because the results are in the past relative to a further action in the past: "When they saw that I *had been entrusted*." When recounting statements indirectly, Greek retains the tense spoken in the original. One can even imagine Paul saying this very sentence at some point during the debate! This then is a pf. retained in indir. discourse. It encapsulates a key argument Paul made in the meeting: God had entrusted him with an important ministry to the Gentiles, just as he had entrusted Peter with a ministry to the Jews.

τὸ εὐαγγέλιον τῆς ἀκροβυστίας. This nous phrase identifies what was entrusted to Paul. The gen. noun τῆς ἀκροβυστίας ("the uncircumcision") functions as a metonymy for ethnic people groups who were uncircumcised, that is, the Gentiles.[71] The next statement, which focuses on Peter's connection to "the circumcised," makes clear that εὐαγγέλιον does not refer to a separate gospel in terms of content, but rather a separate ministry of the gospel with implications that were lived out in different ways among different groups. This language shows that circumcision was the crucial issue at this time (de Boer, 119), but it was also a representative issue as Paul's larger arguments about the Law make clear.

καθὼς Πέτρος τῆς περιτομῆς. With this phrase Paul equates his ministry with Peter's because the source and enablement for each was the same. They had both been entrusted with their ministries by God. Paul places himself on a plane equal with Peter, whose credentials and authority none would deny. The strength of the statement flows from the correlative conj. καθώς, which boldly states the equality. The verb that Paul used previously concerning his own ministry is implied here with reference to Peter: "just as Peter [was entrusted with the gospel] for the circumcised." Just as ἀκροβυστία in the prior phrase was a metonymy for people groups who were uncircumcised, so περιτομή stands in for the Jewish people who were circumcised.

This statement forms a strong defense of Paul's gospel: God had entrusted Peter and Paul equally, Peter with a ministry of the gospel to the Jews and Paul with a ministry of the gospel to the Gentiles. Paul did not simply assert this; the leaders in Jerusalem fully recognized and accepted this equality between their respective ministries. It was the response of the Jerusalem leaders to this equality that Paul wanted to highlight in this verse (cf. Martyn, 203), as that would be a primary defense of his position before

---

70. BDAG, 818.

71. See BDAG, 39.

the Galatians and against his opponents. In essence, this is an example of contextualization of the gospel message. Peter and Paul would have each proclaimed particular emphases to their particular audiences (Burton, 91; Dunn, 106; Schreiner, 128; Moo, 134). Paul would preach to Gentiles that they need not take on circumcision; Peter would preach to Jews that they that they need not abandon circumcision (Burton, 92).

2:8 ὁ γὰρ ἐνεργήσας Πέτρῳ εἰς ἀποστολὴν τῆς περιτομῆς. Here Paul offers the evidence that provides the warrant for his prior statement about the equality of his and Peter's ministry. It amounts to a parenthesis in his larger argument. The subst. ptc. ὁ ἐνεργήσας refers to God. Paul uses the same verb ἐνεργέω elsewhere to describe God's action in believers (1 Cor 12:6; Eph 1:11; Phil 2:13).[72] Here the language points to God's activity of designating Peter as an apostle and making his ministry effective. The use of the ptc. is a rhetorical strategy that keeps the focus not on human action but on God's identity and action in the present moment (Martyn, 202). The force of the dat. case with the noun Πέτρῳ (and the following pronoun ἐμοί) is a little unclear. BDAG argues that this is a dat. of advantage ("the one who was at work *for* Peter")[73] while Wallace considers this a dat. of means/instrument.[74] The dat. of advantage is preferred because the expressed goal of God's activity in the prepositional phrase εἰς ἀποστολὴν τῆς περιτομῆς is an office, not a person. The argument is that God worked on behalf of Peter to establish him in that apostolic office.

The word ἀποστολή only occurs four times in the NT. It shows contours of meaning very similar to the noun ἀπόστολος (see discussion in Gal 1:1) owing to their common root. It can mean an action of sending off or dispatching, and this comports with the particular meaning within the NT context of the office of an apostle.[75] The NT usage is not solely Pauline; Acts 1:25 refers to Judas's vacant place in the group of Jesus's twelve disciples as τὸν τόπον τῆς διακονίας ταύτης καὶ ἀποστολῆς. The other occurrences are in Rom 1:5 and 1 Cor 9:2, and each has a similar meaning to that found here. Paul's point is that God was working for Peter to establish his ministry to the Jews.

ἐνήργησεν καὶ ἐμοὶ εἰς τὰ ἔθνη. In this clause Paul parallels God's work to establish Peter's ministry to God's work to establish his own. Although Paul does not state it with a correlative conj., the point is the same because the

---

72. For an important clarification, see G. B. Winer, *A Treatise on the Grammar of New Testament Greek, Regarded as a Sure Basis for New Testament Exegesis* (Edinburgh: Clark, 1882), 323, who says, "In the verb ἐνεργεῖν we find a distinction in usage between the active and the middle, the active being used by Paul of *personal* (1 C. 12:6, G. 2:8, E. 1:11, al.), the middle of *non-personal* activity (Rom. 7:5, Col. 1:29, 2 Th. 2:7, al.): hence in 1 Th. 2:13 ὅς must he referred, not to θεός, but to λόγος."

73. BDAG, 335.

74. Wallace, *Greek Grammar*, 162–63.

75. BDAG, 121.

adjunctive *καί* drives home the point: God who worked on behalf of Peter worked also for Paul.[76] The aor. indic. ἐνήργησεν states the fact that God worked but without elaboration; Paul likely in the meeting referenced his nascent missionary work undertaken immediately after his conversion. Just as Πέτρῳ was a dat. of advantage, so is ἐμοὶ, and just as εἰς ἀποστολὴν τῆς περιτομῆς indicated the goal of God's activity on Peter's behalf, so εἰς τὰ ἔθνη indicates the goal of God's activity on behalf of Paul (with the noun ἀποστολήν elided). Betz makes much of the absence of the word ἀποστολή applied to Paul (Betz, 98), arguing that later Paul's opponents would use this absence against him (Betz, 99; so Martyn, 203). This deduction is entirely overdrawn, however: The imbalance of v. 7 *contra* Peter—there he is not described with πεπίστευται—shows the imbalance of v. 8 is insignificant (Soards and Pursiful, 70). The best explanation here for the absence of ἀποστολή is brachyology, not a lack of attestation about Paul's apostolic office in the context of the original meeting (so Fung, 98; Schreiner, 129; de Boer, 122; Moo, 135).[77]

There is an important aspect of Paul's argument that should be highlighted: Paul attributes the effective ministry of Peter to God's work, appropriately recognizing that God is at work in a ministry and apostleship other than his own. All would recognize Peter as having an apostolic office from God among the Jews.[78] But his logic does not remain there. Paul's point is that the same God is at work to establish Paul's apostolic office among the Gentiles. If the former is acknowledged, the latter must be acknowledged as well.

2:9 *καὶ γνόντες τὴν χάριν τὴν δοθεῖσάν μοι.* This ptc. phrase is parallel to the one that begins with ἰδόντες in v. 7. The ptc. γνόντες just like the previous one is most likely temporal, but more broadly the dir. obj. here gives the grounds for the positive decision rendered by the leaders. Paul frequently speaks of "the grace that was given to me" (see Rom 12:3; 15:15; 1 Cor 3:10; Eph 3:2, 7, 8); it uniformly refers to his role as an apostle to the Gentiles (so also Bruce, 121; Matera, 77; Hays, 227). The noun χάρις in the construction emphasizes the divine origin of Paul's ministry. Even though the referent here is his apostolic office, the connotations of God's beneficence freely bestowed are

---

76. The nature of this apostolic work is unstated. Bruce, 119, argues for "signs of divine power," but the working may simply have been in the effectiveness of the ministry, that is, the response of the hearers to the gospel. See Lenski, 87, who argues that God worked "by grace and by providence in the widest sense."

77. Bruce, 119, refers to parallels in Rom 1:5 and 1 Cor 9:2 for affirmation that Paul's own mission was indeed an ἀποστολή.

78. Paul seems to write as if the Galatians know clearly about Peter and his ministry (de Boer, 121). This would thus be an important argument for them to process regarding their current situation.

in no way eclipsed.[79] It speaks as well of the fundamental character of Paul's mission to the Gentiles (Martyn, 203), that of grace given freely. The adj. particle δοθεῖσαν is pass. voice. This is a divine passive, which points to God as the agent of the action. With this phrase Paul continues his argument that his gospel had a divine origin, arguing essentially that his apostleship and gospel were inherently connected. The Jerusalem leaders at this critical meeting recognized that God was the one who bestowed Paul's ministry upon him and made him effective for it. The decisive evidence that swayed the Jerusalem leaders is not stated. Likely it was a combination of everything Paul has already discussed in the letter: his conversion, his preaching and evangelistic ministry, and the discussion in the meetings in Jerusalem (Burton, 91; Longenecker, 55). With this new understanding about the origin of his ministry, the decision of the leaders in the meeting regarding Paul and his message could be nothing but affirmative.

Ἰάκωβος καὶ Κηφᾶς καὶ Ἰωάννης. Paul mentions here specifically the three apostles with whom he met and who made the decision to accept his ministry. It is unclear whether Paul met only with the apostles in his private meeting or whether other church leaders were present. In any case the apostles' response to Paul is key, and that is what Paul highlights here. James and Peter had been mentioned before within the context of Paul's first visit to Jerusalem (1:18–19). Paul had not yet seen John; this is the first (and only) time he is mentioned in Galatians. The John mentioned here is the disciple of Jesus who later wrote the Gospel and Epistles that bear his name.[80] Although not as prominent as Peter in the context of Jerusalem, John clearly was a leader among the disciples and in the early church. He is mentioned along with his brother James right after Peter in the earliest list of the disciples (Mark 3:13–19).[81] More to the point of what Paul argues here in Galatians, John was involved in the initial expansion of the gospel outside of Jerusalem when he and Peter were sent to Samaria to follow up with those who had recently

79. See BDAG, 1080, which says, "Paul knows that through the χάρις of God he has been called to be an apostle, and that he has been fitted out w. the powers and capabilities requisite for this office fr. the same source."

80. For a robust defense of this view relative to the Gospel of John, see D. A. Carson, *The Gospel According to John* (Grand Rapids: Eerdmans, 1991). For one relative to the Epistles, see W. H. Harris III, *1, 2, 3 John: Comfort and Counsel for a Church in Crisis* (Dallas: Biblical Studies, 2009).

81. Both Matt 10:1–4 and Luke 6:12–16 alter Mark's wording in various ways in their lists. For a helpful study on the disciples within the context of the historical Jesus, see S. McKnight, "Jesus and the Twelve," in *Key Events in the Life of the Historical Jesus*, ed. D. L. Bock and R. L. Webb, WUNT 247 (Tübingen: Mohr Siebeck, 2009), 181–214.

"accepted the word of God" (Acts 8:14).[82] Coupled with Peter's experience of seeing the gospel expand to the Gentiles (Acts 10–11), John's experience was likely great help to Paul in securing a positive outcome in this meeting. The order of the names is significant as it implies that James at the time of the meeting had become a greater authority than Peter. The order of names in some sense reflected the organization of the leadership of the Jerusalem church (Martyn, 204).

οἱ δοκοῦντες στῦλοι εἶναι. This phrase uses the ptc. form of δοκέω, which Paul has used before (2:2, 6), to describe the Jerusalem leaders with whom he met. The ptc. οἱ δοκοῦντες is in apposition to the three names Ἰάκωβος καὶ Κηφᾶς καὶ Ἰωάννης, so there is more specificity here than in prior uses. The collocation of στῦλοι with οἱ δοκοῦντες shows that Paul calls Peter, James, and John "pillars" with regard to how they are perceived by others. There is no doubt that they were indeed leaders of the Jerusalem church, but Paul's phrasing concerns the human side of the equation, not God's view of things. The noun στῦλος, "pillar," refers literally to a cylindrical architectural support and by metaphorical extension to someone recognized for spiritual leadership.[83] The use of this term in the LXX to refer to literal pillars of the tabernacle and temple could explain why this usage would be applied to Peter, James, and John (so Moo, 136–37), but there are numerous examples from Greek literature of a purely metaphorical sense of the term without religious associations (Longenecker, 57). The Galatians could have easily understood it based upon this usage without any specific allusions to Jewish thought (de Boer, 124). The other Pauline use in 1 Tim 3:15 refers to the church as στῦλος καὶ ἑδραίωμα τῆς ἀληθείας, "a pillar and buttress of the truth" (ESV). In light of 1 Tim 3:16, which focuses on particular revelation about Christ, Paul's use in that epistle would refer to the church's function to preserve that revelation, which has an analogue in the current role Peter, James, and John played at this meeting with Paul.

δεξιὰς ἔδωκαν ἐμοὶ καὶ Βαρναβᾷ κοινωνίας. With this phrase the final decision of this meeting in Jerusalem is proclaimed. Paul masterfully arranges his material in this paragraph so that this decision is anticipated a number of times, but the reader does not hear the actual outcome until this very moment. The key phrase here, occurring in reversed order in what Paul actually wrote, is ἔδωκαν δεξιὰς. This phrase does not occur anywhere else in the NT, but it occurs frequently in the LXX and in classical Greek. It means to come to terms of peace, to cease hostility, and to in some way become friends.[84] See, for example, its use in 1 Macc 6:58, where Lysias encourages his king and

82. The following verses clarify that the key issue of their visit was the reception of the Holy Spirit by these new converts who had "only been baptized in the name of the Lord Jesus" (Acts 8:16).

83. BDAG, 949.

84. Lightfoot, 110, dryly notes, "In the patriarchal times the outward gesture which confirmed an oath was different, Gen. 24:2."

commanders to stop hostilities against the Jews so he can return to Antioch and fight against Phillip, who was attempting to take the kingdom by force:

> νῦν οὖν δῶμεν δεξιὰς τοῖς ἀνθρώποις τούτοις καὶ ποιήσωμεν μετ' αὐτῶν εἰρήνην καὶ μετὰ παντὸς ἔθνους αὐτῶν
>
> Now therefore let us give the right hand to these men and let us make peace with them and with all their nation.

In this context the idiom of "give the right hand" clearly means to come to peaceful terms in a time of battle. Another good example is Xenophon, *Anab.* 1.6.6, where during Orontos's trial for treason Cyrus spoke about how they had come to peace:

> καὶ ἐγὼ αὐτὸν προσπολεμῶν ἐποίησα ὥστε δόξαι τούτῳ τοῦ πρὸς ἐμὲ πολέμου παύσασθαι, καὶ δεξιὰν ἔλαβον καὶ ἔδωκα.
>
> And I, by the war I waged against him, made him count it best to cease from warring upon me, and I received and gave the hand-clasp of friendship.[85]

What is striking in these two examples is the context of war that precedes the giving of the right hand. Paul was not literally at war with Peter, James, and John, but he uses the metaphor to highlight the extreme difficulty he was experiencing in his relationship with them because of the agitation of the false brothers.[86] It speaks to the psychological turmoil Paul experienced relative to this meeting and the importance that it be resolved properly. The word κοινωνία clarifies that equality is in view, not surrender (Lightfoot, 110). It clarifies the idiom that in Jewish texts did not necessarily denote equality (Longenecker, 58). Thus it emphasizes the partnership in the agreement that the meeting had reached (Burton, 95; de Boer, 124).The recipients of the right hand of fellowship were Paul and Barnabas. As the key individuals who were sharing the gospel with the Gentiles, Paul and Barnabas were the analogues to Peter, James, and John. This decision puts their ministries and offices on equal footing. This was an important ratification of Paul's mission, and in Galatians it serves as the final proof that Paul's gospel was divine in origin and was worthy of acceptance.

ἵνα ἡμεῖς εἰς τὰ ἔθνη, αὐτοὶ δὲ εἰς τὴν περιτομήν. This ἵνα clause on the heels of the declaration of détente between Paul and the Jerusalem leaders provides additional details about what the "right hand of fellowship" entailed. This is the practical outcome of the agreement that was reached, founded upon a recognition of Paul's apostleship as legitimate and on par with Peter's. The

85. Greek text and translation taken from Xenophon, *Anabasis*, trans. C. L. Brownson, revised by John Dillery, LCL 90 (Cambridge, MA: Harvard University Press, 1998), 102–3.

86. Compare this to the military metaphors Paul already used in 2:4.

ἵνα here is epexegetical and provides further explanation.[87] The ἡμεῖς is an "exclusive" we,[88] as Paul has in mind himself and Barnabas as opposed to Peter, James, and John. Implied in each of these phrases is something like "might go" or "might preach"; the latter is certainly preferred given the preference Paul has shown for εὐαγγελίζω in this letter.[89] These clauses should not be understood as conditions placed upon the fellowship between Paul and the Jerusalem leaders. Rather, this is the decision about how these apostles would move forward now that the question of the legitimacy of Paul's gospel was answered. Practically this is what they had been already doing; now this arrangement has the approval of all the leaders of the early church. This also has an important place in Paul's argument vis-à-vis the Galatians: The Gentile Galatians are now forced to acknowledge, despite what the opponents have been telling them, that Paul's gospel had the approval of the leaders in Jerusalem. This places those who were working against Paul, supposedly under the auspices of the Jerusalem church, in an extremely negative light, grounding further Paul's call upon the Galatians to return to his gospel.

The general contours of the agreement are best understood as a division of labor along ethnic lines (so Betz, 100; Martyn, 213–16; Schreiner, 131), not a geographic division of territories (argued by Burton, 98; Lenski, 86; Matera, 77; de Boer, 125). That is certainly the implication of the circumcision language, which assumed cultural and religious differences between Jew and Gentile, not geographic ones. As a practical matter, however, it is not likely that there was sharp differentiation between territory and race among Jewish Christians given the overlap between these spheres in the ancient world (Bruce, 125; Fung, 100; Longenecker, 59; Witherington, 141). Other NT passages show that this agreement was neither intended strictly nor followed too rigidly (Schreiner, 131; Moo, 137). The book of Acts indicates that Paul had regular contact with Jews, even on missionary journeys after the Jerusalem Council. If Gal 2 depicts Acts 15, that would be clear evidence that the agreement struck here was not rigidly interpreted.[90] In general then, but not absolutely with strict boundaries, the agreement indicated that Paul and Barnabas would continue their ministry among the Gentiles and the

---

87. See E. D. W. Burton, *Syntax of the Moods and Tenses in New Testament Greek* (1900; repr., Grand Rapids: Kregel, 2000), 91–92: "Complementary or epexegetic limitation of verbs of various significance; the clause defines the content, ground, or method of the action denoted by the verb, or constitutes an indirect object of the verb. ... See also John 9:22; Gal. 2:9; in both these latter passages the ἵνα clause defines the content of the agreement mentioned in the preceding portion of the sentence." BDF, §391(3), implies a conditional sense for ἵνα: "Ὥστε (ἐφ' ᾧτε) 'on the condition that' does not appear in the NT (for which ἵνα G 2:9)," but the context of the final decision of the Jerusalem leaders implies something much stronger than condition.

88. See Wallace, *Greek Grammar*, 398.

89. So also Robertson, *Grammar*, 394; Winer, *Grammar*, 735.

90. See as well Paul's own testimony on this matter in 1 Cor 9:19–23.

Jerusalem apostles would minister among the Jews.[91] This division along ethnic lines would be a simple matter of recognition of both the calling from God upon the individual apostle and a recognition of past effectiveness. This would have a very practical application for the Galatians: According to the agreement, they were under Paul's apostolic care (de Boer, 126). Any efforts to bring them under the auspices of Jerusalem would have been seen as counter to the agreement.

2:10 *μόνον τῶν πτωχῶν ἵνα μνημονεύωμεν*. This *ἵνα* clause functions differently from the previous one. It is similarly a further qualification of the "right hand of fellowship," but stronger, functioning as an impv. (Bruce, 125).[92] It is not an addition to the agreement but rather part of the agreement itself (Burton, 99). A verb of saying of some kind would be implied: "[They told us] only that we must remember the poor." The referent of "the poor" is up for debate. The article here could be generic, indicating that no specific group is in mind. Rather, the poor as a class is intended.[93] Caring for the poor was an important covenantal obligation (Dunn, 113) and part and parcel of Jewish religious sensibility (Oakes, 72). The poor often represented those who were spiritually dependent upon God (Betz, 102). The command here in this context would simply be a reminder to continue exercising care over this group of people who were very important to God, a part of the Christian mission from the start (see, e.g., Acts 6:1–7). Alternatively, the referent of "the poor" could be quite specific: The group in mind could very well be the poor of the Jerusalem church (Bruce, 126; Dunn, 112; Moo, 139). The command here would become very specific with important implications: Remember to care for the poor of the Jerusalem church, the church that is the root from which the Gentile branches have sprung (Fung, 102–103; Longenecker, 60; Martyn, 206).[94] This referent becomes more likely when Rom 15:26 is taken into account (Fung, 102; de Boer, 127). There Paul specifies that specific Gentile churches were happy to give *εἰς τοὺς πτωχοὺς τῶν ἁγίων τῶν ἐν Ἰερουσαλήμ*, "to the poor of the saints in Jerusalem." If this later verse from Romans is allowed to influence Paul's vague reference here in Galatians, the specific referent of the poor in the Jerusalem church could be readily defended. Also important to consider is the general frame of reference for this Jerusalem visit. If Gal 2 depicts the

---

91. Calvin's application of this agreement is classic: "But if Peter's apostleship had a peculiar reference to the Jews, let the Romanists see on what ground they derive from him their succession to the primacy. If the Pope of Rome claims the primacy because he is Peter's successor, he ought to exercise it over the Jews" (Calvin, 58).

92. S. E. Porter, *Idioms of the Greek New Testament* (Sheffield: Sheffield Academic Press, 1995), 224; Wallace, *Greek Grammar*, 477.

93. See Wallace, *Greek Grammar*, 227–30, for discussion.

94. Witherington, 145, argues that the leaders may have seen it as a way for Paul and Barnabas to appear as Law-abiding, while Paul would have seen it as the eschatological tribute of Gentiles to Zion.

same Jerusalem visit as Acts 11, then famine relief was a principal reason Paul was in Jerusalem (so Fung, 103).[95] The balance of the evidence points to "the poor" as having a specific referent here, namely, the poor in the Jerusalem church whom Paul set out to help early in his ministry and continued to help through specific, later collections.

ὃ καὶ ἐσπούδασα αὐτὸ τοῦτο ποιῆσαι. With this phrase Paul emphasizes his desire to serve the poor as already present: "which very thing I was eager to do!"[96] The relative pronoun ὅ refers to the entirety of the preceding sentence.[97] The καί signals both parallelism to and confirmation of what he said previously.[98] The use of τοῦτο here is resumptive, referring back to the ἵνα clause that contains the injunction to remember the poor. This second phrase reiterates the command given in the first, and the emphasis here is quite strong.[99] This shows that the requirement to remember the poor is not an authoritative command but rather an encouragement to continue what Paul was already doing (Moo, 138). Paul, Peter, James, and John were never that far apart on any issue related to the gospel, whether that was the theological foundation of what Jesus accomplished, the outworking of the gospel in Paul's ministry to the Gentiles, or his efforts to support the poor in Jerusalem.

The meeting that Paul described in Gal 2:1–10 was a turning point for Paul. When Paul went to Jerusalem to meet with the church and its leaders, a great deal was at stake. The outcome would determine whether Paul's ministry would continue as it had before with his insistence upon a Torah-free gospel for the Gentiles. A negative outcome would be disastrous, as it would effectively make Paul's ministry null and void, impacting for the worse the unity of the nascent church, this new community God was creating in Christ. Thankfully Paul and the Jerusalem leaders were able to see eye to eye. All recognized that God was at work equally among Jews and Gentiles through Peter and Paul respectively, and all agreed that unity could be maintained while respecting the different spheres of ministry God had granted to each. The meeting affirmed Paul's office as apostle to the Gentiles and provided an important basis for him to persuade the Galatians about the truth of his gospel.

---

95. This emphasis could still be in place if Gal 2 depicts Acts 15, but it would not be nearly as prominent.

96. In keeping with his view that Gal 2 depicts Acts 15, Lightfoot, 111, argues that the switch from the pl. μνημονεύωμεν to the sg. ἐσπούδασα is significant because Paul had parted from Barnabas in Acts 15:39. I prefer to see it simply as an emphasis upon his own actions and motivation, which are his central consideration of the book vis-à-vis the Galatians.

97. Robertson, *Grammar*, 714.

98. S. E. Runge, *Discourse Grammar of the Greek New Testament: A Practical Introduction for Teaching and Exegesis* (Peabody, MA: Hendrickson, 2010), 340–41.

99. Winer, *Grammar*, 185, calls the emphasis here "unmistakable."

Theological Comments

This paragraph creates some difficulties for our understanding of Paul and his psychology, so to speak. At issue is his conviction of the truth of his message juxtaposed with his apparent doubts about whether his ministry would be accepted by the Jerusalem leaders. On the one hand, Paul makes statements that imply that he harbored no doubts whatsoever about the truth of his message, and he references the Jerusalem leaders in ways that minimize their authority. So Paul presents himself as confident and sure about the truth of his message and the authority of his role as the apostle to the Gentiles. But on the other hand, Paul implies that he carried reservations about his ministry and legitimately sought the approbation of the Jerusalem leadership. This is a difficult dichotomy to understand, especially given the popular portrait of Paul as the supremely confident apostle who withstood all onslaughts against his presentation of the gospel. In truth we need not struggle long with this disparity because Paul was simply being human. He knew the truth of his message and was firmly convinced that God had revealed it to him and given him his ministry, and yet he experienced doubts given the intensity of the opposition he received from those who were seeking to lead the Galatians away and the subtle pressure coming from certain quarters that were closely connected to the Jerusalem apostles. To Paul's credit he did not ignore the leaders of the church while blithely going his own way. That course of action would certainly have split the church into two irreconcilable factions, one Jewish and one Gentile, something entirely contrary to Paul's ministry and understanding of Christ's work (see, e.g., Eph 2:11–22). Rather, he sought the counsel of the Jerusalem leaders and ultimately received their affirmation, which ensured that the church would continue to develop and minister as the unified church of God.

Understanding the function of this passage within the book clarifies its theological weight. As stated above, this section serves the larger purpose of proving that Paul's gospel was divine in origin. Paul includes this material not to exalt himself over the Jerusalem apostles, nor to put his Law-free gospel to the Gentiles first over any different contextualization taken by those preaching to Jews. Instead, he describes this meeting and its positive outcome to show the essential unity on the gospel held by all the leaders of the church at that time. This is an important outcome that should not be understated or undervalued. Because of this outcome, Paul could move forward definitively with his Gentile mission without fear of restriction or uselessness. It was now certain that the truth of the gospel could continue to be proclaimed to the Gentiles. And more to the point pragmatically, he could call the Galatians to account on the grounds that by moving away from his gospel they were moving away from this declaration of acceptability on the part of the Jerusalem apostles. Whatever his opponents might say and however they might persuade, it was they who were out of step with Jerusalem, not Paul. This would thus serve to motivate the Galatians to remain loyal to Paul's gospel.

One important theological theme from this text is the unity of the gospel even with diversity of application. Clearly Paul and the Jerusalem leaders preached the same gospel: They all preached Jesus Christ as the crucified and risen Messiah, the savior for the whole world. The Jerusalem meeting held this truth as assumed but still central, and there was absolutely no indication that it was discussed or in doubt. But around this strong unity developed a diversity of application most noticeably along the ethnic division of Jew and Gentile. For the Jew, to believe in Jesus Christ as the Messiah meant a complete fulfillment of all that it meant to be a Jew. To throw off Jewishness would in some sense be a denial of what the Messiah accomplished. But for the Gentile, to believe in Jesus Christ as the Messiah meant full incorporation into the family of God without regard for ethnic distinction. To add Jewishness would be a denial of the global scope of the Messiah's accomplishments. Both Jew and Gentile believed in the same Messiah and accepted the proclamation of the same gospel. But each lived it out differently with regard to their ethnic background. In a real sense the beauty of the gospel is the concord that it attains among diverse peoples who each have faith in the same Messiah.

Application and Devotional Implications

The contemporary church clearly struggles with the issue of unity. One need only catalog denominational differences among Protestants to get a sense of how fractured the Christian church actually is.[100] The rise of various movements and networks in recent times prove that some within the church can be unified around certain themes, doctrines, or practices, but these newer developments have yet to prove their longevity or breadth compared to established denominations. In some sense, the current situation would have shocked Paul, for whom the singular nature of the church was an important theological axiom. At the same time, believers do have legitimate differences theologically and practically that should not be ignored. Paul himself represented a difference of praxis from the Jerusalem church, and he certainly

---

100. David Dockery, in his plenary address at the ETS Southwest regional meeting on March 7, 2014, at Southwestern Baptist Theological Seminary, stated that there are about 30,000 different denominations in the United States today. On the other end of the spectrum, *Yearbook of American & Canadian Churches 2012* (Nashville: Abingdon, 2012), published by the National Council of Churches USA, lists 227 groups under the heading "Religious Bodies in the United States Arranged by Families," which includes many groups widely recognized as denominations. Obviously given the difference in numbers, the definition of a denomination is open to discussion.

expressed his theology in ways that emphasized different aspects of Christ's person and work. The question that this paragraph answers has to do with the bridge between oppressive, monolithic unity on the one hand and crippling, diluting diversity on the other. For Paul the question was, how can I continue in my distinct ministry to the Gentiles while remaining true to the leadership of the Jerusalem church? The answer was found in honestly representing how God was at work in him, recognizing that divine constancy in the ministry of Peter, and affirming their unity around the central affirmation of the kerygma, namely, that Jesus was the crucified and risen Messiah of Israel for the whole world. The fact that Peter and Paul were agreed on the central truth of the gospel coupled with the fact that God was readily at work in both Peter and Paul was the key for Paul's full and final legitimization in the eyes of the Jerusalem leaders. These two parallel points can serve as an important pattern for the contemporary church, too, as we work for unity in the diversity we express. As we affirm the central truth of the gospel and recognize God's legitimate work through others, we can be unified in our diversity.

Focusing on these two parallel points leads to two additional questions of application: What are the central doctrinal affirmations of the church today? How can we tell that God is at work through others? In other words, on which points of doctrine do believers need to agree to be considered unified, and what evidence can we seek to determine if God is at work through others? The first question is the easier one to answer. Christianity has historically acknowledged that certain subjective beliefs stated objectively as doctrines are central to being Christian. These have been classically expressed in the various creeds of the church, such as the Nicene Creed, developed out of the Council of Nicea in AD 325. Evangelicalism in more recent times has developed a theological center around certain distinguishing characteristics. David Bebbington identified four key characteristics that mark evangelicals: biblicism, crucicentrism, conversionism, and activism.[101] Whether one looks to the historic creeds or current definitions of evangelicalism, there are definite, measurable theological contours that have marked the church both historically and in contemporary times, and these shared convictions provide a doctrinal basis for unity within all the contemporary expressions of the Christian church.

The second question concerning evidence for the work of God in another is much more difficult to answer. The central truth that led to a positive decision at this meeting was that God was equally at work within Peter and Paul; he had divinely appointed each to their respective ministries. Within this paragraph Paul does not describe how this assertion was assessed or accepted. Instead, he simply states that it was indeed accepted. The leaders

101. D. Bebbington, *Evangelicalism in Modern Britain: A History From the 1730s to the 1980s* (London: Unwin Hyman, 1989), 2–17. Although these might be considered sociological and not theological, they certainly have a doctrinal basis.

in Jerusalem recognized Paul's ministry to the Gentiles as coming from God (v. 7). They accepted Paul's argument that the same God was at work in Peter and in him (v. 8). They also recognized Paul's apostleship as a divine gift (v. 9). So based upon the text of this paragraph itself, this question remains open, but it need not stay that way given what Paul says elsewhere in this vein. Within Galatians itself, Paul makes an important implicit argument in defense of his gospel. Essentially the work of the Spirit in the lives of the Galatians is given as proof that Paul's gospel, not that of his opponents, is true. Paul argues clearly in Gal 3:1–5 that God's gift of the Spirit to the Galatians because of their belief in the gospel shows that reverting to works of the Law would be detrimental and against God's intentions. This presence of the Spirit proves then to be a central proof of the validity of Paul's ministry. Paul makes a similar statement elsewhere in Rom 15:19 as proof of Christ's work through him. Outside Paul we can turn to the narrative of Peter and Cornelius in Acts 10–11. The key conclusion made by Peter himself is apropos to the current discussion: God gave the same Spirit to the Gentiles as well as the Jews, thus proving that God is at work in both. Although it is not stated explicitly in Gal 2:1–10, the affirming work of the Spirit in the ministries of Peter and Paul would readily have been the confirming evidence needed for the Jerusalem leaders to approve of Paul's ministry.

How then does someone recognize the work of the Spirit today? The Pauline answer is not hard to find. In the same context in Romans where Paul mentioned the power of the Spirit in his ministry, Paul speaks of its effect: He is bringing about the "obedience of the Gentiles" (Rom 15:18), that is, Gentiles are believing that Jesus is the crucified and risen Messiah and they are obeying him as a result. Because of the work of the Spirit in Paul's ministry, Gentiles are professing and obeying the same doctrine that Paul and the leaders in Jerusalem held as central. The Spirit was creating belief in and fidelity to the preached word of Christ. Although not the only measure of the Spirit's work—one may also point to the fruit of the Spirit in Gal 5:22–23 as an important measure—in this context that measure is central.

This paragraph then gives the contemporary church important standards for unity: the consistent confession of the central doctrines concerning the nature of Jesus and his work and the Spirit's affirming work in guiding people to affirm that doctrine and live in obedience to it. When these two dynamics are in place, the church can proclaim unity and claim consistency with Paul and the Jerusalem leaders.

Additional Exegetical Comments

2:1–10 P. F. Esler discusses the social dynamics of this event extensively, applying the broad concept of honor/shame and the more specific concept of challenge/response to his understanding of the text.[102] One of his central goals is to explain the agreement reached here between Paul and the Jerusalem apostles in light of Peter's subsequent behavior in 2:11–14. The basic lines of the argument can be explained as follows: Paul bringing Titus to Jerusalem was a strong challenge to those who advocated for circumcision of Gentiles. They were severely shamed when Titus was not required to be circumcised. Paul made a tactical error by not securing an oath on the part of the Jerusalem leaders regarding their agreement. In an honor/shame culture it is only by oath that one can be certain that another will keep his word, as hiding true intentions behind deception can preserve honor. Subsequently those who were shamed by Paul successfully put pressure on Peter and James to renege from their agreement in order to enact their revenge on Paul. Esler's incisive application of this social construct to the Galatians text does account reasonably for the behavior of many of the players, but the essential argument Paul makes, namely, that it is only God's approbation and action that matter in assessing his gospel, would arguably marginalize the honor/shame matrix in Paul's thoughts and actions.[103] Esler helps account for the behavior of the apostles and Paul's opponents, but he cannot fully account for Paul's actions within that social construct. This is picked up by Oakes, 65, 67, who critiques Esler on a number of counts: The targets of the challenge are the false brothers, not the apostles, and their meeting was private, when honor/shame challenges were generally public. Paul wasn't concerned with his own public honor, so the meeting did not need to be public, but rather only before the "court of public opinion" that mattered on this issue, that is, the Jerusalem apostles.

2:3 B. Orchard argues that the common interpretation of this verse—that the issue of Gentile circumcision arose concerning Titus at this private meeting, and it was decided that he would not be circumcised—misses the mark. Instead, he argues that the issue never even came up.[104] The text and subtext would be along these lines: "Not even Titus who was with me, although he was Greek, was compelled to be circumcised [because the issue did not even come up for discussion]." Verses 4–5 then become a statement about the present situation Paul faces, albeit with an ellipsis of the main verb. This conclusion allows Orchard to equate Gal 2:1–10 with both Paul's famine visit to Jerusalem (Acts 11:30; 12:25) and the Jerusalem Council (Acts 15), the former being parallel to Gal 2:1–3, 6–10, and the latter being parallel to Gal 2:4–5. This hypothesis is attractive in that it does offer a way to synthesize the data of Acts and Galatians coherently, both in terms of the Jerusalem visits and the conflict over circumcision. It also suggests another reasonable

---

102. P. F. Esler, "Making and Breaking an Agreement Mediterranean Style: A New Reading of Galatians 2:1–14," *BibInt* 3 (1995): 285–314.

103. See for further discussion Witherington, 128–31.

104. B. Orchard, "The Problem of Acts and Galatians," *CBQ* 7 (1945): 377–97.

way to understand the question of Titus's circumcision. The difficulty lies in his exegesis of the most difficult verses in the paragraph, vv. 4–5. There is no explicit mention that these verses apply to the present situation facing Paul and the Galatians, which on Orchard's view would soon be solved at the Jerusalem Council; the main clause has to be supplied.[105] Admittedly these verses are difficult because of their choppy grammatical structure, but it is difficult to accept his view absent explicit temporal wording to support it.

2:6 D. Hay presents a helpful analysis of v. 6 that puts the authority of the Jerusalem apostles in proper perspective.[106] "The authority of the Jerusalem leaders is not so important that it could have led [Paul] to change his gospel. ... If these leaders had rejected Paul's message (and persisted in so doing) they would then in his eyes have ceased to be apostles."[107] Similarly J. L. Jaquette (following Betz, 94) argues that Paul here connects to the Stoic topos of indifference, which moves him to disregard the reputation of those apostles and relativize their authority.[108]

2:7–8 There are numerous details here that lead some to argue that Paul is in some way citing an official document that came out of this meeting. First, the phrasing "gospel of the uncircumcision" and "of the circumcision" is not Pauline language. Second, the word ἀποστολή is not applied to Paul. Third, the rough grammar indicates that Paul is not making his own argument but weaving together some preexisting material. None of this stands up to scrutiny. The point of the language here is practical, not theological: Peter and Paul each preached the same gospel of the risen Christ, but to different audiences with appropriate emphases (Fung, 98; Hays, 226). Paul gives no indication that he is quoting any text of an agreement, and there are numerous ellipses in vv. 7–8 (Betz, 97; Matera, 77; Hays, 226). Likely the agreement was oral, not written (Witherington, 142). Arguments that Paul cited a particular document tend to coincide with the North Galatia view, which sees Gal 2 as the same meeting as that detailed in Acts 15 (Longenecker, 55) since there was an official document that was sent out after that consultation. The view that sees Gal 2 as equal to the Jerusalem visit of Acts 11 generally emphasizes the more informal nature of that visit, which would be less likely

---

105. Orchard, "Problem," 382, suggests that 2:4–5 read as follows, with the missing clause that ties these to Paul's current situation in brackets: "(but because of the false brethren privily brought in, who came in privily to spy out our liberty which we have in Christ Jesus, that they might bring us into bondage [the liberty of the Gentiles is now in danger]: to whom we gave place in the way of subjection, no, not for an hour; that the truth of the gospel might continue with you)."

106. D. M. Hay, "Paul's Indifference to Authority," *JBL* 88 (1969): 36–44.

107. Hay, "Paul's Indifference," 36.

108. J. L. Jaquette, "Paul, Epictetus, and Others on Indifference to Status," *CBQ* 56 (1994): 68–80.

to create any official record. No matter the source of Paul's wording, his intended meaning is still clear.

Selected Bibliography

Bacon, B. W. "The Reading of οἷς οὐδέ in Gal. 2:5." *JBL* 42 (1923): 69–80.

Bauckham, R. "Barnabas in Galatians." *JSNT* 2 (1979): 61–70.

Bebbington, D. *Evangelicalism in Modern Britain: A History From the 1730s to the 1980s*. London: Unwin Hyman, 1989.

Burkitt, F. C. *Christian Beginnings: Three Lectures*. London: University of London Press, 1924.

Carson, D. A. *The Gospel According to John*. Grand Rapids: Eerdmans, 1991.

Danby, H. *The Mishnah*. London: Oxford University Press, 1933.

Harris, W. H. III. *1, 2, 3 John: Comfort and Counsel for a Church in Crisis*. 2d ed. Dallas: Biblical Studies Press, 2009.

Hay, D. M. "Paul's Indifference to Authority." *JBL* 88 (1969): 36–44.

Jaquette, J. L. "Paul, Epictetus, and Others on Indifference to Status." *CBQ* 56 (1994): 68–80.

McKnight, S. "Jesus and the Twelve." In *Key Events in the Life of the Historical Jesus*, ed. D. L. Bock and R. L. Webb, 181–214. Tübingen: Mohr Siebeck, 2009.

Neusner, J. *The Mishnah: A New Translation*. New Haven: Yale University Press, 1988.

Orchard, B. "Ellipsis Between Galatians 2:3 and 2:4." *Bib* 54 (1973): 469–81.

———. "Once Again the Ellipsis Between Gal 2:3 and 2:4." *Bib* 57 (1976): 254–55.

———. "The Problem of Acts and Galatians." *CBQ* 7 (1945): 377–97.

Walker, W. O. Jr. "Why Paul Went to Jerusalem: The Interpretation of Galatians 2:1–5." *CBQ* 54 (1992): 503–10.

Xenophon. *Anabasis*. Trans. C. L. Brownson. Revised by John Dillery. LCL 90. Cambridge, MA: Harvard University Press, 1998.

Yearbook of American & Canadian Churches 2012. Nashville: Abingdon, 2012.

Paul's Conflict with Peter (2:11–14)

Textual Notes

2:11 The reading Κηφᾶς is replaced by Πέτρος in the vast majority of manuscripts, but this change is surely secondary. Peter's Aramaic name has impeccable support from Alexandrian witnesses at this point in the text (א A B C 33 81 104 1175 1739 1881), and it is the harder reading. Scribes would very naturally have changed the name here to Peter's more widely used Greek name Πέτρος. For similar textual problems in the book, see 1:18; 2:9, 14.

2:12 NA[28] here reads ἦλθον, a pl. verb that refers to the group of people from James mentioned in the prior clause. A handful of very important witnesses (𝔓[46] א B D* 33 *pc*), however, reads ἦλθεν, a sg. verb that would refer either to James himself or Peter, neither of which makes sense in the context. Despite the value of these witnesses, their reading must be discounted. Scribes were either influenced by the similar wording at the beginning of v. 11 (Ὅτε δὲ ἦλθεν) and harmonized this phrase to the previous one, or they were influenced by the 3 sg. verbs before and after this phrase and modified the original, perhaps as an error of sight or hearing. To account for the strength of the evidence for the variant reading, Lightfoot, 112, argues that Paul intended ἦλθον but the original amanuensis incorrectly recorded ἦλθεν.[1]

2:14 The reading Κηφᾷ is replaced by Πετρῷ in the vast majority of manuscripts, but this change is surely secondary. The Aramaic name should be favored here for the same reason that it is favored in v. 11, namely, it has excellent Alexandrian support and it is the harder reading. For similar textual problems in the book, see 1:18; 2:9, 11.

1. "Such readings are a valuable testimony to the scrupulous exactness of the older transcribers, who thus reproduced the text as they found it, even when clearly incorrect" (Lightfoot, 112).

Translation

11 But when Cephas came to Antioch, I personally took a stand against him
because he had condemned himself.[2] **12** For before certain people from James
arrived, he would regularly eat with the Gentiles. But when they arrived, he
consistently withdrew and separated himself because he was afraid of those
who were circumcised. **13** And the rest of the Jews finally joined with him
in this hypocrisy, so that even Barnabas was carried away by their hypocrisy.
14 But when I saw that they were not walking on the right path toward the
truth of the gospel, I said to Cephas in front of everyone, "If you, although
you are a Jew, live as a Gentile and not as a Jew, how do you compel Gentiles
to live like Jews?"

Commentary

The NT clearly testifies that the early church struggled with how to integrate Gentiles together with Jews into local fellowship, both in practical matters and theological understanding. The early church began as a manifestation of Jewish belief and practice. The central question from the start was how Gentiles should fit within the essentially Jewish movement.[3] There are hints of this tension early on, even before the church began to expand out from Jerusalem into Gentile areas. In Acts 6:1–7 the dispute between Hellenistic Jews and Judean Jews over the inequitable distribution of food to widows was resolved through the appointment of several men to take charge of that task. Nicolas interestingly is identified as a Gentile convert to Judaism from Antioch (Acts 6:5); presumably the other men listed were ethnically Jewish. Highlighting Nicolas as a Gentile convert shows that this ethnic distinction was important, even within the almost entirely Jewish, nascent church.[4] The story of Cornelius's conversion in Acts 10 is an important milestone for the full involvement of Gentiles in the Church. In contradistinction to Nicolas in Acts 6, Cornelius places his faith in Jesus without coming through Judaism.[5] Peter's strong testimony to his fellow Jews about the divine approbation of these Gentile converts resolves the issue for the time being. Paul addresses this question theologically in Eph 2:11–22 where he identifies the church

---

2. This translation, like many others, focuses on the judicial nuance present in the phrase κατεγνωσμένος ἦν. Contrast "he had clearly done wrong" (NET).

3. The contemporary Western evangelical church operates in reverse, that is, churches wonder how to reach out to Jews or how to reflect a more Jewish approach to fellowship. The situation in the early church was entirely the opposite.

4. The Acts 6 passage also shows the solution was to make the multiethnic church work together, not to fragment along ethnic lines. See D. L. Bock, *Acts*, BECNT (Grand Rapids: Baker, 2007), 261.

5. See again Bock, *Acts*, 261. The best interpretation of Acts 10 is that Cornelius was a Godfearer, not a full convert to Judaism.

a new entity made up of the two preexisting groups of Jews and Gentiles. The prior ethnicities are not obliterated but rather incorporated and placed anew within the controlling association of connection with Christ. Suffice it to say that the early church wrestled deeply with how to integrate Gentiles into the primarily Jewish church, and the present passage testifies clearly to the difficulty of that issue.

Enter Peter and Paul onto the same stage at the church in Antioch. Galatians 2:11–14 gives additional evidence of a rift in that church over Jew-Gentile integration. It also portrays the personalities involved and how they themselves handled the issue for good or for ill. Indeed, the passage gains much of its emotional tenor from this dynamic. Center stage at this moment are Peter and Paul, but in the wings are Barnabas, Paul's missionary partner to the Gentiles, and James, the *de facto* leader of the Jerusalem church. These individuals at the close of the Jerusalem meeting detailed in Gal 2:1–10 appeared to be in complete agreement as to how the Gentile integration would proceed, but now further north in the city of Antioch, because of a challenge unforeseen at the time of the prior Jerusalem meeting, they are starkly opposed to one another: Peter, Barnabas, and James on one side and Paul on the other. Paul not only challenges Peter's behavior as inconsistent with the outcome of the Jerusalem meeting, he also implicitly challenges Peter in his role as an apostle because he was leading Gentiles down the wrong path.

This passage is best understood through a variety of lenses. Literarily, Paul details the next important historical event in the timeline of his life after his conversion. As part of the *narratio* this section asserts Paul's independence from Jerusalem apostles while maintaining essential agreement with them (Longenecker, 65). His rebuke of Peter shows that Paul's gospel has authority over the Jerusalem apostles and is authoritative everywhere (Schreiner, 135, 136). The recurrence in 2:14 of the phrase "the truth of the gospel" binds 2:11–14 with 2:1–10 through a common theme and emphasis, namely, Paul's efforts to preserve this truth (de Boer, 128; Moo, 141).

Historically, this passage shows the difficulty of living out the agreement made in the Jerusalem meeting.[6] There was an inherent ambiguity in the outcome of the Jerusalem meeting that essentially led to the problem in Antioch (Moo, 143).[7] It did not address all aspects of Jew-Gentile integration, and thus a new situation in Antioch regarding common meals created a new problem to address.[8] This also provides the historical grounding for the

---

6. For a helpful overview of the sequence of historical events related to this passage, see George, 169; de Boer, 130.

7. See Hays, 232, who highlights the difference in possible interpretations of the agreement between Paul and stricter Jewish Christians in Jerusalem.

8. Because of the ambiguity of ὅτε in comparison to ἔπειτα, occasionally it is argued that 2:11–14 actually preceded 2:1–10; see Longenecker, 64, for sources. This argument fails for a number of reasons, the most important of which is Paul's use of ὅτε to

theological explanation that follows in Gal 2:15–21, providing a framework to understand Paul's language and theological argument that follows, arguably the central affirmation of the entire book.[9]

Socially and culturally, this passage testifies to the ongoing problems related to Jew-Gentile integration in the church. The presenting problem in Jerusalem, due to Paul's action of bringing along Titus, was whether Gentiles should be circumcised. Interpreted broadly, the meeting in Jerusalem decided that Gentiles did not have to be Law-observant to join the church. The situation in Antioch was different: The issue was not whether the Gentile was required to obey the Law but whether the Jewish Christian was released from the obligation to obey (Burton, 101). Paul's interpretation of Peter's unfortunate response to this question showed that Jewish observance of the Law could not help but reflect upon the Gentiles' status within the church. As such, the issue in Antioch, although ostensibly about Jewish food regulations, refracted theologically to become a question of relative status in the new Messianic community.

Rhetorically, through this passage Paul provides further motivation for the Galatians to remain faithful to his gospel by implicit encouragement to resist as he did in the face of Peter's return to Jewish practice. The encounter here is presented as an analogy to the situation in Galatia (de Boer, 129; deSilva, 210). The terseness of the account shows that the Galatians already knew about it; Paul was recounting and emphasizing elements important for their situation (Lenski, 91; Betz, 105). The fact that the account is open-ended is problematic. The reader would naturally think that if Peter had agreed with Paul that Paul would have clearly stated that. On that basis it can be argued that Paul wrote before the matter was fully resolved (Witherington, 149). Despite the historical question, Paul's rhetorical goal is still to persuade the Galatians about the divine origin of his gospel. When the gospel was at stake, Paul could not capitulate, no matter what others did. The Galatians are now presented with their own choice, whether to follow Peter or Paul. They must follow the truth of the gospel, even if they stand alone (Matera, 87–88).

---

indicate chronological sequence in Gal 1:15 (Witherington, 149) and within 2:11–14 (Soards and Pursiful, 75). Every other occurrence of ὅτε δέ in the NT introduces something that follows chronologically from that which precedes (Moo, 145n2). In addition, the strength of Paul's language against Peter in this paragraph makes sense best if the agreement of 2:1–10 were already in place (Moo, 141).

9. This connection is so strong that Hays, 230, argues that 2:11–21 should be considered as a coherent whole, with the speech that Paul begins in v. 14 extending to v. 21. There is no change of addressee until 3:1, and the 1 pl. in vv. 15–17 show that a Jewish audience in view, not the Gentile Galatians. Hays is certainly right to note this connection, but there are important changes in vocabulary, language, and style in vv. 15–21, such that I think it best to treat it as a separate paragraph, an elaboration of the theological point Paul made in Antioch but not a recounting of it.

It is a difficult question whether the current paragraph ends in v. 14 or in v. 21. Paul has written the material in such a way that there is not a clear break at any point. "Text and comment are so blended together that they cannot be separated without violence" (Lightfoot, 113–14). Paul's use of the 2 sg. forms in v. 14 shows that Peter is certainly in view, but his switch to 1 pl. in v. 15 creates some interpretive difficulties. It could reasonably reference Peter and Paul, the Jewish Christians in Antioch, or even Paul and his companions vis-à-vis the Galatians. A change of addressee does not clearly occur until Gal 3:1, when Paul speaks to the Galatians directly. There is certainly some sort of connection between v. 14 and what follows because of the use of the 1 pl., but there is a disconnection as well in light of v. 17, which seems removed from the actual situation in Antioch (Fung, 105). The best interpretation sees Paul as leaving the transition open and the referents ambiguous as part of his rhetorical strategy: He ultimately wants to apply the Antioch incident to the Galatian situation, and the subtle moves he makes in this paragraph support that goal. He moves readily from history to theology to make that application (Burton, 111; George, 182). I have chosen to end the current paragraph at v. 14 and to treat vv. 15–21 as a separate, theological argument, recognizing that the connections here are quite strong; a truly new section of the letter does not begin until 3:1.

2:11 Ὅτε δὲ ἦλθεν Κηφᾶς εἰς Ἀντιόχειαν. Paul begins this section with the conj. δέ to connect to the preceding material in Gal 2:1–10. The conj. is certainly adversative, but it also continues the development of the argument (Burton, 102; Longenecker, 71; Martyn, 231), so there is a closer connection between vv. 1–10 and 11–14 than might initially be understood with an English adversative like "but." Paul positions this paragraph not as an event separate from the Jerusalem meeting, but as a related one that has to be understood in light of the prior meeting. The implied contrast is between what was decided previously in Jerusalem and Peter's later conduct in Antioch.

There were a number of cities that bore the name Antioch in the ancient world,[10] but the two most important for the biblical record are Antioch of Pisidia in what is now south central Turkey and Antioch of Syria east of the Orontes River in what is now extreme southern Turkey, near the border with Syria. The former was one of the sites Paul visited on his first missionary journey (Acts 13; see also Acts 14:21–23). The latter was an important center of early Christianity and the one in view in this event. Paul and Barnabas themselves ministered there because of a large number of new believers (Acts 11:21–26). They were commissioned for missionary work there (Acts 13:1–3), and the city then served as a base for Paul's travels. Interesting for the present

10. Seleucus I Nicator established sixteen cities with the name Antioch in honor of his father Antiochus, one of Philip II of Macedon's generals. See R. K. Harrison and C. J. Hemer, "Antioch (Syrian)," in *New Bible Dictionary,* ed. D. R. W. Wood (Downers Grove: InterVarsity, 1996), 51.

passage with its central presenting concern, Antioch was the recipient of the letter detailing the decision of the Jerusalem Council concerning the place of Gentiles in the church (Acts 15:22–23a). This important city forms the backdrop for the event that Paul details.

In his excursus on Antioch, Longenecker, 65–71, details the importance of this cosmopolitan city in the wider world: During the first century AD it was the third largest city of the Roman Empire with a population of over 500,000. When Roman rule first began over Antioch, Jews within the city generally assimilated well and got along with their Gentile neighbors. Many Gentiles associated with Jewish synagogues in the city, which set the stage for Gentile acceptance of Christianity. This peaceful situation for Jews was shattered in AD 40 when they were the victims of mob violence, likely influenced by Caligula's program of self-aggrandizement. The cultural and religious situation in Antioch made it a likely place for Jews to assert their ethnicity, as seen in this paragraph, over and against the backdrop of Gentile Roman influence.[11] This combination of Jew and Gentile together in close association within the context of early Christianity made Antioch a "time bomb, being the locus in which the two parallel lines of mission threatened to cross in such a way as to pose unexpected problems" (Martyn, 232).[12]

κατὰ πρόσωπον αὐτῷ ἀντέστην. Paul does not hold back in his description of the interaction he had with Peter. He first describes what he did and why in two terse summations, and then he explains the particular events and their content. He presents in essence his interpretation of the event first, ensuring that the Galatians see the events just as he did. The phrase *κατὰ πρόσωπον* normally refers to being in someone's presence. The emotion of this section, however, implies more: Paul got up close and personal in a very literal way with Peter over this issue. He was "in his face" both literally and metaphorically. The use of *πρόσωπον* here provides an important connection to 2:6: Paul himself puts into practice God's impartiality by not respecting the face of another person (Garlington 2007, 125). The verb *ἀνθίστημι* means to "be in opposition to,"[13] so with the dat. pronoun as the obj. of the verb, the phrase can be translated formally as "I stood against him to his face." More functional translations would be "I opposed him to his face"[14] (so many

11. This portrait is similar to that of Betz, 104–5, who points out that Antioch was cosmopolitan, prosperous, cultured, and politically influential.

12. Even with Antioch's importance, it is worthwhile to mention as a counterbalance that Paul's point in this paragraph does not in any way rely on Antioch's size or importance, or the relative ethnic makeup of the church there, aside from the fact that it was mixed with both Jews and Gentiles present. Paul would have stood up to Peter even if his actions affected only a few individuals in a backwater town. The principles are ultimately on display here, not the size or influence of the arena in which they play out.

13. BDAG, 80.

14. BDAG, 80.

English translations) and "I took a stand against him in person." This was not just a casual discussion; it was instead an intense moment of disagreement.[15]

ὅτι κατεγνωσμένος ἦν. This causal ὅτι clause explains why Paul opposed Peter to his face. The phrase κατεγνωσμένος ἦν, "he had condemned himself," is the crux of the matter. Peter's own behavior vis-à-vis his table fellowship with Gentiles condemned him, and Paul had to address him as a result. Unpacking the force of this expression requires attention to both lexical and grammatical details. Concerning the lexeme, the verb καταγινώσκω regularly carries technical, legal denotations of charging someone with a crime or pronouncing a guilty verdict (e.g., Deut 25:1 LXX).[16] Other occurrences, however, involve not a legal, public context but a personal, private one (see 1 John 3:20, 21; Sir 14:2). Given the preceding context in Gal 2:1–10 in which the private meeting in Jerusalem resulted in a formal agreement about the acceptability of Paul's gospel and how Paul and the Jerusalem apostles would divide their labors, and in light of the following context in which Paul makes the case that Peter's public actions in Antioch deserved censure because they were in some sense contradictory to the gospel, the public, legal meaning of "to pass sentence, to condemn" for the verb makes a great deal of sense in Gal 2:11. We need not assume, though, that Paul is actually taking on legal authority of some kind over Peter in this declaration. Very likely Paul is speaking metaphorically, using technical, legal language to drive home the inappropriateness of Peter's behavior.

Concerning the grammar, there are two issues to address, the function of the ptc. and the voice. As a ptc., the impf. of εἰμί with the pf. ptc. denotes the plupf. periphrastic tense (so Burton, 103). This makes excellent sense after the aor. main verb of the preceding independent clause, as this action of Peter's self-condemnation occurred earlier in time, before Paul opposed him to his face. As the ὅτι here indicates, this condemnation was simply the grounds for Paul's public rebuke of Peter. As to the voice, the ptc. could be either midd. or pass. The pass. voice is more common than the midd. as a whole in the NT, but there is no clear indication from the context who would be the agent of this action. Arguments for a divine passive here (Witherington, 152; Soards and Pursiful, 78) with the meaning "condemned before God"[17] are offered without warrant. If Paul thought that God had condemned Peter, why would he not have said that directly? If the ptc. is understood as midd., however, clarity is immediately obtained: With his own actions Peter condemned himself, especially in light of the prior context of the Jerusalem meeting that

15. Dunn, 117, mentions some suggestive background to the phrase: "The use of the idiom in Jewish history (Deut. 7:24; 9:2; 11:25; Josh. 1:5) may suggest a sense on Paul's part that the issue was of epochal significance and its outcome dependent on God's being with him."

16. LSJ, 886–87; MGS, 1046.

17. So U. Wilckens, "ὑποκρίνομαι et al.," *TDNT*, 8:568n51.

in Paul's mind settled the issue of Jew-Gentile relations in the church.[18] This makes especially good sense given the charge of hypocrisy Paul levels in v. 13, which would have a particular focus on Peter's own behavior. This verse then summarizes all that took place in Antioch, from Peter's initial actions to the results it caused to Paul's public challenge of Peter.

2:12 This verse presents a number of tantalizing exegetical problems, certainly the most within this paragraph and perhaps the most within the book, none of which yield ready answers. The relatively secure exegesis of the verse, fair from any point of view, is that Peter over a period of time ate with Gentile believers in Antioch but changed his behavior to eat only with Jewish believers when certain people from James arrived among them. That minimum amount of meaning is enough to make sense of Paul's assertions in the text that follow. What challenges the reader here are the explanations for each part of this minimal picture, readily highlighted by a series of questions: Why was Peter in Antioch at all? What was the nature of the meal he shared with Gentiles? Who were the people from James? Had Paul mentioned them already in the epistle? What did they communicate that caused the change in Peter's behavior? Were they acting at James's behest or contrary to his desires? What was the nature of Peter's withdrawal, and how should we understand his stance toward Law observance before and after the change? Who was Peter afraid of, and why was he afraid of them? Of all the passages in Galatians, this requires the most by way of "mirror reading" in order to answer these questions, which also means that this verse requires the most restraint on the part of the exegete.[19] The data we have, both within the text and from the wider historical, cultural context, do not readily lead to definitive answers to these questions, and some of the questions do not need to be answered to understand the meaning of the text. My goal in commenting on the passage is to assert a clear minimum of meaning from the wording of the

---

18. See also the note by E. Masson on G. B. Winer, *A Treatise on the Grammar of New Testament Greek, Regarded as a Sure Basis for New Testament Exegesis* (Edinburgh: Clark, 1882), 431, which says, "Κατεγνωσμένος ἦν is strictly the pluperfect middle,—had condemned himself, stood *self-condemned*. Paul merely pointed out the flagrant inconsistency of Peter, by contrasting Peter's present with his previous proceedings and expressed views." This interpretation is advocated by Lightfoot, 111; Burton, 103; Bruce, 129; de Boer, 131.

19. See D. A. Carson, "Mirror-Reading with Paul and against Paul: Galatians 2:11–14 as a Test Case," in *Studies in the Pauline Epistles: Essays in Honor of Douglas J. Moo*, ed. M. S. Harmon and J. E. Smith (Grand Rapids: Zondervan, 2014), 112, for a similar sentiment: "We must seek out [mirror readings] that listen sympathetically to the greatest number of texts and that 'fit' these texts as closely and as plausibly as possible. We ought to be least comfortable with those scenarios whose viability depends on dismissing select texts."

text while answering questions important for discerning that meaning based upon an appropriate understanding of the historical context.

πρὸ τοῦ γὰρ ἐλθεῖν τινας ἀπὸ Ἰακώβου. Paul moves to explain the specifics of what occurred between him and Peter in Antioch. As stated previously, it is important to recognize the personal dynamics that drive the narrative of this section. The issue at stake is not understood solely through the articulation of theological propositions, although that becomes an important part of the exegesis. Rather, the retelling focuses on how particular personalities act and how they influence others. With the phrase πρὸ τοῦ ἐλθεῖν τινας ἀπὸ Ἰακώβου Paul identifies a key personality in this conflict who, although not present in Antioch, was keenly involved in the matter. The express function of this phrase demarcates timing through the use of πρό plus an articular inf: "before certain people from James arrived." We do not have much to go on to ascertain why it was important for Paul to mention James. Paul's prior interactions with James had been brief. They met briefly on Paul's first visit to Jerusalem after his conversion (1:19), and then James figures prominently in the Jerusalem meeting along with Peter and John (2:9). Both these mentions are positive and imply that James agreed with Paul regarding Gentile Law observance, if not at first then certainly at the conclusion of the first Jerusalem meeting. The present situation creates difficulties for that interpretation. The fact that Paul mentions James by name with the prep. ἀπό means more than these people were simply associates of James, which could have been conveyed with the simple gen. case. Instead, the language implies that these people were sent from him in some capacity as the leader of the Jerusalem church with his authority and approbation. By extension, then, Peter's actions stemmed from James's influence. How is one to reconcile James's prior agreement with Paul with his stance in the Antioch incident? The answer is the particular issues that were front and center at each point in time. Galatians 2:3, 7 indicate that at the Jerusalem meeting circumcision was the central issue, and the meeting had resolved that particular aspect of Gentile involvement in the church. Without doubt circumcision was not required of Gentiles to fully embrace the gospel. The issue on the table in Antioch was different:[20] It concerned table fellowship, which was a constant issue for personal relationships and fellowship between Jews and Gentiles. This change of issue changed the people group at the center of the debate: Gentiles had no scruples about table fellowship, but Jews did. The locus of attention had thus changed from what was required of Gentiles to what was required of Jews (Burton, 104). Likely James welcomed into fellowship uncircumcised Gentiles who had embraced the gospel, but he still had scruples relative to food preparation and common meals. James cast a long shadow from Jerusalem to Antioch on this issue, and Peter fell under his influence.

The identity of these individuals from James is not specified. They were somehow associated with him, but in what way and to what purpose is not

20. Pun definitely intended.

stated clearly. Very likely they were part of the Jerusalem church where James was active (Lightfoot, 112) and arrived in Antioch to represent him in some way (as argued above from the prep. ἀπό), conveying his beliefs and preferences to the congregation there. Arguments that they abused his authority or acted contrary to his wishes cannot be supported by the wording of the text.[21] Otherwise, why would Paul mention the association with James without any clarification? If Paul knew that these people were acting contrary to James's wishes, would he not say that? Assuming then that these individuals were acting in concert with James, can any inference be made that they specifically acted on James's command to bring Peter's table fellowship to an end, either by bringing him a message to that effect or by assessing the situation and demanding that James's take on the issue generally be applied specifically in Antioch? Based on the wording of this text, we cannot necessarily make this leap. The individuals from James could simply have been innocent bystanders, so to speak, who visited Antioch and as Jewish Christians ate in accordance with the Law (Lenski, 95, 101). Without intending to, their actions may have influenced Peter because of their connection to James. It cannot with certainty at this point be concluded that James demanded anything of Peter because Paul ultimately does not criticize James, only Peter (Schreiner, 140). Suffice it to say that on the basis of this phrase alone, the question of how the people from James influenced Peter must be answered elsewhere. And ultimately Paul's critique of Peter does not rest on the fact that he was influenced by others but on the inconsistency of his own behavior.

μετὰ τῶν ἐθνῶν συνήσθιεν. This phrase describes what Peter regularly did in Antioch before the people from James arrived: He would eat with the Gentiles.[22] The impf. verb *συνήσθιεν* indicates a customary action, that is, something Peter did on a regular basis. Peter had previously undergone some type of change that allowed him as a Jew to regularly share table fellowship with Gentiles without difficulty; Paul did not state it explicitly, but the driving force for this change was surely Peter's experience with Cornelius in Acts

21. George, 175–76, argues through comparison with Acts 15:24 that these individuals could be ultra-conservative members of the Jerusalem church who were connected to James in some way but not acting under his authority (similarly Lightfoot, 112). Betz, 108, and de Boer, 132, argue similarly to my view, namely, that seeing these individuals as "renegades" cannot be supported by the text.

22. The prep. *μετά* is redundant, given the *συν-* prefix on the verb *συνεσθίω*. Other occurrences of this verb in the NT (Luke 15:2; Acts 10:41; 11:3; 1 Cor 5:11) use only the dat. Of three occurrences in LXX, one is with dat. only (2 Kgdms 12:17), and two are with *μετά* (Gen 43:32; Exod 18:12). Given the point of Paul's argument about Peter's prior behavior, it is tempting to regard this redundancy as emphatic, but likely it is simply a move toward explicitness common within Koine Greek.

10–11.[23] Jews were well known for very particular scruples regarding table fellowship.[24] These arose from their commitment to ritual purity in meals and food preparation. It was a matter of logical extension: Jews desired to obey the food laws in the Torah (Lev 11:1–23; Deut 14:3–21), so they would not eat with anyone who did not also follow those same laws to avoid possible impurity because of the intimate nature of sharing meals. Practically that meant that Jews would eat only with Jews. By changing his behavior on this issue, Peter made a strong, multivalent statement. Practically Peter set aside the cultural boundary between Jews and Gentiles that the food laws had demarcated. Theologically he affirmed that Gentiles were full members of the church based solely on their faith in Christ (similarly Moo, 151). Socially he attested that Jews and Gentiles could function together as a cohesive assembly. Personally he validated in Paul's eyes the further implications of the Jerusalem agreement, which had addressed circumcision only. There was tremendous reality and symbolism in table fellowship between Jew and Gentile, which Paul recognized as supporting and leading to inclusion of Gentiles in the church without any requirement for Law observance. Paul became incensed because Peter's change away from this sharing threatened that bedrock of Paul's gospel.

A reasonable inference from this text is that Peter had given up all Jewish food regulations by eating with Gentiles, but the historical situation may have been more complex. Dunn, 117–22, in his well-known argument argues that the social dynamic here revolved around the intra-Jewish debate of how rigorous Jewish Law observance should be, a debate that here caught Gentiles in its crossfire. The argument runs thusly: Jewish food laws were indeed strict, and their importance during this period should not be underestimated because of the influence of the persecution Jews experienced during the Maccabean period. It cannot be argued, however, that Jews as a whole would never eat with Gentiles. Jews and Gentiles were not monolithic entities without variation. Gentiles often crossed the boundaries toward Jews through adoption of Jewish customs, and Jews often welcomed them when they did. The mode of Peter's eating with Gentiles was likely not complete abandonment of his Jewish scruples but simply a moderation of them, keeping in mind basic food rules without being overly strict. His withdrawal from Gentiles then was essentially an intra-Jewish move from less strict observance to stricter, not complete abrogation to observant practice. Dunn has capably argued his case, and his interpretation does have explanatory power. The problem

---

23. The lack of any reference, explicit or implied, to the celebration of the Lord's Supper most likely means that Paul simply speaks generally here about common meals. This picture of Peter would comport with his portrait in Acts 10–11 (Longenecker, 73), and it makes better sense of Paul's challenge to Peter in v. 14b (Fung, 106).

24. See, for example, Jub. 22:16; Josephus, *Ant.* 11.346; *Jos. Asen.* 7:1; John 4:9; and many others.

is that its specificity cannot readily be supported by the text. Paul's challenge that comes later in v. 14b is not that he was essentially Law-observant but lax in some particulars; it was that he was "living like Gentiles," which more readily implies wholesale abrogation of Jewish food laws (Schreiner, 142; Moo, 146).[25] On this basis it is best to acknowledge there were indeed a range of views on this issue among Jews, but Peter himself had essentially become non-observant.

ὅτε δὲ ἦλθον, ὑπέστελλεν καὶ ἀφώριζεν ἑαυτόν. This clause describes Peter's change in behavior that set in motion the negative situation that Paul had to address. The simple temporal clause refers to the arrival of the people from James, which occurred after Peter was regularly eating with Gentiles in Antioch. The words Paul uses to describe Peter's behavior are quite important because of their tense and lexeme. Both ὑπέστελλεν and ἀφώριζεν are impf. These are likely ingressive but could also be customary, the latter of which would better explain the wholesale defection of the remaining Jews in Antioch described in the next verse, which likely took some time.[26] Paul's choice of words is important as well. The verb ὑποστέλλω is cognate to ἀποστέλλω, whose word group has an important function in the book. Note especially Paul's key use of the nouns ἀπόστολος in Gal 1:1 to describe his own ministry and ἀποστολή in Gal 2:8 to describe Peter's.[27] Paul uses ὑποστέλλω here to imply that Peter's action was the opposite of what he should have done as an apostle.[28] The same implication is true for the verb ἀφωρίζω: Paul used that verb earlier in 1:15 to describe God's action of setting him apart from birth for his apostolic ministry. Here Peter "sets himself apart" with disastrous effects.[29] Paul uses these two words with not a little hint of irony as an implicit critique of Peter's exercise of his apostolic office.

φοβούμενος τοὺς ἐκ περιτομῆς. With this clause Paul explains Peter's reason for his withdrawal and separation from the Gentiles. The ptc. φοβούμενος

---

25. See as well the strong critiques of Dunn's thesis in J. L. Houlden, "A Response to James D. G. Dunn," *JSNT* 18 (1983): 58–67; D. Cohn-Sherbok, "Some Reflections on James Dunn's 'The Incident at Antioch (Gal 2:11–18),'" *JSNT* 18 (1983): 68–74.

26. This is also affirmed by the natural expectation that these verbs, both due to the nature of the action described and the flow of the narrative, would be aor. tense here, that is, "when they came, Peter withdrew and set himself apart." Paul must have chosen the impf. to emphasize the extent of the change in Peter's behavior. At first he regularly acted one way; now he regularly acted another.

27. The noun ἀπόστολος occurs in Gal 1:1, 17, 19, to designate the ministry of an apostle. The verb ἐξαποστέλλω occurs in 4:4, 6 to denote God's sending of his Son and the Spirit.

28. Lightfoot, 112, and Betz, 108, argue that ὑποστέλλω is used to describe strategic, military operations, thus it would have important force as a metaphor. *Contra* Moo, 147, who sees no military usage for the term in NT, LXX, Philo, or Josephus.

29. The association of ἀφορίζω with cultic separation from the unclean (so Betz, 108) helps explain why Paul would use this verb here, but it does not exhaust his intention.

gives the cause for the main verbs: Peter withdrew and separated himself "because he was afraid." Paul does not explain exactly why Peter was afraid, nor does he give him the benefit of the doubt by describing him as acting with the right motives (Hays, 234).[30] He disapprovingly attributes Peter's withdrawal from Gentiles to fear. The more challenging part of this phrase is the dir. obj. τοὺς ἐκ περιτομῆς. This nominal phrase consists of the prepositional phrase ἐκ περιτομῆς with the pl. article τούς, referencing a group of people. Grammatically it is imprecise, as Paul does not include the verbal idea that would clarify the meaning of ἐκ he intended. One essential question is the identity of this group. There are four options for the referent: the "false brothers" of Gal 2:4, the "people from James" of Gal 2:12, individuals from the Jerusalem church heretofore unmentioned, or unconverted Jews heretofore unmentioned. The first two options can be readily dismissed. The specific language Paul used to describe the "false brothers" who created problems in the Jerusalem meeting (Gal 2:4) and the disdain expressed toward them through his metaphorical language would surely be repeated here if they were in view in Antioch (similarly Burton, 107). Seeing the "people from James" and "those of the circumcision" as the same individuals does make sense in the context: Peter withdrew from table fellowship with Gentiles because he was afraid of the people from James. The problem is that this is entirely out of concert with Peter's attitude as implied in Gal 2:1–10. There Paul gave no indication that Peter was influenced by the "false brothers," who presented a difficult challenge in that context, so why would he be influenced negatively in Antioch by friendly people from James? It is much more difficult to decide between the third and fourth options. In favor of the third, Paul uses phrasings with ἐκ to indicate a broad notion of "dependence upon"; this becomes a description of standing and character (Longenecker, 73). In Galatians 3:6 Paul cites Gen 15:6 (Καθὼς Ἀβραὰμ ἐπίστευσεν τῷ θεῷ, καὶ ἐλογίσθη αὐτῷ εἰς δικαιοσύνην) and then in vv. 7 and 9 uses the phrase οἱ ἐκ πίστεως. The inferential conj. in v. 7 makes a strong link between Abraham's expression of faith and οἱ ἐκ πίστεως. Logically then οἱ ἐκ πίστεως stands for those who have expressed faith in God in the same way as Abraham did; it identifies those who depend upon faith in God in their relationship with him. By analogy τοὺς ἐκ περιτομῆς would refer to those who rely upon circumcision in their relationship with God. This is also supported by the wording of Acts 11:2, a very close parallel grammatically to Gal 2:12 as it identifies the individuals in view only as οἱ ἐκ περιτομῆς. These people argued with Peter over his table fellowship with Cornelius and his household; context shows them to be part of the Jerusalem church. This would favor seeing these individuals in Gal 2:12 as a Law-observant group in the Jerusalem church who promoted Law

30. DeSilva, 197–98 (and similarly Keener, 147–48) allows for the argument that Peter may simply been acting out of respect for the visitors in order to protect the Jewish mission and the larger Christian mission, but since we do not have Peter's take, this cannot be substantiated.

observance for Gentiles (so Martyn, 234; de Boer, 133).[31] In favor of the fourth option, Acts 10:45 provides a helpful parallel. This verse uses the phrase οἱ ἐκ περιτομῆς πιστοί to refer to Jewish believers. The phrase ἐκ περιτομῆς acts as a broad ethnic identifier while πιστοί is a subset of that ethnic group that has faith: "The faithful from among the circumcision," that is, "the faithful from among the Jews." In addition, Paul's use of περιτομή elsewhere in the epistle to mean "circumcision" points to Jews without specification (Moo, 148). The grammatical parallels for the third option are strong, so that is to be preferred, but there is further evidence to support the view that individuals from the Jerusalem church heretofore unmentioned are the ones causing Peter's fear.

At this point the exegete must think through the historical situation surrounding the incident in Antioch to decide which interpretation can be best defended. Robert Jewett made a suggestion regarding the historical situation in Judea in an article addressing the agitators in Galatia that has found wide acceptance and explains not only this passage but others in the NT as well.[32] Essentially the nomistic missionary effort that touched Antioch and Galatia was a reaction to the troubled political situation in Judea and Galilee from the late 40s to the beginning of the Jewish War in AD 66. During this time the Zealots launched a campaign of terrorism against Rome on the one hand and religious cleansing toward Jews on the other. The goal was both to undermine Rome's control of Israel and to purify Israel in order to hasten the final eschatological kingdom. Jewett's thesis is as follows:

> My hypothesis therefore is that Jewish Christians in Judea were stimulated by Zealotic pressure into a nomistic campaign among their fellow Christians in the later forties and early fifties. Their goal was to avert the suspicion that they were in communion with lawless Gentiles. It appears that the Judean Christians convinced themselves that circumcision of Gentile Christians would thwart Zealot reprisals.[33]

It is important to note that on its face Jewett attempts to explain only the emphasis upon circumcision, and our text deals with the different issue of table fellowship. These issues are of a piece, however, as they were both important for Jewish identity in the midst of persecution. This thesis is very attractive because it offers a reasonable explanation of the details of the text, specifically the different wording τοὺς ἐκ περιτομῆς that shows up here, and for Peter's change of behavior specifically due to fear. It does not solve every difficulty, though, because one might expect if the situation Jewett described pertained that Peter would revert and advocate Gentile Law obedience, when

31. See also Martyn, 236–40, who argues for this interpretation on the basis of language usage in Rom 4:11b–12; Eusebius, *Eccl. Hist.* 4.5.3; and Acts 10:45; 11:2.

32. R. Jewett, "The Agitators and the Galatian Congregation," *NTS* 17 (1971): 198–212.

33. Jewett, "Agitators," 205.

in fact he simply withdrew from table fellowship.[34] Despite this difficulty, Jewett's hypothesis is persuasive. In sum, the arrival of the people from James brought the wider solution of Gentile Christian Law observance to solve the problem of Zealot persecution of the Jerusalem church to bear on the church in Antioch. Peter was not afraid of these particular people from James, but of the larger group in the Jerusalem church that they represented, individuals who were agitating vigorously for Gentile Law observance to protect themselves from the Zealots. Peter was swayed by this enough to alter his habit of common table fellowship with Gentiles.[35]

It is worthwhile at this point to redraw the assertions of this text to have a clear picture moving forward. At first, while in Antioch, Peter regularly ate with Gentiles. Because of what he had learned through the events surrounding the conversion of Cornelius (Acts 10–11), he recognized that Gentiles could be saved by Jesus the Messiah without becoming Jews. The metaphor of no unclean food in his vision had become the reality of his experience in his table fellowship with Gentiles, as he recognized that the food restrictions no longer had any value (Lightfoot, 112; Bruce, 129; Schreiner, 140). But when people from James arrived in Antioch from Jerusalem, they brought news of danger from the Zealots and an emphasis upon Gentile Law observance in order to mitigate that danger. Peter, fearing for the safety of the Jerusalem church, decided to withdraw from Gentiles in order to maintain an outward semblance of Jewish piety, something he likely deemed appropriate in light of his role as apostle to the circumcision.

2:13 *καὶ συνυπεκρίθησαν αὐτῷ καὶ οἱ λοιποὶ Ἰουδαῖοι*. Peter's behavior on its own was bad enough, but the problem was compounded by the fact that all the other Jewish Christians in Antioch "joined him in this hypocrisy" by separating themselves from Gentiles. The verb *συνυπεκρίθησαν* is potent in that it affirms that the withdrawal occurred in line with Peter's actions, but it also casts judgment upon them. The aor. tense is consummative, describing the end point of the process that occurred over time. The subject *οἱ λοιποὶ Ἰουδαῖοι* refers to the remaining Jews in the Antioch church, clearly demarcated culturally from the Gentiles.

34. Presumably Peter could not advocate for Gentile Law observance outright in light of the content of the Jerusalem agreement, so his withdraw from table fellowship was a compromise of sorts.

35. This historical reconstruction is accepted by Bruce, 130–31; Longenecker, 74–75; Witherington, 155–56; Rapa, 579–80; Schreiner, 144; Moo, 148. Carson, "Mirror-Reading," 99–112, carefully considers all permutations of these interpretations and eventually decides upon this view. George, 170–71, similarly sees persecution in play but instead of Zealot influence references the persecution of Jews in Antioch by Caligula (AD 37–41) and similar persecution in Palestine as a possible background.

ὥστε καὶ Βαρναβᾶς συναπήχθη αὐτῶν τῇ ὑποκρίσει. The conj. ὥστε introduces a dependent clause with an indic. verb that shows actual result.[36] This is a strong statement that expresses indignation on Paul's part.[37] Barnabas had been Paul's ministry partner, instrumental in bringing the gospel to the Gentiles (see, e.g., Acts 11:22–26). Barnabas was at the meeting in Jerusalem detailed in 2:1–10; he went as Paul's advocate and was himself party to the agreement. On these grounds his defection in Antioch from table fellowship with Gentiles surprised and even shocked Paul. The ascensive καί brings out this emotional force: "*even* Barnabas!" The verb συναπάγω (here as the aor. pass. form συναπήχθη) means "to be led away"[38] and occurs with the dat. to indicate the instrument that effected the action, in this case τῇ ὑποκρίσει (Burton, 109).[39] Paul does not state that Barnabas himself acted hypocritically. Rather, he was swept up by the powerful groupthink in play.[40]

The centerpiece of Paul's condemnation of this situation is his use of the words συνυποκρίνομαι and ὑπόκρισις with intense effect.[41] The word group in classical Greek showed a wide variation of meaning, often denoting the action of replying or answering, and then in a related vein an explanation or interpretation. Some of the word meanings related directly to oratory, but more importantly for Jewish and Christian literature the words were used within the domain of acting. They were generally neutral and literal, referring to an actor playing a part, but the word meanings could naturally shade into a metaphorical nuance, referring to pretending, and then into a negative connotation, referring to those who pretended for nefarious purposes, that is, deception. The occurrences of this word group in the LXX are

---

36. BDAG, 1107.

37. M. Zerwick, *Biblical Greek: Illustrated By Examples*, trans. J. Smith, Scripta Pontificii Instituti Biblici 114 (Rome: Pontifical Biblical Institute, 1963), 121–22, argues that ὥστε with an indic. is stronger than ὥστε with an inf: "Similarly we may suppose that indignation moved St Paul to use the stronger indicative when he wrote that Peter's ὑπόκρισις was shared by the other Jews ὥστε καὶ Βαρνάβας συναπήχθη αὐτῶν τῇ ὑποκρίσει (Gal 2:13)." Compare to John 3:16, the only other example of ὥστε with an indic. in the NT, which is also a very strong statement but for positive reasons.

38. Betz, 110, and Longenecker, 76, argue that συναπάγω implies an element of irrationality.

39. *Contra* Lightfoot, 113, who argues that τῇ ὑποκρίσει is association.

40. Witherington, 150n194, suggests that Barnabas's being a Levite (Acts 4) may explain his defection as he would certainly understand the importance of following Jewish customs.

41. The verb συνυποκρίνομαι is the shorter verb form ὑποκρίνομαι with the prefixed prep. σύν to indicate association or participation. This word group contains other forms, all of them similar in meaning. U. Wilckens, "ὑποκρίνομαι et al.," *TDNT*, 8:559, includes ὑποκριτής and ἀνυπόκριτος. LSJ, 1885–86, and MGS, 2223, list several other rarer forms.

all decidedly negative: They refer to pretending with intention to deceive and even more generally to being an evildoer.[42] The NT shows the same contours for this word group as the LXX. The words can mean pretending in order to deceive; see, for example, the use of the noun ὑπόκρισις in Mark 12:15 and the use of the verb ὑποκρίνομαι in Luke 20:20. The word group can also simply refer to insincerity as a general term used of those who are evil before the Lord; see, for example, Luke 12:1 and Matt 23:28 where ὑπόκρισις is used as a general descriptor of the Pharisees. The latter passage is especially illuminating as the word is joined with ἀνομία, another somewhat general term that means "lawlessness."[43] One passage from the LXX particularly important for understanding the emotional tone of these terms is 4 Macc 6:12–23.[44] This text shows how incompatible this pretension was to Jews who were faithful to God. In this passage Eleazar is tortured because of his staunch refusal before Antiochus to eat pork. At one point, some of the king's servants implore him to end the torture by simply pretending to eat.

> At that point, partly out of pity for his old age, partly out of sympathy from their acquaintance with him, partly out of admiration for his endurance, some of the king's retinue came to him and said, "Eleazar, why are you so irrationally destroying yourself through these evil things? We will set before you some cooked meat; save yourself by pretending to eat pork [σὺ δὲ ὑποκρινόμενος τῶν ὑείων ἀπογεύεσθαι σώθητι]." But Eleazar, as though more bitterly tormented by this counsel, cried out: "Never may we, the children of Abraham, think so basely that out of cowardice we feign a role unbecoming to us [ὥστε μαλακοψυχήσαντας ἀπρεπὲς ἡμῖν δρᾶμα ὑποκρίνασθαι]! For it would be irrational if having lived in accordance with truth up to old age and having maintained in accordance with law the reputation of such a life, we should now change our course and ourselves become a pattern of impiety to the young by setting them an example in the eating of defiling food. It would be shameful if we should survive for a little while and during that time be a laughingstock to all for our cowardice, and be despised by the tyrant as unmanly by not contending even to death for our divine law. Therefore, O children of Abraham, die nobly for your religion! And you, guards of the tyrant, why do you delay?"

Eleazar regarded even pretending to eat pork as entirely out of keeping with his status as a child of Abraham. It would go against his lifetime of obedience

42. U. Wilckens, "ὑποκρίνομαι et al.," *TDNT*, 8:563, notes the parallelism in Sir 1:28–30 which juxtaposes obedience to the fear of the Lord with being a hypocrite.
43. BDAG, 85.
44. Dunn, 125, notes this passage as well as Sir 32:15; 33:2; Pss. Sol. 4:20, 22; 2 Macc 6:21, 24.

to the Law and set the wrong example for Jewish youth. Indeed, he was willing to die rather than even pretend to be disobedient. The assessment of this passage by Wilkens is very helpful:

> In the par. 4 Macc. 6:12 ff. he gives a similar answer to the advice of well-wishers that he cunningly dissemble (σὺ δὲ ὑποκρινόμενος τῶν ὑείων ἀπογεύεσθαι σώθητι, v. 15): μὴ οὕτως κακῶς φρονήσαιμεν οἱ Ἀβρααμ παῖδες ὥστε μαλακοψυχήσαντας ἀπρεπὲς ἡμῖν δρᾶμα ὑποκρίνασθαι, v. 17. To play such a role in this situation would be to pervert a long life of adherence to the Law and to become an example of iniquity (ἀσεβείας τύπος) rather than of righteousness, v. 19f. In both cases the suggested stratagem of ὑποκρίνεσθαι involves a much worse ὑποκρίνεσθαι: a spectacle of apostasy from God and His Law, i.e., ὑπόκρισις as a sin, which does not befit a son of Abraham.[45]

This passage could very well have been in Paul's mind, given the prominence of the term ὑποκρίνομαι and the appellation "children of Abraham" (οἱ Αβρααμ παῖδες in v. 17, ὦ Αβρααμ παῖδες in v. 22), the latter of which is prominent in Gal 3. If so, he would be using it ironically, even sarcastically: Peter would be a hypocrite not for maintaining fidelity to the Jewish food laws as Eleazar had done but for rejecting what God had so clearly revealed about the inclusion of the Gentiles. At the very least, these allusions from 4 Macc 6 paint Peter in a poor light because he immediately caved when his faithfulness to the gospel was under pressure, unlike Eleazar who remained faithful to the end.[46]

The meaning here in Gal 2:13 is thus not difficult to discern. In describing the actions of Peter and the other Jews with the verb συνυποκρίνομαι and the noun ὑπόκρισις, Paul highlights the inconsistency of their withdrawal from Gentile table fellowship with their confession of the gospel. This is especially important in the case of Peter, whom Paul had described in 2:1–10 as affirming his gospel and the related changes in Jew-Gentile relations. So Peter's culpable actions were twofold: He acted against Gentiles generally by withdrawing from table fellowship, which was out of step with the gospel, and he went back on his word that had been given to Paul in the agreement attained at the Jerusalem meeting. His actions could lead the observer to two theological deductions: Peter believed Gentiles would need to become like Jews in order to fully experience the gospel, and he valued the opinion of men more than the approbation of the Lord. It is precisely on these points that Paul's condemnation of hypocrisy rings true, as it is clear Peter did not

45. U. Wilckens, "ὑποκρίνομαι et al.," *TDNT*, 8:563.

46. Oakes, 78–79, notes that the charge of hypocrisy was also powerful in a Greco-Roman context. Peter instead of acting on principles had changed his actions to please different groups. Hays, 234, sees this as restating the charge of pleasing people from Gal 1:10.

hold to these theological convictions. The problem with the English word "hypocrisy" is that the term has been used so much in contemporary English that it is almost an empty cipher, plus its contemporary usage does not quite capture what Peter was doing. Peter did not intend to deceive anyone with his actions. For example, he did not proclaim to be Law-observant while secretly eating with Gentiles. Nor was he broadly disobedient to God such that this fit him as a general description. Rather, he was not acting in accordance with his true convictions (Bruce, 131; Moo, 149). He truly believed that Gentiles were accepted by God only through faith in Jesus, but he acted as if something more were required (Lenski, 98). Without doubt this was out of character for him. Peter stumbled, but his misstep had tragic theological and social ramifications. In this way Peter the apostle, who should have acted in keeping with the gospel in fidelity to the Lord in all particulars, acted in hypocrisy against it and rightly received Paul's condemnation.[47]

2:14 ἀλλ' ὅτε εἶδον. Paul's decision to oppose Peter contrasts with Peter's own actions. Where Peter was quick to capitulate, Paul was quick to stand up on behalf of the Gentiles. The phrase ὅτε εἶδον is a temporal clause pointing to specific past event. The verb ὁράω refers not to actual sight but rather a mental conclusion, similar to the previous use in Gal 2:7. Indeed, Paul may be alluding to his wording there to further show how wrong Peter's actions were. An intriguing question is when this actually occurred, that is, when did Paul reach this conclusion relative to the events just described. The impf. verbs in v. 12 imply some duration to Peter's improper actions, and the defection of all the Jews in the Antioch church from table fellowship with Gentiles may have taken some time. Paul's description of his own actions follow Barnabas's defection described in v. 13. Perhaps Paul fully recognized the impropriety of the actions of these Jews only when Barnabas, the one who had stood beside him in the Jerusalem meeting, defected with them. In the cold light of that betrayal by his close friend, Paul grasped how their withdrawal would imply the secondary status of Gentiles in the church.

ὅτι οὐκ ὀρθοποδοῦσιν πρὸς τὴν ἀλήθειαν τοῦ εὐαγγελίου. This ὅτι clause that follows contains Paul's assessment of the whole messy situation. This is what he realized about the defections happening all around him. Technically this ὅτι clause is a subst. dir. obj. clause, indicating the content of what Paul recognized. The verb ὀρθοποδέω occurs first in Greek literature here in Gal 2:14, so there are no prior texts to help elucidate the meaning. There were similar terms extant in Greek literature, however, and these can be marshaled to

47. Dunn, 125–26, describes the actions from Peter's viewpoint with four assertions: The Jerusalem agreement required Jews to keep acting like Jews. The appeal to retain Jewish identity would have been strong. Peter's credibility as "apostle of the circumcision" would have been denigrated if the charge of living like a Gentile gained traction. It was not too much to ask that Gentiles act like Jews to satisfy the concerns of James's people. George, 177, argues similarly.

help understand the meaning here. Lightfoot, 113, states that its equivalent in classical Greek is εὐθυπορεῖν, which means "to go straight forward."[48] C. H. Roberts points to a use of ὀρθοποδία in the papyri that has a neutral connotation rather than a moral one: "making progress, advancing."[49] Building upon this work, J. G. Winter points to another occurrence of ὀρθοποδέω in the papyri that also means "make progress." The context in the papyri is rearing a child and the costs that entails, so it is not moral standing in play but simply advancement in that the child is growing as expected (and eating more to boot).[50] This meaning of "make progress, advance" fits well in the context of Gal 2:14, especially given the collocation with πρός, which commonly indicates direction or goal. If the verb has a meaning like "act rightly," πρός would take on a nuance of reference; although this is not impossible, it is uncommon.[51] If ὀρθοποδέω refers to advancement or progress in a particular direction then πρός would take on its common nuance of "to, toward." The latter makes good sense in the context. Paul's assertion would be metaphorical, built upon the literal sense of the verb. In their action of withdrawal, the Jews in the church at Antioch were not making progress toward the truth of the gospel. "In Paul's eyes, they were taking the wrong road" (Bruce, 132).

In this context τὴν ἀλήθειαν τοῦ εὐαγγελίου, the direction in which these Jews were not going, takes on an important nuance. Paul used this phrase in Gal 2:5 to refer to the outcome of the Jerusalem agreement, which combined pragmatic effect with bedrock theological truth: Because the Gentiles were saved by faith in Jesus, they did not need to be circumcised. His repetition of the phrase with reference to the Antioch makes a similar conclusion: Because Gentiles were saved by faith in Jesus, Jewish food laws that separated them within the assembly cannot stand. Essentially the imposition of circumcision on Titus and food laws in Antioch cannot be differentiated (Schreiner, 146). Just as circumcision could not be required of Gentiles, separation of Jews from Gentiles based on food laws could not be maintained. In one sense the central doctrinal truth of the gospel was not under consideration in Antioch. All the people involved would confess that Jesus was the Christ, the Messiah sent from God. At issue rather were the practical ramifications of that truth relative to what requirements would be placed upon Gentiles for full inclusion in the church. The withdrawal of Jews at Antioch from table fellowship with Gentiles was contrary to the gospel in the same way that requiring Gentiles to be circumcised was. And just as in Jerusalem, the practical reality reflected back on the theological foundation, which is why Paul reacted as strongly as he did.

---

48. LSJ, 716; MGS, 848.

49. C. H. Roberts, "A Note on Galatians II 14," *JTS* 40 (1939): 55–56.

50. J. G. Winter, "Another Instance of ὀρθοποδεῖν," *HTR* 34 (1941): 161–62.

51. BDAG, 875. Winer, *Grammar*, 505, accepts this definition and argues that here πρός acts like an acc. of standard.

εἶπον τῷ Κηφᾷ ἔμπροσθεν πάντων. Paul responded to the defection by the Jews from table fellowship with Gentiles with a public admonition of Peter in front of the entire church in Antioch. Very simply he states, "I said to Peter in front of everyone." The use of πᾶς here is literal, not hyperbolic. It is not unreasonable to imagine that the entire Antioch congregation was present. This was a very public confrontation due to a very public problem. It is a reasonable question why Paul confronted Peter on this matter instead of the people who had come from James. The answer is multifaceted. First and foremost, Peter was an apostle, and his behavior had ramifications for the gospel and for the church on a level that others' did not. In addition, Peter had been at the Jerusalem meeting in his role as an apostle and was party to the decision made there. His behavior in Antioch appeared to backtrack on that agreement. Other factors surely came into play as well. Peter was the one who had changed his stance while the people from James had not, and Peter was integrated in the church in Antioch while the people from James were not. His actions were felt deeply by the Gentiles there.

Εἰ σὺ Ἰουδαῖος ὑπάρχων ἐθνικῶς καὶ οὐχ Ἰουδαϊκῶς ζῇς, πῶς τὰ ἔθνη ἀναγκάζεις Ἰουδαΐζειν; This single question serves multiple purposes in Paul's recounting of the conflict with Peter. It highlights the essence of the issue at stake in Antioch, whether Gentiles needed to live as Jews. It serves as a rebuke to Peter by showing his hypocrisy on the matter. It shows the way Paul believes the issue should be resolved by pointing toward Torah-free living by the Gentiles. It also points to the theological issue under the surface, what God requires to be rightly related to him. The sentence as a whole is a first class condition. The protasis highlights Peter's personal stance and actions on the matter of table fellowship before the visitors from James arrived, while the apodosis focuses upon the implied requirement he placed upon Gentiles by withdrawing from them after the visitors arrived. As a first class condition, it asserts a truth for the sake of the argument.[52] One can imagine the rhetorical power it held in the meeting when Paul spoke. The sentence has both logical and practical function. Logically Paul shows the incongruity of Peter's actions, but practically he desires to promote a change in behavior. The answer he imagines on Peter's lips in response to the question is "I cannot so live," which would then provoke a change in Peter's behavior back to what it was previously.

The particular structure of the sentence is worth examining more carefully. The protasis is rather involved, as the main verb has important modifiers that are central to Paul's point. The core of the sentence is εἰ σὺ ἐθνικῶς ζῇς, "if you live like the Gentiles."[53] This is modified by Ἰουδαῖος ὑπάρχων, a concessive ptc. with a predicate nom: "although you are a Jew." The contrast

52. D. B. Wallace, *Greek Grammar Beyond the Basics: An Exegetical Syntax of the New Testament* (Grand Rapids: Zondervan, 1996), 690.

53. BDAG, 276, colorfully translates this phrase as "if you live like the rest of the world."

implied in the concessive ptc. is then made explicit with a negated adv. that modifies the core of the sentence: καὶ οὐχ Ἰουδαϊκῶς, "and [live] not as a Jew." The verb ζάω, "I live," in this context refers to general conduct and pattern of life,[54] and the two adverbs ἐθνικῶς and Ἰουδαϊκῶς highlight two different modes for that conduct.[55] The difference revolves around adherence to Jewish cultural norms that separated them and demarcated them from Gentiles (rightly Dunn, 127). Paul highlights the fact that even though Peter is a Jew, he lives now after the manner of the Gentiles. The immediate referent would be his conduct in table fellowship, but the verb ζάω because it is quite general would imply that Peter had adjusted his behavior in many ways, essentially becoming non-observant toward the Law on other matters as well (de Boer, 137). The apodosis of the sentence presents the logical conundrum: πῶς τὰ ἔθνη ἀναγκάζεις Ἰουδαΐζειν; "How can you compel the Gentiles to live like Jews?" If Peter himself had moved away from normal Jewish practice, despite the fact that he was a Jew, how could he lay any requirement upon Gentiles, who were not Jews to begin with, to take up those practices? The verb ἀναγκάζεις is a conative present because Peter's action of compulsion, whether explicit or implicit, is neither complete nor successful.[56] The noun τὰ ἔθνη is likely not generic but specific, even deictic. Given the context of Paul and Peter facing off in Antioch before the church, Paul could have been pointing at the very people affected by Peter's action.[57] The verb Ἰουδαΐζειν is a complementary inf. to the indic. ἀναγκάζεις; it is the action that is being compelled. The verb means to live as a Jew, which would entail taking on Jewish practices like circumcision.[58] A legitimate question based upon what Paul has stated so far is in what way Peter was compelling the Gentiles. Paul described nothing that could be construed as active compulsion on Peter's part to make Gentiles become Jews. He only described Peter's withdrawal from table fellowship. This is where Paul's critique of Peter's actions as an apostle comes to full flower. As an apostle, indeed as the chief apostle, Peter was central to the life of the church. As he went, so went the church. By withdrawing from table fellowship with Gentiles, Peter by his apostolic authority moved the social boundaries of the church on his coattails. The orbit of the assembly in Antioch had changed from a generous circle that encompassed everyone to a tight ring around only those who were Jewish

54. BDAG, 425–26.

55. Both adverbs occur only here in the NT.

56. So A. T. Robertson, *A Grammar of the Greek New Testament in the Light of Historical Research* (Nashville: Broadman, 1934), 880.

57. This of course would not preclude the theological issue of whether these requirements should be placed upon Gentiles as a whole. The theological issue is certainly driving this particular confrontation.

58. BDAG, 478. For examples see Josephus, *J. W.* 2.454; Esth 8:17 (LXX). Martyn, 236, argues that the verb implies something false, that people act like Jews without true conviction.

or lived as Jews. Before Peter's actions, it would appear that those who were in the church consisted of all those who had believed in Jesus the Messiah. After Peter's actions, it would appear that those who were in the church were those who had confessed Jesus as the Christ but who also were Jewish or living as Jews. The logical corollary was clear: To be in the church, to be among those who confessed the Messiah, one had to become a Jew. The social pressure this placed upon the Gentiles in Antioch to take up Jewish practices would have been immense, as Peter's actions as the chief apostle affected and infected the behavior of all the Jews in the Antioch assembly. When all the Jews followed suit, the powerful majority placed a compulsion upon a weak minority (Martyn, 245). Simply put, this compulsion went against the gospel. Peter had condemned himself as hypocritical, and Paul's carefully worded statement showed why he was wrong.

Because Paul does not say that Peter accepted his rebuke nor does Paul give any indication as to the outcome, Dunn, 130, posits failure on Paul's part to resolve the issue in Antioch and a subsequent break with Barnabas, Jerusalem, and Antioch (similarly Betz, 104; Martyn, 236; Witherington, 159; Hays, 231). One can argue well, however, that Paul was ultimately successful in his challenge. It would have been useless for Paul to appeal to the agreement with the Jerusalem apostles in 2:1–10 in the first place if it had subsequently been nullified through Peter's conduct in Antioch (Schreiner, 145). An ongoing disagreement with Peter cannot be supported because the difference here focuses on conduct, and the following paragraph indicates fundamental theological agreement between Peter and Paul (Moo, 146). Assuming that Gal 2 refers to the Jerusalem visit in Acts 11, Peter's stance in Acts 15 would imply his return to Paul's position (George, 181). The letters that both Paul and Peter wrote later show no signs of schism between the two (George, 181; Schreiner, 146); indeed, the epistles of Peter within the NT were written to mostly Gentile groups. If Paul did fail in Antioch, the high regard for Paul in Acts and the letters of Ignatius would imply that the failure did not endure long at all (Longenecker, 80; Betz, 111).[59]

This leaves the exegete with one final question to answer. What purpose did Paul have in leaving the Antioch incident open? It fits with his purpose for writing the epistle, which was ultimately to motivate the Galatians to return to his gospel. The issue in Antioch was whether Gentiles had to obey the Law in order to have status in the church as full participants, which is

59. Bruce, 134, is essentially agnostic on whether the issue was resolved by the time Paul sent the letter. In favor of Paul's failure, the reader might have expected Paul to say whether Peter or the Antioch church responded positively to his challenge, but he did not. One might have expected that a Gentile church would follow the apostle to the Gentiles, but the church in Galatia did not, hence the need for the epistle. On the other side, Paul's later movement away from Antioch as a base was simply to find a more suitable location to the west and cannot be taken as *de facto* evidence of a schism.

the very issue Paul has to address in Galatia (Moo, 144). This ending to the Antioch incident fits rhetorically because every opponent is rendered silent before Paul's argument about the truth of the gospel (Matera, 90; Witherington, 160). By ending the account in this way, Paul seeks to motivate the Galatians to act in the same way he did, namely, standing strong against any requirement for Gentiles to obey the Law.

Theological Comments

It is not easy for the contemporary, evangelical reader to identify with what is at stake in this particular section of the book of Galatians. There are numerous difficulties, both related to the historical situation and the proper interpretive framework:

> The type of meal from which Peter has withdrawn is unknown, the outcome of the situation is lost to modern scholars and the purpose of Paul's writing has been subsumed in an understanding of Christianity that opposes the "law" and the "gospel" and assumes Paul is normative for understanding not only the historical, but also the theological reality of the situation in Galatia in the 1st century of the common era.[60]

Current readers are faced with two different, overarching interpretations of this paragraph (and the next). Traditionally interpreters have understood these sections to be no less than the heart of the gospel. On this reading Paul defends the gospel of faith alone in Christ alone against any encroachment of a works-based righteousness. Paul is seen as the sole champion who stood against the Judaizers by proclaiming the true gospel message, namely, that man is saved by no action of his own but only by the finished work of Christ. Peter for a brief moment lost sight of that and granted works salvific currency, but Paul withstood him and saved the day. In a related vein these two paragraphs in Galatians are seen to be functionally equivalent to Paul's central theological statement in Rom 3:21–26, which also concerns the heart of the gospel.[61] More recent interpreters have focused less on the grand theological scheme and more closely on the social issues mentioned in the text. On this reading the central issue is how the nascent church is to accommodate both Jews and Gentiles who have decided to follow Jesus the Messiah. On the one hand, Jesus was certainly Jewish, and God had moved among the Jews first to create the new assembly of the faithful. On the other hand, God

---

60. E. C. Stewart, "I'm Okay, You're Not Okay: Constancy of Character and Paul's Understanding of Change in his Own and Peter's Behaviour," *HvTSt* 67 (2011): 2. I include this quotation as an example of the different areas of difficulty scholars identify, not as examples of my own.

61. A difference between the two passages would be the practical situation that arose in Antioch about which Paul writes in Galatians, Romans having no analogy.

had graciously moved among the Gentiles to create Christ-followers from many nations. Did Gentiles have to adopt Jewish practices in order to join this assembly centered upon the risen Messiah? In short, was the issue social or was it theological?

Framed this way, the question is a false choice. Both issues were at stake because there was a very real and present theology driving the actions of all the people involved. Peter and those who followed him gave precedence, if only for a time, to Jewish cultural practices that distinguished between Jews and all other nations. Previously there had been no separation in Antioch between Jews and Gentiles; afterwards there was clear division. The question at stake is whether these cultural practices would be allowed to define who was granted fellowship with the assembly of the faithful. That is a question with both theological and practical sides: Who constitutes the people of God? How are Jews and Gentiles now to live in light of what Jesus has done? As in so many areas of life, the theology underneath drove the actions above.

Paul's rebuke of Peter shows what Peter really believed. Peter had decided to follow Jesus the Jewish Messiah, yet he had also recognized that Jesus was the Messiah for the whole world. Consequently even Gentiles who confessed Jesus as Messiah were welcomed into this new assembly. Peter was both instrumental in bringing Gentiles to the faith (Acts 10) and approving of Paul's Gentile-focused ministry (Gal 2:1–10). He himself crossed the cultural divide presented by food and table fellowship and ate with Gentiles in Antioch, symbolizing their full acceptance by the Lord. When Peter withdrew from that table fellowship, even if for a legitimate reason—because he was afraid of Jewish persecution of the church in Jerusalem—he made a theological statement that was contrary to his own actions and his role as an apostle. By reversing himself, he claimed implicitly that something other than faith in the Messiah was required for admission into the assembly. Paul saw through both the hypocrisy and the theological error and rebuked Peter for his actions. In so doing, Paul championed the singularity of faith for entrance into the assembly, but he did it through the medium of the practical issue of Jewish cultural practices.

Application and Devotional Implications

This short passage presents an important event in the early church, the emotions of which far outweigh the short space granted to it. It is not hyperbole to state that in this moment the nature of the church's identity hung in the balance. Would the church essentially remain a Jewish movement through the maintenance of particular cultural practices, tied closely to the root of Israel from which it sprang? Or would the church become global, allowing for a mixture of all peoples to enter and have fellowship together in Christ? This was not simply a question of theology but of personality. This event played out through the interactions of Peter and Paul, two of the most important leaders of the early church. Both had seen the risen Lord, and both were commissioned as apostles. Whose understanding of the outworking of the gospel would carry the day? Nor was it only a question of personality but of influence. The problem arose in Antioch initially because of James's influence over Peter and then secondarily because of Peter's influence over the Jews in Antioch. On the other side was Paul's own influence as the apostle to the Gentiles. This complex problem is not easily solved, and the testimony of the rest of the NT is that the church continued to struggle with this issue for some time. But the message of Galatians is clear: Only through faith in Christ can anyone becomes a son of Abraham, and as such faith is the only requirement to enter the assembly of the Lord.

In light of this passage, there are two important applications to consider. The first is central to the message of the paragraph: Are we announcing the gospel to all people, without any requirement other than faith in the risen Messiah? To put it another way, are we following in the footsteps of Paul or of Peter? The Protestant church has maintained ever since the time of the Reformation that individuals are saved through faith alone in Christ alone. There is no other requirement, nor is there any other efficacious means. Our attention then should turn not to our profession but our practice. We need only to consider the contemporary caricature of Christianity as a rules-based religion to see where we have failed. Any time someone thinks that they must do something or be something before they can respond in faith to the risen Lord, something has broken down, either explicitly or implicitly, in our communication of the good news. The church must rebuild a better understanding and practice of what it means for the gospel to be a message for all people. We must properly contextualize the gospel as a message that simply asks for a response of faith, not adherence to a particular cultural norm.

The second application recognizes the complexity of this Antioch event. Interesting to note is the convergence of different layers of the early church's experience. Certainly this event was about the theology of the gospel and how it worked out among Jews and Gentiles. But this event was not solely about the theology of the gospel; it was also about the apostolic leadership of the early church and how they handled a divisive issue. But this event was not solely about the apostolic leadership in the early church; it was also about the key personalities of Peter and Paul and how they handled the influence of James. But this event was not solely about a personality play between two key leaders and whose view would win out; this issue was additionally about the influence of those personalities over the believers in the local community of Antioch. The conflict in Antioch was an exceedingly complex event, and we would do well to recognize that many conflicts we experience in the contemporary church are just as complex and multi-faceted. Solving them requires that we exercise discernment and wisdom to know how to approach them appropriately. Yes, a hot take blasted to the Twittersphere might win points with adherents, but it will not necessarily advance the gospel. Instead, we must be willing to take the time to learn both the theology and the personalities involved. Then we will be able to see clearly how to resolve the conflict while maintaining fidelity to the risen Lord and harmony in the church.

Additional Exegetical Comments

2:11–14 One challenge with understanding this passage is its one-sidedness: We have only Paul's position and nothing from James, Peter, or Barnabas on this issue. J. P. Meier in a short, popular-level text presents thoughtful possibilities for what each might have thought on how the Antioch incident played out.[62] Although Meier largely reads between the lines about the thoughts of each of the key players, his essay is valuable for showing in a thoughtful way what some of the issues may have been.

2:11–14 Arguing from the social background of an honor/shame culture, P. F. Esler explains the broad historical incident of Gal 2:1–14 in the following way:[63] Stricter Jewish Christians were shamed when Paul brought Titus to Jerusalem because he was uncircumcised. They restored their honor by forcing James and Peter to go back on their agreement. The problem developed because Paul had not secured an oath from the Jerusalem apostles that they would keep their word. Although this reconstruction provides helpful nuance to what Paul wrote, it remains suggestive and not mandatory for understanding.

2:11–14 J. Taylor makes a persuasive argument that explains the historical background of this text.[64] Essentially James interpreted the decision of the Jerusalem Council in Acts 15 as parallel to the commandments given to Noah after the flood, which did not prevent Gentiles from turning to God but did prevent their fellowship with Jews. Peter then interpreted the decision of the Jerusalem Council as parallel to Lev 17–18, which allowed Gentiles to become resident foreigners within Israel. This is a helpful distinction except that it assumes that the Antioch incident took place after Acts 15.

2:12 Oakes, 77, interprets the issue of common meals in light of a house-church context. House churches would have met individually but also in common on occasion. Peter initially accepted invitations from both Gentile and Jewish hosts into private house gatherings. When the people from James arrived, he ate with them initially but then under their influence ate with them consistently, then exclusively. It was in a plenary meeting of all the house churches that Paul confronted him. Compare Soards and Pursiful, 77, who argue that the best inference from the language is a single church body.

62. J. P. Meier, "Biblical Reflection: The Conflict at Antioch (Gal 2:11–14)," *Mid-Stream* 35 (1996): 471–75.
63. P. F. Esler, "Making and Breaking an Agreement Mediterranean Style: A New Reading of Galatians 2:1–14," *BibInt* 3 (1995): 285–314.
64. J. Taylor, "The Jerusalem Decrees (Acts 15.20, 29 and 21.25) and the Incident at Antioch (Gal 2.11–14)," *NTS* 47 (2001): 372–80.

Selected Bibliography

Bock, D. L. *Acts*. BECNT. Grand Rapids: Baker, 2007.

Carson, D. A. "Mirror-Reading with Paul and against Paul: Galatians 2:11–14 as a Test Case." In *Studies in the Pauline Epistles: Essays in Honor of Douglas J. Moo*, ed. M. S. Harmon and J. E. Smith, 99–112. Grand Rapids: Zondervan, 2014.

Cohn-Sherbok, D. "Some Reflections on James Dunn's 'The Incident at Antioch (Gal 2:11–18)'." *JSNT* 18 (1983): 68–74.

Harrison, R. K., and C. J. Hemer. "Antioch (Syrian)." In *New Bible Dictionary*, ed. D. R. W. Wood, 51–52. Downers Grove: InterVarsity, 1996.

Houlden, J. L. "A Response to James D. G. Dunn." *JSNT* 18 (1983): 58–67.

Meier, J. P. "Biblical Reflection: The Conflict at Antioch (Gal 2:11–14)." *Mid-Stream* 35 (1996): 471–75.

Roberts, C. H. "A Note on Galatians II 14." *JTS* 40 (1939): 55–56.

Stewart, E. C. "I'm Okay, You're Not Okay: Constancy of Character and Paul's Understanding of Change in his Own and Peter's Behaviour." *HvTSt* 67 (2011): 1–8.

Taylor, J. "The Jerusalem Decrees (Acts 15.20, 29 and 21.25) and the Incident at Antioch (Gal 2.11–14)." *NTS* 47 (2001): 372–80.

Winter, J. G. "Another Instance of ὀρθοποδεῖν." *HTR* 34 (1941): 161–62.

The Nature of the Gospel (2:15–21)

Textual Notes

2:16 The text of NA[28] includes the postpositive conj. δέ as the second word of the verse but with brackets, indicating that the editors judge the word to be original but that the decision is difficult. This is an important problem, as the presence or absence of a conj. affects the flow of the argument. Given that this is an important section for the book theologically, that is not an unimportant consideration. The manuscript evidence on this problem is rather evenly divided. The omission is read by 𝔓[46] A 33 1739 1881 𝔐 et al., while the inclusion is read by א B C D* lat et al. The absence of the conj. has solid support from the Byzantine text type, while the presence of the conj. has solid support of the Western text type. The Alexandrian text type splits its attestation with exceptional witnesses on each side. On one hand, the presence of δέ perhaps is to be preferred on the grounds that Alexandrian-Western agreements are often historically solid, but this text type agreement is mitigated by the split of the Alexandrian witnesses. On the other hand, the oldest witness to this text is 𝔓[46] (ca. AD 200), and it lacks the conj. On that basis the absence of δέ could be preferred. Forced to choose on the basis of external evidence, because of the age of 𝔓[46] the shorter reading is to be preferred, but only slightly. Consideration of internal evidence also leads to a split decision. When we consider what scribes would have done with this text, more likely a scribe would have added the conj. to heighten the adversative force between vv. 15 and 16 rather than taken it out to weaken the connection. This also fits the canon of the shorter reading. When we turn to the question of what Paul would have written, there is no clear-cut answer. The conj. δέ was quite common, but Paul was not opposed to asyndeton, especially at points of high emotion (see, e.g., Phil 3:2). The final question is which reading best explains the rise of the others. In my estimation the absence of δέ best explains the inclusion of δέ. Early scribes likely understood v. 16 and following in some sense to contrast with what Paul stated in v. 15, so they naturally added a common adversative conj. when they saw that one was not there originally.

2:17 The particular particle written here is not entirely certain. The particle ἄρα, with an acute accent on the penult, is inferential, drawing a conclusion.

If this particle were intended, the apodosis of the sentence would be a stated inference: "Then Christ is a servant of sin." The particle ἆρα, with a circumflex on the penult, is interrogative, pointing to a debated point. If this particle were intended, the apodosis of the sentence would be a question: "Is Christ then a servant of sin?" Both internal and external evidence favor the interrogative particle. Paul routinely uses the phrase μὴ γένοιτο after a question within tight, logical argumentation, and the vast majority of witnesses support it, so much so that NA[28] lists only a negative apparatus for this problem.[1]

2:20 The variant in this verse is very significant theologically. Instead of ἐν πίστει ζῶ τῇ τοῦ υἱοῦ τοῦ θεοῦ ("I live by the faith of the Son of God"), several important manuscripts read ἐν πίστει ζῶ τῇ τοῦ θεοῦ καὶ Χριστοῦ ("I live by the faith of God and Christ"). This variant reading could imply important theological points—God as well as Christ could be the object of faith—or it might provide further evidence for Christ's faith as Paul's intended meaning in other passages.[2] It would also describe Christ as divine by virtue of a Granville Sharp construction. The variant reading is supported by 𝔓[46] B D* et al., while the text reading is supported by ℵ A C D[1] Ψ 0278 33 1739 1881 𝔐 lat sy co. The variant reading is quite ancient (the combined reading of 𝔓[46] and B is very important) but not preferred. The text reading also has exceptional witnesses, and it has greater geographical distribution among the text types as well as genealogical solidarity in the Western and Byzantine texts. The variant reading likely arose due to scribal error. In majuscule script the text reading would have appeared thusly: ΤΟΥΥΙΟΥΤΟΥΘ̅Υ̅.[3] A scribe could have easily skipped over the words υἱοῦ τοῦ because of the preponderance of upsilons, leaving simply τοῦ θεοῦ. Later scribes then clarified by adding καὶ Χριστοῦ.[4] The variant reading is also the harder reading theologically: Paul does not elsewhere speak of God as an object of the believer's faith,[5] and a Granville Sharp construction with the nouns θεός and Χριστός is unlike the other clear instance of Paul's use of this construction in Titus 2:13. Put more

---

1. Many of the important witnesses for this text lack accentuation here (𝔓[46] ℵ B* C D F G), which makes their support for either variant difficult to determine.
2. This relates to the subj./obj. gen. problem for the phrase πίστις Χριστοῦ. See discussion on the similar phrase in 2:16.
3. Although υἱός was one of the words often written as *nomina sacra*, it apparently was not consistently so written until later in the manuscript tradition. See C. H. Roberts, "Lecture II. Nomina Sacra: Origins and Significance," in *Manuscript, Society and Belief in Early Christian Egypt*, The Schweich Lectures of the British Academy 1977 (London: Oxford University Press, 1979), 26–48. Codex Sinaiticus and Codex Vaticanus both write υἱός out in full in this text, so that is a legitimate option for discussing the rise of the variants.
4. B. M. Metzger, *A Textual Commentary on the Greek New Testament* (New York: United Bible Societies, 1994), 524.
5. Metzger, *Textual Commentary*, 524.

simply, seeing τοῦ θεοῦ καὶ Χριστοῦ in the text, it is hard to see why a scribe would have changed it to τοῦ υἱοῦ τοῦ θεοῦ. But if a scribe saw only τοῦ θεοῦ in his text, the intervening words υἱοῦ τοῦ having been dropped because of an error of sight, a clarifying addition would become very likely. On this basis the NA[28] reading should be preferred.

Translation

15 We are Jews by birth and not sinners from among the Gentiles. **16** Because we know[6] that people are not justified by works of the Law but only through faith in Jesus Christ,[7] even we believed in Christ Jesus, so that we would be justified by faith in Christ and not by works of the Law because no flesh will be justified by works of the Law. **17** Now if while seeking to be justified in Christ we ourselves were also found to be sinners, is Christ then a servant of sin?[8] Absolutely not! **18** For if I presently build up again the things that I previously broke down, I show myself to be a transgressor of the Law. **19** For through the Law I died to the Law so that I would live to God. I have been crucified with Christ,[9] **20** but I no longer live, but Christ lives in me. And the life that I now live in the body I live by faith in the Son of God who loved me and gave himself for me. **21** I do not nullify God's grace. For if righteousness comes through the Law, then Christ died for nothing!

Commentary

To say that Gal 2:15–21 is one of the most important texts within the Pauline corpus is not without warrant. Paul's thoughts are at once practical and immediate, but also sublime and timeless. This paragraph connects Paul to his Jewish heritage and expresses quintessential Christian faith and doctrine. In short, it is almost impossible to overestimate the importance of this passage, and it deserves our utmost attention and effort.

---

6. Some translations treat the ptc. εἰδότες as a main verb: "yet we know that" (NET, ESV, NLT). Compare NIV, which unusually makes the sentence structure cross vv. 15 and 16. This is not the best construal of the syntax, however.
7. Compare "faithfulness of Jesus Christ" (NET). For discussion see excursus "The Meaning of πίστις Ἰησοῦ Χριστοῦ."
8. "Servant of sin" is a formal rendering of ἁμαρτίας διάκονος. Compare the more dynamic translations "one who encourages sin" (NET); "promoter of sin" (CSB); "Would that mean that Christ has led us into sin?" (NLT).
9. Here I follow the versification of NA[28], which includes this clause with v. 19 (so also NRSV). Compare most other translations, which move this clause to the beginning of v. 20. Regardless of the versification, this clause clearly connects with the following material.

The first point of interpretation for this paragraph is its placement in the flow of the epistle's argument. Betz, 114, famously argued that this paragraph was the *propositio*, which sums up the legal content of the *narratio* and transitions to the *probatio*.[10] This helpful assessment, supported to a large extent by the grammar of the passage, explains its suggestive, summary tone and transitional placement within the argument of the book. In short, this paragraph acts both as a theological conclusion to what precedes and as a transition to what follows.[11] In the body of the letter, beginning in 1:11, Paul demonstrates that his gospel has a divine origin by detailing his independence from the Jerusalem apostles following his conversion and then by describing their approbation of his gospel in 2:1–10. In 2:11–14, Paul details his conflict with Peter in Antioch over the implications of his gospel; this paragraph serves to summarize the issues at stake in that conflict, thus proving through theological argument that his gospel came from God and the implications he practiced were the proper ones for both Jews and Gentiles to follow. Following this paragraph, in chapter 3 Paul exposits what it means to be a child of Abraham through faith, filling out the implications of the theological seeds he plants here. This passage summarizes and implies, concludes and previews.

This passage is also central for Protestant expressions of soteriology. Luther in his commentary on this passage says things that the Protestant church has held as central for hundreds of years:

> The true way to Christianity is, first, to acknowledge that we are sinners according to the law and that it is impossible for us to do anything good. Therefore, you cannot earn grace by what you do; if you try, you double your offense, for since you are a bad tree, you can only produce bad fruit—that is, sins. ... The second part is this: if you want to be saved, you must not seek salvation through works. God has sent his one and only Son into the world, that we might live through him. He was crucified and died for you and bore your sins in his own body. ... [H]e will freely give us remission of sins, righteousness, and everlasting life for the sake of Christ his Son. God gives his gifts freely to everybody, and that is the praise and glory of his divinity.[12]

---

10. This is adopted explicitly by many commentators. See, e.g., Longenecker, 80–81; Matera, 98; Witherington, 169; Rapa, 581–82.

11. Longenecker, 80, argues that seeing this paragraph as the *propositio* provides an interpretive key for understanding its compressed language: "For if the *probatio* contains the proofs or arguments introduced by the *propositio*, then we must look to Paul's *probatio* of 3:1–4:11 for an understanding of how to unpack the terms of the *propositio* of 2:15–21."

12. Luther, 87.

Here Luther clearly juxtaposes the futility of righteousness through works with the free grace of the gospel. The human problem is clearly in view: We are sinners who cannot save ourselves, no matter what we do. The solution is freely offered: Christ bore our sins, and God freely offers salvation in him. Luther's comments are evidence that Paul's thoughts are key to many expressions of soteriology and related theological domains.

In addition to its centrality to Protestant theology, this passage is also important for the interpretation of Paul, brought into recent focus especially with the New Perspective on Paul. Ever since the advent of this New Perspective, Gal 2:15–21 has been a *crux interpretum* and with good reason: In these few verses occur all the central lexemes and themes of that debate. Issues of ethnicity are front and center. Justification language occurs throughout the passage. The phrase "works of the Law" occurs six times in Galatians, three of which are in 2:16. Paul interacts in this passage with both his Jewish heritage and his understanding of faith in Christ. Not only is this passage important for wrestling with the New Perspective on Paul, but its similarity with the book of Romans makes for ripe comparison between the two. I have always seen this passage and Rom 3:21–26 as parallel in both thought and function: theological stakes in the ground that Paul uses to ground his entire argument for each letter. The importance of that paragraph in Romans is widely recognized; this paragraph in Galatians takes on equal importance.[13]

Two related questions of macro structure need to be addressed relative to this paragraph for its interpretation to be well grounded. Broadly stated, the connection of the paragraph to what precedes should be elucidated, and the structure of the paragraph itself merits discussion. The presenting question about the context is whether the address to Peter that Paul begins in 2:14 extends in any way into vv. 15–21. There are many reasons commentators argue that Paul's address to Peter extends all the way to v. 21.[14] Verse 15 begins with no apparent disjunction from v. 14.[15] Paul uses 1 pl. pronouns, which would naturally include Peter as an addressee as in v. 14. There is no change of subject or addressee until 3:1. Conversely some have argued that 2:15–21 begins a new argument and should be treated separately from 2:11–14. Todd Scacewater, in an analysis of the phrase "works of the Law," argues that this paragraph is not polemic against Peter but polemic against the agitators in Galatia.[16] Thus the paragraph would introduce a new argument. Many commentators with good reason take a middle position. Dunn, 132, argues

13. For the purpose of this commentary, I do not undertake a thorough investigation of this comparison. My goal has been to examine Galatians on its own terms.

14. See Hays, 230; Schreiner, 150.

15. Lenski, 102, vividly argues this shows a verbatim retelling: "The absence of a connective is to be expected. Paul paused after stating his question, and when Peter offered no answer as he, indeed, could not, Paul continued to speak."

16. T. A. Scacewater, "Galatians 2:11–21 and the Interpretive Context of 'Works of the Law,' " *JETS* 56 (2013): 307–23.

that Paul restates his argument from Antioch but does so in such a way to influence the Galatians. Moo, 153, sees the paragraph as a continuation of Paul's Antioch speech but clearly transitional to the next major section of the letter. Each part of the paragraph, including the beginning volley in vv. 15–16, is tightly bound to what precedes, but key words central to the following argument are also introduced here.[17] Soards and Pursiful, 86, argue that the switch from the 1 pl. in the first section to the 1 sg. in the latter section means that some lines of the paragraph need to be understood as directed to the Galatians directly. Any way the paragraph is construed relative to its connection to the Antioch incident, Paul's rhetorical purpose is still focused on the Galatians and their present moment. Paul recounts the Antioch incident to press his point with the Galatians, writing in such a way that he creates a discourse that functions on two levels at the same time; he weds history and theology perfectly.[18] As Betz, 114, ably says, "Paul addresses Cephas formally, and the Galatians materially."

The structure of the paragraph itself challenges the reader. It is not simply historical review or theological exposition, nor is it simply personal justification or polemical attack. Rather, it is a mix of all these things. Paul is still in the midst of defending himself against Peter concerning the implications of his gospel for Gentile inclusion in the people of God, but Paul makes paradigmatic assertions about any person's relationship to God in Christ to bolster that argument. Paul finalizes his autobiographical argument regarding his apostolic authority, but he does so with an eye on those who oppose him and the arguments they have made. All along the way the paragraph is tightly argued, and moving from one verse to the next with understanding requires a careful explanation of the connections involved. As a whole, the passage emphasizes faith vis-à-vis the Law, reflecting a fundamental reorientation away from the Law to faith in Christ. This faith in Christ results in justification before God and a new spiritual orientation away from obedience to the Law to living to God. This reorientation comes through Christ's spiritual life available to the believer through his mystical union with Christ in co-crucifixion. Indeed, the passage is best understood if forensic and participatory categories on the one hand and salvation history and justification on the other are each recognized and not collapsed into one another (Moo, 155).

---

17. Moo, 153–54, lists these key words and phrases: νόμος, ἔργα νόμου, δικαιόω, δικαιοσύνη, πίστις, πιστεύω, and ζάω, with the caveat that some are used previously in the letter but their use in this paragraph has a distinctive sense taken up in the following argument. I would add to this list σάρξ as well. For similar lists see Matera, 98; Witherington, 171. It might be easier to list words from the passage that do not take on such theological significance!

18. The terminology of "two levels" was originally used by J. L. Martyn to describe Johannine narrative. See J. L. Martyn, *History and Theology in the Fourth Gospel*, NTL (Louisville, KY: Westminster John Knox, 1968).

The best structure for the internal argument of the paragraph is tripartite.[19] In vv. 15–16 Paul addresses the common ground he holds with his fellow Jewish Christians, that of reliance upon Christ for justification, not any works of the Law. In vv. 17–20 Paul addresses the implication this reliance upon Christ has for the Law for entering the people of God and then living as a member of that community by the Spirit. The final verse of the paragraph succinctly summarizes Paul's argument through a powerful deduction that touches both the theology and history of Christ's death on the cross.

2:15 This verse and the next present some challenges to the interpreter, not the least of which is the essential structure of the sentence (or sentences) that they comprise. The central questions are whether v. 15 is an independent clause and how the ptc. that begins v. 16 connects to the context. My interpretation, which will be defended with particulars below, is that both vv. 15 and 16 constitute sentences unto themselves (*contra* NKJV, NIV). Verse 15 is composed of a simple sentence with a compound predicate nom. Verse 16 is composed of a complex sentence, formed with an independent clause with three dependent clauses, one preceding and two following. Consequently I interpret v. 15 as logically related to v. 16, but grammatically independent.

Ἡμεῖς φύσει Ἰουδαῖοι καὶ οὐκ ἐξ ἐθνῶν ἁμαρτωλοί. Paul begins the passage with an affirmation of the common ground he and Peter share. The affirmation would appear to be axiomatic, unnecessary to state in the context, but given the nature of the conflict between Peter and Paul and where Paul goes in his argument, this datum becomes a central point. He asserts something in common with Peter to gain assent, which he then uses to show the impropriety of Peter's position. The asyndeton of this clause marks a turn in Paul's recounting of the Antioch incident, perhaps from quotation to explanation but most certainly from challenge to commonality. The clause does not have a verb, so one has to be supplied. The most natural inference is the copulative verb ἐσμέν, as Greek often left the copula out if the context was clear enough. This clause then becomes an independent assertion: "We [are] Jews by birth and not sinners from the Gentiles." On the other hand, it is possible to construe this phrase as functioning like a pendant nom., identifying the subject of what would be a very long sentence to help focus the argument. On this understanding, Paul would use this phrase to delineate the subject of the ptc. εἰδότες and the aor. indic. ἐπιστεύσαμεν in v. 16 more carefully for his audience. Given that the conflict detailed in vv. 11–14 had ethnicity as a central component, this would not be an unimportant delineation. However, given the repetition of the pronoun ἡμεῖς almost immediately in front of the main verb ἐπιστεύσαμεν, this second option appears somewhat convoluted. The emphasis of καὶ ἡμεῖς in v. 16 is best explained if v. 15 is a complete sentence (Moo, 173). The first explanation is the simpler, better one (Lightfoot,

19. See Longenecker, 82, and Moo, 154, for these essential arguments.

114), namely, that the equative verb is implied and Paul begins his argument with an assertion of the Jewish identity he and Peter shared.

Paul begins by affirming what he and Peter are. The rhetorical function of the argument vis-à-vis the current situation in Galatia, however, allows an even wider referent to be construed for the pronoun ἡμεῖς. This could be seen in the context of Antioch, referring to Paul, Peter, Barnabas, and James (so Garlington 2007, 139), or it could be seen in the context of Galatia, referring to Paul, Peter, and the agitators (so Martyn, 248). Given the rhetorical function of the paragraph, it is better to see a broader referent: Paul basically presents his conceptual agreement with Jewish Christianity more broadly (Fung, 112–13; Longenecker, 83). The noun φύσις here refers to characteristics acquired by birth, the dat. case indicating a point of reference: "With respect to birth, we are Jews."[20] It implies broader connections of ancestry (Garlington 2007, 139) and the benefits that come with being a Jew (Schreiner, 154). Paul reemphasizes this point with the substantive Ἰουδαῖοι, which refers both to ancestry and religion.[21] By virtue of their births, Peter, Paul, and all Jewish Christians had an ancestral, physical connection to Abraham; a moral, spiritual connection to Moses and the Law; and through these connections a special relationship with God who called them as a people.

Paul continues by stating what he and Peter are not. The phrase οὐκ ἐξ ἐθνῶν ἁμαρτωλοί provides a stark contrast on all levels to Ἡμεῖς φύσει Ἰουδαῖοι. The phrase ἐξ ἐθνῶν functions similarly to φύσει to refer to Gentiles by race; the prepositional phrase indicates source or origin generally and ancestry specifically. In this context ἁμαρτωλός, usually translated "sinner," takes on significance beyond the simple assertion of bad behavior. Terms for sin are not common in Galatians,[22] so the use of ἁμαρτωλός here is significant. In classical Greek ἁμαρτωλός was quite rare. As an adj. it meant "erroneous" without any connotation of spiritual or religious failing,[23] but it could also refer generally to poor moral character.[24] These meanings carried over into the Koine period, which gives ample evidence for the term having a secular meaning. The use of the term in the LXX significantly focused the connotation of the term, however, as it was regularly used to translate the Hebrew word רָשָׁע, which means "wicked, guilty."[25] In the Psalms the Hebrew word was used specifi-

---

20. The English translation "by nature" (so NASB, NAB) can communicate this as well, but that phrase can also communicate disposition, which is not in view in this context.

21. BDAG, 478–79.

22. The word ἁμαρτία, normally translated "sin," occurs twice (1:4; 3:22); the related word ἁμαρτωλός, which means "sinful" as an adj. and "sinner" as a substantive, also occurs twice (2:15, 17).

23. See, e.g., Aristotle, *Eth. nic.* 1109a33.

24. See, e.g., Aristophanes, *Thesm.* 1111.

25. *HALOT*, 1295–96.

cally for Jews within Israel who did not orient their lives around complete devotion to Torah (see Ps 1, where this word is used four times). Eventually this influenced the Greek term so strongly within the Jewish context that it could be used simply to refer to Gentiles, who by definition had no relationship to the Law (see, e.g., Tobit 13:8 [LXX]; 1Macc 1:34; 2:48; Jub. 23:24). The NT usage of ἁμαρτωλός reflects this background. Many occurrences refer simply to people who engage in sinful behavior (e.g., Luke 7:37, 39, where the focus is on the woman's immoral conduct), but the term can simply refer to Gentiles (cf. Matt 26:45). Pauline usage as a whole reflects the more general usage of this term without a specific ethnic referent. The four occurrences in Romans (3:7; 5:8, 19; 7:13) and the two in 1 Timothy (1:9, 15) each reflect the general meaning of one who has disobeyed God. The use here in Galatians is different, however; the juxtaposition of Ἰουδαῖοι with ἐθνῶν shows that Paul here is not speaking of ἁμαρτωλοί as people generally culpable before God but rather with reference to ethnicity and the related non-reception of Torah. It encapsulates how Jews generally regarded Gentiles. It is traditional Jewish language that divided the world into two groups: the Jews who had a relation to God by virtue of his election and covenant, and the Gentiles who were outside that covenant.[26] Important to note is the intended irony in Paul's use of this traditional language (Lightfoot, 115; George, 189; Rapa, 583). The language was traditionally used to condemn Gentiles, but Paul uses this language only to debunk it in the following verse with a universal declaration of humanity's sinfulness (Moo, 156). As Martyn, 249, so ably says, "Verse 15 proves, then, to be the baiting of the trap, so to speak, which will be sprung in v 16." Paul jabs with his left in v. 15, then connects with a right hook in v. 16.

2:16 It is not an overstatement to say that Gal 2:16 is one of the most important in the book for a number of reasons. It crystallizes Paul's response to the conflict he experienced with Peter in Antioch, so it has an important textual and rhetorical function. With it Paul expresses his soteriology in a very compact way, which is important theologically but also practically relative to the question of how Jews and Gentiles can join together as the people of God within the church. It provides key evidence for discussion about the New Perspective on Paul, so it has important interpretive value as well. There are multiple exegetical knots to untie in this sentence: the meaning of the term δικαιόω, the referent of ἔργων νόμου, the meaning of the preposition ἐκ with ἔργων νόμου, the meaning of ἐὰν μή and how it relates its clause to the preceding, and the nature of the Ἰησοῦ Χριστοῦ as a gen. noun to πίστεως. In

26. This fact is acknowledged by many commentators. See, e.g., Lenski, 104–5; Betz, 115; Hays, 236; Oakes, 81; Soards and Pursiful, 87. Dunn, 132–33, also notes that this is "characteristic Jewish language" but goes further to argue that this is the language of "typical Jewish factionalism." Given the emphasis upon the Gentiles in this context, it seems only the former can be in view.

order to provide a helpful discussion here, without diving into so much detail that the forest gets lost because of the trees, the discussion here will focus on the flow of the argument, assuming conclusions that are detailed in the excursuses included at the end of the chapter after the selected bibliography.

εἰδότες ὅτι. Given the lack of a main verb in the prior verse and the lack of conj. here,[27] the relationship between the ptc. and the context is ambiguous. Paul uses this ptc. sixteen times in his writings. Each time it is causal, but more often than not it follows the verb it modifies.[28] A causal clarification related to what precedes would be nonsense. In addition, the normal placement for a causal ptc. is in front of the verb it modifies,[29] so Pauline usage in which this ptc. follows the controlling verb would be more unusual. The best construal of vv. 15–16 takes v. 15 as a complete assertion unto itself. Verse 16 begins a new sentence with εἰδότες as causal to the main verb ἐπιστεύσαμεν that follows later (so Burton, 119). Paul with this ptc. then sets up the basis for the main verb, that is, the reason he and Peter believed in Christ Jesus.

Even with the clarity gained when vv. 15 and 16 are regarded as separate sentences, their logical relationship needs to be elucidated, especially in light of the asyndeton. The variant reading δέ would convey adversative force, so this sense could be taken to imply the logical connection between the verses even without a conj. A rather dynamic rendering would be "We are Jews by birth and have a relationship to the Law through covenant, but despite this fact, because we know …" (similarly Schreiner, 154). This is hard to defend for two main reasons, though: It puts a great deal of interpretive weight on an implication rather than on the explicit statements of the text, and it goes against the structural arrangement of vv. 15–16 as a statement of agreement that begins the *propositio*. Paul's logic and rhetoric here are founded not in the *contrast* between his Jewish nature and faith in Christ but rather in their inherent *consistency*. It is thus best to see both sentences as pointing in the same direction, that is, toward faith in Christ, rather than seeing v. 15 as emphasizing the Law and v. 16 as emphasizing faith in Christ. Verse 15 emphasizes the common Jewish heritage that Paul, Peter, and other Jewish Christians share; verse 16 emphasizes their common faith in Christ.

οὐ δικαιοῦται ἄνθρωπος ἐξ ἔργων νόμου ἐὰν μὴ διὰ πίστεως Ἰησοῦ Χριστοῦ. This phrase is the content Paul knows that serves as the cause for the main verb ἐπιστεύσαμεν. In other words, this is the theological assertion that motivated Paul to believe in Christ Jesus. Paul's essential argument is a universal proposition regarding the basis of humanity's justification. People are not justified by God on the basis of any works of the Law they have done; instead God justifies them only on the basis of faith in Christ. The pass. voice of

27. I take the shorter text to be original. See the textual note on v. 16.

28. The occurrence in Gal 4:8 could be taken as temporal (so NET), but this would be redundant with the use of τότε in that clause. Exceptions in which the εἰδότες as causal precedes the modified verb are 2 Cor 5:11; Gal 4:8.

29. Wallace, *Greek Grammar*, 631.

δικαιόω is used in each occurrence in v. 16, which focuses on God's actions to justify (Soards and Pursiful, 94). A great deal of this proposition is carried by the force of the noun ἄνθρωπος. In the prior verse Paul's attention had been on humanity as two separate groups, that is, Jews and Gentiles. This noun levels the playing field, placing both Jew and Gentile before God as human beings without distinction (Bruce, 138; Martyn, 249; Schreiner, 154; de Boer, 151). It anticipates the positive declaration of Gal 3:28 in which ethnic distinctions no longer pertain (Soards and Pursiful, 88).

Paul's assertion about humanity concerns the verb δικαιόω, traditionally translated with the English verb "justify." Writ large, it refers to the future, eschatological declaration by God that an individual is right before him and part of his people. Writ small, it refers to the present forensic status of an individual within the people of God in light of that future declaration. As argued in the excursus below, Paul's use of this word group within Galatians is polyvalent. He has in view both the particular issue of Torah observance relative to an individual's justification, for which his use of this language is the immediate response, and the general principle of humanity's inability to in any way merit God's favorable declaration through action, the theological principle that underlies his particular response in this instance. In this context δικαιόω is both covenantal and forensic: It refers both to the relationship an individual has with God—more specifically, the proof that one is indeed in that relationship—and the basis for that relationship, that is, the right standing granted to the individual before God. Thus translations such as "declared righteous," "justified," "made right," and "vindicated" all have merit, as they all represent a particular facet of the relationship in which an individual stands appropriately before God. Because of Paul's citation of Ps 143:2 later, which functions as a scriptural proof for this theological assertion, I hold that Paul's primary emphasis in the present context is upon the underlying theological principle, so I favor the forensic concepts of "declared righteous" and "justified" as foremost in Paul's mind. Even so, covenantal implications cannot be excluded, nor should they be, as Paul certainly had an eye on an individual's connection to the people of God.

The meaning of the prep. ἐκ with ἔργων νόμου is an important issue as it fundamentally orients the works of the law to the concept of justification. The more common interpretation of the prep. is as reason or basis,[30] that is, Paul here argues that justification does not come to the individual on the basis of the works of the law. Don Garlington has argued, however, that the proper meaning of ἐκ here is "partisan," that is, denoting an intensified idea of origin, that of participation or belonging.[31] Paul's emphasis would thus not be on works of the Law as a means for justification, but rather on works of the Law as a Jewish identifier or social boundary. He paraphrases this

30. BDAG, 297.

31. D. B. Garlington, "Paul's 'Partisan ἐκ' and the Question of Justification in Galatians," *JBL* 127 (2008): 567–89.

phrase as "we know that a person is not justified *by belonging to the arena of Torah-works*."[32] Along with ἐκ πίστεως Χριστοῦ, this forms a strong antithesis with the comment in v. 15 about how Peter and his fellow Jews are not ἐξ ἐθνῶν ἁμαρτωλοί. This interpretation cannot hold, though, in light of the parallel assertion Paul makes with the phrase διὰ πίστεως Ἰησοῦ Χριστοῦ in the following clause and other clear instances of an instrumental meaning for ἐκ, for example, in Gal 3:2, 5. In his critique of Garlington's argument, J. Lambrecht makes an important comparison with Gal 3:10–13: The curse comes because of works *not* done, and thus instrumentality is the best way to understand the force of the Law in 3:12 and the wider context.[33]

The identity of "works of the Law" in this passage is a perennial problem in interpretation. As detailed in the excursus, the wider context of Paul's argument in the epistle, with special reference to 3:10 and 5:3, points not to particular works that were useful in marking out the Jew as faithful, whether with reference to the world at large or to Jews within Judaism. Rather, it refers to the entire Law, that is, what the Law required as a whole of Jews in covenant with God. De Boer, 148, states well that these are "the actions or deeds demanded by the law without distinction and without regard to the manner in which these deeds are performed." Put another way, the phrase refers neither to legalism nor identity badges but to simply what the Law requires.

The problem of the meaning of ἐὰν μή is a thorny one. Fortunately, there are only two options. The phrase can indicate an exception to the prior clause, or it can indicate a contrast. As an exception, it would accept the blanket negation of the prior phrase with the exception of the condition indicated in its own phrase. The sense would run thusly: "No one is justified by works of the law except [when they are justified] through the faith of Jesus Christ." The implication would be that for an individual who has faith in Christ, the negation would not hold. This then would apply directly to Jewish Christian believers who had accepted Jesus as the Messiah but who still sought to follow the Law. Their practice of the Law would be valuable and appropriate as long as it was accompanied by faith in Christ (see Dunn, 137). As a contrast, ἐὰν μή would be equivalent to ἀλλά, indicating something adversative or negated. The sense would run thusly: "No one is justified by works of the law but [instead they are justified] through faith in Jesus Christ." The support for the exceptive view comes from the normal sense of the phrase ἐὰν μή.[34] Some New Perspective interpreters argue that Paul's stance toward the Law was not negative in and of itself, but negative when used to exclude Gentiles from joining the people of God. If this is the background for the statement,

32. Garlington, "Paul's 'Partisan ἐκ,'" 570.

33. J. Lambrecht, "Critical Reflections on Paul's 'Partisan ἐκ' as Recently Presented by Don Garlington," *ETL* 85 (2009): 139.

34. See BDAG, 267–68. A. T. Robertson, *A Grammar of the Greek New Testament in the Light of Historical Research* (Nashville: Broadman, 1934), 1025, argues that it is equivalent to εἰ μή.

ἐὰν μή as an exception could be a legitimate interpretation. The support for the contrastive view is multifaceted, however. The parallel term εἰ μή was on occasion exchanged for ἀλλά, each taking on the meaning of the other.[35] The use of ἐὰν μή as adversative could come from Semitic influence: The phrase כִּי אִם, formally equivalent to ἐὰν μή, often has an adversative meaning in the MT (Schreiner, 163).[36] In addition, Paul restates his thesis in the last two clauses of the verse. The ἵνα clause claims that justification comes from faith in Christ and not through works of the Law, and the ὅτι clause cites Ps 143:2 to deny justification through works of the Law. Both these clauses are statements without exception or qualification. Given these clearer statements toward the end of the verse and the likelihood that Paul was consistent at least within the same verse, the absolute statements should influence the interpretation here. Seeing ἐὰν μή as adversative also fits better with what Paul argues elsewhere about the relationship of faith and Law (Burton, 121; Longenecker, 84; Witherington, 178–79). Thus the contrastive sense is much more likely Paul's intention rather than the exceptive sense. Paul denies that justification comes through works of the Law; he affirms that it only comes through faith in Jesus Christ.

It is possible that these different construals for ἐὰν μή explain part of the conflict Paul had with the Galatian agitators. De Boer, 189–216, makes a strong case that the entirety of this phrase is traditional, accepted by both Paul's Jewish-Christian missionary opponents and Paul himself. The disagreement is not over the meaning or referent of the key ideas (justification language, works of the law, faith in/of Christ) but rather how those ideas relate. Paul's opponents accept a complementary relationship between works of the Law and faith in/of Christ in justification, while Paul disassociates works of the Law and faith in/of Christ, allowing only the latter to have any impact upon justification. Put another way, Paul accepts the same language as his opponents for his nascent Christian theology but realigns it so that the works of the Law are understood as irrelevant to justification. The realignment comes primarily through the phrase ἐὰν μή: Paul's opponents accept this phrase as exceptive, while Paul intends it to be contrastive or exclusive.[37]

The last phrase of this clause is perhaps the most challenging. The first word of the phrase presents no significant problems to the reader. The prep.

---

35. See M. Zerwick, *Biblical Greek: Illustrated By Examples*, trans. J. Smith, Scripta Pontificii Instituti Biblici 114 (Rome: Pontifical Biblical Institute, 1963), 157–58; MHT, 2:468; Moo, 163. For an example of εἰ μή standing in for ἀλλά, see Matt 5:13; 12:4; Rom 14:14. For an example of ἀλλά standing in for εἰ μή, see Mark 4:22.

36. An important caveat, noted by Schreiner, 163, is that the LXX does not translate כִּי אִם with ἐὰν μή.

37. This was originally suggested by J. D. G. Dunn, *The New Perspective on Paul* (Grand Rapids: Eerdmans, 2008), 112–13. See also A. A. Das, "Another Look at ἐὰν μή in Galatians 2:16," *JBL* 119 (2000): 529–39.

διά takes on the same nuance as *ἐκ* earlier in the verse, that of means or basis.[38] The phrase *πίστεως* Ἰησοῦ Χριστοῦ is much more difficult to interpret. The central issue is whether faith should be interpreted as humanity's response of faith or Christ's faithful obedience and whether Christ receives this faith as the object or enacts this faith as the subject. As detailed in the excursuses, I hold that faith here is humanity's proper response to Christ with Christ receiving the faith as its object (see "Excursus: Paul's Use of the *πιστ-* Word Group in Galatians" and "Excursus: The Meaning of *πίστις* Ἰησοῦ Χριστοῦ"). In this clause, then, Paul juxtaposes two different responses of humanity to God's revelation in the present time. On the one hand there are those who seek justification from God on the basis of their obedience to the Law; on the other hand there are those who seek justification from God on the basis of their faith in Christ. For the purposes of his argument at this point in which he details areas of agreement between himself and his interlocutors, Paul places himself, Peter, and other Jewish Christians in this latter camp. The doctrine of justification by faith is part of Jewish Christian theology (Betz, 115). They all know that no one is justified by God by the works of the Law; that declaration comes to individuals only on the basis of their faith in Christ.

καὶ ἡμεῖς εἰς Χριστὸν Ἰησοῦν *ἐπιστεύσαμεν*. With this statement Paul makes the key declaration of the sentence. The *καί* at the beginning is not connective, despite this interpretation by many translations ("and" NET, NRSV; "so" ESV, TNIV). If the *καί* were connective, it would connect this independent clause to the one in v. 15. But if that were the case, the ptc. εἰδότες would then be causal to v. 15, which as stated above would be nonsensical. The better construal of this conj. is ascensive, adding a point of focus to the discussion.[39] This provides a better fit with the main thrust of this first part of the paragraph: Even Peter and Paul themselves, Jews with an ancestral relationship to the Law, have placed their faith in Christ, accepting all that entails vis-à-vis the Law. A better translation of the phrase is "Even we believed in Christ Jesus" (see, e.g., KJV, NASB, RSV). The pronoun ἡμεῖς is somewhat emphatic. Taken together *καὶ* ἡμεῖς points back to the words of v. 15 (Burton, 123; Lenski, 103; Hays, 237). Paul uses it with an exclusive sense to emphasize himself and Peter and by extension other Jewish believers over and against the Gentiles (Moo, 157). The prepositional phrase εἰς Χριστὸν Ἰησοῦν identifies the obj. of the verb *ἐπιστεύσαμεν*, which indicates the response of the individual to the person of Christ revealed by God in the historical event of his death and resurrection (see "Excursus: Paul's Use of the *πιστ-* Word Group in Galatians"). The collocation of *πιστεύω* and εἰς is important theologically. It expands *πίστις* from cognition to volition: "This faith has a cognitive element—a 'believing that' certain things are true—but the language of believing 'into Christ' shows that it is much more, involving both trust and commitment" (Moo, 163).

---

38. BDAG, 224, defines this usage more precisely as "efficient cause."

39. See Wallace, *Greek Grammar*, 670–71.

The sense of the argument at this juncture is important to follow. Paul began the paragraph by identifying the common ground he and Peter shared (and by extension his opponents in Galatia). They would all acknowledge their Jewish ethnicity and heritage, which gave them a certain religious outlook and framework in contradistinction to the Gentiles, who traditionally were identified as sinners because they had no connection to the covenant. In v. 16 Paul changes his focus, identifying the specific reason for the conversion to being Christ-followers he, Peter, and other Jewish Christians all experienced. They all know that justification does not come through the Law; it comes only through faith in Jesus Christ. Paul does not explain how or when he and Peter came to know this, but the fact of the matter is they both recognize it. This leads to the central affirmation of the sentence: Because of this knowledge, both he and Peter have placed their faith in Jesus Christ. Both know that justification comes through faith, not works of the Law, not only in principle but in their very own experience (Dunn, 139). Looking at the situation from the outside, one could understand why Gentiles would place their faith in Christ. They had no connection to God because they had no connection to the Law. When the gospel was made known to them, which allowed a relationship to God solely through faith in Christ, without any requirement for obedience to the Law, they eagerly responded. The Jew was in a different position when the gospel was announced. Already having a relationship to God, with the Law as a central aspect of that relationship, faith in Christ without reference to the Law would seem at best redundant and at worst perverted. Yet despite their ethnic and religious predisposition to privilege the Law, both Paul and Peter placed their faith in Christ. They were both convinced by the truth of the gospel such that they changed their allegiance. This personal testimony is an application of the general statement Paul made previously about humanity to Paul and Peter specifically as Jews (Schreiner, 166). The premise behind this is that Jews needed to be put right with God just as Gentiles did (Witherington, 183). Paul implicitly argues for a fundamental difference between justification through the Law and justification through faith in Christ. Jews would be disposed to privilege the former, Gentiles the latter. Even so, he and Peter placed their faith in Christ. Paul intends for this personal testimony both to attest to the truth of his gospel and to set up further pieces of his argument to follow. Paul's point is that if Jews have to believe in Christ for justification and not rely on works of the Law, then it makes no sense to require Gentiles to obey the Law (Schreiner, 166).

ἵνα δικαιωθῶμεν ἐκ πίστεως Χριστοῦ καὶ οὐκ ἐξ ἔργων νόμου. Paul modifies the main kernel of the sentence, explaining why he, Peter, and other Jewish Christians placed their faith in Jesus Christ. The verb *δικαιόω* is a divine passive, pointing to God's role as the actor in bringing justification. The prep. *ἐκ* continues to convey means or basis. The phrases *πίστεως Χριστοῦ* and *ἔργων νόμου* convey the same meaning as before. The emphasis of this statement is not primarily on the reality of faith in Christ as a bedrock, theological affirmation. Instead, this purpose clause highlights the particular reasons that Paul, Peter, and other Jewish Christians changed the direction of their faith. The conj. ἵνα plus the subjunctive normally indicates either purpose or result for a controlling verb, in this case the ἐπιστεύσαμεν of the prior clause. Purpose is preferred here because it is the more common semantic force of ἵνα plus subjunctive,[40] but it also conveys deeper connections in Paul's logic. Jewish Christians would not necessarily agree with his assertion consciously, but it is implicit in their expression of faith; Paul here makes it explicit (Oakes, 90). By expressing purpose, Paul focuses on the future-looking motivation he and Peter shared in placing their faith in Christ, which pairs well with the retrospective viewpoint he takes up in the following ὅτι clause with the scriptural citation.

ὅτι ἐξ ἔργων νόμου οὐ δικαιωθήσεται πᾶσα σάρξ. This causal ὅτι clause modifies the immediately preceding ἵνα clause. With this clause Paul states the reason he, Peter, and other Jewish Christians purposed to be justified by faith in Christ and not by works of the Law. This clause has language similar to the ptc. clause that began the verse, but at this point Paul is not simply emphasizing through repetition or proving through tautology. Instead, he cites the OT Scriptures, specifically Ps 143:2 (142:2 LXX), to prove his theological point. This serves his argument both in terms of content and function: Even the Jewish Scriptures recognized generally that no one is righteous before God; Paul applies that specifically to mean that no one would ever be justified by works of the Law (so also Keener, 189).[41] This serves to garner both assent to the argument and application of its outcome.

The ὅτι here is causal and connects this clause to the immediately preceding one as grounds for the purpose Paul expressed related to his faith in Jesus. To put it periphrastically and somewhat inelegantly, "We believed in Christ Jesus *with this purpose as our motivation, namely,* that we would be justified by faith in Jesus and not by works of the Law. *The fundamental reason we have this purpose is that* no flesh will be justified by works of the Law." This ὅτι clause serves as a causal justification for the claim that Paul, Peter, and other Jewish Christians sought justification through faith in Christ and not through works of the Law. The phrase ἐξ ἔργων νόμου has the same nuance as earlier in the verse, that of means or basis. The verb δικαιωθήσεται is a fut. pass., indicating what will be true at the future, eschatological moment of justification. More to the point of Paul's argument, because it will be true in the future at the final moment of justification, the argument has universal applicability in the present. Paul uses the phrase πᾶσα σάρξ to refer to all humanity. The noun σάρξ in this instance refers to living beings,

40. Wallace, *Greek Grammar*, 472.

41. See "Excursus: Paul's Use of Psalm 143:2" for discussion of the particulars of Paul's citation.

and the context points to humans in their standing before God.[42] The use of πᾶς with a negated verb is a Semitism.[43] It is functionally equivalent to οὐδείς with a non-negated verb,[44] and the sense is most clearly conveyed in English as "No one will be justified by the works of the law."

Paul's reference to Scripture here is important in two central ways. Within the context of his argument, Paul's citation of this passage is an appropriate application of the theological argument made in the original psalm. This clause states the particular theological presupposition that undergirds the whole of Paul's argument (Betz, 118). Within Paul's broader rhetoric, this citation grounds his argument in the authority of Scripture (Lightfoot, 115; Burton, 124), which would certainly appeal to both Peter and other Jewish Christians. Some argue that Jews would not have read this passage in this way, making this citation evidence of early Christian reinterpretation of Scripture (see Witherington, 183; Oakes, 81). Given the fact that this opening salvo states common ground Paul and other Jewish *Christians* share, this may be a true statement, but Paul's argument rests on what he sees as a true and accurate interpretation of the OT passage. Paul's interpretation may indeed be novel, but it is in concert with the meaning of the original, highlighting its fullest sense.

2:17 After making his central theological affirmation in v. 16, Paul moves on to two logical deductions, one in v. 17 and another in v. 18, both of which address the presenting problem in Antioch and the current issue with his opponents in Galatia. These are points of disagreement between him and other Jewish Christians about the proper place of Law observance in the ethnically mixed community of the Church. Ultimately the disagreement concerns the theological implications of the doctrine of justification by faith for Gentile Christians (Betz, 119). Paul argues against two extremes: nomism for Gentiles on the one hand (Longenecker, 88) and antinomianism and libertinism as overreactions against the Law on the other (Rapa, 585).

The exegesis of v. 17 is challenging because of the ambiguity of the inherent logic of the grammatical structure involved, partly because Paul phrased it as a question. The sentence is a first class condition, presenting something as true for the sake of the argument. This particular conditional sentence contains an evidence-inference argument: The protasis presents the evidence, while the apodosis presents the inference made from that evidence.[45] It is clear from the conclusion of the verse that Paul rejects something, but it is not clear exactly what Paul rejects. There are two possible construals: Paul

42. BDAG, 915. See also Matt 24:22; Mark 13:20; Luke 3:6; Rom 3:20; 1 Cor 1:29; 1 Pet 1:24.

43. MHT, 2:433–34; 4:158.

44. Robertson, *Grammar*, 752.

45. See Wallace, *Greek Grammar*, 683, for discussion on this semantic nuance of conditional sentences.

could in some way reject the truth of the protasis and thus deny that the conclusion follows deductively, or he could accept the truth of the protasis and deny only the conclusion drawn from it.[46] The first construal accepts that the conclusion has properly been deduced from the premise, so the statement as a whole would be an attack on the premise, not on the deduction.[47] The second construal denies that the conclusion has been appropriately deduced from the proper premise, so the statement as a whole would be an attack on the logic involved.[48] Stated in terms of the content, Paul either writes from the viewpoint of an objector who strives to show that his abandonment of the Law was wrong, or he writes from his own viewpoint to show that to abandon the Law is ultimately not sinful. On the whole, the second construal makes better sense of all the data. The first construal could be favored because it maintains the sense of ἁμαρτωλός used in v. 15. Paul's point would be that he has not crossed over to become a sinner like the Gentiles, that is, he has maintained his essential fidelity to the Torah (in spirit if not in letter). The problem with this interpretation is that it creates an awkward transition to the next verse, which implies with its imagery of tearing down a building that Paul has indeed abrogated the Law in some form or fashion, not that he has simply become less strict in his observance. In the better construal Paul acknowledges that the appellation of ἁμαρτωλός is true of himself in some way. In addition, the second construal has much more contextual evidence in its favor. It actually develops fully the irony of ἁμαρτωλός in the context. Paul accepts the moniker because he has abrogated the Law, but there is a fuller sense in play beyond the Jewish use of the term given the use of ἁμαρτία later in the verse. The second construal also agrees with Paul's use of μὴ γένοιτο, which he uniformly uses to deny a wrong conclusion from correct premises. It appropriately prepares the reader for the concept of dying to the Law because it implies that Paul has ceased obeying the Law *qua* Law, and it fits the contours of the first class condition with the aor. indic. εὑρέθημεν, which strongly implies the reality of the protasis. So the second construal, in which Paul accepts the truth of the premise (although perhaps subverting it along the way)[49] but rejects the conclusion drawn should be preferred.[50]

---

46. Lightfoot, 116, helpfully presents the two essential interpretive arguments. What is presented here is largely a summation of his evidence. See also Burton, 127–30, for helpful discussion.

47. In this instance the particle ἄρα (logical conclusion) would thus be preferred to ἆρα (interrogative). See the textual note on this word.

48. In this instance ἆρα (interrogative) is preferred over ἄρα (logical conclusion).

49. Rapa, 585, argues the second presupposition is used ironically in that Paul adopts the view of his opponents.

50. This construal is accepted by Lightfoot, 116; Martyn, 253; Rapa, 11:585; Soards and Pursiful, 96. Betz, 119–20, argues that the second presupposition (εὑρέθημεν καὶ αὐτοὶ ἁμαρτωλοί) is false because it concerns those in the body of Christ who cannot be considered sinners, outside the reach of God's salvation.

εἰ δὲ ζητοῦντες δικαιωθῆναι ἐν Χριστῷ εὑρέθημεν καὶ αὐτοὶ ἁμαρτωλοί. This protasis of the conditional sentence contains two assertions. The first is the participial phrase ζητοῦντες δικαιωθῆναι ἐν Χριστῷ, the second the indic. verb and its modifiers εὑρέθημεν καὶ αὐτοὶ ἁμαρτωλοί. The ptc. ζητοῦντες is temporal, and its adjunct δικαιωθῆναι is a complementary inf. Together ζητοῦντες δικαιωθῆναι connotes a conative idea, but this does not imply a lack of success in the endeavor. Rather, it positions the action as something in process that awaits future completion (so Dunn, 141), as implied by the fut. tense of δικαιωθήσεται at the end of v. 16. The phrase ζητοῦντες δικαιωθῆναι ἐν Χριστῷ recapitulates all that Paul stated in the previous verse. It functions as shorthand for the fuller idea of placing faith in Christ in order to be justified by faith and not by works of the Law. This helps to define ἐν Χριστῷ in context as the basis for the declaration of justification; it is best understood to convey means, showing the external, objective basis for justification (Burton, 124).[51] The verb εὑρέθημεν is the main verb of the protasis and here conveys the meaning "be found, appear, prove, be shown (to be)."[52] As an aor. pass. it points to a past event in which Paul and Peter were contemplated or perceived by others to be sinners, a reference either to the schism in Antioch caused by the attitude of the certain people from James or to the wrangling of Paul's opponents in Galatia. Both καί as adjunctive and αὐτοί as adj. intensive add emphasis to the verb: "If we *ourselves* were *also* found ..." The noun ἁμαρτωλοί here acts as a predicate nom. to εὑρέθημεν given the equative force of that verb in this context. The definition of ἁμαρτωλοί is the same as the first occurrence of the word in v. 15. There the nuance focused on ethnicity and relation to Torah, and the exact same nuance is in play here, except instead of being a "sinner" because of Gentile ethnicity, Paul and Peter become "sinners" because of their association with Gentiles through common meals. Thus Peter and Paul were called sinners by their opponents because in their estimation Peter and Paul did not follow the Law and thus were sinners who did not participate in the covenant. This protasis captures the essential critique from the people who came to Antioch from Jerusalem, a critique that Peter sought to avoid by withdrawing from table fellowship with Gentiles and that Paul's opponents leveled at him because he invited Gentiles to relate to Jesus without any requirement to obey the Law.[53] Paul subverts this use of the word ἁμαρτωλός, however, by accepting the classification while redefining it with the following use of ἁμαρτία in the apodosis. Paul refocuses the lens upon what sin actually is. He accepts that he is a "sinner" in that he no longer obeys the food

---

51. This is *contra* de Boer, 157, who sees the phrase as locative, referring to the territory where Christ is Lord, that is, in the community of people who believe in him.

52. BDAG, 412.

53. Longenecker, 89–90, argues that the key interpretive weight is on the second proposition. In keeping with his overall argument that Paul's opponents were emphasizing Law as a check on libertinism, it is reasonable to see that Paul was here responding to an argument of his opponents.

requirements of the Law, but he prepares his readers to realize that "sin" is much more than that. The force of the denial rests on the different nuances for sin in this context (Burton, 126).

Fleshing out the inherent logic of this protasis enables its full force to be felt. Paul had stated in the prior verse that he had indeed placed his faith in Jesus Christ in order to be justified through faith in him and not through works of the Law, and this purpose was grounded in the scriptural assertion from the Psalms that no one finds justification before God on their own, a truth that Paul applied specifically to works of the Law. On this basis, then, Paul posits this protasis in which he is recognized as a sinner, that is, accused of acting contrary to the Law precisely because he seeks to be justified in Christ and not in the Law. The logical implication of being found a sinner in this fashion is that Paul was wrong to seek justification in Christ, but clearly Paul does not accept this deduction. He quickly moves in the next clause to show how the thinking of his opponents in this regard is fundamentally wrong.

ἆρα Χριστὸς ἁμαρτίας διάκονος; This phrase constitutes the apodosis of the conditional sentence. The interrogative conj. ἆρα strongly emphasizes the logical deduction.[54] This apodosis is verbless; the equative verb ἐστίν is implied. As a proper name, Χριστός is the nom. subject and διάκονος is the predicate nom. The noun ἁμαρτίας is an obj. gen. preceding the word διάκονος to which it relates: "Is Christ then a servant [who serves] sin?"[55] The phrase ἁμαρτίας διάκονος is unique. These words occur together only here in the NT, and there are no other similar collocations in the NT or extrabiblical literature. The word διάκονος refers to one who does something for another. This could be construed as an intermediary, agent, or assistant, depending on the context.[56] Thus sin in this context is personified as a power that can be served (Matera, 95; Dunn, 141; Hays, 241). Certain Jewish traditions saw the Messiah as sinless; see Pss. Sol. 17:36; T. Jud. 24:1 (Garlington 2007, 162). So this question is a natural one to ask given that the opponents' stance cast doubt on Paul's role as a proclaimer of this Messiah. But Paul redefines the question by presenting sin as a power, setting the stage for a bigger discussion than just the individual's relationship to the Law. It becomes a global question of the power of sin and how Christ has defeated it with his sacrifice on the cross, which Paul develops in the central theological section of the letter.

μὴ γένοιτο. With this phrase Paul crisply and clearly denies the conclusion drawn from the premises. Paul regularly uses this phrase to deny an

---

54. BDAG, 127, states this is a "marker of a tone of suspense or impatience in interrogation."

55. Some translations focus on the inherent action implied in διάκονος: "is Christ then one who encourages sin?" (NET); "is Christ then a promoter of sin?" (CSB). One could put it very dynamically, "Does Christ then serve sin?"

56. BDAG, 230–31.

improper conclusion framed as a question and drawn from valid premises.[57] Paul was found to be a "sinner" in the eyes of his opponents because his new understanding of life based in Christ affected relationships between Jew and Gentile in the church vis-à-vis the Law. He ceased obeying food laws and as such became a "sinner." Both Paul and his opponents accept this construal of the situation. The difference is in the conclusion each draws. Paul's opponents deduced that his disobedience toward Torah in service to faith in Christ would make Christ a servant of sin. Their standard of how to live toward God was Torah; all else must be subservient to it. Paul subverted their thinking by orienting his new life toward Christ, who in his death and resurrection reframed himself as the anchor point for life toward God. By definition, then, in Paul's mind Christ could never be a servant of sin, so his new stance was not in fact disobedience toward Torah but obedience to Christ and the new state of affairs he began. Christ was the new authority who determined how those related to him should live; the Torah had been subjugated. The opponents saw non-observance of the Law as an indictment of Paul's view of the Messiah; Paul's view of the Messiah necessitated a theological revision of the requirements of Law observance.

2:18 *εἰ γὰρ ἃ κατέλυσα ταῦτα πάλιν οἰκοδομῶ, παραβάτην ἐμαυτὸν συνιστάνω.* This verse explains the previous one, fleshing out the inherent logical argument (Dunn, 142). As in v. 17, Paul uses a first class condition to offer an argument for consideration. The semantic relationship between the two parts is again evidence-inference. The grammar of the sentence is relatively clear. The relative clause *ἃ κατέλυσα* acts as a noun, a pendant nom. brought forward in the clause for emphasis and resumed by *ταῦτα* as the dir. obj. of *οἰκοδομῶ*: "For what things I broke down, if I build these things up again ..." The pronoun *ἐμαυτόν* is the dir. obj. of *συνιστάνω*, and *παραβάτην* is the obj. complement to *ἐμαυτόν*: "I show myself [to be] a transgressor." Paul speaks circumspectly and metaphorically with the protasis but more clearly with the apodosis, placing the primary difficulty in the former.[58] What are the "things that [Paul] destroyed"? How would he build them up again? Answering these questions requires thinking through the two-level nature of Paul's argument. In the context of the problem in Antioch, the things in view

---

57. The lone exception in the fourteen occurrences of the phrase in Paul is Gal 6:14 in which Paul uses the phrase almost as an oath. The other occurrence in this book is Gal 3:21.

58. It is possible that Paul chose some of this language because it was proverbial. Similar language occurs in *b. Ber.* 63A with general force. The context is a debate over what objects are clean or unclean. One interpreter had previously lauded his interlocutors, but when they disagreed over this issue, he derided them. They responded thusly in light of this change in attitude, after which they continued their debate: "You have already built [us up], and you cannot now destroy [us], you have already made a fence, and you cannot now destroy it."

would be the food laws as a metaphorical wall that protected Israel (Dunn, 142), representative of the Torah as a whole. Peter felt pressure to withdraw from table fellowship with Gentiles under influence from the Jerusalem faction, in effect rebuilding the wall that had previously been torn down to celebrate common meals in Antioch. Relative to Paul's ministry in Galatia, the agitators advocated circumcision for Gentiles, rebuilding a key marker of Torah observance that Paul had torn down. Both in Antioch and in Galatia Paul rejects any rebuilding of the Law. He rejects any requirement for Jews to maintain ritual purity relative to Gentiles and food, and he does not require circumcision of his Gentile converts. Thus the referent of ἃ κατέλυσα is best understood generally: "what things [Paul] destroyed" would be the behavioral requirements revealed in the Torah for Jews to obey as part of keeping the covenant, whether food regulations, circumcision, or something else. This clarifies the protasis: "If I build these things up again" would mean that Paul reverses his previous position on these matters, requiring separate tables for Jews and Gentiles, circumcision of his Gentile converts, and Law observance more broadly. It would mean taking up again a stance toward the Law that he had set aside when he fully understood what Christ had done for humanity in his death on the cross. Theologically it would be an admission that the Law remained in force for all believers, even considering the death of Christ. If Paul reversed his position and "built these things up again," it would prove that the faction from James and the agitators were right—that he was indeed a lawbreaker and wrong to go down this path to abrogation of the Law.[59] The essence of his point in this conditional sentence, however, is that he is not a lawbreaker. The conditional sentence has to be regarded as hypothetical or unreal. Paul is not building these things back up again, and he will not go back to his previous attitude toward the Law. Christ affected a definitive change vis-à-vis the Torah, and a new age has begun. To acquiesce would prove that those who favored the Torah were right, and Paul will not take that step. Here is where the irony of ἁμαρτωλός in the prior verse becomes clear in light of the noun παραβάτης, the latter removing the ambiguity of the former (Burton, 131). Paul accepts that he is a "sinner" in that he no longer obeys the letter of the Law, but he rejects that he is a "transgressor," that he actually violates the Law, because this would assume the Law has present force over the believer (Witherington, 187).

The use of the 1 sg. verbs here would presumably mean that Paul utters this statement with reference to his own status before the Law. This interpretation, however, is not automatic given the way that the 1 sg. can function in Koine Greek. The 1 sg. here could be generic and equivalent in a sense to the

59. The noun παραβάτης more generally means "one who deviates from or transgresses a standard or norm" (*NIDNTTE*, 3:606), but the context here relates specifically to transgressing the Law. See the other NT uses of the word, where the Law is also clearly in the context: Rom 2:25, 27; Jas 2:9, 11.

indefinite pronoun τις, "someone."[60] Given that Paul's experience of this issue was real and present, growing out of the Antioch incident and affecting his ministry to the Galatians directly, it is very reasonable to construe that "I" here concretizes the "we" previously and serves to represent Jewish Christians generally, but perhaps with special reference to Peter (see Moo, 166). Even so, Paul himself comes into view with this statement, as does any Christian who lives in such a way that the Law no longer holds sway over their actions.

Important to grasp in this verse is Paul's underlying theological argument. In the revelation of Christ's death the Law is torn down (Witherington, 187). Paul's abrogation of the Law is the only proper stance in the present time. To explain his stance Paul speaks in salvation-historical terms (Schreiner, 170), thinking of his life as different eras marked by different attitudes toward the Law. Dunn, 142, explains it well, using Paul's own metaphor of the Law as a wall or fence: "Paul in effect divides his life into three possible phases: the time when his life was protected by a wall; the time when he tore that construction down; and the possibility of rebuilding it again. The point is that his tearing down was an essential part of the complete turn-around which his encounter with the risen Christ on the Damascus road entailed." Thus the Law no longer holds in the present era. This has direct application to each situation Paul references here. He casts one eye back on Antioch, where Peter "rebuilt" the Law by no longer eating with Gentiles. Paul intends the 1 sg. pronoun to apply to himself hypothetically, but he also refers to Peter's actual behavior. But Paul also casts one eye toward Galatia, where the agitators argue for Law observance, specifically through the avenue of circumcision. Anyone who advocates for observance of the Law anywhere has grasped neither the full import of Christ's death as the Messiah nor the true role of the Law, a stance Paul will flesh out more fully in the central, theological portion of the book.

2:19 In this verse Paul moves from conditional and hypothetical stances, dealt with in the prior two verses, to the real and actual situation of his own relationship with God. The argument turns from deductive reasoning to theological, personal truth. From here until the end of the paragraph Paul's language is intensely personal, yet at the same time he intends it to be universal, applicable to all believers (Betz, 121; George, 198; Schreiner, 170; Moo, 168). Essentially Paul describes his conversion in which he was confronted by the risen Lord, in which his understanding of and relationship to the Law

60. Robertson, *Grammar*, 402, says, "Sometimes indeed the first and second persons are used without any direct reference to the speaker or the person addressed." See also his statement on p. 678: "Sometimes the first person singular is used in a representative manner as one of a class (cf. the representative article like ὁ ἀγαθός)." MHT, 3:39–40, argues similarly: "Paul instances both himself and his reader in a vivid way to illustrate a point, not intending to apply what is said literally to himself or his reader."

was completely changed (Dunn, 143). This paradigm becomes the norm for all believers, serving Paul's rhetorical purpose of challenging the Galatians as they flirt with the Law, enabling them to interpret their own conversion experiences vis-à-vis the Law in the same way (Witherington, 188).

Before describing the particulars of the wording, some broad strokes of the arrangement of Paul's phrasing in the larger paragraph is in order. Verses 19–20 are two sentences marked by asyndeton. The first sentence, found in v. 19ab, has two parts: a statement of Paul's changed relationship to the Law and then a result of that change. The second sentence, found in v. 19c and 20, explains the preceding. A simple chart offers a more visual explanation:

Original statement	Explanation
ἐγὼ γὰρ διὰ νόμου νόμῳ ἀπέθανον (v. 19a)	*Χριστῷ συνεσταύρωμαι* (v. 19c)
ἵνα θεῷ ζήσω (v. 19b)	*ζῶ δὲ οὐκέτι ἐγώ, ζῇ δὲ ἐν ἐμοὶ Χριστός· ὃ δὲ νῦν ζῶ ἐν σαρκί, ἐν πίστει ζῶ τῇ τοῦ υἱοῦ τοῦ θεοῦ τοῦ ἀγαπήσαντός με καὶ παραδόντος ἑαυτὸν ὑπὲρ ἐμοῦ* (v. 20)

Another way to express this arrangement would be to restate the passage periphrastically as follows: "For through the law I died to the law. How did I die to the Law? I have been crucified with Christ. This was done so that I might live to God. What does living to God look like? It means Christ lives in me and I live by his power." Thus vv. 19–20 consist of a tight theological statement followed by an explanation of that statement.

ἐγὼ γὰρ διὰ νόμου νόμῳ ἀπέθανον. The *γάρ* here is causal; this verse offers the logical justification for the hypothetical argument of v. 18. Paul has torn down the Law, never to rebuild it again, because he has died to the Law. This verse conveys the reality that gives the theological warrant for v. 18. If Paul were to again submit to the Law, he would be living in reverse, seeking to revive something that was dead. It also further proves that he has not actually transgressed the Law (Rapa, 586). The pronoun *ἐγώ* here truly points to Paul. He explains his own personal experience that in turn becomes paradigmatic for all believers. The prepositional phrase *διὰ νόμου* indicates the instrument by which the action of the verb *ἀπέθανον* is carried out: Paul died "through/by means of" the Law.[61] The dat. noun *νόμῳ* is a dat. of reference: Paul died "regarding/with reference to" the Law.[62] The verb *ἀπέθανον* is an aor. indic., here consummative, expressing the finality of the action. The aor. tense is significant because in the indic. it references a past action. Paul uses it to

---

61. BDAG, 284, classifies this verse under the category of "efficient cause," that is, something external to the object that causes motion or change.

62. BDAG, 111, states that *ἀποθνήσκω* occurs "w. dat. of pers. or thing fr. which one is separated by death, however death may be understood."

refer holistically to his conversion. In both uses in this clause the noun νόμος is anarthrous but definite on the grounds that it is monadic.[63] In this phrase Paul encapsulates his prior and present relationship to the Law: Through the means of the Law itself, Paul has died to the Law.

The problem for interpretation of this clause concerns the phrase διὰ νόμου. The meaning of the dat. νόμῳ presents no problems: To die to the law means that the Law no longer exercises power over the individual. The phrase διὰ νόμου is confusing on its face, though, because it is not clear how the Law itself was the means for Paul's death to it and ultimate release from its requirements. Paul does not state here how abandoning the Law was made clear to him by the Law itself (Burton, 133). In what way was the Law the efficient cause for Paul's abandonment of it? A fair response is that Paul does not explain the theological mechanism of how this works; he states simply that the separation from Law has occurred. Paul's ultimate point is *that* the Law no longer has control over him, not *how* (Hays, 242–43).[64] This stance does not do justice, however, to the central place this paragraph has in the theology of the letter. As with other issues, this needs to be unpacked both in light of Paul's entire argument and to shed light on it as well.

There are two primary directions for interpretation of how the Law itself was the means for Paul's death to it and release from it, one of which centers on Paul, the other of which centers on Christ. The focus on Paul itself has two options. The first concerns the Law's moral effect. The Law identified and punished sin without offering any solution or means of escape. Thus Paul lived a life of ultimate frustration and failure in living up to its demands. This interpretation can be favored on the basis of parallels to the latter half of Rom 7, a classic *crux interpretum* in which Paul describes his struggle with the Law, and Gal 3:10, where Paul describes the Law's own condemnation upon those who do not obey it fully (so Lightfoot, 118; Moo, 169).[65] The second option for a Pauline focus concerns his intense devotion to the Law. Paul's adherence to the Law put him on the Damascus road where he met the risen Christ (Bruce, 143; de Boer, 160). In this way the Law was the means that affected his conversion, which changed his allegiance, metaphorically referred to as "death to the Law." The interpretation that focuses on Christ concerns the role of his death in abolishing the Law. In his death Christ bore the

---

63. Robertson, *Grammar*, 796, says, "In general when νόμος is anarthrous in Paul it refers to the Mosaic law, as in ἐπαναπαύῃ νόμῳ (Ro. 2:17)." But note G. B. Winer, *A Treatise on the Grammar of New Testament Greek, Regarded as a Sure Basis for New Testament Exegesis* (Edinburgh: Clark, 1882), 152n4, where differing views are noted. This is *contra* Lenski, 114, who argues that anarthrous νόμου is generic: "everything that is 'law.' "

64. Hays, 242–43, does prefer the view that connects διὰ νόμου to the curse of Gal 3:13.

65. This interpretation comes under fire regularly within New Perspective interpretation because of parallels like Phil 3:6, in which Paul describes his relationship to the Law in positive terms.

curse of the Law, exhausting it and thus ending its reign (Fung, 123; Martyn, 257; Schreiner, 169–70). This interpretation relies heavily upon Gal 3:13, where Paul describes Christ as becoming a curse because of his crucifixion in accordance with the wording of Deut 21:23. By association with Christ's crucifixion, believers are cursed by the Law just as he was, so just as the Law condemned Christ it condemned all those in Christ, effectively killing them with the same curse and severing their relationship with it. The same idea would be expressed in the present passage but in seminal form to be fleshed out later in Paul's theological argument. Based upon the larger context of Galatians, the interpretation that relies upon the Law's moral effect can be set aside. Even if Rom 7 refers to Paul's struggle to live up to the standards of the Law before his conversion, a view I do not presently accept, that is not a *topos* within Galatians.[66] Paul does refer to the Law's difficult demands globally, but he does not apply them to himself. Between the other two interpretations, the latter with its Christological focus is preferred both because of its logic and because of its connection to what follows. As stated above, this paragraph states in compact form the theological arguments to come. It would make much better sense to see Paul allude to a forthcoming argument rather than look back to his autobiographical material. Thus in nascent form Paul makes an important theological argument: He was co-crucified with Christ and bore the same curse as he. Just as Christ was then resurrected to be free from the Law, Paul himself was raised with Christ and now lives free from the Law's demands.

ἵνα θεῷ ζήσω. The conj. ἵνα here indicates result: Living to God is a result of dying to the Law. As with the dat. νόμῳ in the prior phrase, θεῷ is a dat. of reference.[67] Paul's point of reference for his life is no longer himself or the Law; it is God, and by extension Christ, who is the locus of God's revelation in the present time. The concept of living to God has some intriguing parallels in extrabiblical literature. It occurs in 4 Macc 7:19; 16:25 as a reference to the resurrection, the latter quite vivid as it occurs in the context of an encomium for the mother of the seven sons who refused to disobey Jewish laws even while being tortured by Antiochus:

> Διὰ τούτων τῶν λόγων ἡ ἑπταμήτωρ ἕνα ἕκαστον τῶν υἱῶν παρακαλοῦσα ἀποθανεῖν ἔπεισεν μᾶλλον ἢ παραβῆναι τὴν ἐντολὴν τοῦ θεοῦ, ἔτι δὲ καὶ ταῦτα εἰδότες ὅτι οἱ διὰ τὸν θεὸν ἀποθνῄσκοντες ζῶσιν τῷ θεῷ ὥσπερ Αβρααμ καὶ Ισαακ καὶ Ιακωβ καὶ πάντες οἱ πατριάρχαι.
>
> By these words the mother of the seven encouraged and persuaded each of her sons to die rather than violate God's commandment.

---

66. At present I would argue that Rom 7 refers to the Christian's post-conversion struggle with sin, but as with many difficult passages next week might be different!

67. See MHT, 3:264, which says, "When Paul means *to live to*, and not *in the sphere of*, he uses the simple dat."

> They knew also that those who die for the sake of God live to God, as do Abraham and Isaac and Jacob and all the patriarchs.

In this passage "living to God" refers to the future resurrection in light of the reference to the ancestors of Israel's past. Philo uses the same wording in *Names* 213 but with an ethical tone:

> τοῦ μὲν γὰρ κατ᾽ ἀρετὴν βίου, ὅς ἐστιν ἀψευδεστάτη ζωή, μετέχουσιν ὀλίγοι, οὐχὶ τῶν ἀγελαίων φημί—τούτων γὰρ οὐδεὶς τῆς ἀληθοῦς ζωῆς κεκοινώνηκεν,—ἀλλ᾽ εἴ τισιν ἐξεγένετο τὰς τῶν ἀνθρώπων φυγεῖν σπουδὰς καὶ θεῷ μόνῳ ζῆσαι.
>
> For the life of virtue, which is life in its truest form, is shared by few, and these few are not found among the vulgar herd, none of whom has part or lot in true life, but are only those to whom it is granted to escape the aims which engross humanity and to live to God alone.[68]

Paul's expression of the concept is both soteriological and ethical (Betz, 122; Moo, 170). It expresses a hope for future, eschatological justification as well as a recognition of present, transforming power.

Χριστῷ συνεσταύρωμαι.[69] This statement offers a parallel to the beginning of v. 19, where Paul states ἐγὼ γὰρ διὰ νόμῳ ἀπέθανον. Paul restates, albeit with new content, the same theological reality. The verb συσταυρόω is only found in Christian writings. It occurs four other times in the NT. The three uses in the gospels are literal, referring to the thieves who were crucified with Jesus (Matt 27:44; Mark 15:32; John 19:32). The two Pauline uses are metaphorical, referring to the believer's spiritual union with Christ (Rom 6:6 and here).[70] The sense of the phrase is easy to understand: Paul identifies himself as crucified with Christ. The σύν prefix on the verb σταυρόω implies association with or joining together in the activity of the verb. Verbs with this prefix routinely take a personal noun in the dat. to indicate with whom the

---

68. Greek text and translation taken from Philo, *On Flight and Finding. On the Change of Names. On Dreams*, trans. F. H. Colson and G. H. Whitaker, LCL 275 (Cambridge, MA: Harvard University Press, 1934), 252–53.

69. Many modern English translations place the verse division in front of this phrase (so NET, ESV, NASB, NIV). This is more natural, as it reflects the asyndeton of this statement, implying a sense division of some kind, and it keeps this phrase with what follows, which is a further elaboration of the topic. I have chosen to retain the versification of NA[28] since the Greek text is the basis of my exegetical discussion (so also HCSB [but not CSB], NRSV), but I agree with the argument that this phrase is best taken with what follows. *Contra* Moo, 170, who argues that this phrase connects with both prior and following material.

70. It is an intriguing possibility that the Gospel uses are earlier and influenced the Pauline usage both lexically and theologically, but that is difficult to say with certainty, especially given an early date for Galatians, and can only be suggestive.

activity was done.[71] Paul speaks metaphorically, using the image of co-crucifixion to refer to a very real connection to Christ Paul experienced in his conversion. The following wording in v. 20 demonstrates that Paul sees the believer's life as mirroring Christ's death and resurrection: As Christ died and was resurrected, so in connection with Christ the believer dies and is resurrected to new life. While Paul uses this verb to speak of the believer dying to sin in Rom 6:6, here the focus is on death to the Law. Co-crucifixion with Christ is the means by which Paul through the Law died to the Law. The exact means by which Christ accomplished this will be discussed more fully in the central theological section of the epistle.

2:20 ζῶ δὲ οὐκέτι ἐγώ, ζῇ δὲ ἐν ἐμοὶ Χριστός. With this statement Paul further explains the purpose clause he wrote in v. 19b, ἵνα θεῷ ζήσω. Verse 20 as a whole amplifies what Paul means by the concept of living to God: It is a life grounded and empowered by Christ. This flows out of the affirmation of co-crucifixion with Christ and the attendant reality of co-resurrection with him, explaining exactly what is involved in co-crucifixion: "the participation of the believer in the benefits of Christ's experience, a spiritual fellowship with him in respect to these experiences, and the passing of the believer through a similar or analogous experience" (Burton, 135). Because of the implied, attendant co-resurrection, Paul in essence presents himself as the paradigm of the new, eschatological humanity created in Christ (Martyn, 258). The conj. δέ marks this clause as continuing the argument begun in the prior phrase. Paul's use of the 1 sg. pronoun and progressive pres. tense verb ζῶ refers to the life he presently lives, but he intends his experience to be representative of all believers. The key word of the first clause is οὐκέτι, "no longer." The moment of his unification with Christ at his conversion was a turning point. Prior to this moment he himself was living as a Torah-observant Jew; after this point that individual was dead. With the second clause Paul describes the life that replaced that of the Torah-observant Jew: Christ now lives in him. The key words of the second clause are ἐν ἐμοί. The intended sense is spatial but metaphorical: Christ lives "in Paul" in that he so totally controls Paul's being, Paul can speak of him as being "in me."[72] The natural result of being co-crucified with Christ is that Paul is controlled and guided by Christ's resurrection life. Identification with Christ's death not

71. Even though this is routine, it is not the only way to indicate the idea of association. Other prepositional prefixes and verb lexemes can indicate this idea. See Wallace, *Greek Grammar*, 159.

72. See BDAG, 327–28, where this verse is listed in two places. First is under category 4.a: "fig., of pers., to indicate the state of being filled w. or gripped by someth.: *in someone*=in one's innermost being." Second is under category 4.c: "esp. in Paul. or Joh. usage, to designate a close personal relation in which the referent of the ἐν-term is viewed as the controlling influence: *under the control of, under the influence of, in close association with*."

only affects the believer's relationship with Law but also with the individual ego (Longenecker, 92). As Paul affirms in the next line, however, the human personality is not replaced. Rather, the union with Christ effects a renewal and fulfillment of the human person. It is Paul in Adam that no longer exists (Schreiner, 172).

ὃ δὲ νῦν ζῶ ἐν σαρκί, ἐν πίστει ζῶ τῇ τοῦ υἱοῦ τοῦ θεοῦ. Paul explains his present mode of being further by identifying the grounds for his present life in his earthly body. The nominal clause beginning with the acc. relative pronoun acts as a cognate acc. to the verb ζῶ.[73] This is an unusual construction to occur with the verb ζάω. There is no place in the NT where ζωή acts as the dir. obj. of ζάω. A construction similar to this one occurs in Rom 6:10 with reference to Christ: ὃ δὲ ζῇ, ζῇ τῷ θεῷ.[74] Despite its rarity, it is easy enough to understand that the relative pronoun refers to the concept of living: "So the life I now live in the body" (NET); "And the life I now live in the flesh" (ESV); "and the life which I now live in the flesh" (NASB); "The life I now live in the body" (NIV). The prepositional phrase ἐν σαρκί means "in the flesh, in the body," that is, in the sphere of natural, present existence as opposed to spiritual or eschatological existence; the adv. νῦν helps clarifies this point. The prepositional phrase ἐν πίστει indicates means or instrument in this context. The verb ζῶ is again a progressive pres., focusing on present life and existence. Paul lives his present life by means of faith. The phrase τῇ τοῦ υἱοῦ τοῦ θεοῦ is a third attributive position construction that modifies πίστει, identifying specifically which kind of faith is in view. The entire phrase πίστει τῇ τοῦ υἱοῦ τοῦ θεοῦ is functionally and semantically equivalent to the πίστις Χριστοῦ language that occurs earlier in the paragraph.[75] Paul lives his present life by means of the faith he has in Christ, the Son of God.

τοῦ ἀγαπήσαντός με καὶ παραδόντος ἑαυτὸν ὑπὲρ ἐμοῦ. This phrase is adj. to τοῦ υἱοῦ τοῦ θεοῦ, further describing Christ. Paul describes Christ with the ptc. τοῦ ἀγαπήσαντός με, "who loved me."[76] This verse and 5:14 are the only places in Galatians where Paul uses the verb ἀγαπάω,[77] but Paul's use of the term is significant. The verb means "to love, cherish," with a wide variety of nuances determined by the context.[78] Important here is the assertion that Christ is the one who loves; Paul uses the word to denote the actions of Christ on his

73. So also Robertson, *Grammar*, 715, but see Winer, *Grammar*, 209, who argues that this is an adv. acc., "with regards to what I live ..."

74. This grammatical parallel also provides an important conceptual parallel to the current passage.

75. See the excursus for a defense of this language as objective, that is, Paul's intent is to discuss faith directed toward Christ. Witherington, 191, argues that the variant reading at this point in the text supports an objective meaning.

76. Cf. Rom 8:37 and 2 Thess 2:16, where similar constructions are used with God as the referent.

77. Neither is the noun ἀγαπή common (see 5:6, 13, 22).

78. BDAG, 5.

behalf, which in turn shows in what the divine love for mankind consists. Paul fleshes out the content of Christ's love by describing Christ with the ptc. παραδόντος, referring to Christ's sacrifice of self on the cross. The verb means "to hand over, deliver," and in this context refers to the particular action of handing over a person in a judicial context.[79] Paul uses the verb regularly to refer to Jesus's betrayal as an integral part of his passion.[80] The juxtaposition of these terms connects Christ's love for the believer with his death as substitution, the one defining the other. Thus it is appropriate to say that Christ's sacrificial death on the cross is the way in which he showed his love for us.[81] Jesus's love is "an *enacted* love, a love that was made manifest in action and in suffering" (Hays, 244). The ptcs. here hearken back to the introduction of the book, where Paul describes Jesus in 1:4 in a similar way. There Paul uses the verb δίδωμι and περί with sin as the obj. of the prep.[82] Here Paul uses the verb παραδίδωμι and ὑπέρ with himself as the obj. of the prep. In this context ὑπέρ with a personal obj. denotes substitution (Lenski, 118), which is more explicit than the idea expressed with περί. This fits well with the idea of representation present in the context: Paul personally appropriates Christ's love for the whole world (Lightfoot, 119), and in turn, this reflects the universal experience of Christ's love in which all believers partake.

2:21 Οὐκ ἀθετῶ τὴν χάριν τοῦ θεοῦ. After his short discourse on the new nature of his current life of faith in Christ, Paul returns to the matter at hand, that is, the issue of the Law vis-à-vis Gentile believers. Despite the asyndeton, this statement functions as a conclusion of sorts. God's grace has been displayed fully in and to Paul. To turn away from that grace by returning to the Law would essentially nullify it. Thus Paul does not, will not, cannot turn away. He does not nullify God's grace; he embraces it and follows its implications to their logical end. The verb ἀθετῶ generally means "to reject, nullify,"[83] and the NT uses routinely it to refer to "irreligious acts."[84] The phrase τὴν χάριν τοῦ θεοῦ is easily translated as "the grace of God," but the precise referent is not immediately clear. There are three basic options. First, this grace could be God's grace toward Israel in the giving of the Law (Burton, 140; Longenecker,

---

79. BDAG, 761–62.

80. Paul's use of the term shows some interesting variation. The pass. voice with Christ as subject occurs in Rom 4:25; 1 Cor 11:23. God as subject with Christ as object occurs in Rom 8:32. Christ as subject with the reflexive pronoun occurs in Eph 5:2, 25. The uses in Eph 5 are interesting parallels to Gal 2:20 because each joins ἀγαπάω and παραδίδωμι as here.

81. For a similar understanding elsewhere in the NT, see R. H. Gundry and R. W. Howell, "The Sense and Syntax of John 3:14–17 with Special Reference to the Use of οὕτως … ὥστε in John 3:16," *NovT* 41 (1999): 24–39.

82. I accept the reading περί as original over ὑπέρ. See the textual note on Gal 1:4.

83. BDAG, 24.

84. *NIDNTTE*, 1:161.

94; Rapa, 587). This is supported primarily by the reference to the Law in the next clause. It would also be implied if Paul was responding to the objections of some of his nomistic opponents, but that is not certain. Second, this grace could be a reference to Paul's calling and ministry (Dunn, 147). Two times in Galatians χάρις refers to Paul's apostolic ministry to the Gentiles (1:15; 2:9). This interpretation could be preferred on the grounds that this paragraph and indeed this verse summarize the autobiographical section of the letter with its strong focus on Paul's apostleship. Third, this grace could refer broadly to God's salvific grace toward believers in Christ (Betz, 126; Schreiner, 173; Moo, 173; Soards and Pursiful, 103). This is the referent of other occurrences of χάρις in Galatians (1:3, 6; 5:4; 6:18). It is also supported by the immediate context: Paul has just described his new life in Christ, and immediately following he references δικαιοσύνη, which refers to matters of soteriology as opposed to ministry. The third option should be preferred on the basis of the immediate context in the paragraph. This verse is a conclusion to his larger argument about why Paul behaves the way he does vis-à-vis the Law. His abrogation of the Law is founded on matters of his spiritual life in Christ. By standing firm against Peter, by staying steadfast in his dedication to Christ, Paul did not nullify the grace of God extended to him in Christ that created new spiritual life within.

εἰ γὰρ διὰ νόμου δικαιοσύνη, ἄρα Χριστὸς δωρεὰν ἀπέθανεν. As Paul has done already in vv. 17 and 18, he uses a conditional sentence to advance his argument, explaining why Paul does not nullify the grace of God. This condition is second class, which means that Paul is expressing something unreal, often called "contrary to fact," in order to draw a conclusion. The protasis of this conditional sentence has an implied verb, perhaps ἦλθον ("if righteousness arrived through the Law"), although others like γέγονεν ("if righteousness came about through the Law") could be supplied just as easily.[85] The noun δικαιοσύνη is the nominal cognate to the verb δικαιόω, used before frequently in the paragraph. As with the verb, without complete exclusion of other concepts, Paul intends primarily the forensic ideas of "declaration of righteousness" and "justification" with this term. The prepositional phrase διὰ νόμου expresses means: "For if righteousness [comes] by means of the law ..." With the protasis Paul highlights the essential theological point made by the people from James and his opponents in Galatia. They argue, whether explicitly through teaching or implicitly through social persuasion, that the Law is sufficient to bring righteousness. In keeping with the force of the second class condition, Paul's conclusion in the apodosis is reached only on the assumption that something untrue is in fact true.[86] The deduction is

85. Cf. "if righteousness could be gained through the law" (NIV).

86. This is an example of a second class condition without ἄν, as seen elsewhere in the NT (Witherington, 192–93).

strengthened by ἄρα, which here indicates a logical result.[87] The verb ἀπέθανεν as a constative aor. refers to the simple fact of Christ's death, but the echo of Paul's equation of Christ's death with God's grace still resonates in the air and influences the connotations understood by the reader. The word δωρεάν acts as an adv. acc. with negative connotations in this context: If the Law could bring righteousness, Christ's death would have been "in vain" or "needless."[88] If Paul's opponents are right and the Law does indeed bring righteousness, then Christ's death, which Paul understands to be the apocalyptic turning point of all history, ceases to have any meaning whatsoever. It becomes instead an empty act, communicating nothing and bearing no fruit. But that is not at all the case! Paul's conviction is that Christ's death was bursting with meaning and significance. The affirmation of the value of Christ's death then works in the opposite direction: The death of Christ itself proves that it was not needless, which in turn proves that righteousness through Law was not God's plan, thus refuting the implication that denying the Law sets aside God's grace (Burton, 141). Paul's applicational stance for the Galatians is clear: The value of Christ's death to bring righteousness means that requiring obedience to the Law on the part of Gentiles must be fully and soundly rejected.

Paul uses this final conditional sentence to explain his refusal to nullify the grace of God, which encapsulates the argument Paul makes in the entirety of this paragraph. The historical and spiritual reality that serves as his epistemological and religious foundation is the death of Christ. All other interpretations of reality must be measured, accepted, or rejected based on their comportment with the centrality of this event. The proper role of the Law in the mixed Jewish and Gentile communities Paul founded must be understood relative to the apocalyptic reality of Christ's death and resurrection, which Paul learned and experienced so powerfully in his conversion. This foundational reality colors everything for Paul, including the logic he uses to argue his points in this section. "If the law suffices, Christ is superfluous. And if the law suffices, grace is nullified" (Schreiner, 174). Said another way, since Christ suffices, the Law is now superfluous.

Theological Comments

This paragraph in Galatians is central to many different aspects of Paul's theology. Because of the early date of Galatians in relation to Paul's other writings, this can reasonably be regarded as his first statement on many of

87. So BDAG, 127, but *contra* Robertson, *Grammar*, 1190, who argues for inference. Result makes this a stronger statement than inference because it points to the tangible implications of Peter's behavior in Antioch.

88. Hays, 245, translates δωρεάν as "gratuitously" to bring out the word play with "gift."

these theological issues. This does not automatically mean, however, that this passage can be the standard by which all others are measured. Some regard Paul's wording here to be suggestive, while his wording elsewhere, most specifically in Romans, is fuller and more exact on many of the same issues. Crowding around the words of the text is the historical occasion and situation of the letter: Paul was wrestling with an issue that was very important to him, namely, the full inclusion of Gentiles into the nascent church. His words are not a dispassionate, pedagogical treatise separate from a real-world situation. Rather, they are meant to stop the Galatians in their tracks and force them to reevaluate the flirtatious overtures they had made toward the Law. Suffice it to say that because of this tangible context, any abstraction of what Paul thought about theological matters presents some challenges. Paul fully intended for his views to have concrete consequences, and he says what he says in order to accomplish something real and powerful.

Without starting a historical discussion about how this passage compares or coheres to Paul's theology generally, I wish simply to describe the theological import of what Paul says. My intention is in no way to make a full statement on these important theological issues. Rather, I want to describe theologically what Paul does say here specifically and occasionally.

First and foremost, whatever one decides about the New Perspective on Paul and how he viewed the works of the Law specifically or the Law holistically, Paul regards faith, not the Law, as central to his new life in Christ. Faith is now the central mode of existence for those who seek to relate to God, replacing and displacing any other mode of existence. The Law, whether understood negatively as representative of legalism or positively within the context of covenantal nomism, has been superseded. The Law, whether particular instances of obedience or a general principle of human effort, accomplishes nothing before God. Faith is now front and center as the mode of existence by which the individual has a relationship with God.

Second, whatever one decides about the centrality of justification to Paul's theology, faith—now central to life with God—enables a mystical union with Christ that Paul describes here as co-crucifixion. It is by this co-crucifixion with Christ that an individual believer is co-resurrected to live to God. This new resurrection life is achieved by the willing death of Christ in the place of the individual. The seminal idea of substitutionary atonement—Christ dying for the individual so that there might be a true spiritual change within—makes itself felt in this passage. More to the point of what Paul states here, Christ gives a very real and present spiritual power to the believer for their present life through union with him. The very power of the resurrected Lord resides within the individual. This is so much more than having "Jesus in my heart," as I would often hear in churches of my youth. It goes far beyond that: The impotent life of the individual is replaced with the efficacious divine presence. As with faith, it is an entirely new mode of existence that enables a life oriented toward, concerned with, and governed by God.

Third, whatever one thinks about the basis for final justification, Paul conceives of everything he describes—justification, faith, union with Christ—as a gracious gift. As a matter of personal behavior and responsibility, he is supremely concerned with enabling that gift to have its full effect. He avoids any behavior that would muddy the meaning of this gracious gift or limit its effectiveness or application to anyone. God has acted graciously in Christ to enable all people to enter a relationship with him by means of faith. As an apostle of that grace, Paul dedicates himself to a complete proclamation of it and a full realization of its effects.

Application and Devotional Implications

The primary applicational problem with Pauline texts is whether we as contemporary readers are to imagine ourselves in Paul's situation or the situation of his readers. Generally speaking, the latter is more appropriate. There is no biblical warrant to argue that Paul's mantle of apostolic authority transfers to us in any objective or subjective sense, no matter our role in the contemporary church. Rather, we are to understand ourselves as continuing the task of working out of Paul's instructions to his readers as we receive his apostolic instruction and are shaped by it. Despite that general stance, however, this paragraph offers a different paradigm because Paul offers his own spiritual experience as paradigmatic for all who follow the Lord Jesus. In this passage Paul's spiritual autobiography as paradigm comes to fruition. Even so, this does not violate the basic principle of application I advocate, namely, that application is more appropriately drawn from our relations to Paul's readers rather than Paul as author. We are justified in drawing application from Paul's life in this text because that is what he intended his original readers to do as well. The central theological assertion in this text is that belief in Christ leads to justification and enables the believer's union with him. Appropriate applications can be made from each link in this argument.

Paul argues that faith in Christ is the new mode of existence for those who relate to God. Put another way, faith in Christ governs everything about how the believer lives. Faith starts the Christian life, it is the key for growth in one's relationship with God, and it is the consummation of all the believer hopes for in spiritual development. For those who believe in the Lord Jesus Christ, faith in him is not simply a key that unlocks the door to our new existence. Rather, it is the air we breathe, the ground upon which we walk, and the very essence of our existence. Faith cannot be underestimated or undervalued, and we should seek to grow in it at every point of our lives. Practically, though, how is that to occur? Daily life teaches us that there are opportunities to nurture faith everywhere, in things both little and large, and believers should pray that we can maximize our faith wherever we can. My natural, human response when difficult circumstances arise is anxiety, and part of my growth as a believer has come by praying for and practicing a different reaction. When I feel anxiety encroaching, I consciously choose to pray aloud and state my faith in God, who is sovereign and controls all my circumstances. This simple yet tangible response has markedly increased my faith in our great God.

Justification has been taught since the time of the reformation as the declaration that a believer has right standing before God, that is, justification is being declared righteous, which the believer attains by expressing faith in Christ. This is true as a statement of systematic theology, but without proper care to Paul's argument, dependence on this idea might flatten out Paul's expression in this paragraph. There is certainly a past dimension to justification: God's declaration that I am righteous occurred at the moment I expressed faith in his Son. But this precludes neither a present nor future aspect to justification. Paul's description of his co-crucifixion with Christ is most certainly related to the present life of the believer, but it grows out of the justification attained through faith. Paul uses a fut. tense verb to describe justification in Gal 2:16, so we can state with confidence that justification also concerns God's future declaration about my forensic standing before him. Justification in Paul is a richer concept than often understood. The proper response for the believer is to realize how deeply their justification affects their life before God in all its aspects. Justification is the past declaration of our righteous standing before God, but it is also the foundation for Christ's power presently available for living today and the grounds for our future salvation.

The believer's union with Christ, presented in this passage with the imagery of co-crucifixion, is the intimate, personal connection of the believer to Christ attained through faith in him. As imagery it is designed to explain the reality to which it points in a powerful way. The image of co-crucifixion is visceral. It means that from the divine viewpoint believers were on the cross with Christ as the moment of his crucifixion. We were placed as well in the unused tomb, our bodies overlapping his. And triumphantly we exited the tomb with the risen Lord to enter new life. Paul's primary point of explaining this union with Christ is to provide the theological basis for the spiritual power that believers now have to live their lives each day. The life presently lived in the bodies we have is none other than the power of the resurrected Lord, who gave himself on the cross out of his love for us. This power is not motivational or imitational as much as it is real and practical. The proper response of the believer is to yield to that power, accessing it through the continual exercise of faith, and in this way the empowered daily life reinforces the means of justification that opened the way for co-crucifixion in the first place.

An overarching applicational point relates to the believer's stance toward what God has done for the individual through Christ's loving self-sacrifice. Paul at the end of the paragraph recognizes that this blessed situation for the believer is a gracious gift from God. He states, "I do not nullify God's grace." As argued above, the word "grace" has as its referent all that has preceded, that is, God's activity in Christ on behalf of the believer. But the point of the word is not just its referent but also what it signifies in Paul's mind. He views the salvation believers receive as an act of grace from God. This is in keeping with God's gracious character, his calling of believers, and his appointment of Paul as an apostle to the Gentiles. Paul with this use of the word connects the salvation believers receive to all those things, and it establishes the character of what they receive as godly in a very tangible sense of the word. It should provoke thanksgiving and worship on the part of the believer. The proper response to God's grace is an acknowledgement of his greatness in giving it, our lack of worth to receive it, and thankfulness for his loving disposition toward us. Paul's description of salvation here should motivate us to thankful worship of the God who freely gives it to us in Christ.

Additional Exegetical Comments

2:15–21 T. A. Scacewater has helpfully argued how this paragraph should be understood vis-à-vis the Antioch incident and the Galatian context.[89] Essentially the paragraph is not a polemic against Peter but against the Galatian opponents. Peter's problem in 2:11–14 was ethnocentrism manifested as a sociological action. His inappropriate response to the men from James, which involved withdrawing from Gentiles, threatened the unity of the church, relegating Gentiles to second class status. Paul rebuked him for this but then uses this as a springboard in 2:15 to turn his attention back to the Galatian opponents, not Peter. The opponents had truly distorted the gospel by demanding circumcision; Peter had done nothing of the sort. So "works of the Law" in Gal 2:16 should not be read backwards to the Antioch incident as a sociological issue, but forward to his extended theological argument about how one enters the family of God. Works of the Law are in this context not sociological as the New Perspective has claimed, but required actions for justification and thus certainly soteriological.

2:16 D. Hunn has argued that ἐὰν μή in this verse is adversative through an examination of extant Greek literature and through a comparison to Gal 2:16 of the logical structure of the sentences in which ἐὰν μή occurs.[90] The three possible views grammatically are that ἐὰν μή is exceptive of the entire preceding statement, that it is exceptive of only the principal part of the preceding statement, or that it is adversative. With examples from extrabiblical Greek, Hunn provides grammatical evidence that the latter two options—the more traditional views of the meaning here—are not common but are legitimately possible. The difference between the latter two is one of emphasis, and Hunn argues that here ἐὰν μή is adversative because the context sets up

89. Scacewater, "Galatians 2:11–21," 307–23.

90. D. Hunn, "Ἐὰν μή in Galatians 2:16: A Look at Greek Literature," *NovT* 49 (2007): 281–90.

a clear contrast between the prepositional phrases ἐξ ἔργων νόμου and διὰ πίστεως Ἰησοῦ Χριστοῦ.

2:17 Discussions about whether Paul refers to pre- or postconversion status (see Schreiner, 168 and Moo, 164, for representative examples) miss the point of Paul's argument. That distinction puts too fine of a point on what Paul is arguing, as Paul makes his argument here in light of timeless truth founded in the OT but also verified in the present time. Either viewpoint could make sense of what Paul argues since he does not develop any sort of chronological argument, but given that his goal here is to address the presenting situation in Antioch and the current situation in Galatia, if a choice has to be made a postconversion viewpoint is best.

Selected Bibliography

Das, A. A. "Another Look at ἐὰν μή in Galatians 2:16." *JBL* 119 (2000): 529–39.

Garlington, D. B. "Paul's 'Partisan ἐκ' and the Question of Justification in Galatians." *JBL* 127 (2008): 567–89.

Hunn, D. "'Ἐὰν μή in Galatians 2:16: A Look at Greek Literature." *NovT* 49 (2007): 281–90.

Lambrecht, J. "Critical Reflections on Paul's 'Partisan ἐκ' as Recently Presented by Don Garlington." *ETL* 85 (2009): 135–41.

Martyn, J. L. *History and Theology in the Fourth Gospel*. NTL. Louisville, KY: Westminster John Knox, 1968.

Philo. *On Flight and Finding. On the Change of Names. On Dreams*. Trans. F. H. Colson and G. H. Whitaker. LCL 275. Cambridge, MA: Harvard University Press, 1934.

Roberts, C. H. "Lecture II. Nomina Sacra: Origins and Significance." In *Manuscript, Society and Belief in Early Christian Egypt*, 26–48. The Schweich Lectures of the British Academy 1977. London: Oxford University Press, 1979.

Scacewater, T. A. "Galatians 2:11–21 and the Interpretive Context of 'Works of the Law.'" *JETS* 56 (2013): 307–23.

Excursus: Paul's Use of Psalm 143:2

In Ps 143 (142 LXX) David entreats the Lord for help in light of attacks from his enemies.[91] Because of these attacks, David despairs of life. He requests the Lord's help to vanquish his enemies and restore him to safety and security. The phrase Paul quotes comes from the beginning of the psalm, forming part of David's rationale for his request. It appears in the MT as כִּי לֹא־יִצְדַּק לְפָנֶיךָ כָל־חָי. The particle כִּי here acts as a causal conj., offering an explanation for Paul's

91. The LXX adds a clarification to the title: ὅτε αὐτὸν ὁ υἱὸς καταδιώκει.

request that the Lord not judge him. The verb צדק is here a Qal impf.; it is possible that this could refer to a specific future situation, but the most natural construal of this verb is as a habitual non-perfective, roughly equivalent to a gnomic idea,[92] which also fits with the referent of the subject, כָל־חַי. The sense of the verb צדק is "to be right/righteous."[93] Whether this word as a whole refers to legal standing or covenantal faithfulness is an open question, but given that the previous phrase refers to God's judgment upon the individual, the forensic meaning is entirely feasible here.[94] The prepositional phrase לְפָנֶיךָ has the sense "according to the opinion of, in the view of."[95] The generic subject כָל־חַי is meant to be universal: all the living, all people. The phrase thus acts as a justification for David's plea that God not judge him: If God did so, David would be condemned and have no standing in his request for God's help because no living person is righteous before God. So David has asked for the Lord's help (1a), basing his request on the Lord's righteousness (1b), not on his own. Understanding his need for mercy, David asks that the Lord not judge him (2a) because no person is righteous before God (2a).

The translation of these two verses in the LXX is essentially literal. In the LXX the pertinent line reads ὅτι οὐ δικαιωθήσεται ἐνώπιόν σου πᾶς ζῶν. The literalism in this instance extends even to the word order. There are two nuances introduced with the translation of the verb, however, that affect the meaning of the line. The verb δικαιωθήσεται is a fut. pass., negated here as in the MT. The fut. is a common way the LXX translates the Hebrew impf. This might imply a future, eschatological nuance for the statement in the LXX, but that need not be the case, as the gnomic fut. is feasible in this instance. What is true at any time will be true in a future time, so the essential meaning is unchanged. The pass. voice is different, though, from the stative nuance of the Qal stem. In Greek the pass. voice indicates that the subject receives the action of the transitive verb; the agent of the action may or may not be explicitly mentioned. Here the action of the verb in the LXX is construed as being directed toward the subject πᾶς ζῶν; the verb δικαιόω has to be considered transitive, not stative, in this instance. So for the LXX the meaning "to be right/righteous" found in the MT would not hold. Instead, the meaning has to be transitive, such as "to make righteous, vindicate, acquit, justify" or the like.

Paul's wording of the line in question in Gal 2:16 is different enough that there is some doubt whether this is a citation of Ps 143:2 at all.[96] In NA[28] the

---

92. See B. K. Waltke and M. O'Connor, *An Introduction to Biblical Hebrew Syntax* (Winona Lake, IN: Eisenbrauns, 1990), 506.

93. So *HALOT*, 1003, who cites Ps 143:2 under this category of meaning.

94. This would mean that the root צדק would be used with a different meaning in v. 1, where it certainly refers to God's faithfulness to his covenant promises.

95. *HALOT*, 942.

96. For example, NA[27] lists Ps 143:2 in the margin at Gal 2:16, indicating that an allusion is present, while NA[28] does not.

clause reads *ὅτι ἐξ ἔργων νόμου οὐ δικαιωθήσεται πᾶσα σάρξ*. On the face of it this is different enough from the text of the LXX that doubting the presence of an allusion has merit, but there are several factors that favor this association. The wording *οὐ δικαιωθήσεται* makes a strong connection. The phrase לֹא־יִצְדַּק occurs only here in the MT. Similarly, the phrase *οὐ δικαιωθήσεται* only occurs four times in the LXX (Ps 142:2; Sir 23:11; 26:29; 31:5), and none of the other verses have *πᾶς ζῶν*, *πᾶσα σάρξ*, or anything similar as the subject. The phrase כָּל־חַי only occurs five times in the MT (Gen 3:20; 8:21; Ps 143:2; Job 12:10; 28:21). Only in Gen 8:21 and Ps 143:2 is there anything close to Paul's wording.[97] Semantically Paul's phrasing is similar to both the MT and the LXX, as in each there is a negated main verb, the subjects are similar, and there is a prepositional modifier to the verb. There is also an intra-Pauline reason to favor the association: In Rom 3:20 Paul more clearly cites Ps 143:2. There he says *διότι ἐξ ἔργων νόμου οὐ δικαιωθήσεται πᾶσα σὰρξ ἐνώπιον αὐτοῦ*. More clearly than in Gal 2:16 Paul cites the LXX form of Ps 143:2 and adds a key theological clarification with the prepositional phrase *ἐξ ἔργων νόμου*. Even so, the wording of Gal 2:16 is similar enough to the wording of Rom 3:20 that Paul likely drew from a common source for each. When everything is considered, it is more likely that the wording of Gal 2:16 is a citation of Ps 143:2, albeit modified somewhat, than it is not.

In the context of Galatians this clause serves as a theological justification for the reason Paul placed his faith in Jesus. The meaning of the phrase is similar to the MT and identical with the LXX: No living thing finds justification before God apart from his mercy. Paul clarifies the means of this justification with the addition of the prepositional phrase *ἐξ ἔργων νόμου*, specifying an entailment of the general sense of the original passage and applying it to his current context. The original context of the psalm—David's petition for rescue from his enemies—is not invoked in Galatians. Paul's concern is the theology undergirding David's intense request. Paul has lifted what David said from its context, but in no way has he violated the meaning. His wording is similar enough that the meanings of the two utterances coincide, and the meaning of the original utterance fits quite well in Paul's theological argument.

Describing Paul's hermeneutics here in the citation of Ps 143:2 is not difficult. He has used a theological statement regarding humanity's standing before God in a new context but in a perfectly appropriate and understandable way in concert with the intention of the original. There is an analogy in play: Just as David knew that no one standing before God would ever find justification on their own, Paul knew that neither would anyone standing before God on the merit of their obedience to works of the Law find justification. The difference is that in Paul's expression of the analogy he makes explicit the means of justification in question, that is, works of the Law.

97. Interestingly in Gen 8:21 the translation is *πᾶσαν σάρκα ζῶσαν*.

Paul has taken David's theological expression and applied it rightly to his own context.

Excursus: Paul's Use of the δικ- Word Group in Galatians

In addressing the exegetical question of what Paul means when he says in Gal 2:16 that "no one is justified by works of the Law but only through faith in Jesus Christ"—and the subsequent restatements that follow that use similar wording—one must first wrestle with a host of other attendant issues. Lexical issues come to the fore: Hebrew antecedents are clearly in view in Paul's formulations, and how the Greek terms he used overlap with the Hebrew terms or distinguish themselves from them are of primary concern. Alongside this discussion of the meaning of terms one must discuss their development and use through history. Second Temple Judaism saw important applications of these terms that may have had a ready impact upon Paul's thoughts as he wrote. The interpreter must also address theological concerns, as Paul was seeking to explain not only the present circumstances of his Galatian converts vis-à-vis their place in the church, but he was also seeking to explain how God was at work at present in the world in Christ through the Spirit, an effort that extends to all his letters. In short, this is a complex problem that requires the analysis and synthesis of a great deal of data, material that is still under intense discussion and debate within the current scholarly setting. My goal with this short excursus is twofold: First, I will survey in a very brief fashion the current state of discussion on the above issues with a goal of describing Paul's use of the δικ- word group in Galatians. My emphasis in this survey will be on "New Perspective" interpretations of the data, most notably those of J. D. G. Dunn and N. T. Wright, and the use of the terms and concepts in Galatians itself, not in Paul broadly or even in contradistinction to his admittedly similar usage in Romans. Second, I will offer a hermeneutical suggestion for interpretation of Paul's meaning that might allow a closer alignment of more traditional interpretations and those offered under the New Perspective.

Paul's uses of the δικ- word group is ultimately founded in the Hebrew root צדק, which is capable of a wide range of meanings. Although somewhat reductionistic, it is helpful to see the root as connoting "conformity to an ethical or moral standard."[98] This is confirmed by comparison to related roots in cognate languages: "The term appears to be used to refer to right comportment: status or behavior in accord with some implied standard."[99] The root exists in multiple forms that show a great deal of overlap; evidence shows that the verb and noun forms are used somewhat interchangeably.[100]

98. H. G. Stigers, "צָדֵק," *TWOT*, 2:752.

99. D. J. Reimer, "צדק," *NIDOTTE*, 3:746.

100. D. J. Reimer, "צדק," *NIDOTTE*, 3:746.

The verb form has a range of meanings depending upon the stem. It can mean "to be right/just," "to declare right," or "to vindicate," among others. The related nouns exhibit similar semantic flexibility. They can refer to God's righteous character, the righteous action of a judge, or loyalty and honesty within the context of a community.[101] In sum, the concept of צדק undergirds much of the OT thought on how God and humanity relate:

> The *ṣedeq-ṣĕdāqâ* of the community and the individual is comportment according to God's order in every area of life, in just and proper social order (justice to the helpless, the poor, the oppressed, the widow, the orphan, the resident alien), in legal procedure, in the ritual of worship, all effected by God's *ṣedeq-ṣĕdāqâ*.[102]

It is during the Second Temple period that the δικ- word group becomes strongly associated with the Hebrew root צדק. There is a natural semantic overlap between the terms, and the LXX creates a strong connection between the two in translation. For example, the noun form צְדָקָה occurs 159 times in the Hebrew MT; it is translated by the Greek term δικαιοσύνη 135 times. This connection creates a strong link theologically between the word groups. The difference is that the δικ- word group has a stronger emphasis upon legal and forensic denotations,[103] while the Hebrew use of the צדק word group emphasizes covenantal relationships more prominently. This stronger emphasis upon the legal connotations carries into the NT as well,[104] but the moral aspect is not absent. In short, the צדק and δικ- word groups can be used quite broadly to refer to a wide range of human experience under the rubrics of covenant, conformity, and legal standards.

Paul's particular use of the δικ- word group is also equally varied. One cannot argue that his use of the terms springs from a single source, for example, from OT exegesis or from his polemical debates with opponents. Rather, Paul uses the words widely, in keeping with the breadth of the underlying terms, and with novelty, applying them to his own particular, new situation, which requires theological, social, and cultural insight. He clearly uses the terms in the context of soteriology and ethics, but he also connects the δικ- word group closely to faith. He uses the words generally, such that for him they embody theological principles, but he also understands them very particularly, exegeting their meaning in several contexts that involve his own close reading of prior texts. In Galatians Paul uses only three words from this word group: δικαιόω (verb, 8x: Gal 2:16 [3x], 17; 3:8, 11, 24; 5:4), δικαιοσύνη (noun, 4x: Gal 2:21; 3:6, 21; 5:5), and δίκαιος (adj., 1x: Gal 3:11). His use of the words is concentrated in the theological ending to his personal narrative (Gal 2:15–21) and the central theological argument of the epistle (Gal 3), so

101. See the entries for צֶדֶק and צְדָקָה in *HALOT*, 1004–7; BDB, 841–42.

102. J. J. Scullion, "Righteousness: Old Testament," *ABD*, 5:736.

103. See J. Reumann, "Righteousness: Early Judaism," *ABD*, 5:737.

104. See entries on δικαιοσύνη and δικαιόω in BDAG, 247–49, as examples.

it is fair to say that for Paul within Galatians these words are distinctly theological. Even the uses outside this section (5:4, 5) have a distinct theological cast to them. In 2:15–21 Paul piles the uses of this word group one on top of the other. This powerful redundancy serves the emotion of his rhetoric, but it also supports the logical inference that his readers likely understood what he meant. The theological discussion that follows in chapter 3 is not an explanation of the terms as such but rather a specific example of exegesis, in this instance of Gen 15:6, that supports his theological affirmations. Paul may very well have developed these ideas in his original preaching to the Galatians so that he did not need to explain them in this literary moment but simply chose to repeat and reaffirm. Thus one must think more broadly to understand Paul's intention in using the terms.

Enter the New Perspective, which has served to expand the conceptual boundaries of what Paul had in mind when using the δικ- word group. Put simply, the traditional interpretation of Paul on this matter has focused on the legal and forensic meanings of the terms. Said another way, justification (the English term most often associated with the δικ- word group) has been discussed as a forensic matter regarding God's declaration regarding the individual's standing before him. Two contemporary scholars have changed the discussion by forcing exegetes to see the broader nuances associated with the word group. J. D. G. Dunn has emphasized the social and cultural issues in play with the concept, and N. T. Wright has explained justification not just as a present, individual matter but also as a holistic way of understanding God's past, present, and future work in the world. Dunn has written extensively on this issue, but an easy entrée to his thought is his book *The Theology of Paul the Apostle*.[105] Here he devotes chapter 14 to the topic of "Justification by Faith" and addresses not only Paul's use of these important terms but also related issues of history and theology. His argument can be encapsulated thusly: Paul's use of the δικ- word group cannot be understood apart from the Hebrew background of covenant faith associated with the צדק root nor apart from the intense nationalism that developed within Judaism during the Second Temple period. As a Pharisee, Paul measured righteousness in the currency of covenant distinctiveness, both against fellow Jews and against Gentiles. The "badges" prescribed by the Law—circumcision, Sabbath, food regulations—that Judaism had followed in obedience to God were also used as "boundaries," marking clearly who was in the covenant and thus accepted by God and who was outside the covenant and thus under his judgment. After Christ revealed himself to Paul, Paul realized that it was only faith in Christ, the Messiah, that marked covenant distinctiveness; the badges and boundaries of the Law no longer held. Thus justification through faith was the only marker that mattered and the only way to distinguish between who was in and who was out. Gentiles thus could have full acceptance into the

105. J. D. G. Dunn, *The Theology of Paul the Apostle* (Grand Rapids: Eerdmans, 1998).

church, the new community of the covenant, on that basis alone without any need to follow the works of the Law.

N. T. Wright has also written extensively on this issue.[106] One way to access his thought on this matter is through a section in his recent work *Paul and the Faithfulness of God*, where he discusses the issue of "Faith, Justification, and the People of God" by first discussing "The Shape of Justification," a theological overview of how justification worked in Paul's thought, and then by working through particular passages.[107] The extent and depth of Wright's argument defies simple summary, but suffice it to say for present purposes that Wright argues quite ably that justification should not simply be understood as the end goal of Paul's theology, as if he was concerned only with the individual's legal standing before God. Rather, justification is part of a much larger complex of thought that concerns God's remaking of this present world by finally putting humanity right, that is, dealing with its sin through covenant in the person of the Messiah. As Wright says in multiple places in this work and elsewhere, justification is eschatological, forensic, participatory, and covenantal. Thus Paul's terminology serves multiple purposes and connects to several theological assertions all at once. What is helpful in these examples of New Perspective thought, particularly in Wright, is the expansion of the idea of justification into broader, biblical areas of meaning without a denial of the traditional emphasis upon the forensic connotations. Based upon these two authors, it is appropriate to argue that when Paul used the δικ- word group he was certainly interested in an individual's legal standing before God, but he was also interested in much more, including the individual's connection to God's covenant community, a community now delineated by faith in his Messiah, not in observance of works of the Law.

The constant battle when interpreting Paul on this issue has to do with discerning the difference between what should be understood as a timeless principle of his text and what should be taken as something that is culturally bound within his particular situation. When thinking through Paul's use of key terms related to justification, especially in light of recent New Perspective discussions, it is fairly easy to see where particular interpretations fall. The traditional interpretation broadly speaking sees Paul's justification language as referring to forensic justification, that is, an individual's legal standing before God, which Paul uses to counter a legalistic righteousness based upon works. This interpretation regards Paul's statements as timeless principles. God has always dealt with humanity by justifying on the basis of faith; witness his dealings with Abraham! Paul thus makes general statements that are still directly applicable to humanity today. Interpretations within the New Perspective, even though they cannot be necessarily unified under this rubric, operate somewhat differently. They regard Paul's particular context

106. In all honesty, this is likely the epitome of understatement.

107. N. T. Wright, *Paul and the Faithfulness of God* (Minneapolis: Fortress, 2013), 925–1037.

as paramount. He spoke from a Jewish background of covenant, and he was in debates that pitted observant Jewish Christians against Gentiles on the matter of obedience to Torah as a stipulation for inclusion in the church. Paul pointed to justification as the defining basis for Gentile inclusion in the nascent Christian community; witness Paul's dispute with Peter over eating with Gentiles and justification through faith as the answer! Paul thus used justification as an answer for the particular social problem he faced.

I humbly offer here a hermeneutical suggestion that might provide a way for further dialogue on this matter. Christians for centuries have recognized that particular aspects of the biblical text are indeed culturally bound, and those discussions are still with us.[108] But this recognition of cultural situation was never an end in itself. Indeed, a proper hermeneutic examines the cultural context to determine the theological principle operating under the surface that can then be elucidated, discussed, and applied in the contemporary moment. Perhaps this model might prove helpful here. Paul was struggling with a particular cultural context of a Jewish Christian community that needed to figure out the place of Gentiles in its midst. Justification through faith alone, not by works of the Law, was his answer to that problem. But that culturally bound answer points to a deeper theological principle of how God is at work through Christ to solve the human problem and create his community. Entrance to that community, into relationship with God, is not gained through any thing that the individual does. It rests solely upon God's gracious acceptance of that individual, one aspect of which is certainly forensic. In my opinion the traditional interpretation and New Perspective interpretations of Paul's justification language are both right. The former has majored on the timeless principle, and the latter upon the cultural moment in which Paul was situated. They both end up in the same place, however, and they both can aid understanding of Paul's texts.[109]

Excursus: Paul's Use of the πιστ- Word Group in Galatians

It perhaps borders on oversimplification to say that the essence of the Christian message and life can be reduced to the principle of faith, but that is not an unreasonable or indefensible position to take given the breadth and depth of that concept within the NT. The Christian life begins, continues,

108. Witness the well-known example of W. J. Webb, *Slaves, Women & Homosexuals: Exploring the Hermeneutics of Cultural Analysis* (Downers Grove, IL: InterVarsity, 2001), who either advanced the discussion or aggravated it, depending on whom you ask.

109. For a similar argument, see J. R. McGahey, " 'No One is Justified By Works of the Law' (Galatians 2:16a): The Nature and Rationale of Paul's Polemic against 'Works of the Law' in the Epistle to the Galatians" (Ph.D. dissertation, Dallas Theological Seminary, 1996).

and ends with the individual's response of faith to the Creator God who has revealed himself definitively in the ministry, death, and resurrection of Jesus Christ. Faith encompasses the totality of humanity's responsibility in salvation and entails much of what can be subsumed under other rubrics, such as discipleship, maturity, and sanctification. Although less debated in contemporary scholarship than the δικ- word group, the πιστ- word group is no less important for Paul's argument in Galatians. The verb πιστεύω and the noun πίστις are used in very important passages, most notably the central theological statement of Paul's argument in 2:15–21; as such the word group requires careful study. The purpose of this excursus is to examine Paul's use of the πιστ- word group in Galatians and describe how it fits within the message and argument of the book.

The use of this word group is widely attested in extrabiblical Greek but with a less specific semantic domain than the NT uses of the word. The word group is quite ancient: The adj. πίστος is found in Homer (8th century BC), the noun πίστις is found in Hesiod (approximately 6th century BC), and the verb πιστεύω is found in Aeschylus (5th century BC). Although there are legitimate nuances that can be differentiated in particular contexts, the general meaning of the word group is trust or confidence, owing to the derivation of this word group from the verb πείθω/πείθομαι ("persuade" and "obey" respectively). The expression of trust referred to by the particular words in the group can be active or passive: It can be trust directed outwardly toward an object, or it can refer to a quality that engenders trust in or receives trust from others. These nuances can be seen in the different categories of meaning possible for the verb πιστεύω: trust, put faith in; comply; believe that, feel confident that; have faith; entrust; confide; accept as true; be persuaded.[110] The noun πίστις "connotes persuasion, conviction, and commitment, and always implies confidence, which is expressed in human relationships as fidelity, trust, assurance, oath, proof, guarantee."[111] The adj. πιστός reflects these same nuances and can generally mean "faithful, trustworthy" in the passive sense or "believing, relying on, loyal" in the active sense.[112] One important distinction from a contemporary understanding is that the πιστ- word group was not primarily focused on cognition or what could be termed mental assent. Rather, it primarily focused on conduct. The earliest uses of this word group concern an agreement or bond and thus have a social orientation.[113] Nor was it solely a religious term as in the NT. The word group was used in religious contexts but not primarily; this context was not central or foundational as it came to be in the NT.[114]

110. LSJ, 1407–8; MGS, 1668–69.

111. *TLNT*, 3:110.

112. BDAG, 820–21.

113. *NIDNTTE*, 3:760.

114. G. Barth, "πίστις, πιστεύω," *EDNT*, 3:92; R. Bultmann, "πιστεύω et al.," "Greek Usage: Classical Usage," *TDNT*, 6:179.

The LXX uses this word group to translate the verb אמן, especially the Hiphil and Niphal stems, and related cognate words, such as אֱמוּנָה. This presents a slightly skewed picture if this is the only evidence considered, though, as אמן was only one of many words to describe the relationship between man and God. Other words like בטח ("trust, be confident"), חסה ("take refuge"), קוה ("await, hope"), יחל ("wait, cause to hope"), and חכה ("to wait for, be patient") were also used commonly to express the breadth and depth of the human-divine relationship.[115] Even so, the use of the πιστ- word group in the LXX and its central focus in the NT is lexically and semantically warranted:

> The LXX and NT were right when they related their term for faith (πιστεύειν) to the OT stem אמן, for in this word is expressed the most distinctive and profound thing which the OT has to say about faith. ... The significance of the OT view of faith may be seen in the fact that, as an expression of the particular being and life of the people of God which stands both individually and collectively in the dimension of a vital divine relationship, it embraces the whole span of this form of life, even to the final depths which are disclosed only when, under the threat to human existence, certainty in God releases new energies of faith and life.[116]

The simplest meaning of אמן is "to be firm, trustworthy, safe."[117] The Niphal of אמן means "to be reliable, faithful," which is applied to both God and humans in the OT.[118] The related noun אֱמוּנָה similarly means "steadfastness, trustworthiness, faithfulness."[119] Important theological uses are found in Isa 7:9 and 28:16; in each instance there is a call to trust within difficult circumstances, which then leads to a future beyond the present.[120] This prefigures well the important NT nuances of the terms. It is a fair summary that "the אמן word group describes a living act of trust, and also the dimension of human existence in a historical situation. The terms do not step outside the realm of the personal."[121]

The πιστ- word group in the NT exhibits a semantic domain similar in in scope to that of אמן in the OT. The verb πιστεύω can mean "give credence to a message and/or its bearer."[122] This meaning can be used in a non-reli-

---

115. G. Barth, "πίστις, πιστεύω," *EDNT*, 3:92; A. Weiser, "πιστεύω et al.," "Old Testament Concept: General Remarks," *TDNT*, 6:183; J. P. Healey, "Faith: Old Testament," *ABD*, 2:744.

116. A. Weiser, "πιστεύω et al.," "The Old Testament Concept: Summary," *TDNT*, 6:196.

117. *HALOT*, 63.

118. *NIDNTTE*, 3:762.

119. *HALOT*, 62, which notes other meanings as well.

120. *NIDNTTE*, 3:762–63.

121. *NIDNTTE*, 3:764.

122. G. Barth, "πίστις, πιστεύω," *EDNT*, 3:92.

gious sense, but the religious context clearly dominates. For example, God is frequently the object, important to note in contradistinction to a message or messenger. The noun πίστις can mean "that which elicits trust, faith," which in certain contexts would mean "faithfulness, dependability" and "trust which one puts into practice, faith."[123] Because of this range of meanings, this word group has a strong connection to several important OT concepts, including belief, obedience, trust, hope, and faithfulness.[124] Even so, the word group developed some specific meanings within the Christian context of the NT, including the content of that which is believed, the total attitude of life that could wax and wane with the human condition, and a specific orientation toward the act of God in Christ.

> In all these areas faith is the act in virtue of which a man, responding to God's eschatological deed in Christ, comes out of the world and makes a radical reorientation to God. It is the act in which the new eschatological existence of Christians is established, the attitude which is proper to this existence. As this attitude which constitutes existence, πίστις governs the whole of life.[125]

For Paul πίστις begins with the general idea of "the acceptance of the proclamation of God's salvation activity in Christ," but he makes it more theologically central:

> Though faith does, indeed, find its basis in proclamation of God's salvation activity, Paul thinks through the consequences of this event in a much more radical fashion: If God has acted for salvation once and for all in Christ's cross, then the human response can only consist in obedient acceptance, in trust in God's χάρις, and in receiving this gift with and in a life lived from within the gift itself. Thus πίστις belongs together with χάρις (Rom 4:4f., 16) and for the same reason is antithetical to ἔργα νόμου (Rom 3:28; 9:32; Gal 2:16) and to the νόμος understood as the principle of performance (Rom 3:21f.; Gal 3:12; Phil 3:9).[126]

Thus faith is the only means to receive the gracious salvation gift of righteousness. Paul understands it to be the central goal of the OT message, as evidenced by his central use of Gal 15:6 and Hab 2:4 in Galatians and elsewhere. Faith is the central guiding principle of the Christian life as the

---

123. G. Barth, "πίστις, πιστεύω," *EDNT*, 3:92–93.

124. R. Bultmann, "πιστεύω et al.," "The πίστις Group in the New Testament: General Christian Usage: The Continuation of the Old Testament and Jewish Tradition," *TDNT*, 6:205–208.

125. R. Bultmann, "πιστεύω et al.," "The πίστις Group in the New Testament: General Christian Usage: The Relation of Christian Faith to That of the Old Testament," *TDNT*, 6:216.

126. G. Barth, "πίστις, πιστεύω," *EDNT*, 3:95.

individual and the larger community respond to the revelation of God in Christ and his continued work in their midst by the Spirit.

In summary, it is fair to say that the NT takes the foundation laid in the OT with אמן and related terms and focuses the concept, making the response of the individual to the person of Christ revealed by God in the historical event of his death and resurrection a central *topos* for the term. This is shown well in Paul's use of the terms in Galatians, most of which without doubt refer to the individual's attitude of trust toward God. Exceptions would be 1:23, in which πίστις refers to Christian faith as a religious system *per se*; 2:7, in which Paul uses πιστεύω with the sense "entrust"; and 5:22, where Paul emphasizes the related nuance of "faithfulness" in personal relationships. The uses of πίστις in Gal 3:23, 25 might seem to be used differently than this majority within Galatians, perhaps referring to Christ himself, but upon closer inspection these uses also find their foundation in the individual's attitude of trust toward God. They are personified and expanded without losing the central semantic anchor: They refer to a whole complex of events within salvation history that lead to faith, specifically the coming of Christ—his death, resurrection, and call to faith embodied in the gospel.

Excursus: The Works of the Law in Galatians

In tandem with other lexical and theological issues in Gal 2:15–21 is the conundrum concerning the phrase "the works of the Law," appearing for the first time in this book in 2:16 in the phrase ἐξ ἔργων νόμου. Although not that common in Galatians—or elsewhere in Paul, for that matter—the phrase carries certain exegetical and theological weight. Within Galatians it occurs solely in Paul's theological argumentation: first in the theological closing to his personal narrative, then in his rebuke of the Galatians, which serves as a transition to his theological discussion proper, then once in the theological discussion itself. But the theological placement of the term does not deny its very practical character. Paul's use of the term in 2:16 is a foil to the practical issues of circumcision and food regulations that create the tension in the first part of that chapter. So understanding the meaning and referent of the phrase is of utmost importance for understanding Paul's argument in Galatians and indeed his theology as a whole.

Even though the lexical and syntactical issues surrounding the phrase are not complex, a short review will set the stage for further discussion to follow. The phrase occurs six times in Galatians (2:16 [3x]; 3:2, 5, 10), each time in the form ἐξ ἔργων νόμου.[127] Important to note for contrast is that in

127. The phrase occurs elsewhere only three times in Romans (2:15; 3:20, 28). The first occurrence is articular (τὸ ἔργον τοῦ νόμου); the second two are anarthrous (ἐξ ἔργων νόμου and χωρὶς ἔργων νόμου respectively). Arguably the sg. ἔργον in Rom 2:15 has a meaning different from the pl. ἔργων in the other occurrences, but that is not a

Galatians Paul does not use ἔργον by itself in any way that readily implies "works" as a general principle. The two occurrences of this word in Galatians not in collocation with νόμος clearly mean something different.[128] In each anarthrous instance of ἔργων νόμου, ἔργον is pl. while νόμος is gen. sg. The gen. νόμου is best understood as a poss. gen., gen. of production, or possibly gen. of source. Despite the lack of the article in this construction, both ἔργων and νόμου are definite: The context prior to this use in 2:16 points to "works of the Law" as specific requirements for Jewish conduct and practice found in the Torah. Paul referenced circumcision relative to Titus in 2:3; the conflict over Peter arose because of food. This is *prima facie* evidence that supports Dunn's argument that in principle "works of the Law" meant all the Law required, but in practice there were particular works that were more important (Dunn, 136). The wider context points, however, to a holistic conception for "works of the Law." Paul states in Gal 3:10 that the curse comes upon those who do not do πᾶσιν τοῖς γεγραμμένοις ἐν τῷ βιβλίῳ τοῦ νόμου, "all that is written in the book of the Law." In 5:3 he states that accepting circumcision obligates a man to do ὅλον τὸν νόμον, "the whole Law." So within Galatians "works of the Law" does not refer simply to the well-known requirements of the Torah, such as food regulations and circumcision. It must refer generally to all the Law requires of the Jew in covenant with God (so Longenecker, 86; George, 195; de Boer, 145–48; Schreiner, 161; Moo, 158; Oakes, 84, 86).

The bigger question relative to these works of the Law concerns whether they functioned within primarily a salvific or social context.[129] The traditional interpretation of these "works of the Law" in Paul's argument is that they served a salvific function, that is, Jews practiced said works to merit salvation before the Lord. Paul thus juxtaposes these works against faith as a contrary principle of how an individual's relationship with God fundamentally works. God does not justify based on works but graciously on the basis of faith. More recent interpretations, specifically within the framework of the New Perspective on Paul, regard these works of the Law as having instead a social

---

major problem for Galatians as such since the sg. does not occur in that book. See J. D. G. Dunn, *Romans*, WBC 38AB (Dallas: Word, 1988), 100, who correctly argues that "the work of the Law" in this context is a positive, commendable attitude of the heart.

128. In Gal 5:19 Paul writes of "works of the flesh" (τὰ ἔργα τῆς σαρκός), pointing to recognizable actions that stem from the sinful nature of the flesh. In Gal 6:4 he says, "But each one should examine his own work" (τὸ δὲ ἔργον ἑαυτοῦ δοκιμαζέτω ἕκαστος), an admonition for humble self-examination within the context of supporting those caught in sin. Romans, however, has several passages in which "works" could be considered a general principle, not tied directly to the Law; see Rom 2:6, 7; 3:27; 4:6; 9:12, 32; 11:6.

129. Yes, this is an overly simplistic way to explain the issue, but my intention is to show clearly the differences between the two interpretations. This language impresses me as helpful in meeting that goal.

function, that is, proper practice of them marks one out as a faithful member of God's covenant community, while improper practice of them marks one as outside that community. J. D. G. Dunn is well known for his argument that works of the Law acted as "badges" or "boundary markers"; he relies heavily on similar phrasing within the Dead Sea scrolls to affirm this social function.[130] This is similar to the arguments made by Wright concerning the attitudes of the Jewish Christians who had come to Galatia after Paul. They themselves were already marked as part of God's covenant community by virtue of their proper obedience to the Law; they had believed in Jesus as well. Their requirement of the Galatians was essentially to get the first marker right, and then the second would have value for them as well.[131]

Determining the proper meaning of "works of the Law" in Paul's argument in Galatians is not easy, as much of the background to the term relevant for its interpretation is left unspecified. Paul does use it in this particular context within a particular flow of argument that does give clues to how he intends it to be understood. When Paul first uses the phrase in Gal 2:16, it is in response to the particular issues that provoked his visit to Jerusalem and the conflict with Peter in Antioch: circumcision and food laws. These are indeed well-known requirements of the Torah that marked an individual

---

130. See Dunn, *Romans*, 154; J. D. G. Dunn, "4QMMT and Galatians," *NTS* 43 (1997): 147–53. The connections of Galatians with 4QMMT are striking, and Dunn's conclusion (p. 153) is not unreasonable: "MMT preserves a vocabulary and manner of theologising which left its mark on a wider spectrum of Jewish thought and practice, and that it was just this sort of theologising and practice which confronted Paul in Antioch and which he wrote Galatians to counter." My initial response is that the fundamental social situation in Antioch (a mixed-ethnicity social group within a predominately Gentile environment) or within Galatia for that matter did not match the one implied by 4QMMT (a singularly Jewish, separatist group), so the connection between the motivations of Peter and company in Antioch may have been quite different. Even so, the connections Dunn notes on the whole have merit and are persuasive. See also M. G. Abegg, "Paul, 'Works of the Law' and MMT," *BAR* 20 (1994): 52–55.

131. See N. T. Wright, *Pauline Perspectives: Essays on Paul, 1978–2013* (Minneapolis: Fortress, 2013), 429, which is a reprint of N. T. Wright, "Justification: Yesterday, Today, and Forever," *JETS* 54 (2011): 49–63, where this argument occurs on p. 55. This is a particularly potent argument, in my view. Traditional exegesis has viewed Paul's opponents in Galatia as Jewish Christians who had placed their faith in Christ but also were requiring a work. They were Christian brothers who were fundamentally wrong in adding a requirement to faith in Christ. But the exegetical and historical data makes much more sense to view these individuals as Jews who had never left their adherence to works of the Law behind. They had professed faith in Christ but never changed their thinking regarding the importance of works of the Law. Their fundamental theological flaw was not in adding works to faith, but in adding faith to works.

as connected to the covenant. But Paul does not leave the discussion there: The flow of his argument in v. 16 moves from current praxis (οὐ δικαιοῦται ἄνθρωπος ἐξ ἔργων νόμου ἐὰν μὴ διὰ πίστεως Ἰησοῦ Χριστοῦ) to past act (καὶ ἡμεῖς εἰς Χριστὸν Ἰησοῦν ἐπιστεύσαμεν) to intended purpose for past act (ἵνα δικαιωθῶμεν ἐκ πίστεως Χριστοῦ καὶ οὐκ ἐξ ἔργων νόμου) to scriptural justification (ὅτι ἐξ ἔργων νόμου οὐ δικαιωθήσεται πᾶσα σάρξ). Paul moves from the specifics of his current praxis with the Gentile Galatians through his personal experience to a theological, timeless warrant, and the works of the Law do not fit anywhere within his argument on any level. The better interpretation does not restrict works of the Law within Paul's argument to simply social or only salvific. Rather, they are legitimately both, and Paul rejects their function in both contexts. Paul refuses their function as restrictive markers of who is within God's covenant community; faith in Christ is now the only badge those within the covenant should wear. Paul also refuses any value or merit of these same works before God; his citation of Ps 143:2 proves that it is only God's mercy on which the individual can hope. For Paul "works of the Law" point to the requirements of the Torah that do have an important social function within Judaism, but he affirms that they have no value before God, who responds to individuals mercifully only because of their trust in him.

Excursus: The Meaning of πίστις Ἰησοῦ Χριστοῦ

In Gal 2:16 is one of the most difficult problems of interpretation in the entire book and indeed in the broader work of Pauline studies. Simply put, does the phrase πίστεως Ἰησοῦ Χριστοῦ mean "faith in Christ" or "Christ's faith"? In its most reduced form the problem is a question of grammar. Because the noun πίστις is a verbal noun, that is, it embodies a verbal idea (as reflected in the related verb πιστεύω), the related gen. noun Ἰησοῦ Χριστοῦ could be interpreted either as an obj. gen. or as a subj. gen. It is either the obj. of the verbal action, receiving the expression of faith, or the subject of the verbal action, exercising faith in some way. In its broadest form the problem is a question of Paul's theology. At issue would be his solution when arguing about the basis of a believer's justification. The answer lies either in humanity's proper response to God or what God has done through Christ to secure justification and thus salvation. The import of this problem for understanding Paul's text is profound and far reaching. It becomes a question of emphasis: Does Paul focus on humanity's response to God or God's actions on behalf of humanity? The phrase πίστις Ἰησοῦ Χριστοῦ also sets up an important contrast to works of the Law, but exactly what is contrasted is not clear. Is it a proper response from man or God's work in Christ ? The objective view implies that Paul makes an essentially anthropological argument. At issue is the proper response of humanity to God's actions through Christ. The subjective view implies that Paul makes an essentially salvation-historical argument. At issue is the change in economy from the Law to the faithful ministry of Christ. Thus the subjective view shifts the argument from anthropological to salvation historical (Moo, 160). It reestablishes priorities (Matera, 94), realigning the human response of faith under the more important datum of Christ's own faithfulness to the call of God.

My goal in this excursus is limited. Because I cannot be exhaustive, I will present a limited survey of the problem as discussed within commentary literature. Citations are included so the reader can follow up directly with the evidence presented there. The citation of a particular author under discussion of a particular view does not imply that the author holds that view. Many authors fully present both sides of the discussion, so the citation simply notes where that evidence was found in the literature. My primary focus is on the text of Galatians. This is not a holistic examination of the phrase within Paul, although discussion of the evidence does sometimes point to parallels elsewhere within Paul and the broader NT. I will close with the view I hold, why I hold it, and how it affects the meaning of the passage.

The obj. gen. view is the view traditionally held regarding this phrase. It holds that πίστις Ἰησοῦ Χριστοῦ refers to faith in Christ, that is, humanity's response of faith properly directed toward Christ as its object in contrast to reliance upon works of the Law. Following is evidence in support of this view:

1. The obj. gen. is the more natural reading of the language. It would be naturally understood as opposed to the subj. gen. The subj. gen. requires a fair bit of unpacking, which Paul does not do in Galatians (Dunn, 138) or elsewhere (Keener, 180).
2. The natural expectation by virtue of the common root is that phrases with the verb πιστεύω would be equivalent to phrases with the noun πίστις (Dunn, 139; Fung, 115; Moo, 160).
3. In other passages with verbal nouns a gen. Χριστοῦ refers to Christ as obj. For example, in Phil 3:8 the phrase τῆς γνώσεως Χριστοῦ Ἰησοῦ τοῦ κυρίου μου certainly means "knowledge of Christ Jesus our Lord," with Χριστοῦ Ἰησοῦ as an obj. gen. The same situation pertains in 1 Thess 1:3, where Paul writes τῆς ἐλπίδος τοῦ κυρίου ἡμῶν Ἰησοῦ Χριστοῦ, "the hope of our Lord Jesus Christ" (Schreiner, 165; Soards and Pursiful, 91–92).
4. A gen. object with πίστις is clear in Mark 11:22 and Jas 2:1 (Schreiner, 165).
5. Outside the disputed texts, a divine name occurs as a gen. after πίστις only six times. In five of those texts, the best interpretation of the gen. is obj. (Moo, 44).
6. Relevant parallels with πίστις plus a prepositional phrase support the objective view. "When, therefore, NT authors take the opportunity to make explicit the connection between πίστις and Christ by means of a preposition, they never suggest that the πίστις in question is exercised by Christ" (Moo, 45).
7. It is an almost universal pattern in the NT that humans are the subject of the related verb πιστεύω. Only in John 2:24 is Jesus the

subject, and there the verb has a different meaning than "have faith" (Moo, 45).

8. Paul's citation of Gen 15:6 in Gal 3:6 implies an obj. gen. in 2:16, since the issue there is Abraham's justification through his response of faith in God (Dunn, 139; Moo, 160; deSilva, 231).
9. Construing this wording as obj. fits with Paul's citation of Hab 2:4 (Moo, 160).
10. "Faith in Christ" shows the alternative (and proper) human response to "works of Law," which under any construal refers to human effort and obedience (Dunn, 139; Rapa, 584). Paul often contrasts works and faith, both construed as human activities (Schreiner, 165; Moo, 47).
11. The main verb of the sentence, ἐπιστεύσαμεν, focuses on faith exercised by individuals toward Christ (Rapa, 584).
12. The redundancy with the construction ἐπιστεύσαμεν εἰς is emphatic (Schreiner, 165; Soards and Pursiful, 91–92).
13. The whole of Galatians is about God's initiative versus human efforts in salvation (George, 195).
14. The christological substructure in Galatians concerns Christ acting in relation to people, not God (Oakes, 88–89).
15. No early church fathers read the passage as subj. They do not seem to be aware of that interpretation as an option (Soards and Pursiful, 92). They normally interpret it as an obj. gen. (deSilva, 233; Keener, 178).
16. Paul nowhere else speaks of Christ's faithful life of "obedience" with the word πίστις (Schreiner, 165).
17. Reliance upon the salvation-historical reading of Gal 3:22, 25 for the subjective view is problematic because it pits redemptive history against anthropology. They can be held together as complementary with the objective view: "Faith in Christ becomes a reality when he arrives and fulfills God's saving promises" (Schreiner, 165).
18. Reliance upon the salvation-historical reading of Gal 3:22, 25 for the subjective view ignores the primacy of Abraham's faith for Paul's argument. It points both forward and backwards in the text, controlling references to faith from Gal 2:16 to 3:22 (Moo, 47).

The subj. gen. view is the more recent interpretation. It construes the gen. name as the subject of the verbal idea in the noun πίστις. The translation "faith of Christ" is itself somewhat ambiguous, so this concept is normally unpacked as "Christ's faithfulness," that is, the faithfulness that Christ exercised, his faithful ministry that accomplished God's redemptive activity. Following is evidence in support of this view:

1. It parallels well the "faith of Abraham," that is, the faith he exercised toward God, as Paul discusses it in Gal 3:6–9 (deSilva, 230).
2. In Rom 3:3 τὴν πίστιν τοῦ θεοῦ clearly means "the faithfulness of God" (Schreiner, 164).

3. In Rom 4:12 the phrase πίστεως τοῦ πατρὸς ἡμῶν Ἀβραάμ means "the faith which our father Abraham exercised" (Schreiner, 164).
4. A subj. gen. here would be parallel to ἐκ πίστεως Ἀβραάμ, "the faithfulness of Abraham," in Rom 4:16 (Soards and Pursiful, 92).
5. Construing πίστεως Ἰησοῦ Χριστοῦ as a subj. gen. avoids redundancy with the construction εἰς Χριστὸν Ἰησοῦν ἐπιστεύσαμεν, the main assertion of the sentence (Soards and Pursiful, 92; deSilva, 230).
6. Construing this as subjective points to an objective act, namely, his death on the cross (de Boer, 148–50), which Paul has referenced already in Gal 1:4 and will reference in 2:20, the immediately following context.
7. In 3:22 the phrase πίστεως Ἰησοῦ Χριστοῦ is used. The context following that passage seems to personify "faith" as Christ himself. By extension then πίστεως Ἰησοῦ Χριστοῦ would refer to Christ's redemptive activity, requiring the subj. gen. (Matera, 101; Schreiner, 164; de Boer, 148–50; Moo, 46–47).
8. The subj. gen. highlights contrast between Israel's unfaithfulness and Christ's faithfulness in Galatians (Soards and Pursiful, 92).
9. The larger antithesis is not "works of Law" versus "faith in Christ" but Law versus Christ, that is, what the Law accomplishes contrasted with what Christ accomplishes (Witherington, 182).
10. The faithfulness of Christ leading to his death is an early theme in Christian preaching (Soards and Pursiful, 92).
11. Holistic use of the phrase in Paul shows that it refers to the objective basis of the gospel found in Christ's ministry. "Paul uses πίστις Ἰησοῦ Χριστοῦ in his writings to signal the basis for the Christian gospel: that its objective basis is the perfect response of obedience that Jesus rendered to God the Father, both actively in his life and passively in his death" (Longenecker, 87).
12. The broad theological grid of justification is God working through Christ, not human response to that work (Schreiner, 164; Soards and Pursiful, 93–94).
13. The subjective view is preferred as an allusion to the story of Christ's ministry, death, and resurrection. He was faithful even unto death on the cross, and in so doing achieved salvation for humanity (Witherington, 182; Schreiner, 164; Moo, 217).[132]
14. Against the objective view, there is no linguistic requirement that related nouns and verbs get used in the same way (Witherington, 180).
15. Paul does explain the phrase when he uses it in Phil 3:9, which contextually refers to Phil 2:5–11 (Witherington, 180).

---

132. This encapsulates the argument of R. B. Hays, *The Faith of Jesus Christ: An Investigation of the Narrative Substructure of Galatians 3:1–4:11*, SBLDS 56 (Chico, CA: Scholars, 1983). A revised edition of this work was published in 2002.

Even a cursory survey of the evidence briefly presented above shows that this is a very difficult problem to solve. Neither interpretation at present carries the day, and neither has a preponderance of the evidence. Deciding between the two interpretations requires the exegete to weigh the evidence in an exercise of reasoned judgment. Broadly speaking, the evidence can be divided into three types: linguistic, contextual, and theological. The exegete first has to make a judgment call on which type of evidence is most persuasive and then which particular arguments are convincing. In this situation, my approach to exegesis favors linguistic and contextual arguments over broad theological ones on the grounds that the former are more appropriately foundational, immediate, and relevant to the meaning of an utterance.[133] When Paul communicated with the Galatians, he could not rely on their knowledge of what he wrote in Romans because he had not written it yet. Neither could he rely on their understanding of his theological thinking on justification more broadly because they did not know it. He relied instead primarily upon the words as contained in the text of the letter framed on one side by the general Greek linguistic milieu of his time and on the other by the specific relationship and history Paul shared with the Galatians. When push comes to shove, then, as it does here, I favor linguistic arguments proven from their shared Koine milieu and contextual arguments provable from the text of Galatians. On these grounds I favor the objective view, which sees faith directed toward Christ as the referent of the phrase. I find most convincing the linguistic arguments about the similarity of meaning for πίστις and its related verb πιστεύω (#2 above under the objective view), the contextual arguments regarding the balance between "faith of Christ" and "works of the Law" as different human responses to God (#10 above under the objective view), and the primacy of Abraham's faith in God to the argument of the book (#18 above under the objective view). The most difficult evidence against my view is the personification of faith in Gal 3:22, which very likely could refer to Christ himself (#6 above under the subjective view). Ultimately, though, I do not see Christ as the referent in those instances in Gal 3 but instead the individual's response to God in keeping with the broader use of the word πίστις (see "Excursus: Paul's Use of the πιστ- Word Group in Galatians"). Thus I favor the traditional, objective view for πίστεως Ἰησοῦ Χριστοῦ in Gal 2:16. I understand it to mean humanity's response of faith directed toward Christ alone as the basis for a declaration of justification.[134]

---

133. I do not mean that theological arguments never come into play in exegesis. They do so constantly. But when a difficult problem requires that linguistic and contextual evidence be weighed against theological, as is somewhat the case here, I give more weight to the former.

134. For further investigation, a recent, helpful study on this problem is M. F. Bird and P. M. Sprinkle, *The Faith of Jesus Christ: The Pistis Christou Debate: Exegetical, Biblical, and Theological Studies* (Peabody, MA: Hendrickson, 2009).

The Proof of the Spirit (3:1–5)

Textual Notes

3:1 The phrase τῇ ἀληθείᾳ μὴ πείθεσθαι is added in a number of manuscripts, adding the idea of result to the verb ἐβάσκανεν: "Who bewitched you so that you do not obey the truth?" Most likely the addition is secondary. Strong Alexandrian and Western manuscripts support the NA[28] text and omit the phrase (א A B D 33 81 1739 lat sy[p]). Scribes likely added this phrase intentionally as an assimilation to 5:7, as noted in the NA[28] text. As the shorter reading, the text better explains the rise of the variant reading than vice versa. The meaning of the passage is not greatly affected. The addition of the phrase simply makes clear what is obvious from the context.

3:1 The phrase ἐν ὑμῖν is added following the verb προεγράφη in a number of manuscripts. The addition is supported by the Western (D F G it sy[h]) and Byzantine texts. However, the omission of the phrase is supported by many reliable Alexandrian manuscripts (א A B C 33 81 104 1175 1739 1881). Internal considerations are somewhat evenly divided. A scribe may have added the phrase for clarity, but at the same time given the clear use of the relative pronoun to refer to the Galatians a scribe may have removed it as redundant. On the basis of the Alexandrian support for the text reading and the fact it is shorter, the NA[28] text should be accepted as more likely original.

Translation

1 You foolish Galatians![1] Who cast a spell on you for envy?[2]—you before

1. The translation "O foolish Galatians!" (so ESV) although more literal is not clear, contemporary English.
2. With this translation I seek to bridge the gap between a formal rendering of the Greek text—"Who has bewitched you?" (see ESV, NRSV, NASB, NKJV, NIV); "Who has cast a spell on you?" (see NET, CSB, NLT)—and its meaning in context.

whose eyes Jesus Christ was vividly portrayed as crucified![3] **2** This one thing[4] I want to learn from you: Did you receive the Spirit based upon the works of the Law or upon faith in what you heard? **3** Are you so foolish? Having begun by the Spirit, are you now finishing by the flesh? **4** Have you experienced so many things to no avail? **5** So the one who gives you the Spirit and works miracles among you, does he do this based upon the works of the Law or upon faith in what you heard?

Commentary

This paragraph marks a major turning point in the flow of the book. Up to this point Paul was focused on defending his gospel through a recollection of his personal conversion and subsequent activities as an apostle, all of which clarified the nature of his gospel. Here he abruptly shifts his attention to the presenting problem that caused him to write this epistle in the first place. The Galatians had listened to the opponents in their midst. Their allegiance had begun to shift away from Paul's gospel. This defection allowed Paul to highlight the fundamental theological problem that undergirded their defection. In a sense, then, this short, punchy section becomes an introduction, albeit a minor one, to the central topics that he discusses in the remainder of the epistle.

Front and center in this section is the persuasion the opponents exercised on the Galatians, which Paul views as entirely negative. Paul uses the metaphor of witchcraft in v. 1 to show how pernicious the opponents are in pulling the Galatians away from the gospel Paul proclaimed. Both the Galatians and the opponents are castigated for the present state of affairs: the latter for pulling the Galatians away, the former for allowing themselves to be enticed. This implicitly contrasts with Paul's persuasion of the Galatians to believe his gospel, a theme that Paul has touched upon briefly already in the letter (1:10), and one he will broach specifically later (4:13–20).

The fundamental logic of the paragraph centers around the role of the Spirit. The Galatians' reception of the Spirit through faith in Paul's gospel has already invalidated the new direction the opponents want the Galatians to go. The Galatians had begun their new lives in God's family through faith in Christ, and God graciously gave them the Spirit. This gift serves as proof that Paul's gospel was right and the gospel of the opponents was wrong. The work of the Spirit, given graciously by God, showed they were on the

3. In the Greek text this entire sentence is a question, but I have separated the relative clause to showcase its adj. function. Many translations create an entirely new sentence, as NET "Who has cast a spell on you? Before your eyes Jesus Christ was vividly portrayed as crucified!"

4. This translation for τοῦτο μόνον (cf. "just one thing" in NIV) is appropriately emphatic.

right track and had now veered off course. This mention of the Spirit also previews the central argument Paul makes in the next two chapters, namely, the importance of the Spirit within the present work of God in Christ. This is Paul's trump card. No one would deny the work of the Spirit in the midst of the Galatians; their own experience should have convinced them of the truth of Paul's gospel (Dunn, 151). Paul constructs his argument such that the Galatians themselves, because of their own experiences, will have to affirm his gospel (Soards and Pursiful, 119).

A fundamental interpretive problem with this section is how v. 6 connects: Does this verse connect to the preceding material, so that the first paragraph is vv. 1–6, or is it better to take it with the following material so that the first paragraph is vv. 1–5? In either case there is strong continuity between this paragraph and the next; no division should be regarded as a strong disjunction. Taking v. 6 as connected to the previous material construes it as a conclusion to vv. 1–5. The adv. καθώς would naturally link v. 6 with vv. 1–5 in a comparison (so deSilva, 266). The Galatians had received the Spirit, and by implication had been justified, just as Abraham had been justified by faith. The example of Abraham in v. 6 would confirm the truth in vv. 1–5 that the Galatians received the Spirit by faith, not by works of the Law. One strength of this view is that it understands καθώς to be functioning as a comparative adv., drawing on thoughts in context, which is a usual function for this word.[5] Here the comparison would be between the Galatians' reception of the Spirit and Abraham's justification. Another strength of this interpretation is that it reflects the close, conceptual connection between v. 6 and vv. 1–5. Paul has just explained that the Galatians received the Spirit by faith, which was confirmation of their justification (Moo, 188). Abraham was justified the same way—by faith. One weakness of this view is that Paul speaks specifically of the reception of the Spirit, something Paul does not attribute to Abraham. This makes the connection looser than καθώς might naturally imply. Another weakness is the presence of the inferential particle ἄρα in v. 7. This particle makes a strong connection between vv. 6 and 7, which consequently draws v. 6 more closely to the following material.

Those who take v. 6 to be more closely connected with the following material differ on their reasoning. Longenecker, 112, takes καθώς here as an *exemplum*, that is, Paul is saying, "take Abraham for example." Even if this is a legitimate category, it is rare.[6] As such, this option seems unlikely. Another view understands καθώς to be a shortened form of an introductory formula καθώς γέγραπται, "just as it is written" (Betz, 140). However, Paul does not do this elsewhere with καθώς. Furthermore, that would mean that "Abraham" is the first word of the quotation. This is possible, but the verb precedes Abraham in the LXX text. One view understands καθώς "to connect

5. BDAG, 493.

6. Neither MGS, 1009, nor BDAG, 493–94, lists this as a category. LSJ, 857, does not list this under καθώς, but it is possible under καθά (p. 848).

what he has just said to what he will now say" (Martyn, 296), the prior material forming some logical basis for the following. Verses 6–9 would all hang together by using Abraham as the example and basis for arguing that justification and reception of the Spirit are by faith and not works. Since vv. 7–9 have Abraham as their focus, it also seems natural to include v. 6 with them, which begins the argument from Abraham's example. The weakness of this view is that *καθώς* is normally used to compare to prior thoughts in the context (Moo, 187). However, this weakness can be overcome when one sees v. 6 as a "Janus" in that it faces both directions, connecting closely to the preceding and following material at the same time (Moo, 187). It certainly is drawing on thoughts in the prior context, but it shows a tighter logical and grammatical connection with following material. Taking v. 6 as more closely connected with vv. 7–9 on the whole seems preferable. This does not deny a connection with prior material. It indeed presents a basis for Paul's statements in vv. 1–5, but it is primarily connected with vv. 7–9.

3:1 *Ὦ ἀνόητοι Γαλάται, τίς ὑμᾶς ἐβάσκανεν.* Verse 1 begins with the interjection Ὦ, indicating a high level of emotion.[7] The interjection indicates Paul's astonishment that the Galatians are beginning to take on the Law. This statement revisits his initial emotion expressed in 1:6–9. The remainder of this paragraph spells out why the Galatians' movement toward observing the Law was so astonishing. The adj. *ἀνόητος* means "unintelligent, foolish, dull witted."[8] Paul uses this same adj. in Titus 3:3 to describe the "intellectual and spiritual condition of people before becoming Christians."[9] The Galatians, who should know better, have begun to lapse into their prior condition before conversion.[10]

To put a point on his feelings, Paul asks the Galatians a powerful rhetorical question: *τίς ὑμᾶς ἐβάσκανεν*, "Who cast a spell on you for envy?" There are two options for the meaning of the verb *ἐβάσκανεν* here. It can refer to bewitching, as with the evil eye.[11] The point of the word would be the speed of the Galatians' defection from the gospel. It was so quick and astonishing to Paul (see 1:6) that it was as if they had come under someone's spell. There are good reasons, however, to argue that Paul is using the word here in the sense of "envy."[12] This is the meaning of the word group in the LXX (see Prov 23:6;

---

7. See D. B. Wallace, *Greek Grammar Beyond the Basics: An Exegetical Syntax of the New Testament* (Grand Rapids: Zondervan, 1996), 56–58.

8. BDAG, 84.

9. BDAG, 84.

10. Longenecker, 100, identifies an important parallel to Paul's wording in Luke 24:25, where *ὦ ἀνόητοι καὶ βραδεῖς τῇ καρδίᾳ* ("you foolish and slow of heart") stresses "lack of discernment regarding the prophetic word."

11. BDAG, 171.

12. BDAG, 171.

28:22; Sir 14:6, 8; Deut 28:54, 56).[13] It is used to translate the phrase רע עין, "evil eye," which refers to looking on something with envy. Josephus, Philo, and the Apostolic Fathers use the word with that sense,[14] and this meaning occurs in wider Koine literature.[15] In light of that wide usage, it seems best to see this verb as ultimately meaning "cast an envious eye." The point of the metaphor would be the harm that the envious eye can cause upon the one on whom it is cast, which is certainly the case here. The false teachers have seen the freedom the Galatians had in Christ, specifically in their experience of the Spirit without obedience to the Law (so Dunn, 152); they "cast an envious eye upon" them and thus convinced them to put themselves back under the Law.[16]

οἷς κατ' ὀφθαλμοὺς Ἰησοῦς Χριστὸς προεγράφη ἐσταυρωμένος; This relative clause further grounds Paul's attitude and emotion, giving a reason why the harmful effect of the "envious eye" of the false teachers upon the Galatians was so astonishing. The Galatians are described as those "before whose eyes Jesus Christ was publicly portrayed as crucified." Paul's presentation of the gospel to the Galatians was so clear, it was as if they had been eyewitnesses to the crucifixion of Christ. They had previously been inoculated; how could they now succumb to this sickness? Paul uses the noun ὀφθαλμούς here in contrast to the "envious eye" of the false teachers. This is rhetorically useful: The solution to the effect of the evil eye is found in what the Galatians saw with their own eyes, so to speak (similarly Lightfoot, 134; Moo, 182). The verb προεγράφη can simply mean "to write beforehand, previously,"[17] which is the sense Paul uses for the word in Rom 15:4 and Eph 3:3, the only other occurrences of this word in his writings. However, that meaning does not fit the context here given the focus on his own oral proclamation among the

---

13. The possible exception of Wis 4:12 should still be given the sense of "envy, begrudge," since the following line concerns "roving passions."

14. *NIDNTTE*, 1:491–93.

15. See, e.g., Strabo, *Geogrraphy* 14.2.7.

16. See J. H. Elliott, "Social-Scientific Criticism: Perspective, Process and Payoff: Evil Eye Accusation at Galatia as Illustration of the Method," *HTS Teologiese Studies/Theological Studies* 67 (2011): 1–10, and Oakes, 101–2, for arguments that the actual evil eye is in view. For the opposite view, see Burton, 144; Betz, 131; Hays, 250; de Boer, 170; Soards and Pursiful, 120; deSilva, 267. It is highly unlikely that Paul would have in mind here literal, actual magic given the very Jewish nature and practice of his opponents, their emphasis upon the Law, and the Law's admonitions against witchcraft. But this does help interpret his metaphor: It is as if his opponents had indeed practiced witchcraft. The metaphor rails against them as much as it does against the Galatians. For a similar view see Witherington, 201–4.

17. BDAG, 867.

Galatians.[18] The word can mean "to proscribe, mark out for judgment."[19] This is the meaning in Jude 4, clarified there by the presence of the prepositional phrase εἰς τοῦτο τὸ κρίμα.[20] That meaning is not likely here because no such clarification exists in Gal 3:1. It seems best then to understand προεγράφη in this passage to mean "to set forth publicly, to placard."[21] Paul uses the aor. tense to point back to his public portrayal of Christ when he preached in Galatia. The sense would be that Christ had been so clearly proclaimed to the Galatians through Paul's preaching that they had perceived the equivalent of a ubiquitous public notice, like a huge billboard that cannot be missed as one heads down the freeway. With this word there also comes condemnation, as the Galatians could not blame their defection on any misunderstanding or lack of knowledge. The message was crystal clear. "This is the indictment against the Galatians: all this placarding was so plain to the eye, and yet they acted as though they could not see, had no sense to read, could not think what this meant" (Lenski, 124).

The ptc. ἐσταυρωμένος which ends this clause finalizes the rhetorical punch of Paul's admonition. The word acts as a predicate adj., asserting an attendant truth about Jesus Christ. He was not simply proclaimed to the Galatians; he was publicly portrayed before their eyes as "having been crucified." The pf. tense of the ptc. conveys the completed act of Christ's crucifixion with the ongoing result presented vividly as him still on the cross. It is feasible that Paul used the concept of crucifixion as a catchphrase of sorts. His intent was not to focus on the crucifixion alone without the attendant resurrection. Rather, Paul intends "a narrative substructure that recounted the redemptive ministry of Jesus of Nazareth" (Longenecker, 101). Even so, Paul's choice of the pf. ptc. of σταυρόω still carries significance within the argument of Galatians. Paul's emphasis on crucifixion here and elsewhere within Galatians explains theologically the believer's life with God vis-à-vis the world.[22] Relevant for the Galatians' present situation, they needed to see and understand clearly the implications of the crucifixion on their current dalliance with the Law (cf. 2:21; 3:13). The crucifixion proves that the Law

18. *Contra* Hays, 250–51, who argues that Paul uses προγράφω elsewhere to refer to things "written beforehand" in Scripture, e.g., Rom 15:4. Paul may then use this verb to refer to preaching of Christ through interpretation of OT texts, specifically the lament psalms, since the Gospel narratives would not have been written. My impression is that this interpretation is overly subtle. It would be stronger if Paul alluded to a particular passage here.

19. LSJ, 1473; MGS, 1753.

20. BDAG, 867.

21. BDAG, 867. See as well LSJ, 1473, and MGS, 1753, for numerous examples of this meaning.

22. This emphasis in no way denies the importance of the resurrection to Paul. He clearly views the resurrection as essential for salvation (Rom 4:25; 1 Cor 15), and he assumes its central importance throughout the book of Galatians.

no longer pertains to any who would relate to God; Christ completed its work when he died upon the cross. This theological motif both explains Paul's position on the Law and points to the particular practice he desires the Galatians to resume, that is, a Law-free existence because of the power of the gospel. "Paul again invests the fact of the crucifixion with considerable significance. When truly appreciated, the cross of Christ, the manifestation of God's wisdom, power, and grace, should rule out of court the kind of human-oriented law program that the agitators are perpetrating" (Moo, 182).

3:2 τοῦτο μόνον θέλω μαθεῖν ἀφ' ὑμῶν. After castigating the Galatians for turning from his vivid gospel, Paul appeals to their experience of receiving the Spirit from their faith in the gospel, not by the Law, to prove the foolishness of the opponents' promotion of obedience to the latter. The pronoun τοῦτο is an example of *constructio ad sensum*, referring to a conceptual postcedent.[23] It focuses the readers' attention on the rhetorical question to follow. The adj. μόνον here functions adverbially,[24] indicating that the one answer to this question will resolve completely the implied debate Paul has with the Galatians concerning justification and the Law (similarly Bruce, 148; Matera, 112; Hays, 251). The pres. tense verb θέλω is a pres. progressive, focusing on Paul's desire as he writes.[25] It adds emotional presence and power to this context. The prepositional phrase ἀφ' ὑμῶν reidentifies the Galatians as the ones from whom Paul desires the information.[26] By drawing their attention to the question, Paul exercises an important rhetorical strategy: He knows the answer to the question he is about to ask, and the Galatians know it, too. By focusing their attention, he draws them into the discussion, preparing for an affirmative response to the following rhetorical question.[27]

ἐξ ἔργων νόμου τὸ πνεῦμα ἐλάβετε ἢ ἐξ ἀκοῆς πίστεως; This questions presents a crux of Paul's argument, and its importance cannot be overstated. Paul now introduces the Spirit into his interaction with the Galatians. The point of the question is that they are no stranger to the Spirit's work, and their undeniable reception of the Spirit proves that Paul's gospel is right and the agitators' gospel is wrong. The prepositional phrase ἐξ ἔργων νόμου indicates

---

23. See Wallace, *Greek Grammar*, 333–34; S. E. Runge, *Discourse Grammar of the Greek New Testament: A Practical Introduction for Teaching and Exegesis* (Peabody, MA: Hendrickson, 2010), 66.

24. BDAG, 659.

25. B. M. Fanning, *Verbal Aspect in New Testament Greek*, OTM (New York: Oxford University Press, 1990), 201.

26. BDAG, 106; A. T. Robertson, *A Grammar of the Greek New Testament in the Light of Historical Research* (Nashville: Broadman, 1934), 579.

27. Soards and Pursiful, 121, also note this as a rhetorical device because Paul could have easily furnished this information himself.

means.[28] It is placed at the front of the clause for emphasis.[29] Paul desires to contrast ἐξ ἔργων νόμου with the prepositional phrase that completes the sentence. The aor. ἐλάβετε refers to the time in the past when the Galatians received the Spirit; this would have been at their conversion when they first believed the gospel Paul preached.[30] The concept of "receiving the Spirit" was essentially a technical term to refer to conversion and the beginning of Christian discipleship (Dunn, 152–53). This reception of the Spirit on their part was incontrovertible proof that God had accepted the Galatians and nothing more needed to be done (Dunn, 153). So any preaching that required further action on their part to enter the company of God's people or fully participate in his blessings was proven wrong from the start.

The phrase ἢ ἐξ ἀκοῆς πίστεως presents the alternative means of receiving the Spirit in obvious contrast to the Law. The sense of the first two words is not debated. The disjunctive conj. ἤ proposes an opposite to ἔργων νόμου. The prep. ἐκ is functioning in the same way as previous uses, indicating means. The latter two words of the phrase, however, are debated regarding both meaning and grammar. The noun ἀκοῆς could indicate either "the act of hearing" or "the proclamation, message, or report as proclaimed (active) or as heard (passive)."[31] The noun πίστεως could indicate either "the human act of believing" or "that which is believed, meaning the gospel message."[32] The relationship between the two can be understood in a variety of ways: a gen. of quality ("faithful hearing"; Moo, 182–83),[33] a gen. of product ("hearing that produces faith"),[34] a subj. gen. ("a hearing that comes of faith"; Lightfoot, 135), an obj. gen. ("a hearing of faith"),[35] or a gen. of apposition ("hearing that is faith"; Burton, 147; Witherington, 212–13). Resolving these issues requires a number of exegetical decisions. It seems best to view ἀκοή in the passive sense, meaning, "that which is heard" because of clear usage with that sense in Rom 10:16–17 and 1 Thess 2:13 (Martyn, 288; de Boer, 175; Soards and Pursiful, 122).[36] The meaning of the noun πίστις in Galatians arguably is more

28. See H. W. Smyth, *A Greek Grammar for Schools and Colleges* (Cambridge: Harvard University Press, 1956), 378; *contra* BDAG, 297, which categorizes the present usage under cause.

29. See BDF, §472(2).

30. The implied question works because of this clear chronology (George, 211). For this grammatical force of the aor., see Fanning, *Verbal Aspect*, 255–56.

31. See BDAG, 36, and de Boer, 174.

32. BDAG, 819–20. See also de Boer, 174.

33. See BDF, §165.

34. See Wallace, *Greek Grammar*, 106.

35. See BDF, §163.

36. In light of Rom 10:16, Paul's use of ἀκοῆς πίστεως here could ultimately allude to Isa 53:1 (Bruce, 149). The use of ἀκοή in 1 Cor 12:17 refers to the faculty of hearing because of the body metaphor, as does the use in 2 Tim 4:3–4 with its metaphor of "itching the ear." This is *contra* Lightfoot, 135, who argues that ἀκοῆς is best taken as

slippery than one would hope. The first occurrence of the term in 1:23 refers broadly to a system of belief or perhaps even more generally to a way of life as a Christian. Most all other uses in the book are debated as to their meaning. In this present context, the clearest argument for the meaning of πίστις comes from the example of Abraham mentioned in 3:7. The focus there is on the faith he exercised toward God, so the best interpretive option is to consider the same meaning here, that is, faith in Gal 3:1–5 is humanity's response to God when he reveals himself (so also Moo, 182–83; Oakes, 104; Soards and Pursiful, 122). Based on these lexical decisions, the sense of the gen. would be subj: "From the hearing of faith" would mean "through faith exercised toward what you heard." This construal is consistent with the argument Paul makes in the context where he contrasts alternate modes of responding to God. Paul points out that the Galatians previously received the Spirit (v. 2) and that God presently supplies the Spirit and works among them (v. 5) by means of their belief. This also connects to the model of Abraham that Paul mentions in 3:6. He believed what God said to him, and he was declared righteous. Paul's point is that the Galatians have experienced essentially the same thing as Abraham. They believed what God said through Paul's proclamation of the gospel, and they were justified as evidenced by their reception of the Spirit. The obvious answer to the question Paul poses to the Galatians is the latter option he gives: The Galatians received the Spirit by believing in what they heard, not by obeying the Law. Their pneumatological experience is proof that Paul is right and the agitators are not, and it serves as motivation to return to his gospel from obedience to the Law.[37]

3:3 οὕτως ἀνόητοί ἐστε; Paul castigates the Galatians further with another rhetorical question. He repeats the adj. ἀνόητος, found in v. 1 earlier in the paragraph, to describe them again. Paul does not take up this negative description of the Galatians in the abstract. It is practically applicable to them because of their behavior. The adv. οὕτως can function one of two ways. It is either intensive, emphasizing the extent to which the Galatians exhibit the quality of foolishness, or it could refer to the material that follows and indicate manner, describing the way in which the Galatians are foolish, that is, attempting to continue their spiritual life by the flesh.[38] Within the context of this paragraph, given the clarity with which Paul expresses exactly what the Galatians have done by turning to the flesh, it seems best to view οὕτως as emphasizing manner. It expresses the way in which the Galatians are

---

"hearing," not "report," on the grounds that it provides a better contrast with ἔργων and its emphasis on the Galatians' actions.

37. Calvin, 81, and Schreiner, 182, each note that the same argument about the reception of the Spirit is used by Peter in Acts 10:47 and Paul and Barnabas in Acts 15:2, 12. This would suggest an essential unity on this question among the apostles and early church, not immediately clear from a limited reading of Galatians.

38. See BDAG, 742, for both possibilities.

foolish, pointing to the following material (so also Lenski, 127). A somewhat awkward translation that clarifies this nuance is, "Are you foolish in this way, that beginning by the Spirit you now finish by the flesh?"

ἐναρξάμενοι πνεύματι νῦν σαρκὶ ἐπιτελεῖσθε; With this clause Paul identifies the central problem with the Galatians' defection from his gospel: Their flirtation with the Law is illogical, contradictory, and dangerous because it means they are turning from the Spirit who was part and parcel of their salvation through the gospel. The first half of this clause details how they began their spiritual life; the latter half depicts where they are now. Paul does not intend to convey an *ordo salutis* with this phrase, as later he will argue that the Spirit is the blessing given to those who believe in Jesus the Messiah.[39] Rather, this is a general statement about the holistic role of the Spirit in the Galatians' conversion through his preaching and their subsequent growth as a church.[40] Their belief in Paul's gospel ushered in the work of the Spirit in their midst; now they are illogically turning from that, swayed by the opponents. The latter half of the clause focuses on their present situation, emphasized by the adv. νῦν. The dat. noun σαρκί is opposite to πνεύματι, indicating an entirely different mode for living out belief in Christ. The verb ἐπιτελέω means "finish" or "complete."[41] This form could be either midd. or pass. Given the focus on the Galatians' activity relative to their own salvation, it is best to see it as midd. with the emphasis on their own human effort in the context of keeping the Law (so also Lenski, 128).[42] Likely the verb does not have any theological connotations, such as might pertain to sanctification or an eschatological completion of their lives in Christ. Rather, ἐπιτελέω simply provides a contrast to the beginning of the Galatians' faith.

The noun σάρξ conveys many important concepts within the epistle. Paul used it previously in the idiomatic phrase σάρξ καὶ αἷμα to refer to mortal human beings (1:16). The other two prior uses refer to the human life as physical, bodily existence (2:16, 20). The usage at this point in the epistle, however, becomes theologically significant as Paul invests it with more meaning. There are two important points to state here regarding the term. First, Paul intends σάρξ here to be understood figuratively. As a metonymy, flesh

---

39. Similarly Longenecker, 103, who states that this ptc. "takes it for granted that the beginning of the Christian life and the reception of God's Spirit are coterminous."

40. *Contra* Lenski, 127, and Burton, 148, who argue that the lack of the article means that πνεύματι here cannot refer to the Holy Spirit; since both datives lack the article, both are qualitative. However, anarthrous does not equal qualitative. Anarthrous nouns can be indefinite or definite if the context allows. The context in my view is specific enough to make each of these nouns definite, equal to "the flesh [of circumcision]" and "the Spirit [of God]."

41. BDAG, 383.

42. See Lightfoot, 135, who cautiously accepts this as midd. based on extrabiblical comparisons and context, which seem to require a transitive verb. But he acknowledges the midd. voice of this verb is not found elsewhere in the NT or LXX.

in context first refers to the act of circumcision that is done to the flesh (so also Burton, 148; Martyn, 285; de Boer, 177). Paul had previously implied in the discussion of his Jerusalem visit the importance of circumcision to the opponents (see 2:3). Later in the subscription to the epistle he will mention this again explicitly (see 6:12–13). So here he hints at the importance of that issue as a current problem among the Galatian congregations. But circumcision itself refers further to the broader concept of obedience to the Law. Paul will ultimately bring the entirety of the Law into the discussion (see, e.g., 3:10), so circumcision here is not an issue unto itself but a readily recognized requirement of the Law that ultimately invokes the whole of it.[43] Second, by itself the term *σάρξ* within Galatians should not be construed automatically as having a negative connotation that the Galatians would have readily understood. The uses of the term prior to this point in the book would have been understood with neither positive nor negative connotations. The same neutral force is in play here, in this context referring to the physical body, more specifically the foreskin removed through circumcision. As Paul develops his argument in the coming chapters, *σάρξ* will indeed take on negative connotations, but these will be strictly and contextually defined. The Galatians would not have understood those only from the use of the word itself. The point here is to emphasize that the Galatians needed to be educated about the negative power of the flesh; they did not automatically understand that through the use of the term *σάρξ*.[44]

This brings up the related issue of exactly what the opponents were teaching the Galatians. Paul describes it as "finishing by the flesh," but more specificity is needed. Based on the way Paul references circumcision elsewhere in the book (see 2:3; 5:1–6; 6:11–16), they were teaching the Galatians to follow through with circumcision, but exactly how that fit into their theological framework requires further explanation. A general consensus is that the opponents were not denying Paul's gospel outright. Rather, they argued that it was incomplete or immature, such that the Galatians needed to add Law observance to fully become and participate in the people of God. The exact nuances of how Paul's gospel was incomplete are subject to debate. The opponents may have taught that the Mosaic covenant completed the Abrahamic, thus arguing the Law was an important complement to faith in the Messiah (Betz, 136; Rapa, 591). They did not deny "Christ crucified" or the work of the Spirit in their midst. Rather, they claimed the gospel

43. This is *contra* many interpreters who see *σάρξ* as a reference to human effort; see Luther, 128; George, 212; Moo, 184; Soards and Pursiful, 124. I do think Paul ultimately argues that human efforts come to naught before the Lord, but I do not think he does that here with this specific word.

44. *Contra* authors who see a fully formed, Pauline anthropological term here, referring to unregenerate human effort and weakness (Bruce, 149; Fung, 134; Schreiner, 184). Moo, 184, argues that *σάρξ* is best explained with "the typically Pauline sense of human existence, usually set in contrast to the spiritual realm."

proclaimed by Paul was insufficient to complete God's work among them (George, 212–13). This position may have been taken under the influence of the teaching of Jas 2:22, which says ἐκ τῶν ἔργων ἡ πίστις ἐτελειώθη (Betz, 134), or perhaps from a Rabbinic connection between perfection and circumcision in Abraham found in *m. Ned.* 3.11 (Hays, 252). Whatever the foundation for their teaching, the agitators argued that something more needed to be done by the Galatians, in this instance circumcision, to achieve what God wanted for them. Paul's response points out that their reception of the Spirit proves that nothing else is required beyond the faith they had already expressed in the Lord Jesus Christ.

3:4 τοσαῦτα ἐπάθετε εἰκῇ; Paul uses another question to focus the Galatians' attention on their experiences up to this point. At issue is whether the experiences Paul mentions should be understood as positive, neutral, or negative, and this question revolves around the meaning of the term πάσχω. The verb is in the act. voice, but it functions like the pass. form of ποιέω,[45] referring to the subjective experience of some activity. On the one hand, there is evidence that supports the argument that πάσχω is negative, that is, that Paul references some suffering on the part of the Galatians (Lightfoot, 135; Lenski, 129; George, 213; Luther, 129; Hays, 252; Schreiner, 185; Moo, 185).[46] Elsewhere in the New Testament πάσχω means "to suffer" with specific reference to the sufferings of Jesus in the crucifixion.[47] The wider usage of this term in the NT and LXX is uniformly negative (Soards and Pursiful, 125). There are clues that suffering may have been in the background of Paul's interactions with the Galatians. Later in the book in 4:29 and 6:12 Paul mentions persecution; the former is perhaps directed at the Galatians while the latter concerns what the opponents want to avoid. Paul suffered as well when he and Barnabas founded the Galatian churches (Acts 13:50; 14:2, 5, 19; 2 Tim 3:11). Paul even tells the Galatians in Acts 14:22 to expect suffering. This wider context, although not clearly mentioned in the book, suggests with good warrant that the Galatians did experience suffering of some kind, which Paul would have in mind here. On the other hand, the immediate context suggests here a neutral or perhaps even positive meaning of "experience" (Burton, 150; Fung, 133; Matera, 113; Martyn, 285). Paul mentions the Galatians' prior experience of the Spirit in v. 3 and their current experience of him in v. 5. A reference in v. 4 to an experience without any further qualification would naturally rely upon the surrounding verses for semantic content. Relying upon references to suffering in the book is not ultimately helpful because they are only suggestive. The reference to suffering in 4:29 is not decisive for the meaning of the

45. MHT, 3:53.

46. See also J. A. Dunne, "Suffering in Vain: A Study of the Interpretation of Πάσχω in Galatians 3.4," *JSNT* 36 (2013): 3–16.

47. See Matt 16:21; 17:12; Mark 8:31; 9:12; Luke 9:22; 17:25; 22:15; 24:26, 46; Acts 1:3; 3:18; 17:3. Interestingly this verb does not appear at all in the Gospel of John.

term in 3:4 because there the persecution mentioned has a specific meaning within the analogy Paul uses, referring to the interactions of the Galatians with the opponents, not suffering from persecution because of their faith more broadly. The reference to persecution in 6:12 fits within the context of Judea, not Galatia, and those who promote circumcision are the objects of the persecution. Making a decision on this problem forces one to weigh all these factors with none solving the problem decisively. At present I am swayed by the immediate context. Paul gave no clue that persecution was in view, and he did speak clearly about experiencing the Spirit. Given that πάσχω can mean "experience" with a neutral connotation, which fits well the immediate context of the paragraph, that meaning is preferred. With πάσχω, then, Paul refers to the Galatians' experience of the Spirit.[48]

The pronoun τοσαῦτα emphasizes degree, here occurring without a substantive.[49] It can have a qualitative meaning ("such great things") or a quantitative one ("so much, so many things").[50] Here it is more likely qualitative since the emphasis is not on the number of things the Galatians experienced but on their quality, especially in regards to their connection to the Spirit. The adv. εἰκῇ which modifies ἐπάθετε means "without success or result."[51] Paul's intent with this language is not to cast doubt upon the veracity of their initial experience of the Spirit but rather to show up their own obstinance in rejecting his work. Since Paul believes that the Galatians genuinely received the Spirit, it is striking to him that the Galatians would accept the message of the opponents, in essence rejecting that same Spirit. Paul is not satisfied with people believing in Christ but then not progressing in their new existence with God in Christ. For the Galatians not to adhere to Paul's gospel would mean they had experienced the Spirit (v. 3) and God's work among them (v. 5) with no effect.

εἴ γε καὶ εἰκῇ. With this short phrase Paul expresses a complex, implied argument. He writes the protasis of a second class, contrary-to-fact condition: "if indeed without result ..." The main verb of the protasis is itself implied. Likely Paul intends the central affirmation of the prior line to be implied here: "if indeed [you experienced such things] without result." The apodosis of this conditional sentence is not expressed at all. Based upon the context there are two likely options for Paul's logic: Paul's ministry among the Galatians was itself in vain, or the Spirit's work among the Galatians was in vain. The latter is preferred given the emphasis on the Spirit in this paragraph. In order to sort out what Paul intends to convey, the logical function of the second class condition should be considered. The second class condition asserts a non-reality in the protasis, something contrary to fact, in order

---

48. See M. Silva, *Interpreting Galatians: Explorations in Exegetical Method* (Grand Rapids: Baker, 2001), 57–58, for a helpful discussion of this problem.

49. Robertson, *Grammar*, 710.

50. BDAG, 1012.

51. BDAG, 281.

to draw a non-real logical conclusion in the apodosis that itself is contrary to fact. The rhetorical function of the second class condition then inverts these ideas: The converse of the apodosis is actually affirmed, which in turn affirms the converse of the protasis. In this case, the converse of the unfruitful work of the Spirit is affirmed, which in turns casts doubt upon the reality of the protasis, that is, it is doubtful that the Galatians did indeed experience these things to no effect. The argument of the logic could be laid out in the following manner with brackets indicating implied elements:

> What Paul states with the second class condition:
> IF: you experienced the Spirit without result
> [THEN: the Spirit's work among you was in vain.]
>
> What Paul implies further with the second class condition:
> [BUT: the Spirit's work among you was not in vain.]
> [Implied Warrant: because you are now really in God's family.]
> [SO: You did not experience the Spirit without result!]

So Paul's ultimate affirmation is that the Galatians did indeed experience the Spirit with blessed results. The presence of *γε καί* serves to intensify the expression.[52] That there is an unwillingness to believe on the part of the speaker may be true (Lightfoot, 135; Longenecker, 104–5), but Paul's use of the same phrase in 2 Cor 5:3 shows this may not be the case. Paul holds out hope that the Galatians have not believed in vain and that they will listen to Paul and resist the agitators on the basis of what God had already done in their midst through the Spirit.

3:5 *ὁ οὖν ἐπιχορηγῶν ὑμῖν τὸ πνεῦμα καὶ ἐνεργῶν δυνάμεις ἐν ὑμῖν.* With this sentence Paul draws a conclusion to his preceding argument. It both summarizes and recapitulates vv. 2–4 (Moo, 186). Paul intends to show again the illegitimacy of the Galatians' turning to the Law by tracing his logic back to the action of God himself. The use of this question here helps Paul's argument, as the Galatians must answer in the affirmative (Betz, 135). The first part of the verse focuses squarely on God's activity in their midst. The central grammatical construction is a TSKS[53] construction: The ptcs. ἐπιχορηγῶν and ἐνεργῶν are each governed by the single article ὁ. The Granville Sharp rule applies here because neither substantive is impersonal, pl., or a proper name.[54] Therefore, both ptcs. refer to the same entity (so also Longenecker, 105),[55] namely God, whom Paul will later identify in this chapter as the one who gives the Spirit as fulfillment of the blessings promised to Abraham. So at the same time Paul references both what God did among the Galatians and what he does presently through fulfillment of his promises. The verb ἐπιχορεγέω is

---

52. BDF, §439(2).

53. See n46 on page 79.

54. Wallace, *Greek Grammar*, 272.

55. Wallace, *Greek Grammar*, 274–75.

often used to indicate the fulfillment of a responsibility, implying that God giving the Spirit is in perfect accordance with his nature and plan (Dunn, 157). The acc. noun δυνάμεις is the dir. obj. of the substantive ptc. ἐνεργῶν; it here means "powerful act, miracle."[56] Paul identifies God's miraculous acts among the Galatians as proof of the veracity of his gospel.[57] The pres. tense of the ptcs. is significant given Paul's emphasis upon the Galatians' past experiences earlier in the paragraph.[58] With them Paul vividly highlights God's present actions among the Galatians.

ἐξ ἔργων νόμου ἢ ἐξ ἀκοῆς πίστεως; As in v. 2, Paul juxtaposes the two central ideas that come into conflict in this epistle: obedience to the works of the Law on the one hand, and a simple response of faith to his gospel on the other. For discussion on the first phrase, see the commentary on 2:16. For discussion of the latter phrase, see the commentary on 3:2. These phrases are connected to the prior ptc. phrases logically as the two alternates means by which God realizes his actions on behalf of the Galatians. The main verb for the entirety of the verse must be supplied; since the focus is on the basis of God's activity, something like ἐποίησεν is appropriate. Paul asks a question concerning the basis upon which God supplied the Spirit and worked wonders among the Galatians. The answer to this question gives further evidence to support Paul's overarching purposes in the epistle. The obvious answer to Paul's question is again the second of the two choices: The means by which God acts among the Galatians was their belief in Paul's gospel. Thus Paul affirms his gospel, defends his apostleship, and supplies further motivation for the Galatians to remain faithful to his gospel.

Essential to understanding Paul's point in this paragraph are some underdeveloped elements of his logic. First, the awesome work of the Spirit in the midst of the Galatians is assumed, not argued or explained. Paul does not delve into this point with any detail because both he and the Galatians know to what he refers. At a minimum, in response to the Galatians' belief in Paul's gospel, there was a tangible, identifiable manifestation of the Spirit in their congregations. He can point to this as a plank of his argument without any supporting evidence, implying that there was mutual agreement that this was a reality without dispute. Second, Paul regarded the reception of the Spirit and his work in the midst of the Galatians as evidence of their salvation. This reception of the Spirit took place at the beginning of their Christian lives when Paul preached among them; it was based on their faith in his gospel. There is a direct connection between belief in the gospel, the salvation granted, and the work of the Spirit. Third, depending upon removal of the foreskin of the flesh for continuation of the spiritual life is antithetical

---

56. BDAG, 262.

57. Burton, 151, argues as well that Paul has in mind the "charismatic manifestation of the Spirit," but Paul also attributes inward, moral change to the Spirit (5:22–23), so the latter cannot be totally excluded.

58. See προεγράφη in v. 1, ἐλάβετε in v. 2, ἐναρξάμενοι in v. 3, ἐπάθετε in v. 4.

and contradictory to the work of the Spirit and by extension to the gospel Paul proclaimed. Indeed, dependence upon the flesh negates the work of the Spirit. All of these points lead to Paul's astonishment at the Galatians: It makes no sense having begun with the Spirit to attempt to complete their salvation by the flesh.

Theological Comments

Much of the spiritual reality of what Paul expresses in this passage can be summarized in the statement, "God through Christ sends the Spirit to believers in response to faith in the gospel." In this passage Paul highlights the tangible results of the reception of the Spirit due to the Galatians' faith in the gospel as an implicit proof that his gospel is God-ordained. As such, there are some very important theological deductions to draw regarding what Paul has claimed.

First, the work of God among the Galatians is expressly Trinitarian in description and outworking. Each member of the Godhead is involved in bringing the Galatians into God's family. This shows the full extent of God's divine plan to redeem his people and ultimately the world. It is clear in Paul's mind that God the Father is ultimately behind the salvation of the Galatians. Paul intends God the Father in v. 5 as the referent of "the one who gives the Spirit and performs miracles among you." Paul explains to the Galatians that the wonderful events that transpired as a result of their faith in the gospel come directly from God himself. The proclamation of the gospel centers upon Christ crucified, and it is in him the Galatians placed their faith. It is his work on the cross that opened the door for the Galatians to believe, and it is his person in whom the Galatians now live. The result of faith in the crucified Christ is the Galatians' reception of the Spirit. God the Spirit provides the confirmation of the salvation graciously granted in Christ.

Second, there is a strong focus on God's activity in the Galatians' receipt of the gospel. Often the work of God can be described as mysterious, but here Paul describes him as acting in discernible ways. The work of God is pneumatic, by which I mean that it is focused on the Spirit. Wrestling with pneumatology, and Paul's own expression of that teaching, is often challenging in the biblical text, but not here. In response to the Galatians' faith God sends the Spirit, and as Paul will soon explain this marks the fulfillment of all God's promises to Abraham. The sending of the Spirit is a decisive moment in salvation history that cannot be ignored, minimized, or mitigated. The work of God is also miraculous. Paul specifically mentions "miracles" among the Galatians, wrought by God. He offers no explanation as to what these miracles were, nor by what means they came, but his theological explanation clearly sees them as a work of God.

Third, the tangible presence of the Spirit among the Galatians is proof of two very important points. It is implicit proof of the Galatians' salvation—that through Paul's gospel, which they believed, God had worked his intended effect, saving them from the effects of their sin, from the false gods to which they had been enslaved. It is also explicit proof that Paul's gospel was the only gospel. The false gospel of the agitators that required obedience to the Law offered nothing in return, while God through Paul's gospel offers the life-giving Spirit.

Application and Devotional Implications

Continuing with the statement "God through Christ sends the Spirit to believers in response to faith in the gospel," the proper response of believers to this truth can be identified through interaction with its constituent parts.

First, *God ... sends.* Paul does not know a god who has disconnected himself from his world, passively watching it work as a watchmaker might gaze upon a complication. Instead, he presents God as active, a being with goals and intentions who works to bring them about. God is intimately involved in this world, working specifically in the lives of the Galatians. God continues to work in our lives today. He is immanent and active, seeking to save those he created in accordance with his will.

Second, God sends *through Christ.* The central focus of God's work in the world is the ministry of Christ. It is he who is proclaimed in the gospel, offered to the Galatians and by extension to the world as the savior. It was he who was "publicly placarded" before the Galatians as the crucified Lord, and it is he who brings salvation to those who believe.

Third, God through Christ *sends the Spirit to believers.* It is important to note that Paul does not simply describe God as saving the Galatians, without means or mode. Rather, God acts in specific ways. God's action of sending the Spirit to the Galatian believers places the Spirit as a central reality of the Christian life, the primary means and mode. To be Christian, "in Christ" as Paul expresses it, means that God gives the Spirit to powerfully affect and change the destiny of the individual. The Spirit's influence is measurable, tangible, and undeniable.[59]

Fourth, God through Christ sends the Spirit to believers *in response to faith in the gospel.* Something very real had transpired among the Galatians as a result of their expression of faith in Christ through the gospel Paul preached to them. This becomes on the one hand a powerful proof that the gospel they had heard was God-ordained and approved and on the other hand an implicit argument against any other means to access this eschatological blessing of God in Christ. This is a central truth directly applicable

59. Hays, 253–54, argues that Paul points to the experience of the Spirit as "independently self-validating," which is shocking to Christians who have not had "a living experience of the power of the Spirit." This power of the Spirit becomes the means by which to organize the Christian experience instead of race, nation, gender, or any other human characteristic.

to believers today. Our life from God in Christ with the Spirit is rooted, enabled, and advanced only through faith in the gospel Paul preached. Any requirement for action in order to manifest that life is misguided, placing the behavioral cart before the soteriological horse.

Additional Exegetical Comments

3:1 Moo, 181, argues the true meaning of *βασκαίνω* lies in between literal witchcraft on the one hand and simple metaphor on the other. In his view, Paul does not mean they were under the influence of a sorcerer or any type of magic, but there likely was "an evil spiritual influence" behind their quick defection. Beyond the subtlety of this view, the difficulty lies in the fact that Paul never uses this language elsewhere to discuss what he regards as true, evil, spiritual influences.

Selected Bibliography

Dunne, J. A. "Suffering in Vain: A Study of the Interpretation of Πάσχω in Galatians 3.4." *JSNT* 36 (2013): 3–16.

Elliott, J. H. "Social-Scientific Criticism: Perspective, Process and Payoff: Evil Eye Accusation at Galatia as Illustration of the Method." *HTS Teologiese Studies/Theological Studies* 67 (2011): 1–10.

Fanning, B. M. *Verbal Aspect in New Testament Greek*. OTM. New York: Oxford University Press, 1990.

The Identity of "Sons of Abraham" (3:6–14)

Textual Notes

3:7 The NA[28] text reads οὗτοι υἱοί εἰσιν Ἀβραάμ while the majority of manuscripts have the word order οὗτοι εἰσιν υἱοί Ἀβραάμ. The latter reading is certainly the more natural one, as it does not separate the predicate nom. υἱοί from its gen. adjunct Ἀβραάμ. It is also clearer: It can be understood only as "These are the sons of Abraham," but the text reading could be either "These sons are of Abraham," which weakens Paul's logical deduction, or more naturally "These are sons of Abraham." The variant word order is found in ℵ² A C D 33 1739 1881 𝔐 latt; the reading of NA[28] is found in 𝔓⁴⁶ ℵ* B 81 326 2464 and a few others. The variant has geographical distribution across all text types and strong genealogical solidarity in the Western and Byzantine texts. It is also Alexandrian, but the witness of A and C puts this within the secondary Alexandrian stream. This evidence shows that the variant is certainly an ancient reading, but it is not the absolute best in terms of pedigree. The reading of NA[28] finds strong support, though, in the primary Alexandrian stream with the support of 𝔓⁴⁶ ℵ* and B and could be preferred on those grounds alone.[1] What makes the text reading an even stronger candidate

1. Secondary Alexandrian is the term currently used to describe manuscripts that exhibit Alexandrian readings as a whole but at the same time show readings that align with a pre-Byzantine, non-Western text. B. F. Westcott and F. J. A. Hort originally used the terms neutral and Alexandrian to refer to what are now commonly known as the primary Alexandrian and secondary Alexandrian text types; see B. F. Westcott and F. J. A. Hort, *Introduction to the New Testament in the Original Greek* (Cambridge: Macmillan, 1881), 126–32. K. Aland and B. Aland have used the terms Alexandrian and Egyptian respectively; see K. Aland and B. Aland, *The Text of the New Testament: An Introduction to the Critical Editions and to the Theory and Practice of Modern Textual Criticism*, trans. E. F. Rhodes (Grand Rapids: Eerdmans, 1989). Practically speaking, when the Alexandrian text splits into primary and secondary streams within any one particular textual problem, as it does here, the primary Alexandrian should be favored over the secondary Alexandrian because of its purer, less contaminated text.

for the original is that it better explains the rise of the other: Scribes would very naturally change the ambiguous word order to the clearer reading of the variant rather than introduce ambiguity where none was before. So on the basis of both external and internal evidence, the reading of NA[28] should be preferred as more likely original.

3:14 In his conclusion to this extended argument from Scripture, Paul includes two purpose statements, the first of which speaks of "the blessing of Abraham," the second of which speaks of "the promise of the Spirit." Several manuscripts read instead *τὴν εὐλογίαν τοῦ πνεύματος*, "the blessing of the Spirit." This variant presents a significant difference in meaning: The former implies predetermination on the part of God and a prophetic connection to the OT; the latter removes these nuances and focuses solely on the present experience. The variant reading is supported by a small but significant number of witnesses (𝔓[46] D[*,c] F G b vg[ms], Marcion, Ambrosiaster). It could readily be dismissed as simply a Western reading were it not for the witness of 𝔓[46], one of the oldest Alexandrian witnesses to Paul's text. Even so, the reading "promise of the Spirit," the text of NA[28], has more extensive support across all text types (א A B C K L 33 1739 𝔐 lat et al.) and should be preferred on external grounds. The internal logic of the variant does warrant consideration: Paul previously in 3:5 spoke of God giving the Spirit to the Galatians, without any reference to promise in that context. "Blessing" would be an appropriate noun to use then in the conclusion of this argument. This logic does not overcome two important factors, however: The importance of "promises" in Paul's subsequent argument argues for its originality here, and scribes would be more likely to change *ἐπαγγελίαν* to *εὐλογίαν* under the influence of the first purpose clause in v. 14, which creates symmetry between the clauses, than to change in the other direction, removing the repetition. So on both external and internal grounds the reading *ἐπαγγελίαν* is preferred as the original reading.

Translation

6 Just as Abraham believed God, and it was counted to him as righteousness,
7 thus you know that those who are justified by faith, these people are sons
of Abraham! **8** And the Scripture, because it knew beforehand that God
justifies[2] the Gentiles by faith, announced the good news beforehand to
Abraham that "all the nations will be blessed through you."[3] **9** Thus those
who are justified by faith are blessed along with believing Abraham. **10** For as

2. The wording "would justify" is used by many translations in keeping with contemporary English style. However, given that Paul's use of the pres. tense here is intentional (see the exegesis), I chose the pres. tense in English to convey its importance.

3. The translation "through you" (see also CSB, NIV, NLT) conveys means more clearly than "in you" (NET, ESV, NRSV, NASB, NKJV).

many who are justified by works of the Law are under a curse, for it is written, "Cursed is everyone who does not remain in all the things that are written in the book of the Law to do them." **11** And that no one is justified before God by the Law is clear because "the righteous will live by faith."[4] **12** And the Law is not based on faith. Rather, "the one who does them will live by them." **13** Christ redeemed us from the curse of the Law by becoming a curse for us (because it is written, "Cursed is everyone who is hung on a tree") **14** so that the blessing of Abraham would come to the Gentiles in Christ Jesus, so that we might receive the promise of the Spirit through faith

Commentary

With this paragraph Paul begins the central argument of the book, which amounts to an exegetical, theological, and hermeneutical defense of his insistent stance that the truth of the gospel means that Gentiles can be incorporated into God's people without any requirement of obedience to the Jewish Law. The first major part of his argument, which took up the first two chapters of the book, was based on his personal experience and authority as an apostle. This second major part of the argument, also extending for two chapters, dives into the authoritative texts both he and the opponents regarded as foundational and determinative.[5] Paul argues exegetically about the meaning of key biblical texts to support his assertions about the exclusivity of faith as the means for the Gentiles' personal experience of and relationship to God.[6] Paul's argument is also theological because he reads these texts in light of the entire revelation of God in Christ. He finds evidence to support his stance within Abraham's story itself to assert that the only requirement to become part of God's people is to be a child of Abraham, but this relationship to Abraham is established only on the basis of faith in Christ, not because of obedience to the Law. Paul also interprets these passages with a hermeneutical stance distinct from his opponents, but one arguably and appreciably better. He and the opponents agree on textual meaning in key places, but Paul properly organizes the meaning in light of God's entire actions in Christ, arriving

4. This translation is similar to NASB and NKJV in that it clearly treats the ὅτι clause as the subject and δῆλον as the predicate.

5. Dunn, 159, regards this new section as Paul's third line of argument: "first, the agreement on the gospel reached at Jerusalem (2:1–10); second, their own experience of the Spirit (3:1–5); and now, third, the proof from scripture (3:6–4:31)." I regard 3:1–5 as more closely connected to 3:6–14 because of the concluding reference to the Spirit in v. 14 (so also Longenecker, 109).

6. Martyn, 295, argues that Paul's writing here is "fundamentally exegetical."

at a different conclusion.[7] Paul plays ball on his opponents' court by using their terminology and concepts—indeed Paul founds his argument on the very biblical story to which they likely referred to support the requirement of circumcision—but he plays better ball than they do (similarly Longenecker, 109). Paul takes the same story and the same evidence but interprets it properly to show that his opponents are in fact wrong in their conclusions about the gospel and he is right.[8]

It has been argued that here Paul is in the midst of one of the more important sections of rhetorical discourse called the *probatio* in which proofs and evidence for the assertions advanced by the speaker are given. In Galatians this would be the second part of this important section (Betz, 128, 137; Longenecker, 108). However, it is also evident from the content itself that Paul has changed his emphasis and moved to a new rhetorical strategy. His citation of Scripture before this point was practically non-existent.[9] Now in chapter 3 Paul cites Scripture multiple times (vv. 6, 8, 10, 11, 12, 13, 16). These Scriptures connect key concepts in his argument (Dunn, 159). He moves from the language of his reality and experience to the language of citation and argumentation.[10] Even though there is good evidence that the structure of Galatians does indeed follow this convention of classical rhetoric, this convention need not be understood explicitly to follow Paul's argument.

Paul's central thesis is that Gentiles are sons of Abraham by faith, proof of which is in the promised blessing, namely, their receipt of the gift of the Spirit.[11] The argument progresses with three sense units (de Boer, 185): In vv. 6–9 Paul identifies those who have faith in Jesus as sons of Abraham; in vv. 10–12 he identifies those who depend on the Law as under a curse; in vv. 13–14 he points to the redemption accomplished by Christ that removes

---

7. See Hays, 254, although he sees the major section as extending only through the end of chapter 3. Martyn, 296, essentially agrees that hermeneutics is in play when he states that through his exegesis Paul shows he has a fundamentally different "frame of reference" than the opponents.

8. See C. K. Barrett, "Allegory of Abraham, Sarah, and Hagar in the Argument of Galatians," in *Rechtfertigung: Festschrift für Ernst Käsemann z 70 Geburtstag* (Tübingen: Mohr Siebeck, 1976), 1–16, for the argument that most all of Paul's citations of the OT in Galatians (save Deut 21:23 in Gal 3:13) are corrections of exegesis of his opponents. This article has confirmed my thinking on many points regarding this issue.

9. The only citation that occurs before this section is Ps 143:2 in Gal 2:16, which is part of the closing theological argument for his personal narrative. That citation is subtle enough that it is debated as to whether it is a citation at all.

10. Longenecker, 108, notes that Paul moves from a Greco-Roman *exemplum* argument to explicitly Jewish argumentation. The takeaway is that Paul is now on a very different track to accomplish his purposes.

11. It is not so much an issue *that* the Gentiles are included in the blessing but *the means* of their inclusion (Moo, 193).

the curse and provides the Spirit. Paul makes this argument both positively and negatively, juxtaposing those who are of faith and those who are of works of the Law. He addresses the positive situation of the former first by referring to two different Scriptures central to Abraham's story, Gen 15:6 and 12:3. Then Paul draws a logical deduction both informed by the present situation of the Gentiles' faith and drawn from the meaning of the Scripture citations themselves to assert that Gentiles are sons of Abraham solely on the basis of that faith, not in any way because of their obedience to the Jewish Law. They need nothing further from the opponents to maintain or perfect that relationship (Longenecker, 124). Then he turns to address the logical corollary, namely, the negative situation of those who are of works of the Law by citing Deut 27:26; Hab 2:4; and Lev 18:5. His interpretation of these Scriptures shows that the stance of his opponents is self-defeating and self-condemning. The conclusion of this argument draws together these disparate threads with a citation from Deut 21:23 to show that God's salvific purposes for all people are accomplished in the redemption Christ brought through his death and are effective through the connection by faith to Abraham, not the Law.[12]

3:6 At first reading it is not entirely clear whether this verse should connect to what precedes, dividing 3:1–6 from 7–14, or to what follows, dividing 3:1–5 from 6–14. Verse 5 makes a logical, final statement both in terms of structure and content, then v. 7 begins with a natural use of the conj. ἄρα, implying the beginning of a new deduction in the argument. The conj. καθώς could readily connect v. 6 either to what precedes or to what follows in this context. There are a number of arguments to support placing v. 6 with the following material (so NA[28], NET, NIV). Concerning the function and meaning of καθώς, BDAG places this occurrence of the conj. under the very first category of meaning: "of comparison, just as, w. οὕτως foll." A clarification is supplied, however: "The accompanying clause is somet. to be supplied fr. the context."[13] If this assessment is accurate, the implied sentence could be inferred from what follows as an intermediate step in the logic: "Just as Abraham believed God, and it was counted to him as righteousness, [so also us.] Therefore you know ..." This would create a strong, logical tie with the following material. Another argument for taking v. 6 with what follows is content: The topic shifts at this point from the Galatians' errors to the faith of Abraham, which is central to the entirety of the discussion that follows. This citation would thus serve to illustrate the solution to the problem that Paul highlights in vv. 1–5 and then transition to the major topic for this part of his argument. In this construal καθώς would retain its relatively normal function

12. I am greatly persuaded on the shape and extent of Paul's argument, which finds practical expression in my division of the paragraph into vv. 6–14 as opposed to vv. 6–9 and 10–14, by M. Silva, *Interpreting Galatians: Explorations in Exegetical Method* (Grand Rapids: Baker, 2001), 218–22.

13. BDAG, 493.

of comparison: Paul would compare Abraham's faith in God, which leads to justification, to the same reality for himself and other believers. Other arguments connect v. 6 with what precedes (so UBS[5], ESV). The wording of v. 7 could be seen as creating a new part of the argument. "The disclosure formula of 3:7 (γινώσκετε ἄρα ὅτι, 'you know, then, that'), which draws a conclusion from the quotation of Gen 15:6 in 3:6, provides a transition to the extended argument from Scripture in 3:6–4:10" (Longenecker, 11). Since the disclosure formula makes a strong beginning, v. 6 more naturally brings the preceding material to an end. Similarly, the conj. ἄρα very often indicates a new discourse segment that draws a conclusion from the preceding material. Its normal use is not to draw a conclusion from a dependent clause, although it can be used in that fashion on occasion (e.g., Gal 2:21). Also, in numerous places Paul concludes an argument with a καθώς clause, frequently with a Scripture citation, although these are mitigated somewhat because almost all use the verb γέγραπται as well.[14] A decision here is not easy, but I am swayed by the similar content in v. 6 and what follows: Abraham's faith and its result is highlighted through the citation in v. 6, and faith and its benefits for all are highlighted in the argument that follows.[15] On that basis I favor the arrangement of the NA[28] text, which has v. 6 joined to the material that follows, but this should not be construed as a strong disjunction.[16] Paul's argument flows almost imperceptibly from one point to another; the reader must recognize that in essence he makes a single, continuous argument.

The citation from Gen 15:6 identifies central evidence for Paul's position on the exclusivity of faith for the Gentiles as the means for a relationship with God. The person of Abraham is the linchpin on which Paul's argument rests. This is certainly in keeping with his Jewish heritage, but Paul emphasizes something about Abraham differently than his tradition. As the progenitor of the Jewish people, Abraham was a frequent *topos* in Jewish literature. Generally two things about him were emphasized: his obedience to the Law, and his conversion to God from idolatry (Dunn, 160; de Boer, 187–88; Garlington 2007, 155; Witherington, 225). Judaism did not ignore Abraham's faith, but it was always joined to keeping covenant: "For Judaism, then, trust in God and obedience to the law were inseparable" (Longenecker, 111). For example, in 1 Macc 2:49–64, Mattathias encourages his sons to remain faithful to the Law, extolling the Law obedience of many OT luminaries, including Abraham (v. 52). The connection between faith in God and

---

14. See Rom 1:17; 2:24; 3:4, 10; 4:17; 8:36; 9:13; 9:29, 33; 10:15; 11:8, 26; 15:3, 9, 21; 1 Cor 1:31; 10:7; 2 Cor 6:16; 8:15; 9:9.

15. Similarly based on content, Schreiner, 189, argues that there is a looser connection with the preceding material than the following because Paul would not argue that Abraham had the Spirit, the gift of the new age (similarly Soards and Pursiful, 127).

16. On this reading the broad semantic range of καθώς allows Paul to use it as a bridge between the two sections (Longenecker, 112). Moo, 187, goes so far to say this verse is a Janus (similarly Oakes, 104).

Law obedience in this passage practically makes them identical. In v. 61 he states, "And so observe, from generation to generation, that none of those who put their trust in him will lack strength" (NRSV), while in v. 64 he states, "My children, be courageous and grow strong in the law, for by it you will gain honor" (NRSV). Sirach 44:19–21 similarly exalts Abraham, specifically because "he kept the law of the Most High, and entered into a covenant with him; he certified the covenant in his flesh, and when he was tested he proved faithful" (v. 20, NRSV). Rabbi Nehorai stated, "We find that the patriarch Abraham kept the entire Torah even before it was revealed, since it says, Since Abraham obeyed my voice and kept my charge, my commandments, my statutes, and my laws (Gen. 26:5)" (*m. Qidd.* 4:14). Numerous other texts make this same point.[17] Paired with this emphasis on obedience was Abraham's conversion from idolatry. Philo makes this point in *Abraham* 60–88 (de Boer, 187), as he traces Abraham's exit from idolatrous astrology. Josephus, *Ant.* 1.154–55, emphasizes his conversion to monotheism. Other texts emphasize the same.[18] The dual emphasis upon obedience to Law and conversion from idolatry likely made Abraham a ready example for the opponents to use as they taught the Galatians, seeking the same on their part.[19] Indeed, Abraham's conversion from idolatry could have been an important theme to Paul in light of his own Gentile mission (Soards and Pursiful, 127). However, in spite of this strong tradition, Paul emphasizes something different about Abraham. If Abraham is the linchpin on which Paul's exegesis rests, his interpretation of the Abraham story itself rests on the central linchpin of Gen 15:6, which speaks solely of Abraham's faith in God and God's response to him. Paul's emphasis is only on Abraham as righteous because of his response of faith to God (Longenecker, 111). Abraham's faith in God was sufficient, and this relationship of trust was the foundation for God's dealings with Abraham, not the Law that came later (Keener, 224). Betz makes a very helpful argument to highlight Paul's point: In Jewish thought Abraham's faith was not opposed to deeds. It was his trust plus his steadfastness that constituted his works and qualified him as fitting for the reward of righteousness. Paul differed from this construct by separating Abraham's faith from his obedience to Torah, and thus Abraham becomes the prototype of the Gentile-Christian believer (Betz, 139). Indeed, on this basis Paul essentially shows himself as a better interpreter of the Scripture. "Paul's approach seems more faithful to the progression of the narrative than

17. Jub. 17:15–16; 23:10; 24:11; *Pr. Man.* 8; 2 Bar. 57:1–2; and many others. For further citations see Betz, 139–40; Longenecker, 110–12; Garlington 2007, 155; Schreiner, 191–92; Soards and Pursiful, 128.

18. For further citations see Garlington 2007, 155; Dunn, 160.

19. Their teaching would have included a reference to Gen 17:4–14, which established circumcision as a sign of the covenant between God and Abraham (Longenecker, 110; de Boer, 187), but since Paul did not specifically reference circumcision he may have known about their teaching only in broad outline (Witherington, 218–19).

the anachronistic approaches found in Sirach and other early Jewish sources" (Witherington, 225). Indeed, the following narrative is about how God accepts Abraham's basic faith and then patiently cultivates it (Keener, 224).

Καθὼς. As stated above, the meaning of this conjunction in this context is one of comparison and connection: Just as the assertion made in this first sentence is true, the following assertion is also true. Thus the conj. serves to link the larger pieces of Paul's argument: the faith of Abraham and its result in his life on the one hand and the Galatians' experience of faith and its result in their lives on the other. The content that Paul uses as the basis of the comparison is the citation from Gen 15:6. Paul uses this verse as a central theological affirmation about Abraham's spiritual life before God that leads to a generalizing deduction about how all believers relate to God. This movement from affirmation in v. 6 to deduction in v. 7 is set up with his use of this conj.

Ἀβραὰμ ἐπίστευσεν τῷ θεῷ. This part of the citation is not complex grammatically, but it is profoundly important for Paul's theology. The simple force of the Greek grammar matches the Hebrew original of the citation, which is a narrative summary of Abraham's progress of faith in his dealings with God. In the MT Gen 15:6 begins with the verb הֶאֱמִן, not the name אַבְרָהָם. The LXX includes the name Αβραμ after the verb.[20] Paul places Ἀβραάμ before the verb, emphasizing him (so also Rapa, 594). Important to note for Paul's theological argument is the constancy of the meaning of the verb πιστεύω (and the noun πίστις) in this context. There is no difference between the meaning of the verb here and its meaning earlier in 2:16. In fact, the power of Paul's argument rests on the uniformity: There is no difference between the faith that Abraham expressed in God and the faith that Paul and other believers presently express in Christ.

καὶ ἐλογίσθη αὐτῷ εἰς δικαιοσύνην. The second half of the citation, taken from the LXX as opposed to translated from the Hebrew MT, details what ensued after Abraham expressed faith, indicating either logical consequence or actual result (Schreiner, 192). The verb ἐλογίσθη is pass. voice, significant as an example of the so-called "divine passive."[21] God is the agent of the action, explicitly so in the OT passage but implicitly here.[22] This leads to a related question about the grammatical subject of this verb. It is not Abraham, as he

---

20. Paul uses the name Abraham here, which would be appropriate for later texts, not Abram, which would have been appropriate at this point (Soards and Pursiful, 128). Paul most certainly did this because of convention; the name Abram (as opposed to Abraham) occurs nowhere in the NT.

21. See Wallace, *Greek Grammar*, 435–38, for a discussion on the reasons why pass. verbs lack expressed agents. The divine passive fits within this category, and Wallace offers some helpful clarification that goes beyond the traditional explanation of reticence to use the divine name.

22. The LXX might have changed the sentence structure for a number of reasons: to avoid redundancy; to have a simpler sentence structure, given the requirements

is referenced with the pronoun αὐτῷ, nor is it God as he is the agent of the action but not the grammatical subject. Rather, the subject is the concept referred to by the previous statement, that is, that Abraham believed God. The verb λογίζομαι is well known as "a mathematical and accounting term."[23] The dat. pronoun αὐτῷ shows to whose account the transaction applies. The prep. εἰς is used here to replace the predicate nom. Stating the ideas more explicitly, the sentence could be paraphrased as "God credited 'Abraham's-faith-in-God' to Abraham as righteousness." God considers Abraham's faith to be righteousness, and he credits that righteousness to Abraham's account, a metaphorical way to express his justification. "God graciously viewed Abraham's faith as having in itself fulfilled all that God expected of Abraham in order for him to be in the right before God" (Moo, 188).

Even though this citation makes an important theological assertion on its own about the patriarch Abraham, because of the conj. καθώς the sentence points forward in comparison. Paul does not cite Gen 15:6 as a theological lesson unto itself. Rather, it becomes comparative proof in Paul's larger argument about what God is doing presently regarding the Gentiles and their response of faith to the gospel. God's gracious action of crediting Abraham's faith to him as righteousness is replicated now in Gentiles as they believe in Christ. This is especially important when considering Paul's opponents and their stance toward circumcision, which they presumably required because God subsequently required it of Abraham. Paul goes deeper into Abraham's story to strike closer to its theological heart. God's gracious stance toward Abraham was because of his faith, not because of his circumcision. And it is this same gracious stance toward Gentiles that God now takes because of their faith in Christ, which is of a piece with Abraham's faith.

3:7 γινώσκετε ἄρα ὅτι. Paul moves into the contemporary half of the analogy begun in v. 6 with this introductory formula. Paul shifted to the 2 pl. verb γινώσκετε in 3:1 and then reemphasized it here to get the Galatians' attention, reminding them that they know the same essential facts that Paul and Peter do, the facts emphasized in 2:15–16. The verb γινώσκετε could be pres. indic., focusing on the present state of knowledge that the Galatians do indeed have, or pres. impv., in essence a command bringing them to the proper realization. The latter can be preferred based on parallels with didactic literature (Betz, 141) and the rhetorical force of the sentence that seems to present something that the Galatians had previously not understood properly (Schreiner, 193), but the former should be preferred because of the strong force of ἄρα as indicating a real conclusion (Lightfoot, 137; Witherington, 226; Soards and Pursiful, 129) and the role of the phrase as a disclosure formula "that serves more to remind readers of what is known than to exhort"

---

of the verb λογίζομαι to have two objects; or to keep strong focus upon Abraham as the subject of the discourse.

23. BDAG, 597.

(Longenecker, 114; so also Martyn, 299). The difference in meaning is minor (so also Schreiner, 193), as in either construal the conclusion Paul himself draws is clear and forms the primary point of the utterance. The rhetorical force of the statement is a logical conclusion, not simply a reflection on the Galatians' present state of knowledge. The conj. ἄρα is strong in this regard, acting as a "marker of an inference made on the basis of what precedes."[24] The particle ὅτι then indicates the content of what they know. The coupling of this affirmation and the unadorned use of the citation in v. 6 imply that the Galatians were familiar with this verse in some capacity. Paul does not explicitly flesh out his argument about its application to the Galatians, leaving the affirmation stated simply as a general deduction. It is possible that Paul's opponents (or the Galatians themselves) had used Gen 15:6 as *illustrative* of the role of faith in the life of those who approach God but then used other passages, most likely those concerning Abraham's circumcision, as *definitive* for governing that relationship. Paul's argument reverses that stance: He uses this verse instead as *definitive*, making Abraham's faith paradigmatic for all who come to God.

οἱ ἐκ πίστεως. Paul collapses his language, becoming terse and cryptic. The first place the phrase ἐκ πίστεως occurs is Gal 2:16. There it is used in collocation with the idea of justification, expressed with the verb δικαιόω, to proffer a disparate basis for justification vis-à-vis the other in contention, ἐξ ἔργων νόμου. As far as the grammar is concerned, the article οἱ makes the prepositional phrase ἐκ πίστεως function as a substantive, and it serves anaphorically to point to the previous use of the concept. The phrase οἱ ἐκ πίστεως thus becomes a shorthand for those who are marked by the idea expressed in full in the previous argument: "those who are justified by faith in Jesus Christ." As with the example of Abraham, this faith forms the foundation for life with God. A survey of different explanations of this phrase's referent confirms this basic point:

> "they whose starting-point, whose fundamental principle is faith" (Lightfoot, 137)
>
> "those who believe and whose standing and character are determined by that faith" (Burton, 155)
>
> "those whose existence before God is based upon (ἐκ) faith" (Betz, 141)
>
> "those who are justified by faith in Christ and whose life is guided by the principle of faith" (Fung, 138)
>
> "those whose identity is derived from faith" (Martyn, 299)
>
> those for whom faith is their "basic life orientation, the basic or guiding principle by which one lives" (Witherington, 226)

24. BDAG, 127.

> those who are " 'marked by' or 'characterized by' " faith, those whose identity before God and relationship to God are defined by faith (Moo, 197)

The nom. case here functions as a pendant nom., resumed by the following demonstrative pronoun οὗτοι. This is slightly unusual in that the word that normally resumes the pendant nom. is more often an oblique case,[25] but even so Paul's use here conforms to normal usage in that it heightens the emphasis upon the referenced individuals as the topic of concern. The prep. ἐκ as before in 2:16 points to reason or basis. The act of justification for which faith is the reason or basis is only implied, unlike the prior context.[26] The noun πίστεως takes on the same nuance as it did in 2:15, the individual's response of trust, in this instance toward Christ as expressed in Paul's gospel.

οὗτοι υἱοί εἰσιν Ἀβραάμ. This sentence is simple grammatically, but it is quite profound theologically within Paul's argument. This is the conclusion Paul draws about those who have faith in Jesus concerning their relationship to God: They are related to Abraham, and thus they are right with God. Paul uses this to dispute the arguments of the opponents who had referred to Abraham in their preaching to influence the Galatians (Longenecker, 114; Martyn, 299; Hays, 255).

The phrase "sons of Abraham" is the central spiritual conclusion Paul makes about those who have faith in Christ. Interestingly, this phrase is not that common in the biblical text, even though similar phrases with τέκνον also occur. The most natural understanding of the phrase would seem simply to be a designation for ethnic Jews, but the sole time the phrase is used with that meaning is in Acts 13:26, and in that passage there are explicit contextual factors that inform that understanding, namely, the inclusion of the noun γένος in the construction, which focuses on race, and the additional category of God-fearers mentioned by Peter in the context, which implies that υἱοὶ γένους Ἀβραάμ is an ethnic designation. Otherwise, the meaning of the phrase is different—perhaps more restrictive—than ethnic Israel: It refers to those *within* Israel who are properly related to God *spiritually*, focusing not on race but on relationship. This is present in Matt 3:9 // Luke 3:8;[27] John 8:39; and Rom 9:7.[28] The sg. use with reference to Zacchaeus in Luke 19:9 is a bit harder to sort out: σήμερον σωτηρία τῷ οἴκῳ τούτῳ ἐγένετο, καθότι καὶ αὐτὸς υἱὸς Ἀβραάμ ἐστιν, "Today salvation has come to this house because even he

---

25. See Wallace, *Greek Grammar*, 51.

26. MHT, 3:260, calls this use instrumental.

27. The wording here in the Gospels is grammatically different than elsewhere. Here John the Baptist speaks of God raising up children "for" Abraham, τέκνα τῷ Ἀβραάμ. The dat. is used to show the recipient of God's action in this instance; the idea of genetic relationship is still intact.

28. Paul here makes a negative argument: οὐδ' ὅτι εἰσὶν σπέρμα Ἀβραὰμ πάντες τέκνα. This is the same basic argument as he makes in Gal 3:7, but expressed negatively.

himself is a son of Abraham." The context shows that this is a spiritual designation rather than an ethnic one, as the use of καθότι shows that being a son of Abraham is causal to salvation arriving in his house. The sentence would make no sense if "son of Abraham" was an ethnic designation, as that aspect of Zacchaeus' identity was not altered by his interaction with Jesus.[29] In sum, then, in the biblical text the phrase "son of Abraham" is not automatically an ethnic designation. More often it is a spiritual one, showing that the one called thereby is related to God properly, as Abraham was.[30]

To this spiritual emphasis Paul adds a grammatical spin. As noted above, υἱοί comes before the copulative verb in this sentence, separated from Ἀβραάμ, even though they are conceptually and grammatically connected. The current state of research shows that generally predicate nominatives that precede the verb are qualitative in force, that is, they do not designate a specific member of a class (definite), nor do they designate any member of a class (indefinite), but rather they emphasize the traits or character of the entities that make up that class (qualitative).[31] Paul thus moves this predicate nom. forward to make an important grammatical point in tandem with the spiritual emphasis of the phrase "sons of Abraham": These who are justified by faith are not "the sons of Abraham" (definite), which could be construed to mean that they have replaced Jews in this category of existence, nor are they "any sons of Abraham" (indefinite), with little to no emphasis upon how they fit within that group. Rather, they are "sons of Abraham" (qualitative) in that they exhibit the character traits of those who are indeed spiritual sons of Abraham, defined by background and current context as those who exercise faith toward God. This grammatical emphasis plays hand in hand with the spiritual designation of the phrase and further emphasizes Paul's argument about the exclusivity of faith for establishing a relationship with God. With this statement Paul plants his flag. Faith is what connects people to Abraham and thus to God. The Law and adherence to it does not factor into the

29. The use of θυγατέρ Ἀβραάμ in Luke 13:16 is more likely an ethnic designation, although the proper response of the woman to her healing—καὶ ἐδόξαζεν τὸν θεόν—might imply that Jesus uses this phrase with a spiritual referent.

30. This is not unheard of in Jewish literature. See *b. Beṣah* 32B: "[This means that] anyone who has compassion for others is [through his actions] known to be of the progeny of Abraham our father. But anyone who does not show compassion to others is known not to be of the progeny of Abraham our father."

31. See Wallace, *Greek Grammar*, 256–63, who summarizes the research of E. C. Colwell, "A Definite Rule for the Use of the Article in the Greek New Testament," *JBL* 52 (1933): 12–21; P. B. Harner, "Qualitative Anarthrous Predicate Nouns: Mark 15:39 and John 1:1," *JBL* 92 (1973): 75–87; P. S. Dixon, "The Significance of the Anarthrous Predicate Nominative in John" (Th.M. thesis, Dallas Theological Seminary, 1975).

equation. The spiritual attitude of heart and mind is central and primary. This is the theological truth that drives the balance of Paul's theological discussion.[32]

3:8 προϊδοῦσα δὲ ἡ γραφή. Paul adds here an assertion concerning the Scripture that spoke about Abraham. The ptc. προϊδοῦσα modifies the verb προευηγγελίσατο, indicating cause: προοράω describes a mental state prior to the proclamation (either logically or conceptually) that grounds or motivates the proclamation. The verb προοράω can refer on the one hand to mental consideration in the present time or on the other hand to prophetic foresight.[33] In this context the latter meaning is clearly intended by Paul, given the pres. tense of the verb in the ὅτι clause that follows. The verb is not common in the NT, occurring only four times (Acts 2:25, 31; 21:29; here). Similar to the current use is Acts 2:31 where Peter attributes prophetic knowledge to David in his writing of Ps 16. In the current text Paul attributes prophetic knowledge to the Scriptures in Gen 12:3. The assertion here is very bold: The Scripture knew what God would do in the present time in which Paul lives.

The use of the word γραφή here is quite complicated. Paul uses γραφή fourteen times, usually with the meaning "Scripture," the referent being the sacred writings of the OT.[34] In this instance Paul uses γραφή figuratively for God. The product (the sacred writing, the Scripture) stands in for the producer (God, the one who wrote or inspired the Scripture). This figurative use makes two related, important, theological (perhaps even hermeneutical) assertions. First, God is the ultimate author of the OT passage cited. Second, God through that passage speaks to the present situation.[35] From these assertions the usage of γραφή in Gal 3:8 can be fleshed out further. A literal translation reads as follows: "Now because the Scripture foresaw that God justifies the Gentiles by faith, it announced the gospel beforehand to Abraham that 'All the nations will be blessed in you.'" Paul uses γραφή metaphorically; he personifies it, giving it understanding and intention.[36] But Paul's ultimate intention is not to claim that the Scripture *qua* Scripture knew what God was going to do. His assertion goes to the divine intention (similarly Bruce,

32. For this argument in full, see M. H. Burer, "'Sons of Abraham' in Galatians 3:7 as a Spiritual, Qualitative Designation," *BSac* 173 (2016): 337–51.

33. LSJ, 1476; MGS, 1780.

34. This is the meaning in Rom 1:2; 4:3 (which also cites Gen 15:6); 11:2; 15:4; 16:26; 1 Cor 15:3 (2x); Gal 4:30; 1 Tim 5:18; 2 Tim 3:16.

35. This is the usage in Rom 9:17; 10:11 (possibly; this citation of Isa 28:16 could be construed differently, but since the Lord is speaking in the Isa passage, this makes good sense); Gal 3:22.

36. Personification of Scripture was typical of high view of inspiration and authority of the text (Dunn, 164). Martyn, 300, argues vividly that the Scripture is not passive here: "On the contrary, it is alive, having, as it were, eyes and intelligence and a mouth."

155–56): The words of the passage cited are God's own words in the OT context, so Paul shows that *God* knew what he was going to do in the future and in light of that spoke to Abraham in a particular way in the past. When Paul uses γραφὴ, the ultimate referent is God: Because God foreknew what he was going to do, he spoke these particular words to Abraham.

With this short phrase, Paul offers scriptural support that those who are justified by faith are sons of Abraham. The Scripture cited becomes the first link in a rather long argument. Paul argues that God knew he would ultimately justify the Gentiles the same way he justified Abraham, that is, by faith. So Paul notes that because God knew that he was going to do this, he announced this beforehand to Abraham with the words, "All the nations will be blessed in you." God's ultimate meaning was sure because God knew what his ultimate action would be. The surety of this prior knowledge is revealed by what God actually does in the present time noted in the ὅτι clause that follows.

ὅτι ἐκ πίστεως δικαιοῖ τὰ ἔθνη ὁ θεὸς. This ὅτι clause expresses the content of what the Scripture saw previously. The phrase ἐκ πίστεως links back to the shorthand phrase οἱ ἐκ πίστεως used in the prior verse, the difference here being that the verbal idea associated with it is expressed fully as it was originally in 2:16. So ἐκ πίστεως has the same meaning as before, that of grounds or basis.[37] The verb δικαιοῖ has the same meaning here as when Paul first used it in 2:16–17, that is, "to justify" or "declare righteous." The use of the pres. tense at this point is quite interesting. From the standpoint of grammar, the tense expected here is fut. because the context of the original utterance would require it logically; this would be a fut. retained in indir. discourse.[38] It is possible that because this indir. discourse follows a secondary tense the fut. has been altered to the pres. (Burton, 160; Longenecker, 115; Moo, 199), but this is not usual.[39] So the pres. tense is intentional on Paul's part and points to the present reality of the Gentiles' justification (so also Lenski, 137). The point is that the present reality enacted through Paul's ministry—justification of the Gentiles through their belief in the gospel of Christ—is something God foreknew when he initially spoke to Abraham.[40] God saw exactly what would

37. G. B. Winer, *A Treatise on the Grammar of New Testament Greek, Regarded as a Sure Basis for New Testament Exegesis* (Edinburgh: Clark, 1882), 514, categorizes this as either source or means because either fits theologically.

38. E. D. W. Burton, *Syntax of the Moods and Tenses in New Testament Greek* (1900; repr., Grand Rapids: Kregel, 2000), 140.

39. A. T. Robertson, *A Grammar of the Greek New Testament in the Light of Historical Research* (Nashville: Broadman, 1934), 1029.

40. Winer, *Grammar*, 331, argues about the pres. tense here differently: "Hence the present tense—which expresses present time in all its relations (and especially in rules, maxims, and dogmas of permanent validity, compare Jo. 7:52)—is used for the future in appearance only, when an action still future is to be represented as being as good as already present, either because it is already firmly resolved on, or

happen in Paul's ministry to the Gentiles and spoke to Abraham based on that foreknowledge. One other grammatical note is that ὁ θεὸς is the explicit nom. subject of δικαιοῖ, which provides an interesting contrast to the pass. voice used in all other occurrences of the verb in the balance of the book (see Gal 2:16, 17; 3:11, 24; 5:4). Here Paul speaks very directly about God as the agent of the Gentiles' justification to emphasize his point.

προευηγγελίσατο τῷ Ἀβραὰμ. The rare verb προευηγγελίασατο is the main verb of this clause, occurring only here in the NT.[41] The noun ἡ γραφή is its subject, and the proper name τῷ Ἀβραὰμ is the dat. indir. obj. The article is used with the proper name because this name is indeclinable; otherwise, there would be confusion as to which case is intended.[42] Abraham thus received the proclamation that the Scripture announced beforehand. The dir. obj. of the verb is the ὅτι clause that follows, in this case direct discourse of a Scripture citation.

The verb προευαγγελίζομαι is not at all common in the NT or in Greek literature more broadly.[43] The only uses contemporary to the NT are three occurrences in Philo (*Creation* 1:34; *Names* 1:158; *Abraham* 1:153), who uses the word not with a religious sense but rather with a neutral one. This fits with its etymology: The meaning of the verb εὐαγγελίζω is "to announce good news, bring good tidings,"[44] and the prefixed prep. προ- adds the meaning "before" relative to time, a common meaning for this prep. So the meaning of προευαγγελίζομαι is "announce (good news) in advance." The citation from *Creation* 1:34 is a good example of this meaning:

> οὗτοι δ' εἰσὶν ἑσπέρα τε καὶ πρωΐα, ὧν ἡ μὲν προευαγγελίζεται μέλλοντα ἥλιον ἀνίσχειν, ἠρέμα τὸ σκότος ἀνείργουσα
>
> These barriers are evening and dawn. The latter, gently restraining the darkness, anticipates the sunrise with the glad tidings of its approach.[45]

The translation "anticipates" here is fairly literal but appropriate nonetheless. Philo's other two uses of the verb embody the same basic idea of giving evidence beforehand or making known in advance. Paul's use of the term is

---

because it must ensue in virtue of some unalterable law (exactly. as in Latin, German, etc.)." Lightfoot, 137, argues similarly. They treat the pres. tense here like the Hebrew prophetic pf. Bruce, 156, and de Boer, 194, argue for a gnomic pres. here.

41. The related term εὐαγγελίζομαι occurs much more frequently (54x).

42. So Winer, *Grammar*, 141.

43. In the NT it occurs only in Gal 3:8. The TLG shows only 39 instances of the verb: the three uses in Philo contemporaneous with the NT, the others after the NT from the third century AD.

44. See LSJ, 704–5; MGS, 836.

45. Philo, *On the Creation. Allegorical Interpretation of Genesis 2 and 3*, trans. F. H. Colson and G. H. Whitaker, LCL 226 (Cambridge, MA: Harvard University Press, 1929), 26–27.

similar to the uses in Philo, but beyond that he uses the term with a clear religious nuance. This arises from the non-prefixed form εὐαγγελίζομαι elsewhere in the book, which refers specifically to Paul's proclamation of the gospel about Jesus Christ (for key uses see 1:8, 9, 16). So the meaning of προευαγγελίζομαι here is almost technical, building upon the more common verb: "to proclaim the gospel of Jesus Christ in advance or before in time." Paul's point is that in the promise God made to Abraham—"all the nations will be blessed in you"—God proclaimed the gospel of Jesus Christ beforehand. Paul connects God's ultimate, specific intention toward the gospel of Jesus Christ to the giving of this generic promise about blessings for the Gentiles. From Paul's perspective these words were not simply a general promise about generic blessing that would come to the nations through Abraham. It was a specific promise explaining how that blessing would come about, namely, through the proclamation of Jesus to the Gentiles and by implication their acceptance of this gospel through faith.

ὅτι Ἐνευλογηθήσονται ἐν σοὶ πάντα τὰ ἔθνη. This ὅτι clause indicates the content of the good news that was announced to Abraham in advance by God. The statement is a citation from Gen 12:3, but similar wording is found in Gen 18:18; 22:18; 26:4; 28:14; Sir 44:21 (cf. Acts 3:25). Its reuse within the Genesis narrative and elsewhere speaks to the theological importance of this utterance. Here Paul conflates Gen 12:3 with other promises that mention πάντα τὰ ἔθνη, Gen 18:18 being the most likely direct source (Bruce, 156; Witherington, 228; Schreiner, 194; Moo, 199). This modification puts emphasis upon the Gentiles (de Boer, 195; Soards and Pursiful, 131). It becomes an explicit interpretation of the passage (Burton, 160; Moo, 199), possibly rising out of his own mission to the Gentiles (Soards and Pursiful, 131). Contrary to expected grammatical convention ἐνευλογηθήσονται is pl. With a neut. pl. subject (here πάντα τὰ ἔθνη) the expectation would be for the verb to be sg. This lack of traditional concord shows an emphasis not on the Gentiles as a group, but as individuals.[46] The agent of this pass. verb is without doubt God; he is explicitly mentioned previously in the verse, therefore he is implied here. The prepositional phrase ἐν σοὶ most likely conveys impersonal means (so also Fung, 139), as ἐν plus the dat. frequently occurs with pass. verbs with this nuance.[47] This does not mean that Paul conceives of Abraham as impersonal. It simply means that in this construction Abraham is an instrument used by God; there is no emphasis on his volition or personal involvement in the process. The best translation to bring this out is "by/with you." Some argue that incorporation is in view because of the following argument where incorporation and seed become important (Lenski, 139; Matera, 123; Martyn, 301; Oakes, 107). Against this is Paul's follow up in v. 9 where association is key, not incorporation.

---

46. MHT, 3:313, says, "The NT usually breaks the class. rule with words used in a personal sense (ἔθνη, τέκνα, δαιμόνια)." This is essentially the same argument.

47. See Wallace, *Greek Grammar*, 434–35.

The point of this citation is to argue that the current state of affairs in Paul's ministry—Gentiles expressing faith in Christ—is a movement of God. Paul's argument links the current state of affairs with a scriptural, theological basis: The Scripture knew that in Paul's time God would justify the Gentiles on the basis of faith. On the basis of this foreknowledge, God announced to Abraham the proclamation that "all the nations will be blessed with you." The gospel was universal from the very beginning (Garlington 2007, 158). Paul saw his gospel as the working out of all aspects of this original promise for both Jews and Gentiles; his mission to the Gentiles was simply the fulfillment of Israel's mission (Dunn, 165). This statement is both generic and specific: It is clear on who receives the blessing and by whom the blessing is received, but is generic on what the blessing actually is.[48] Generic when given to Abraham, the promise in Paul's thought now refers to a specific content, namely, Gentiles believing in Christ through the gospel. Because God knew that he would ultimately justify the Gentiles on the basis of faith, not Law, he announced beforehand to Abraham the promise that all Gentiles would be blessed by him. Through this scriptural citation, Paul shows that God's present action vis-à-vis the Gentiles was promised long beforehand to Abraham. This proves that Paul's position regarding the Gentiles and the Law is the right one.

3:9 *ὥστε οἱ ἐκ πίστεως εὐλογοῦνται σὺν τῷ πιστῷ Ἀβραάμ.* This clause amounts to a minor stop in the larger flow of Paul's argument. In this short section Paul has intended to show the legitimate connection to Abraham of those who are justified by faith. His conclusion draws together the argument to make the final minor point. The clause is constructed around ὥστε plus the indic. verb εὐλογοῦνται. The conj. ὥστε indicates a conclusion or inference,[49] and the indic. marks the nature of this statement as a logical deduction rather than a natural result.[50] The phrase οἱ ἐκ πίστεως is the same shorthand as before: "those who are [justified] on the basis of faith." It identifies those who are the subject of the utterance, which contrasts with the beginning of the next paragraph in v. 10, ὅσοι ἐξ ἔργων νόμου εἰσὶν, "as many who are [justified] by works of the Law." These two nominal clauses—οἱ ἐκ πίστεως in v. 9 and ὅσοι ἐξ ἔργων νόμου εἰσὶν in v. 10—are topical frames that highlight information that

48. Betz, 142, helpfully notes that Judaism recognized some blessings given to all nations because of Abraham, e.g., creation and continuance of the world and scientific knowledge. Paul obviously goes further by connecting it to grace and justification.

49. BDAG, 1107, states that this conj. can connect clauses by "introducing independent clauses *for this reason, therefore, so.*"

50. Winer, *Grammar*, 377, makes the following argument relative to ὥστε plus the indic. vs. ὥστε plus the inf: "In the better writers indeed the distinction may be, that ὥστε with the indicative joins the facts together merely objectively as facts, as *præcedens* and *consequens*, whilst ὥστε with the infinitive brings them into closer connexion and represents one as proceeding out of the other."

was already made important because of the contrast due to content. These topical frames provide a way for Paul to add even more emphasis, ensuring that his readers catch the shift in topic from v. 9 to v. 10.[51] The verb εὐλογοῦνται is pres. indic., and similarly to Paul's use of the pres. tense in v. 8 with the verb δικαιοῖ, this use of the pres. tense refers to the present reality of the Gentiles' experience of faith. So this phrase is both a logical deduction and a simple affirmation. The nuance of the prep. σύν is difficult to determine but important given the place of Abraham in this conclusion to Paul's argument. The first inclination is to treat this as association,[52] but based on the prior verse, which highlights God speaking through Scripture and the possibility of Abraham represented there as impersonal means, means could be a possibility here for σύν.[53] However, even though means is semantically possible, it does not get at the heart of what Paul argues. His point is that there is a tangible, spiritual connection between what God said to Abraham before and what is taking place now among believing Gentiles. That connection is weakened if σύν is understood to indicate simply means. If the prep. is understood to mean association, which is in fact a common meaning for it with personal objects, the point would be the real, spiritual connection those who have faith in the present time share with Abraham. "Hence it is especially used of spiritual fellowship, as that of believers with Christ (Rom. 6:8, Col. 2:13, 20, 3:3, 1 Th. 4:17, 5:10), or that of believers with Abraham (G. 3:9), σύν denoting in all these instances, not a mere resemblance, but a real association."[54] The point then would be not simply an analogy—"Abraham believed God and now Gentiles similarly believe"—but a real, organic connection—"Abraham believed and Gentiles believe with him, therefore God treats them as part of the same family." This is reinforced by Paul's use of the adj. πιστός, which has an active nuance of "believing, trusting" in keeping with the meaning of πίστις and πιστεύω in context (Lenski, 140; Burton, 162; Longenecker, 116; de Boer, 197) and Paul's interpretation of the Abraham narrative (Bruce, 157; Moo, 200).[55]

With this first half of the paragraph Paul makes his initial theological assertion to support his gospel. He relies both upon the reality of the present experience of the Gentiles—whom God had clearly justified in Christ, proven by the work of the Spirit in their midst—and a fundamental argument from

---

51. S. E. Runge, *Discourse Grammar of the Greek New Testament: A Practical Introduction for Teaching and Exegesis* (Peabody, MA: Hendrickson, 2010), 279–80.

52. So BDAG, 962.

53. BDAG, 962, might support this interpretation given the second definitional category for σύν, "marker of assistance." LSJ, 1690, could support it as well with "7. of the instrument or means, with the help of, by means of."

54. Winer, *Grammar*, 488.

55. This statement mirrors the pres. tense affirmation of God's relation to the patriarchs made by Jesus in Matt 22:32 (and parallels) applied to the Jews. That same living relationship is made between Abraham and Gentiles on the basis of faith.

Scripture, which linked Abraham's faith to faith in the gospel Paul preached. Either one was sufficient to make his case, but he links them together, thus showing the divine nature of these events. Abraham's own experience validates what occurs when an individual believes in Christ without any reliance upon the Law. The narrative of Abraham's belief in Genesis shows that faith was the exclusive requirement to please God then as well as now. The only logical conclusion to draw is that it is those who are justified by faith are associated with Abraham, blessed just as he was.

3:10 In this next subsection of the paragraph, Paul approaches the question of identity from the side opposite faith. He proceeds in a logical fashion: Following his assertion about who is part of Abraham's family and receives blessing, he discusses who is not part of that family and receives cursing. The explicit question in Paul's mind is the sentence of condemnation that comes from the Law: "Those who claim on the basis of scripture that justification is by law must on the same basis admit that the actual sentence of law is one of condemnation" (Burton, 163). The implicit question is how can God's blessing come to Gentiles in view of the curse that separated them from the covenant (Dunn, 170).

Ὅσοι γὰρ ἐξ ἔργων νόμου εἰσὶν, ὑπὸ κατάραν εἰσίν. The opening statement of this subsection parallels the central affirmation of the first (*οἱ ἐκ πίστεως, οὗτοι υἱοί εἰσιν Ἀβραάμ*), providing a contrast to further this negative argument. The *γάρ* connects vv. 6–9 to 10–14 (Longenecker, 116); the fundamental problem of the Law's curse grounds Paul's argument about the priority of faith. This causal argument is based on the logical contrast between the two parts.[56] In a sense this is a logical corollary of the prior argument. Within the context of v. 10 the phrase *ὅσοι γὰρ ἐξ ἔργων νόμου εἰσὶν* is the subject and the focus of attention. The prepositional phrase *ὑπὸ κατάραν* describes *ὅσοι γὰρ ἐξ ἔργων νόμου εἰσὶν*. In the simplest construal it indicates location, but more completely it conveys a sense of control or authority, as *εἰμί* or *γίνομαι* plus *ὑπό* can mean "to be placed in subjection to."[57]

The phrasing *ὅσοι ἐξ ἔργων νόμου εἰσὶν* needs to be considered carefully, as Paul chooses it deliberately to focus his argument. This phrase stands in contrast to *οἱ ἐκ πίστεως*, which he uses earlier in v. 7. There the phrase identified those whose relationship with God was defined by faith; it is those individuals who were in fact justified. Here Paul uses a more expanded construction to make his contrasting point. When used absolutely *ὅσος* can have a meaning similar to *πᾶς*.[58] Paul intends to cast a wide net with it. The prepositional phrase *ἐξ ἔργων νόμου* provides the important qualification. This phrase was first used in 2:16, and the use there governs the use here (Bruce,

56. See M. Zerwick, *Biblical Greek: Illustrated By Examples*, trans. J. Smith, Scripta Pontificii Instituti Biblici 114 (Rome: Pontifical Biblical Institute, 1963), 159.

57. Winer, *Grammar*, 507; see also BDAG, 1036.

58. So BDAG, 729.

157). Similarly to ἐκ πίστεως, the shorthand here points to those who depend upon and base their existence upon ἔργων νόμου. Thus this nominal clause means " 'those who are of works of law,' whose character is founded on works of law" (Lightfoot, 138). With this phrase, then, Paul has delineated two distinct groups: those who derive their existence and identity from faith, and those who derive their existence and identity from the Law (Lenski, 141; Longenecker, 116). In this instance the implied justification is surely conative, not actual; the sense "those who rely on works of the Law for justification" in contrast to "those who are justified by faith" is acceptable. So this phrase as a whole can be taken to mean "as many as are characterized by justification by/reliance upon works of the Law."

Paul now broaches again the concept of curse, applying it to those who depend upon the Law.[59] If certain people are blessed because of what God has declared about them because of their faith, then certain people are cursed because they have depended upon the Law. Galatians 3:6–14 is the only place where Paul uses the noun κατάρα or the adj. ἐπικατάρατος. These two words are not general terms for Paul. Rather, they are specific and exegetical, arising from their use within texts upon which he depends. In the ancient world curses (as well as blessings) were understood to have real power with real effect. Pronouncement of a curse was meant to access supernatural power that then had a real, tangible effect upon the recipient.[60] Within biblical thought, curses were not arbitrary or magical, but rather a real expression of the unavoidable judgment of God, already weighing down upon the individual because of sin.[61] Thus Paul's use of κατάρα and ἐπικατάρατος is not simply wishful thinking or angry denouncement. It is an expression of the actual judgment upon individuals who depend upon the Law and not faith. Blessings and curses figure prominently within Israel's theology, as they were an integral part of Israel's renewal of the covenant before entrance into Canaan (see Deut 11:29; 27:1–28:68).[62] Simply put, blessings would come for obedience to the Law, curses for disobedience. Paul asserts with this language that those who depend upon the Law in the present moment are

---

59. Paul had used language similar in force in Gal 1:8–9 when he declared those who preached a different gospel ἀνάθεμα. His use there was theological and general. Here the use is exegetical, drawn from the specific passages he cites to support his argument. There may be a connection in Paul's mind, but his argument in each place progresses well without assuming the other.

60. *NIDNTTE*, 1:382. Our modern mindset struggles with this worldview, but without it many biblical narratives make no sense. Why would Balak hire Balaam to curse Israel, for example, and then get angry when Balaam could only bless if these were simply wishes or hopes, without real power?

61. F. Büchsel, "κατάρα," *TDNT*, 1:449.

62. This theological construct was so powerful that after the incident with Achan and the ultimate defeat of Ai Joshua reenacted this renewal (Josh 8:30–35) to restore fidelity to God.

the ones actually falling under its curse. The prep. ὑπό here carries a specific connotation, being under an authority or power (Longenecker, 116). "To be 'under a curse' is to be under God's judgment for failure to live up to his covenant requirements" (Moo, 201). The citations that follow show proofs from the Law itself that allow Paul to make this judgment. As in Gal 1:8–9, Paul does not make this determination himself, but rather as an apostle he simply recognizes that these individuals are acting contrary to what God has revealed and thus are under judgment. As an apostle, he simply states aloud what is already true in God's eyes.

γέγραπται γὰρ ὅτι Ἐπικατάρατος πᾶς ὃς οὐκ ἐμμένει πᾶσιν τοῖς γεγραμμένοις ἐν τῷ βιβλίῳ τοῦ νόμου τοῦ ποιῆσαι αὐτά. Paul uses this citation as the theological grounding for his assertion in the prior line; the conj. γάρ functions causally. Those who rely upon the Law are under a curse because of the testimony of this Scripture. Paul regularly uses γέγραπται to identify a citation from the OT.[63] This particular citation is from Deut 27:26, the twelfth and final curse pronounced over the twelve tribes by the Levites after they crossed over the Jordan, but it has linguistic similarity to Deut 28:58 and 30:10. Paul's citation follows the LXX, which adds emphasis with πᾶς, and then he further generalizes by substituting πᾶσιν τοῖς γεγραμμένοις ἐν τῷ βιβλίῳ τοῦ νόμου (Fung, 141). The adj. ἐπικατάρατος is the predicate nom. of the sentence. Even though the placement of the word is due to the citation, its position in the clause serves Paul's purpose because it creates a more prominent linguistic link with the prior clause. The remainder of the citation is the subject, the one who is "cursed." πᾶς functions as an adj., modifying the relative clause beginning with ὅς, "everyone who," acting here as an indefinite pronoun with no particular antecedent.[64] Thus this statement is generic and gnomic. The main verb of the clause is ἐμμένει; it is a customary pres. with an obviously important negation. The prefixed prep. on this verb emphasizes the state or location in which one "remains," which the next phrase identifies: πᾶσιν τοῖς γεγραμμένοις ἐν τῷ βιβλίῳ τοῦ νόμου, "in all that is written in the book of the Law." This is a noun phrase built upon the subst. ptc. γεγραμμένοις, "that which is written." πᾶσιν and ἐν τῷ βιβλίῳ τοῦ νόμου modify that phrase by showing extent and location. The final phrase of this sentence is key to the entire point Paul makes: τοῦ ποιῆσαι αὐτά modifies ἐμμένει, getting beneath the issue of obedience to the inner, spiritual motivation of the individual. As a modifier its exact sense is difficult to pin down. It could be an epexegetical

63. Paul uses γέγραπται thirty-one times. The only time the word does not cite the OT directly is Gal 4:22, but even there the referent is a well-known OT narrative. Rom 2:24 is the only place where γέγραπται follows the citation; everywhere else it precedes.

64. So Robertson, *Grammar*, 719–20, 744.

inf.,[65] but it could also be result or even purpose.[66] This is an exceedingly important qualifier, which Paul is going to highlight later at the end of the book. One cannot simply remain in the Law by any means or for any reason; one must remain in the Law with the intention and outcome of fulfilling it.

Needless to say this citation has engendered intense debate in Pauline interpretation for two primary reasons: Paul appears to use the verse in a way contrary to its original, contextual meaning, which says that obedience avoids the curse, while Paul says doing the Law brings it (Moo, 202), and there is an underlying assumption in Paul's argument that is difficult to elucidate. In its original context Deut 27:26 was the last of the curses pronounced over Israel during the covenant ceremony; as such it served as a summary of them (Lightfoot, 138; Longenecker, 117; Schreiner, 203; deSilva, 286). Thus even within its original context this verse served a generalizing function (Bruce, 158). The modifications Paul makes to the citation serve to generalize it further, making his scope the entirety of the OT Law (Hays, 258; Schreiner, 203; de Boer, 199). Paul cites the verse as applicable to the entirety of the Law, making explicit what was implicit in the OT passage originally, namely, the expectation of obedience to all God revealed and required. Also made explicit in Paul's citation is the particular intention of the individual vis-à-vis the Law: The individual must "remain" in everything written "in order to do them." The intent of the heart is not divorced from the action in Paul's mind; they are both in view in what Paul writes. This leads quite readily into the issue of the content of the underlying assumption driving his argument. In this case, what fits best is to argue that the curse comes because of a lack of complete and total obedience to the Law. I accept this for three reasons. First, this explains Paul's alterations to the citation, which emphasize the complete obedience required to the totality of the Law. Second, this creates a very logical syllogism:

> The Law curses those who do not obey it completely.
> [Implied:] People do not ever obey the Law completely.
> Therefore the Law curses all people.

Third, this coheres with what Paul wrote elsewhere. Later in Gal 5:3 he reminds those who intend to submit to circumcision that their obedience cannot stop there; they actually become obligated to obey the whole Law. In 6:13 he calls out the opponents for their lack of obedience to the Law despite their circumcision.[67] In Paul's thinking, then, the Law set a high bar of complete obedience to all its requirements. Those who do not obey all

---

65. So Robertson, *Grammar*, 1086.

66. MHT, 3:136, argues for result; Robertson, *Grammar*, 1088, argues for purpose! Note J. L. Boyer, "The Classification of Infinitives: A Statistical Study," *GTJ* 6 (1985): 12n25, who identifies this inf. in Gal 3:10 as ambiguous in this regard.

67. A similar theological stance is found in the argument that disobedience to one point of the Law means one has disobeyed all of it; see Jas 2:10; 4 Macc 5:20–21.

that is written in it are cursed. People do not obey the Law completely, and thus they are cursed by it.[68]

The strongest argument against the construal I have explained here is that it does not cohere well with our current understanding of Judaism as a system of covenantal nomism.[69] The Law was designed to maintain Israel's relationship with God, and the Law itself had measures to account for human sinfulness. The sacrificial system by its very existence acknowledged that people would not obey the Law completely. As such, then, Paul must have implied something else. I believe Paul would have accepted this pushback completely, but his theology did not rest simply on what Judaism understood about human nature and the Law. He now saw "the universality and radicality of human sinfulness as seen from the perspective of the cross" (George, 231).[70] In addition, this implied premise was not unheard of in Judaism (Betz, 145; Longenecker, 118). Even the OT itself taught that all people sin (Schreiner, 205) and that the depth of human sinfulness is beyond comprehension (Jer 17:9); the OT prophetic witness regularly highlighted Israel's failure to keep the Law (Keener, 237). It does not stretch credulity to see Paul connecting these dots to recognize in the clarity given to his theological mind by the cross of Christ that humanity will never be able to live up to what God required in the Law, and thus humanity stands condemned under its curse.

3:11 ὅτι δὲ ἐν νόμῳ οὐδεὶς δικαιοῦται παρὰ τῷ θεῷ δῆλον. With this phrase Paul moves to a new assertion within his argument about the nature and status of those who rely upon the Law. How the particle δῆλον relates to the ὅτι conjunctions in the verse is debated. There are two options. The first clause could be construed as causal with the particle δῆλον connected to what follows. In this instance the second ὅτι would indicate content (so Hays, 259):

> And *because* no one is justified by the Law before God
> it is clear *that* the righteous by faith will live.

68. I have chosen to cast my statement here simply in terms of actual obedience, not ability, contrary to many who argue for this view. I do think that Paul would argue that people are unable to keep the Law because of their sinfulness, but this is not an argument he brings up here. That is developed further in his epistle to the Romans.

69. Hays, 257, minces no words when he decries the assumption of perfect obedience as "a ridiculous caricature of Judaism" and states that this view is "read into the text."

70. This to me is a fair explanation for Paul's stance in Phil 3:6, commonly pointed to as problematic for the implied assumption that people cannot obey the Law (as in Soards and Pursiful, 134). The only sense in which Paul was "blameless according to righteousness in the Law" would have been from the limited viewpoint of Judaism before the cross. Paul goes on in vv. 7–11 to argue that in light of the cross he realizes that those gains were in fact losses.

Alternatively the first clause could be construed as the content connected to δῆλον. In this instance the ὅτι conjunctions would reverse roles, the first being content and the second causal (so many commentators and translations):

> And it is clear *that* no one is justified by the Law before God *because* the righteous by faith will live.

Paul uses the word δῆλον one other time in his writings in 1 Cor 15:27, but the structure there is different and cannot be marshaled as a parallel. It would make sense that δῆλον would normally be followed by content,[71] but the flexibility of Greek word and clause order should force the case to be proven in each instance.[72] In this passage, the latter clausal structure conveyed above should be favored primarily on the argument that in this section Paul appears to place the Scripture citations after his assertions for support (Schreiner, 210; Moo, 205). Thus it fits the flow of the unit more readily and fits with his exegetical approach in this paragraph.

The force of the first clause of v. 11, then, is to show a clear conclusion drawn from the following Scripture citation. The content here recalls what Paul wrote in 2:16. The prepositional phrase ἐν νόμῳ indicates means, indicating the way in which the main verb δικαιοῦται is accomplished. It is functionally equivalent to the phrase ἐκ ἔργων νόμου that Paul used previously (Longenecker, 118; Rapa, 597). Here the idea is negated: "by the Law" is not the means by which anyone is justified before the Lord. With the noun νόμος Paul intends the Law. The lack of the article in this instance does not support a general sense of "law" because Paul uses this term as a monadic noun. In addition, within prepositional phrases Paul often omits the article from definite nouns.[73] The pronoun οὐδείς is the nom. subject of the sentence; this indefinite pronoun along with the pres. tense verb δικαιοῦται creates a gnomic statement (similarly Schreiner, 207). The prep. παρά indicates whose judgment is in view.[74] This statement is thus a timeless distillation of the relationship of justification to the Law in God's sight. In establishing his

71. Both LSJ, 385, and BDAG, 222, highlight this semantic situation in some way.

72. Case in point: As part of my research here, I undertook a search in the TLG database for all occurrences of δῆλον preceded by ὅτι within ten words. My hunch was that in the 711 hits I would not readily find any references where this ὅτι was the content related to δῆλον, but lo and behold, the third hit fit. In Hippocrates, *De Corde* 11:8 we read ὅτι δὲ οὐ τρέφεται βλεπομένῳ αἵματι [ἡ μεγάλη ἀρτηρίη] δῆλον ὧδε· ἀποσφαγέντος τοῦ ζώου ..., "That it (the left ventricle) is not nourished by visible blood is made clear here: when an animal is slain ..." This example is a good parallel to Gal 3:11 and helps prove that the first ὅτι could indeed be content. If this commentary gets to a second edition, perhaps I'll have my interns sort through the other 708 examples I didn't look at!

73. When using a prep. with νόμος, Paul omits the article about three times as often as he uses it.

74. See BDAG, 757.

case against those who rely upon the Law for justification, Paul makes this general assertion about how justification before God is obtained. His clear conclusion is that it is not by Law.

ὅτι Ὁ δίκαιος ἐκ πίστεως ζήσεται. The second clause of v. 11 is a citation from Hab 2:4. Paul introduces the citation with a causal ὅτι, which connects this citation to the previous gnomic assertion as its grounds. This citation is another thorny problem in Pauline interpretation because of differences between Paul's rendering, the MT, and the LXX and because of ambiguity in meaning regarding the words and syntax.

Without putting it too simply, the primary textual difference between Paul's rendering, the MT, and the LXX concerns personal pronouns. The MT reads וְצַדִּיק בֶּאֱמוּנָתוֹ יִחְיֶה, "The righteous will live by his faithfulness." Here the 3 sg. masc. suffix refers back to צַדִּיק, "the righteous/faithful one." A translation that would bring out this connection is "The righteous one will live by his own faithfulness." The LXX changes the pronoun to 1 sg., which refers to God: ὁ δὲ δίκαιος ἐκ πίστεώς μου ζήσεται, "The righteous will live by my faithfulness." Paul avoids the pronouns entirely: ὁ δίκαιος ἐκ πίστεως ζήσεται, "The righteous by faith will live." Because of the difference in emphasis between the MT and the LXX, the perennial question is what Paul intended here: Did he intend to focus on the individual's response to God or God's faithfulness to the individual? This then leads to the questions concerning the ambiguity of meaning of the elements.

In this short little phrase every element is called into question. The primary problems concern what appear to be divergences between the original context of the utterance and Paul's use of it in the current context, and how within the context meaning is defined by Paul's other uses. The first question concerns the adj. δίκαιος, here used substantivally. In the OT the word צַדִּיק often emphasized faithfulness to the covenant, but moral connotations were not absent. As I argued above for the use of δικαιόω in 2:16, Paul uses the term here with both covenantal and forensic meanings.[75] The second question concerns the referent of the term πίστις in context, whether it means "faith" or "faithfulness" and whether it refers to humanity's response to God or God's faithfulness toward man. As I argued above for the use of πίστις in 2:16, Paul uses the term regularly in Galatians to refer to the individual's response of trust toward God. Prior uses of πίστις and πιστεύω point to human faith in this context (Moo, 206), especially given the contrast Paul now draws between ἐκ πίστεως and ἐκ ἔργων νόμου. This can even be argued from Habakkuk: The culmination of the book in Hab 3:17–18 emphasizes continued trust in God, not faithfulness (Schreiner, 208–209). A third question concerns where the prepositional phrase fits: Does it modify the subst. adj. ὁ δίκαιος or the verb ζήσεται? This justification before God could refer to righteous standing ("The one righteous by faith, that one will live") or righteous behavior ("The one who is righteous will live by faith"). Given

75. *Contra* Burton, 166; George, 234; Schreiner, 207; who argue for forensic only.

the import of the MT, with its focus on the individual's faithful life to God in light of his revelation, it is very reasonable to connect the prepositional phrase to the verb (so de Boer, 205).[76] This also works because ἐκ πίστεως is parallel to ἐν νόμῳ, and the latter modifies a verb (Moo, 207).[77] This is an important exegetical question, but an answer here does not change the conclusion Paul has drawn from it. Either construal supports Paul's assertion in the prior line, whether faith is the basis for how the person is righteous or whether it is the basis for how one lives. Within the context of his argument, Paul desires to show that faith is the basis for God's approbation, not obedience to the Law. Whether that connection is between righteous standing and faith on the one hand or living and faith on the other does not change the Scripture's essential support of Paul's generic assertion that no one is justified before God by the Law. The fourth question is the meaning of the verb ζήσεται. The context of the MT concerns preservation of physical life in light of the coming geopolitical crisis at the hands of the Babylonians. The original context used "live" as a call to "steadfast faithfulness" in present time, but here "live" has deeper theological significance (Moo, 206). The central question of this paragraph is the relation of the individual to Abraham, a question that has eternal consequences. Thus ζάω takes on eschatological significance, referencing the final declaration of right standing before God.

It is sometimes easy when working on an exegetical problem to punt and say that the author intended both meanings. That is not usually acceptable given normal modes of communication, but this passage is one of the few places where that interpretive strategy may be valuable. It is entirely feasible that Paul adopted a textual reading that allowed both forensic and covenantal elements, both a response of faith and a life of faithfulness to be construed. Paul does not intend to drive a wedge between these. Rather, "he wished to characterize the relationship as constituted by 'faith' through and through" (Dunn, 174; so also Longenecker, 119; George, 234; Witherington, 234). Both faith and faithfulness are necessary, both operate within the salvation God brings to individuals, and most importantly for Paul's argument, both prove that relying upon works of the Law will not bring justification.

3:12 ὁ δὲ νόμος οὐκ ἔστιν ἐκ πίστεως. This next assertion in Paul's argument posits a fundamental difference between the Law and faith. This statement on the face of it is not entirely clear. It is difficult to know whether Paul is stating an objective, theological truth, pointing to a substantial difference in essence, or whether he is referring to a chronological, dispensational distinction.

---

76. This is also supported by the accentuation of the MT (Lenski, 143–44).

77. Some argue that normal word order for an adj. prepositional phrase would be ὁ ἐκ πίστεως δίκαιος, so this construction is likely adv. (Schreiner, 209; Oakes, 111). I would largely concur, but the better argument would be that the first attributive position is more common and certainly clearer, but not necessarily so much more common to be considered the default.

Based upon his use in the immediate and farther context, it is fair to argue that he is using Law and faith here in the former sense. This Law, that is, the doing of it (mentioned before and clarified in the next line), is not based on, characterized by, or founded in faith toward God. The mistake was to confuse the role of the Law in maintaining one's relationship with God, which was proper, with the role of faith as the basis for that relationship (Dunn, 176).[78]

ἀλλ' Ὁ ποιήσας αὐτὰ ζήσεται ἐν αὐτοῖς. Paul cites Lev 18:5 to support his assertion that the Law is in no way based on faith. The citation serves to show that the Law itself requires obedience to its prescribed works, not faith (Longenecker, 120), but this requirement is entirely inappropriate and inadequate now, given the advent of Christ. Paul links this citation with the prior one because of similar wording and structure, but the conj. ἀλλά contrasts this statement with the preceding. Paul cites Lev 18:5 to prove that doing the particular commands of the Law is what the Law itself requires; this then supports his assertion that the Law is not in any way based on faith. Lev 18:5 helps Paul prove that the Law sets up *doing* as the key condition to receive the covenant promises, which contrasts noticeably with his use of Hab 2:4 (Moo, 209; see also Bruce, 162).

It is a legitimate question what Paul is doing hermeneutically with Lev 18:5, as on the surface Paul appears to misappropriate it. In the original context Lev 18:5 was a thankful response of obedience on the part of those already in covenant (Schreiner, 212). In other words, this verse from the Law is a classic statement of covenantal nomism (Garlington 2007, 163). Paul recognizes it as a genuine promise for those who were in covenant with God under the Law, but it held that positive status only until the coming of Christ. Now it is "an empty promise" pointing to a "scheme now rendered inoperative by the death of Jesus" (Hays, 259–60). It is "a merely human way to attain eschatological life" and thus entirely inadequate.[79] Paul's redemptive-historical reading means that going back to the Law as a basis for justification before God is turning the clock backwards (Schreiner, 213).

3:13 This verse begins the closing movement of Paul's exegetical argument in this paragraph, a sentence that actually spans this verse and the next. This verse contains the main assertion concerning Christ's redemptive work, followed by a ὅτι clause that provides scriptural support for the assertion. The next verse contains two ἵνα clauses that express purposes for Christ's action as indicated here.

Χριστὸς ἡμᾶς ἐξηγόρασεν. The noun Χριστός begins the verse as the nom. subject. The OT theological context that informs this section invests this

---

78. Another way of saying this is that Paul was arguing against a perversion of covenantal nomism.

79. P. M. Sprinkle, *Law and Life: The Interpretation of Leviticus 18:5 in Early Judaism and in Paul*, WUNT 2.241 (Tübingen: Mohr Siebeck, 2008), 164. See pp. 133–64 for his entire discussion of Paul's citation of this verse in Gal 3:12.

name with more than simple identification. In this instance the theological category of messiah is also in view: Jesus as the Messiah redeemed humanity from the curse. The personal pronoun ἡμᾶς then follows as the dir. obj. of the verb ἐξηγόρασεν. The extensive debate here is whether this pronoun is exclusive, referring to Jews alone (so Lightfoot, 139 and others), or inclusive, referring to Jews and Gentiles (so Lenski, 148; Longenecker, 121; and others). Either is possible on the face of it, so the answer has to come from which fits the context better. The best argument in my mind is the universality that undergirds the entire paragraph: Paul intends to show that Gentiles are "sons of Abraham" on the basis of faith alone. They were included all along in the promise God gave to Abraham. They were even implicated in the curse of the Law because of their disobedience: It was a truism that they failed to keep the Law and thus fell under its curse (Fung, 148–49; see the traditional language in 2:15), but they also had innate knowledge of right and wrong, an internal law that they broke, thus coming under the curse (Bruce, 167). The use of ὅσος in 3:10 is universal in its condemnation (Schreiner, 215), so the solution found in Christ must be universal in its application. So Gentiles are also in view here as objects of Christ's redemptive work. The main verb ἐξηγόρασεν describes Christ's work on the cross as an act of redemption. The simple form ἀγοράζω refers routinely to commercial transactions related to buying or purchasing, but it is used metaphorically on occasion in the NT to refer to a spiritual purchase related to salvation.[80] The form ἐξαγοράζω with the prefixed prep. ἐκ changes the meaning in relatively transparent ways: "buy up, buy back, redeem, deliver" are all within the field of meaning of this compound form.[81] Paul is the only author to use the compound form ἐξαγοράζω, and he does so rarely (Gal 3:13; 4:5; Eph 5:16; Col 4:5). The two uses in Galatians both have the meaning of "redeem, deliver" because they refer to God saving the individual from judgment for sin. In Gal 3:13 Paul refers to being delivered from "the curse of the Law." The wording in Gal 4:5 refers to the Law more generally ("in order that he might redeem those under the Law") but the same idea is in mind: The Law has cursed all for their disobedience. God delivers individuals from this curse through Christ's ministry of redemption by his death and resurrection.

The background for this concept of redemption is slavery and manumission in the ancient world. Adolf Deissmann is well known for connecting Paul's thought here to the practice of sacral manumission.[82] This is a rich background for understanding Paul's use of the redemption concept, but it does not match the biblical picture in every particular. Sacral manumission was clearly a legal fiction, as the god made no real payment to secure the

80. *NIDNTTE*, 1:140. See 1 Cor 6:20; 7:23; 2 Pet 2:1; Rev 5:9; 14:3.

81. BDAG, 343.

82. A. Deissmann, *Light From the Ancient East: The New Testament Illustrated By Recently Discovered Texts of the Graeco-Roman World*, trans. L. R. M. Strachan (1927; repr., Peabody, MA: Hendrickson, 1995), 326.

freedom of the slave; the god was simply used as the means for the manumission to proceed based upon a payment the slave had made. In Pauline thought God makes a real payment to secure the redemption—the death of Christ—and the subsequent relationship to God is real in all respects,[83] and the slave does nothing and pays nothing (Lenski, 150–51). Paul's use is still metaphorical, but it ceases to be a legal fiction to the same extent as explained by Deissmann. In addition, in this verse Paul does not connect slavery and redemption as he does elsewhere.[84] Paul instead focuses upon the inescapable judgment brought by the Law. He will later discuss the Law in terms that evoke slavery (see Gal 4), but here the connection is not as clear.

ἐκ τῆς κατάρας τοῦ νόμου γενόμενος ὑπὲρ ἡμῶν κατάρα. The prepositional phrase ἐκ τῆς κατάρας τοῦ νόμου describes the thing from which Christ redeems the individual. Jews and Gentiles alike were held by the curse of the Law, and Christ redeemed them from that. The ptc. γενόμενος is means (so also Schreiner, 216; de Boer, 211), showing how Christ redeemed those under the curse. The prepositional phrase ὑπὲρ ἡμῶν indicates substitution (Schreiner, 217; cf. 2:20).[85] The noun κατάτα is the predicate nom.; it shows what Christ became. This metaphorical language replaces the cause for the effect: The legal cause (curse) stands in for the legal effect (punishment).[86] Jesus represented humanity by taking on the curse of the Law in death, exhausting its power (Dunn, 177). This phrase describes in seminal form the doctrine of substitutionary atonement, focusing specifically on Christ taking on the punishment intended for mankind.

ὅτι γέγραπται· Ἐπικατάρατος πᾶς ὁ κρεμάμενος ἐπὶ ξύλου. The content of this citation from Deut 21:23 modifies the ptc. phrase γενόμενος ὑπὲρ ἡμῶν κατάρα, explaining the grounds for Paul's assertion that Christ became a curse. The ὅτι clause is causal, giving the logical grounds or basis for viewing Christ's crucifixion as placing the curse of the Law upon him. Paul introduces the citation with the verb γέγραπται, which is his common practice. The predicate adj. ἐπικατάρατος means "to be under divine condemnation"—put simply, cursed.[87] Paul modified the original wording of the LXX from the ptc. κεκατηραμένος to the adj. ἐπικατάρατος to show linguistically the theological connection he had made between the two citations from Deuteronomy

83. F. Büchsel, "ἐξαγοράζω," *TDNT*, 1:126; G. S. Shogren, "Redemption: New Testament," *ABD*, 5:655.

84. See 1 Cor 6:20 and 7:23 for two picturesque examples elsewhere in Paul.

85. Zerwick, *Biblical Greek*, 30; MHT, 3:271; S. E. Porter, *Idioms of the Greek New Testament* (Sheffield: Sheffield Academic Press, 1995), 176–77; Robertson, *Grammar*, 631 (although some of his literal language about the prepositions is off the mark); Wallace, *Greek Grammar*, 387.

86. This could also be *abstractum pro concreto* (abstract for the concrete), where the curse as an abstract idea stands in for the bearer of the curse as the concrete idea (Fung, 148).

87. BDAG, 373.

he uses in this paragraph. He interprets Deut 21:23, an earlier passage cited here, in light of Deut 27:26, a later one cited in 3:10, through the technique of *gezerah shawah*, that is, a verbal analogy (Fung, 147; Rapa, 596).[88] The nominal phrase πᾶς ὁ κρεμάμενος, "everyone who is hanged," is the subject of the sentence. This use of πᾶς plus a pres. ptc. is generic and gnomic. The prepositional phrase ἐπὶ ξύλου is locative, indicating where the person is hanged. In the original context this citation applied to the body of someone already dead from capital punishment. The body was placed on a tree after the death (Deut 21:22) as a public sign. Moses instructed the people not to leave the body on the tree overnight because the one hung in such a manner was cursed by God. Leaving the body on overnight would defile the land (Deut 21:23). By the time of the NT this passage had also applied to impalement or crucifixion.[89] Paul applies this retroactively to Christ in a striking theological development, possibly developed by early Christians and used here by Paul as a confessional formula (Longenecker, 122; Hays, 261). Paul before his conversion would have never thought that God would allow the Messiah to be crucified (Schreiner, 217). In light of Deut 21:23 Paul sees Christ as cursed because he was crucified. But Christ had been resurrected, and Paul had to reconcile the contradiction of death under a curse with resurrection as a sign of God's approbation (see Bruce, 166, and similarly Fung, 151; Martyn, 320). The only way to reconcile Jesus as Messiah dying under a curse was willing substitution. "The only explanation could be that the Messiah had willingly taken upon himself the dreaded curse that rightly belonged to others" (George, 240). This curse was not from his own doing, but as the substitute for those who were under the Law's curse.

3:14 This verse provides two purpose clauses that relate back to the main verb of v. 13, but it also concludes the larger argument of 3:6–14 by joining together several concepts mentioned throughout the paragraph.[90] Paul again mentions Gentiles, Abraham, the Spirit, and faith. It is not immediately clear how the second ἵνα clause relates to the preceding context. It could be construed as parallel to the first, both modifying the main verb ἐξηγόρασεν in v. 13 (so most commentators), or it could be understood as modifying the first, providing a purpose for the Gentiles' reception of the blessing of Abraham (so Lightfoot, 139). One way to answer this question is to clarify the relationship Paul intends between ἡ εὐλογία τοῦ Ἀβραὰμ in v. 14a

88. This is a hermeneutical move similar to what Paul did relative to Gen 15:6 and 12:3. For a concise list and definition of the seven rules of Rabbinic interpretation traditionally ascribed to Hillel, see R. N. Longenecker, *Biblical Exegesis in the Apostolic Period* (Grand Rapids: Eerdmans, 1999), 20–21.

89. J. A. Fitzmyer, "Crucifixion in Ancient Palestine, Qumran Literature, and the New Testament," *CBQ* 40 (1978): 493–513.

90. M. Silva, "Abraham, Faith, and Works: Paul's Use of Scripture in Galatians 3:6–14," *WTJ* 63 (2001): 218–22.

and τὴν ἐπαγγελίαν τοῦ πνεύματος in v. 14b. If we begin with the reasonable assumption that the second ἵνα clause is dependent upon what immediately precedes, this would imply that ἡ εὐλογία τοῦ Ἀβραὰμ and τὴν ἐπαγγελίαν τοῦ πνεύματος are different, the latter subsequent to the former either logically or chronologically. God would give "the blessing of Abraham" to the Gentiles in Christ so that he could also give "the promise of the Spirit." The problem with this view is that it minimizes the role of the Spirit in what God has done for the Gentiles. In Gal 3:1–5 Paul discusses the Spirit as a central sign of the Galatians' salvation. In Gal 4:6 the presence of the Spirit in the believer is a sign of sonship. In Gal 5:5 the Spirit enables proper confidence in future justification. In Gal 5:16 and following the Spirit is the God-ordained means for living appropriately as a believer. So on this basis, the Spirit is a (if not *the*!) central manifestation of what God has done for Gentiles. This means it is better to equate the reception of the Spirit with "the blessing of Abraham" rather than to see them as distinct. Through the progress of revelation, the promise of the Spirit was given as a key sign of God's work, and thus Paul understood it as the central affirmation of God's action in the present time. The Spirit becomes the specific manifestation of the more general blessing of Abraham (Betz, 152; Bruce, 167).[91] So the best way to construe the second ἵνα clause is as parallel to the first, restating the content differently but still modifying the main clause in 13a.[92]

ἵνα εἰς τὰ ἔθνη ἡ εὐλογία τοῦ Ἀβραὰμ γένηται ἐν Χριστῷ Ἰησοῦ. As a ἵνα clause this expresses purpose, modifying the central statement Χριστὸς ἡμᾶς ἐξηγόρασεν from v. 13. Christ redeemed believers in order that the blessing of Abraham might proceed to the Gentiles. Paul identifies Gentiles explicitly in keeping with his larger purpose in this section of showing how they are connected to Abraham by faith alone. The phrase ἡ εὐλογία τοῦ Ἀβραὰμ refers to the promises given to Abraham about blessings for him, his progeny, and the nations.[93] As elsewhere in Galatians ἐν Χριστῷ Ἰησοῦ is sphere, indicating a close association with, even incorporation into (Oakes, 114), Christ.[94] The Gentiles experience the blessing of Abraham ἐν Χριστῷ Ἰησοῦ alone; no other means is available (Moo, 215). The assertion of the clause is that Christ was crucified so that the blessing of Abraham might be extended to Gentiles. With this Paul connects Christ's death to the Abrahamic covenant,

91. Burton, 177, describes the second final clause as epexegetic to the first: "In that case the apostle refers to the promise to Abraham and has learned to interpret this as having reference to the gift of the Spirit."

92. This construal provides confirming evidence that the "we" in v. 13 is inclusive of Gentiles, and the Gentiles in v. 14a would have to be included in the "we" of v. 14b for this to hold.

93. Some link "the blessing of Abraham" specifically to Gen 28:4 (Matera, 120; Martyn, 321), but this phrase is best understood as referencing the entire context of the Abraham story in Genesis.

94. See BDAG, 327–28.

identifying it as its foundation and means for fulfillment. This completes the circle of argument Paul began in v. 6 by referencing Abraham, his faith, and the promise to him: Abraham had faith in God regarding his promise about descendants and blessing to the world. As Gentiles believe in Christ Jesus, finding salvation in a relationship with God, they receive the blessing God intended all along. This line of divine intention circumvents the Law entirely. Indeed, the Law was never intended to fulfill in any way the promises God gave to Abraham.

ἵνα τὴν ἐπαγγελίαν τοῦ πνεύματος λάβωμεν διὰ τῆς πίστεως. Had Paul stopped with the previous clause, his argument would have been complete in itself. But he continues, expanding his argument with theological clarification and development by making connections between the Spirit and the Abrahamic promises. In short, the promise of the Spirit is received by means of faith, not through the Law. The concept of "receiving the Spirit" is fairly common in the NT (John 14:17; 20:22; Acts 8:15, 17, 19; 10:47; 19:2; Rom 8:15; 1 Cor 2:12; 2 Cor 11:4), but that terminology is simply descriptive of the event. The noun τοῦ πνεύματος that modifies τὴν ἐπαγγελίαν is a gen. of apposition: "the promise, that is, the Spirit" or "the promise which is the Spirit" (Schreiner, 218; de Boer, 215). This is theologically significant, as essentially Paul equates the fulfillment of the promise given to Abraham with the manifestation of the Spirit in the present time. This is a biblical, canonical, and theological argument. Paul equates the reception of the Spirit with the fulfillment of the promises God gave to Abraham, promises that meant blessing for Abraham, his descendants, and all the nations. This affirmation completes the circle of argument Paul began at the beginning of the chapter (so also Witherington, 239): The Galatians had received the Spirit, an experience all could see and confirm as real. This event is the fulfillment of what God promised, accomplished by means of Christ's redemptive work on the cross. The blessing is thus the Spirit that the Galatians have received (similarly Betz, 153). Paul thus confirms in a theologically augmented way that God's promises never needed the Law for fulfillment. Rather, they required only faith in Christ as the means for their realization.

Theological Comments

With this paragraph Paul launches into his central theological argument to support his position about the exclusivity of faith; that theological argument becomes the second major section of the book in chapters 3–4. The topics Paul introduces here play an important role in terms of method and content. Essentially this paragraph is a discussion of how faith connects the Gentiles to Abraham and how reliance upon works of the Law brings cursing. Each part of that topic merits some attention.

One cannot understand Gal 3:6–14 without recognizing the importance of Abraham and the Abrahamic Covenant to Paul's argument. Abraham's faith in God was graciously considered by God as righteousness (3:6); in other words, God considered Abraham to have done what he was required to do within the bounds of the covenant simply on the basis of his trust, without regard to anything he actually did. The promise given to him about his descendants extends beyond his ethnic connections to those who believe in God just as he did (3:7). The covenant given to him originally, which stated that God would bless others in the world outside his family, stands as the foreshadowed proof of how God worked in Paul's time among the Gentiles (3:8). All of this then leads to an important deduction about the relationship that those of faith share with Abraham. They are connected to God because they exercise faith as Abraham did and become recipients of those covenant blessings. God graciously gave Abraham an important place in his redemptive work and primacy of place to his covenant, which still has validity and merit even today.

Paul's use of the term ἔθνος in Galatians is concentrated carefully in the first two chapters of the book, which makes very good sense: As the apostle to the Gentiles, when Paul discussed his ministry, he would naturally focus upon them and his interactions with them. After that initial biographical review of his ministry, Paul uses the term ἔθνος only twice more (Gal 3:8, 14). But these uses are not without import. Here the Gentiles are mentioned in the context of the promise given to Abraham. Paul points to the Gentiles coming to faith in Christ as a fulfillment of that promise. This shows that God is concerned not simply for his people Israel but for all whom he created in keeping with the covenant he promised to Abraham. Even at the moment of the genesis of the people of Israel, God had his eye on the whole world, and he has kept his eye on the world ever since. The entirety of the human race God created has a part in God's plan for redemption. As the present events surrounding Paul's ministry show, the nations' part in these covenant promises is played through faith in the Lord Jesus Christ.

The meaning of the πιστ- word group was discussed earlier in the excursus for Gal 2:15–21, so those particular details need not be repeated here. All that needs to be stated now is the clear, positive, exclusive emphasis faith holds in Paul's argument. Faith was Abraham's response to God on which God based his declaration of righteousness. It is faith that connects individuals to Abraham as his children. Faith is the basis of God's present justification of Gentiles, just as it was the basis of God's justification of Abraham. Faith is what joins individuals to Abraham so that they might be blessed with him. In short, Paul argues particularly well and with repeated emphasis that faith is the exclusive human attitude and response to God that God regards positively. Thus Paul argues more explicitly here what he began in 2:15–21: People are justified by faith in Christ, not by works of the Law. This emphasis by contrast shows the theological value of the second half of the paragraph, which presents numerous challenges for interpretation. Despite the intrinsic difficulties, there is an important affirmation in Paul's argument that remains clear: The Law does not justify anyone in God's sight, and indeed, by its own affirmations the Law condemns those who rely upon obedience to find that justification. In a sense Paul undercuts those who would depend on the Law by showing that they do not fully understand the import of the Law's own strictures. Justification and life are not found in the Law because the Law required obedience; justification and life come only through faith, which Abraham exercised in response to God's promises.

Application and Devotional Implications

In this paragraph of Scripture Paul engages in the first part of a larger argument with a goal of convincing the Galatians about the validity of the gospel that he preached to the Gentiles in contradistinction to the message of others that obedience to the Law is required. He seeks to persuade cognitively, to convince the Galatians to think a certain way, so that ultimately they will reaffirm both their assent and commitment to the gospel he preached. The applications drawn from this section are thus cognitive as well. We do well to rethink and reaffirm the foundations of our own faith periodically to ensure that our faith grows and matures and that our praxis retains a devotional and doxological character. Here I suggest two things for believers to consider in response to this paragraph.

First, we must recognize God has long been at work to redeem humanity. Paul's argument at this point reaches deep into the OT to the very beginning of Israel's story. Abraham believed God within the context of the covenant he promised, and God credited that faith to Abraham as righteousness. God's gracious response to this primordial faith is the foundation for the relationship present believers have with God. God's redemptive work did not begin with the twenty-first century church. It did not even begin with Israel. It began with Abraham, and consequently we need to cast our eye wider than our own lives to see the full scope of what God has done to redeem humanity. We should appreciate and value Abraham's story. It is not simply a wonderful narrative about faith; it is the beginning of our own story. We should recognize our place in Abraham's story through faith, as our present lives of faith flow directly from his own. Even further, we should know the OT foundation for our NT story. Abraham's life as the first patriarch of Israel became the central pillar of the OT story. The rest of the OT flows out from him and becomes the foundation for our NT story. We should know the OT, just as Paul did, as a foundation for our own lives of faith.

Second, Paul's emphasis upon Abraham's faith challenges us to reassert the primacy of faith in our own lives. As Abraham lived by faith, so should we. It cannot be emphasized enough: Faith is the ground upon which Christians walk, the air we breathe, and the height to which we attain. Paul emphasizes Abraham because of his faith. He is the model of the gospel Paul preached. As such, he is to be emulated in all we do. We should reaffirm faith as the foundation of our relationship with God. We should never allow ourselves any reliance upon works to please God. God responds to faith, and we should constantly affirm its foundation in our lives. We should also in faith cross human boundaries. Paul emphasizes here how God knew beforehand how he would justify the Gentiles by faith. Faith from the outset was what God was going to use to build his people Israel and what he would use to unite Jew and Gentile in the church. Faith thus crosses any human boundaries. We should recognize the implications of this and be people who enable and engender faith in those different from ourselves.

Additional Exegetical Comments

3:6 De Boer, 190–91, makes a distinction here between πιστεύω with the dat. and πιστεύω εἰς, citing BDAG, 816–17, for support. The former means to give credence to someone, believe something is true. The latter means to place one's trust in someone. The former is limited in scope, while the latter is broad and holistic. His point is to restrict what Paul says about Abraham: He believed God's promise was true and reliable. Abraham is an analogy for the Christian, but an imperfect one. Abraham believed God's promise; Christians trust in Christ. Paul's point is simply to affirm believing and justification are found in the story of Abraham. Even if de Boer is right about the limit of the analogy, Paul interprets Abraham's more restricted belief as acceptable to God and foundational for their relationship. A lesser-to-greater argument would be in play as he transfers his attention to belief in Christ.

3:6 The citation of Gen 15:6 as an example of the central tenet of faith illustrated in the OT is somewhat problematic given the shape of the Abraham narrative, especially given the climactic place of Gen 22 in displaying Abraham's faith in God and God's response with a divine oath (Gen 22:16–18). In other words, Paul appears to misread the narrative by referring to a passage that comes earlier rather than later as a central text; one might have expected him to cite something instead from Gen 22. In R. B. Chisholm's examination of the Abrahamic covenant within Genesis,[95] he presents a narratival understanding of the outworking of the covenant. He argues "(1) that all of God's promises to Abraham were conditional at the time they were originally stated, (2) that by solemn oath God progressively ratified all of these promises during Abraham's lifetime, and (3) that all conditions associated with the promises either were met by Abraham or refer to the fulfillment, not the ratification, of the promises."[96] Taken as a whole, then, the narrative shows God working out the ratification of conditional promises to Abraham, making them permanent by oath in light of Abraham's faith. Paul's citation of Gen 15:6 likely has this narrative outworking of the covenant in mind; it serves as a shorthand for all God graciously did in response to Abraham's faith throughout the narrative. This interpretation is helped by the fact that

---

95. R. B. Chisholm, "Evidence From Genesis," in *A Case for Premillennialism: A New Consensus,* ed. D. K. Campbell and J. L. Townsend (Chicago: Moody, 1992), 35–54.
96. Chisholm, "Evidence From Genesis," 36.

following Abraham's response of faith in Gen 15:6 is the first of two divine oaths in the narrative (Gen 15:18–21). Thus Gen 15:6 as a single verse in the narrative displays the entire pattern of the narrative as a whole and serves Paul's purposes well of using Abraham as a model of faith.

3:7 The close collocation with ἀκοῆς πίστεως in 3:5 and an emphasis on Abraham's faith in 3:6 lead D. Hunn to argue for the obj. gen. here, which would then influence the interpretation of the original statement in 2:16.[97]

3:7 Burton, 155, argues that πίστις is here not specifically faith in Jesus but rather faith as broad and qualitative. "Here, as in Rom 3:31ff, Paul distinctly implies the essential oneness of faith, toward whatever expression or revelation of God it is directed." I do not think this argument holds exegetically, given the entire context of Paul's argument and its focus on Christ, but I do think the argument holds theologically, given the analogy he draws with Abraham's faith.

3:7 In his excursus "Sons of Abraham," Burton, 156–59, argues that based solely on exegesis, Paul's opponents would be more in the right in their reading of the entire scope of the Genesis passages. Instead, Paul appeals to a single passage, Gen 15:6, and the scope of the entire OT concerning acceptance with God. Paul in essence addresses the larger question from a canonical viewpoint.

3:8 In interaction with the prior work of F. Watson and V. Robbins,[98] J. Dodson seeks to classify Paul's Scripture citation here based upon the presence of personification and the present import of the text for the readers.[99] He presents helpful discussion but ultimately misses some important hermeneutical moves on Paul's part by dismissing the traditional view, that is, that here Scripture is essentially standing in for God's will or intention.

3:11 Citing E. P. Sanders, Martyn, 312, emphasizes well that Gen 15:6 and Hab 2:4 are the only OT passages to link justification and faith, and Paul links them in this catena.[100] This is an important point hermeneutically, as

---

97. D. Hunn, "Πίστις Χριστοῦ in Galatians 2:16: Clarification from 3:1–6," *TynBul* 57 (2006): 23–33.

98. F. Watson, *Paul and the Hermeneutics of Faith* (Edinburgh: T&T Clark, 2004); V. K. Robbins, *Exploring the Texture of Texts: A Guide to Socio-Rhetorical Interpretation* (Valley Forge, PA: Trinity Press International, 1996); V. K. Robbins, *The Tapestry of Early Christian Discourse: Rhetoric, Society and Ideology* (New York: Routledge, 1996).

99. J. R. Dodson, "The Voices of Scripture: Citations and Personifications in Paul," *BBR* 20 (2010): 419–31.

100. E. P. Sanders, *Paul and Palestinian Judaism: A Comparison of Patterns of Religion* (London: SCM, 1977), 484.

it shows Paul's exegetical method in keeping with the Rabbinic practice of linking passages through common words, but it also shows his theological framework for interpreting these passages.

3:11 A nexus of ideas here and in Romans 2 allow for the implication that Paul's statement is universal in scope, which would then reflect back on the curse in v. 10 as also universal, applying equally to Jews and Gentiles. In short, in Rom 2:11–12 Paul discusses God's impartiality by using the prep. παρά and the correlative ὅσοι to emphasize equal condemnation of both Jew and Gentile. The use of ὅσος in Gal 3:10 and the use of justification language with the phrase παρά τῷ θεῷ in Gal 3:11 could refer to the same concept of impartiality, which would mean Jew and Gentile are both in view relative to the curse. This would support the implied assertion that no one, Jew or Gentile, is able to obey the Law, thus all fall under its curse.[101]

3:12 Martyn, 316n99, identifies two ancient texts that tie Lev 18:5 to Gentiles. *Sipra*, Achrei Mot, Perek 13:12, states that Lev 18:5 refers to Gentiles because of the word הָאָדָם, and *b. B. Qam.* 38a takes the verse as a promise to Gentiles. This provides some tangential support to the argument that Gentiles were under the curse of the Law as well.

3:13 Some texts associate specific sins with the curse of Deut 21:23: Blasphemy is highlighted in *m. Sanh.* 6.4 and Josephus, *Ant.* 4.402. Traitors to Israel are highlighted in 11QTemple 64:6–13. This provides support for an assertion made by Dunn, 178, that the citation from Deut 21:23 may have been used in early anti-Christian polemics; Paul doesn't dispute the charge but turns it to his own ends. On a tangential note, Philo, *Posterity* 26, makes a classic allegorical argument: "On which account he says, in another place, 'Cursed of God is he that hangs on a tree'; because one ought to hang upon God."

3:14 Hays, 261, argues that "Paul has creatively expanded the actual content of the promise." The original referent of the blessing in the OT was the gift of land and descendants, but in the NT context Paul argues the blessing is the church's experience of the Holy Spirit. Paul makes this move based on the image of the Spirit in the OT in passages like Isa 44:1–5. The only thing I take issue with is Hays' use of the term "creatively," which could imply that Paul saw something that was never intended to be there. I prefer language that incorporates the divine intention: In light of Christ's redemptive work, Paul now sees what God intended all along.

101. Many thanks to my intern Chris Frost for suggesting this argument to me.

Selected Bibliography

Aland, K., and B. Aland. *The Text of the New Testament: An Introduction to the Critical Editions and to the Theory and Practice of Modern Textual Criticism*. Trans. E. F. Rhodes. 2nd ed. Grand Rapids: Eerdmans, 1989.

Barrett, C. K. "Allegory of Abraham, Sarah, and Hagar in the Argument of Galatians." In *Rechtfertigung: Festschrift für Ernst Käsemann z 70 Geburtstag*, 1–16. Tübingen: Mohr Siebeck, 1976.

Boyer, J. L. "The Classification of Infinitives: A Statistical Study." *GTJ* 6 (1985): 3–27.

Chisholm, R. B. "Evidence From Genesis." In *A Case for Premillennialism: A New Consensus*, ed. D. K. Campbell and J. L. Townsend, 35–54. Chicago: Moody, 1992.

Colwell, E. C. "A Definite Rule for the Use of the Article in the Greek New Testament." *JBL* 52 (1933): 12–21.

Deissmann, A. *Light From the Ancient East: The New Testament Illustrated By Recently Discovered Texts of the Graeco-Roman World*. Trans. L. R. M. Strachan. 4th ed. New York: George H. Doran. 1927. Repr. Peabody, MA: Hendrickson, 1995.

Dixon, P. S. "The Significance of the Anarthrous Predicate Nominative in John." Th.M. thesis, Dallas Theological Seminary, 1975.

Dodson, J. R. "The Voices of Scripture: Citations and Personifications in Paul." *BBR* 20 (2010): 419–31.

Fitzmyer, J. A. "Crucifixion in Ancient Palestine, Qumran Literature, and the New Testament." *CBQ* 40 (1978): 493–513.

Harner, P. B. "Qualitative Anarthrous Predicate Nouns: Mark 15:39 and John 1:1." *JBL* 92 (1973): 75–87.

Hunn, D. "Πίστις Χριστοῦ in Galatians 2:16: Clarification from 3:1–6." *TynBul* 57 (2006): 23–33.

Longenecker, R. N. *Biblical Exegesis in the Apostolic Period*. Grand Rapids: Eerdmans, 1999.

Philo. *On the Creation. Allegorical Interpretation of Genesis 2 and 3*. Trans. F. H. Colson, and G. H. Whitaker. LCL 226. Cambridge, MA: Harvard University Press, 1929.

Robbins, V. K. *Exploring the Texture of Texts: A Guide to Socio-Rhetorical Interpretation*. Valley Forge, PA: Trinity Press International, 1996.

———. *The Tapestry of Early Christian Discourse: Rhetoric, Society and Ideology*. New York: Routledge, 1996.

Sanders, E. P. *Paul and Palestinian Judaism: A Comparison of Patterns of Religion*. London: SCM, 1977.

Silva, M. "Abraham, Faith, and Works: Paul's Use of Scripture in Galatians 3:6–14." *WTJ* 63 (2001): 251–67.

Sprinkle, P. M. *Law and Life: The Interpretation of Leviticus 18:5 in Early Judaism and in Paul*. WUNT 2.241. Tübingen: Mohr Siebeck, 2008.

Watson, F. *Paul and the Hermeneutics of Faith*. Edinburgh: T&T Clark, 2004.

Westcott, B. F., and F. J. A. Hort. *Introduction to the New Testament in the Original Greek*. Cambridge: Macmillan, 1881.

Excursus: Paul's Hermeneutic in Gal 3:6–14

When discussing Paul's hermeneutics and more specifically his use of the OT, there is likely no more contested passage than Galatians 3:6–14. My goal in this excursus is not to make a definitive argument for how Paul has interpreted these specific texts from the OT. Rather, I simply want to highlight Paul's approach more generally to provide further context for the commentary discussion.

The common critique of Paul's citations in this section is that he appears to take some of the citations, most notably Deut 27:26, out of context. That is, the meaning he intends with their use here is not the same as their meaning in the original context; he perhaps even contradicts them. Much of the exegetical work done in this area consists of aligning these intended meanings either through a better explanation of the original context, the context of Galatians, or the implied logic of Paul's argument. For example, one argument given often, especially within the broader discussion of the New Perspective, against the thesis of the implied argument that the Law required perfect obedience and no one was able to fulfill that is that this thesis runs entirely contrary to the Judaism of Paul's day. If he were to make that argument, he would be entirely out of step with his Jewish context. I think that argument is not that far off the mark and in a sense explains Paul's hermeneutic in this passage.

It is reasonable to expect that Paul would think and argue in concert with his Jewish context. In many places we see that he does just that, using arguments and techniques that are right at home in his Jewish worldview. But that does not and cannot explain everything Paul does. Some of his arguments and techniques can be explained only as revolutionary, making sense only in light of the death and resurrection of Jesus Christ. That situation pertains well with his citation of the OT in this paragraph. All of these passages had an original, textual context that made sense in light of the place of the Law in Jewish thought. Gen 15:6 was interpreted in light of Abraham's ultimate faithfulness, Hab 2:4 was understood as a call to faithfulness to the covenant, etc. Paul's interpretive anchor point as a reader, however, had changed. It was no longer centered on the supremacy of Law but on the sufficiency of Christ. This caused him to read and interpret differently. In light of Christ Gen 15:6 becomes a testimony to the centrality of faith in God. Hab 2:4 repeats that theme. Deut 27:26 becomes evidence for the singular power of the Law to condemn. These were revolutionary interpretations vis-à-vis Paul's Jewish worldview, but they made perfect sense in light of Christ.

For those who have a high regard for Scripture, the question then becomes how to hold these differing interpretive moments together. Each citation is different and has to be examined on a case-by-case basis, but generally speaking we can recognize the constant desire of the divine author to reveal his intention over time while at the same time acknowledging the progress of revelation and the limited horizon of earlier texts that get developed in later passages. Paul's citation of Gen 12:3 in Gal 3:8 is a helpful example of this. In my opinion, the exegesis of the OT passage in its original context does not convey the full intended sense of the NT meaning: One cannot readily say from the evidence of the OT itself that Moses as the author (or even Abraham as the original recipient) would have understood that the ultimate fulfillment of this promise would be Gentiles placing their faith in the Messiah, Jesus Christ, who would ultimately come as the key descendant of Abraham—indeed, the key agent of God—to fulfill this promise. Put another way, there is not a straight-line, prophetic fulfillment between Gen 12:3 and Paul's use of it in Gal 3:8. Another possible connection is that the promise was given in generic language whose referent is more clearly specified through the progress of revelation. The difficulty with this view is that Paul's language in Gal 3:8 implies a much stronger connection than a simple specification of referent. He indicates that God intended to "announce the gospel beforehand," and in Paul's mind that gospel had a very specific content, namely, the death and resurrection of Jesus and full inclusion of the Gentiles in the people of God. So a simple specification of referent is not sufficient to explain the nature of this citation. A better argument is that God intended something beyond what the OT author of Gen 12:3 knew or understood but certainly in keeping with what he had revealed to him at that time and the meaning conveyed through the language used; Paul's citation of the passage focuses on the divine intention latent in the original citation. In this way Paul's hermeneutic is indeed revolutionary, as the death and resurrection of Christ laid bare this latent divine intention. Paul could cite passages in ways that were out of step with his Jewish context but perfectly in keeping with the entirety of revelation as given by God in the OT and fulfilled in Christ in the NT.

The Permanence of Promise (3:15–18)

Textual Notes

3:16 The relative pronoun ὅς shows variation in the manuscript tradition. It is replaced in D* F[c] 81 1505 with the neut. pronoun ὅ, also reflected in the Latin translation of Irenaeus, and in F* G with the gen. sg. pronoun οὗ, likely neut. in this context. Each of these can be readily explained as scribal modifications away from the masc. nom. sg. pronoun. Strictly following the norms of Greek grammar, the pronoun should be neut. in agreement with the antecedent σπέρμα, but as it stands it exhibits *constructio ad sensum*, showing gender agreement with the trailing referent Χριστός. The neut. pronoun can be explained as a scribal correction to make the gender of the relative pronoun agree with the antecedent, and thus the masc. pronoun gave rise to the neut. The gen. pronoun οὗ is likely a scribal correction to the sense of the phrase, meaning something like "from whom is the Christ," but this should not be regarded as original: It is practically a singular reading, given the almost constant agreement of F and G, and it is counter to the sense of Paul's argument. The reading of NA[28] stands as the reading that most likely gave rise to the others, and thus is most likely original.

3:17 Both the Western text (supported by D F G it) and the Byzantine text have a longer reading at this point, adding the phrase εἰς Χριστόν to clarify the goal or end for which God ratified the covenant: "The law … does not void a covenant previously ratified by God for/to Christ." This is an important reading, but it is not the best candidate for the original reading. The shorter reading in NA[28] has exceptional support from the Alexandrian text (𝔓[46] א A B C 33 81 1175 1739 1881). Despite the ancient pedigree of the longer reading, it bears the marks of an intentional addition because adding "for/to Christ" to describe the goal of the Abrahamic covenant would make Paul's theological point clearer. The shorter reading best explains the rise of the longer reading, so the shorter reading should be considered more likely original.

Translation

15 Brothers and sisters,[1] I now speak with a human example:[2] Even though it might be simply a human will properly ratified, no one sets it aside or modifies it. **16** And the promises were spoken to Abraham and to his seed. It does not say, "And to seeds," referring to many, but referring to one, "and to your seed," which is Christ.[3] **17** Now I say this: The law that came 430 years later does not nullify the covenant previously ratified by God so that the promise would be nullified. **18** For if the inheritance came through Law, it is no longer through promise, but God gave it to Abraham through promise.

Commentary

In the previous paragraph in this central section of the letter, Paul argued exegetically. His goal was to show that the Law itself—the Scriptures that Israel regarded as given by God and containing his revelation—precluded any dependence upon itself for justification. That justification comes only through Jesus Christ, who was the divinely intended means for the Abrahamic promises to be extended to all, both Jew and Gentile. In this present paragraph, Paul continues the same essential argument, now adding the analogy of a human legal principle to make a point about the proper interpretation of redemption history (Moo, 224). His topic is the proper relationship of the Law to the Abrahamic covenant (Dunn, 181). His point is that the promises given to Abraham were like a ratified will that cannot be altered by anything that comes later. Thus the Law changes nothing about what God promised to Abraham. The Law cannot be God's intended means of fulfillment for the promises, so any arguments that allow the Law to take precedence over promise are automatically wrong. Paul develops the argument further with a new warrant to support the primacy of the promises, namely, the theological fulfillment of the Abrahamic promises in Christ. In a famous bit of exegetical argumentation,[4] Paul relies upon the grammatical number of one particular word in the Genesis text to make his point that Christ was the recipient of the promises and as such the only conduit through which God acts to fulfill those promises. The Law is set aside through, for, and because of Christ. In this way Paul continues to guide the Galatians

1. Here I follow recent scholarship that sees the pl. ἀδελφοί as referring to all members of the group regardless of sex; see BDAG, 18.
2. Some translations prefer an even more dynamic rendering here: "I offer an example from everyday life" (NET); "I'm using a human illustration" (CSB); "I speak in terms of human relations" (NASB).
3. Some translations use the referent instead of the word "seed": "descendants ... descendant" (NET); "offsprings ... offspring" (ESV, NRSV); "children ... child" (NLT).
4. Or infamous, depending upon your viewpoint!

back to his gospel and away from those who would entice them to observe the Law as a way to relate to God.

The essential arguments of this paragraph are likely a response to some specific teachings of Paul's opponents that demonstrated a particular hermeneutical stance toward the biblical story. Jewish tradition viewed the Law as preexistent before human history and sometimes even eternal.[5] Abraham was pictured as keeping the Law even though it was not given to Moses until much later (Longenecker, 133).[6] The means by which Abraham knew the Law was variously ascribed,[7] but the applicational point in Jewish thought was that the Law was definitive for anyone's relationship to God: Despite the difference in time, even Abraham kept the Law, and his example applied to the present day. It is very likely that Paul's opponents in Galatia would have capitalized on this line of argument and would have even made a specific application to the Galatians with reference to Abraham's circumcision in Gen 17:9–14. If Abraham implicitly knew and kept the Law as shown in his circumcision, the Galatians should keep it, too, as his spiritual progeny. In response to this likely argumentation, Paul inverts the interpretation, giving priority to the promises that came first, not the Law that came later. "Paul turns the traditional Jewish view upside down: instead of attributing to Abraham a foreknowledge of the Torah, Paul deprives the Sinai Torah of any significance" (Betz, 159), establishing the Abrahamic promises as the foundation of God's activity in the world. Paul makes a salvation-historical

5. One interesting passage in this regard is *b. Šabb.* 88B, where the angels challenge Moses before God when Moses entered God's presence to receive the Torah: "And said R. Joshua b. Levi, 'When Moses came up on high, the ministering angels said before the Holy One, blessed be He, "Lord of the world, what is one born of woman doing among us?" He said to them, "He has come to receive the Torah." They said before him, "This secret treasure, hidden by you for nine hundred and seventy-four generations before the world was created, are you now planning to give to a mortal? 'What is man, that you are mindful of him, and the son of man, that you think of him, O Lord our God, how excellent is your name in all the earth! who has set your glory upon the heavens' (Ps. 8:5, 2)!" Here the Torah is said to exist exactly 974 generations before the creation of the world. Subsequent to this challenge, God guides Moses in his responses to the angels, helping him prove that the Law was made to help man follow God, not as a help for angels.

6. A helpful example is Jub. 24:8–13, which recounts the story in Gen 26 of Isaac settling in Gerar. When recounting God's promises to Isaac, Jub. 24:11 clarifies that the basis of God's blessing was Abraham's obedience to the Law: "And all of the nations of the earth will bless themselves by your seed because your father obeyed me and observed my restrictions and my commandments and my laws and my ordinances and my covenant."

7. Betz, 158, cites texts that show that Abraham knew the Law implicitly (*Gen. Rab.* 61:1), he knew it from secret writings (Jub. 21:10), and he knew it from special revelation from God (*Mek. Exod.* 20:18; *Gen. Rab.* 44:21).

argument, arguing that there is no certain, straight connection between the Abrahamic covenant and the Law (Schreiner, 223). He de-emphasizes the circumcision commandment in Gen 17:9–14 on the grounds that God's promise to Abraham about offspring preceded the command to circumcise (de Boer, 221).

Paul begins by stating his legal analogy in v. 15, and then he makes his logical deductions from this legal analogy in vv. 17–18, focusing both on the timing and character of the Law vis-à-vis the promise. The discussion regarding the promises and their recipients in v. 16 is a parenthesis that supports the central argument of the paragraph, but it is not necessary for the full affirmation of the logic. This argument foreshadows a move Paul will make in full in the following paragraphs.

3:15 Ἀδελφοί, *κατὰ ἄνθρωπον λέγω*. Paul introduces his argument with a statement designed both to get the attention of his listeners and to explain how his argument is going to proceed. The noun *ἀδελφοί* grabs the attention of his readers by alerting them to a new part of the letter structure (Longenecker, 126) but also by its warm, relational tone (Lightfoot, 140; Lenski, 156; George, 244). The prepositional phrase *κατὰ ἄνθρωπον* indicates the nature of the language and concept that Paul is about to express, that is, Paul speaks in a human way, with reference to everyday affairs, with an "analogy from human life" (Bruce, 169). Paul uses the phrase to alert his readers that he is using a different category of evidence than his previous citations of Scripture, a rhetorical move to help his readers follow his argument.

ὅμως ἀνθρώπου κεκυρωμένην διαθήκην οὐδεὶς ἀθετεῖ ἢ ἐπιδιατάσσεται. Paul's intended sense of this statement is relatively clear and serves the point of his argument without confusion: No one changes a ratified will because it has fixed legal standing. The legal analogy relates to the permanence of the Abraham covenant: Nothing that comes later changes the promises God made to Abraham in any respect. That being said, the exegetical problems in this passage are quite involved, centering around the function of ὅμως, the meaning of διαθήκη, and the legal background for the concepts.

The function of the word ὅμως here is ambiguous with two primary options for meaning. First, ὅμως could act an adversative conj., marking an antithesis between *ἀνθρώπου κεκυρωμένην διαθήκην* and *οὐδεὶς ἀθετεῖ ἢ ἐπιδιατάσσεται*. This accords with the meaning of ὅμως but not its location in the clause. One would expect it to be placed in front of *οὐδεὶς ἀθετεῖ ἢ ἐπιδιατάσσεται* in this construal. Second, ὅμως could function as a comparative conj. with the meaning "likewise, similarly." This accords with the location of ὅμως in the clause but not its normal meaning. One either has to assume the accentuation ὁμῶς (a much rarer term meaning "equally, likewise") or a meaning akin to ὅμοιος (so Moo, 227).[8] Paul uses this conj. elsewhere only in

8. The TLG database shows 634 occurrences of the term ὁμῶς, while it shows 25,089 occurrences of ὅμως.

1 Cor 14:7 where he makes a comparison; this leads some to argue for the comparative force here (Moo, 227; Witherington, 243).[9] There are two other points of consideration, though, that ultimately argue for the adversative sense. First, the word order brings the phrase ἀνθρώπου κεκυρωμένην διαθήκην forward when it more naturally would follow the verbs. This likely is meant to highlight the antithesis, which forms the basis for Paul's analogy. Second, Paul argues from a lesser to greater, which supports the adversative nuance (Schreiner, 226). Here a translation indicating some type of emphasis of concession would bring out the adversative force: "Even though it is only a human covenant that is ratified, nevertheless no one annuls or adds to it" (similarly Lightfoot, 141; Lenski, 156).

Front and center in discussion of this verse is the meaning of the noun διαθήκη and to what exactly Paul intended to refer. The noun had a range of meaning that included the general idea of "compact, agreement" on the one hand and specific types of compacts on the other. It could mean more generally "covenant," that is, a binding of two parties together for a particular purpose, or more specifically "will" or "testament," that is, a legal contract designed to dispose of property and estate upon death.[10] It is clear that Paul has one of the more specific meanings in mind, but which of these is less certain. There is good evidence in favor of the meaning "covenant." Normally in the NT διαθήκη means "covenant" under the influence of the LXX, which consistently uses that word to translate בְּרִית, the Hebrew term regularly used both for human and divine covenants.[11] Paul's other uses of the term, even later in the paragraph in v. 17, have this meaning (so Moo, 227). On the other side of the question, there is also good evidence that Paul intended "will" here. Usage of διαθήκη as a whole in Greek literature is more commonly "will."[12] Paul's use of technical, legal terms would make "will" more likely (Martyn, 338).[13] In Heb 9:16–17 the sense of διαθήκη is without doubt "will" or "testament,"[14] and this parallel would support that meaning here. The meaning "will" is more likely than "covenant" based on the entire semantic situation: the legal terminology, the commonness of that meaning in Greek literature as a whole, the "human analogy" Paul makes, and what his audience was most likely to understand. Paul clearly plays on the double meaning of the

---

9. See also BDAG, 710; BDF, §450(2).

10. See LSJ, 394–95; MGS, 487.

11. See *HALOT*, 157–59, for evidence on the Hebrew term. A search of the Tov-Polak Hebrew/Greek Parallel Text in BibleWorks found 257 places where ברית is translated by διαθήκη. A search of Rahlf's Septuagint with Logos morphology found this in 245 verses. The LXX uses the related term συνθήκη, "treaty," only once for the Hebrew term in 4 Kgdms 17:15 (J. Behm, "διαθήκη," *TDNT*, 2:126).

12. J. Behm, "διαθήκη," *TDNT*, 2:124.

13. Legal terms like these are also used with covenants (Schreiner, 227), so that evidence is moderated somewhat.

14. H. Hegermann, "διαθήκη," *EDNT*, 1:299.

term (Matera, 126; Hays, 263). It allows him to use terminology that connects both to the biblical argument and the life experience of his readers, further convincing them that his argument is correct. His analogy emphasizes the irrevocable nature of a properly ratified will; the covenant God made with Abraham is as permanent.

Another problem with understanding Paul's statement is the lack of clarity regarding the legal background he had in mind. The essential problem is that Paul's absolute statement does not match either the Roman or Greek legal situation, as there are no clear examples of wills in either case that could never be modified or revoked (Moo, 227).[15] Likely Paul was dealing with an implication that only the testator could modify the will, never a third party, and this would fit with Paul's point that God has not modified his original covenant with Abraham in any way (de Boer, 219–20). Ernst Bammel famously argued for the Jewish custom of מתנת בריא (*mattenat bari*), in which a living person could make an irrevocable disposition to another while still alive.[16] This possible connection is weakened, however, by the simple fact that the Gentile Galatians would not necessarily understand an entirely Jewish practice without further explanation (so Betz, 155).[17] Given this lack of precision in identifying a particular legal situation, the better tack is to argue that likely Paul has no specific situation in mind. Rather, he is speaking generally about how a will is a permanent document (Oakes, 118). It cannot be changed willy-nilly by anyone on a whim once it has been ratified (Betz, 156; Garlington 2007, 176). A ratified will is permanent in character; this general assertion makes the point of Paul's analogy.

Having cleared the ground of exegetical underbrush, we can now work the soil a little. The essential kernel of the sentence emphasizes what cannot be done: No one can modify a ratified will. The dir. obj. of the sentence, ἀνθρώπου κεκυρωμένην διαθήκην, has been brought forward for emphasis to help Paul make the analogy. The sense of the phrase is "a human will that has been properly ratified" (cf. NIV "a human covenant that has been duly established"; CSB "a validated human will"). Placing the gen. noun before the head noun marks ἀνθρώπου as emphatic and "arises from an express antithesis,"[18] here due to the comparison of the human and divine in Paul's thought. In this

---

15. See Longenecker, 128–30, for an extensive review of the possible legal background for Paul's statement.

16. E. Bammel, "Gottes DIATHĒKĒ (Gal 3:15–17) und das jüdische Rechtsdenken," *NTS* 6 (1960): 313–19.

17. Evidence has been found that this practice was current in Greek contexts, too. See S. R. Llewelyn and R. A. Kearsley, *New Documents Illustrating Early Christianity: A Review of the Greek Inscriptions and Papyri Published in 1980–81* (Macquarie University: Ancient History Documentary Research Centre, 1992), 44–47. This means the Galatians may have understood the practice from their own background.

18. G. B. Winer, *A Treatise on the Grammar of New Testament Greek, Regarded as a Sure Basis for New Testament Exegesis* (Edinburgh: Clark, 1882), 240.

context the noun ἀνθρώπου is qualitative (Burton, 179); it is not a particular person's will that is in view, but human wills generally speaking. The ptc. κεκυρωμένην is adj. to διαθήκην and functions as an intensive pf., emphasizing the results of the past action: "a covenant that stands ratified." Paul's assertion regarding this properly ratified will concerns its permanence: οὐδεὶς ἀθετεῖ ἢ ἐπιδιατάσσεται, "no one changes or adds [to it]." This gnomic statement uses two technical terms to describe what cannot be done to a will that has been properly executed. The verb ἀθετέω means to annul or invalidate, and the verb ἐπιδιατάσσομαι means to add a codicil.[19] Paul thus argues both positively and negatively that a properly ratified will is permanent.

By using these terms with legal denotations, Paul makes a comparison between the promises of God and the legal example of a will, affirming the permanence of each when properly ratified. The argument is lesser-to-greater (Lenski, 162; Longenecker, 127; George, 245; Rapa, 598): Just as a human will cannot be modified once ratified, God's promises to Abraham do not change no matter what comes later. What is true in the human realm about our documents is certainly true when it comes to God and his promises.[20] The analogy works simply to associate permanence and inviolability of wills in the known, human realm with covenants in the divine. The fact that Paul invokes a will does not mean that he also invokes the death of the testator or other attending factors (Lenski, 157).[21] It is simply an analogy marshaled for the sake of explanation.

3:16 With this verse Paul writes perhaps one of the most intriguing arguments in the entire book of Galatians. The verse amounts to a parenthesis. The legal analogy of v. 15 is applied to the Abrahamic Covenant and the Law in v. 17; this intervening verse could be removed without affecting the logic of the paragraph at all. So the exegesis of v. 16 should bear in mind that this verse is an ancillary proof of Paul's argument, not a necessary one. Even so, the sentence is pregnant with meaning and needs careful examination because it is significant to his overall argument about the way the Abrahamic promises come to Gentiles (Moo, 229).

---

19. BDAG, 24; BDAG, 370. The midd. voice of ἐπιδιατάσσεται is likely an indir. midd. with the implication that a person would add a codicil to a will for personal benefit. This word could very well have been coined by Paul. A TLG search shows Gal 3:15 to be the first occurrence of the word in extant Greek literature. The word διατάσσω in the midd. voice means "make testamentary dispositions ... order by will"; adding the prefixed prep. ἐπί would logically alter the meaning to place upon or add to a will in this instance.

20. See Calvin, 94, who says, "If human bargains be so firm that they can receive no addition, how much more must this covenant remain inviolable?"

21. See also J. Behm, "διαθήκη," *TDNT*, 2:129. By way of contrast, the author of Hebrews clearly does make this point in his use of the term.

τῷ δὲ Ἀβραὰμ ἐρρέθησαν αἱ ἐπαγγελίαι καὶ τῷ σπέρματι αὐτοῦ. Paul continues his argument by identifying the recipients of the promises God gave. This identification of Abraham links this paragraph to the previous one. Even though he now discusses the issue of permanence through the analogy of the will, Paul still attends to what God has done for the Galatians through the patriarch. His implication begins to assemble the argument he will make from the previous analogy: The Law is invalid in the present time because the promises were given to Abraham outside any Law-oriented framework.

The conj. δέ continues the argument from the prior sentence. Returning to the topic of promises from the legal analogy warrants a translation of "Now," further emphasizing the parenthetical nature of the verse, but that should not be taken to imply any disjunction between this sentence and the previous one. Paul simply begins to elaborate on the point of the comparison, namely, the promises of God. The indir. obj. τῷ Ἀβραὰμ comes first in the sentence, emphasizing him as the first recipient in time of the promises God spoke. Paul adds τῷ σπέρματι αὐτοῦ as another indir. obj. to the verb ἐρρέθησαν, a thought that he will develop carefully in the next half of the verse. Paul thus identifies the recipients of the permanent promises God gave, Abraham and his seed.

The key word in this sentence is ἐπαγγελίαι, "promises." The use here points back to the first use in the book in 3:14, where Paul connected promise and Spirit. In that earlier reference Paul only introduced the concept of promise; from this point forward he elaborates it.[22] The meaning of the noun ἐπαγγελία is easy to grasp: "declaration to do something with implication of obligation to carry out what is stated," that is, a "promise" or "pledge."[23] Interestingly the noun is quite rare within the LXX, but it is an appropriate word to describe what God does through covenant in the OT (Moo, 228; so also Witherington, 244; de Boer, 216).[24] More difficult to determine are the specific promises that would be in view and thus the specific text in mind in the following argument. Paul refers to the OT text with two phrases. The first, τῷ σπέρματι αὐτοῦ, is conceptual, while the second, καὶ τῷ σπέρματί σου, is handled as an exact citation. Based upon these two phrases, allowing for some grammatical variation in wording that does not change the sense, there are numerous potential candidates for what Paul has in mind:

MT
וּלְזַרְעֲךָ: Gen 13:15; 17:7, 8; 26:3; 28:4, 13; 35:12; Num 18:19
לְזַרְעֲךָ (without the waw conjunctive): Gen 12:7; 15:18; 24:7; 26:4; 48:4

---

22. The noun ἐπαγγελία occurs 10x in Galatians, starting at 3:14.

23. BDAG, 355.

24. For a thorough study on this matter, see K. P. Conway, *The Promises of God: The Background of Paul's Exclusive Use of "Epangelia" for the Divine Pledge*, BZNW 211 (Berlin: De Gruyter, 2014).

בְּזַרְעֲךָ (with prefixed prep. בְּ): Gen 22:18; 26:4
וּבְזַרְעֲךָ / וּבְזַרְעֶךָ: Gen 28:14; Deut 28:46; 2 Kings 5:27

LXX
καὶ τῷ σπέρματί σου: Gen 13:15; 17:8; 24:7; 26:3; 28:4, 13; 35:12; 48:4; Num 18:19
τῷ σπέρματί σου (without the conj. καί): Gen 12:7; 15:18; 26:4
ἐν τῷ σπέρματί σου: Gen 22:18; 26:4
καὶ ἐν τῷ σπέρματί σου: Gen 28:14; Deut 28:46; 4 Kgdms 5:27

If Paul intends to be understood strictly, the choices are limited, as Abraham has to be the recipient and καί has to be part of the quotation (so Lightfoot, 142). The inclusion of Abraham as a specific recipient of the spoken promises reasonably restricts the references to the Abraham narrative in Genesis. Strictly following the latter requirement to include the conj. would focus attention on Gen 13:15 or 17:8, while allowing for some laxity in the presence of the conj. opens the choices further to Gen 12:7; 13:15; 15:18; 17:7, 8; 22:18; 24:7.[25] Paul's use of the pl. ἐπαγγελίαι would seem to lean to a broader reference, perhaps to a group of texts, reflecting the reiteration of the promises inherent in the Genesis text itself. The very fact that Paul cites different forms of the wording supports this as well. So Paul was thinking conceptually, focusing broadly on the concept of the seed of Abraham and its outworking in the Genesis text.

There are two important observations about these Genesis texts that impact Paul's argument. First, the promises are made first to Abraham as an individual. His role as an individual recipient is never eclipsed by any subsequent restatement of the promise.[26] Indeed, when the seed is in view, it is always identified as "your seed" with a specific reference to Abraham. This is reflected in Paul's language, where he emphasizes Abraham equally as a recipient of the promises. This citation reiterates Paul's emphasis on Abraham as an important example for the Galatians. Second, the promises made to Abraham and to his seed are multifaceted, involving the possession of land, a relationship with God, being an agent of blessing, and an eternal timeframe. Each of these can be seen as entailments of the original promise made to Abraham in Gen 12:2–3. Understood within the context of Paul's argument, though, is an implicit connection of promise and Spirit as in v. 14. In Paul's thought the Spirit and OT promises converge. This is argued convincingly by S. Williams: The OT promises involve numerous descendants for Abraham and possession of the world, but since God fulfills this pledge through the Spirit, the promise of numerous descendants and promise of possessing the world merge into the promise of the Spirit. The promise becomes a promise of the particular means by which sons of Abraham would be created out of

25. Hays, 264, sees this as a particular reference to Gen 17:8 due to the use of διαθήκη in that text.

26. This is rightly emphasized by Lenski, 158.

an enslaved people and the means by which the redeemed people bring the world under the Lordship of Christ. The Spirit accomplishes both of those promises in God's people.[27]

οὐ λέγει· Καὶ τοῖς σπέρμασιν, ὡς ἐπὶ πολλῶν ἀλλ' ὡς ἐφ' ἑνός· Καὶ τῷ σπέρματί σου, ὅς ἐστιν Χριστός. Paul in the second part of the verse focuses his attention upon the one seed, Christ, who is the ultimate recipient of the promises. Paul acts like a probate judge, interpreting the language of the διαθήκη as closely as possible (Hays, 264). The phrase οὐ λέγει serves to dissect the particular wording of the Scripture to which he alludes. The verb is not impersonal (i.e., "it does not say"); instead it refers to the implied agent of the previous phrase: "he does not say." It could even be made explicit: "God does not say ..." (so also Burton, 181; Longenecker, 131).[28] It is well known that Paul points to the sg. σπέρματι to argue that Christ was in view in these promises. This is the conclusion of the final, emphatic point of the line: ὅς ἐστιν Χριστός.[29] The central point Paul makes relies upon the Greek noun σπέρμα and the Hebrew noun זֶרַע. Each of these is a collective noun, most often sg. in number but pl. in referent. Paul focuses upon the sg. number to emphasize the ultimate seed of Abraham, whom he identifies as Christ. His point is that the promises were given to Abraham and also to Christ. This means Christ is able to distribute the intended blessings to all who are connected to him by faith.

27. S. K. Williams, "Promise in Galatians: A Reading of Paul's Reading of Scripture," *JBL* 107 (1988): 709–20.

28. MHT, 4:109, says, "This impersonal use of 'he says' is quite rabbinical and also Pauline (1 Cor 6:16; 15:27; 2 Cor 6:2; Gal 3:16; Eph 4:8); numerous examples of rabbinical precedent are quoted by S.-B. III 365f e.g. weʾômêr (Aboth 6,2.7.9.10.11)." But note Winer, *Grammar*, 656, who argues that God is implicitly in view: "The formulas of citation—λέγει, 2 C. 6:2, G. 3:16, E. 4:8, al.; φησί, 1 C. 6:16, H. 8:5; εἴρηκε, H. 4:4 (compare the Rabbinical ואומר); μαρτυρεῖ H. 7:17 (εἶπε, 1 C. 15:27)—are probably in no instance impersonal in the minds of the N. T. writers. The subject (ὁ θεός) is usually contained in the context, either directly or indirectly: in 1 C. 6:16 and Mt. 19:5, φησί, there is an apostolic ellipsis (of ὁ θεός); in H. 7:17 the best authorities have μαρτυρεῖται."

29. This phrase exhibits *constructio ad sensum* with the masc. relative pronoun, agreeing with Χριστός instead of the neut. relative pronoun, which would agree with σπέρματι. Winer, *Grammar*, 207, states, "It would seem that the relative usually takes the gender of the noun that follows (1) Where this is regarded as the principal noun; as when the relative clause gives the proper names of things which in the principal clause were mentioned in general terms ... especially in the case of personal names." D. B. Wallace, *Greek Grammar Beyond the Basics: An Exegetical Syntax of the New Testament* (Grand Rapids: Zondervan, 1996), 338, says, "It occurs when the focus of the discourse is on the predicate nom.: the dominant gender reveals the dominant idea of the passage."

Paul's exegesis in this verse is thought of as rather rabbinic in character, and this is not in and of itself an unfair characterization. Places where points are made in a similar fashion, based on the grammatical number of a noun, are well known.[30] Paul knows the functional difference between the collective sg. and a singular reference, as evidenced by his argument in 3:29 (Bruce, 172; Moo, 229), so he is making a deliberate choice to focus on the number of the noun in this instance. As with much rabbinic exegesis, Paul uses a technique that suits his argument in a somewhat *ad hoc* fashion. But rabbinic exegesis also made theological connections, and Paul does as well in this context. Paul thinks theologically regarding the role of a particular descendant of Abraham who represents the Jewish people as a corporate personality, an approach that was also known in Judaism.[31] This theological move may itself have been built upon the meaning of the OT text, as in places the noun "seed" could legitimately have a singular referent (Bruce, 173),[32] perhaps even Isaac, which then expanded out from there to other descendants. The ambiguity between sg. and pl. was built into the original declaration (Witherington, 244), and Paul capitalizes on this to make his theological point. But there is more to add. To declare Paul's exegesis rabbinic does not say enough about what he has done. Paul knows that the entire storyline of the Bible leads to a single son of Abraham who will fulfill God's plan, a storyline that finds its fulfillment in Jesus (Schreiner, 230). Thus Paul is not thinking simply exegetically or making theological connections that are only latent in the OT text. In a real sense he is working through the redemption history of the entire biblical canon, reading its texts in light of the current revelation in Christ. God revealed Christ to Paul as the agent through whom the promises to Abraham would be realized. Christ is the ultimate recipient and thus the distributor of the promised blessings to those who have faith in him.

3:17 τοῦτο δὲ λέγω. Paul uses this metacomment to bring the readers' attention back to the main idea that follows. This confirms that the preceding verse is a parenthesis of sorts: Paul now resumes for further explanation an idea already expressed (Burton, 180–82). Paul returns from his generic statement about the validity of a will in v. 15 to the specific issues of the promises and the Law.

διαθήκην προκεκυρωμένην ὑπὸ τοῦ θεοῦ ὁ μετὰ τετρακόσια καὶ τριάκοντα ἔτη γεγονὼς νόμος οὐκ ἀκυροῖ εἰς τὸ καταργῆσαι τὴν ἐπαγγελίαν. The word order of this long phrase is convoluted from the standpoint of English, but it functions well to emphasize particular parts of Paul's argument similarly to what

30. See *m. Šabb.* 9.2; *m. Sanh.* 4.5; Philo, *Names* 145.

31. Jub 16:16–18 identifies a single descendent of Abraham who would become a "holy seed"; this represents a messianic expectation centered upon a single individual, who in turn creates a nation dedicated to God as a special possession.

32. See Gen 4:25; Gen 21:12, 13; 2 Sam 7:12–15; Ps 89:3–4.

he has done before.[33] The phrase διαθήκην προκεκυρωμένην ὑπὸ τοῦ θεοῦ is the dir. obj. of the negated verb ἀκυροῖ brought forward for emphasis. This "previously ratified will" is the promise of God given to Abraham; for Paul's argument to work the referent of διαθήκη has to be the Abrahamic covenant (Moo, 230). Moving διαθήκη and its modifiers forward in the sentence keeps a rhetorical focus on the covenant instead of upon the Law. The nom. subject of the clause occurs next but with an extensive modifier in first attributive position: μετὰ τετρακόσια καὶ τριάκοντα ἔτη γεγονὼς, "which came after 430 years." This means that the reader has to work through extensive language about time first before getting to the actual grammatical subject, the noun νόμος. This has the effect of further minimizing the Law. The kernel of the sentence, ὁ νόμος οὐκ ἀκυροῖ, comes next and emphasizes what the Law does not do by virtue of the fact that the covenant had been ratified earlier. The verb ἀκυρόω means "to cancel, set aside, invalidate"; it is a legal technical term that fits the analogy Paul uses throughout this paragraph.[34] Chronological order and priority here are important to Paul, and he constructs the sentence to emphasize that the promises came first, then the Law. The last phrase of the sentence, εἰς τὸ καταργῆσαι τὴν ἐπαγγελίαν, is an inf. of result. The result here, though, is not actual but rather hypothetical given the flow of Paul's argument. He negates this result to argue that there is no way this result could actually occur.

The point of Paul's argument is to give priority to the Abrahamic covenant because it came first in time before the Law. The essence of Paul's argument flowing from v. 15 to here is a syllogism (Burton, 183; Fung, 157). The major premise is found in v. 15: "no one adds to a ratified covenant." The minor premise is "the Law came 430 years later." The conclusion is that the Abrahamic covenant cannot be set aside by the later Law. This becomes a theological argument as well. Jewish thought usually saw the Abrahamic covenant as the first stage of God's revelation, which was then expanded in the Mosaic covenant (Martyn, 337; Moo, 230). Paul severs any connection between the two on the basis of the temporal priority of the first. The length of time Paul states here for the interval between the covenants is a traditional number, drawn from Exod 12:40–41. Paul is not concerned with the exact length of the sojourn in Egypt as much as he is concerned with the fact of the extended interval between the giving of the covenants. The exact number has no real import to Paul's argument (Burton, 184; Fung, 157n26; Longenecker, 133). His sole point is that the Law is "subordinate and interim" to the Abrahamic covenant (Schreiner, 231). This is emphasized by the negated result clause εἰς τὸ καταργῆσαι τὴν ἐπαγγελίαν. This is a result that cannot occur, a result excluded by definition. The promise God gave to Abraham cannot be nullified by anything that came later. It cannot

33. A similarly unusual word order occurs in 3:15 when Paul introduces the legal analogy.

34. LSJ, 59; MGS, 80; *EDNT*, 1:56.

change its wording, nor can it alter its character (Dunn, 185). The point of Paul's analogy is to treat the Law like an illegitimate codicil because of its late arrival: The Law is "both irrelevant and impotent" with regard to the promise (Soards and Pursiful, 145).

3:18 *εἰ γὰρ ἐκ νόμου ἡ κληρονομία, οὐκέτι ἐξ ἐπαγγελίας.* This sentence provides additional logical grounding for the prior statement in v. 17 regarding the inability of the Law to annul the earlier covenant.[35] The word *κληρονομία* is the focus of the first clause.[36] This word means "inheritance" or "property, possession" in most occurrences in extant Greek literature.[37] Within the OT the concept of inheritance began with the promises to Abraham and involved descendants who would possess a particular land; see, e.g., Gen 17:8, Exod 32:13.[38] During the Exile, this concept was expanded to universal proportions with messianic connections; see, e.g., Ezek 47; Dan 12:13.[39] This eschatological expansion is reflected in the NT in the parable of the tenant landowners in Mark 12:1–12.[40] Thus the ideas of inheritance and heir became eschatological. Paul saw Christ as the messianic recipient of these promises, the heir *par excellence*, and his firm assertion is that the eschatological promises are given to others on the basis on connection to this one heir. The connection is so strong that those thus connected may also be called heirs themselves. So in this term Paul does not see simply reception of promised blessing, but also eschatological fulfillment, which is of a piece with his understanding of Christ's role in salvation history both in himself and in his work among the Gentiles. Paul had connected these OT blessings directly to the promises of God to Abraham. God had promised these blessings to the nations through Abraham, which Paul has now identified with the Spirit.

In this conditional Paul posits that the inheritance could come by means of Law observance. Previously Paul used the phrase *ἐκ νόμου* to show the means or basis for justification. He hypothetically applies that idea here to the receipt of the Abrahamic promises and follows it to its logical conclusion in the apodosis. The phrase *ἐξ ἐπαγγελίας* indicates means in parallel to *ἐκ νόμου*. Paul's logic is clear and quite sound: If the inheritance comes through the Law, then it no longer comes by means of promise. This would reflect a fundamental reconfiguration of inheritance and promise. If those who have

35. Dunn, 186, argues that the *γάρ* shows that the argument of v. 17 did not rely only on "the more dubious argument that priority means superiority."

36. This is the first (and only) time Paul uses the term *κληρονομία* in the book; he uses the noun *κληρονόμος* three times (3:29; 4:1, 7) and the verb *κληρονομέω* twice (4:30; 5:21).

37. LSJ, 959; MGS, 1138.

38. J. H. Friedrich, "*κληρονομέω* et al.," *EDNT*, 2:298.

39. J. H. Friedrich, "*κληρονομέω* et al.," *EDNT*, 2:298.

40. W. Foerster, "*κλῆρος* et al.," *TDNT*, 3:781–82.

faith in Christ receive the Spirit through obedience to the Law, then God's promise is no longer in effect.

τῷ δὲ Ἀβραὰμ δι' ἐπαγγελίας κεχάρισται ὁ θεός. Paul now gives evidence to deny the hypothesis of the prior conditional sentence. Explicitly he denies the truth of the apodosis, namely, that God gave the inheritance not through the promise. Implicitly this affirms the negation of the protasis, namely, that inheritance comes through the Law. The verb κεχάρισται has two possible senses here. If the verb is treated as transitive, the meaning would be "give freely" with the dir. obj. τὴν κληρονομίαν implied; if the verb is treated as intransitive, the meaning would be "show oneself gracious to someone."[41] Either one fits the context well with little difference between the results, but given the emphasis in the prior sentence on κληρονομία, the former option is preferred. The translation for clarity should make this dir. obj. explicit: "But God graciously gave the inheritance to Abraham through promise."[42] The force of the pf. tense here is quite vivid, as the present results of the past action are in full force; indeed, Paul reinforces the present application of those promises through the pf. tense.[43] Taken altogether, the phrases make a tight, logical argument that can be represented as follows

> Hypothesis:
> IF P :: If the inheritance came through Law,
> THEN Q :: it is no longer through promise
>
> Reality:
> NOT Q :: God gave it to Abraham through promise.
> THEN NOT P :: [implied: The inheritance does not come through Law.]

Thus Paul reiterates an argument that began at the beginning of the chapter where he emphasizes the Galatians' reception of the Spirit through faith, not Law. Since in Paul's thought the inheritance is the Spirit, he logically makes the same point there and here.

In this short paragraph Paul emphasizes the enduring validity of the promises given to Abraham by God in contrast to the time-bound nature of the Law. A general principle drawn from human affairs makes his point quite well: After a will has been ratified, it cannot be changed. Similarly the promises God gave to Abraham, received by faith and not works, cannot be changed by the advent of the Law at a later time. Even further, Christ is the recipient of those divine promises. His advent ushers in their fulfillment without any need for the Law. On these grounds Paul continues his effort

---

41. BDAG, 1078.

42. Most English translations make the dir. obj. explicit with a pronoun "it," e.g., NASB "But God has granted it to Abraham by means of a promise."

43. Wallace, *Greek Grammar*, 582, classifies this as pf. of allegory, defined thusly: "The perfect tense can be used to refer to an OT event in such a way that the event is viewed in terms of its allegorical or applicational value" (581–82).

to persuade the Galatians that any reliance upon the Law is misguided and indeed dangerous to their relationship with God.

Theological Comments

The character of God is a central *topos* within the biblical text, and his character manifests itself in his actions. The particular acts of making promises to Abraham and giving the Law to Israel are on display in this paragraph, and they reflect back on God's character to give a fuller picture of who he is and how he works in the present time. Paul's opponents likely argued that the Law superseded the promise. But the implication underlying this argument reflects critically on God's character: If the Law supersedes the promise, then the Law has effectively annulled it. God's promise would no longer be sure, thus he would be capricious (Matera, 130). Paul's central assertion, drawn from the primacy of promise in redemption history, is that the promises God made to Abraham are perpetually sure and cannot be revoked, modified, or vacated, not even by God's own subsequent action in the giving of the Law. This assertion becomes a commentary on God's character: God's promises are sure because he himself is sure. Paul emphasizes this aspect of God's character in the final line of the paragraph, where he describes God's actions as a gracious act of giving. The gracious grant of the inheritance to Abraham through promise is testimony of God's gracious character, on full display in Galatians through the fulfillment of the promises in Christ.

In the flow of thought in this paragraph, the latter half of v. 16 is a parenthesis that confirms Paul's argument. There he argues that Jesus is the promised seed of Abraham to whom the promises were given. Paul with this argument thinks theologically, working backwards from Christ to the promises, delving into the divine intention of the original utterance more deeply. The connection of Jesus Christ to the promises given to Abraham clarifies both referent and means. Jesus is the one who receives the promises of Abraham because he is the promised seed; he is the descendant of Abraham God promised. At the same time he is the means by which the promises are extended to all people. As people of all nations place their faith in him, they become Abraham's descendants, recipients of the blessing of the Spirit God freely gives.

Application and Devotional Implications

Arising directly from the actions of God that accurately reflect his character is the admonition to trust him generally in all things and specifically regarding the gospel of Jesus Christ. Paul reminds the Galatians that they had experienced the blessings of the Spirit through Christ because God had promised it to Abraham. Their experience proves that God faithfully delivers on that promise. There is no reason on earth to turn to anything else—whether Law or false gods or aesthetic practice or ritualistic obedience—because God is faithful. He delivers on his promises by giving graciously to those who have faith. Trusting him in all things is the only logical response to his faithfulness to deliver on his promises.

The specific object of our trust is the one through whom God fulfills his promises, the Lord Jesus Christ. God has delivered on his promises through the life, death, and resurrection of Jesus of Nazareth, whom God has revealed to be the recipient and means of the Abrahamic promises. Faith as a human response or posture is not sufficient in and of itself, as it requires an appropriate object. Faith in God as Creator and Father is preparation for a relationship with him, but that alone is not sufficient. The only proper object of faith in the present time is the Lord Jesus Christ, whom Paul identifies as the risen Lord who receives the promises of Abraham. Trusting God by trusting in Christ is the full, complete, necessary response for all who seek to relate to him.

Additional Exegetical Comments

3:15 Some commentators argue that Paul uses the phrase *κατὰ ἄνθρωπον* to signal that he knows the weakness of the analogy of a human will or covenant to the Abrahamic covenant; see Dunn, 181; Hays, 263; de Boer, 218. This may be true in some sense, but it would be true of any analogy. Any analogy is weak in some sense because it makes a limited point of comparison. Paul does not attempt to make the analogy work in all respects, but that limited use does not impinge upon its effectiveness in the salvation-historical argument Paul makes. He simply uses the analogy to convey the permanence of the promises. He uses the conceptual tool appropriately, and it does not break in his hands. For a similar argument see Witherington, 241, who says, "Paul is not signaling the weakness of the analogy, only the humanness of the argument," that is, humanness is the domain from which he draws the concept.

3:16 Oakes, 121, makes a helpful observation that from here to 3:29 Paul uses time as an important structural factor. He moves carefully from the time of Abraham to the time between Moses and Christ to the time since the arrival of Christ. This observation helps frame Paul's argument here (and even into chapter 4).

3:17 Paul states the time interval between the giving of the Abrahamic covenant and the giving of the Law to Moses was 430 years, but this figure is problematic for a number of reasons. Elsewhere the biblical text has a figure of 400 years (Gen 15:13; cf. Acts 7:6), but this is likely an approximation as a round number. In the MT the interval between Abraham's initial reception of the promise at age 75 and the Exodus was 645 years (Bruce, 173); this includes all the time that he, Isaac, and Jacob lived in Canaan before traveling to Egypt when Jacob was 130 years old.[44] The LXX attempts to solve the issue in Exod 12:40 by adding the phrase "and in Canaan," but this creates other problems with the chronology by making either the time in Canaan or the time in Egypt too short.[45] Very likely Paul is simply citing a traditional number drawn from the biblical text itself that serves to understate the time and thus emphasize his point about the lateness of the Law all the more.

Selected Bibliography

Arndt, W. F. "Galatians 3:17 Once More." *CTM* 20 (1949): 374–77.

Bammel, E. "Gottes DIATHĒKĒ (Gal 3:15–17) und das jüdische Rechtsdenken." *NTS* 6 (1960): 313–19.

Conway, K. P. *The Promises of God: The Background of Paul's Exclusive Use of "Epangelia" for the Divine Pledge*. BZNW 211. Berlin: De Gruyter, 2014.

Llewelyn, S. R., and R. A. Kearsley. *New Documents Illustrating Early Christianity: A Review of the Greek Inscriptions and Papyri Published in 1980–81*. Macquarie University: Ancient History Documentary Research Centre, 1992.

Williams, S. K. "Promise in Galatians: A Reading of Paul's Reading of Scripture." *JBL* 107 (1988): 709–20.

Excursus: The Spiritualization of the Land Promises

An important question arises in this particular section of Paul's argument, a question that Paul himself does not address and the answer to which he does not state: What happened to the land promised to Abraham's seed? Stated another way to better fit our hermeneutical interests, has the land promised to Israel in the OT been spiritualized in the NT?[46] It is a fair question worth investigating simply because of the abundance of the idea in the OT passages that enumerate the promises God made to Abraham and his descendants and the dearth of the idea in the NT discussion of inheritance, as here.[47] It takes on even greater weight when discussed as part of theological systems, like dispensationalism or covenant theology, the lenses through which many discuss the issue. Add to that the hermeneutical stances the question entails and you end up with a rather complicated interpretive problem not easily solved.

There are three basic ways to understand the connection between the OT land promises and their expression in the NT: literal, spiritualized, and

44. W. F. Arndt, "Galatians 3:17 Once More," *CTM* 20 (1949): 375.

45. This understanding of the 430 years as including Abraham's time in Canaan is also reflected in traditional Jewish understanding of this passage (Longenecker, 133).

46. I use the term *spiritualized* because it is commonplace, not because it is particularly useful. Like the word *literal*, the word itself demands explanation.

47. See, e.g., Gen 12:7; 13:15; 15:18; 17:7–8; 24:7, and others.

typological. I will explain all three and offer a few arguments for why the reader should accept the last as the best viewpoint. All of them see the concept of inheritance as having clear roots in the OT and original reference to the land, but each differs in the way to comprehend how the NT treats the issue and how the idea transfers between the testaments.

A *literal* understanding of the land promises argues that the "land" of the OT is a fixed entity, the meaning (and boundaries) of which does not change between the OT and the NT. It argues that God promised the land of Canaan to Abraham and his descendants unconditionally. Since God will not go back on his promise and since the promise has not yet been fully realized in Christ, there must be a future fulfillment of the land promise yet to be made, usually seen as completed in Christ's reign over Israel in the millennial kingdom. Thus when Paul speaks in Galatians of inheritance in the present time, he refers to an entirely different concept than the inheritance of land promised to Abraham. This is the viewpoint found in more traditional forms of dispensationalism.[48]

A *spiritualized* understanding of the land promises argues that the "land" of the OT is not a fixed entity. In the context of the OT it referred to the physical land of Canaan, but in the NT the land promises fade from view or expand to include the entire world (see Rom 4:13). The related concept of inheritance now refers exclusively to the spiritual blessings of salvation found in Christ. When Paul discussed inheritance, he uses the OT concept but has replaced the original referent of land with blessings in Christ. This is the viewpoint found in covenant theology as a rule.[49]

A *typological* understanding of the land promises argues that the "land" of the OT is a fixed entity, but during the progress of revelation the referent expands outward to include not only the land of Canaan but the entirety of the earth, even creation itself. Thus the physical land of Canaan is not replaced or eclipsed in the NT but rather is subsumed into the larger reality of Christ's perfect reign over all creation. It still holds an important place as a real and future inheritance for the people of Israel, but it must be viewed alongside the entirety of redeemed creation as an inheritance for the people of God. This is the viewpoint espoused by progressive dispensationalism and progressive covenantalism.[50]

Despite my revised dispensational upbringing, I presently hold to the typological view because it best accounts for the data of the text. It is difficult to read the OT texts and get any sense other than God was promising

48. See, e.g., L. S. Chafer, *Systematic Theology* (Wheaton, IL: Victor, 1988), 2:494.
49. See, for example, M. J. Glodo, "Dispensationalism," in *Covenant Theology: Biblical, Theological, and Historical Perspectives,* ed. G. P. Waters, J. N. Reid, and J. R. Muether (Wheaton: Crossway, 2020), 339–40.
50. See especially P. J. Gentry and S. J. Wellum, *Kingdom Through Covenant : A Biblical-Theological Understanding of the Covenants* (Wheaton, IL: Crossway, 2012), 703–16.

a particular piece of land to his people.[51] This is the historical, literal starting place for the concept. As time progressed, especially during the Second Temple period, the concept took on a broader referent than just the physical land.[52] The concrete, physical referent of the land was at root anticipatory of a broader concept that included the entire world; "to speak of an inheritance, then, is another way of describing the possession of eschatological salvation" (Schreiner, 231).[53] For Paul the concept of inheritance had become spiritualized in that the referent shifted from solely land to include as well the blessings of salvation in Christ (see 1 Cor 6:9–10; Eph 5:5; Col 3:24; Longenecker, 134). But the physical land should not be excluded from Paul's mind, even though he does not address it directly. The proof would be Paul's attitude toward the people of Israel themselves: The descendants in view in the original promises have not been excluded.[54] So Paul sees both the physical land and the spiritual blessings in view with the concept of inheritance, but his primary expression of it here as elsewhere in his writings concerns the spiritual more than the physical.[55]

---

51. This is acknowledged understandably by commentators such as Burton, 185; Schreiner, 231; but even by commentators such as Dunn, 186; Longenecker, 134.

52. Dunn, 186, mentions Pss. Sol. 14:10; 1 En. 40:9, as two good examples, among others. He mentions Ps 37:9 and Isa 54:17 as having "eschatological reference," but I find that less convincing. Burton, 185, among others identifies Pss. Sol. 7:2; 14:3; which I find convincing, but he also mentions 2 Chr 6:27, which I do not think meets this pattern. (Longenecker, 134, mentions the same passages as Burton.)

53. Schreiner, 231, identifies as important in this regard Pss 22:27–28; 47:7–9; 72:8–11; Zeph 3:9–10; Sir 44:21; Jub. 22:14; 32:19; 2 Bar. 14:13; 51:3; 1 En. 5:7.

54. Witness Rom 9–11 and parts of his argument in Galatians, even on a very charitable stance toward a spiritualized reading.

55. For a recent study that addresses the question of the land promises in Galatians, see E. McCaulley, *Sharing in the Son's Inheritance: Davidic Messianism and Paul's Worldwide Interpretation of the Abrahamic Land Promise in Galatians*, LNTS 608 (London: T&T Clark, 2019). McCaulley argues that Paul expands the land promises to include the whole earth on the grounds that as the messianic seed of Abraham and David, Jesus receives the whole world as his inheritance and kingdom.

The Purpose of the Law (3:19–22)

Textual Notes

3:19 There is quite a bit of textual variation in the first half of v. 19, all appearing to arise from scribal error:

> Τί οὖν ὁ νόμος; τῶν παραβάσεων χάριν προσετέθη, "Why then the Law? It was added because of transgressions ..." (This is the reading of NA[28].)
>
> Τί οὖν ὁ νόμος τῶν πράξεων; "Why then the Law of deeds?" (𝔓[46])
>
> Τί οὖν ὁ νόμος; τῶν παραδόσεων χάριν ετέθη, "Why then the Law? It was established because of traditions ..." (D*)
>
> Τί οὖν ὁ νόμος τῶν πράξεων; ετέθη, "Why then the Law of deeds? It was established ..." (F G it and others)

The shortest reading in 𝔓[46] creates a nonsensical reading, as it omits the verb of the second sentence, leaving the relative clause without connection: "Why then the Law of deeds? Until when the seed would come." The variation exhibited in the Western text likely arose from the reading in D, which appears to be an unintentional error on the part of a scribe who remembered the text incorrectly,[1] and then from an intentional error as scribes corrected that reading to make better sense of the passage, leading to the creation of the reading in F G it. The reading of NA[28] is solidly Alexandrian and Byzantine, and it makes the best sense in the context. On these grounds it should be considered most likely to be original.[2]

3:19 Instead of the reading ἄχρις οὗ ἔλθῃ τὸ σπέρμα ᾧ ἐπήγγελται, "until which [time] the seed to whom it was promised should come," several important

1. Burton, 188, argues that the apparent contradiction between promise and Law led to the reading ἐτέθη in the Western text, apparently making this an intentional change.

2. For a full discussion of the readings that contain τῶν πράξεων as "orthodox corruptions" and Latin impact upon 𝔓[46], see J. A. Staples, "Altered Because of Transgressions? The 'Law of Deeds' in Gal 3,19a," *ZNW* 106 (2015): 126–35.

witnesses (B 0278 33 1175 2464 Clement) read ἄχρις ἂν ἔλθῃ τὸ σπέρμα ᾧ ἐπήγγελται, "until the seed to whom it was promised should come." The difference is one of emphasis: The former emphasizes the time of arrival, the latter the seed itself.[3] Both are reasonable readings in the context, and ἄχρι is used frequently in non-biblical Greek with both οὗ and ἄν, so on the basis of internal evidence either reading could be original.[4] Ultimately the former should be preferred as original on the basis of strong external support from all major text types (𝔓[46] ℵ A C D F G K L 81 104 1739 1881 𝔐).

3:21 At this point in the text an important variation arises. Two very important, ancient, Alexandrian witnesses omit τοῦ θεοῦ (𝔓[46] B).[5] It is possible that scribes would have added the words based upon the flow of the argument in context and under influence from similar wording in Rom 4:20 and 2 Cor 1:20.[6] The strength of the external evidence supporting the longer reading is substantial, however, coming from all major text types with significant depth (ℵ A C D K L 33 81 1175 1739 1881 𝔐 lat). On this basis the longer reading should be considered original.

3:21 The NA[28] text reads ὄντως ἐκ νόμου ἂν ἦν ἡ δικαιοσύνη, "certainly righteousness would be based on the Law." The textual apparatus in NA[28] lists seven different readings at this point in the text, all of which have essentially the same meaning. The most significant variation is between ἐκ νόμου and ἐν νόμῳ, but both in this context would indicate the means by which righteousness would be attained. The other variation concerns the presence and placement of ἄν and ἦν; either could be readily implied, and the meaning remains the same regardless of location in the clause. The text reading is

---

3. The relative pronoun can be used in expressions of time in place of a word for time; see BDAG, 727.

4. This is the only place in Paul where the Hellenistic spelling ἄχρις occurs. Everywhere else he uses the Attic spelling ἄχρι; see BDAG, 160. Burton, 189, states, "Ἄχρις ἂν is the reading of B33, 1912 Clem. Eus. All others apparently read ἄχρις οὗ. Both ἄχρις ἂν and ἄχρι οὗ are current forms in the first century ... but Paul elsewhere reads ἄχρι[ς] οὗ (Rom. 11:25; 1 Cor. 11:26; 15:25). In Rom. 11:25 and 1 Cor. 15:25 mss. vary between ἄχρι and ἄχρις before οὗ and in 1 Cor. 11:26; 15:25 a considerable group add ἂν after οὗ, yet none apparently read ἄχρις ἄν. It is improbable, therefore, that this reading is the work of the scribes."

5. F and G omit τοῦ, but this could be explained possibly as an error of sight because of the similar endings of τοῦ and θεοῦ in majuscule script.

6. See B. M. Metzger, *A Textual Commentary on the Greek New Testament* (New York: United Bible Societies, 1994), 525. Soards and Pursiful, 153, prefer the shorter reading on the grounds that it is more likely that scribes added the words for clarification.

preferred slightly on the grounds that it fits Paul's emphasis, it follows more conventional Greek word order, and the manuscript evidence for it is strong.[7]

Translation

19 Why then did the law come?[8] It was added for transgressions, until the time when the seed to whom the promises were made should arrive. It was set in order through angels by the hand of a mediator.[9] **20** Now a mediator is not for one person only, but God is one. **21** Is the Law therefore contrary to God's promises? Not at all![10] For if a law had been given that could give life, certainly righteousness would have been based on the Law. **22** But the Scripture imprisoned everything under sin[11] so that the promise might be given on the basis of faith in Jesus Christ to those who believe.

Commentary

As a Pharisee Paul had an intimate knowledge of the Law that God had given to Israel in the Pentateuch through Moses. Indeed, his own personal devotion to the Law exceeded that of his contemporaries. He held his devotion at such a pitch that he could describe himself with a term like zealot (Gal 1:14) with no sense of hyperbole. In the Law he saw the purpose and plan of God for Israel, and through it he lived to bring that purpose and plan to fruition. This ardent devotion abruptly changed when Paul was confronted by the risen Lord Jesus and became a Christ follower. As a believer who had come to see Jesus Christ as the purpose and plan of God for Israel and the world beyond, he no longer gave the Law the same place of prominence as before. That primacy of place had been taken by the risen Lord, and Paul

---

7. My ulterior motive for discussing this problem is to undercut the argument that the sheer number of variants in the NT manuscript tradition creates a problem for the certainty of the original text. Here there are seven variants, none of which affect the meaning. Examples like this show that on its face this argument does not properly represent the nuances of the variations present in the manuscript tradition.
8. Cf. "Why the Law then?" (NASB); "What purpose then does the Law serve?" (NKJV); "Why, then, was the Law given at all?" (NIV).
9. In this sentence I added the words "It was" to make clear that the last clause without doubt modifies ὁ νόμος from the very first phrase. Without that connection the English translation would be unclear.
10. In my view this translation best captures the rhetorical sense of Paul's use of μὴ γένοιτο here.
11. Some translations make explicit the nuance of ὑπό plus the gen. to indicate control or power: "under sin's power" (CSB), "under the power of sin" (NRSV), "under the control of sin" (NIV). Compare the more ambiguous "But the Scriptures declare that we are all prisoners of sin" (NLT).

had to wrestle with this newly understood reality, namely, that the Law had never been God's central plan or purpose for Israel all along. This short paragraph in the middle of Paul's theological argument in Galatians shows Paul wrestling with that issue and coming to a conclusion about the Law's function that integrated it with God's promises made to Abraham that find fulfillment in Christ.

Up to this point in the epistle Paul has mentioned the Law frequently. Some occurrences refer to particular acts the Law required of faithful Israelites (ἔργων νόμου, Gal 2:16 [3x], 3:2, 5, 10), while other occurrences speak of the Law without any modifier, addressing how it works and functions holistically (Gal 2:19, 21; 3:11, 12, 13, 17, 18). Paul's discussion in the present paragraph is in the latter vein: In light of the fact that the promises of God have temporal and functional priority—that is, the promises are the sole means by which God delivers the inheritance to Abraham, his seed, and the nations—what purpose does the Law serve? If it is not a vehicle to deliver God's promises, what purpose does it have? Paul argues that the Law does not work against the promises; rather, it works with them. The negative, temporary purpose of the Law to confine humanity under sin works in tandem with the positive, permanent function of the promises to give life to those who believe in Jesus Christ. This theological point on the purpose and function of the Law demonstrates how Paul has reordered his Jewish thinking in light of the revelation received from God about Jesus, and as such this paragraph augments his exhortation to the Galatians not to turn to the Law.[12]

The extent of the paragraph under consideration and its relationship to the context is open to different interpretations. De Boer, 225, regards vv. 19–22 as connected to the preceding unit, 3:15–18, which was concerned with relationship of promise and Law. Since that same issue remains here, he does not see a new paragraph division at v. 19. Other commentators see the paragraph division as vv. 19–25 (Rapa, 600; Moo, 232), that is, this passage is more tightly connected to what follows. Paul's argument throughout this section is wound so tightly that the reader would not be misled by a different paragraph division than the one I have chosen, but I do think there are good reasons for treating vv. 19–22 as a separate paragraph. Concerning its beginning, Paul's take on salvation history discussed in 3:15–18 sets the stage for the questions he answers here: "He holds to a single, continuous history of salvation" but the coming of Christ introduces "a significant shift in the history of salvation" (Moo, 225).[13] The import of this shift is essentially the argument between him and the opponents, which he takes head-on by questioning the purpose for the Law. Seeing the beginning of the paragraph at

12. Similarly Longenecker, 135, who argues that Gal 3:19–25, although often treated as a digression, is actually central to Paul's argument since it deals with the function of the Law vis-à-vis the nomism his opponents espoused.

13. Moo makes his point *contra* Martyn, 161–79, who argues that Paul highlights the antithetical contrasts so strongly that continuity in salvation history is lost.

v. 19 recognizes the focus on that import. Regarding the end, Paul's mention of faith in 3:23 creates a slight pivot in the discussion, such that seeing a paragraph division between v. 22 and v. 23 makes logical sense. In addition, the opening question focuses on the purpose of the Law, such that the ἵνα clause in 3:22b forms a logical *inclusio*.

3:19 Τί οὖν ὁ νόμος; Paul begins this paragraph with a very logical question, given the conclusion he reached in v. 18 that the promise is the means by which God gives the inheritance: "Why then the Law?" The conj. οὖν connects this question to the prior argument of 3:1–18, an argument that seems to leave the Law without any purpose in God's plan (Longenecker, 137; Witherington, 253; Rapa, 600).[14] Paul essentially asks, "Given the primacy of the promises, why did the Law come?" This is the essential problem of Paul's postconversion, theological development. If God acted in accordance with the promises given to Abraham apart from and before the Law—and indeed still does through Christ to the Gentiles, as evidenced by the salvation of the Galatians themselves—why did he give the Law at all?[15] What function does it serve within God's purpose and plan, within salvation history?

τῶν παραβάσεων χάριν προσετέθη. With this short phrase Paul answers his question about the reason the Law was added, reflecting a fundamental change in the purpose of the Law from his Jewish way of thinking.[16] Determining the sense of the phrase presents some challenges. The pass. verb προσετέθη is generally recognized as a divine passive (Betz, 167; Witherington, 255; Schreiner, 239; Moo, 233), with God as the implied agent of the action. This is an important nuance, as it affirms that God was at work in giving the Law but allows Paul to redefine exactly what his purposes were in accordance with his present argument. That to which the Law relates is indicated by the prepositional phrase τῶν παραβάσεων χάριν.[17] The word παραβάσις here is the second occurrence of this word group in the book of Galatians. The word group regularly refers to violation of a legal statute, and that is the obvious sense here. Paul had already used the related noun παραβάτης in Gal 2:19 to hypothetically refer to his relationship to the Law if he were to reestablish it relative to his behavior and eating with Gentiles.[18]

The key issue in this phrase is the sense of χάριν, which could be interpreted one of two ways. On the one hand, the prep. could indicate the reason

14. Cf. George, 251, who connects the logic of the question to Paul's essential theological argument developed from 2:16 onward.

15. De Boer, 226, argues that the form of the question reiterates that God had nothing to do with the giving of the Law.

16. Betz, 165, argues that Paul's viewpoint is essentially non-Jewish.

17. The phrase exhibits the generally unusual word order of the obj. preceding the prep., but with χάριν this is actually normal word order. See BDAG, 1078.

18. Paul does not use the related verb παραβαίνω; it is rare in the NT, used only three times in Matt 15:2, 3; Acts 1:25.

or grounds for an action. With this sense the Law was added in response to transgressions, restraining them or checking them in some form or fashion. The sense would be essentially positive in the argument since the Law would in God's good purposes provide an antidote for sin. Alternately, the prep. can indicate purpose or goal. In this sense the Law was added for the purpose of transgressions, either to promote awareness of transgressions or to create an environment in which they could flourish (Longenecker, 138).[19] Put another way, if *χάριν* is causal the Law has a "preventative function"; if it is telic, it has a "provocative function" (George, 255). The positive function of the Law to provide a solution for sin makes good sense given its presentation of the atonement provided by the sacrificial system (Dunn, 189). The contextual description of the Law as a power to control and the dangerous presence of sin also supports this (Oakes, 123). Against this view is the fact that if Paul were arguing that the Law properly restrained sin, he would play right into the hands of the opponents (Schreiner, 240). The negative function of the Law to provoke sin can be preferred because that idea is represented in Rom 4:15 and 5:20 and would be in concert with Paul's negative imagery of the Law as a jailer in Gal 3:22 (Lightfoot, 144; similarly Bruce, 175). The relative clause that follows focuses on the extent of time the Law would have validity after its arrival, so in this context *χάριν* looks forward to indicate a purpose or goal. The very meaning of the word *παραβάσις* as the breaking of an established command implies that the giving of the Law created the environment that produced the transgressions (Martyn, 354; de Boer, 230).[20] With everything considered, the negative function makes better sense here.[21] The Law was given to provoke transgressions and clearly establish their existence.[22] With

19. Longenecker, 138, prefers the cognitive emphasis, not the causative one, because it "fits the contextual imagery of a supervisory custodian (the *παιδαγωγός* of 3:24–25 or the *ἐπίτροποι* and *οἰκονόμοι* of 4:2) and provides an answer to why being *ὑπὸ νόμον* ('under law') results in being *ὑπὸ κατάραν* ('under a curse') in Paul's earlier discussion at 3:10." I do not see a need to delineate between cognitive and causative here on the grounds that each would reinforce the other. Longenecker, 139, appears to argue similarly to my thinking. See also Matera, 132, who favors the cognitive view.

20. Moo, 234, cogently argues that the Law turned existing sin (general) into transgression (specific). " 'Sin' is worthy of punishment; but the particular form of sin known as 'transgression' evokes greater punishment because it involves conscious violation of a known law of God."

21. Luther, 165, argues for both positive and negative purposes here: The law has a civil purpose, to restrain and punish unrighteousness, and a spiritual purpose, to reveal sin,

22. See BDAG, 1079, which states, "*τῶν παραβάσεων χάριν* for the sake of transgressions, i.e. to bring them about and into the open." Similarly Witherington, 256, who states that "the Law turns sin, which certainly already existed before and apart from the Law, into transgression." Commentators often separate the knowledge or recognition of sin from the provocation to sin (so Schreiner, 239–40; Moo, 233; Fung,

an explicit Law in place, humanity would thus violate it specifically and be more and more guilty of transgressions against it. In other words, God gave the Law to create a context for the clear delineation of transgressions within Israel particularly and humanity generally. The Law creates specific culpability from general sinfulness because under its watchful eye transgressions can neither be avoided or denied.[23]

ἄχρις οὗ ἔλθῃ τὸ σπέρμα ᾧ ἐπήγγελται. With this phrase Paul identifies the specific time frame within which the Law was operative. ἄχρις οὗ commonly has the force of a temporal conj., with the particular word for time implied; it can readily be translated "until the time when."[24] The subjunctive verb ἔλθῃ emphasizes the future contingency relative to the timing of the event, not to its actual occurrence; it was unknown from the standpoint of the OT promises when τὸ σπέρμα, the promised seed, would finally arrive. Based upon his argument in Gal 3:16–18, Paul clearly has in mind Jesus's arrival as the fulfillment of this statement. The subject of verb ἐπήγγελται is unexpressed, but the verb itself and the larger context implies "the promises"; this is confirmed by Paul's explicit mention of them later in v. 21. Thus the Law was added to the promises until the arrival of Christ, the seed to whom the promises were given. The pf. tense of ἐπήγγελται should not be overlooked: It emphasizes the continual validity of the promises (Bruce, 176), especially in contradistinction to the temporality of the Law (Burton, 189). This argument operates both from the context of the OT promises themselves and reflectively as Paul looks back upon the OT relative to the Christ event. The Law was added temporarily; God never intended it to remain in place once Christ came.[25]

The nature of Paul's argument here is revolutionary in light of Second Temple Judaism, which never argued that the Law was temporary. On the contrary, the Law was viewed as eternal (see, e.g., Wis 18:4; 2 Esd 9:37; 1 En. 99:2; Bar 4:1), and in some cases preexistent (see, e.g., *b. Šabb.* 30B, where R. Yannai appears to argue that the Torah existed before the sun).[26] "Certainly the Judaizers of Galatia argued along these lines. Viewing matters from a Christocentric perspective, however, Paul thought otherwise, and here he

---

159; among others), but given Paul's general stance of sin as a controlling power, I do not believe he would argue for such a distinction. To know sin and transgression, to recognize them as such through the Law, is in fact to be under their control.

23. This contrasts with the normal Jewish view, in which the Law was a guard against sin, designed to prevent it. See M. Wolter, "παράβασις et al.," *EDNT*, 3:14.

24. So BDAG, 160–61.

25. Longenecker, 139, states, "The whole clause beginning with the temporal conjunction ἄχρι 'until' (ἄχρις before a vowel) sets the *terminus ad quem* for the law, just as προσετέθη set its *terminus a quo*. Thus the Mosaic law, for Paul, was intended by God to be in effect for God's people only up until the coming of Christ."

26. See Betz, 168; Longenecker, 139; Schreiner, 241; who list numerous other references.

makes his point as to the law's intended duration" (Longenecker, 139). Paul may have developed this viewpoint through theological reflection upon Christ's coming (Matera, 133), or perhaps even more personally through his Damascus Road experience (Bruce, 176). In any case, Paul's prior understanding of the Law in conformity with Judaism at large gave way to a different understanding through his new Christocentric lens, modified by his undeniable experience of Christ personally and in the Gentiles to whom he preached and bolstered by his exegesis of the relevant OT texts.

διαταγεὶς δι' ἀγγέλων ἐν χειρὶ μεσίτου. Paul now clarifies through the end of the next verse how the Law was established, and in so doing augments his argument that the Law was only temporary, never intended by God to be permanent. The means by which the Law was established, contrary to the means by which the promises were made, show the temporary nature of the Law. The word διαταγείς is an adj. ptc. from διατάσσω, further describing the Law mentioned at the beginning of v. 19. The verb means "to order, direct, arrange," so the adj. ptc. in the pass. voice describes the Law as "ordered, directed, arranged." It is appropriate, as with the indic. verb προσετέθη, to take the pass. ptc. as a divine passive (Schreiner, 241), pointing to God as the ultimate agent of the action. The more interesting elements in this phrase are the prepositional phrases δι' ἀγγέλων and ἐν χειρὶ μεσίτου, which specify different types of agency relative to the action of the ptc. The former indicates the intermediate agent for the action of διαταγείς and the latter the instrument, that is, the angels are the entity used by God, the ultimate agent, to establish the Law, and the instrument used to accomplish this action is the hand of the mediator.[27]

The mention of angels and a mediator in the context of the giving of the Law on Mount Sinai as told in the book of Exodus further shows how Paul differs from the Judaism of his day in his approach to the function and purpose of the Law. The latter term is the easier to process. The word μεσίτης is rare in the NT, only occurring six times (Gal 3:19, 20; 1 Tim 2:5; Heb 8:6; 9:15; 12:24). It can fairly be translated as "mediator" or "arbitrator" in the limited sense of a party that goes between two other parties to accomplish some purpose, but the contemporary connotations of compromise or coming to agreement through mediation or arbitration are not necessarily present.[28] The referent of the "mediator" is Moses, readily understood from the OT text itself. His role as a mediator is seen in Exod 20:19 and Deut 5:5 (Lightfoot, 146; Fung, 161), and the phrase ἐν χειρὶ Μωϋσῆ is used frequently

---

27. See D. B. Wallace, *Greek Grammar Beyond the Basics: An Exegetical Syntax of the New Testament* (Grand Rapids: Zondervan, 1996), 431–35, for discussion of different types of agency. Interestingly Hays, 267, and Moo, 235, argue that διά indicates instrumentality, so Paul's emphasis is not on angels as final authority but simply as instruments.

28. Lenski, 170, states helpfully that the sense of "mediator" here is simply one who transmits.

in the LXX to describe the Law (Betz, 170; Longenecker, 140; Moo, 235; Soards and Pursiful, 151). Second Temple texts also use the same word μεσίτης to describe Moses; see Apoc. Mos. 1.14; Philo, *Moses* 2.166; *Spec. Laws* 1.116 (Betz, 170; Bruce, 178; Longenecker, 140). Some interpreters have seen Christ as in view here, likely under the influence of 1 Tim 2:5, where Paul uses the term with Christ as a clear referent.[29] This would make no sense in this context, however, where Paul argues that Christ is the seed of the Abrahamic promises—indeed, their end and goal—not the mediator of the Mosaic covenant (George, 257).

Paul's specific identification of angels is the more difficult phrase to understand, both in terms of the referent and Paul's use of it in his argument. Essentially Paul sees angels as intermediate agents involved in the giving of the Law on Mount Sinai. Although not explicit from the Exodus passage itself, the OT texts that refer to this event, when taken as a whole, could imply angelic presence. Exodus 19:16–19 mentions amazing phenomena that accompanied the event: thunder, lightning, a thick cloud, the blast of a trumpet. Deuteronomy 33:2 (MT) reads וְאָתָה מֵרִבְבֹת קֹדֶשׁ מִימִינוֹ אֵשְׁדָּת לָמוֹ, a somewhat unclear text. At issue is the word אֵשְׁדָּת, which appears to be a compound of אֵשׁ ("fire") and דָּת ("law"). *HALOT*, 93, suggests without confidence the translation "fire a law for them." The LXX of this same passage reads καὶ κατέσπευσεν ἐξ ὄρους Φαραν σὺν μυριάσιν Καδης, ἐκ δεξιῶν αὐτοῦ ἄγγελοι μετ' αὐτοῦ.[30] This appears to be an explicit association of angels with the giving of the Law (Bruce, 176; Longenecker, 139; Schreiner, 241); it likely arose because the MT was unclear. Following these developments in the OT, Second Temple literature often associated angels with the giving of the Law (e.g., *y. Meg.* 74D; As. Mos. 1:14; Josephus, *Ant.* 15.136).[31] So Paul's argument fits both OT exegesis and Second Temple theological development. The point of the reference, however, is more difficult to ascertain. The purpose of the theological development that saw angelic presence at the giving of the Law certainly served to elevate the Law, but in the flow of Paul's argument, which contrasts the Law with the promises, noting the angelic presence as well as the "hand of a mediator" serves the opposite purpose of denigrating the Law (so Burton, 189; Longenecker, 140; Fung, 161; and others).[32]

29. Lightfoot, 146, argues that Origen's misunderstanding here influences a host of later commentators.

30. Similar language occurs in Ps 68:17 MT (67:18 LXX) but without the specification of ἄγγελοι in the LXX. This text refers to the chariotry of God, which became important in later Rabbinic thought as a reference to angels (Longenecker, 139–40; Schreiner, 241).

31. For other texts, see Lightfoot, 145; Burton, 189; Longenecker, 139–40; Dunn, 190; Schreiner, 241–42.

32. Paul's emphasis here contrasts with Stephen's mention of angels in Acts 7, which serves to exalt the Law (Lightfoot, 145). Paul uses the Jewish tradition to draw a different conclusion about the role of the Law (Betz, 162; Oakes, 124).

Paul's emphasis provides a further point of distinction between the Law and the promises: Unlike the promises, which were given directly by God to Abraham, the Law was given to Israel through various intermediaries, namely, the angels of God's presence and Moses, not by God directly (Betz, 170). Thus the Law was given in a manner inferior to the promises (Lenski, 167), showing that it was not God's final, definitive word (Witherington, 257).

3:20 ὁ δὲ μεσίτης ἑνὸς οὐκ ἔστιν, ὁ δὲ θεὸς εἷς ἐστιν. This enigmatic phrase adds a second premise, drawn from the fact just stated that the Law was given through a particular intermediary. The Law is in view in the first clause, the repeated reference to the mediator tying this content to the prior verse. Paul speaks of God's character in the second clause. What is unclear is how the second clause interacts with the first.[33] The grammar of the first clause is not difficult to understand. The article with μεσίτης is anaphoric, pointing back to its prior mention at the end of the last verse.[34] The specific mention of a mediator in v. 19 referred to Moses, but here the assertion is more general; it could perhaps be paraphrased as "the role of the mediator." The gen. ἑνός indicates a generic reference: "with reference to one [party]."[35] The sense is that the mediator always works with reference to two parties. He never acts with reference to only one; otherwise, he would not be needed. Although somewhat tautologous, the point serves Paul's argument well. Concerning the giving of the Law, Moses served as a mediator between two parties, God

33. Regarding the enigmatic meaning of this verse, Lightfoot, 146, reports that "the number of interpretations of this passage is said to mount up to 250 or 300. Many of these arise out of an error as to the mediator, many more disregard the context, and not a few are quite arbitrary." He does not enumerate the interpretations he is able to summarily dismiss, and for that I am thankful. Bruce, 178, and Moo, 236, both state the difficulty lies not in interpreting each clause but in how they should be understood together.

34. The article could be generic; see S. M. Baugh, "Galatians 3:20 and the Covenant of Redemption," *WTJ* 66 (2004): 64–65. See Wallace, *Greek Grammar*, 227–30, for discussion of the generic article.

35. The ambiguity for the referent of the "one" has generated some discussion over the years. Even G. B. Winer, *A Treatise on the Grammar of New Testament Greek, Regarded as a Sure Basis for New Testament Exegesis* (Edinburgh: Clark, 1882), 741, discussed a possible implication of υἱός with ἑνός, stating helpfully, "A word can be left out only when the idea which it expresses is supplied by the context, or may be supposed to be familiar to the reader. But he who writes 'the mediator is not of one' has not given even the most remote indication that 'son' is the idea he would have the reader supply." For this essential interpretive reason, I do not concur with scholars who posit specific referents for εἷς in this context; see, e.g., Bruce, 179, who argues that the "one" in each half of the sentence refers to God; N. T. Wright, *The Climax of the Covenant: Christ and the Law in Pauline Theology* (Minneapolis: Fortress, 1993), 169–70, who argues that "one" refers to the one unified family of God.

and Israel. Thus the Law can be construed as inferior because it was indirect (Burton, 190–91; Longenecker, 142) and by implication contingent as both parties have to fulfill the contract (Lightfoot, 146; Schreiner, 243).

As with the first clause, the grammar of the second clause is not difficult. The δέ serves here to provide a contrast. The article marks θεός as the subject, making εἷς the predicate nom: "but God is one." It is very reasonable to see this phrase as an allusion to the Shema in Deut 6:4. The text of the LXX in that verse reads *κύριος ὁ θεὸς ἡμῶν κύριος εἷς ἐστιν*; interestingly the words Paul uses occur in the same order in the LXX. Paul seems at least to be alluding to this passage, if not citing it directly.[36] But what purpose does the citation serve? Unfortunately there are some links in the argument that Paul leaves implied.[37] Given that the Shema is a statement about God's character, it appears that Paul contrasts the nature of the mediator, who deals with a plurality of persons, with the character of God, who is singular and acts without reference to any other entity. Given the contrast that Paul makes consistently in this theological section between the Law and the promises (see most notably 3:17–18), it is quite apropos to see the same contrast in play here. When God gave the promises to Abraham, he acted unilaterally, directly, and unconditionally (similarly Longenecker, 142; Witherington, 258).[38] Paul argues thusly that the Law is implicitly inferior to the promises because of the way it was delivered compared to the way the promises were given, solely by God himself.

3:21 *Ὁ οὖν νόμος κατὰ τῶν ἐπαγγελιῶν τοῦ θεοῦ; μὴ γένοιτο.* Paul now transitions to a logical deduction from his prior argument. By pointing to the means by which the Law had been established, through intermediaries in contrast with the establishment of the promises by God himself, Paul subjugates the Law to the promises. This implies a different purpose for the Law than traditionally understood within Judaism, and Paul broaches the possibility that the Law

---

36. Lightfoot, 147, argues that this resembles the Shema but is not connected to it, against most other commentators.

37. Burton, 191, states that "God is one" is the minor premise to the preceding major premise. The unexpressed conclusion is that the giving of the Law involved another party besides God. De Boer, 227–28, argues similarly that the underlying point appears to be that a mediator is needed when the party that initiates a transaction is a plurality. Since Moses mediated the Law for the angels (*contra* my view on the role of the angels), he could not have mediated it for God, since God is one.

38. The latter is emphasized by Lightfoot, 147; George, 258. Lenski, 171, states it succinctly: "God is one person and can act for himself." Dunn, 191, states it with a little shade thrown toward the author: "Paul was probably attempting a not very successful (as subsequent confusion has shown) epigrammatic play-off between the thought of God's oneness and the fact that mediation implies more than one (between whom to mediate)." Bruce, 178, argues that it is natural to think that Paul refers to God's grace-filled, unilateral action, but this is an odd way to state that.

had in fact purposes contrary to the promises. It is possible that Paul takes this tack in response to accusations from the opponents: "His opponents might understandably portray Paul as a renegade Jew in rebellion against God's Law—a proto-Marcionite theologian who paints the Law as an evil power working against God" (Hays, 268). The argument he advances here would then be a means to protect his readers from inappropriate conclusions about the relationship between the Law and the promises (Longenecker, 143). This is not a necessary condition to establish Paul's meaning, however, as the logic he traces is clear enough and could very well be his own (Moo, 237). The conj. οὖν is inferential, showing that Paul is operating on the level of logical deduction. He uses κατά with the gen. to indicate a contradiction, which is a fairly common use of that prep.[39] The phrase τῶν ἐπαγγελιῶν τοῦ θεοῦ in this context refers to the promises of God given to Abraham; this is the same focus as in the prior section (see Gal 3:16, 18). Paul thus poses the logical deduction as a question: Given that the Law is inferior to the promises because it is indirect while they are direct, is the Law in fact contrary to the promises? Paul answers the question with his well-known negation μὴ γένοιτο to strongly deny the implication of the previous clause.[40] With this statement Paul essentially affirms the opposite of the stated logical deduction. Stated a different way, the Law is in no way contrary to the promises God gave to Abraham.

εἰ γὰρ ἐδόθη νόμος ὁ δυνάμενος ζῳοποιῆσαι, ὄντως ἐκ νόμου ἂν ἦν ἡ δικαιοσύνη. In order to explain how the Law is not contrary to the promises of God, Paul begins to explain what exactly the function of the Law was. The thought he begins here will be finished in essence through the remainder of this theological section of the book. Paul begins this line of argument with a second class condition that as a whole concerns the inability of the Law to give life or bestow righteousness. The second class condition is contrary to fact; it reaches a logical conclusion that is unreal, thereby affirming the opposite logical assertion.[41] The protasis of this second class condition concerns the ability of the Law to give life. The subject νόμος is anarthrous to emphasize the non-reality of the proposition; it generically refers to any law given by God (Longenecker, 143; Moo, 238). The subject is modified in the third attributive position by ὁ δυνάμενος ζῳοποιῆσαι, the key element of the phrase, "that was able to make alive / give life." The verb ἐδόθη is a divine passive, pointing to God as the ultimate giver of the Law. This clause thus asserts the non-reality of the Law's ability to give life; that kind of law was not given by God. The

39. See BDAG, 511.

40. This occurs twice elsewhere in Galatians: in 2:17, whereas here Paul denies a possible deduction from a prior argument, and in 6:14, where Paul expresses a wish that he not boast except in the cross.

41. M. Winger, "Unreal Conditions in the Letters of Paul," *JBL* 105 (1986): 110–12, argues helpfully that since Paul has essentially argued this point already at length, the unreal form serves to ensure that his readers do not misunderstand his point.

apodosis of the second class condition uses the adv. ὄντως to emphasize the certainty of that conclusion.[42] The prepositional phrase ἐκ νόμου takes on the meaning here that it has had throughout its previous occurrences, that of means or basis. The articular δικαιοσύνη is the subject. This clause asserts the non-reality of righteousness being based on the Law. Thus the text and subtext of this condition should be understood in the following way:

> If a law was given that was able to give life [but this kind of law was not given],
>
> then certainly righteousness would have been based on the Law [but it is instead based on the promises].[43]

The logic thus circles back around to affirm the opposite of the protasis: The Law is not able to give life as the promises do.

Paul uses two terms here with important theological meaning. In the first clause is the verb ζῳοποιέω, in the second the noun δικαιοσύνη. Paul has used the latter already at key points in the epistle (2:21; 3:6). As argued in the excursus on 2:15–21, Paul uses the δικ- word group deftly to refer both to the traditional notion of a right forensic standing before God but also to the cultural issues at play about who can be rightly related to God. Here it is a shorthand for that right standing before God that brings the individual into the community of God's people. Interestingly, the occurrence of the noun in 2:21 is cast similarly to this use in a conditional: εἰ γὰρ διὰ νόμου δικαιοσύνη, ἄρα Χριστὸς δωρεὰν ἀπέθανεν. The underlying assumption there and here is the same, namely, that righteousness is not in any way obtained with, through, or by the Law. The verb ζῳοποιέω proves more challenging to grasp. The word is a compound of ζωός and ποιέω,[44] and its meaning comports with its etymology, "to make alive." Within the context of biology it refers to breeding or producing live young.[45] Within the LXX usage primarily centers upon God and his unique ability to give life as the Creator.[46] The NT usage is

---

42. Other Pauline uses of ὄντως are found in 1 Cor 14:25; 1 Tim 5:3, 5, 16; 6:19; although none of these passages are a conditional as here.

43. It is an open question whether this conditional sentence refers to present or past time. See A. T. Robertson, *A Grammar of the Greek New Testament in the Light of Historical Research* (Nashville: Broadman, 1934), 1015, who says, "It is not always certain that the present reference of ἦν can be insisted on, since there was no separate aorist form of εἰμί. Sometimes ἦν is aorist." I favor the past time viewpoint given Paul's consistent insistence that the Law is no longer in force, that is, it is in the past (so also Lenski, 174). Whether with past or with present reference, the implications of Paul's logic are the same.

44. BDAG, 431.

45. LSJ, 759; MGS, 897.

46. In Judg 21:14 LXX it refers to sparing a human life.

very similar: Almost every passage refers to God's unique power to give life.[47] The context varies between present spiritual life and future resurrection life (Lightfoot, 147; Martyn, 359–60; de Boer, 233),[48] and God, Jesus, and the Spirit are equally in view. Even so, the unique focus upon God as the one who gives life is clear.

How then are the concepts of "giving life" and "righteousness" to be related in Paul's thinking? On the one hand they could be synonymous (so Bruce, 180). This is reasonable on the surface, especially given the structure of this conditional sentence, but the use of ζῳοποιέω with physical, biolog ical referents does not allow that to be an easy fit.[49] A better view sees the first as focusing on the process, the second resultant status (Moo, 238); the first as effect, the second cause (Fung, 163). Paul uses the first in essence metaphorically to refer to the new spiritual life that only God can give; the second refers to the status that those who have that new life possess. It is here that Paul begins to show how deeply the theology of his Jewish mind has been altered by the revelation of Christ to him. It is clear that God gave the promises to Abraham to bestow life. Indeed, the fundamental proof of the promise was the life of his son Isaac, born to him and Sarah when their bodies were well past the age to engender life through normal conception and pregnancy. But the same could be said of the Law within a Jewish framework. One need not go beyond the famous exhortation of Moses in Deut 30:15–20, where obedience to Law and the blessing of abundant life in the land are inextricably linked, to see how Law and life would be connected in Jewish thought. What Paul does is correct an inappropriate deduction from this connection: The Law was intended to regulate life, but it could not give it, a power reserved for God and his Spirit alone (Dunn, 192–93).

The question with which Paul wrestles is important from the standpoint of the Law and his current challenge to the Galatians, but it is also critical from the standpoint of theology proper. If God gave both the promises and the Law, any conflict between them becomes a true theological problem. Fortunately for his readers, Paul knows where he is going and signals immediately that any problem is in perception only, not reality. Paul had just recited the Shema in the prior verse, confessing the oneness of God. The God who gave the Law is the same God who gave the promises, and thus

---

47. First Corinthians 15:36 would appear to be the lone exception, but even there the analogy of sowing a grain so that a plant will live fits the general contours of the rest of the NT usage.

48. Matera, 135, prefers to see only resurrection life in view.

49. Longenecker, 144, goes so far as to say, " 'Being made alive,' 'being in Christ,' 'being led by the Spirit,' and 'being righteous (both forensically and ethically)' are for Paul cognate expressions (cf. 2:20; 5:16, 25)." I would prefer to say that they all refer to different aspects of the same fundamental reality.

the former must serve the latter in some way (see Bruce, 175; Longenecker, 143; George, 259).[50]

3:22 ἀλλὰ συνέκλεισεν ἡ γραφὴ τὰ πάντα ὑπὸ ἁμαρτίαν. Having established that the Law was not able to give life or bestow righteousness, Paul now describes what the Law in fact did that ultimately supports the promises: The Law imprisoned everyone under sin. This assertion parallels his earlier statement that the Law was added for transgressions. The prior statement focused on individual transgressions, while here Paul focuses on sin generally. The conj. ἀλλά denotes a contrast with the non-real presupposition of the second class condition in the prior sentence, namely, that the Law could give life; here Paul presents the reality of what the Law was about (Burton, 195). The subject of the sentence is ἡ γραφή, "the Scripture." The verb συγκλείω means "hem in, enclose, confine, imprison"; it describes both a judicial and punitive action (George, 262). The verb is modified by the prepositional phrase ὑπὸ ἁμαρτίαν, "under sin." The neut. τὰ πάντα ultimately refers to people but with some nuance.[51] So the general sense of the passage is fairly easy to ascertain, but particular elements require clarification.

In an unusual move Paul uses the noun ἡ γραφή to personify God as he acts through the Scripture generally and through the Law specifically. Previously in 3:8 he used γραφή to refer to the Scriptures that contained the promises to Abraham, with ultimate reference to God who gave both the Scriptures and the promises. Using the same word here with similar force promotes continuity with that prior occurrence. However, it is possible that Paul intends a specific scriptural reference here, likely Deut 27:26 due to its citation in 3:10 and the content, which focuses on punishment for disobedience to the Law (so Luther, 179; Burton, 195; Longenecker, 144; Soards and Pursiful, 155–56).[52] It is also possible that Paul intends γραφή to be synonymous with νόμος (Oakes, 126) or with the Scripture as a whole (Dunn, 194; Schreiner, 244; Moo, 239).[53] But my preference for γραφή as a personification of God rests on the nature of the image as a whole; here the Scripture acts with intention and with powerful result for humanity.

---

50. This theological current is strong enough in this section that I fail to understand how some commentators, such as de Boer, 232, argue that Paul's point is to disassociate God from the Law.

51. See MHT, 3:20: "As in class. Greek the neuter gender may refer to a person (e.g. τὸ γεγεννημένον Jn 3:6 1 Jn 5:4, cp. masc. 5:1), provided that the emphasis is less on the individual than on some outstanding general quality."

52. Lightfoot, 147, presents cogent arguments that the sg. γραφή always refers to a particular passage, but ultimately I think Paul's rhetorical power here overrides the normal idiom.

53. Lenski, 176, argues cogently that γραφή was a better word than νόμος because the former extends back to Adam through whom sin entered the world as mentioned in Rom 5:12.

Similarly in 3:8 the Scripture spoke with intention, bringing great blessings. The message of the Scripture, not just a particular text nor the Law strictly defined, is that all are sinners (Fung, 164). Paul ultimately refers to the God who spoke Scripture, who gave the Law, who acted with intention to accomplish his purposes for his creation (see similarly Lenski, 175; George, 261).[54]

The neut. τὰ πάντα is somewhat unexpected because based on the flow of the argument, one would expect instead the masc. τοὺς πάντας, which is exactly what Paul writes in Rom 11:32: συνέκλεισεν γὰρ ὁ θεὸς τοὺς πάντας εἰς ἀπείθειαν ἵνα τοὺς πάντας ἐλεήσῃ.[55] The neut. here does not refer to something other than humanity, but it refers to more than people themselves. It expands upon the referent to include mankind and everything that pertains to them (Lenski, 175). It refers to the whole world, humanity's entire existence, especially the Jew/Gentile distinction that defined Jewish life (Calvin, 105; Bruce, 180; Dunn, 194; George, 263).[56] For this reason, Longenecker, 144, prefers the translations "all people" or "everyone without distinction" to emphasize humanity as an entity (see also Burton, 196).

Taken as a whole, this clause shows a theological shift in the way Paul conceives of sin and how it operates. In the two prior uses of the term ἁμαρτία in the book, Paul used the word in fairly traditional ways: In 1:4 it refers to the particular acts that make one culpable before God, and in 2:17 it refers to disobedience to Torah requirements specifically. From a Jewish mindset, sin was simply disobedience to the Law. Here Paul uses ἁμαρτία in an altogether different sense, and the function of the Law vis-à-vis sin changes in two major ways. First, Paul emphasizes sin as the primary problem, the Law playing a supporting role. Instead of referencing individual acts, sin instead becomes a controlling power. The Law serves as a jailer, in a sense, who locks everyone up under sin's power (see Martyn, 361). People are thus culpable but powerless to act without sin exerting its influence. Second, Paul emphasizes the universality of sin. The totality of this statement regarding Jew and Gentile, with emphasis on τὰ πάντα, cannot be denied. Even though the Law was given to Israel, it exercised its function over all humanity: over Israel by virtue of disobedience, over Gentiles by virtue of disassociation. Hays, 269, states that the Law illuminates Israel's condition and *a fortiori* "the universal human condition—of bondage to the power of Sin."

ἵνα ἡ ἐπαγγελία ἐκ πίστεως Ἰησοῦ Χριστοῦ δοθῇ τοῖς πιστεύουσιν. This ἵνα clause describes why the Law confined humanity under the power of sin, supporting Paul's larger argument of how the Law and the promises are in

54. Matera, 135, argues that the parallel in Rom 11:32 supports the interpretation that γραφή equals the "personification of God's will."

55. Hays, 268, notes this as a helpful parallel to this verse, given that Paul uses God as the subject with the same verb.

56. Moo, 239, argues that this can refer to persons, but a comparison to Rom 11:32 leads to the conclusion that this is a broad reference to the entire cosmos. I see the personal element as paramount (so also Schreiner, 245).

step and how the Law serves God's bigger purposes in the promises. In so doing, Paul immediately redeems the Law from a negative assessment of its worth. He does not do this so the Law can become the current standard for obedience, something his opponents would certainly argue, but so that his readers would gain a fuller understanding of God's purposes in history. The ἵνα clause could indicate purpose (Moo, 240), result (Matera, 135), or purpose-result (de Boer, 236); purpose is preferred because of the emphasis on God's intentionality in the use of personified ἡ γραφή in the prior clause. In the context, promise refers either to the inheritance promised to Abraham in light of v. 18 or to justification by faith and reception of Spirit in light of v. 14 (Fung, 165). I do not think it is unfair to say that given the flow of Paul's argument he intends both; they are beginning to coalesce in his presentation. The prepositional phrase ἐκ πίστεως indicates basis or means as it has elsewhere in the book; it describes the verb δοθῇ, not the noun ἡ ἐπαγγελία.[57] The gen. Ἰησοῦ Χριστοῦ is related to πίστεως and expresses the same idea as in prior similar occurrences (see Gal 2:16). The ptc. τοῖς πιστεύουσιν is substantive and here refers to those who believe in Jesus; it is functionally equivalent to the ἐκ πίστεως expressions Paul used earlier. This phrase thus expresses why God used the Law to confine people under sin: so that the promise given to Abraham might ultimately be given to those who believe on the basis of their faith in Jesus, not obedience to the Law, which could never bring righteousness.

It would not be surprising if Paul's opponents thought he had painted himself into a corner with his arguments about the Law. As a Pharisee himself, Paul exalted the Law and obedience to it as the primary means to worship God and accomplish his will in the present time. So his statements about the inability of the Law to justify anyone (3:10–14) and its temporary nature (3:15–18) would demand a deeper explanation. The leading question of Gal 3:19 is perfectly logical and appropriate given Paul's background on one hand and contemporary Jewish thought on the other. Paul responds that the Law's function is properly understood only with regard to its relationship to sin. The Law was added with the goal of increasing transgressions. It served to confine everyone under sin until the promised seed would arrive. In this way the Law was not the endgame but rather a servant to God's greater purposes revealed in the promises given to Abraham. "Here again it is the limited power of the law which is in view: it was not so ultimate or important a factor in the divine purpose as grace and Spirit, as promise and inheritance received through faith; nor so ultimate and powerful as sin" (Dunn, 195). God intended all along to defeat the totalizing power of sin with grace and Spirit, the Law simply assisting that process, not guiding it.

---

57. Fung, 165, argues that first attributive position would be required to connect the prepositional phrase to the noun. I appreciate the argument, but it certainly is not airtight. In Galatians, for example, see 1:8 ἄγγελος ἐξ οὐρανοῦ. The better argument here would simply be the overall logic of Paul's argument.

"Thus we cannot move from Abraham to Christ, from promise to fulfillment, without going through the law after all. However secondary and subordinate in God's overall economy of salvation, the law nonetheless has a necessary and irreplaceable role to play. For, as Luther said, 'God wounds in order to heal; he kills in order to make alive' " (George, 264).

Theological Comments

As a believer who has placed his faith in the Lord Jesus Christ, I am in a position similar to Paul in that I wrestle with the present function of the Law. On the one hand, I believe and affirm that the Law is revelation from God. The NT discussions of Scripture had in view the entire scope of OT writings. When Paul wrote to Timothy in 2 Tim 3:16 that "all Scripture is inspired and profitable," he likely wrote in the mid to late AD 60s at a time when the NT was not yet complete. His intended referent for *πᾶσα γραφή* was the OT Scriptures. When Peter wrote in 2 Pet 1:21 that "no prophecy was ever borne of human impulse; rather, men carried along by the Holy Spirit spoke from God" (NET), his most likely referent was the prophetic word of the OT Scriptures. So the NT witness is clear that the OT is inspired by God and presently profitable for believers. On the other hand, there are central aspects of the Law that are clearly no longer in force. Circumcision is not required of believers to enter God's family. Most evangelical believers worship on Sunday, not Saturday, which is the original referent of the Sabbath commandments. On Sunday after worship I can eat whatever food I wish; I am not restricted by the OT food regulations. I wrestle with the Law because at the same time I respect it as revelation but minimize it as regulation. It is Paul's teaching in this paragraph (and indeed in Galatians as a whole) that leads to this dichotomy. He at the same time acknowledges the value of the Law to accomplish God's purposes, but minimizes its function to presently govern believers.

Does this dichotomy cause theological problems for the believer? Is there a sense in which we are inconsistent in our handling of Scripture if we approach the Law in this manner? Clearly the answer is no. It is important to remember that the Law in Paul's framework is not coextensive with the entire OT witness. Indeed, his central argument is that the promises of God given to Abraham in Gen 12 are presently valid; the Law is a distinct revelation with a different function. So we should remember first that Paul uses *νόμος* with a very specific literary and historical referent of the Mosaic Covenant, given to and accepted by Israel in Exod 19. We should also remember the global function of the Law still has merit: The burden of Paul's argument in this paragraph is to show that humanity was controlled by sin, a power that the Law could not break. This domineering force could be removed only by the promises of God, distributed by Abraham's chosen seed, Jesus Christ. The theological force of the Law is still in place, while its regulatory function has been vacated.

Application and Devotional Implications

Given Paul's argument about the Law, a valid question for application is how believers are presently to handle the Law. He at the same time argues that it does not govern behavior but that it served God's purposes in history to magnify sinfulness. What does this mean for interpretation of the Law? It means that the Law appropriately shows humanity's sinfulness, but it has no governing power *per se* as Law. An easy way to demonstrate this is with reference to homosexuality. A common argument heard in this discussion runs as follows: "If you condemn homosexuality based on passages in Leviticus, you should also then condemn football, lobster thermidor, and most modern fabrics." In a sense this argument has merit. Leviticus prohibits all kinds of behaviors that we now accept. Touching a pig carcass is prohibited by Lev 11:7–8, shellfish is prohibited by Lev 11:9–12, and fabrics made from different types of threads are prohibited by Lev 19:19. The person who argues against homosexuality from Leviticus but does not prohibit these other things is indeed open to the charge of inconsistency. More to the present point, Leviticus particularly and the Law holistically have been superseded by faith in Christ. But that does not mean the Law has nothing to say to our present situation. As believers in a new dispensation, we must be nuanced in how we discuss this. If we present this passage as something that must be obeyed simply because it is in the Bible or it is part of the Law given by God, then we say too much. This approach would essentially be theonomy or reconstructionism, which are inappropriate given Paul's teaching on the temporary purpose of the Law. We must say fairly and directly that the Law no longer holds any place as a law that governs the actions of God's people. At the same time, if we ignore it altogether (the opposite problem of antinomianism), we say too little, because the Law certainly serves to illustrate humanity's extreme sinfulness. Our use of the Law needs to represent that nuance: Passages from the OT law can prove our sinfulness, showing sin to be an extremely dominant power, exercising total control over our every desire and action. But the Law gives way to the blessings bestowed by Christ in fulfillment of the promises given to Abraham by God. Therein lies the source of conviction and restoration for all in this present age.

Although Paul does not address here specifically his theology of sin, it certainly lies under the surface, informing his discussion of salvation history at this point. Paul knows that sin is a controlling, consuming power, and the Law served to reveal it as such. Sin is the central problem of the human condition that the Law revealed and Christ solved. We would do well to remember this as we reflect on our own spiritual condition today. The Law does not have authoritative power, but it stands as a witness against our sinfulness, showing it to be the destroying power that it is:

> While it is latent, sin stirs but slightly. It is like a lion who is asleep or is moving about quietly. Apply the stick of the law to it, prod it a little, and its fangs flash, its rages and roars, it tries to rend

> and tear, it displays what a wild beast it really is. That stick does not make the beast a beast; it cannot kill or change the beast; all it can do is to make it show what it is. (Lenski, 167–68)

Believers can rejoice because Christ through his death has killed this raging beast, and as Paul will discuss in later chapters, because the Spirit guides the believer to victory over it each day.

Additional Exegetical Comments

3:19 Paul's opening question is rather cryptic because the verb is missing: Τί οὖν ὁ νόμος; On the basis of comparison to Rom 3:1 and 1 Cor 3:5, Betz, 162n9, argues this question should be understood as "What then is the Law?" Each passage has a similar question that begins with τί οὖν; the verb ἐστιν occurs in the latter and is reasonably implied in the former. Burton, 187, discusses the different meanings "why is," "what is," and "what signifies," arguing that the difference in meaning is not great. "Why the Law?" is included in "what signifies?" which is Paul's key thought.

3:20 Hays, 267–68, argues that Paul's point here is only about the nature and essence of God, linking to other important aspects of singularity in God's program: "The oneness of God in v. 20b is to be linked with the singularity of the 'seed' in v. 16 and the oneness of the people of God in v. 28. The deficiency of the Law, therefore, may be related to its divisive character, its inability to bring Jews and Gentiles together into a single new people."

Selected Bibliography

Baugh, S. M. "Galatians 3:20 and the Covenant of Redemption." *WTJ* 66 (2004): 49–70.

Chafer, L. S. *Systematic Theology*. Abridged ed. Wheaton, IL: Victor, 1988.

Gentry, P. J., and S. J. *Wellum. Kingdom Through Covenant: A Biblical-Theological Understanding of the Covenants*. Wheaton, IL: Crossway, 2012.

Staples, J. A. "Altered Because of Transgressions? The 'Law of Deeds' in Gal 3,19a." *ZNW* 106 (2015): 126–35.

Wright, N. T. *The Climax of the Covenant: Christ and the Law in Pauline Theology*. Minneapolis: Fortress, 1993.

The Arrival of Faith (3:23–29)

Textual Notes

3:23 Most all manuscripts read the pf. ptc. συγκεκλεισμένοι (C D[1] K L 365 630 1175 𝔐), while several important manuscripts read the pres. ptc. συγκλειόμενοι (𝔓[46] ℵ B D* F G P Ψ 33 81 104 1241 1739 1881 2464). The latter has strong Alexandrian witnesses on its side, most notably 𝔓[46] ℵ B 33 1739, but their support is mitigated somewhat by the testimony of C for the pf. tense. A choice on internal evidence is not clear cut. Either tense makes good sense in the context. The pf. tense fits the meaning of the verb συγκλείω quite well, but this does not solve the problem; Paul may have used the pf. originally, or scribes may have changed the pres. tense to the pf. Altogether the pres. ptc. should be preferred as the reading more likely to be original. It has better external evidence, and it is more likely that a scribe would change the pres. to the pf. than vice versa.

3:26 The NA[28] text reads διὰ τῆς πίστεως ἐν Χριστῷ Ἰησοῦ while 𝔓[46] 6 sa read διὰ τῆς πίστεως Χριστοῦ Ἰησοῦ and 1739 1881 sy[p] read διὰ τῆς πίστεως Ἰησοῦ Χριστοῦ. Despite the importance of these witnesses that read the name in the gen. case, that reading is likely a scribal change to comport with other occurrences within the book of πίστις plus a gen. which refer to Christ (see Gal 2:16, 20; 3:22).[1]

3:28 There are some interesting variations at this point in the text:

> πάντες γὰρ ὑμεῖς εἷς ἐστε ἐν Χριστῷ Ἰησοῦ (This is the reading of NA[28], supported by excellent and numerous witnesses.)
>
> πάντες γὰρ ὑμεῖς ἐστε ἐν Χριστῷ Ἰησοῦ (ℵ*)
>
> πάντες γὰρ ὑμεῖς ἐστε Χριστοῦ Ἰησοῦ (𝔓[46] ℵ[c] A)
>
> πάντες γὰρ ὑμεῖς ἕν ἐστε ἐν Χριστῷ Ἰησοῦ (F G 33)

1. R. B. Matlock, "ΠΙΣΤΙΣ in Galatians 3.26: Neglected Evidence for 'Faith in Christ'?," *NTS* 49 (2003): 433–39, argues helpfully that the reading of 𝔓[46] should be understood as evidence for the obj. gen. interpretation of πίστις Χριστοῦ. Essentially the scribe understood the words ἐν Χριστῷ as modifying πίστεως and then replaced the words with the normal Pauline idiom of the simple gen.

Each of these readings other than the first can be explained as scribal error.[2] The reading of ℵ* can be dismissed as too difficult because in majuscule script the letters ЄN would be ambiguous (either the prep. ἐν or the neut. form of the number one). The other readings are slight variations in the sense. The text reading has the best external support and makes the best sense in the context.

Translation

23 Now before faith[3] came we were confined under the power of the Law,
imprisoned until the coming faith would be revealed. **24** For this reason the
Law became our guide[4] to Christ so that we would be justified on the basis of
faith. **25** And because faith came, we are no longer under a guide. **26** For in
Christ Jesus you are all sons of God through faith. **27** For as many of you as
were baptized in Christ, you were clothed with Christ. **28** There is neither Jew
nor Greek. There is neither slave nor free. There is neither male nor female.
For in Christ Jesus you are all one. **29** And if you are Christ's, then you are
Abraham's seed;[5] you are heirs according to the promise.

Commentary

Throughout the exegetical, theological discussion in this central section of the letter, Paul writes for a very practical purpose. He has to explain on a fundamental level why his admonitions to the Galatians, which effectively abrogate and vacate the present validity of the Law to govern the behavior of those who are related to God in Christ, are in keeping with God's plans, purposes, and character. To advance that broader purpose, Paul introduces a metaphor in this paragraph that explains his admonition relative to the Law both in function and timing. Here Paul clearly breaks from his Jewish roots; it is here that his theology truly shows itself to be Christian, seen in bold relief against the Jewish views of his opponents. His essential argument is that the Law served not a permanent purpose, but a temporary one. The Law was not the final goal of God's revelation, but rather a servant to what

---

2. B. M. Metzger, *A Textual Commentary on the Greek New Testament* (New York: United Bible Societies, 1994), 526.

3. Some translations translate as "this faith" (CSB, NIV), recognizing the anaphoric force of the article. The NLT fills out the conceptual referent: "Before the way of faith in Christ was available to us."

4. Translations vary here and in v. 25 based on the precise nuance of παιδαγωγός seen in Paul's argument: "guardian" (NET, CSB, ESV, NIV, NLT); "disciplinarian" (NRSV); "tutor" (NASB, NKJV).

5. Some translations use the referent instead of the word "seed": "descendants" (NET, NASB); "offspring" (ESV, NRSV); "children" (NLT).

God would ultimately reveal in Christ. The Law was not where God's people ultimately would land; instead, it led them to their final destination. In this way Paul supports his admonitions to the Galatians to turn from the false gospel proclaimed to them that required obedience to the Law. Seen from the standpoint of God's revelation in Christ, obeying the Law is moving backwards in time and purpose, away from God's intended goal for his people.

Paul orders his thoughts in this section chronologically, dividing salvation history into two eras: before and after the arrival of faith and the promises given to Abraham. In many ways Paul thinks dispensationally: There is a distinct change in God's administration of the relationship to his people brought about by new revelation given by God. The central focus in this chronological division is the function of the Law; a secondary emphasis is the resultant structure of the people of God relative to their inclusion in his family.

The extent of this paragraph is tied to the extent of the previous paragraph (3:19–22). Obviously my decision there affects the starting point here. The shape of this paragraph is governed by Paul's discussion of the role of the Law, not its purpose as in the prior paragraph. Paul introduces the Law's prior role as a guardian, shows that this role is now defunct, and then shows the reason that role is now defunct. The final verse of the paragraph, while logically tied to the preceding material, also serves to summarize Paul's main theological argument in this chapter. Some commentators (e.g., Martyn, 374) treat 3:26–29 as a new paragraph in which Paul directly addresses the Galatians and takes them back to their moment of baptism, usually relying heavily upon the shift to the 2 pl. pronoun in v. 26. There is a reasonable logic to this approach, but I am persuaded that there is a tighter connection between vv. 23–25 and 26–29 because of the γάρ and the content expressed.

A key element for Paul in this paragraph is the theological statement of v. 26 and the baptismal imagery of v. 27. Some commentators regard these clauses as the central key for the passage that unlocks its meaning. Betz, 181–85, argues extensively along these lines, stating that the form of vv. 26–28 springs from "early Christian baptismal liturgy" and that the baptismal formula concerns "eschatological status before God in anticipation of the Last Judgment"; Paul shows how that status changes current social and religious standings and responsibilities. Longenecker, 154–55, describes vv. 27–28 as confessional formulae from the early church that Paul has taken up to explain the Gentiles' new situation in Christ, to support his assertion in v. 26, and to apply it to the Galatians. Martyn, 374, argues that Paul's point is to show how the Law played no role whatsoever in their baptism. These theses are certainly thought-provoking, but ultimately I am agnostic about the origin of this material. We need not be agnostic, however, about the theology that Paul expresses explicitly, the thought that undergirds Paul's argument, and the importance of baptism as a sign of the spiritual reality that believers now experience in Christ.[6]

3:23 Πρὸ τοῦ δὲ ἐλθεῖν τὴν πίστιν ὑπὸ νόμον ἐφρουρούμεθα. Paul begins this section with a distinct grammatical form that focuses on antecedent time (πρό plus an articular inf.). The action of the main verb ἐφρουρούμεθα ("we were confined") occurs prior to the action of the inf. phrase τοῦ ἐλθεῖν τὴν πίστιν ("before faith came"). The primary difficulty in explaining Paul's language is the referent of the noun τὴν πίστιν. This word has been used before in the epistle to mean an individual's particular response of trust in God, but Paul cannot mean that here because he argues clearly in Gal 3:6–9 that Abraham had that very response of faith to God's revelation of the promises. To understand Paul's meaning, we must first acknowledge the article with πίστιν is anaphoric and refers back to the faith just mentioned in v. 22, ἐκ πίστεως Ἰησοῦ Χριστοῦ, and thus refers to not just faith in a divine object but faith specifically in Jesus Christ (so Burton, 198; Lenski, 178; Schreiner, 246).[7] With a rhetorical figure Paul uses the noun πίστις to stand in for its arrival of its ultimate object, the Lord Jesus Christ.[8] This enables us to see that Paul speaks broadly concerning God's interactions with humanity. The noun "faith" takes on the larger connotations of salvation history, the mode and means by which God works with humanity as a whole, so Paul can address the overall function and place of the Law within the framework of God's promises to Abraham. The referent of the noun here is the full revelation of the place of faith in Jesus Christ, which was not fully shown until the ministry, death, and resurrection of Jesus were complete. That function of faith with its fully revealed object is now available to all on the basis of the promises of God to Abraham, only now fully grasped by Paul in the apocalyptic revelation of Jesus to him by God. So it is not without reason that Bruce, 181, argues that the "coming of faith" can be understood both as salvation-historical and personal.

The main verb of this clause is ἐφρουρούμεθα, "we were held in custody." This is the only place where Paul uses the verb φρουρέω in Galatians.[9] The word in this context means "to detain, confine, guard, hold in custody."[10]

---

6. In keeping with my Southern Baptist roots, I consider baptism to be an outward sign of an inward change and an ordinance as opposed to a sacrament.

7. As would be expected, commentators who argue that πίστις Χριστοῦ refers to the "faithfulness of Christ" see that here. See Longenecker, 145; Dunn, 197; de Boer, 238.

8. Witherington, 268, describes Paul's figure here as the reverse of personification: "here a person is described as the very definition of an abstract concept faith or faithfulness, and that person is Christ." See similarly de Boer, 238, who describes this as a metonymy of a trait standing in for the whole person.

9. He uses it twice elsewhere (2 Cor 11:32; Phil 4:7). It occurs only once elsewhere in the NT (1 Pet 1:5).

10. BDAG, 1067; *EDNT*, 3:440.

The impf. tense works very well here to indicate continuous time in the past; this was the ongoing situation for the "we." The decisive turn in Paul's logic comes with the prepositional phrase ὑπὸ νόμον, brought forward in front of the main verb for emphasis. The image here is entirely negative: In tandem with the prior argument about the function of the Law to magnify transgression (3:19), Paul here describes the Law as a jailer who confines humanity to sin, in and of itself offering no resolution for the problem it highlights (similarly Witherington, 268; Burton, 199, who points to the ptc. συνκλειόμενοι as supporting this negative connotation; Moo, 246–47).[11] In v. 22 Paul had argued that the Scripture confined everyone under sin, and now he speaks of the Law as having that function. Bruce, 181–82, cheekily says this is "a distinction without much of a difference. ... To be 'under law' is in practice to be 'under sin'—not because law and sin are identical, but because law, while forbidding sin, stimulates the very thing that it forbids."[12] The use of the 1 pl. here for the main verb is significant: Paul uses it as an exclusive "we" to differentiate between the experience of Jews and Gentiles (similarly Longenecker, 145).[13] He will turn to the 2 pl. in vv. 26–29 to emphasize the proper understanding of the place of Gentiles in God's plan, but for now he focuses on the condition of the Jewish people. This supports his central goal with ultimate application to the Gentiles, however: They should not go back into a situation from which Jews themselves have been delivered. Any movement toward Jewish behavior on the part of Gentiles is logically and chronologically absurd, given the change of state for Jews themselves in light of Christ's advent. There is even a larger theological point in play: As Lenski, 179, argues in light of Rom 3:19, this particular assertion involves Jews, but it also impacted the whole world: "What this law did for the Jews had its bearing on the whole world, also on all the Gentiles who did not have the Mosaic law."[14]

---

11. See BDAG, 1067, which says relative to this use of the verb, "The terminology is consistent w. the Roman use of prisons principally for holding of prisoners until disposition of their cases." One need not see this exact cultural background in play in Paul's use, but it does emphasize the vivid imagery Paul uses. This is *contra* Dunn, 197, who argues that Paul intends a positive function of the Law as a "custodian."

12. Luther, 186, goes a bit further: "The law's true function, then, is to show us our sins, to make us guilty, to humble us, to kill us, to bring us down to hell, and finally to take away all help and comfort; yet this is wholly in order that we may be justified, exalted, brought to life, carried up into heaven, and obtain everything good. Therefore, the law does not just kill, but it kills in order that we may live."

13. See D. B. Wallace, *Greek Grammar Beyond the Basics: An Exegetical Syntax of the New Testament* (Grand Rapids: Zondervan, 1996), 397–99, for discussion of this grammatical feature.

14. de Boer, 238, makes the same point by arguing that the situation of Jews under the Law represented all of humanity. Schreiner, 246, and Moo, 241, both argue that Gentiles are not entirely excluded because as Paul argues later in 4:1–11 Gentiles are

συγκλειόμενοι εἰς τὴν μέλλουσαν πίστιν ἀποκαλυφθῆναι. This participial phrase further augments the idea of the main verb by showing how the action of confinement was carried out. The ptc. συγκλειόμενοι is a pres. ptc. of means that modifies the main verb ἐφρουρούμεθα: "[we were held in custody] by being confined." Most normally the verb συνκλείω has a negative meaning (Schreiner, 246), which fits well with Paul's argument here. The modifying prepositional phrase εἰς τὴν μέλλουσαν πίστιν ἀποκαλυφθῆναι is a rather complex construction.[15] The central grammatical component of the modifying phrase is the core of the prepositional phrase, εἰς τὴν πίστιν. The prep. in this context could indicates an extension in time up to a point,[16] but a telic force would not be unreasonable (Moo, 242–43).[17] The fem. ptc. μέλλουσαν is in the first attributive position to πίστιν. This is emphatic, pointing to the undisputed reality of the future arrival of the faith from the standpoint of the confinement. Open to debate is how the aor. inf. ἀποκαλυφθῆναι is to be construed. It could logically modify μέλλουσαν. In that case, the meaning would be the future surety of the action indicated by the inf.[18] A reasonable translation would be "by being confined until the faith which was destined to be revealed [appeared]." A different option for ἀποκαλυφθῆναι is to take it as epexegetical to πίστιν, offering a clarification or explanation of which faith was in view. A reasonable translation of this construal would be "by being confined until the coming faith, that is, the faith that was to be revealed."[19] In this case the faith would be qualified twice: It is coming, and it is to be revealed. The difference between the interpretations is slight, and the latter is preferred because it more naturally flows from the word order and comports well with the preferred referent for πίστιν at the beginning of the verse. As there, the article here is anaphoric, pointing back to the faith expressed in v. 22; this is "faith in its distinctly christological dimension" (Moo, 241).

---

under the Law as well as Jews. Fung, 167, argues differently, stating that anarthrous νόμος means a "general principle of law" and "we" refers to all people, presumably because all people are beholden to a principle of law in some form or fashion.

15. The word order and choice is somewhat unexpected. One might have expected third attributive position, εἰς πίστιν τὴν μέλλουσαν ἀποκαλυφθῆναι, which would be a simpler way to describe the noun faith.

16. BDAG, 289.

17. Moo, 242–43, prefers the telic force on the grounds that a temporal force for εἰς is rare in Paul, and the telic force fits his argument quite nicely. Soards and Pursiful, 161, see εἰς as a temporal parallel to ἄχρις in 3:19.

18. See BDAG, 628, which says, "w. aor. inf. ἀποκαλυφθῆναι that is destined (acc. to God's will) to be revealed Gal 3:23."

19. This translation puts into English what Lenski, 180, argues: " 'About to be revealed' is a periphrastic substitute for the future tense and is not often found with the aorist infinitive (R. 857), but is punctiliar in the case of this aorist infinitive (R. 878)."

It is not without import that the inf. ἀποκαλυφθῆναι is pass. voice. As a divine passive and in keeping with Paul's other uses of this word group, the revelation decisively comes through the action of God. Martyn, 362, argues that the inf. ἀποκαλυφθῆναι points to "God's eschatological act" (similarly Soards and Pursiful, 161). Even though he only implies it here, Paul still maintains his focus on the activity of God in salvation history throughout his argument. This even explains the way Paul uses his key terms. As Dunn, 198, says, "The contrasting epochs can be summed up simply by their most characteristic features—law (for Israel) and faith. Faith (the faith of Abraham, and faith in Christ) brackets the interim epoch of the law." Put rather simply, Paul describes the "inauguration of a new era in redemptive history" (Schreiner, 245).

3:24 ὥστε ὁ νόμος παιδαγωγὸς ἡμῶν γέγονεν εἰς Χριστόν. This clause makes a logical deduction regarding the function of the Law from the standpoint of the arrival of the full revelation of faith in Christ Jesus described in v. 23. The conj. ὥστε when introducing independent clauses can mean "for this reason, therefore, so" with an inferential force (so Schreiner, 248; *contra* Soards and Pursiful, 161, who see this as result).[20] This conclusion on Paul's part is a decidedly Christian deduction in light of the flow of salvation history. It shows that the Law was not the full revelation of God to his people; that full revelation was only attained finally in Christ. In light of that later, full revelation, the Law now takes on a different role than that previously understood in Jewish thought. The extensive force of the pf. tense γέγονεν makes sense in this regard; it is used essentially like a historical aor. (Lenski, 181–82; Longenecker, 146). Paul discusses the situation pre-faith at this point: Note the pattern πρὸ τοῦ δὲ ἐλθεῖν τὴν πίστιν in v. 23 and ἐλθούσης δὲ τῆς πίστεως in v. 25. So this pf. is confined to the action of the past.

In describing the function of the Law relative to God's dealings with humanity in history, Paul introduces a metaphor of the παιδογωγός to describe both the function of the Law and its temporary nature vis-à-vis faith. Paul is the only NT author to use this metaphor: The word παιδαγωγός occurs only within this paragraph in the book of Galatians, and only elsewhere in 1 Cor 4:15. Essentially the παιδαγωγός was a guardian or supervisor of a minor child, approximately from ages 6 to 16, who had the responsibility to accompany the child to school and provide general guidance and instruction in social mores and manners.[21] Once the child became an adult, the service of the παιδαγωγός was no longer required. The word occurs from the 5th century BC onward, and this particular servant function was well known throughout the Hellenistic world. The more difficult question with

20. See BDAG, 1107; Wallace, *Greek Grammar*, 673.

21. See LSJ, 1286; MGS, 1518; J. H. Moulton and G. Milligan, *Vocabulary of the Greek Testament* (Peabody, MA: Hendrickson, 1997), 473; BDAG, 748. See Witherington, 264–65, for a helpful overview of the many functions of a παιδαγωγός.

this word is whether the connotation of the παιδαγωγός is positive or negative.[22] From the standpoint of the παιδαγωγός itself, there was a distinction made between the generally corrective function of this role and the positive, educational function of the διδάσκολος (Lightfoot, 148; Longenecker, 146; de Boer, 240).[23] The παιδαγωγός did indeed serve to instruct the child under his care in proper social and ethical conduct, but Paul's language elsewhere of the Law's function is entirely negative: He speaks of the Law guarding (φρουρέω) and confining (συγκλείω).[24] The function of the Law as παιδαγωγός is seen only vis-à-vis the full arrival of faith in the coming of Christ. If the ultimate revelation of God's dealings with humanity is found in faith at the coming of Christ, in Paul's thought the Law could only serve a negative function. Any ascription of positive value to it would in a sense preempt the faith in Christ to be revealed. So Paul intends the metaphor of the παιδαγωγός to serve only as a negative one in the sense that he only is concerned with the limiting, restrictive nature of that servant's function in the life of the minor child. Stated directly, relative to the revelation of Christ, the Law served only to highlight sin and restrict Israel's behavior. Longenecker, 148, argues helpfully in this regard:

> The point of the analogy here is not that the Mosaic law was a positive preparation for Christ, though in terms of piety and education that cannot be doubted in other contexts. Rather, the focus here is on the supervisory function of the law, the inferior status of one under such supervision, and the temporary nature of such a situation in the course of salvation history.

In this light the force of the prepositional phrase εἰς Χριστόν can be understood best as temporal in keeping with the emphasis on salvation history (so most commentators). The Law was a tutor not toward Christ but only until the coming of Christ. Thus Paul highlights the temporary, negative function of the Law in light of the full revelation of faith in Christ. The Law served a limited, negative function in the flow of salvation history in that it restricted and confined the Jewish people until the full revelation of Christ appeared; once that revelation appeared, the Law as παιδαγωγός was no longer needed.

ἵνα ἐκ πίστεως δικαιωθῶμεν. A legitimate question here is which phrase this *ἵνα* clause modifies. It logically could modify any of the clauses preceding in vv. 23–24. Based both on the prior contrasts Paul has made between faith

---

22. *TLNT*, 3:1, highlights the generally negative portrait these servants had within the classical period and then their generally positive reputation within Hellenistic Greek, but Paul makes no direct claim on this score.

23. Oakes, 127, argues that the παιδαγωγός is positive because even though the Law was not a διδάσκολος, neither was it a δεσμοφύθλαξ, a jailer. So there must be some positive connotation in its use here.

24. De Boer, 240, highlights the latter verb as negative, which impacts the meaning of the metaphor.

and the Law and the general grammatical rule that dependent clauses are more likely related to what immediately precedes, the best argument is that the ἵνα cause modifies the preceding ὥστε clause. In essence then this clause fleshes out the purpose of the Law as a παιδαγωγός: to lead to justification by faith for God's people. With this short phrase, essentially a shorthand for other arguments Paul has made earlier in the book (e.g., 2:16), Paul reminds the Galatians of their present status as fully incorporated into God's people by virtue of their faith in Christ. They have fulfilled the ultimate purpose God intended through the Law. The pass. voice of δικαιωθῶμεν, another divine passive (Soards and Pursiful, 163), shows that these are God's purposes for his people (de Boer, 241). This argument serves Paul well in his admonition to the Galatians. The Law was a guide until Christ came, not an end unto itself. Its purpose was always to lead to justification on the basis of faith. Once the full revelation of faith in Christ appeared, the Law was no longer needed, so it makes no sense in any way for the Galatians to desire to be under the Law again. "The Law was compelled to serve God's intention simply by holding all human beings in a bondage that precluded every route of deliverance except that of Christ" (Martyn, 363). This preclusion applied even to itself.

3:25 ἐλθούσης δὲ τῆς πίστεως. With this phrase Paul moves from a discussion of the past situation under the Law to the present reality out from under the Law with the decisive change made at the coming of faith. The aor. ptc. points to an action in the past relative to the main verb. As in prior verses in this paragraph, the article with πίστεως is anaphoric, referring ultimately back to the faith mentioned in v. 22.[25] So Paul is referring here to the full arrival of faith in Christ at his first advent. Although often temporal in force, this gen. abs. is causal, providing important background information to understand the affirmation of the main clause.[26] Paul has just affirmed that the Law was indeed a guardian until faith was revealed; in order for his following affirmation to ring true, he needs to establish the background information that faith has indeed come as a basis for that affirmation.

οὐκέτι ὑπὸ παιδαγωγόν ἐσμεν. The cause expressed in the preceding gen. abs. clause now has its present effect in the main clause of the sentence: "we are no longer under a guardian." The adv. οὐκέτι is temporal, emphasizing the new state in time (Schreiner, 249). The prepositional phrase ὑπὸ παιδαγωγόν is functionally equivalent to ὑπὸ νόμον in v. 23 (Burton, 201; Bruce, 183). The Law had its proper function at the proper time, but now that the full revelation of faith in Christ has come, humanity is no longer under the Law; it has ceased to function as a jailer. Here is where Paul's disagreement with his

25. Burton, 201, calls this article restrictive, but the point of his meaning is the same as anaphoric.

26. See L. K. Fuller, "The 'Genitive Absolute' in New Testament/Hellenistic Greek: A Proposal for Clearer Understanding," *JGRChJ* 3 (2006): 142–67, for a discussion of this function of the gen. abs.

opponents comes to a head (Witherington, 269). He decisively argues that the Law no longer has validity as a guardian to regulate the faith of God's people (Longenecker, 149). "Thus the Galatians' new desire for the Law and Law observance is not only inappropriate; it is also dangerous because it is a failure to recognize the time in which believers are living—a new time of independence from sin and the Law" (Soards and Pursiful, 164).

3:26 *πάντες γὰρ υἱοὶ θεοῦ ἐστε διὰ τῆς πίστεως ἐν Χριστῷ Ἰησοῦ*. Paul now switches his attention from the Jews to the Gentiles. For the next four verses he uses the 2 pl. instead of the 1 pl. to highlight the current situation of the Gentiles in the family of God. In many ways these verses serve as a conclusion to the entire argument begun in 3:6. Paul's goal has been to show that the Gentiles are within God's family, recipients of the promises given to Abraham, only on the basis of faith and not obedience to the Law. Here Paul reemphasizes this reality and highlights the new unity found within the people of God. The conj. *γάρ* serves to show that this phrase is the cause or grounds for the immediately preceding one; it is the proof that his assertion about the Law is true (Matera, 141).[27] In this instance, the connection is made through the repetition of the noun *πίστις*. The grounds to argue that faith has come, and thus the services of the guardian are no longer needed, is the present sonship of Gentiles, attained through faith in Jesus Christ. That spiritual reality that none can deny, proven by the work of the Spirit among the Galatians (3:1–5), proves Paul's assertion that no one is any longer under the guardianship of the Law. Because of this reality, Paul can confidently say that the Law is no longer in force, thereby undermining the arguments of his opponents. This verse is thus not a central conclusion, but rather an affirming proof, drawing on prior elements of the argument.

The most notable grammatical feature of this verse is the change from 1 pl. to 2 pl., from "we" to "you." Even though there is a change in referent, Jews versus Gentiles, in the flow of Paul's argument this is a distinction without any difference. Lightfoot, 149, notes helpfully that 1 Thess 5:5 shows a similar change of pronoun, there within a single verse. Burton, 202, argues that the change in pronoun means Paul is applying v. 25 to his readers; this is a helpful idea, as it shows that the experience of Jews is meant to be a paradigm for all people. The classic statement of v. 28 has to have an impact here, meaning that the second pl. does not ultimately exclude Jews (de Boer, 242). Paul even later in chapter four blurs this distinction further.[28] Consequently very little

27. Moo, 250, regards *γάρ* here as inferential rather than causal. To be causal, "sons of God" would have to denote difference between youth and adult, which it does not, and Paul would have to regard Gentiles as under the Law in the full sense of the language, which they were not.

28. George, 274, helpfully states, "However, even in Galatians 4, Paul would move from 'we' to 'you' language with no discernible difference in meaning. He could do this because the fundamental human reality is the same for Jews and Gentiles

should be made of the switch. What is true of Jews in this new era of faith in Christ is also true of Gentiles and vice versa.

Paul begins his assertion with πάντες, here emphatic both by its placement first in the sentence and because of the following emphasis upon universality from here to the end of the paragraph (Longenecker, 151; Martyn, 374; Hays, 271).[29] As before when discussing the promises given to Abraham, the term υἱοί figures prominently in this assertion, but an escalation has occurred. Before Paul asserted that the Gentiles were υἱοί Ἀβραάμ (Gal 3:7), but now he asserts that they are υἱοὶ θεοῦ (see also Martyn, 374–75). The OT often references the idea of Israel as the son of God. A helpful example is Hosea 2:1 (1:10 ET), where God promises an eschatological renewal for Israel:

> וְהָיָה בִּמְקוֹם אֲשֶׁר־יֵאָמֵר לָהֶם לֹא־עַמִּי אַתֶּם יֵאָמֵר לָהֶם בְּנֵי אֵל־חָי
>
> Although it was said to them, "You are not my people," it will be said to them, "You are sons of the living God!"

The themes of kinship, eschatology, and exclusivity are strong in this text and others like it.[30] Essentially the idea of sonship was exclusive to Jews alone, representing their special relationship with God (Witherington, 269–70; Dunn, 202).[31] The NT takes up this idea but escalates it by applying it to all believers. The phrase occurs elsewhere in the NT in Matt 5:9; Luke 20:36; Rom 8:14, 19. Paul uses the phrase here to highlight the connection of all believers to God within an eschatological framework. The Gentiles have received the promises made to Israel by God for an intimate, renewed relationship. The fact that υἱοί is anarthrous and pre-verbal marks it as qualitative; this emphasizes the spiritual reality without obliterating the ethnicity of those in view.[32] The phrase διὰ τῆς πίστεως indicates the means by which the sonship of believers occurs. As with other occurrences of πίστις in this section, the article makes this anaphoric, referring ultimately back to v. 22 and the totality of the revelation of faith in Christ (Lenski, 185; Soards and Pursiful, 168–69). It is not immediately clear in this sentence what the phrase ἐν Χριστῷ Ἰησοῦ modifies. It could either modify the immediately preceding πίστεως, indicating where the faith is placed, or it could modify the main verb

---

alike. The Scripture has concluded all under sin, all under the curse, all in bondage. Conversely, the redemptive work of Christ and incorporation into his body have relativized the former distinctions of race, rank, and role."

29. Moo, 249, argues that the emphatic placement of πάντες means both Jews and Gentiles are in view in this section.

30. This is the only place in the OT where the term בְּנֵי אֵל occurs. The collocation also occurs with forms of אֱלֹהִים but the contexts are different from that in Galatians. See Gen 6:2, 4; Job 1:6; 2:1; 38:7.

31. Betz, 185–86, notes that this honorific is reserved for Jews at the last judgment.

32. See M. H. Burer, " 'Sons of Abraham' in Galatians 3:7 as a Spiritual, Qualitative Designation," *BSac* 173 (2016): 337–51. The same construction is in view here; see discussion at p. 349n37.

ἐστε, showing the sphere in which this assertion is true, that is, "in Christ Jesus you are all sons of God through faith." Ultimately the latter is preferred (so most commentators). The former is logical based upon the word order since prepositional phrases most naturally modify that which immediately precedes, but the latter is ultimately preferred on several grounds. The clear use of the same phrase in v. 28 to indicate sphere would imply sphere here in v. 26. When Paul connects faith to Christ he usually prefers the gen. *πίστις Χριστοῦ* (so Bruce, 184). If this prepositional phrase modifies *πίστεως* this would be the only place in his writings where the object of faith is specified with the prep. ἐν. The metaphor of baptism and clothing following in v. 27 also supports a broader idea of sphere here. So believers become sons of God through incorporation into Christ, God's Son (Martyn, 375). The "in Christ" idea is common in Paul and is a central aspect of his soteriology. "Being 'in Christ' is, for Paul, communion with Christ in the most intimate relationship imaginable, without ever destroying or minimizing—rather, only enhancing—the distinctive personalities of either the Christian or Christ. It is 'I-Thou' communion at its highest" (Longenecker, 154). Within the context of Galatians, this idea is reflected in the intimate, personal relationship of Christ in the believer (2:19–20); the believer "in Christ" represents the other side of the coin. There is a "new relational identity" (Rapa, 602); the believer is no longer defined by the Law but by being in Christ, which makes him God's Son. "Our relationship with God is established by our union with Christ Jesus, and that union is in turn secured by our faith" (Moo, 251).

3:27 *ὅσοι γὰρ εἰς Χριστὸν ἐβαπτίσθητε, Χριστὸν ἐνεδύσασθε.* In order to explain his blanket assertion in v. 26 about the place of believing Gentiles within the family of God, Paul delves more deeply into the underlying spiritual reality. This statement is a prime example of Paul's language of incorporation. His conception of the nature of the spiritual life is fundamentally that of a connection to Christ that alters the very mode and realm of the believer's existence. The metaphorical language of getting dressed into Christ implies that the believer joins with Christ in a way that can only be described with difficulty; it is mysterious and powerful, and Paul only scratches the surface of the concept. The conj. *γάρ* connects this phrase to the previous as its grounds with special emphasis on the phrase ἐν Χριστῷ Ἰησοῦ at the end of v. 26 (Lightfoot, 149; Matera, 142; Dunn, 202). Paul is confirming the partial thesis of v. 26 ("You are all sons of God … in Christ Jesus") with the confessional material of vv. 27–28 (Longenecker, 154). The verse begins by restating the idea expressed by *πάντες* in the prior verse; *ὅσοι* modifies the implied subject of the verb *ἐβαπτίσθητε*: "as many of you who were baptized." This is the only place Paul mentions baptism within Galatians, but that in no way undermines its importance. The complete idea Paul uses here is to be baptized into Christ (*εἰς Χριστὸν ἐβαπτίσθητε*). The prep. *εἰς* could be equivalent to *ἐν*, indicating sphere (Lenski, 186–87), or it could indicate reference (Burton, 203; Longenecker, 155). The former is preferred because of the emphasis on sphere in this context. Paul's reference to the physical ritual of baptism as a public sign of conversion points to the spiritual reality he describes in the following phrase.[33] Baptism represents a fundamental change in the spiritual existence of the believer, so the importance and symbolism of the act itself cannot be underestimated. It becomes paradigmatic for the new life of the believer, "a vivid picture of being incorporated into Christ" (Schreiner, 257).[34]

Paul then extends the argument with the second half of the sentence, Χριστὸν ἐνεδύσασθε. The verb ἐνδύω refers to the process of dressing, either oneself or another, depending upon the voice.[35] The pass. voice is appropriate here given the emphasis throughout on God's activity in the life of the believer.[36] The metaphor of using ἐνδύω to describe the believer getting dressed with Christ as one puts on a garment points to the complete transformation of the individual due to their incorporation into Christ. The figure involves taking on the characteristics of the person mentioned (Burton, 204; Longenecker, 156). This image implies much that Paul does not flesh out here: a new nature, new behavior, substitution, perhaps even imputation. Even so, the image highlights the full inclusion in God's family of all who are baptized into Christ. Indeed, it interprets the significance of the baptism event (Hays, 271). All who are baptized into Christ are clothed with Christ, and all who are clothed with Christ are sons of God through faith. Calvin, 110–11, perhaps said it best: "He employs the metaphor of a garment, when he says that the Galatians have put on Christ; but he means that they are so closely united to him, that, in the presence of God, they bear the name and character of Christ, and are viewed in him rather than in themselves."

3:28 *οὐκ ἔνι Ἰουδαῖος οὐδὲ Ἕλλην, οὐκ ἔνι δοῦλος οὐδὲ ἐλεύθερος, οὐκ ἔνι ἄρσεν καὶ θῆλυ.* This verse flows naturally in Paul's thought from the previous two. If all who believe are sons of God in Christ through faith because all who are baptized have been clothed with Christ, then the human divisions that occur naturally—ethnic, social, and physical distinctions—no longer pertain in God's family. Stated another way, the incorporation of the Gentiles into Christ proves that Christ's ministry had universal scope and equal blessing for all. The present realization of that universal scope means that human divisions have fallen away in this present age of salvation history and must be made to fall away in our present experience as far as availability of salvation is

33. Moo, 251, argues that baptism was more than symbol: "It is the capstone of the process by which one is converted and initiated into the church." Thus it becomes a shorthand for the entire conversion experience.

34. See Oakes, 130, for a helpful discussion of baptism as an entry ritual with a high cost but with universal opportunity.

35. BDAG, 333.

36. See BDAG, 334, which says, "The mid. sense is not always clearly right; the pass. is somet. better."

concerned. Thus this statement is both indicative and imperative, the reality and the expectation, theology and call to action.

The rhetorical import of the verse is helped grammatically by its asyndeton. It makes a strong pronouncement with deep emotional feeling, and the lack of conj. would make this pronounced for the Greek reader. The first pair (Jew/Greek) is Paul's central point in the argument; the second (slave/free) and third (male/female) are elaborations that hint at Paul's theology and ethic but go beyond his specific argument for the Galatians (Longenecker, 157; Dunn, 206). The three sentences each have the same basic shape with the phrase οὐκ ἔνι negating the existence of each pairing. The word ἔνι was originally a strengthened form of the prep. ἐν; it came to be used as a variant of ἔνεστιν, and here it is an emphatic equivalent of ἐστιν (Lightfoot, 150; Bruce, 187; Longenecker, 156). The first sentence, οὐκ ἔνι Ἰουδαῖος οὐδὲ Ἕλλην, is expected given the topic of Paul's writing up to this point. The primary issue with which he wrestles is the ethnic distinctions between Jews and Gentiles relative to inclusion within the church.[37] Because of the primacy of faith in Christ, because of each believer's participation in Christ, because of the abrogation of the Law at Christ's arrival, because of the Law's temporary role—because of all these things, the salvific distinction between Jew and Gentile is no more. Both are equally in God's family and equal in God's family.

The second and third sentences are surprising, as Paul has not discussed these distinctions up to this point in the epistle. They point to areas of life that the gospel impacts but upon which Paul does not elaborate. These negated pairs hint suggestively at the all-encompassing scope of Christ's work in the gospel. The second sentence, οὐκ ἔνι δοῦλος οὐδὲ ἐλεύθερος, focuses on the primary social division in the ancient world between freedom and slavery.[38] Just as ethnic distinctions no longer pertain in Christ, this societal difference falls away as well. The master and the slave are no longer defined as such in Christ; they are now in Christ together on equal footing. The third sentence, οὐκ ἔνι ἄρσεν καὶ θῆλυ, focuses on the physical, human division between male and female, more often than not used to create divisions within God's family. Paul breaks down this barrier instantly by extending the clothing metaphor to cover even gender.[39] The wording of this third sentence differs slightly from the previous by using καί between the pairing instead of οὐδέ. Paul does this under the influence of the original wording of the phrase in Gen 1:27 (LXX). The grammar would naturally require οὐδέ, but the

37. For a helpful overview of the social tension between Jews and Greeks as ethnic groups during this period, see C. D. Stanley, " 'Neither Jew Nor Greek': Ethnic Conflict in Graeco-Roman Society," *JSNT* 19 (1997): 101–24.

38. Paul does use this slave/free terminology elsewhere in Galatians, but every other time it refers to spiritual realities, not the social divisions of Greco-Roman society.

39. This is especially fitting given that clothing is used to cover the parts of the physical body that distinctly mark the human person as male or female.

mnemonic force of the original wording is so strong that the καί prevails. The essential point of this verse cannot be missed: The spiritual change wrought in humanity by incorporation into Christ is all encompassing. Inclusion in God's family, in the promises given to Abraham and fulfilled in Christ, extends to all equally. No ethnic, social, or physical distinction can stand in the face of its universal reach.[40]

πάντες γὰρ ὑμεῖς εἷς ἐστε ἐν Χριστῷ Ἰησοῦ. This statement serves as the grounds for the negated pairings just described, the conj. γάρ exercising its common function of explanation. The statement explains why the removal of these common human distinctions is an appropriate deduction from the baptismal clothing metaphor. It expresses the logical middle term between all believers being clothed in Christ and the removal of human distinctions vis-à-vis salvation: All are clothed in Christ, and therefore all are one in Christ, and if all are one in Christ, human distinctions no longer pertain. Paul uses similar wording here as in v. 26. Each clause emphasizes the unity of believers as a result of salvation in Christ; the repetition of the prepositional phrase ἐν Χριστῷ Ἰησοῦ is significant. The wording πάντες ὑμεῖς is emphatic; Paul intends that none of the Galatian Gentile believers be left out of this assertion. The number εἷς could be understood "distributively and qualitatively, or inclusively and numerically" (Burton, 207). The former means that distinctions vanish; it is as if the same person always comes to God. The latter means that those in Christ merge into a single personality. Burton prefers the second because it provides a middle term between Christ as seed in v. 16 and those of Christ as Abraham's seed in v. 29. I prefer the former on the grounds of the pre-verbal word order and in light of the distinctions just mentioned. Thus unity is a shared experience of being in Christ regardless of their individual characteristics. It is possible that the imagery of the body undergirds this metaphor and clarifies its meaning: Oneness does not abolish distinctions, but integrates them into a common participation, a common life "in Christ" (Dunn, 207–8). Understanding Paul's statement, however, does not require the body imagery to be present; the same conclusion is clear regardless. In a sense Paul is working counter to his opponents because he aims to preserve social diversity, not eliminate it. Paul's opponents wanted to remove diversity by making Gentiles become Jews, but "being in Christ brings oneness, unity, across these polarities" (Oakes, 128).

40. For a similar constellation of concepts see 1 Cor 12:13; Col 3:11. See Moo, 252–53, for discussion with a helpful chart of comparisons. See also M. E. Boring, K. Berger, and C. Colpe, eds., *Hellenistic Commentary to the New Testament* (Nashville: Abingdon, 1995), 468–69, for a discussion of a second or first century BC inscription from Philadelphia regarding the worship of Dionysis that emphasized equality of men and women, slaves and free. They also cite Philostratus, *The Life of Apollonius of Tyana*, letter 67, in the same vein.

3:29 *εἰ δὲ ὑμεῖς Χριστοῦ, ἄρα τοῦ Ἀβραὰμ σπέρμα ἐστέ, κατ' ἐπαγγελίαν κληρονόμοι.* With this first class conditional sentence Paul concludes the argument of this short paragraph and indeed the entire section that began at 3:6 (Hays, 273). His goal has been to show that the Galatians, by virtue of their faith in Christ, evidenced by the work of the Spirit in their midst, are certainly in God's family. They are without doubt related to Abraham in Christ and receive the promises given to him with the Law playing no role whatsoever in the process. "Paul has already clarified that the only genuine son of Abraham is Christ himself (3:16). The law could not produce true sons of God, for the law only precipitated more sin. Therefore, the only way one can legitimately be called the offspring of Abraham is if one belongs to Christ" (Schreiner, 259).

The conj. *δέ* links this conclusion directly with his prior assertion, providing a final emphasis for the discussion. The protasis of the conditional sentence is quite short: *εἰ δὲ ὑμεῖς Χριστοῦ*. The key piece is the gen. *Χριστοῦ*, which indicates possession with a view toward identity (Lightfoot, 151). This is an important clarification in light of the prior context, which delineated the three social distinctions that are removed in Christ: "[No matter where you fit in these prior categories,] if you are Christ's ..." In the apodosis the conj. *ἄρα* provides a strong conclusion, fitting for the rhetorically important conclusion Paul makes here. The central conclusion to which he leads is *τοῦ Ἀβραὰμ σπέρμα ἐστέ*. The gen. *τοῦ Ἀβραάμ* is brought forward for emphasis to align this conclusion with Abraham's central role in salvation history. The word *σπέρμα* is a pre-verbal anarthrous predicate nom.; the emphasis is on the qualitative nature of noun, which here marks "standing and privilege" (Burton, 209). This allows Paul to assert that the Galatians fulfill this promise in their experience, but neither are they the only fulfillment of it. The noun *κληρονόμοι* is parallel to *σπέρμα*, a second predicate nom. which also asserts nature and essence. The prepositional phrase *κατ' ἐπαγγελίαν* indicates the standard by which the assertion is made: heirs according to the promise. This is the first time Paul uses the word *κληρονόμος* in Galatians; it builds upon his use of *κληρονομία* in 3:18, used to refer to the blessings promised by God to Abraham. The heir is the one who receives those blessings. In this verse Paul concludes definitively that the Gentiles who are sons of God through faith are also Abraham's seed and recipients of the promises, just as Jews are.

Here Paul concludes a major portion of his theological argument to support his assertion to the Galatians that they need not devolve into obedience to the Law. They have received sonship to God apart from the Law. They have become the seed of Abraham through faith without obedience. They are heirs of the blessings because they are now party to the promises. On this firm foundation, established through faith in Christ, they can stand. Any movement toward the Law runs contrary to what God had planned and indeed to what God had actually done in their hearts through Paul's preaching.

Theological Comments

For all of my adult life I have been a dispensationalist. The theological system I hold views Scripture through the lens of different dispensations organized by God to reveal himself to mankind and govern mankind's response to him. This passage presents a primary argument in favor of this theological viewpoint, as it describes definitive changes in the way God revealed himself to humanity and how humanity was to respond properly to that revelation. Paul clearly sees the Law as now removed from its primary role governing the behavior of God's people because of Christ's ministry, death, and resurrection. This change is a hallmark of dispensational thought and has strong warrant based on this passage and many others.

For the latter part of my adult life, however, I have been a progressive dispensationalist, with emphasis upon the progressive nature of revelation and a small "d" on dispensation.[41] By this I mean that the progress of revelation shows some unexpected changes in the administrations. This passage also presents a primary argument in favor of this viewpoint, especially related to the place of the Gentiles in God's plan and purposes. No one denies that the Abrahamic covenant promised blessings to the Gentiles through Abraham's seed, but no one expected that the Gentiles would become Abraham's seed, as Paul states clearly here in his conclusion to the paragraph. To be clear, the Gentiles have not replaced Israel in any form or fashion (hence the importance of certain nouns as qualitative in the discussion), but they have been added as heirs to the blessings in a way unexpected from the viewpoint of the original promises.

In short, I believe the best exegesis of the biblical text acknowledges changes in the way God reveals himself and governs his relationship to humanity. These changes can often be unexpected from the standpoint of the original revelation, but they are always in keeping with it. My responsibility is always to read and understand the text carefully as written, adjusting my theological framework to what is revealed there, submitting in humility to the guidance of the Holy Spirit in the process.

Application and Devotional Implications

It is difficult to process everything that transpired in the ministry, death, and resurrection of Jesus. In a real sense all of Scripture serves to explain the meaning of that event. This is especially so in this particular paragraph, as Paul relates the coming of Christ to the function of the Law over Israel; to the present sonship, seedship, and heirship of Gentiles; and to human

41. I am borrowing deliberately from D. L. Bock, "Why I Am a Dispensationalist with a Small 'd,'" *JETS* 41 (1998): 383–96. Dr. Bock is a friend and colleague, and I don't think he will mind my blatant theft.

divisions that have restricted some from full access and inclusion in God's family. Each of these leads to a clear application presently for the Church.

Because the Law functioned in a temporary role over Israel, it now has no role functionally over the people of God. Now that Christ has come, the Law no longer governs behavior as it did previously. This does not mean that it no longer holds a place as God's revelation. Rather, its function to control behavior and thus magnify sin is no more. Any move to require people to obey the Law is moving backward in God's revelatory scheme, not forward. People now relate to God on the basis of faith in Christ. That should be what we proclaim to others in the present time.

A central argument in this paragraph is that by virtue of faith Gentiles are now fully related to God, just as Jews were. They now have a central seat at the table, so to speak, which was God's plan all along. In response to this we should worship God for his universal love to all mankind and commit to proclaim that love to all through evangelism and missions. There is no part of humanity that is not included in this promise. We must proclaim this truth to all so the promised blessings may extend to all as God intended.

Paul argues from this theological foundation that with regard to access to salvation, the ethnic distinctions between Jew and Gentile exist no more. He then extends that to new areas. The social distinction between slave and free has been torn down, as owner and owned both have the same access to salvation through faith in Christ. The physical distinction between male and female no longer governs access to God as it did in Judaism; both man and woman through faith experience adoption equally. This Scripture not only states the reality but it calls it into being. We must impress this new reality into our thoughts and actions: All have equal access to God as the call to faith in Christ extends equally to all. No human division should ever keep any one from full inclusion in God's family any more.

Additional Exegetical Comments

3:23–26 B. Schliesser argues that these verses are helpful to illuminate a "third view" on the πίστις Χριστοῦ problem.[42] He regards the gen. neither as obj. nor subj., but as something even more complex. These verses point to πίστις Χριστοῦ as having an "event-character": Paul conceives of this neither as an individual's attitude toward Christ ("faith in Christ") or Christ's own disposition ("faithfulness of Christ") but as referencing an eschatological event.[43] I appreciate the suggestive nature of this interpretation, but I do not

---

42. B. Schliesser, " 'Christ-faith' as an Eschatological Event (Galatians 3.23–26): a 'Third View' on Πίστις Χριστοῦ," *JSNT* 38 (2016): 277–300.

43. In his article Schliesser references as prior work in this vein P. M. Sprinkle, "Πίστις Χρίστου as an Eschatological Event," in *The Faith of Jesus Christ: Exegetical, Biblical, and Theological Studies,* ed. M. F. Bird and P. M. Sprinkle (Peabody, MA:

see how it would work in other passages where πίστις Χριστοῦ occurs, nor do I see how it accounts for the metaphorical use of πίστις in this paragraph.

3:23 T. Wilson argues that ὑπὸ νόμον is rhetorical shorthand coined by Paul in Galatians and that it refers to being under the curse of the Law (3:10, 13).[44] Moo, 246, presents the best argument in my opinion against this view: If this were true, it is not clear why the Galatians would now seek to be "under the Law." They must have expected some blessing to Law observance as opposed to simply a curse.

3:24 D. Gordon models careful examination of the immediate context in his discussion of the meaning of the παιδαγωγός metaphor.[45] He argues that Paul intends the metaphor to focus on the guardian's protective role in keeping his charge from harm. Although I do not agree with all of his interpretive conclusions, his work is worthy of consideration.

3:27 D. Hunn argues with force that baptism here should be understood not as water baptism, nor as a metaphorical reference to the rite (essentially the view I hold), but as a reference to baptism in the Spirit.[46] Her argument has merit, but I am ultimately dissuaded from this view on the grounds that without further clarification, baptism would most naturally for the Galatians refer in some way to their baptism in water as a sign of conversion.

3:28 In contrast with most exegetes and commentators, B. Lategan makes a cogent argument that this tripartite formula was not a preexisting formula but rather created by Paul.[47] He also helpfully discusses potential conflict with other Pauline writings, arguing that the full implications of this truth, which Paul recognized as an implication of Abraham's justification through faith alone, could only emerge over time.

Selected Bibliography

Bock, D. L. "Why I Am a Dispensationalist with a Small 'd.'" *JETS* 41 (1998): 383–96.

Hendrickson, 2009), 165–84, who himself references several prior authors.

44. T. A. Wilson, " 'Under Law' in Galatians: A Pauline Theological Abbreviation," *JTS* 56 (2005): 362–92.

45. D. T. Gordon, "A Note on παιδαγωγός in Galatians 3:24–25," *NTS* 35 (1989): 150–54.

46. D. Hunn, "The Baptism of Galatians 3:27: A Contextual Approach," *ExpTim* 115 (2004): 372–75.

47. B. C. Lategan, "Reconsidering the Origin and Function of Galatians 3:28," *Neot* 46 (2012): 274–86.

Boring, M. Eugene, Klaus Berger, and Carsten Colpe, eds. *Hellenistic Commentary to the New Testament*. Nashville: Abingdon, 1995.

Fuller, L. K. "The 'Genitive Absolute' in New Testament/Hellenistic Greek: A Proposal for Clearer Understanding." *JGRChJ* 3 (2006): 142–67.

Gordon, D. T. "A Note on παιδαγωγός in Galatians 3:24–25." *NTS* 35 (1989): 150–54.

Hunn, D. "The Baptism of Galatians 3:27: A Contextual Approach." *ExpTim* 115 (2004): 372–75.

Lategan, B. C. "Reconsidering the Origin and Function of Galatians 3:28." *Neot* 46 (2012): 274–86.

Matlock, R. B. "ΠΙΣΤΙΣ in Galatians 3.26: Neglected Evidence for 'Faith in Christ'?" *NTS* 49 (2003): 433–39.

Schliesser, B. " 'Christ-faith' as an Eschatological Event (Galatians 3.23–26): a 'Third View' on Πίστις Χριστοῦ." *JSNT* 38 (2016): 277–300.

Sprinkle, P. M. "Πίστις Χρίστου as an Eschatological Event." In *The Faith of Jesus Christ: Exegetical, Biblical, and Theological Studies*, ed. M. F. Bird and P. M. Sprinkle, 165–84. Peabody, MA: Hendrickson, 2009.

Stanley, C. D. " 'Neither Jew Nor Greek': Ethnic Conflict in Graeco-Roman Society." *JSNT* 19 (1997): 101–24.

Wilson, T. A. " 'Under Law' in Galatians: A Pauline Theological Abbreviation." *JTS* 56 (2005): 362–92.

The Redemption of the Heir (4:1–7)

Textual Notes

4:6 Many manuscripts here read ὑμῶν instead of ἡμῶν, presumably referring to Gentiles only (D² K L Ψ 33 81 365 630 1505 2464 𝔐). This is very likely an intentional alteration on the part of scribes for concord with the 2 pl. verb ἐστε in the earlier part of the verse. The 1 pl. pronoun has excellent support from the Alexandrian and Western witnesses (𝔓⁴⁶ ℵ A B C D* F G P 0278 104 1175 1241 1739 1881 lat), and it more likely gave rise to the other variant than vice versa. The argument against the 2 pl. pronoun is that it creates a reading that could be too hard. Tracking the referent of the pronouns in this verse is difficult, as it is throughout much of the epistle. Paul moves from referring to the Gentiles with the 2 pl. to an inclusive "we" with the 1 pl. Even so, Paul is prone to alternate readily between the first and second person, so this quick alternation is not without precedent. In addition, this verse does not emphasize cause as much as it makes an inference between the sonship of Gentiles and the arrival of the promised Spirit.[1] Within an inferential framework a switch between persons would not be too hard to understand.

4:7 There is a dizzying amount of variation at this point in the text:

> δια θεου 𝔓⁴⁶ ℵ* A B C* 33 1739*vid lat bo; Cl
> δια θεον F G 1881
> δια Χριστου 81 630 sa
> δια Ιησου Χριστου 1739c
> θεου δια Χριστου ℵ² C³ D K L 0278 104 365 1175 1241 2464 𝔐 ar
> θεου δια Ιησου Χριστου P 6 326 1505 sy
> κληρονομος μεν θεου, συγκληρονομος δε Χριστου Ψ

The reading that most likely gave rise to the others is διὰ θεοῦ. On the face of it, because διά with the gen. case often indicates means, it would appear that Paul mentions God here as an intermediate agent when he should have mentioned Christ. The more logical prepositional phrase here in keeping

1. So M. Zerwick, *Biblical Greek: Illustrated By Examples*, trans. J. Smith, Scripta Pontificii Instituti Biblici 114 (Rome: Pontifical Biblical Institute, 1963), 143.

with the argument would have been ὑπὸ θεοῦ, indicating that God was the ultimate agent. Paul uses the phrase διὰ θεοῦ only once (Gal 1:1); much more often he refers to a mediating aspect of God's person, e.g., διὰ θελήματος θεοῦ (Rom 15:32; 1 Cor 1:1; 2 Cor 1:1; 8:5; Eph 1:1; Col 1:1; 2 Tim 1:1). Thus much of the variation is an attempt to remove this apparent difficulty in the text. The NA[28] reading is supported by strong Alexandrian attestation, so it is to be preferred on external grounds, too. The phrase διὰ θεοῦ can be understood as shorthand for God's actions, which Paul clearly describes in the prior verses as his sending the Son and the Spirit.

Translation

1 Now I say that as long as the heir is a minor,[2] he is no different from a slave,
even though he is master over everything, **2** but he is under guardians and
managers[3] until the time appointed by the Father. **3** So also we, while we
were young, were enslaved to the basic things[4] of the world, **4** but when the
fullness of time came,[5] God sent his Son, one born from a woman, one born
under the Law, **5** so that he might redeem those under the Law, so that we
might be adopted as sons.[6] **6** And this shows that you are sons:[7] God sent

---

2. Some translations use the word "child" (CSB, ESV, NASB, NKJV) to focus on the age of the individual in view as opposed to legal status. The NIV splits the difference with "underage."

3. Some translations use the word "trustees" (CSB, NRSV, NIV), which does get at the sense of Paul's argument. I chose not to use that term because of the more limited financial connotations of the term in my American context.

4. The translation of τὰ στοιχεῖα τοῦ κόσμου varies in the translations because of the exegetical difficulties associated with the phrase: "the basic forces of the world" (NET); "the elements of the world" (CSB, NKJV); "the elementary principles of the world" (ESV); "the elemental spirits of the world" (NRSV); "the elemental things of the world" (NASB); "the elemental spiritual forces of the world" (NIV); "the basic spiritual principles of this world" (NLT).

5. Some translations focus on the appropriateness of the time as opposed to its completion: "when the appropriate time had come" (NET); "when the right time came" (NLT).

6. The Greek term υἱοθεσία and the co-occurrence of the gendered term υἱός in the following verses present problems for translation. The noun υἱοθεσία in its ancient context applied only to males, but Paul clearly uses it more broadly for all believers regardless of sex. To make that application clear, some translations use "child" and its cognates in this section (see NRSV, NLT). The NIV splits the difference: "adoption to sonship" (v. 5); "Because you are his sons" (v. 6); "you are ... God's child" (v. 7); "since you are his child" (v. 7).

7. This translation treats the ὅτι clause as subst., while most translations treat it as causal: "because you are sons."

the Spirit of his Son into our hearts, a Spirit that cries, "Abba! Father!" 7 So
you are no longer a slave but a son, and if you are a son, then you are also an
heir through God.

Commentary

Paul's most basic goal in this central theological section of the epistle is to show that the Law no longer has any power over believers; it no longer confines them so that their sin is magnified, nor does it govern any aspect of their relationship to God. This fits within his overarching goal of motivating the Galatians not to follow those who were encouraging them to become Law-observant and thus reject his gospel. To meet this end Paul relies upon very specific arguments about the time and function of the Law. In light of the original promises given to Abraham, in light of Jesus's ministry, death, and resurrection, in light of the flow of salvation history, the Law can only be understood as temporary. In the prior paragraph Paul made this argument with a focus upon the Law itself, referring to it as a *παιδαγωγός*, a common household servant who had a temporary role of guardianship over the minor child. In this paragraph Paul extends that metaphor by examining the other side of that analogy, namely, the minor child who is under guardianship. As the guardian is to the minor, so the Law is to humanity. Just as the role of the guardian ends because the child reaches the age of majority, so the role of the Law is set aside as God ushers in a new relationship for humanity, that of true children, by sending Jesus who redeemed humanity and made them sons and by subsequently sending the Spirit who confirms the sonship through his testimony. This paragraph then connects certainly to what precedes in 3:23–29 as an explanation, elaboration, and extension (see Fung, 179; Dunn, 210; Hays, 281; Garlington 2007, 235; Schreiner, 262; Moo, 257), but it also serves to conclude the argument begun in the beginning of chapter 3 (so Betz, 202; Martyn, 384; de Boer, 249).

The difficult interpretive matters here concern the source and function of the extended metaphor Paul uses to make his central point. Commentators have discussed the social background to the legal language at length, whether it is Roman, Hellenistic, particular to the Galatian region, or something else (see, e.g., Lightfoot, 165–66; Betz, 202–4; Longenecker, 161, 163). I am persuaded that none of these apply specifically in all respects. Rather, Paul is developing the metaphor in an *ad hoc* fashion and not attempting to be exact in his representation of the legal situation that serves as the vehicle for the metaphor (similarly Martyn, 386; Soards and Pursiful, 190). As a metaphor, the simplest interpretive path is to focus on a primary point of comparison. We need not make the metaphor walk on all fours, so to speak, at every point in the discourse. This metaphor, as metaphors regularly do, serves to make one central point of comparison even though it is extended in its literary application. In addition, the metaphor makes better sense along these lines when we understand it from Paul's Christian perspective. As argued before,

Paul in this section makes decisively Christian theological moves that are understood best from the later standpoint of Gentile inclusion in the family of God. The advent of Christ and Gentiles' faith in him with their subsequent inclusion in the church is the central theological datum with which Paul works. This metaphor serves to organize Paul's understanding of chronology in light of that theological *a priori*.

This paragraph brings Paul's argumentation in this center section of the book to a close. In the next paragraph he changes his strategy and pleads directly with the Galatians to return to his gospel. Its structure supports its function. Following Schreiner, 263, and similarly Fung, 181, I see vv. 1–2 as presenting the analogy, vv. 3–5 as applying the analogy, and vv. 6–7 as drawing out theological implications for believers. Many have argued that vv. 4–5 are not original with Paul but rather borrowed from the kerygma of the early church due to the language of sending and the chiastic structure (see, e.g., Bruce, 195; Longenecker, 166). Much of this discussion strikes me as speculative and essentially unprovable. The statement is understandable regardless of origin. I prefer the stance taken by Soards and Pursiful, 194: No matter the origin, the idea of God sending his Son for the benefit of humanity is truly remarkable.

4:1 Λέγω δέ, ἐφ' ὅσον χρόνον ὁ κληρονόμος νήπιός ἐστιν. With this line of discussion, Paul extends the metaphor of the Law as guardian. Paul had introduced the concept of the guardian and the heir in the prior paragraph (3:23–29). Here he adds more information to that argument. The conj. is not contrastive but rather expansive as Paul moves the metaphor in a new direction; the translation "now" is appropriate. The phrase ἐφ' ὅσον χρόνον as a prepositional phrase focuses upon the extent of time.[8] It almost has the force of a condition: As long as the situation in this clause—the implied protasis—is valid, the situation of the following clause—the implied apodosis—is valid, too.[9] The assertion Paul makes expands the metaphor, building off the idea of heir introduced in 3:29 (so also Moo, 258), now focusing on the heir's age. The article with the noun κληρονόμος is anaphoric, referring back to the anarthrous κληρονόμοι in 3:29. With this use Paul focuses not on the individual heir but on the entire class of individuals.[10] The word νήπιος, technically an adj. but used frequently as a substantive, has a wide range of meaning but overlaps fairly well with the senses of the English word "child." In Greek literature it referred to a wide range of ages, from a fetus in the womb to

8. So BDAG, 729.

9. See Paul's other uses in Rom 7:1; 1 Cor 7:39.

10. See G. B. Winer, *A Treatise on the Grammar of New Testament Greek, Regarded as a Sure Basis for New Testament Exegesis* (Edinburgh: Clark, 1882), 132; A. T. Robertson, *A Grammar of the Greek New Testament in the Light of Historical Research* (Nashville: Broadman, 1934), 757.

teenagers.[11] Usually it referred to the age of the individual, but it could also reference an implied level of maturity (see, e.g., Prov 1:32 LXX where it is used negatively in that regard). In this passage the word is a legal technical term, referring to the status of a minor child who has not yet reached the age of adulthood.[12] Paul is only making a point about the time when the heir is young, not yet at the age of majority. This is not a comment about the nature or development of the heir. Paul does not intend the metaphor to imply that humanity has evolved, or that Judaism was a primitive form of religion. The metaphor only makes a point about the time frame of a minor's status, and that is the only analogy he makes with reference to humanity and the Law.

οὐδὲν διαφέρει δούλου κύριος πάντων ὤν. This phrase serves as the apodosis of the implied condition. As long as the heir is a minor, this situation pertains, namely, he is no different from a slave despite his real status as master of all. The verb *διαφέρω* in this context simply focuses on difference without judgment as to value.[13] The indefinite gen. noun *δούλου* indicates the point of comparison, and the neut. acc. pronoun *οὐδέν* functions adverbially to show the extent of comparison. Taken together these terms show the totality of the heir's situation: He differs from the servant in no respect. The participial phrase *κύριος πάντων ὤν* is concessive: "although he is master of all." This acknowledges the underlying reality of the minor child's status as an heir, but that reality is only potential because of the heir's minor age.[14] Paul looks at the situation through the metaphor as before but now from a different angle. His prior view was from the inside looking out, from the viewpoint of the child who was essentially enslaved; now he looks from the outside in, from the viewpoint of one who can see that the child is really the heir (de Boer, 259).

4:2 *ἀλλὰ ὑπὸ ἐπιτρόπους ἐστὶ καὶ οἰκονόμους ἄχρι τῆς προθεσμίας τοῦ πατρός*. Paul describes further the status of the minor heir, with *ἀλλά* indicating contrast between his prior assertion about the real state of the heir as lord over all versus the current state of the heir as a minor. The essential assertion of this verse concerns the freedom of the child: The heir is essentially enslaved under guardians and managers until he reaches the age of majority. The key phrase is *ὑπὸ ἐπιτρόπους … καὶ οἰκονόμους*. This describes the sphere in which the heir exists while he is a minor; the emphasis falls upon the prep. *ὑπό*, which

11. LSJ, 1174; MGS, 1396; BDAG, 671.

12. See BDAG, 671.

13. BDAG, 239.

14. Dunn, 211, makes a suggestive comment regarding this concept: "The idea of the (Jewish) child as 'lord of all' may well reflect and affirm the tradition already well established which interpreted the land promised to Abraham as the whole earth (e.g. Sir. 44:21; Jub. xxii.14; xxxii.19; 1 Enoch v.7; Philo, Mos. i.155)." Although potentially right, this connection goes beyond what can be shown from the text, and it makes the metaphor work beyond what Paul intended.

indicates that one entity has a "controlling position" over another.[15] The key is the heir is under authority (Hays, 281). The word ἐπίτροπος generally refers to someone who has been entrusted with responsibility to manage something.[16] When the responsibility involves children, the meaning "guardian" is quite appropriate.[17] Within the flow of Paul's argument, this is practically a synonym for παιδαγωγός (Longenecker, 162; Witherington, 284). The second word οἰκονόμος generally means a manager or administrator, but specifically refers to the person charged with the duties of managing a household.[18] Often a slave, this person could be in charge of a wide swath of daily life, from finances to personnel to labor and production to goods and services.[19] In this context the individual manages the estate with reference to the minor child; the contemporary legal role of trustee would be analogous. Taken together, these terms cover the entire life experience of the minor heir: He is guarded and managed during the time of his minority. This was a common situation in the ancient world.[20] That Paul uses the pl. of these terms and they overlap somewhat in meaning shows that Paul describes the situation generally and comprehensively. He is not trying to explain a particular legal situation (see Lightfoot, 166; Dunn, 211).[21]

The situation in which the minor child finds himself is only temporary, as indicated by the following prepositional phrase, ἄχρι τῆς προθεσμίας τοῦ πατρός. The prep. ἄχρι indicates continuous time up to a point designated by the noun in gen. case. The word προθεσμία generally refers to a time fixed or appointed for a particular purpose. Within legal discourse it served as what amounted to a statute of limitations, after which further legal action was denied.[22] Within Hellenistic Greek it was a legal technical term associated with the coming of age of the minor child and the ending of guardianship.[23]

---

15. BDAG, 1036; cf. Winer, *Grammar*, 507.
16. LSJ, 669.
17. This word is used commonly with this nuance; see J. H. Moulton and G. Milligan, *Vocabulary of the Greek Testament* (Peabody, MA: Hendrickson, 1997), 249.
18. LSJ, 1204; MGS, 1433; BDAG, 698.
19. See *TLNT*, 2:568–72, for copious examples.
20. See, for example, 1 Macc 3:32–33; 6:17; 2 Macc 11:1; 13:2; 14:2. The passages from 2 Macc even use the term ἐπίτροπος, "guardian," as here.
21. Burton, 213, and Longenecker, 164, cite Demosthenes, *Naus.* 12.988, which uses the phrase ἐπίτροπος καὶ κηδεμών ("guardian and caretaker/protector") for the single person Aristaechmus, to argue these words could be synonyms. Burton, 214, concludes that it is best to understand that the two terms designate different functions, not persons, and the plurals are qualitative.
22. LSJ, 1481; MGS, 1764, under the entry for προθέσμιος.
23. *EDNT*, 3:156. Bruce, 192, points to P. Oxy. 491.8–10 as an example of a time set by the father. The context is a will written by Eudaemon. He instructs that money is to be given to his sons when they reach the age of 20 and restricts them from selling any part of their inheritance until they reach the age of 25. What is helpful

Here it serves Paul's chronological focus. Just as a father determined when his minor children no longer needed a guardian—τοῦ πατρός is a subj. gen. to προθεσμίας—God determined when humanity would no longer be governed by the Law.

4:3 οὕτως καὶ ἡμεῖς, ὅτε ἦμεν νήπιοι, ὑπὸ τὰ στοιχεῖα τοῦ κόσμου ἤμεθα δεδουλωμένοι. With this sentence Paul brings the analogy home by applying it to human experience broadly conceived within the flow of salvation history. Just as the minor heir is like a slave, controlled by guardians and managers, so also humanity was under the control of an external power for a period of time. The conj. οὕτως explicitly draws the comparison of humanity's situation with that of the minor child mentioned in 4:1–2, and the καί emphasizes the place of the "we" in the comparison. It is reasonable to argue that the pronoun ἡμεῖς is an exclusive "we"—that is, Jews—in light of Paul's prior uses of the 1 pl. (so Longenecker, 165; see Gal 2:15–16; 3:13–14; 23–25) and his likely reference to the Law here (Bruce, 193). However, Paul uses equivalent expressions for both first and second persons; for example, see "we were enslaved" in v. 3 and "you are no longer slaves" in v. 6 (Burton, 215; Fung, 181). In addition, the following discussion in vv. 6–7 and in 4:8–11 shows that both Jews and Gentiles lived in a period of "minority" under a controlling power (similarly Hays, 282; Schreiner, 267). Paul switches pronouns but does not as readily switch referents. The experience of Jews and Gentiles are similar in this regard, and the language does not explicitly at this point refer to one or the other exclusively.

The conj. ὅτε plus impf. means "a period of time coextensive with another period of time."[24] Thus the period of time in view is when "we were minors." This raises a logical question: In what sense were Jews and Gentiles "minors"? The metaphor should not be pressed beyond what Paul intended it to do. He did not intend to explain the nature of Jews or Judaism on its own merits, in essence declaring it immature or unevolved. Nor did he seek to argue that Gentiles on the whole were immature in their spiritual understanding. Rather, he intended to describe them from the standpoint of post-Easter reflection, the metaphor showing that Jews and Gentiles were simply under restrictions as minors normally are.

The main assertion in this verse regards the enslavement of humanity to an external power. The verb phrase ἤμεθα δεδουλωμένοι shows that the indicated state was simultaneous to the temporally dependent one.[25] During the time that all humanity were minors, they were enslaved. The prepositional phrase ὑπὸ τὰ στοιχεῖα τοῦ κόσμου indicates as before the sphere of a

---

here is not the particular words, which do not match what occurs in Galatians, but the concept.

24. BDAG, 731.

25. See D. B. Wallace, *Greek Grammar Beyond the Basics: An Exegetical Syntax of the New Testament* (Grand Rapids: Zondervan, 1996), 585.

controlling power,[26] which leads to one of the most well-known interpretive problems in all of the book, the meaning and referent of στοιχεῖον.[27] The essential problem concerns whether Paul had in mind a form of Hellenistic religion that worshiped the stars as cosmic forces, and if so how this could in any way be applied to the Law. The word στοιχεῖον across many of its uses has the meaning of "basic component" or "element." This relates conceptually to other words within this semantic domain: στοῖχος means "row," and στοιχέω means "to place or order in a row," so from the idea of something ordered in a row flows the concept of "element." But as such this could refer to any number of things.[28] In the realm of language it referred to simple sounds, the first component of the syllable, or letters. In the realm of cosmology it referred to the components of which matter consists—the elements, so to speak.[29] In logic it referred to the elements of a proof or an elementary or fundamental principle. With reference to astronomy it referred to the fundamental components of constellations, that is, stars and planets, and then by extension to the spiritual beings that those stars and planets represented. Philo, *Decalogue* 53, is cited often in this regard:

> ἐκτεθειώκασι γὰρ οἱ μὲν τὰς τέσσαρας ἀρχάς, γῆν καὶ ὕδωρ καὶ ἀέρα καὶ πῦρ, οἱ δ᾽ ἥλιον καὶ σελήνην καὶ τοὺς ἄλλους πλανήτας καὶ ἀπλανεῖς ἀστέρας, οἱ δὲ μόνον τὸν οὐρανόν, οἱ δὲ τὸν σύμπαντα κόσμον·
>
> For some have deified the four elements, earth, water, air and fire, others the sun, moon, planets and fixed stars, others again the heaven by itself, others the whole world.[30]

Another colorful example is T. Sol. 8:1–2. Even though this is likely later than the NT, it illustrates the cultural force at work:

> Again, I glorified God, who gave me this authority, and I commanded another demon to appear before me. There came seven spirits bound up together hand and foot, fair of form and graceful. When I, Solomon, saw them, I was amazed and asked them,

26. Note that agency is not in view since the gen. is not used.
27. Of course many commentators discuss this problem at length. For more extensive discussions see Betz, 204–5; Longenecker, 165–66; George, 295–98; Martyn, 393–406; Witherington, 284–86; Moo, 260–63. The word occurs 7x in the NT: here and Gal 4:9; Col 2:8, 20; Heb 5:12; 2 Pet 3:10, 12. The latter three uses are fairly clear to interpret; the Pauline uses show interpretive difficulty similar to here.
28. See LSJ, 1647; MGS, 1967; BDAG, 946.
29. See, for example, Josephus, *Ant.* 3.183.
30. Text and translation are taken from Philo, *On the Decalogue. On the Special Laws, Books 1–3*, trans. F. H. Colson, Loeb Classical Library 320 (Cambridge, MA: Harvard University Press, 1937), 32–33.

> "Who are you?" They replied, "We are heavenly bodies, rulers of this world of darkness."[31]

This wide semantic range does not immediately lead to a clear sense in the present passage. Compounding this uncertainty is the question of the background that Paul had in mind: Is he drawing on a Jewish context, a Hellenistic context, or both? Paul has been straddling the Jew/Gentile divide throughout this letter, and indeed the fundamental issue at play involves both groups. The rapid switch between pronouns here and in the next paragraph shows that Paul may not have one referent or context solely in mind. Thus it is not without warrant to argue that Paul might draw upon a Hellenistic image to connect the two but not rely solely on the Hellenistic image to make his case:

> More likely Paul uses this term, known to him from (Stoic) popular philosophy, on his own initiative to designate collectively both the Jewish Torah, which the false teachers understood as a path to salvation and advised the Galatians to follow at least in part (5:3), and the previous Gentile piety of the Galatians (4:3f., 8f.). He considered both to be manifestations of that power presently enslaving human beings (4:3, 5, 8f.), a power that nonetheless appears "beggarly" compared to the *υἱοθεσία* (v. 5); such power was the basis of human religious existence before Christ.[32]

So Paul uses a Hellenistic phrase somewhat generally with two referents in mind: He points to the Law with reference to the Jews and to deity worship with reference to Gentiles, designating both as emanating from the bygone era of the minor. Both should be set aside in light of the current sonship that Christ brings. This take is adopted by Longenecker, 166; Dunn, 213; Witherington, 286; Martyn, 401.[33] This is not meant to designate Gentile pagan worship as equivalent in some way to Torah observance. The metaphor only serves to show that both should be left behind in light of what God has now done through Christ. The emphasis here falls not primarily on to what humanity was enslaved, but rather the fact of the enslavement. This is the force of ὑπό here, just as it has been used before in the epistle (so

---

31. D. C. Duling, "Testament of Solomon: A New Translation and Introduction," in *The Old Testament Pseudepigrapha,* vol. 1, ed. J. H. Charlesworth, Anchor Bible Reference Library (New York: Doubleday, 1983), 969–70. The textual note here states, "Gk. *esmen stoicheia,* 'we are heavenly bodies.'" See as well T. Sol. 18:2. For the Greek text of the Testament of Solomon, see C. C. McCown, *The Testament of Solomon: Edited From Manuscripts at Mount Athos, Bologna, Holkham Hall, Jerusalem, London, Milan, Paris and Vienna* (Leipzig: J. C. Hinrichs, 1922).

32. E. Plümacher, "στοιχεῖον," *EDNT*, 3:278. See a similar conclusion in *NIDNTTE*, 4:380.

33. *Contra* Rapa, 605, who sees a clear identification of τὰ στοιχεῖα with the Law; and *contra* de Boer, 251; Oakes, 135; who see a clear reference to pagan religious beliefs and practices in Galatia.

Witherington, 284; Schreiner, 269; see 3:22–25; 4:1–2). Paul's assertion is that all humanity, both Jew and Gentile, were just like the heir: While a minor, they were enslaved to something basic and temporary, now left behind because the age of majority has come in Christ.

4:4 ὅτε δὲ ἦλθεν τὸ πλήρωμα τοῦ χρόνου, ἐξαπέστειλεν ὁ θεὸς τὸν υἱὸν αὐτοῦ. This verse and the next showcase the heir's transition from a minor to an adult. Paul steps outside the metaphor somewhat at this point in two ways: He references God's action to send Jesus and not simply the passing of time, and he makes no explicit connection to the heir reaching the age of majority. Even so, it is clear that this decisive event corresponds to the heir reaching adulthood, so this becomes the high point of the analogy and indeed of the paragraph. The conj. δέ supplies new consideration for the discussion; it is contrastive because of the context, that is, Paul discusses the key event that moved salvation history to the present situation, creating a strong difference from the way things were. Previously Paul focused on the state of enslavement, but now he focuses on the transition to freedom, God sending the Son being the means. In the opening dependent clause the focus is upon time as in the extended metaphor. The conj. ὅτε plus aor. indicates a point in time in the past. The meaning of the phrase τὸ πλήρωμα τοῦ χρόνου depends on the force of the gen. τοῦ χρονοῦ. Reasonable options would be attributed ("when the full time arrived"), poss. ("when time's fullness arrived"), or reference ("when the fullness with reference to time arrived"). The gen. of reference is the best option in the context; it would show the frame of reference in which the fullness should be understood, and it reemphasizes Paul's focus on chronology in this section. This is functionally equivalent to τῆς προθεσμίας τοῦ πατρός from v. 2. This is simply part of the imagery Paul uses to make his point. "The fullness of time" argues simply that "the coming of Christ was fixed in the purpose of God" (Longenecker, 170; similarly Fung, 183). It should not be understood as anything other than the analogy of the metaphor of the minor child reaching the age of majority. The fullness of time was reached only because of the divine will, not anything external to that.[34] Some argue for an eschatological nuance with this phrase (so Betz, 206; Matera, 150; de Boer, 261). Mark 1:15 does provide a suggestive parallel, but it is better to see any eschatology coming from the events associated with this language, not the language itself.

The description of what God did to bring humanity into the age of majority is powerful: "God sent his Son." This is a reassertion, indeed a theological development, of what God accomplished through Jesus in his life

34. For this reason in my opinion arguments about the time of Jesus's first advent being appropriate because of the political conditions of the *pax Romana*, the ease of movement because of Roman roads, the ease of communication because of Greek as a *lingua franca*, or the like fall flat. Paul takes into account nothing other than the will of the Father in determining what was in fact "the fullness of time."

and ministry. At the time he determined, God sent his Son; this served as the definitive event to move the humanity as the heir from slavery to freedom.[35] At the same time the phrase portrays the definitive action of God on the part of humanity and the role of Jesus in that action. The central interpretive issue is whether it involves a "sending formula" that evokes ideas about the preexistence and sending of Wisdom from God and by implication whether preexistence of the Son is implied.[36] J. D. G. Dunn has argued against this idea with his well-known emphasis on Adam Christology, which did not involve preexistence but rather emphasized prophetic sending by God.[37] It is certainly true that Paul does not emphasize preexistence here. Rather, his focus is on the human life of Jesus and how he accomplished God's purposes in the action of being sent, which involved his birth and life (see the following participial phrases). However, it is clear that God sends the Son, a personal entity as opposed to an impersonal characteristic like Wisdom (so Witherington, 288; Schreiner, 270). Paul may have had the preexistence of the Son in mind, but that is not necessary for his argument to work (see Bruce, 195; Fung, 181).

γενόμενον ἐκ γυναικός, γενόμενον ὑπὸ νόμον. Paul at this point qualifies the noun τὸν υἱόν with two similar ptc. phrases, each beginning with γενόμενον, each attributive acting substantivally (Burton, 218). The best sense of the verb γίνομαι in these phrases is "born."[38] The first occurrence is modified by the prepositional phrase ἐκ γυναικός, "one born from a woman." Ostensibly ἐκ here would indicate source, although agency is possible.[39] This common wording refers to a human person, emphasizing the commonality of our similar starting point in life.[40] Just like every other human, Jesus entered the world in the usual way (Witherington, 288). The point of the wording is to emphasize Jesus's true humanity in connection with those whom he freed

35. Prior occurrences of "sending" language do not occur in Galatians except with the noun ἀπόστολος (1:1, 17, 19; 2:8) and the verb ὑποστέλλω used negatively of Peter in 2:12.

36. For the seminal work in this regard, see E. Schweizer, "Zum religionsgeschichtlichen Hintergrund der Sendungsformel," *ZNW* 57 (1966): 199–210. For a fair discussion of Schweizer's work, see Longenecker, 167–68.

37. See J. D. G. Dunn, *Christology in the Making: A New Testament Inquiry into the Origins of the Doctrine of the Incarnation* (London: SCM, 1980), 39–43.

38. BDAG, 197, Interestingly, note KJV "made of a woman, made under the Law," and NLT "born of a woman, subject to the Law."

39. Robertson, *Grammar*, 820.

40. See, e.g., Matt 11:11 οὐκ ἐγήγερται ἐν γεννητοῖς γυναικῶν μείζων Ἰωάννου τοῦ βαπτιστοῦ. This phrase uses the verb γεννάω, but the sentiment is exactly the same, given the "well-attested use of γίνομαι as a quasi-passive of γεννάω" (Bruce, 195). *Contra* Burton, 218, who argues that the ptc. in the second phrase should not be taken as "born." The first one implies that but only from the prepositional phrase, not the ptc. Paul could have used γεννηθέντα in the second phrase to indicate the idea of birth.

from slavery (Lenski, 199; Longenecker, 171; Martyn, 390; Schreiner, 270). In a few Jewish texts, the phrase "one born of woman" emphasizes the lowliness of humanity compared to God (1QS 11.21–22; *b. Šabb.* 88B), but that is not Paul's emphasis here. The second occurrence of γενόμενον occurs with the prepositional phrase ὑπὸ νόμον, which again indicates a controlling power. Jesus was born in the same condition as all of humanity, under the control of the Law. The emphasis on birth in these phrases means "under Law" here does not mean "under the curse of the Law" but more simply "subject to the Law" (Moo, 266).[41] Just as all humanity was under the Law—Jews by covenant with and Gentiles by exclusion from—Jesus lived under the Law so that he might fulfill its requirements and bear its curse (Longenecker, 171), thus securing redemption from it. "It was by his sharing in Israel's subjection to the law during his life, as by his sharing in the status of the outcast from the law in his death (3:13), that his death and resurrection were able to effect redemption for both Jew and Gentile" (Dunn, 216).[42] This verse is quite rich in its theological affirmations: Jesus was God's Son, yet human. Jesus was born under the Law, yet sent to bring freedom in keeping with God's purposes and promises. In short, as Betz, 208, states, "this anthropological definition is given a christological purpose."

4:5 ἵνα τοὺς ὑπὸ νόμον ἐξαγοράσῃ. With this clause Paul focuses on Christ's role vis-à-vis the Law in the analogy he has been developing. This ἵνα clause indicates the purpose for the verb ἐξαπέστιλεν in the prior verse. God sent his Son in order that the Son might redeem those under the Law. The article in the phrase τοὺς ὑπὸ νόμον conceptualizes the prepositional phrase, making it into a substantive: "those under the Law." As in prior uses in the book, the prep. ὑπό emphasizes being under a controlling power. That τούς is masc. focuses on the personality of those in view, referencing humanity as persons. A natural impulse would be to regard this as referring only to Jews, but as argued above, Paul switches pronouns and argues in such a way that most likely all humanity is in view (see Moo, 267). "The universal scope of God's redemptive activity in Christ thus corresponds to—and addresses—the universal scope of the human predicament" (de Boer, 264). Paul had used the verb ἐξαγοράζω before in 3:13 with reference to the curse of the Law, which hung over humanity because of our absolute inability to obey the Law. Here the verb has the same nuance, to liberate those enslaved under its controlling power.[43] Now Paul has widened the image to refer not just to the curse of the Law, but the Law *en toto*. The parallel with 3:13 also indicates

41. Similarly and helpfully Bruce, 196, who notes that Jesus was under the Law but not under sin.

42. Similarly Martyn, 390, who argues that ὑπὸ νόμον refers to that "malignant orb in which all human beings have fallen prey to powers inimical to God and to themselves."

43. BDAG, 343.

that the redemption was achieved through Christ's death. Paul thought of Christ's coming in soteriological terms, his death being the price to pay for freeing humanity from their slavery to the basic forces (Dunn, 216; similarly Schreiner, 270).

ἵνα τὴν υἱοθεσίαν ἀπολάβωμεν. This ἵνα clause is parallel to the prior one, stating another purpose for the verb ἐξαπέστειλεν in the prior verse.[44] God sent his Son for the additional purpose of granting sonship to believers. It is a valid question whether this clause, instead of modifying the main clause, could modify the action of deliverance in the prior purpose clause. In other words, these two ἵνα clauses could be successively dependent rather than parallel (so Fung, 182). The logic of the content does not mandate a particular connection between the phrases, and in 3:14 Paul uses successive ἵνα clauses as parallel, both modifying the prior phrase. The content of this clause focuses on the human side of the analogy Paul has been developing in this section and in a sense completes it. God's sending of his Son allows those who are not related to the Father to be adopted into his family just like the Son. This extends outside the thought-world of the metaphor up to this point. Adoption would mean that the people in view were not even minors under the care of servants, but they are now brought fully into the family with full rights as sons. The 1 pl. verb here is evidence that Paul cannot mean only Jews when he uses the 1 pl., as the whole point of Galatians is that Gentiles are adopted into God's family, too, just like Jews (Schreiner, 271).[45]

The term υἱοθεσία referenced the action of adoption, the transaction that created a legal parent-child bond between two individuals that was regarded to be the same as a biological bond.[46] This legal fiction primarily involved sons since the concern was often to secure an heir; thus the primary focus of ancient adoption was often practical and legal, not humanitarian and moral as it is in the present day.[47] This fits quite naturally into Paul's argument since his focus is the securing for the heirs the promises given to Abraham.[48]

---

44. *Contra* de Boer, 264, who argues that the first ἵνα clause is purpose, the second result.

45. *Contra* Longenecker, 172, who sees these two clauses as both describing Jewish Christians.

46. For helpful background on adoption in the Greco-Roman world, see the articles "Adoption: Greek" and "Adoption: Roman" in *OCD*, 12–13, but it is also possible that key OT concepts may have influenced Paul's thinking (Bruce, 197; Fung, 183). For the argument that Paul had only the concept of Roman adoption in mind, see F. Lyall, "Roman Law in the Writings of Paul: Adoption," *JBL* 88 (1969): 458–66.

47. For example, Julius Caesar was Octavius's maternal great uncle, but Caesar's will established him as an adopted son and heir. When Octavius died he was succeeded by Tiberius, who was his adopted son, but also his stepson and former son-in-law.

48. Burton, 220, notes that Paul's use of the adoption concept is not necessarily uniform. After a review of Pauline uses, he says, "ἡ υἱοθεσία is, therefore, for Paul, God's reception of men into the relation to him of sons, objects of his love and enjoying his

Even so Paul also speaks counter-culturally. He makes no distinctions in the gender of those adopted. He expands the term to include everyone, not simply sons. This divine act of adoption was rooted not solely in the need to secure heirs, but in the love of God for humanity. The adoption of humanity into God's family encompassed not only the practical and legal realm but also the loving will of the Father.

Taken as a whole these two clauses describe in rich language the purposes God had for sending Jesus, what he intends for those whom he loves. God sent Jesus so that he could redeem humanity from under the Law and so that those who believe could be adopted into God's family as sons, just as Jesus is God's Son. The two clauses inform each other. The first ἵνα clause references the objective aspect of our salvation, the second the subjective (Lenski, 203).[49] Put another way, the second enriches the first: "Those whom Christ has set free from the power of the Law are the same as those whom he has caused to receive his Spirit" (Martyn, 390). The OT background of Israel as God's son (e.g., Exod 4:22) shows that Paul means not only that Christians are adopted into God's family but they have become his people, inheriting the same status and blessings promised to Israel (Moo, 268).

4:6 ὅτι δέ ἐστε υἱοί. Here δέ indicates the addition of new information, a development in the argument. Paul switches to the 2 pl., which would appear to focus on the Gentiles, but by the end of the verse he switches back to the 1 pl. As with prior verses in this paragraph, he appears to be casting a wide net with his referents, referring most likely to all people, not just Jews or Gentiles. The connection between the previous verse and this is the mention of the related terms υἱοθεσίαν and υἱοί. The force of the conj. ὅτι that begins the clause is an open question. It could be causal (Betz, 209),[50] a common nuance for the word; if so, it would be somewhat loose, bordering on inferential. The implication would not simply be a cause-effect relationship, that is, because believers have now received sonship in Christ, God sent his Spirit to them. Rather, the scope would be larger: Because believers now receive sonship, which is indicative of the arrival of the great eschatological moment, God sent his Spirit. However, causal would run against Paul's basic argument that the Spirit is the beginning of the Galatians' relationship with God and

---

fellowship, the ultimate issue of which is the future life wherein they are reclothed with a spiritual body; but the word may be used of different stages and aspects of this one inclusive experience." Here it is used holistically and globally.

49. Longenecker, 172, conceives of this slightly differently: God's sending the Son in v. 4 and believers' reception of adoption in v. 5 balance God's action and humanity's response.

50. See also MHT, 3:345; Wallace, *Greek Grammar*, 461.

demonstrates their full acceptance by God (Dunn, 219).[51] Construing the ὅτι as subst. is preferred based on the general flow and content of Paul's argument. The emphasis is on the proof that shows that believers are indeed sons, now included in God's family, redeemed out from under the Law, the proof being God's sending of the Spirit. This interpretation essentially vacates the problem of the logical order of sonship and sending of the Spirit some have seen in this verse (for discussion see Longenecker, 173; George, 306; Hays, 285). This is supported by the tense of the verbs as well: What is true presently—Ὅτι δέ ἐστε υἱοί, pres. tense—is affirmed by a past event—ἐξαπέστειλεν ὁ θεὸς τὸ πνεῦμα τοῦ υἱοῦ αὐτοῦ, aor. tense. The essential point is logical and evidentiary: The reception of the Spirit affirms the sonship of believers (Schreiner, 272). "For Paul the sonship of believers becomes evident in the experienced fact that God sent forth the Spirit of his Son into their collective hearts" (de Boer, 265).

ἐξαπέστειλεν ὁ θεὸς τὸ πνεῦμα τοῦ υἱοῦ αὐτοῦ εἰς τὰς καρδίας ἡμῶν. Taking the prior phrase as subst., this phrase establishes the proof that validates the prior phrase as true. The past action of God sending the Spirit into the lives of the Galatian believers is proof that they are indeed presently sons of God, no Law being necessary. The verb ἐξαποστέλλω refers to the act of sending someone away, but it can carry the connotation of a purpose or mission to accomplish.[52] Given the broader purposes mentioned in the context about God's actions relative to humanity, the full sense of mission or purpose should be understood here. The sending of the Spirit fully accomplished the purposes of God subsequent to yet in tandem with the sending of the Son. Here God acts and he does so decisively with the wonderful blessing of the Spirit as the result. Not only did God send Jesus his Son, he sent το πνεῦμα τοῦ υἱοῦ αὐτοῦ. This has trinitarian implications by showing both Jesus and the Spirit as sent by God to accomplish his purposes. The prepositional phrase εἰς τὰς καρδίας ἡμῶν indicates the location to which the Spirit was sent. Use of the pl. καρδίας for a group is the normal Greek idiom.[53] This references the intimate relationship the believer now has with God, hearkening back to Paul's original statements along these lines in Gal 2:19–20.

There are two striking theological questions about this verse. The first concerns the relationship of the Spirit to Jesus, and the second concerns the timing of this act of sending. The Spirit is most normally connected to God the Father, but here the connection is to Jesus. This is not the only occurrence of such an idea, but it is rare (see Acts 16:7; Rom 8:9; 2 Cor 3:17, 18; Phil

51. Dunn, 219, argues that this ὅτι clause should be considered as explanatory "to show or prove that." This nuance is referenced by BDAG, 732, but the examples given generally appear to be anaphoric, referencing either a stated or implied demonstrative, which is not the case here.

52. Note the first and third definitions for this term in BDAG, 345–46: "to send someone off to a locality or on a mission" and "to send someth. off in an official sense."

53. So MHT, 3:23.

1:19; 1 Pet 1:11). This phrasing mutually informs the nature of both Jesus and the Spirit. By connecting Jesus with the Spirit when the normal expression connects the Spirit to God, Paul affirms implicitly the deity of Christ. By connecting the Spirit to Jesus, Paul affirms the Spirit as in full continuity with Jesus's work. This implicitly argues for trinitarianism and for the personality of the Spirit. Indeed, it relates the present experience of the Spirit to the historical person of Jesus, connecting them ontologically and soteriologically (Dunn, 220). The second issue concerns the timing of this event and its identification. The sending of the Spirit here could refer either to Pentecost or to the sending of the Spirit in the moment of salvation. Given Paul's emphasis on the work of the Spirit in the lives of the Galatians (see 3:1–5; Betz, 210) and his reference to the hearts of the Galatians (Longenecker, 174), the latter is preferred. The sending referred to is the receipt of the Spirit in the lives of the Galatians at the moment of salvation, shown through the continued word of the Spirit in their midst. That sending of the Spirit was from God and proves the Galatians' place as his sons.

κρᾶζον· Αββα ὁ πατήρ. This short phrase explains what the Spirit does to prove that believers are sons of God: He cries out in testimony to God. The Greek word *αββα* is a transliteration of the Aramaic term אַבָּא which means "father." It is found only three times in the NT: in Mark 14:36 on the lips of Jesus in the garden of Gethsemane and then in Rom 8:15 and here, the latter two similar in use. Paul's use of the term here is evidence that the Aramaic word found traction within the early church, likely because Jesus's own use of the term resonated within the bilingual early church (Longenecker, 174). The phrase *ὁ πατήρ* is a translation of the term *αββα*; technically it is a nom. for voc. (Lightfoot, 170).[54] Thus the two terms ultimately refer to the same idea. The Spirit within the believer cries out to God and calls him "Father!" This proves the paternal relationship the Father now has to the believer and is the objective proof of the believer's sonship. "The fact that Christians call God 'Abba,' using the same word as Jesus used, is a token that they are indwelt by the same Spirit as indwelt him" (Bruce, 199). On this basis the sonship of the Galatians is firmly established: The infallible witness of the Holy Spirit within them testifies to a relationship with God, a relationship of sonship just as Jesus had. It is important to remember the implicit argument along these lines Paul made in 3:1–5. There he asks the Galatians *ἐξ ἔργων νόμου τὸ πνεῦμα ἐλάβετε ἢ ἐξ ἀκοῆς πίστεως;* The receipt of the Spirit comes only through faith, not through observance of the Law. In 4:6 Paul nuances the argument differently, referencing the proof of sonship through the Spirit, but the root is the same. Faith, not Law, establishes the sonship of the believer and is proven through the testimony of the Spirit. The Law is nowhere to be found in this complex of ideas. This proves via another route Paul's admonition to the Galatians that the Law holds no place over them in the present time. It also reinforces the Spirit/Law distinction common throughout the

54. See further Zerwick, *Biblical Greek*, 11.

book while also setting up the Galatians to understand better his paraenesis to come regarding the Spirit in 5:13–26.

4:7 ὥστε οὐκέτι εἶ δοῦλος ἀλλὰ υἱός. Paul now brings his argument to a close with a logical inference that applies the extended metaphor he has been using to explain the spiritual history of the Galatians and the reality of their present existence.[55] Paul uses the pres. tense verb εἶ to describe the movement from past to present reality: They are no longer slaves, rather they are sons. The verb is sg., emphasizing with distributive force all the Galatians and by extension all individual believers (similarly Witherington, 292; Schreiner, 272n44). This phrase makes an explicit contrast between δοῦλος ("slave") and υἱός ("son"). Describing the past state of the Gentiles with the former term is unexpected. Paul's only mentions of slavery relative to the Gentiles up to this point in the book are in passing: In 3:28 he mentions δοῦλος versus ἐλεύθερος as a social barrier that is now broken down in Christ, and δοῦλος is part of the extended metaphor regarding the minor child used in 4:1. In neither place does Paul specifically say that Gentiles were slaves. However, this is the clear implication of Paul's meaning from the metaphor itself and by implication from their redemption from under the Law in v. 4. This is a new, suggestive idea that he will discuss briefly again in 4:9 in a particular way appropriate to the Gentiles' experience. The Gentiles were slaves—to whom or what is not elucidated here—but becoming sons of God in Christ has freed them.

εἰ δὲ υἱός, καὶ κληρονόμος διὰ θεοῦ. This short conditional sentence closes the loop on the entire argument, establishing that the Gentiles, without any obedience to the Law, are now heirs to the promises God gave to Abraham. The sonship of the Gentiles, established in full in the prior verses, is the evidence that points to the inference that the Gentiles are also heirs. This means that the promises are at work in full in them (3:29). They are no longer in a position of servitude but rather in freedom (4:1). God has brought his full plan of salvation to fruition in them in the present time. The prepositional phrase διὰ θεοῦ would usually indicate means, but having θεός as the obj. is entirely unexpected.[56] Here διά plus the gen. would appear to be indicating the ultimate, not intermediate, agent.[57] Paul in a sense moves from the more easily understood theological proposition to the more difficult one. It was clear to all that the Galatians had received the Spirit because of their faith in Christ. In this way the fact of their sonship was readily established. On the face of it, however, this state of affairs did not answer the question of their relationship to Abraham and the Law. So Paul closes the loop with

55. Longenecker, 275, argues that this verse concludes all Paul has said from 3:1 onward.

56. See the textual problem here as evidence of the unusual nature of this expression.

57. See Winer, *Grammar*, 473–74: "Διά is sometimes, but only seldom, used in reference to the *causa principalis* (as in 1 C. 1:9, G. 4:7 *v. l.*), and might appear here to be synonymous with ὑπό or παρά." See also BDF, §223.

this inference. Sonship truthfully implies being an heir, so the Galatians are heirs to the promises of Abraham, proving definitively that the Law has no hold over them and that they are equally part of God's family as Jews are.

With this paragraph Paul cements the theological argument of the present status of Gentiles within the family of God apart from any role of the Law. He thus continues to support his admonition to the Galatians not to depart from the gospel he had preached to them—a gospel that itself solidified their place as sons as testified by the Spirit. The function of the extended metaphor he uses is clear. Those who have trusted in Christ are no longer minors but adults, no longer slaves but sons, and by implication then they are heirs of the promises of God. Gentiles receive everything they need through the gospel; thus there is clearly no need for them to obey the Law.

Theological Comments

Theology proper concerns God: his nature, characteristics, attributes, and actions. It is an investigation into who God is and how he acts in the world. A constant confession of orthodox Christians throughout the ages has been God's trinitarian existence. Classically defined, the Trinity describes God existing as three distinct persons—Father, Son, Holy Spirit—who share the same essence. It is a foundational statement about who God is, but as many passages in the Bible show, it is also a foundational statement about how God acts. In the present passage each person of the Trinity is present and active in God's interaction with humanity to deliver everyone from slavery to the elemental things of this world and to bring the promises given to Abraham to everyone in Christ. Said in the language of the extended metaphor about the minor child, God the Father determined the time to bring the minor out from his restricted existence. God the Father sent God the Son to deliver those who were enslaved under the Law, to be an agent through whom adoption as a son was extended to all. God the Father also sent God the Spirit, here identified as the Spirit of the Son, to indwell those who trust Jesus and to testify to God the Father that they are indeed his sons. Thus the salvation that all experience—redemption, adoption, inheritance apart from the Law—occurs by, through, and in the Triune God as each person of the godhead acts to bring it about.

Theology also concerns humanity and our place in the world. We practice theology so we can understand God and how he works vis-à-vis our past, present, and future situation. A constant confession of orthodox Christians throughout the ages has been that we are sinful people who need God to act for our salvation. Paul describes this sinful state here as slavery: Before God sent Jesus, humanity was enslaved to the elemental things of this world. God had created us to be children—indeed, his heirs—but our position under guard prohibited us from living out the existence for which we were made. But then God acted. He sent his Son, who delivered us and enabled us to be adopted as God's children. God sent his Spirit, who indwells us and testifies to him that we are his children. In the final argument of this paragraph Paul shows clearly the endgame of our salvation: We are not simply sons, but we are heirs. We expect and anticipate the blessing of future inheritance. There is more to come, which God will graciously bring at the appropriate time. This passage confirms the classic Christian confession that humanity is fallen and in need of salvation, and it confirms the picture of salvation as something that not only changes our present state but also secures our future.

Application and Devotional Implications

Certain biblical passages evoke a sense of wonder and awe at our God and the way he works in our midst. Many believers rest in the quiet comfort offered by Ps 23 and its image of God as shepherd who guides and comforts his people. Paul extols the godly shape of love in 1 Cor 13, calling believers to emulate it. This passage makes me marvel because it shows so clearly how God is sovereign over the broad flow of history and how he works out his plan of salvation for humanity in his time. An important framework for understanding this passage is that it discusses salvation writ large. It is less about the particular salvation of any one individual and more about the salvation of humanity as a whole into which our individual lives fit. This passage brings the reader to worship because it shows the marvelous actions of God taken at the appropriate time in history to redeem mankind. And these actions of massive historical sweep find their cause not in any worth of our own: We were enslaved! We could offer nothing to God of value! Yet God determined, because of his promises to Abraham, to act on our behalf. He sent his Son to deliver us and the Spirit of the Son to indwell us. The proper response to reading this is simply thankfulness to our great God who delivers mankind from the slavery of this world and frees mankind to live as his heirs with confident hope in the future.

As this passage describes the broad sweep of God's actions in history to save mankind, it is clear that Paul intends these words to have a very personal impact. God has acted in history, and thus he effects salvation for individuals. Paul paints a picture of the change this salvation brings in the last verse of this section by describing what we were and then what we are. We were slaves, under the control of other powers that restricted our freedom and magnified our misery. But God through Jesus extends to us adoption so that we become his children, moving from bondage to freedom. And not only are we children, we are heirs to the promises God gave to Abraham, the promises that began the whole flow of salvation history, promises that secure our future and give us hope. This flow of salvation history has great magnitude, but it also has personal effect. All believers have each been brought from the slave's quarters to the Son's table where we can see the blessings the Father plans to bestow upon us. May our hearts resonate with thanksgiving and praise to our great God, Jesus his Son, and the Spirit who testifies that we are indeed his children!

Additional Exegetical Comments

4:1–2 For a defense of the traditional view of Paul's metaphor here as taken from a Greco-Roman background as opposed to an allusion to the Exodus, see articles by J. K. Goodrich.[58]

4:3 E. Schweizer argues from a review of several pertinent texts that τὰ στοιχεῖα τοῦ κόσμου refers to the actual elements of the world (earth, air, fire, water), which could come into disharmony with terrible effect.[59] They could be personified, but they were not necessarily conceived of as demons or powers. These powers were feared but not necessarily worshiped.

Selected Bibliography

Duling, D. C. "Testament of Solomon: A New Translation and Introduction." In *The Old Testament Pseudepigrapha*, vol. 1, ed. J. H. Charlesworth, 935–87. New York: Doubleday, 1983.

Dunn, J. D. G. *Christology in the Making: A New Testament Inquiry into the Origins of the Doctrine of the Incarnation*. London: SCM, 1980.

Goodrich, J. K. " 'As Long as the Heir Is a Child': The Rhetoric of Inheritance in Galatians 4:1–2 and P.Ryl. 2.153." *NovT* 55 (2013): 61–76.

———. "Guardians, Not Taskmasters: The Cultural Resonances of Paul's Metaphor in Galatians 4.1–2." *JSNT* 32 (2010): 251–84.

Lyall, F. "Roman Law in the Writings of Paul: Adoption." *JBL* 88 (1969): 458–66.

McCown, C. C. *The Testament of Solomon: Edited From Manuscripts at Mount Athos, Bologna, Holkham Hall, Jerusalem, London, Milan, Paris and Vienna*. Leipzig: J. C. Hinrichs, 1922.

Philo. *On the Decalogue. On the Special Laws, Books 1–3*. Trans. F. H. Colson. Loeb Classical Library 320. Cambridge, MA: Harvard University Press, 1937.

Schweizer, E. "Slaves of the Elements and Worshipers of Angels: Gal 4:3, 9 and Col 2:8, 18, 20." *JBL* 107 (1988): 455–68.

———. "Zum religionsgeschichtlichen Hintergrund der Sendungsformel." *ZNW* 57 (1966): 199–210.

58. J. K. Goodrich, "Guardians, Not Taskmasters: The Cultural Resonances of Paul's Metaphor in Galatians 4.1–2," *JSNT* 32 (2010): 251–84; J. K. Goodrich, " 'As Long as the Heir Is a Child': The Rhetoric of Inheritance in Galatians 4:1–2 and P.Ryl. 2.153," *NovT* 55 (2013): 61–76.

59. E. Schweizer, "Slaves of the Elements and Worshipers of Angels: Gal 4:3, 9 and Col 2:8, 18, 20," *JBL* 107 (1988): 455–68.

A Challenge Not to Turn Back (4:8–11)

Textual Notes

4:9 The NA[28] text reads in this relative clause the pres. inf. verb δουλεύειν. The manuscripts ℵ and B instead read the aor. inf. δουλεύσαι. This difference is difficult to bring out in English translation. The pres. tense would emphasize the ongoing nature of the servitude, while the aor. would emphasize the simple fact of it. (Adding an adv. like "continually" helps clarify the sense of the former.) Both make good sense in the context. Even though ℵ and B are excellent witnesses, the pres. inf. should be preferred primarily on the overwhelming support of the rest of the manuscript evidence.

4:11 Here the vast majority of manuscripts read the pf. tense verb κεκοπίακα, while 𝔓[46] 1739 1881 read the aor. tense ἐκοπίασα. The difference between the verbs focuses on how Paul describes the entire situation relative to its timing. The aor. would simply refer to the action in the past, while the pf. would refer to the present results. The latter fits the context quite well: Paul not only labored in the past for the Galatians, but he feels those results in the present (acutely as he writes this very letter!). Add to this the overwhelming support from the rest of the manuscript evidence, and the pf. tense verb should be judged as most likely to be original.

Translation

8 But formerly, when you did not know God,[1] you served things that were by nature not gods, **9** but now, even though you have begun to know God[2]—rather, you are known by God![3]—how can you turn back again to

1. The CSB treats this ptc. clause as causal: "since you didn't know God."

2. I have translated this ptc. clause as concession. Compare CSB "since you know God"; NKJV "after you have known God."

3. The intent of my translation is to catch the shock of this concept in the context. Compare NLT: "So now that you know God (or should I say, now that God knows you)."

the weak, poor, basic things[4] that you want to serve all over again? **10** You
carefully observe days and months and seasons and years! **11** I am afraid for
you perhaps that I have labored for you in vain.

Commentary

The rhetorical power of the Epistle to the Galatians shines brightest when Paul writes most personally. The book proves that Paul does not see himself as a detached, modern theologian, simply commenting on the Galatians' situation in the abstract. Rather, he is involved personally and deeply in the lives of these individuals, even from a distance, and his words flow from his own emotions about them and their apparent defection from the truth. This short paragraph is one such emotional proof within the larger constellation of the book. Paul is personally concerned about what is going on in Galatia. He is deeply involved with these individuals; indeed, his own ministry is at stake in how they have acted and how they will respond to his letter. No doubt his emotions flow from his theological convictions about what God has done in the lives of the Galatians, proof of what God is doing on the broad stage of salvation history. So Paul is not emotional simply for emotions' sake. Instead, his emotions flow naturally from the truth that God has acted for the Galatians and the discord between that truth and the Galatians' behavior.

This paragraph marks a new phase within Paul's writing. He concluded an important theological argument in 4:7 when he affirmed the Galatians are fully sons and heirs of God. Now his writing takes on a more personal tone with direct appeals to the Galatians from here to the end of the chapter (see also Moo, 273). Longenecker, 178, argues that this small section is similar to 3:1–5 in the use of questions, thus these verses form an *inclusio* with 3:1–5. Although that is not an unreasonable view, Paul does change his content and tone somewhat here. The better argument is that, as with other places in the epistle, Paul makes this a transitional paragraph (Moo, 273). Here as almost everywhere, though, Paul does not compartmentalize his thought. The theology Paul expressed previously flows naturally into this exhortation, and the exhortation he presents finds its existence only within the scope of that theology. The danger of the Galatians' present behavior becomes fully apparent in light of their sonship and status as heirs. Paul's own thinking

4. The translation of τὰ ἀσθενῆ καὶ πτωχὰ στοιχεῖα of course varies in the translations because of the exegetical difficulties associated with the noun στοιχεῖον: "the weak and worthless basic forces" (NET); "the weak and worthless elements" (CSB; cf. NKJV); "the weak and worthless elementary principles of the world" (ESV); "the weak and beggarly elemental spirits" (NRSV); "the weak and worthless elemental things" (NASB); "those weak and miserable forces" (NIV); "the weak and useless spiritual principles of this world" (NLT).

and feeling become more prominent as he describes his reactions to the Galatians' predicament.

4:8 Ἀλλὰ τότε μὲν οὐκ εἰδότες θεὸν ἐδουλεύσατε τοῖς φύσει μὴ οὖσιν θεοῖς. Paul begins this more personal section by setting up a contrast between the past and present relative to the Galatians' spiritual existence. Part of his goal has been to fully inform the Galatians of their spiritual realities, what they were before and what they are now. The contrast centers around status and behavior: Paul has just declared that the Galatians were heirs—the social, moral, and practical opposite of slaves, their prior state. The Galatians' desire to submit to the Law is tantamount to reverting back to slavery. That discord launches Paul into this emotional paragraph.[5] "The image of slavery (4:8–9) connects this paragraph with the preceding analogies in 3:23–25 and 4:1–7, depicting the Galatians' contemplated course of action as an unthinkable, unnatural, and wholly unnecessary return to a most disadvantageous condition."[6]

Paul's grammatical setup for this paragraph is somewhat complex, as each of the three words that begin the verse has an important function. The conj. ἀλλά provides a strong contrast with the conclusion of the prior section in 4:7, namely, that the Galatians are full sons and heirs of God.[7] The adv. τότε indicates the time prior to the Galatians' receipt of the gospel; in this verse Paul describes the contrast to the Galatians' status as heirs in terms of time in keeping with his focus on chronology as a central theme. The conj. μέν correlates with δέ in v. 9; it presents the first of two facts Paul juxtaposes in this paragraph. In this instance μέν presents the past, setting up the δέ clause that focuses on the present.

The sentence that makes up the first assertion of the paragraph consists of a participial clause followed by the main clause. The ptc. εἰδότες introduces the important concept of knowing God. More precisely, negation of the same summarizes the Galatians' existence prior to the gospel.[8] Ignorance of God and consequent idolatry is a common theme in Jewish literature (Matera, 152; Dunn, 224; Martyn, 410; de Boer, 273), but Paul is not simply using a trope. Rather, he intends to convey the stark reality of the Galatians' prior

---

5. The contrast is strong enough that Burton, 227, labels it an antithesis.

6. D. A. deSilva, *Galatians: A Handbook on the Greek Text*, Baylor Handbook on the Greek New Testament (Baylor University Press, 2014), 84.

7. *Contra* Lenski, 209, who argues that "Ἀλλά is merely copulative."

8. Bruce, 201, notes that this is a rare instance of classical οὐ plus the ptc.; in Hellenistic Greek there was a steady drift toward μή with ptc.

experience.[9] Paul uses οἶδα rarely in the epistle (2:16, here, 4:13).[10] Paul does not frequently speak of someone knowing God: θεός is the obj. of οἶδα in Gal 4:8; 1 Thess 4:5; 2 Thess 1:8, and θεός is the obj. of γινώσκω in Rom 1:21; Gal 4:9.[11] The concept of "knowing God" in Paul is rare and on that basis quite potent. It conveys knowledge of God as a person with the implication of a relationship. In this particular verse the ptc. could be either causal or temporal. The latter is preferred as Paul seeks simply to describe the Galatians' experience. He does not attempt to explain the reason for the prior status of servitude but only to state the fact of its existence. The aor. main verb ἐδουλεύσατε refers to the Galatians' prior life before hearing the gospel. The verb δουλεύω means "to act as a slave, serve, obey."[12] It acts as a synonym for worship similarly to 1 Thess 1:9 (de Boer, 272). By using the aor. indic., Paul neatly summarizes the whole scope of the Galatians' former existence: They served non-gods. This affirmation fits perfectly with the syntactical emphases of the first three words of the verse.

The interpretive weight in the sentence is on the following phrase, which indicates exactly what the Galatians did serve in their prior state: τοῖς φύσει μὴ οὖσιν θεοῖς, "things that were by nature not gods."[13] This phrase presents grammatical and referential problems. Grammatically it is unclear if the dat. pl. article relates to the ptc. οὖσιν or to the noun θεοῖς.[14] Connecting it to the former makes οὖσιν a dat. subst. ptc., which is negated by the adv. μή. The noun θεοῖς would then be a predicate dat., matching the case of the ptc. This phrase as a whole would then focus on the nature of the things that the Galatians served prior to their conversion: "[You served] things that by nature were not gods." This would emphasize the reality of the situation from a post-conversion viewpoint. The other option has a different viewpoint: Connecting it to the latter makes the noun the object of service, which is then modified by the ptc: "You served gods that were not that by nature,

9. As Moo, 275, notes, Paul speaks of nonbelievers—whether Jew or Gentile—as "not knowing God." See 2 Thess 1:8; Titus 1:16. However, note 1 Thess 4:5, where Paul refers to Gentiles with this traditional language.

10. The synonym γινώσκω is only slightly more frequent: Paul uses it four times within the book (2:9; 3:7; 4:9 [bis]). Although some interpreters have argued for a difference in meaning between οἶδα and γινώσκω (see, e.g., Lightfoot, 171), the use of both in this immediate context implies no essential difference in meaning (see, e.g., Bruce, 202).

11. This occurs outside Paul in 1 John 4:6, 7, 8 (cf. 1 John 4:2 where "Spirit of God" is the obj.).

12. BDAG, 259.

13. Similar language in the OT (2 Chr 13:9; Isa 37:19; Jer 2:11) may indicate an allusion here, but the differences are significant enough that this is not certain. In any case, this language was common in Jewish polemic (Bruce, 201, who cites Deut 32:21 for comparison).

14. The dat. is used with the verb δουλεύω to indicate the person served.

that is, not in reality." This would emphasize the perception the Galatians had regarding the objects they formerly worshiped. The difference in meaning is slight, but the latter is preferred because of the parallel in 1 Cor 8:5 (Burton, 229) and Paul's emphasis on the Galatians' prior state of ignorance. The referential question concerns the actual entities that the Galatians did in fact serve previously, whether these were false gods that did not exist at all or whether they were demonic forces (Dunn, 224). On its own this passage is not clear on the question. Pauline parallels in 1 Cor 8:5–6; 10:19, 20; Col 2:15 seem to indicate that he conceived of them as actually existing, so that by extension could apply here (Burton, 228; Witherington, 297; Moo, 275). Seeing τὰ στοιχεῖα as ultimately referring to the elements controlled by demonic powers would also support this (Betz, 215; similarly Hays, 287).[15]

Referring to the deities of the Anatolian religions that formed the Galatians' cultural background, which they left at the moment of their conversion, Paul here uses a potent argument particular to the Galatians as Gentiles.[16] From his standpoint as a Jew, the Galatians did not serve the one true God. Paul's statement was designed to make them think: If the spiritual realities they served were not gods, what in fact were they? What does this mean for that to which they now desire to turn? The whole point concerns their return to their prior state. Their prior condition was horrendously bad; they were enslaved, not free, and the beings that they served were not gods but something far less, something sinister. This creates strong implications against their present desire to be Law-observant.

4:9 νῦν δὲ γνόντες θεόν, μᾶλλον δὲ γνωσθέντες ὑπὸ θεοῦ. Paul turns from the past to the present to complete the contrast begun with μέν in the prior verse. The prior clause introduced the fact of the Galatians' existence in servitude. Now Paul follows the logic based on their present relationship to Christ. The leading dependent clauses also present the simple facts of their existence, this time in the present, and the main clause that follows introduces the logical inconsistency of the Galatians' behavior given these facts. The conj. δέ correlates with μέν in v. 8; in this instance the emphasis falls here on the second part of the correlation, focusing on the contrast.[17] Paul uses νῦν

15. "He reminds them of this fact, that the gospel had removed the aura of divinity from the beings they had once worshiped, reducing the stoicheia to the merely natural phenomena they in fact always were (cf. Wis 13:1–3)" (de Boer, 272).

16. For research into these deities, see S. Mitchell, *Anatolia: Land, Men, and Gods in Asia Minor* (Oxford: Oxford University Press, 1993); S. Elliott, "Choose Your Mother, Choose Your Master: Galatians 4:21–5:1 in the Shadow of the Anatolian Mother of the Gods," *JBL* 118 (1999): 661–83; S. Elliott, *Cutting Too Close for Comfort: Paul's Letter to the Galatians in Its Anatolian Cultic Context*, LNTS 248 (London: T&T Clark, 2003).

17. I would classify this use as "without any real concessive sense on the part of μέν, but adversative force in δέ" (BDAG, 630).

to focus on the present time in contrast to τότε of v. 8. As Moo, 275, notes, this "but now" contrast is typical for Paul.[18] The verb γινώσκω here refers to knowledge with a personal object, as does οἶδα in the prior verse. The ptc. is concessive because it contrasts with the main assertion of the sentence, and the aor. tense is ingressive, emphasizing the beginning of the action (Lenski, 210; Bruce, 202; Fung, 189). My translation is designed to emphasize both those elements: "even though you have begun to know God." The second occurrence of δέ indicates development in the argument without contrast or negation. The adv. μᾶλλον in this instance does not negate the prior information but instead adds to it.[19] The ptc. γνωσθέντες is also concessive; the primary importance is the shift to pass. voice with ultimate agency expressed by the prep. ὑπό.[20] This second ptc. serves an important role in the argument. An immediate correction of the prior statement is a figure of speech called epidiorthosis; it serves to intensify the logic of the argument without negating the former statement (Bruce, 202). Both of these ptc. phrases are true, but the latter is more important for the argument, and indeed for the reality of the Galatians' experience (similarly Lenski, 211; Longenecker, 180). "God knows us" is the more important idea, overshadowing (but not negating) the fact that "we know God." The latter ptc. shows where the locus of attention should be theologically in the relationship between God and humanity. A relationship with God certainly requires action by both parties, but God's knowledge of the individual is the only real way the relationship occurs (see Lightfoot, 171; Dunn, 225). These ptcs. are very important for Paul's logic. "Knowledge of God (or being known by God), in Paul's view, should not have led to the action represented by the main verb, namely 'turning back to the weak and wretched elements.' "[21]

πῶς ἐπιστρέφετε πάλιν ἐπὶ τὰ ἀσθενῆ καὶ πτωχὰ στοιχεῖα; With this phrase Paul moves to logical deduction. The prior statements leading up to this clause indicate facts that Paul and all his readers, even the opponents, would agree upon: The Galatians had served non-gods in the past, but they now both know and are known by God. But now Paul parts ways with them rhetorically. The incredulity Paul expresses with this rhetorical question arises naturally from the discord between these agreed-upon facts and the Galatians' present desire to become Law-observant. The particle πῶς indicates surprise on the part of Paul given the facts of the case; in English the phrasing "How can you ... ?" is appropriate to bring out this nuance. The pres. tense verb ἐπιστρέφετε is progressive, describing the action of turning

18. See Rom 6:19, 21–22; 7:56; 11:30; Gal 1:23; Eph 2:12–13; 5:8; Col 1:21–22; 3:7–8; Phlm 11.

19. See BDAG, 614: "for a better reason, rather, all the more."

20. The voice of the ptc. is in full force and is not mitigated by the non-finite form; see A. T. Robertson, *A Grammar of the Greek New Testament in the Light of Historical Research* (Nashville: Broadman, 1934), 1110–11.

21. DeSilva, *Galatians: Handbook*, 84.

back as in progress (so also Burton, 231; Lenski, 212), but the lexeme itself has conative implications. Indeed, the whole argument of the book implies that Paul is persuading the Galatians not to follow through with what they have started.[22] This is the only occurrence of ἐπιστρέφω in Galatians, but the concept is strikingly similar to the use of the pres. tense of μετατίθημι in 1:6 (Lightfoot, 171). It can simply mean "turn back" to where one was before, but it also carries the connotations of conversion or even apostasy, turning away from God (Longenecker, 180; Dunn, 225; Garlington 2007, 247). Paul uses it here sarcastically to reference another "conversion" (Martyn, 411; Hays, 287). The prepositional phrase with ἐπί indicates the direction to which the turning occurs. The phrase τὰ ἀσθενῆ καὶ πτωχὰ στοιχεῖα presents an interpretive problem primarily because of the noun στοιχεῖον. The adjectives themselves are not difficult to grasp. The elements are weak in that "they have no power to save or justify"; they are beggarly "because they have no spiritual riches to bestow" (Fung, 192). The problem is the association in the context of στοιχεῖον with τοῖς φύσει μὴ οὖσιν θεοῖς. On the face of it, Paul seems to mean that the Galatians are returning to serve false gods. This creates some type of association in Paul's mind between the Law and false gods. The best argument for understanding the connection is an implied analogy: Turning to servitude to the Law in the present time would be analogous to returning to servitude to false gods from the Galatians' former religions. The key is the flexibility of the word στοιχεῖον: Within a Jewish context it could refer to the Law, and within a Gentile context it could refer to the deities the Galatians used to worship. Serving either the Law or deities in the present time, in light of the full revelation of God in Jesus, is turning back from the one true God to something far less, thus Paul's incredulity that the Galatians could even fathom such a move.

οἷς πάλιν ἄνωθεν δουλεύειν θέλετε; The following relative clause further describes τὰ στοιχεῖα. The syntax of the relative clause is challenging. Some translations separate it into a different question (so NET, NIV, CSB, NRSV), but that confuses the argument, as a question here would imply that Paul is uncertain about their desire to serve τὰ στοιχεῖα again. Paul's emphasis with the pres. tense θέλετε is that they do indeed want to serve them again. Any question hangs on the mode of their turning with the interrogative πῶς, not in the reality of their desire. So instead of a question, this relative clause is an indictment: The Galatians do want to return to servitude, and Paul is incredulous that they can take even one step in that direction given the reality of their present spiritual experience of being known by God. The synonymous terms πάλιν and ἄνωθεν are used together for emphasis.[23] The inf. δουλεύειν is complementary to θέλετε, which should be taken as a progressive pres. that conveys the actual state of affairs. This statement corroborates what Paul has

---

22. Robertson, *Grammar*, 879, calls this the "descriptive" pres., by which he means the action is in progress; current terminology would be progressive.

23. See BDAG, 92: "Oft. strengthened by πάλιν ... Gal 4:9."

already argued. Coupled with 1:6–10, the reality of their desire is assured, hence the need for Paul's direct language here and elsewhere. Any veneration of the elements, no matter what form they may take, is enslavement to them (de Boer, 274). "Whatever leads one away from sole reliance on Christ, whether based on good intentions or depraved desires, is sub-Christian and therefore to be condemned" (Longenecker, 181). The rhetorical power of this statement should not be underestimated. As Hays, 287, states:

> This is perhaps the most stunning sentence in this entire confrontational letter. Paul is suggesting that Judaism's holy observances are, in effect, no different from paganism's worship of earthly elements. He could hardly have said anything more calculated to arouse the outrage of the Missionaries, but the rhetorical shock value of his question is surely calculated. He is trying to jolt the Galatians out of the hypnotic spell of the Law-gospel.

4:10 ἡμέρας παρατηρεῖσθε καὶ μῆνας καὶ καιροὺς καὶ ἐνιαυτούς. With this sentence Paul offers evidence that the Galatians had indeed turned back in some fashion to "the elemental things" (so also Bruce, 204). In Jewish life alongside circumcision was the calendar. Paul's opponents must have encouraged obedience to particular Jewish days and celebrations, and Paul presents the Galatians' observance of such days as a fact.[24] The main verb παρατηρεῖσθε means to observe or follow carefully a custom or tradition.[25] The midd. voice occurs with the acc. to indicate the involvement of the individual in the action. The subject is not detached, as if observing from a distance, but personally involved, as in observing a ritual (see Lightfoot, 172; Bruce, 205; Martyn, 412).[26] The referent of these nouns is subject to interpretation. They are arranged from shorter, more precise periods to longer ones. The noun ἡμέρας ("days") most likely refers to the weekly Sabbath, while the noun

---

24. Josephus's use of the verb παρατηρέω in relation to Torah observance supports this connection (Longenecker, 182; Moo, 277–78). See *Ant.* 3.91; 11.292; 14.264; *Ag. Ap.* 2.282.

25. BDAG, 771.

26. Robertson, *Grammar*, 810, and D. B. Wallace, *Greek Grammar Beyond the Basics: An Exegetical Syntax of the New Testament* (Grand Rapids: Zondervan, 1996), 421, call this an indir. midd.; cf. also G. B. Winer, *A Treatise on the Grammar of New Testament Greek, Regarded as a Sure Basis for New Testament Exegesis* (Edinburgh: Clark, 1882), 317. This is *contra* Longenecker, 182, who says, "In the secular uses of παρατηρέω in the NT, the active and middle voices are used interchangeably with the same meaning, and that is how we should undoubtedly understand παρατηρεῖσθε here as well (i.e., middle in form but active in meaning)." However, as he states, those uses are secular; this context is different enough to warrant a different understanding of the midd. voice. For the other uses, all of which are in non-religious contexts, see Mark 3:2; Luke 6:7; 14:1; 20:20; Acts 9:24.

μῆνας ("months") refers to the monthly new moon.[27] The referents of the two latter, broader periods καιροὺς ("seasons") and ἐνιαυτούς ("years") are harder to determine. The words could retain their distinct meanings, referring to seasonal and yearly events,[28] or they could be a hendiadys that refers to the sabbatical year.[29] The problem in this argument is the rarer nature of the latter, less frequent events. It is not entirely clear how the Galatians could have become observant regarding these times in the relatively short time period of their defection, but perhaps the issue is one of intention instead of realization. Although the referent of the exact events is difficult to determine, the import of Paul's accusation is not. By following these calendrical events, the Galatians had reverted back to a prior state in salvation history and were in effect becoming pagan again. "In so doing, they were submitting themselves to the authority of the stars and other heavenly bodies again. For Paul, this amounted to a return to idolatrous service to things that were not in themselves divine."[30]

4:11 φοβοῦμαι ὑμᾶς μή πως εἰκῇ κεκοπίακα εἰς ὑμᾶς. Paul gets to the heart of the matter with the final sentence of this paragraph. He expresses his own personal feeling and evaluation of the Galatians' situation, namely, fear that the Galatians' defection proves that his labor as an apostle among them was ultimately for nothing. The verb φοβοῦμαι in the context this is not raw, primal fear, but rather regret or longing for a different situation and a different outcome. Paul is not afraid of the Galatians but for the Galatians, with reference to them. The pronoun ὑμᾶς is brought forward in the sentence in a structure called prolepsis; this is in anticipation of the obj. of the subsequent clause (so Burton, 234).[31] The phrase follows the verb to indicate its obj.[32] The pf. of κοπιάω is appropriate in this subsequent phrase since the action is done and the present state is in question. The prepositional phrase with εἰς indicates the goal or beneficiary of the work. The fact that the indic. is used here is significant, as it shows that in Paul's mind the outcome is actually decided; he does not know what that outcome is, but it is already a *fait accompli*.[33] Lightfoot, 172, states the indic. mood is used "because the speaker suspects that what he fears has actually happened." His apprehension

---

27. Lightfoot, 171, offers Col 2:16 as evidence for this interpretation.
28. So deSilva, *Galatians: Handbook*, 85, referencing Burton, 233–34.
29. See BDAG, 337. Dunn, 228, rejects the sabbatical year as a referent because that would not be relevant outside of Palestine.
30. DeSilva, *Galatians: Handbook*, 85.
31. This is a rarer form of prolepsis; see BDF, §476(3).
32. See BDAG, 901: "in object clauses, after verbs of apprehension *that perhaps, lest somehow* ... Referring to someth. that has already taken place, w. pf. ind. Gal 4:11."
33. See E. D. W. Burton, *Syntax of the Moods and Tenses in New Testament Greek* (1900; repr., Grand Rapids: Kregel, 2000), 96; MHT, 3:99; Robertson, *Grammar*, 995; BDF, §370.

about the Galatians is now entirely independent of his will or actions. The tragedy of the statement is not simply in the possibility of wasted labor and effort on Paul's part. Front and center in Paul's mind is his role as the apostle to the Gentiles. His labor among the Gentiles was ordained by God in his calling and ratified by the Galatians' receipt of the Spirit. Their defection back to Law observance would indicate that Paul's preaching of the crucified and risen Savior in their midst was for nothing. This would be a tragedy far beyond the wasted effort of an ineffective preaching tour. It would be a rejection of God's work on their behalf to make them sons and heirs. It would be a rejection of Christ crucified and resurrected, who gave himself for their sins. It would be a renunciation of the Spirit's work within them, who testifies to their place within God's family. On this basis, Paul's vain effort would be a tragedy with eternal consequences.

With this short yet powerful transitional paragraph, Paul sets the stage for his potent, personal appeal to follow. He highlights the inherent danger of the Galatians' desire to become Law-observant. That would return them essentially to idolatry, which by analogy is like their pre-Christian lives (Rapa, 607). It would be essentially equivalent to their prior state when they were ignorant of God (Martyn, 410). By reminding the Galatians of their past, he thereby urges them to stop toying with Law observance and to remain faithful to the gospel he preached to them (Moo, 273).

Theological Comments

Within this initial paragraph, which begins his very personal arguments toward the Galatians, Paul makes an important argument relative to salvation history. God had worked to bring the Gentile Galatians into his family apart from the Law. They were truly under a new dispensation. The faith they expressed in Jesus was sufficient to introduce them into God's family and to maintain their inclusion; there was no other requirement to know God and be known by him. Moving from the worship of false deities to the worship of the one true God was a monumental change in their spiritual existence. An essential argument Paul makes here is that God's salvation-historical clock cannot be turned back without terrible consequence. The Galatians were turning to the Law as the primary mode of existence for their relationship to God. This was analogous to them turning back to worship the demons that governed their prior existence. God had opened the way for all to become Abraham's children through faith in Christ. Turning back from that would have terrible consequences because there is simply now no other way to relate to God other than through faith in Jesus Christ, his Son.

As Paul discusses the power of the salvation-historical clock, he uses two simple phrases to describe the entirety of the Galatians' new spiritual experience. He states as evidence that proves the insanity of their defection that they now know God and are known by God. The simplicity of these phrases belie their profundity. The Galatians went from worshiping false deities to knowing the one true God. They went from outside God's family to being known intimately by him. The import of knowing God and being known by him cannot be underestimated. It is the key that unlocked the door for their entrance into his house as sons, and it is the ledger in which their inheritance as heirs is written. That is what makes their defection all the more tragic. How did they come to know God? Through Paul's preaching to them of Jesus Christ crucified and risen, through faith in him for righteousness. Turning back to the Law as a means to know God means they have effectively rejected Christ, and as Paul argued, Christ is the only means for righteousness. Thus their adherence to Law, in spite of what Paul's opponents might have said, did not help them know God better. Rather, it shut the door God had opened to them and even further barricaded it with requirements that would never fulfill what the Galatians intended.

Application and Devotional Implications

In this emotional appeal to the Galatians, Paul makes an analogy between observance of the Law and servitude to false deities. The Galatians had left slavery to false gods (v. 8) to enter a relationship with the one true God through faith in his Son Jesus Christ (v. 9a). His question to them—in light of their new spiritual existence, how could they turn back to the elemental things?—creates this analogy. The Galatians' prior existence was marked by servitude to things that were not God, things that were powerless to save, things that through their slavery brought only ruin. In Paul's mind servitude to the Law brought the same negative effects. The Law could not bring righteousness. It could not save as the promises did. It was intended to work in concert with the promises, never to replace them, by bringing awareness of sin (3:21–22). By returning to the Law, the Galatians were returning to something as powerless to save as the false deities they had previously renounced. An equation of servitude to the Law with servitude to demons is shocking, but it proves Paul's point well: Neither the Law nor demons have the power to make one righteous. That comes only through faith in Jesus Christ.

This analogy forces believers to examine our own attitude toward the Law. We must think of it as Paul did. It was revelation from God that showed humanity's sinfulness, but it was not a vehicle for righteousness or salvation. That came only through the promises to Abraham, received by faith, ultimately given to the Lord Jesus Christ who then distributes them to all on the basis of a similar faith. When we teach the place of the Law, we must remember that it no longer holds any place to govern a relationship with God. We should not treat it as if it is still a Law to be obeyed. That role for the Law is gone forever. In its place is a new Law, centered on Christ and his love, which governs how we are to live. Hays, 292, states it well from the standpoint of proclamation:

> The task of the preacher working with this text is to reflect deeply on the ways in which our congregations today unaccountably

reject God's gift of adoption and liberation, choosing instead familiar destructive patterns of life and religiosity. Then, after identifying such analogies and patterns, our next task is to reproclaim the good news of 4:3–7: God has sent the Son to set us free and has given us the Spirit as a sign that we are children and heirs of God.

Additional Exegetical Comments

4:8 Both Lightfoot, 170, and Lenski, 209, argue that the ἀλλά here connects not to the nearer ἐδουλεύσατε but the farther ἐπιστρέφετε in v. 9. This appears to be supported by the μέν … δέ construction that would intervene between the ἀλλά and its related verb, but it is mitigated by the logic of the πῶς introducing a question logically deduced from the flow of the argument presented by the μέν … δέ clauses.

4:8 Burton, 228, argues that the anarthrous θεόν is qualitative. This would provide a suggestive sense and is somewhat appropriate given the way in which Paul describes the Galatians' past: "When you did not know *anything that was truly God*, you served things that were in reality not gods." It would in a sense reemphasize their ignorance.

Selected Bibliography

deSilva, D. A. *Galatians: A Handbook on the Greek Text*. Baylor Handbook on the Greek New Testament. Baylor University Press, 2014.

Mitchell, S. *Anatolia: Land, Men, and Gods in Asia Minor*. 2 vols. Oxford: Oxford University Press, 1993.

Proper Imitation of Paul (4:12–20)

Textual Notes

4:14 The variation at this point in the text exists primarily because of the difficulty of the original reading: *καὶ τὸν πειρασμὸν ὑμῶν ἐν τῇ σαρκί μου οὐκ ἐξουθενήσατε*, "And you did not disdain *your* trial in *my* flesh." The use of ὑμῶν is unexpected; it sounds odd for Paul to say that his flesh was the sphere for the Galatians' trial. The variations that occur make the phrasing more logical in the context:

> *καὶ τὸν πειρασμόν μοῦ τὸν ἐν τῇ σαρκί μου*, "and my trial in my flesh" (C*vid D¹ K L P Ψ 365 630 1175 1505 𝔐 and some versions)
>
> *καὶ τὸν πειρασμόν μοῦ ἐν τῇ σαρκί μου*, "and my trial in my flesh" (𝔓⁴⁶)
>
> *καὶ τὸν πειρασμὸν τὸν ἐν τῇ σαρκί μου*, "and the trial in my flesh" (א² 0278 81 104 326 1241 2464)

These can be rejected as scribal alterations on the grounds that ὑμῶν is the harder reading and scribes would more likely remove the 2 pl. pronoun than introduce it. Add to this the excellent manuscript testimony for this pronoun (א* A B D* 6 33 1739 1881 bo), and the reading of NA²⁸ can reasonably be regarded as original.

4:15 Variation exists at this point in the text with reference to the time frame of Paul's question. The majority of manuscripts read *τίς οὖν ἦν ὁ μακαρισμὸς ὑμῶν;* "What then was your blessing?" (D K 630 𝔐 Ambrosiaster); this question forces the Galatians to focus on the past.[1] Several ancient, important witnesses read *ποῦ οὖν ὁ μακαρισμὸς ὑμῶν;* "Where [is] your blessing?" (𝔓⁴⁶ א A B C P Ψ 0278 6 33 81 104 365 1175 1241 1739 1881 2464); this question makes the Galatians consider their present experience. (The reading of F G is *ποῦ οὖν ᾖ ὁ μακαρισμὸς ὑμῶν;* "Where then might your blessing be?" which is similar in meaning.) Either makes good sense in the context, so this problem can be decided primarily on external grounds. On the basis of the

1. See Lightfoot, 175–76, for discussion about alternate meanings for this variant.

more ancient and important manuscripts, the reading *ποῦ οὖν ὁ μακαρισμὸς ὑμῶν;* is preferred as original.

4:18 Very important witnesses (א[2] B 33 lat) have an indic. verb here: *καλὸν δὲ ζηλοῦσθε ἐν καλῷ πάντοτε*, "and you are always being sought well for good." Despite the excellent witnesses, this reading fails on internal grounds because it does not make sense in the context. This positive statement about the Galatians' current situation would contradict everything else Paul has written in the letter. NA[28] accepts the shorter reading with the anarthrous inf.: *καλὸν δὲ ζηλοῦσθαι ἐν καλῷ πάντοτε*, "and it is good always to be sought for good." This generic statement makes better sense. The vast majority of the manuscript tradition has an articular inf. instead, but this is likely a scribal clarification of the grammar. The inf. is supported over the indic. in any case, and the meaning would be the same. The reading *ζηλοῦσθε* likely arose because of an error of hearing; a scribe could have confused the two vowel sounds, exchanging *ε* for *αι*.

4:19 The reading *τέκνα μου* ("my children") is more likely original than the reading *τεκνία μου* ("my little children," which uses the diminutive form of *τέκνον*) primarily on external grounds, as it is supported by strong Alexandrian and Western manuscripts (א* B D* F G 1739). Internal evidence is not as clear cut. The diminutive form is a Johannine idiom (John 13:33; 1 John 2:1, 12, 28; 3:18; 4:4; 5:21). Scribes could have changed the reading here under the influence of these other passages. But the diminutive is emotionally charged and fits the context. See Lightfoot, 178, who says, "Here the diminutive, expressing both the tenderness of the Apostle and the feebleness of his converts, is more forcible. It is a term at once of affection and rebuke." Along these lines Longenecker, 195, argues that the diminutive is the harder reading, and scribes may have changed it to comport with Paul's normal practice. All things considered, the reading *τέκνα μου* should be considered original but with some degree of reservation.[2]

2. Even though Lightfoot argues strongly and persuasively, he also shows a measure of reserve here: "The reading *τέκνα* however is very highly supported and may perhaps be correct" (Lightfoot, 178).

Translation

12 Be like me because I became like you, brothers and sisters,[3] I beg you! You harmed me in no way.[4] **13** You know that because of a physical illness[5] I preached to you at first, **14** and you did not scorn the difficulty you experienced in my body, nor did you shield yourself from it, but you welcomed me as an angel of God, as Christ Jesus! **15** Where then is your blessing? For I testify to you that if possible you would have given your eyes to me by tearing them out! **16** Therefore I have become your enemy by telling you the truth![6] **17** They are not devoted to you in the right way. Rather, they want to exclude you so that you will in turn be devoted to them! **18** But it is good to be sought after for good always and not only when I am with you. **19** My children, for whom I suffer birth pains until Christ is formed in you! **20** I wanted to be with you now and to change my tone because I am confused about you.

Commentary

In the prior paragraph Paul began to show more fully his emotions regarding the Galatians. He closes that paragraph with a very personal remark that displays his concern both for the Galatians and for the status of his own ministry: "I am afraid for you perhaps that I have labored for you in vain." Having opened his heart to them in that way, Paul now bares his soul with a deeply moving appeal to the Galatians. The depth of the relationship they had shared previously was intense and real, and that relationship had led the Galatians to a full acceptance of the gospel that he had proclaimed to them. Turning from the gospel at the insistence of the opponents means that the Galatians have also turned their back upon Paul. This gives Paul the chance to contrast the intense desire both he and his opponents have toward the Galatians. Theirs is wrong because it is self-directed and manipulative, while his is right because it is focused on the good of the Galatians and the gospel.

In his pursuit of the Galatians, Paul uses every weapon in his arsenal. He has been biographical and theological; now he gets personal. This may strike

3. Here I follow recent scholarship that sees the pl. ἀδελφοί as referring to all members of the group regardless of sex; see BDAG, 18.

4. The verb ἀδικέω can refer to physical harm or some type of moral or social wrong. Paul clearly meant the latter, and translations differ on the best way to phrase this: "You have done me no wrong" (NET, NRSV, NASB; cf. CSB, ESV, NIV); "You have not injured me at all" (NASB); "You did not mistreat me" (NLT).

5. Difficulty with the phrase ἀσθένειαν τῆς σαρκός leads to a variety of translations: "physical illness" (NET); "weakness of the flesh" (CSB); "bodily ailment" (ESV); "physical infirmity" (NRSV, NKJV); "bodily illness" (NASB); "illness" (NIV; cf. NLT)

6. This is translated as a statement *contra* most Bible translations, which treat this as a question, certainly under the influence of NA[28].

the contemporary reader as odd in some fashion, but that is likely due to our modern predisposition toward dispassionate argumentation. This appeal by Paul, full of raw emotion, reminds us that truth is holistic in its breadth and relational in its effect. The Galatians must come to grips with the fact that their relationship with Paul had previously guided them to accept the gospel he preached. Now their relationship with his opponents has caused them to turn from Paul, his gospel, and the God of that gospel (de Boer, 277). Paul wants the Galatians to face that fact squarely and to acknowledge the pain it has caused him. By so doing he might just motivate the Galatians to return to their original state.

This change in tone and content leads some commentators to argue that Paul now changes to a new section of the letter. Arguments about the tone center on the grammar and genre. Based upon the occurrence of imperatives and hortatory subjunctives from this point onward in the letter, Rapa, 610, argues that this is the second major section of the letter.[7] Lenski, 215, argues somewhat similarly but on the basis of the admonition's content.[8] Longenecker, 184–87, argues that in 4:12 Paul switches from forensic to deliberative rhetoric, beginning the *exhortatio* of the letter, while Witherington, 304, argues differently, stating that 4:8–11 and 4:12–20 are both deliberative rhetoric, "two parts of a well integrated and rhetorically effective appeal to experience, drawing heavily on emotional language to persuade the audience." Arguments about content deal with the *topos*. Betz, 221, argues that Paul switches to the theme of friendship,[9] while Witherington, 306, argues that Paul refers to family, a relationship more intimate than friendship, as he plays the role of a "wounded, and potentially rejected" parent. This fluidity of focus among commentators is a sign that Paul is perhaps more sublime than we expect. As with many structural issues in the book, there are good reasons to see a greater connectedness between sections; Paul flows quite naturally from one argument to another without a clear demarcation of new sections. This "personal parenthesis" (George, 319) makes perfect sense emotionally, even if the logic of the flow is a bit unclear. This section is marked by *pathos* (Moo, 280), which gives the readers time to digest the dense theological argument that preceded (Matera, 163).

4:12 Γίνεσθε ὡς ἐγώ, ὅτι κἀγὼ ὡς ὑμεῖς, ἀδελφοί, δέομαι ὑμῶν. Paul begins the paragraph with a personal, intimate appeal for the Galatians to imitate him.

---

7. He argues for apostolic admonition in 1:6–4:11 and apostolic appeal in 4:12–6:10.

8. He argues based upon Paul's approach to legalism: "From this point onward the epistle is admonitory yet with a difference: 4:12–5:12 deals with dropping legalism itself, while 5:13 to the end deals with the evidence that it has been dropped, the Christian life exhibiting this fact." Even if one does not agree with Lenski's take on legalism here, his argument has some merit.

9. Matera, 163, rightly argues that the friendship theme does not fully explain the passage since Paul functions as the authority for the Galatian churches.

The impv. γίνεσθε is highlighted in two ways: There is no conj. to introduce it, and it resides at the very front of the sentence when normally it would follow the verb δέομαι (so Moo, 281).[10] Lenski, 216, argues that γίνεσθε is best understood as a customary pres. impv: "Be (ever) like me."[11] But given that the Galatians were not acting like Paul, a better understanding would see this as ingressive-progressive: "Become and remain like me."[12] The ground for this entreaty is Paul's own imitation of the Galatians. The ὅτι here is causal, and the καί (contained in the form κἀγώ, made by crasis) is intensive, bringing special focus to the basis for the impv. There is a verb implied here as in the first phrase, most naturally a form of γίνομαι: "because even I [became] as you."[13] The noun ἀδελφοί is a nom. for voc. and draws specific attention to the Galatians and their relationship to Paul, thus heightening the emotion of the utterance. The verb δέομαι means to ask or request; in tone and placement it marks this utterance not as a command but as an intense entreaty. Paul pleads with the Galatians to imitate him now just as he imitated them when they were together before, during his time of ministry among them.

A challenge of this particular sentence is the nature of the imitation Paul desires.[14] In what way did he intend for the Galatians to imitate him?[15] Paul makes this same call in other letters (see 1 Cor 4:16; 11:1; Eph 5:1 [with God as object]; Phil 3:17), and in those passages the nature of the imitation is clear from the context. This admonition in 4:12 is more difficult to pin down, however, because it is mutual: Paul enjoins the Galatians to become like him because he became like them (see George, 320; Soards and Pursiful, 205).[16] The immediate context of the paragraph does not flesh this out, so

---

10. Many commentators point out that this is the first impv. of the book. Technically this is not true, as ἔστω occurs previously (2x in Gal 1:8–9). However, the spirit of the point is true in that it is the first impv. in the 2 pl., directed toward the Galatians in common paraenetical fashion. Even so, the whole import of the epistle is for the Galatians to stop their defection away from Paul's gospel to the Law. I don't think the Galatians started thinking about how to act in response only at 4:12. See, e.g., Oakes, 145, who notes that Paul has already used himself as a paradigm in 2:19–21 (and will again in 6:14), which implies a command to change behavior.

11. He uses the phrase "durative present imperative."

12. See D. B. Wallace, *Greek Grammar Beyond the Basics: An Exegetical Syntax of the New Testament* (Grand Rapids: Zondervan, 1996), 721, for discussion of this category of impv.

13. Longenecker, 189, points to ἐγενόμην in 1 Cor 9:20–21 as evidence for this argument.

14. Bruce, 208, argues that the plea to "become as I am" is not an *imitatio Pauli* in light of the following phrase. Rather, it is a call to a connection like father to children.

15. *Contra* Lightfoot, 174, who states that there is no dispute on the meaning (yet also discusses two different interpretations!).

16. As with many concepts in Galatians, this is a seminal representation of something that receives more explicit, clear explanation in later letters.

the reader has to rely upon the broader context of the letter to fill in the exact nature of the imitation Paul desires. The central issue at hand is the Galatians' relationship to the Law, and Paul himself addresses his own stance toward the Law at various points. He speaks of his former way of life in Judaism (1:13). Through the Law he died to the Law (2:19). He is no longer under the guardianship of the Law (3:25). In short, he abandoned the Law as the proper way to attain righteousness before God (Moo, 281). In this sense he became like the Galatians, Gentiles who had no (and needed no) relationship to the Law.[17] Thus Paul's entreaty is for them to return back to that Law-less state, rather than move toward the Law as they are presently. Paul never states specifically how he became like them when he was among them, but it is not unreasonable to assume that food would have been a central issue just as it was in Antioch, and perhaps Sabbath as well if Paul was among them for an extended period of time. While among the Galatians, Paul either modified or dropped those Torah-centric practices and announced a Law-free gospel to these Gentiles. He now begs them to become like him and not turn back to something that he had left behind.

οὐδέν με ἠδικήσατε. As with the prior sentence, this one also begins abruptly with asyndeton. The verb ἠδικήσατε is a constative aor. with reference to past time in contrast to what is occurring in the present. The verb ἀδικέω when transitive means "to harm, injure."[18] The word had a broad denotation; here Paul refers generally to negative behavior that the Galatians did not undertake when he was among them: "You harmed me in no way!" By stating that they did nothing in this vein, Paul emphasizes the opposite, positive reception he received among the Galatians during his initial visit. This is shown especially well in the next verse where Paul shows positively how much the Galatians cared for him (so Lenski, 217, who identifies this as a litotes). His point is that the prior relationship he shared with the Galatians was based on kindness and proper concern. The nature of their interaction had changed because of the influence of Paul's opponents over the Galatians, and this attestation of their concern for him forms a basis for a call to that prior attitude of heart.

In this paragraph Paul balances what he desires for the Galatians in the present with what occurred in their relationship in the past. The previous admonition asked for a change in present behavior based upon nature of the connection between Paul and the Galatians in the past, and with this phrase Paul elucidates more clearly what that past relationship looked like. It is unclear whether Paul intends this phrase to connect with what precedes or with what follows. If it connects with the preceding material, it would be a description of the Galatians' response to Paul becoming like them: He dropped Jewish practices mandated by the Law, and in response

---

17. Both Hays, 293; Garlington 2007, 253; and Moo, 281–82, point to 1 Cor 9:21 as a helpful parallel.

18. See LSJ, 23; MGS, 32; BDAG, 20.

the Galatians did not harm him in any way (so Moo, 282), which presumably would involve rejecting him in some fashion as hypocritical or inconsistent. If the phrase connects with what follows, it begins the description of how the Galatians received him relative to his physical ailment when he was among them (so Schreiner, 285). The full description that follows this phrase of how the Galatians cared for Paul is very much in concert with this short assertion. Thus it is most likely that this phrase connects with what follows. With it Paul begins to describe more fully the past relationship he had with the Galatians. Their part in this relationship was not marked in any way by injury to Paul by them.

4:13 οἴδατε δὲ ὅτι δι' ἀσθένειαν τῆς σαρκὸς εὐηγγελισάμην ὑμῖν τὸ πρότερον. Paul continues his positive description of the interaction he had with the Galatians when he first preached to them by describing an important aspect of his part in the relationship. The verb οἴδατε reminds the Galatians of what they know, and the ὅτι marks the content of what was known. This metacomment serves to highlight this information and make it a mutual point of agreement between Paul and the Galatians. In some ways this is a setup of sorts: His goal at present is to focus on the strength of their relationship as a motivation to return from the path they are on, and this information they hold in common shows the depth of that relationship, strengthening the call to return.

Paul uses this content clause to describe his physical condition when he preached to the Galatians, the key phrase being δι' ἀσθένειαν τῆς σαρκός, "because of a physical illness." The noun ἀσθένεια means "weakness, feebleness, illness."[19] On its own it does not convey whether the "weakness" is physical or moral, but Paul's use of the gen. modifier τῆς σαρκός shows that he refers to some sort of physical impairment. This is confirmed by his description in v. 15 of the Galatians' desire to help him, even to the point of tearing out their own eyes; they wished to help Paul in his weakness, and a physical impairment fits this context best. The prepositional phrase as a whole indicates cause (so Burton, 238; Fung, 196), not state or condition.[20] Lightfoot, 174, helpfully clarifies that the phrase δι' ἀσθένειαν should not be explained as if it were δι' ἀσθενείας or ἐν ἀσθενείᾳ. The phrase τὸ πρότερον is an adv. use of the adj. πρότερος and in this instance simply refers to a prior time, "before, formerly."[21] Thus Paul describes what he and the Galatians both know is the reason he preached to them before: Paul had a physical illness of some kind.

Two central interpretive issues present themselves in this verse: the event Paul refers to as his prior preaching, and the nature of his physical illness. Regarding the time frame of his prior preaching to the Galatians, the referent Paul had in mind is not entirely clear, and it is intertwined with the

19. BDAG, 142.

20. See G. B. Winer, *A Treatise on the Grammar of New Testament Greek, Regarded as a Sure Basis for New Testament Exegesis* (Edinburgh: Clark, 1882), 499.

21. See BDAG, 889; BDF, §62. MHT, 3:30, calls this comparative for elative.

dating and recipients of the epistle. At issue is how many times he visited the Galatians to preach to them, and whether the letter itself is included as one of these events. Lightfoot, 175, argues that Paul refers to the first of two visits before the letter was written, but this requires τὸ πρότερον to mean "on the former of two occasions," which was not the normal meaning of this phrase during the Koine period. Burton, 240, argues similarly but on contextual grounds, namely, that communication between Paul and the Galatians could readily have occurred between his initial preaching and the letter, and linguistic grounds, namely, that Paul never refers to his letters as preaching. Longenecker, 190, argues that a more general meaning for τὸ πρότερον and the immediate context where Paul contrasts the Galatians prior attitude toward Paul with their present attitude would lead to understanding the former event as his initial preaching to them. Many commentators argue that the data is simply not clear enough to determine exactly what Paul intended (see, e.g., Dunn, 233). I favor a simpler understanding of the situation: Paul simply refers to his prior preaching to them without any implied reference to other visits between that time and the writing of the letter.

The nature of this physical illness or weakness and how exactly it related to Paul's arrival among the Galatians are not at all clear. Many different things have been suggested over the history of interpretation: a physical sickness, persecution or opposition, sinful longings, or spiritual trials. Commentators who see a physical sickness here have spoken of headaches or some type of seizure disorder like epilepsy. William Ramsay famously postulated that Paul had contracted malaria.[22] If the following verse is taken as determinative, then perhaps Paul was suffering from an eye disease. What he says later in Gal 6:11 about the size of his handwriting could confirm this thesis. The difficulty with this thesis, though, is it is only suggestive; Paul does not describe himself directly or clearly as having impaired vision or being sick in that way. His famous discussion in 2 Cor 12:7–10 of his "thorn in the flesh" focuses as well on the term ἀσθένεια, so there is a possible connection between the two ideas, but Paul also mentions "insults, hardships, persecutions, and calamities" (2 Cor 12:10 ESV), which could imply that his "thorn" was not physical but social or experiential, referring to the constant trouble he experienced in his ministry. The time difference between the events could prove problematic (Witherington, 308), but the text of 2 Corinthians is unclear itself on the time difference between the vision of 2 Cor 12:2–4 and the reply of 12:9, or even when Paul himself learned this valuable lesson (Dunn, 233).[23] Even if the two ideas in Galatians and 2 Corinthians are meant to be connected in

22. W. M. Ramsay, *St. Paul the Traveller and the Roman Citizen* (New York: G. P. Putnam's Sons, 1896), 94–97.

23. This uncertainty is *contra* Lightfoot, 189, who argues that Paul had an initial attack of the illness in AD 44. It also occurred when he first preached in Galatia in 51 or 52. Then he had a fresh attack around 57 or 58 when he wrote Galatians and 2 Corinthians. For similar arguments, see Bruce, 208.

some way, the nature of the connection is unclear except to perhaps render the weakness as enduring (Moo, 282). The narrative of Paul's visits to Galatia in Acts offer no additional information. Assuming a destination in south Galatia, Paul was physically harmed while there (see Acts 14:19); the phrase *ἀσθένειαν τῆς σαρκός* could just as easily refer to an injured body as a diseased one, so perhaps Paul intends to refer to the physical harm he suffered from persecution. Assuming a destination in north Galatia, Paul mentions no causal factor related to an ailment, only a restriction from the Holy Spirit to not go to Asia (Acts 16:6). The short of the matter is that the nature of this "weakness" or "illness" cannot be determined, but the exact nature of the condition is not crucial to Paul's point (similarly Longenecker, 191; Martyn, 420). At the time he came to the Galatians, he suffered from some sort of physical problem, such that his presence among the Galatians proved to be a difficulty for them, a difficulty that they overcame.[24]

4:14 *καὶ τὸν πειρασμὸν ὑμῶν ἐν τῇ σαρκί μου οὐκ ἐξουθενήσατε οὐδὲ ἐξεπτύσατε.* The conj. *καί* continues the progression of the argument. The noun *τὸν πειρασμόν* is the dir. obj. of the two main verbs, brought forward for emphasis. The gen. pronoun *ὑμῶν* is an obj. gen. to *πειρασμόν* (Burton, 241; Lenski, 219). The prepositional phrase *ἐν τῇ σαρκί μου* is local but obviously metaphorical, replacing cause (Paul's flesh, which is a metonymy for his physical problem) for the effect (the difficulties the Galatians had as a result). The Galatians were on the receiving end of some sort of difficulty because of Paul's physical condition when he was with them. The term *πειρασμός* is well known to mean "test, trial." This can be neutral, along the lines of a "difficulty" or "challenge," or negative, referencing a "temptation," depending upon the context.[25] In this instance, the term carries the negative nuance of temptation given the words that follow (Fung, 198; Moo, 284). When Paul arrived among the Galatians, he suffered from some sort of physical ailment. The response of the Galatians to Paul could have been one of rejection and self-protection, implied in the phrase *οὐκ ἐξουθενήσατε οὐδὲ ἐξεπτύσατε* (Longenecker, 191). Given the positive response the Galatians had to Paul with regard to his physical illness, he regards them to have positively responded to this temptation.

The two verbs of this clause, which come at the end of the utterance, present some challenges for interpretation. The words *ἐξουθενέω* and *ἐκπτύω* are similar enough in meaning that they are difficult to distinguish in terms

24. Soards and Pursiful, 240n36, helpfully note the theme in Paul's thought that weakness enables demonstration of God's power; see 1 Cor 1:18–25; 2 Cor 4:7–12; 12:7–10. Schreiner, 286, argues that Paul's sickness was a corollary of Christ's sufferings and could not be separated from his calling as an apostle. This weakness was the "pathway" for Christ's strength.

25. For a clear negative example, see Luke 4:13; for a neutral example, see Jas 1:2. See as well Heb 3:8–9, where God is the one who is tested.

of English translation.[26] The best way to differentiate between them is to regard the first as the mental attitude and the second as the resultant action from that attitude.[27] The verb ἐξουθενέω means "regard as nothing, reject, disdain." It reflects the mental attitude toward something regarded poorly. The verb ἐκπτύω is a compound of the prep. ἐκ and the verb πτύω, which means to spit or spit out. Spitting was regarded as a way to ward off evil in the ancient world, frequently done when confronted with an illness.[28] At issue is whether Paul intends this to be literal or figurative. Either would fit the context. Given the religious culture of the Galatians, literal spitting is not out of the question, especially if Paul was very sick at the time of his introduction to them. The use of βασκαίνω in 3:1 would lend credence to this interpretation, given the association of that term with witchcraft (Moo, 284). Given that both verbs convey negative ideas, and that the οὐκ ... οὐδέ construction negates them both, the assertion is ultimately positive. The Galatians' reaction to Paul when he was among them was in no way negative. Ultimately then there are two ideas present in this affirmation: The Galatians did experience some sort of difficulty because of Paul's condition, but they did not react negatively to him because of it.[29] Betz, 225, states it clearly: "The temptation therefore was to let superstition and prejudice judge the matter of the gospel," which the Galatians did not do.

ἀλλὰ ὡς ἄγγελον θεοῦ ἐδέξασθέ με, ὡς Χριστὸν Ἰησοῦν. With a bit of sanctified hyperbole, Paul describes positively the reception he received from the Galatians. The Galatians did not react negatively to Paul; on the contrary, they reacted extremely positively to him. The phrase ὡς ἄγγελον θεοῦ is the second acc. in an obj.-complement construction.[30] Paul brings it forward in the sentence to emphasize it. It is very possible that ἄγγελος should be construed as "messenger" here, given his use of εὐαγγελίζομαι in the prior verse, but his prior use of ἄγγελος in 1:8, with definite reference to an angelic being, ought to influence the interpretation here. The gen. θεοῦ indicates source, so the entire idea could be fleshed out as "the angel sent from God."[31] The concept points to angels as exalted messengers from God (Moo, 285). The verb δέχομαι is quite strong in this context. It refers to the holistic way the Galatians accepted Paul into their midst. The ancient world prized hospitality to individuals, especially those who were regarded as divine messengers in

---

26. Note, for example, that BDAG, 309, 352, list the definition for both as "disdain."

27. Witherington, 311, understands the omission of οὐδὲ ἐξεπτύσατε by 𝔓[46] as the scribe removing a redundancy, thus implicitly defining the meaning of the second term. Although this interpretation is possible, omission by homoioteleuton should not be ruled out.

28. See H. Schlier, "ἐκπτύω," *TDNT*, 2:448; BDAG, 309.

29. See *NIDNTTE*, 3:699; BDAG, 352.

30. See Wallace, *Greek Grammar*, 184.

31. Note Apollonius' Corollary in play with ἄγγελον θεοῦ. The most logical implication grammatically is that ἄγγελον is as definite as θεοῦ.

some capacity, and to welcome or receive someone in this context would entail both acceptance of the message and the person, caring and providing for them.[32] Thus Paul describes a fully positive, emotional, social, and personal response on the part of the Galatians to his arrival among them. They received him as if he were an angel sent from God, better than they would have received him as a human in his own right. But Paul extends the comparison and ups the ante with the next clause ὡς Χριστὸν Ἰησοῦν. They received Paul as if he were Christ Jesus! This emphasizes the full acceptance of his gospel message and him as the bearer of that message (Betz, 226; Dunn, 235).[33] It is as if there was no difference between Paul and Christ in this regard in the Galatians' thinking. To receive and accept one was to receive and accept the other. Whatever the underlying issue or difficulty was, Paul's point is that the Galatians went beyond normal cultural expectations in receiving him and providing for him (Oakes, 147). Indeed, they accepted his message fully.

4:15 *ποῦ οὖν ὁ μακαρισμὸς ὑμῶν;* Once Paul reminds the Galatians of their extremely positive acceptance of him and his message, he springs the trap, so to speak, by bringing them back to the present state of difficulty and tension with a sharp contrast. Here he asks them a blunt question designed to help them diagnose what went wrong between then and now. The conj. *οὖν* draws an inference from the implied difference between their past and present state. The interrogative pronoun *ποῦ* asks "where?" implying that their prior positive attitudes are now lacking. The noun *μακαρισμός* is the key idea: The "blessing" they had previously is no longer present, and Paul wants them to think about where and why it has gone. The word *μακαρισμός* means "blessing" or "declaration of favor."[34] It has a decidedly spiritual nuance, drawing upon the use of the adj. *μακάριος* in the beatitude formula that figures prominently both in the Greek OT and NT.[35] Based on the immediate context in which Paul references the way the Galatians received him initially (v. 14) and now their present regard for him as an enemy (v. 16), the blessing to which Paul refers would most likely be a state of happiness or positive disposition toward him (Longenecker, 192).[36] With this meaning the pronoun *ὑμῶν* acts as an obj. gen. (Burton, 243; Lenski, 221), identifying the ones who receive the blessing. A paraphrase to bring out this idea would be "Where is the positive attitude toward me that blessed you?" Moo, 285–86, and Hays, 294, interpret the phrase differently. While seeing the context as emphasizing the state of their relationship, they see *μακαρισμός* as a pronouncement of blessing on Paul by the Galatians on the basis of their positive relationship.

---

32. For a full, helpful discussion of hospitality in the ancient world, see G. Stählin, "ξένος et al.," *TDNT*, 5:17–25.

33. De Boer, 281, emphasizes Paul as "the embodiment of Christ's self-giving love."

34. BDAG, 611.

35. See, e.g., Ps 1:1; Sir 14:1–2; Matt 5:3–12.

36. So *NIDNTTE*, 3:208.

This emphasizes the Galatians' attitudes toward Paul. Another option would be seeing in μακαρισμός the blessings of the Spirit in the life of the believer. The larger contextual argument Paul made in 3:6–4:7 mentions synonymous ideas of blessing and ultimately points to the manifestation of the Spirit as the blessing the Galatians had received. The implication would be that because of their changed attitude toward Paul and his gospel, the work of the Spirit had been minimized in their midst. The latter idea could certainly be in play here, but the utterance makes better sense as a reference to the relationship between Paul and the Galatians given the explicit relational ideas present in the context that Paul has begun to press in earnest.

μαρτυρῶ γὰρ ὑμῖν ὅτι εἰ δυνατὸν τοὺς ὀφθαλμοὺς ὑμῶν ἐξορύξαντες ἐδώκατέ μοι. This clause (and the next in v. 16) emphasize the change in relationship between Paul and the Galatians. This one focuses on how intensely positive their relationship was initially. The phrase μαρτυρῶ ὑμῖν ὅτι is a metacomment that focuses the readers' attention on Paul's own take on the situation. The content Paul affirms is striking. Cast as a contrary-to-fact condition, the sentence emphasizes exactly how far beyond normal human expectations the Galatians would have gone to love and care for Paul had they been able to do so. The protasis is short, focusing ultimately upon the inability of the Galatians to do what they desired: εἰ δυνατὸν, "if it had been possible [but it was not]." Their inability, as made clear in the next clause, was not from any failing on their part but simply because of natural, physical limitations. The apodosis describes the Galatians' willingness to hurt themselves physically in order for Paul to receive relief from his physical illness. The ptc. ἐξορύξαντες indicates means to the main verb ἐδώκατε: "by tearing out your eyes you would have given [them] to me." At issue here is the referential nature of the statement: Is it literal, referring to the Galatians' desire to give Paul their healthy eyes to replace his sick ones? Or is it idiomatic hyperbole, referring simply to their intense desire to help Paul in his physical illness?[37] It makes very good sense for this to be interpreted hyperbolically (so Lenski, 221; Longenecker, 193). Betz, 228, points to Lucian, *Toxaris* 40–41, as a story about friendship and eyes that embodies this motif.[38] Even so, this metaphor is uncommon, and it is not clear why Paul would have chosen it (Moo, 286). All things considered, given the lack of clarity concerning the details of Paul's illness, it is best to treat this as idiomatic conveying the intense depth of feeling the Galatians had for Paul, which is clearly conveyed no matter the referent. The Galatians' initial feelings toward Paul were so fully positive that they desired to do something superhuman for him.

---

37. An analogue in English is the phrase, "I would give my right arm [for something]!"
38. In the relevant passage a man named Dandamis allows his eyes to be gouged out by the Sauromatae to secure the release of his friend Amizoces, whom they had captured in battle. When the battle was over, Amizoces could not bear to see while his friend could not, so he gouged out his own eyes in sympathy.

4:16 ὥστε ἐχθρὸς ὑμῶν γέγονα ἀληθεύων ὑμῖν. This short verse tersely changes direction and describes the present negative relationship between Paul and the Galatians by encapsulating the damage done to their relationship in the present time. It is a strong assessment of the Galatians' attitude toward Paul at the moment (Burton, 244; Longenecker, 193). The conj. ὥστε shows inference or logical result. It is a legitimate question whether Paul intends a statement or a question. Almost every translation treats this as a question (so also Schreiner, 288), likely under the influence of the Nestle-Aland text. However, every other occurrence of ὥστε in the NT introduces an inference in the form of a statement (so most commentators; *contra* Moo, 286, who argues this would not be an unprecedented way to begin a rhetorical question). Even if construed as a question, though, the result of the clause is the same: Paul overstates his case to make the Galatians confront their role in the deterioration of their relationship, signaling bitterness at their betrayal by going over to the opponents (Dunn, 236). The emphasis here falls on the word following the conj. The adj. ἐχθρός referenced hostility between entities and could convey either active/subjective ("hating, hostile") or passive/objective ("hated") meanings depending upon the context. These meanings coalesced in the substantive use of the term to mean "enemy, opponent."[39] Paul uses the term nine times in his epistles. Often it has a theological tone, describing an antagonistic relationship on the part of humanity to God or the gospel (see Rom 5:10; 11:28; 1 Cor 15:25; Phil 3:18; Col 1:21). Twice Paul uses it somewhat generically to describe negative human relationships (Rom 12:20; 2 Thess 3:15). This occurrence in Galatians is the only place where he uses it to describe himself, and it speaks of a very negative relationship between him and the Galatians, the exact opposite of what their relationship was before. The sense would more likely be active, that is, the Galatians were "hating, hostile to" Paul; Burton, 244, notes that elsewhere in NT and in classical authors ἐχθρός plus the gen. has this active sense. Grammatically the noun ἐχθρός is a predicate nom. to the pf. verb γέγονα: "I have become your enemy!" The use of the pf. tense draws attention to the present state of the relationship based on a prior action. The ptc. ἀληθεύων indicates the means by which this transformation occurred. The verb ἀληθεύω simply means "to tell the truth," but in this context it takes on a significant referent of Paul's proclamation of the gospel. In Galatians Paul uses the verb ἀληθεύω only this one time and the related noun ἀλήθεια three times (2:5, 14; 5:7). The use of the noun is clearly related to Paul's proclamation of the gospel: In the first two occurrences the noun is modified by the gen. τοῦ εὐαγγελίου. The entire phrase ἡ ἀλήθεια τοῦ εὐαγγελίου in these instances does not refer only to the content of the proclamation, that is, the historical data about Christ's death and resurrection, but rather to the implications that truth has for the Galatians and its outworking in their full inclusion in the church without any basis in Law observance. The use of the verb ἀληθεύω evokes that same

39. See LSJ, 748; BDAG, 419.

context (Matera, 161; Moo, 286). Paul thus expresses surprise and dismay that his relationship with the Galatians has changed because he spoke to them truthfully and accurately about the implications of the gospel for them. Some scholars argue that this ptc. would refer to prior contact between Paul's initial preaching and this letter (similarly to the reference of τὸ πρότερον in v. 13; see Lightfoot, 176; Burton, 245). However, given the ambiguity of this evidence, it is better to see the ptc. as referring to Paul's initial preaching of the gospel to the Galatians (Bruce, 211; Fung, 199). Under the surface of this statement is of course the influence of the opponents, who had pulled the Galatians away from their initial acceptance of this truth and likely had disparaged Paul in their view, such that he had become *persona non grata* in the opinion of the Galatians. The Galatians had become convinced under the influence of the opponents that Paul was not their friend but rather their enemy (Martyn, 419).

4:17 ζηλοῦσιν ὑμᾶς οὐ καλῶς. The influence of the opponents implied in v. 16 now comes to the fore as Paul addresses them directly and negatively. Paul rarely takes the opponents head-on in the epistle, as his desire is to influence the Galatians more through a positive presentation of their actual, truthful situation in Christ. When he does take on the opponents, though, Paul pulls no punches. The first phrase of v. 17 describes the opponents' eager desire for the Galatians in a negative way. It is cast in the present tense: "They are not devoted to you in the right way." The verb ζηλόω is important in this context because Paul uses it to describe his own attitude toward the Galatians as well as that of his opponents. Broadly speaking the verb ζηλόω refers to intense emotions directed toward something or someone; whether this is positive or negative is determined by the context. In other words, the "jealousy" mentioned here is morally neutral (George, 327; Oakes, 149). It can refer to positive or negative feelings oriented toward an individual, like admiration or esteem on the one hand or jealousy on the other.[40] It can also highlight the intensity of the feelings directed toward a thing; again, whether this is positive ("earnestly desire") or negative ("envy, be jealous for") is determined by the context. See, for example, 1 Cor 12:31, where Paul uses this verb positively with reference to particular spiritual gifts. When this intense desire is directed toward an individual, as here, the verb can take on the meaning "to court someone's favor" or "be deeply interested in someone."[41] This describes well the juxtaposition of attitudes Paul describes. Both he and his opponents have a deep, emotional interest in the Galatians. The validity of that desire is measured by the intended outcome. The opponents are interested in the Galatians but οὐ καλῶς, "not in the right way." Their desire is negative because they seek not the fulfillment of God's call or purposes but their own exaltation in eyes of the Galatians. Paul, however, constantly and always is

---

40. See, e.g., Sophocles, *Electra* 1027; Ps 72:3 LXX.
41. So LSJ, 755; MGS, 892; BDAG, 427.

interested in the Galatians ἐν καλῷ, "for good" (see v. 18), evidenced both in his presence and in his writing. His interest is apostolic, oriented toward God's purposes for the Galatians, that "Christ might be formed in you" (see v. 19).

ἀλλ' ἐκκλεῖσαι ὑμᾶς θέλουσιν, ἵνα αὐτοὺς ζηλοῦτε. This sentence describes more specifically how the opponents have a negative desire for the Galatians. The inf. ἐκκλεῖσαι is complementary to θέλουσιν, brought forward for emphasis. Together they express what the opponents desire to do: "They want to exclude you." As with many of Paul's arguments in this book, the meaning of the word ἐκκλεῖσθαι itself is not difficult to discern; the challenge comes rather with determining his exact use in the context. This particular verb is a compound of the prep. ἐκ and the verb κλείω. In this instance the etymology of the word conveys its meaning: ἐκκλείω means "to shut someone out from something."[42] What is unexpressed here in Galatians is from what exactly his opponents desire to exclude the Galatians; this has to be gleaned from the argument of the surrounding paragraph. Based on the extended argument from 3:6–4:7, the entity from which the opponents wanted to exclude the Galatians is the family of God (Witherington, 314), that is, the group of people identified as sons of Abraham. The irony, though, is palpable. The final conclusion of Paul's extended argument is that the Galatians are in that group by virtue of their faith, while the opponents are not because they have set themselves up against Paul and the gospel he preaches! The trailing ἵνα clause expresses the intended goal the opponents had for shutting out the Galatians, that is, the opponents intended the Galatians to have the same fervor of devotion toward them. Paul shows in this verse quickly and clearly that the desire the opponents had for the Galatians was not good because it worked counter to the actions of God in history. Instead, the desire the opponents had was manipulative and self-serving (Soards and Pursiful, 211).

4:18 καλὸν δὲ ζηλοῦσθαι ἐν καλῷ πάντοτε. After denigrating his opponents by laying bare their selfish motives among the Galatians, Paul now speaks about his own motivations toward the Galatians. καλόν is a predicate adj. ascribed to the subject ζηλοῦσθαι. The pres. tense of the inf. is possibly gnomic, but it could also be progressive given that the referent could be Paul's own writing to the Galatians.[43] Here the inf. is the subst. subject of implied ἐστιν. The prepositional phrase ἐν καλῷ denotes "kind and manner,"[44] that is, "in a good way"; it serves as a periphrasis for the adv. καλῶς which Paul used in prior sentence. The affirmation comes across as somewhat tautologous: "Being sought after in a good way is always good." The redundancy is not problematic, however, because Paul here speaks less to logic and more toward relationship. Some argue that this statement is an aphorism (Longenecker,

42. See Herodotus, *Histories* 1.144, for a colorful example.

43. Wallace, *Greek Grammar*, 521, considers this iterative.

44. See BDAG, 330.

194), but even if so, Paul uses it to describe his own action of seeking the Galatians (Burton, 247). This is a positive assessment of his own attitude and desire toward the Galatians, which is made even clearer in the following line.

καὶ μὴ μόνον ἐν τῷ παρεῖναί με πρὸς ὑμᾶς. Paul now validates his own concern for the Galatians on the grounds of its constancy. The phrase *μὴ μόνον* provides an adv. specification in contrast to *πάντοτε*. The construction *ἐν τῷ* plus the inf. indicates contemporaneous time.[45] The prepositional phrase *πρὸς ὑμᾶς* here is static, showing location, in conj. with the verb *πάρειμι*: "when I am present with you."[46] Paul's point is that he always had the right attitude of heart toward the Galatians, even when he was away from them. He gave evidence for that earlier in the book when he described his trip to Jerusalem on their behalf (2:1–10), and the present evidence is the very letter that the Galatians are reading from him. Paul has not wavered in his proper desire for the Galatians. This constancy of purpose differs from the opponents, who were concerned about the Galatians only when they could be with them to selfishly influence their thinking and behavior. This shows that Paul's attitude toward the opponents is not mere jealousy. If someone were helping the Galatians in the right way and teaching them the right things, he would have rejoiced (Martyn, 423). Lenski, 227, argues powerfully that this puts Paul's constancy in direct contrast with the Galatians' flippancy:

> In a flash Paul makes the Galatians see themselves. He was the one who was once so zealously sought by them when he labored in their midst. He was the one whom they should ever seek because of the honorable thing he honorably brought them. But now that he had left them to pursue his honorable work elsewhere, what had they done? They had begun to listen to men who dishonorably wanted the Galatians to seek them to the exclusion of Paul. Is Paul no longer to be honorably sought by the Galatians? Is his mere absence to end their honorable course?

Paul potently hits many notes in this verse, contrasting himself with all the other players in the drama. The opponents are degraded for their selfish motives, and the Galatians are chastised for pining after another gospel.

4:19 *τέκνα μου, οὓς πάλιν ὠδίνω μέχρις οὗ μορφωθῇ Χριστὸς ἐν ὑμῖν*. Without a doubt this deeply emotional, theological statement encapsulates almost more than the words can contain about Paul's ministry, his relationship to the Galatians, their response to his ministry, and the spiritual reality at stake. Properly understood, this interjection encapsulates several key themes of the book, the most immediate of which are Paul's intense concern for the Galatians and his role as the apostle who seeks to accomplish Christ's work

---

45. See Wallace, *Greek Grammar*, 611.

46. See Wallace, *Greek Grammar*, 358–60, for discussion of motion and state relative to prepositions.

among them. There is some debate whether v. 19 should be grouped with the immediately preceding material (as in NA[28]) or whether it should begin a new paragraph. The former appears best on the basis of the grammar. The δέ in v. 20 would be difficult to explain if v. 19 began a new sentence (see Lightfoot, 178; Burton, 248; Matera, 161). The latter appears best on the basis of the tone of the utterance (Longenecker, 195). De Boer, 284, argues for the former based on the repetition of παρεῖναι πρὸς ὑμᾶς in both v. 18 and 20, and that repetition sways me as well. Moo, 289, points out that the δέ in v. 20 shows that v. 19 is a fragment. In essence, then, v. 19 is something of a parenthesis, and v. 20 continues the argument of v. 18.

This utterance is powerful both because of the grammar and the metaphors. It begins with an intensely personal interjection. The noun τέκνα is a neut. nom. pl. functioning as a voc. The gen. pronoun μου is poss. This is the first time Paul uses the noun τέκνον in the book, and it is the only time he uses it to describe his own relationship to the Galatians. Paul uses this powerful metaphor of family relationship to make an emotional connection to the Galatians and to create distance between the Galatians and his opponents. What follows is a relative clause that is adj. to τέκνα, further defining them. With the relative clause Paul extends the metaphor of family relationship to the specific vehicle of a mother giving birth to her child. The relative pronoun οὕς functions as the dir. obj. to the verb ὠδίνω. This verb refers to experiencing the pains of childbirth; it is frequently used metaphorically to describe experiencing great pain or anguish.[47] Here it is a progressive pres., emphasizing Paul's present suffering on behalf of the Galatians. The pronoun οὕς is masc., even though the antecedent τέκνα is neut. This is a good example of *constructio ad sensum* (so Bruce, 212).[48] Together the verb and dir. obj. describe the intense pain of giving birth to a child: "whom I painfully bear in anguish again." The metaphor focuses on the pain Paul feels as he seeks to avert the Galatians' defection. The anguish a mother feels during the pain of childbirth is set beside the anguish Paul presently feels in the implied comparison. The adv. πάλιν adds to the shock of this sentence. Paul is not distressed at simply having to experience this pain, but rather that he has to experience it again, after they had been "born" already.[49] Paul's reference to the pain a mother experiences during birth is a powerful metaphor. This image—at once intimate and tender, yet also frightening—shows how deeply Paul cares for the Galatians but also how dangerous their current dalliance with defection actually is. The pain of childbirth in the ancient world was a potent reminder of its dangers. Paul uses this moment to remind the Galatians that just as the

---

47. See BDAG, 1102.

48. So also MHT, 3:312; BDF, §296; Winer, *Grammar*, 176; Wallace, *Greek Grammar*, 337–38.

49. The suggestion that Paul's distress is not at the repetition of the pain but at the extended duration (see Dunn, 240) can be dismissed on the grounds that Paul would have used ἔτι as the adv. rather than πάλιν.

life of mother and baby were in danger during childbirth, so they were too in danger until their return to his gospel was complete.

In the next phrase, Paul uses the metaphor in a different way, creating "a complexity that far exceeds what is commonly called a mixed metaphor" (Martyn, 427). Paul intends to shock the Galatians (Schreiner, 289), part of his rhetorical strategy. The phrase μέχρις οὗ functions as a conj. meaning "until," that is, the prior phrase is valid continuously up to the second phrase.[50] The verb μορφόω means "to shape, form something" and can be used to described the formation of a baby inside its mother's womb.[51] Here it is pass. voice, which fits naturally with the meaning. The subject of the clause is the noun Χριστός, and the location where the formation occurs is denoted by the prepositional phrase ἐν ὑμῖν. The phrase ἐν ὑμῖν could be individual or communal, that is, it could reference Christ being formed in the individual believer or within the community of the church. The former is preferred because Paul is writing to a group of churches; it would be harder to conceive of this as communal (Witherington, 316). In addition, Paul uses similar imagery in 2:20 with an individual focus. Paul uses the pass. verb μορφωθῇ without expressed agent. He might intend a divine passive, but given the context with its focus on his ministry among the Galatians he likely regards himself as the agent of the verbal action. The metaphor of Christ being formed among the Galatians is best understood with reference to the context of the letter's occasion. It is not a reference to salvation *per se* but rather to the Galatians living out Christ's presence fully in their lives, something they are not presently doing given their desire to return to the Law. The image theologically is very similar to what Paul says about his own spiritual relationship with Christ in 2:20 (similarly Bruce, 212; Witherington, 316). This internal realization of the life of Christ in the believer is what Paul means when he speaks of Christ being formed in the Galatians. This life cannot be realized, though, without a full separation from the Law. The context to Paul's prior statement earlier in 2:19 drives this home. There he states, "For through the Law I died to the Law so that I would live to God," hence the birth pains that Paul experiences on behalf of the Galatians. He desires that the Galatians fully live out the life of Christ, that it be completely evident among them, but this cannot occur until they die to the Law. This requires a complete and total reversal of their present attitude.

4:20 ἤθελον δὲ παρεῖναι πρὸς ὑμᾶς ἄρτι καὶ ἀλλάξαι τὴν φωνήν μου, ὅτι ἀποροῦμαι ἐν ὑμῖν. Paul now expresses his desire to be with the Galatians and to correct the problems that had arisen in their relationship. The verb ἤθελον is impf. indic., but it is an unusual use. Normally the indic. would indicate the author's desire to portray something as real in past time, but given that Paul cannot be with the Galatians and that he speaks of his present attitude

50. So BDAG, 644; MHT, 3:111.

51. See, e.g., Philo, *Spec. Laws* 3.108.

in the ὅτι clause, there is some sense in which this verb is unfulfilled.[52] The infinitives παρεῖναι, modified by the prepositional phrase πρὸς ὑμᾶς and the adv. ἄρτι, and ἀλλάξαι with its dir. obj. τὴν φωνήν μου are both complementary to ἤθελον. They express what Paul would like to do but cannot because present circumstances hinder him. The evidence is not clear enough to know exactly why Paul was prevented from visiting the Galatians; for different theories see Matera, 162, and Witherington, 314. The phrase ἀλλάξαι τὴν φωνήν μου is an idiom that means "to change my tone."[53] Its ultimate referent is the relationship Paul and the Galatians share. Paul wants to change his tone in speaking to the Galatians because he has had to say harsh and difficult things to them. He wants to be with them to heal their relationship and change his tone of voice with them. The conj. ὅτι is causal to ἤθελον; it expresses why Paul wanted to be with them and to change his tone. The verb ἀποροῦμαι is midd. voice, which marks this verb as intransitive, but that voice also focuses on the emotional involvement of Paul in this action.[54] The prepositional phrase ἐν ὑμῖν indicates cause or grounds.[55] The reason Paul desires to be with the Galatians and change his tone of voice with them is because their actions have left him perplexed and confused. This refers to the obvious difficulty Paul experienced because of the Galatians' defection away from him and his Torah-free gospel to the Law-abiding gospel of his opponents.

Paul closes this paragraph with something of a rhetorical *inclusio*. He began the section with earnest speech designed to shake the Galatians out of their fealty to the Law. Here he references that earnest speech, expressing a desire to change from the serious words he has used to comforting ones more fitting to what he desires for their relationship. In a sense he hedges his bets: "Paul may be afraid here that his Galatian friends will concentrate on the uncompromising severity of his language and overlook the underlying concern and affection" (Bruce, 213). So he reminds them of his ultimate

---

52. M. Zerwick, *Biblical Greek: Illustrated By Examples*, trans. J. Smith, Scripta Pontificii Instituti Biblici 114 (Rome: Pontifical Biblical Institute, 1963), 123, calls this the impf. in place of the potential optative, which is the optative for "modest assertion." Wallace, *Greek Grammar*, 552, calls this a conative impf. (so also MHT, 3:65), which makes sense since it is impossible to fulfill the desire of this action (see also BDF, §360). E. D. W. Burton, *Syntax of the Moods and Tenses in New Testament Greek* (1900; repr., Grand Rapids: Kregel, 2000), 16, says, "In Gal. 4:20 it is probably the impossibility of realizing the wish that leads to the use of the Imperfect, and ἤθελον παρεῖναι may be rendered, *I would that I were present*" (see also MHT, 3:91). Robertson, *Grammar*, 919, says, "In Gal. 4:20, ἤθελον δὲ παρεῖναι πρὸς ὑμᾶς ἄρτι, Paul is speaking of present time (cf. ὅτι ἀποροῦμαι). He puts the statement in the imperfect as a polite idiom."

53. So BDAG, 45.

54. See BDAG, 119.

55. See BDAG, 329.

desire to restore their relationship, but only through their return to his Law-free gospel.

Theological Comments

In the beginning of this paragraph Paul urges the Galatians to imitate himself in his approach to the Law (Gal 4:12). When with them Paul had stopped following specific Torah practices that would have inhibited his fellowship with them as Gentiles. Paul now encourages them in light of their desire to take up the Law to imitate him by going a different direction. Contrary to contemporary sensibilities, which often view a call to personal imitation of another with suspicion, the NT call to imitation of godly people is an appropriate response for believers who seek to follow Christ. Occurring frequently in paraenesis in the NT, calls to imitation are most frequently found in Paul, but he is not alone in his use of the concept. Paul commands the Corinthians to imitate him because he is their spiritual father in Christ by virtue of the gospel (1 Cor 4:16). Paul commends the Thessalonians because they imitated him by receiving the gospel with joy in the midst of affliction (1 Thess 1:6). Paul commands imitation of his own example of ministry (Phil 3:17; 2 Thess 3:6–12). Paul is not the only center of attention, however. Paul commends the Thessalonians for their endurance under suffering in imitation of the churches in Judea (1 Thess 2:14). The author to the Hebrews encourages imitation generally of those who show faith and patience (Heb 6:12) and specifically of leaders whose lives embody faith (Heb 13:7). John encourages imitation of those who do good because good comes from God (3 John 11). The key theological link in this call to imitation is not simply reduplication of another's character; that is simply an intermediate step. The ultimate goal is the believer reproducing the character of God himself. Paul mentions this specifically on two occasions, once referencing Christ (1 Cor 11:1) and once referencing God (Eph 5:1). Thus the call to imitation has the ultimate goal of reproducing the character of God in the believer by means of following the example of godly individuals who in turn have imitated God.[56] A very natural way to develop and learn, imitation in the NT becomes a sanctified means to practice holiness and develop godliness.

Front and center in this emotional appeal to the Galatians is a triad of relationships. Paul first emphasizes his own relationship with the Galatians by appealing to them to imitate himself (4:12) and by reminding them of how deeply they cared for him when he was first among them preaching the gospel (4:14, 15). Then he focuses on the relationship the Galatians have with his opponents, but he brings no praise for it. Rather, he excoriates his opponents

56. See *NIDNTTE*, 2:429, which says, "The Pauline statements contain a certain tendency to build *imitatio* into a hierarchical system (ranging downward from God to Christ, Paul, the congregation, and other congregations)."

because their zeal for the Galatians is designed to exclude them from the family of God and to serve their own ends (4:17). Surely the Galatians feel the sting of that critique, too, because they could not see through the façade the opponents presented. Paul then contrasts himself with the opponents, emphasizing his constant, proper desire for the Galatians in keeping with the gospel (4:18, 19). Paul is emphatic about these relationships because of their power to embody and actualize truth or falsehood. In their proper function, relationships are *incarnational* because they personify God and realize his truth. This is the theological foundation for the *imitatio Pauli* at the beginning of this paragraph. By reigniting the fervor of the relationship he and the Galatians shared originally, Paul uses a divinely ordained tool to bring them back to a proper relationship with Christ. Used wrongly, however, relationships are not incarnational but destructive. They have the power to lead away from God and his revelation in the gospel. By guiding the Galatians to themselves, the opponents were in fact destroying them. Relationships have power, and whether that power is good or bad depends on whether the relationship is properly oriented to God.

Application and Devotional Implications

When I entered seminary, I was a traditionally evangelical believer with some fundamentalist leanings. My most important spiritual concerns were personal: An individual's personal relationship to Christ was paramount. I endeavored day by day to understand the Bible and to live by it in my particular circumstances. I desired to grow in love for Christ my Savior and maintain a fervent devotion of heart. As I began my studies, though, I learned that the spiritual universe I inhabited was rather small. God was concerned not only with the state of my soul but also with the fate of the world. Like a miniature big bang, my universe expanded enormously when I learned the full scope of biblical teaching. Take, for example, the concept of the kingdom of God. In my Southern Baptist upbringing the kingdom of God was in practice equated with the work of the church. My attitude was remade as I discovered more fully of what the kingdom of God consisted (short answer: everything!) and where it was found in the Scriptures (short answer: everywhere!). My spiritual universe became much larger than before. But just as a cooling contraction follows a hot expansion, I faced the danger of losing my focus on the personal. It was a real temptation to jettison my prior emphases for the ones I had more recently learned. Paul's utterance in Gal 4:19, however, and many others like it, would not let me do this. This verse shows clearly that God's concern for the state of the individual soul remains an appropriately biblical emphasis. Paul emphasizes here that he endures birth pains for the Galatians "until Christ is formed in you." As stated previously in the commentary, this image is of Christ being formed inside the individual, much as a baby forms inside her mother. When Christ is fully formed in the Galatians, they will act in accordance with Paul's teaching and choose not to be bound to the Law.

Instead, they will fully embrace faith as the only means to relate to Christ and enter the family of God. They will each think and act differently, in accordance with God's will and character. I cannot avoid the fact that Paul speaks clearly of an internal reality, a spiritual change of character, that is the work of the gospel in the Galatians. He was desperate for that change to occur in them so they would make the proper choice to return back to his fold. Certainly the gospel Paul preached had global, apocalyptic effects, but it also drove deep into the heart of the individual to change thoughts and decisions. Let us never forget that God in his omniscience has his eyes both on the world and on the individual. And by saving and sanctifying the latter, God testifies that he will ultimately redeem the former.

Additional Exegetical Comments

4:13–14 T. W. Martin offers an intriguing interpretation: When Paul mentions ἀσθένειαν τῆς σαρκός, he refers not to his own illness or persecution (two central avenues of interpretation) but to the Galatians' own flesh, which was not circumcised.[57] More to the point, the fact that Paul was circumcised and they were not did not become a hindrance to the Galatians accepting Paul's gospel; they did not reject him because of his circumcision. Paul now calls them back to that same attitude, namely, to consider circumcision of no consequence in their attitude toward his gospel.

4:19 Much has been made of the possible apocalyptic nuances of the birth imagery (see Martyn, 429–30; Hays, 296; de Boer, 284).[58] This is not outside the realm of possibility, given other apocalyptic emphases within the epistle. It impresses me, however, that the better solution here is the simpler one: Paul's use of birth pains as a metaphor is not meant to evoke apocalyptic themes as much as it simply fits his desire to fully bring forth the new life of Christ in them (so also Oakes, 151).

57. T. W. Martin, "Whose Flesh? What Temptation? (Galatians 4.13–14)," *JSNT* 21 (1999): 65–91.

58. See especially B. R. Gaventa, "The Maternity of Paul: An Exegetical Study of Galatians 4:19," in *The Conversation Continues: Studies in Paul and John in Honor of J. Louis Martyn,* ed. R. T. Fortna and B. Gaventa (Nashville: Abingdon, 1990), 189–201; B. R. Gaventa, *Our Mother Saint Paul* (Louisville: Westminster John Knox Press, 2007), 29–39. For one response to Gaventa's work, see J. P. Davies, "What to Expect When You're Expecting: Maternity, Salvation History, and the 'Apocalyptic Paul,'" *JSNT* 38 (2016): 301–15.

Selected Bibliography

Davies, J. P. "What to Expect When You're Expecting: Maternity, Salvation History, and the 'Apocalyptic Paul.'" *JSNT* 38 (2016): 301–15.

Gaventa, B. R. "The Maternity of Paul: An Exegetical Study of Galatians 4:19." In *The Conversation Continues: Studies in Paul and John in Honor of J. Louis Martyn*, ed. R. T. Fortna and B. Gaventa, 189–201. Nashville: Abingdon, 1990.

———. *Our Mother Saint Paul*. Louisville: Westminster John Knox Press, 2007.

Martin, T. W. "Whose Flesh? What Temptation? (Galatians 4.13–14)." *JSNT* 21 (1999): 65–91.

Ramsay, W. M. *St. Paul the Traveller and the Roman Citizen*. New York: G. P. Putnam's Sons, 1896.

Proof from the Old Testament (4:21–31)

Textual Notes

4:23 The final prepositional phrase in Gal 4:23 shows some variation of wording in the manuscript tradition. The majority of manuscripts read δι' τῆς ἐπαγγελίας, "through the promise" (B D F G K L P 365 630 1175 1739 1881 𝔐 Origen). Even though this manuscript support has ancient, strong witnesses and is distributed across the text types, the addition of the article is likely a scribal addition to specify the Abrahamic promise, as opposed to promise generally. The reading *κατ' ἐπαγγελίας* found in 323 and 945 is also very likely a scribal change to make this latter phrase parallel to the previous one, *κατὰ σάρκα*. The reading of NA[28], δι' ἐπαγγελίας, is supported by excellent Alexandrian witnesses (𝔓[46] ℵ A C Ψ 33 81 104 1241 2464). It is also the shorter reading and the harder one, on the grounds that it is slightly ambiguous compared to the articular reading. When all evidence is considered, δι' ἐπαγγελίας is the reading most likely to give rise to the others. Thus it should be considered original.

4:25 The short sentence in the beginning of 4:25 shows a great deal of variation, a sign that Paul's argument here was somewhat hard to grasp (so Martyn, 437; Moo, 302):[1]

> τὸ δὲ Ἁγὰρ Σινᾶ ὄρος ἐστὶν ἐν τῇ Ἀραβίᾳ (A B D 323 365 1175 2464 sy[hmg] bo[pt]; this is the reading of NA[28])
>
> τὸ γὰρ Σινᾶ ὄρος ἐστὶν ἐν τῇ Ἀραβίᾳ (ℵ C F G 1241 1739 lat)
>
> τὸ δὲ Σινᾶ ὄρος ἐστὶν ἐν τῇ Ἀραβίᾳ (𝔓[46])
>
> τὸ γὰρ Ἁγὰρ Σινᾶ ὄρος ἐστὶν ἐν τῇ Ἀραβίᾳ (K L P Ψ 33 81 104 630 1881 𝔐 sy bo[mss])
>
> τὸ γὰρ Ἁγὰρ ὄρος ἐστὶν ἐν τῇ Ἀραβίᾳ (d)

The essential differences between the readings concern whether the name Ἁγάρ is present and whether the conj. is δέ or γάρ. The canon of which reading

1. A small consolation to those who seek to understand it!

most likely gave rise to the others leads immediately to the reading of NA[28].[2] The presence of the name Ἁγάρ could have easily confused scribes such that they added the conj. γάρ in some form to the text. Between the variants with δέ, the longer one is preferred in this instance because of the strength of its external support.

4:26 The majority of manuscripts add πάντων before ἡμῶν (א² A C³ K L P 81 104 365 630 1175 𝔐 vg^mss sy^h), presumably to emphasize the certainty of Gentile inclusion in Paul's argument. This addition can be reasonably considered a scribal alteration, plus the evidence for the shorter reading is exceptional (𝔓⁴⁶ א* B C* D F G Ψ 6 33 1241 1505 1739 1881 2464 lat).

4:28 The text of NA[28] in 4:28 reads Ὑμεῖς δέ, ἀδελφοί, κατὰ Ἰσαὰκ ἐπαγγελίας τέκνα ἐστέ, "and you, brothers, are children of promise according to Isaac." This reading is supported by a very strong group of witnesses, with several important Alexandrian and Western manuscripts (𝔓⁴⁶ B D* F G 6 33 365 1175 1739 1881). The majority of witnesses, several of which are important and ancient, read instead the 1 pl. here: Ἡμεῖς ... ἐσμεν, "we are [children of promise]" (א A C D² K L P Ψ 81 104 630 1241 1505 2464 𝔐 lat sy bo). On the face of it, a decision between the readings is difficult. The 2 pl. reading is more likely original based on its more solid Alexandrian evidence and on the grounds that scribes may have changed the 2 pl. utterance to first under the influence of the 1 pl. pronoun ἡμῶν at the end of v. 26.[3]

4:30 The text varies at this point between the fut. indic. κληρονομήσει and the aor. subjunctive κληρονομήσῃ. The former is supported by 𝔓⁴⁶ א B D H P 6 33 81 326 1175 1241 2464, and the latter is supported by A C F G K L Ψ 104 365 630 1739 1881 𝔐. On external grounds the fut. indic. should be preferred because of its support from the older Alexandrian manuscripts. On internal grounds, since the aor. subjunctive would be expected here with the emphatic negation of οὐ μή, scribes would be much more likely to change the fut. to the subjunctive than the other way around. So the fut. indic. is more likely original. The meaning of the utterance does not change, plus this replacement of the aor. subjunctive with the fut. indic. in not unheard of elsewhere in the NT.[4]

4:31 The conj. that begins v. 31 varies in the manuscript tradition. The strongest contenders are διό (supported by א B D* H 33 365 1175 1739 1881) and ἄρα

---

2. Lightfoot, 192–93, favors the reading τὸ γὰρ Σινᾶ ὄρος ἐστὶν ἐν τῇ Ἀραβίᾳ as the reading that best explains the rise of the others, likely because γάρ would be somewhat odd in this context, while Lenski, 239, favors it on the grounds it best fits the sense.
3. So B. M. Metzger, *A Textual Commentary on the Greek New Testament* (New York: United Bible Societies, 1994), 528.
4. See D. B. Wallace, *Greek Grammar Beyond the Basics: An Exegetical Syntax of the New Testament* (Grand Rapids: Zondervan, 1996), 468.

(supported by $\mathfrak{P}^{46\text{vid}}$ D^{2} K L 104 630 $\mathfrak{M}$). Both conjunctions mark inference, and both make good sense in the context. There is not much rationale for scribes to change from one to the other, so on the slightly better external support διό is preferred.

Translation

21 Tell me, you who want to be under the Law, do you not understand
the Law? **22** For it is written that Abraham had two sons, one by the slave
woman and one by the free woman, **23** but the one by the slave woman has
been born according to the flesh,[5] and the one by the free woman through
the promise. **24** These things are interpreted allegorically,[6] for these are
two covenants, one born from Mount Sinai into slavery, which is Hagar.
25 Now "Hagar" is Mount Sinai in Arabia, and she corresponds to the present
Jerusalem, for she is enslaved with her children. **26** But the Jerusalem above
is free, which is our mother. **27** For it is written, "Rejoice, you barren one
who does not bear, shout out mightily, you who does not bear children in
pain, because the children of the desolate one are many, much more than
those of her who has a husband!" **28** And you, brothers and sisters,[7] are
children of promise like Isaac. **29** But just as then the one born according to
the flesh persecuted the one born according to the Spirit, so also even now!
30 But what does the Scripture say? "Throw out the slave woman and her
son, for the son of the slave woman will never inherit with the son of the
free woman." **31** Therefore, brothers and sisters, we are not children of the
slave woman but of the free.

Commentary

Paul was a master of the Hebrew Scriptures. He knew their content and could readily recall passages as needed to support his arguments. More fundamentally, he understood their meaning and implication on a number of levels. He certainly understood what the text meant in terms of the original context and authorial intent, but he also knew the meaning of the passage within the flow of the entire narrative and canon. He also knew what significance

5. The translation "by natural descent" (NET) is a clear rendering, but it lacks the lexical connection to Paul's larger argument in the book concerning the flesh. See also v. 29.

6. Translations vary in how they treat the phrase ἅτινά ἐστιν ἀλληγορούμενα: "These things may be treated as an allegory" (NET; cf. ESV, NRSV, NASB); "These things are being taken figuratively" (CSB, NIV); "which things are symbolic" (NKJV); "These two women serve as an illustration" (NLT).

7. Here and in v. 31 I follow recent scholarship that sees the pl. ἀδελφοί as referring to all members of the group regardless of sex; see BDAG, 18.

a passage had for his present situation. He could readily cite any passage as needed to accomplish whatever his purpose might be, all of which was in keeping with the meaning and intent of what he cited. In Paul's citation of OT Scripture we see his understanding of Scripture as a Jew meet his conviction that Jesus was the Messiah; then we see him merge those to apply that conviction about Jesus to his present situation.

Such is the case here with Paul's retelling of one particular facet of the Abraham story. He focuses on the births of Abraham's sons Ishmael (Gen 16) and Isaac (Gen 21:1–7) and their contentious rivalry (Gen 21:8–14). Paul intends to extend the argument in chapter 3 about what it means to be "sons of Abraham." He adds to that argument by discussing the two lines of descent from Abraham (Moo, 292), both of which issued in sons but only one of which fulfilled God's promise. Paul retells the story for the Galatians and against his opponents, emphasizing its theology and applying it to the present situation in which they find themselves. Despite the history of interpretation around this passage, Paul's interpretation is not fanciful or allegorical, strictly speaking. Rather, he retells the story with full trust in its historicity. It is the historicity of the theological reality of both slavery and promise that gives the story applicational power to the present situation.

Paul's purpose in discussing this story is the most important point for its interpretation. With these words he wrestles intensely with the Galatians, seeking to overcome their desire to take on various aspects of Law observance. He has just bared his soul to them, basing his call to return upon the deep bond he had with them (4:12–20). Now with an understanding of the Law better than that held by the Galatians and even his opponents, because it is an understanding in keeping with the Scripture's intent, Paul shows how the Law itself works against the position the opponents have advocated and the Galatians have embraced. Paul does not add any new material here. Rather, what he cites serves to illustrate the point he has already made throughout the epistle (Dunn, 243; Rapa, 615; similarly Burton, 268). Embedded in the narrative about Ishmael and Isaac is the theological seed that would bear fruit in the very situation of the Galatians. Paul's recitation forces the Galatians to realize that their present situation is untenable. Full acceptance of what the Law teaches, their supposed position now as those who are becoming Law-observant, forces one to acknowledge that the Law requires that one be born through promise, but being born through promise means there is no place for the Law. The Law contains within itself a sunset provision enacted when the promise to Abraham is fully realized. The testimony of the Law itself regarding the Galatians is that they are connected to Abraham through the covenant of promise, not through the covenant of Law, and they are therefore free, not in slavery. "The Law-free mission to the Gentiles is in fact prefigured in the Torah itself" (Hays, 300). Paul proclaims this to ensure that the Galatians act accordingly and turn from the path down which they have started. He also prepares them well for his admonition to stand firm in their freedom that follows in 5:1 (deSilva, 391–92).

4:21 Λέγετέ μοι, οἱ ὑπὸ νόμον θέλοντες εἶναι, τὸν νόμον οὐκ ἀκούετε; This bold question challenges the Galatians' (and by extension the opponents') fundamental understanding of the Law. Paul's implied point in the rhetorical question is that those who desire to obey the Law are fundamentally out of step with the Law itself. They want to claim obedience to the Law, but the Law itself shows that their position is untenable. The asyndeton helps to mark the beginning of a new section,[8] but the abrupt change of content and tone also clearly shows that Paul has taken a new tack. Paul shows his emotions, doing so to get their attention (Burton, 252). The phrase οἱ ὑπὸ νόμον θέλοντες εἶναι identifies those who desire to submit to the Law and be controlled by its mandates. Paul addresses all within the Galatian churches, not just a subset (Longenecker, 206), so arguably Paul has his opponents in his sights, too. The wording could be interpreted, however, to refer to those who have not yet fully adopted the Law (Burton, 252; Longenecker, 206; Matera, 168). Because Paul addresses desire, not practice, he is casting his net widely here, entrapping all who desire to obey the Law, whether Galatian or opponent. The challenge to the Galatians comes in the question τὸν νόμον οὐκ ἀκούετε. The verb ἀκούετε here means "understand."[9] The question is clearly rhetorical and expects a negative answer: They actually do not understand the Law! In contrast to what they think they have understood, they actually do not fully understand the Law to which they have committed themselves! This is a direct challenge to the thinking of both the Galatians and the opponents. Being faithful is not simply about obedience to the Law and its regulations. It is also about understanding the theology of the Scripture in which the Law is found and living it out in the present age in light of Christ (see Betz, 241; Martyn, 433). Thus the Law can have both a negative and positive use: The Law as controlling power is to be rejected, but the Law as that which communicates the truth of God's promise (see Soards and Pursiful, 215) is to be fully accepted.

4:22 γέγραπται γὰρ ὅτι Ἀβραὰμ δύο υἱοὺς ἔσχεν, ἕνα ἐκ τῆς παιδίσκης καὶ ἕνα ἐκ τῆς ἐλευθέρας. Paul reviews in summary fashion from the Law itself the well-known narrative about the births of Ishmael and Isaac, which accomplishes two purposes from his larger argument from 3:6–4:7: It reiterates the promise as the proper way to relate to God, and it connects all who have faith, even Gentiles, to Isaac and then by extension to Abraham. Paul begins with the short introductory phrase γέγραπται γὰρ ὅτι to introduce the retelling of the story.[10] The pf. tense γέγραπται is quite common with scriptural citations, but here Paul does not cite the Scripture as such but rather summarizes it (so also Moo, 297). The conj. γάρ provides the grounds for Paul's prior challenge

8. So G. B. Winer, *A Treatise on the Grammar of New Testament Greek, Regarded as a Sure Basis for New Testament Exegesis* (Edinburgh: Clark, 1882), 673.

9. So BDAG, 38.

10. See Gal 3:10, 13 for other strong, scriptural arguments.

in v. 21; by introducing the scriptural citation, the conj. shows that it contains the argument that proves that the Galatians have not really understood the Law they presumably seek to obey. The ὅτι then indicates content, showing what was written in the Scripture. What follows is a terse summary of the rather involved narrative from Genesis. The initial statement identifies the fact of the births with the aor. ἔσχεν.[11] The following statement clarifies the first with more detail. The two uses of the pronoun ἕνα are acc. pointing to the antecedent δύο υἱούς. This double use of εἷς is a Semitic idiom.[12] The sense is "one … another," the latter occurrence taking on the sense of ἕτερος.[13] The first statement refers to Ishmael and the second to Isaac. The prep. ἐκ in each indicates origin or source. It is not unheard of for this prep. to be used with reference to the mother's role in birth.[14] The articles with παιδίσκης and ἐλευθέρας are well-known articles, well known from the narrative itself (Moo, 298).[15] The terms themselves refer respectively to Hagar, Ishmael's mother, and Sarah, Isaac's mother. There is an interesting disparity in Paul's use of these two terms. The noun παιδίσκη refers to a female slave. This term occurs frequently in the LXX in the Genesis narrative to refer to Hagar directly (see Gen 16:1, 2, 3, 5, 6, 8; 21:10 [2x], 12, 13; 25:12), so this is drawn directly from the text itself. The term to describe Sarah, though, is not. The adj. ἐλεύθερος is never applied to Sarah in that way. This statement has exegetical warrant, but it is interpretive nonetheless.[16] One wonders whether this is part of the opponents' argument that Paul uses against them, but there cannot be certainty on that matter. What can be said is that Paul juxtaposes slavery and freedom, giving clear preference to the latter. This becomes a very important part of his total argument in this paragraph, but the full import of the term does not become clear until his statement in Gal 5:1: "For freedom Christ has freed us; therefore stand firm and do not again be subject to the yoke of slavery." The implication here—that freedom is God's design and the result of the promise—becomes explicit there. The implication here helps signal the interpretive approach Paul will take with this passage (Moo, 298), developing it further starting in v. 24. He reintroduces the theme of who has the right to be considered a son of Abraham, but he does so in a way that leaves him free to make some important distinctions from his opponents' exegesis (Dunn, 246).

---

11. This shows quite well the power of the aor. to summarize without commenting on the nature of the makeup of the action.

12. See MHT, 2:438; 4:70.

13. BDF, §247; Winer, *Grammar*, 216.

14. See Matt 1:3, 5; Gal 4:4. See BDAG, 296, for meanings associated with giving birth.

15. See also Wallace, *Greek Grammar*, 225.

16. The term appears previously in the book in Gal 3:28, but there it is not connected directly to any part of Paul's argument.

4:23 *ἀλλ' ὁ μὲν ἐκ τῆς παιδίσκης κατὰ σάρκα γεγέννηται, ὁ δὲ ἐκ τῆς ἐλευθέρας δι' ἐπαγγελίας*. A reader might assume that, given the fact that the same man had two sons, that the sons would be equal in all respects. Instead, this deduction is far from the truth: In addition to the fact they were each born to a different kind of woman, they were conceived through entirely different means (so also Lenski, 234; Moo, 298) and thus are spiritually, theologically, and applicationally very different. Thus the conj. *ἀλλά* creates a strong, logical disjunction here. The phrases that follow are linked with a *μέν* … *δέ* construction, displaying perfectly in this instance the disjunction between the two sons that Paul wants to emphasize and within that disjunction highlighting positively the latter son. The phrases *ὁ ἐκ τῆς παιδίσκης* and *ὁ ἐκ τῆς ἐλευθέρας* are each a prepositional phrase made into a substantive by the presence of the article. The masc. articles are anaphoric, pointing back respectively to the sons mentioned previously. The pf. tense verb *γεγέννηται* could be used simply in keeping with the verb *γέγραπται* in v. 22, emphasizing the enduring nature of the Scripture, but more likely Paul truly intended the sense of the pf., that is, a past action has yielded a present result. The effect of these births remains, which is why Paul brings them up as applicable to the Galatians (see Burton, 253; Lenski, 234). Wallace identifies this as a pf. of allegory, which focuses upon the present application of the OT text: "The perfect tense can be used to refer to an OT event in such a way that the event is viewed in terms of its allegorical or applicational value. … Sometimes it focuses on the paradigmatic significance of the OT event."[17] Key to the distinction Paul makes here are the modifying prepositional phrases: Ishmael was born *κατὰ σάρκα* while Isaac was born *δι' ἐπαγγελίας*. The prep. *κατά* in the phrase *κατὰ σάρκα* indicates "in accordance with, in keeping with." Paul uses *σάρξ* frequently in Galatians with varied nuances; here the emphasis is not simply on human flesh, as Isaac was a biological child of Abraham like Ishmael, but rather the nature of his conception: Ishmael was born through natural, human means (so Lightfoot, 180; Bruce, 217; Moo, 299; *contra* Dunn, 246; Schreiner, 299).[18] The birth of Ishmael *κατὰ σάρκα*, "according to the flesh," contrasts with Isaac's birth as *δι' ἐπαγγελίας*, "through the promise." This latter phrase figures prominently earlier in Galatians at 3:18, but the whole of the central argument supports the same idea: Relationship to God is through promise as opposed to any other means. Specifically within the context of this paragraph, the birth of Isaac results from the promise that God gave to Abraham. Here *διά* indicates means (or instrument as Moo, 299, argues), and *ἐπαγγελίας* refers to God's promises to Abraham. Isaac was born as a fulfillment of those promises due to God's intervention while Ishmael was not. Paul's retelling of the Scripture uses his

---

17. Wallace, *Greek Grammar*, 581–82. See also BDF, §342; M. Zerwick, *Biblical Greek: Illustrated By Examples*, trans. J. Smith, Scripta Pontificii Instituti Biblici 114 (Rome: Pontifical Biblical Institute, 1963), 52.

18. Indeed, the whole Abraham-Sarah-Hagar cycle shows at various points exactly how human each person was.

own terminology, but it still rests upon what amounts to a plain reading of the Genesis text (similarly Betz, 242). The interpretive development that follows works only because of Paul's fundamental connection to the plain historicity and exegesis of the Genesis narrative.

4:24 ἅτινά ἐστιν ἀλληγορούμενα. Paul now expounds on the basic details of the narrative that he has just explained. The neut. pronoun ἅτινα refers broadly to the things Paul has just described, not any one specific part of the narrative, and it does so with reference to types or class: "such class of things" (Lightfoot, 180; Lenski, 235).[19] The verbal construction ἐστιν ἀλληγορούμενα is periphrastic ("such things are spoken [or interpreted] allegorically").[20] The big interpretive elephant in the room is the verb ἀλληγορέω, which means "interpret allegorically" or more precisely "to use analogy or likeness to express something."[21] The challenge for exegesis at this point is whether Paul's use of the verb should be understood simply within the context of the paragraph, with its rather ambiguous meaning, or whether it should be understood in light of its broader use literarily and philosophically, in which it takes on a more technical meaning of "allegorize." This verb and its related noun ἀλληγορία are well known for their presumed connections to the literary form of allegory and the hermeneutical method of allegorical interpretation, but it is not at all clear that Paul used the term in that sense. Indeed, even though Philo, a rough contemporary with Paul, was well known for his use of the term and the interpretive method, there is no clear connection between his mode of thought and that which Paul exhibits. Note, for example, Philo's classic statement about why allegorical interpretation is necessary in *Posterity* 49–51. When discussing Gen 4:17, in which the text speaks of Cain building a city, Philo spends a fair bit of time discussing how this assertion is contrary to common sense. His determination is clear: "For it is plain that it is not only extraordinary, but utterly contrary to all reason, that one man should build a city." This leads Philo to the hermeneutical mode of allegorical interpretation to make sense of the text: "Perhaps, therefore, since all these ideas are inconsistent with truth, it would be better to look upon the statement as an allegory (βέλτιον ἀλληγοροῦντας λέγειν ἐστίν), and to say that Cain determined to build up his own doctrine like a city." There is somewhat of a straight line between Philo and later allegorical interpreters like Clement and Origen,[22] but there is no clear evidence that Paul intersects

19. See also BDF, §293(4). This is an important distinction given the stance I will take on Paul's interpretive method here.

20. So A. T. Robertson, *A Grammar of the Greek New Testament in the Light of Historical Research* (Nashville: Broadman, 1934), 881; BDF, §353; MHT, 3:88. MHT, 4:89, clarifies that this is done with no emphatic force.

21. LSJ, 69; MGS, 92; BDAG, 45.

22. So *NIDNTTE*, 1:251.

with that line at any point.[23] Indeed, in this particular instance, the historicity of the events surrounding the birth of Abraham's two sons is paramount in the larger flow of Paul's argument (see the discussion of v. 23). The very fact that Paul mentions the two women implies that he does not view the story as allegorical; the use of ἀλληγορέω refers in some sense to his interpretation (Moo, 299). And as Longenecker, 209, notes, the practice of allegorical interpretation was not unheard of in Palestinian rabbinic traditions. So the nuances of Philonic allegory are not mandated here and Paul's language has merit to stand on its own. Thus there are three essential options for the meaning of ἀλληγορέω in Gal 4:24: (1) literarily, that the Genesis story itself is an allegory; (2) hermeneutically, that Paul is using allegorical interpretation; (3) generically, that Paul is speaking figuratively in some fashion.[24] The last option should be preferred given the generic nature of the verb's meaning and Paul's dependence upon the original historical meaning of the text (similarly Keener, 407). The nature of the figure—whether Paul intends analogy, illustration, typology, etc.—has to be determined on the particulars of this case. Some argue for some type of typology here (so Bruce, 217; Schreiner, 293). This is not unreasonable given Paul's efforts to show the pattern from Genesis being repeated in the lives of the Galatians, but ultimately this fails because in Paul's argument there is no sense of anything potential in the original narrative being fulfilled in the present time (similarly Lenski, 236–37). Paul is not interpreting the Genesis narrative allegorically or typologically but analogically (see, e.g., NIV and CSB "These things are being taken figuratively"). His entire effort is to show how the current situation in Galatia is illuminated by a proper understanding of the Genesis narrative, that is, the situations are analogous. They certainly do connect on a deep, theological level given the role Isaac had in fulfilling the Abrahamic covenant, but Paul's primary concern is how the details of that narrative match and illuminate the details of the situation in front of him. That by definition, since there is no sense of fulfillment, is analogy.

αὗται γάρ εἰσιν δύο διαθῆκαι, μία μὲν ἀπὸ ὄρους Σινᾶ εἰς δουλείαν γεννῶσα, ἥτις ἐστὶν Ἁγάρ. In this way Paul explains his analogy: The two women—Hagar who bore Ishmael according to the flesh and Sarah who bore Isaac through promise—represent two covenants. The demonstrative pronoun αὗται is fem. because of the concord with διαθήκη and the association with the women. The verb εἰσιν could be translated as "represent" in this instance (so NIV, NET, CSB); the verb εἰμί is quite flexible with its denotations, as one might expect. It does not automatically indicate equation of identity

23. Lightfoot, 200, explains quite well the difference between Paul and Philo on this score: "With Philo the allegory is the whole substance of his teaching; with St Paul it is but an accessory. He uses it rather as an illustration than an argument, as a means of representing in a lively form the lessons before enforced on other grounds. It is, to use Luther's comparison, the painting which decorates the house already built."

24. *NIDNTTE*, 1:252.

on the one hand or figurative correspondence on the other; that has to be decided from the context. Covenants were mentioned previously in Gal 3:15, 17, first generically by example and then with specific reference to the covenant God made with Abraham and its attendant promises. Here Paul expands his discussion of covenants to reference not only the Abrahamic covenant but also to include the Mosaic Covenant. Only the former was present in the Genesis passage, so Paul overlays the latter on the narrative as part of his analogy to combat his opponents (Martyn, 436). After this analogical association of the births with covenants, Paul explains the nature of the covenants more clearly. The conj. *μέν* is correlative with the *δέ* in v. 26; up to that point he associates Hagar with the restrictive covenant, and from that point forward he associates Isaac with the liberating covenant. The phrase that begins with the adj. *μία*, here with the force of an ordinal, "the first,"[25] ultimately refers to the Mosaic Covenant. The word *μία* is modified by the aor. ptc. *γεννῶσα*, which Paul uses to pivot from the analogy of the physical births to the creation of the covenants. This ptc. is then modified by two prepositional phrases. The first is *ἀπὸ ὄρους Σινᾶ*, referring to source or origin. This identifies the covenant under consideration as the Mosaic Covenant, given from Mount Sinai (Exod 19). The second is *εἰς δουλείαν*, indicating goal or destination. This is an interpretive comment made from Paul's present assessment of the Law and what the opponents were teaching about it. Paul is working backward through the analogy from his present situation to Genesis because there is no reference to Sinai in the Genesis narrative (Martyn, 436). The similar situation between promise and Law represented by Sarah and Hagar on the one hand and freedom in Christ and the Torah observance of the opponents on the other allows Paul to make the analogy (Rapa, 616). The relative clause that concludes this verse provides clarifying information about the nature the situation in view. The birth of Ishmael corresponds to the Mosaic covenant, which finds a ready example in Hagar, his mother, all three of which are linked through the concept of slavery (Schreiner, 301). Such is the force of *ἥτις* in this instance.[26] The focus upon Hagar, using the metaphor of covenant as "mother," reinforces the nature of these two covenants as the controlling source from which people derive their spiritual life and relationship to God. Paul never mentions the covenant that contrasts with Mount Sinai; the overall context, with its emphasis on the birth of Isaac, points to the Abrahamic (Moo, 301).

4:25 τὸ δὲ Ἁγὰρ Σινᾶ ὄρος ἐστὶν ἐν τῇ Ἀραβίᾳ. The conj. *δέ* continues the discussion of this first covenant by supplying additional analogical interpretation. The word choice at the beginning of the clause is a bit unusual because Paul uses the neut. article with a fem. proper name. He does this likely to focus

25. MHT, 3:187.

26. So Zerwick, *Biblical Greek*, 69; so also BDF, §293(4), which states that here "ἥτις = ἡ τοιαύτη."

on Ἁγάρ as a word cited from the biblical narrative, not on her as a person as such (Burton, 258; Matera, 170; Hays, 302).[27] The verb ἐστίν here is flexible in meaning as before, indicating correspondence as opposed to identity. The prepositional phrase ἐν τῇ Ἀραβίᾳ is locative. Paul adds this information to inform in case his readers did not know it but also to transition to the *topos* of geography, which allows him to introduce Jerusalem in the next clause. Paul had previously stated that the women who gave birth to Ishmael and Isaac were analogous to two covenants. The first came from Mount Sinai and led to slavery (v. 24); this corresponds to the birth of Ishmael to Hagar. Thus to extend the analogy Paul connects Hagar to Mount Sinai by virtue of both leading to slavery. Arguments that connect Hagar with Mount Sinai on the basis of linguistic connections or traditions about the location of Mount Sinai as somewhere other than the Arabian peninsula (for examples, see Betz, 244; Longenecker, 211; Witherington, 333; de Boer, 299) are ultimately unconvincing but also unnecessary. Paul makes the connection based upon the association of both with slavery; that is sufficient for the analogy to work. It is difficult to see how Paul's Gentile readers would understand any association based on Arabic or on subtle traditions about geography (so Schreiner, 302; Moo, 302). More likely the point of the phrase is to provide a context that enables the next step in the analogy to work, that is, the association of Hagar with Jerusalem. So this phrase acknowledges a well-known fact about geography that Paul marshals to prepare for the next step in the argument, which contrasts with what he had just said in the prior verse (so Moo, 303).

συστοιχεῖ δὲ τῇ νῦν Ἰερουσαλήμ, δουλεύει γὰρ μετὰ τῶν τέκνων αὐτῆς. With this statement Paul extends the analogy even further, into the present time and situation. His ultimate goal is to show the Galatians that the Law itself testifies to its own obsolescence in the present era after Christ has come. So Paul must connect the analogy to the current situation and apply it to his opponents and those who seek to be bound by the Law. The verb συστοιχεῖ is pres. progressive, perhaps even gnomic, and means "corresponds." Lightfoot, 181, focused on the literal meaning of the term, "to belong to the same row or column," common in military contexts. This led him to create a chart of connections, which was then followed by several other commentators (see, e.g., Burton, 261–62; Dunn, 252; Martyn, 438; Hays, 303). Whether Paul had in mind comparative columns as such is hard to say, but the idea does fit the context and enables the analogical connections to be clear (Moo, 303). The primary import of the verb, however, is that it advances the argument by pointing out the analogical nature of the connection. Its subject is Ἁγάρ from the previous clause. The dat. τῇ νῦν Ἰερουσαλήμ is the entity to which Ἁγάρ is analogous. The adv. νῦν is in first attributive position and acts as an adj., meaning "present, contemporary." This refers to the city of Jerusalem, which, as the center of Jewish life, by metonymy stands for a Judaism that still holds tightly to the Law, the immediate referent being Jewish Christians

27. See also Robertson, *Grammar*, 411; Winer, *Grammar*, 223; BDF, §267.

who currently hold to Law observance as required for becoming part of the people of God. This analogy works well because their center of activity was indeed the city of Jerusalem. Note that the problems in Antioch began when people from James arrived, and James was without doubt active, even paramount, in Jerusalem. Paul's opponents likely referred to Jerusalem as a cipher for the church there (Martyn, 439; Witherington, 333) with great deference. So the image of "the present Jerusalem" is an indictment against those whose emphasis on Law observance ran counter to the gospel Paul preached (Bruce, 220). The next phrase is key to Paul's entire analogy. Why does Hagar correspond to Jerusalem? Because "she is enslaved with her children." Both the birth of Ishmael through Hagar and the Mosaic Covenant from Mount Sinai ultimately lead to slavery under the Law. It is unclear whether Ἁγάρ or Ἰερουσαλήμ is the subject of δουλεύει. Both the logic and more recent reference imply Ἰερουσαλήμ is the subject, plus the following context in v. 26 describes a new Jerusalem that is free. This verse helps elucidate the flow of Paul's argument. Paul ultimately works from the present situation—Jerusalem enslaved, demanding that everyone submit to the Law—back to the Scripture, which supports this understanding.

4:26 ἡ δὲ ἄνω Ἰερουσαλὴμ ἐλευθέρα ἐστίν, ἥτις ἐστὶν μήτηρ ἡμῶν. The conj. δέ is the second part of a correlative pair, the first being the μέν after the word μία in v. 24. This occurrence of δέ begins the focus on the second covenant Paul wishes to discuss, but he does not pick up at the same point in the analogy. Instead, he goes a few steps further. The noun phrase ἡ ἄνω Ἰερουσαλήμ has ἄνω in first attributive position, corresponding to τῇ νῦν Ἰερουσαλήμ, which he mentioned in the prior verse. Paul switches from νῦν, a word expressing time, to ἄνω, a word expressing location. Neither one, however, should be understood strictly in their literal sense, as Paul invokes them with an eschatological nuance. Indeed, the mixing of temporal and spatial ideas was common in apocalyptic (de Boer, 302); here the mixing serves Paul's purpose to emphasize the present outworking of the apocalyptic reality (Moo, 305). In Jewish thought the present age was very often contrasted with the future age, the age to come; Paul himself uses this figure often, and it grounds much of his theology. In addition, the earth below was contrasted with the heavenly realm above (see Dunn, 253–54, for helpful discussion). By using the word νῦν Paul emphasizes the present, evil side of the eschatological dichotomy, and by using the word ἄνω Paul emphasizes the divine, heavenly side of the location dichotomy. The Jerusalem above is described as ἐλευθέρα in contrast with the verb δουλεύει from the prior verse. The relative clause ἥτις ἐστὶν μήτηρ ἡμῶν plays with the analogy further and identifies "the above Jerusalem" as "our mother." This maintains an association similar to that made with Hagar in the prior part of the argument. As ἥτις previously helped to identify an example, as opposed to being a cause in the analogy, so it does here.

The image of the Jerusalem above, the heavenly Jerusalem, is found in a number of Jewish and Christian writings (for references see Longenecker,

214; Martyn, 440; Hays, 304; de Boer, 301). The language does not always match what Paul says here, nor does the image serve the same function in context, but the concept was common enough and highlighted both the eschatological and ontological difference from what exists presently. Arguably this image of the heavenly Jerusalem finds its roots in the biblical text, as Ezek 40–48 sees the prophet describing a rebuilt temple in a renewed Jerusalem (George, 343). The image found further development in Jewish apocalyptic literature of the first few centuries AD.[28] In the biblical text this imagery is used explicitly in Heb 11:10; 12:22; 13:14; and developed at length in Rev 21. The spatial and temporal imagery associated with heavenly Jerusalem are linked and cannot really be considered separately from each other.[29] Thus Paul's combination of the two through the use of νῦν and ἄνω is quite appropriate and shows that his use of Jerusalem is not simply practical or occasional but also eschatological. Thus Paul uses the imagery of the Jerusalem above to emphasize the proper, present role of faith in contradistinction to the Law in relating to God and the eschatological, even apocalyptic nature of that faith. Referencing Jerusalem as "mother" was a common image in Jewish literature (for references see Betz, 247–48; Longenecker, 215). As Burton, 263, explains well, there are two transformations here in the analogy: Since the seed of Abraham are not Jews but believers in Christ, the new Jerusalem is not the city but the believing community, and since this community is a heavenly community in terms of destination and life, the Jerusalem that is to be becomes the Jerusalem above.

4:27 *γέγραπται γάρ. Εὐφράνθητι, στεῖρα ἡ οὐ τίκτουσα, ῥῆξον καὶ βόησον, ἡ οὐκ ὠδίνουσα.* Paul now cites Isa 54:1 to support the connection those of faith have to the Jerusalem above. The *γάρ* is explanatory, positioning the citation as the basis for the previous statement in v. 26 about how Jerusalem above is free and "our mother." The first line of the citation speaks to the city of Jerusalem; in Paul's new setting, the addressee is the New Jerusalem. The verb *εὐφραίνω* as a pass. means "be glad or delighted, be glad, enjoy oneself, rejoice, celebrate."[30] The force of the aor. impv. in this context is ingressive. The voc. noun *στεῖρα* is the one to whom the command is given; this is applied ironically to the New Jerusalem. This noun is modified in third attributive position by the negated pres. ptc. *τίκτουσα*. This description of *στεῖρα* seems tautologous, but the point is emphasis through poetic repetition: "Rejoice, barren one who does not give birth." The second line calls the Jerusalem above to break out into joyous shouting. It begins with two aor. act. imperatives, also ingressive, from *ῥήγνυμι* and *βοάω*. The use of the two verbs here is likely a hendiadys:

---

28. J. Neusner, A. J. Avery-Peck, and W. S. Green, eds., *The Encyclopaedia of Judaism*, vol. 2 (Leiden: Brill, 2005), 527. See 2 Bar. 4:1–3; 4 Ezra 7:26, 8:52–53, 10:44–50.

29. K. Son, *Zion Symbolism in Hebrews: Hebrews 12:18–24 as a Hermeneutical Key to the Epistle*, Paternoster Biblical Monographs (Milton Keynes: Paternoster, 2005), 59.

30. BDAG, 414.

"Break out and shout" means "Shout out mightily." The second phrase in the line, ἡ οὐκ ὠδίνουσα, is a subst. ptc. which parallels στεῖρα ἡ οὐ τίκτουσα from the prior line: "you who does not bear children in pain."

ὅτι πολλὰ τὰ τέκνα τῆς ἐρήμου, μᾶλλον ἢ τῆς ἐχούσης τὸν ἄνδρα. This line begins with a causal ὅτι which explains why the barren woman should break out into rejoicing. What follows is a sentence with only a predicate adj. and subject; the main verb is implied: "Because the children of the desolate woman [are] many." The last line of the citation expands the emphasis of the whole by intensifying the degree to which the barren woman now has children. The comparative adv. μᾶλλον modifies πολλά from the prior line: "much more." This functions to clarify further the statement already made in the prior line.[31] The particle ἤ shows to what the children of the barren woman are compared. The gen. phrase τῆς ἐχούσης τὸν ἄνδρα modifies an implied noun τέκνα, assumed because of the context of the prior line. The articular ptc. τῆς ἐχούσης is subst., and τὸν ἄνδρα is an acc. dir. obj: "much more than the one who has a husband."

Isaiah 54:1 LXX in its original context served as a rousing promise to Israel that God would restore her fortunes, using the person of Sarah from the Genesis narrative as a figure to make the application. Understandably this passage would be used in Jewish eschatological contexts to point to the future glory of Zion.[32] Even with this antecedent usage, though, the connections Paul makes with the text appear to be his own (de Boer, 303). Just as Sarah was barren but through the work of God gave birth to Isaac and ultimately to a great nation, so Israel who previously had been barren, an image referring to her destitution and agony in exile, would now have many children, an image referring to blessing and prosperity through her restoration into the land. Paul does not cite this passage in order to indicate that it has been fulfilled regarding the people of Israel. Rather, as with his use of the Genesis narrative earlier in the paragraph, the connection is one of illustration (Lightfoot, 182) and analogy. In the Genesis narrative the woman with children was Hagar, and the barren woman was Sarah. In Isaiah the barren woman was exiled Jerusalem and the woman with children was returned Jerusalem. In the analogy Paul draws to his current situation, Sarah ultimately represents the mother of the numerous people of God who in the present time have a relationship with God through faith in Christ. The citation from Isaiah thus shows that just as God will graciously bless Israel and multiply her after her exile is complete because of the promises he long ago made to Abraham and realized through Sarah, similarly God in the present time is multiplying his people through Paul's ministry among the Gentiles based upon those same promises. As such, then, this promise to Israel shows that God is at work in the present time in the same way that he promised originally in Genesis, pictured in Isaiah, and will fulfill again in the future. It is important to note

31. See LSJ, 1076.

32. See Str-B 3:574–75.

that Paul does not intend his citation to indicate fulfillment of the original intent of the promise. If that were so, then the new Jerusalem would stand in the same place as the old and be barren in some capacity, but this makes no sense in Paul's argument. The connection is simply an analogy based on the principle of multiplication of descendants, and the barrenness that applies to Israel does not apply to the Jerusalem above in any way. This is seen as well in the way Paul reuses the OT imagery. The citation in the context of Isaiah speaks to Jerusalem as if the city were a young, barren mother, ultimately referring to Israel as a people and nation. Paul takes this citation and applies it to the Jerusalem above, which is no longer connected to Israel alone but to all those who relate to God through faith in Jesus Christ. So the complex image of the OT gets reapplied and reused to the people of God now in Christ, expanded to include all people, regardless of race.

4:28 ὑμεῖς δέ, ἀδελφοί, κατὰ Ἰσαὰκ ἐπαγγελίας τέκνα ἐστέ. After the citation that makes an important connection to the Genesis narrative by positioning Sarah, not Hagar, as the mother of the present people of God, Paul now completes the analogy by asserting that the Gentiles are the numerous children whom God promised to give. Paul does this by positioning them as similar to Isaac in the analogy, that is, they are children born from promise, not from the flesh. This is a return to his central idea in the theological section of the argument (Dunn, 256). It amounts to an application of the analogy to his readers (Burton, 265). The nom. pronoun ὑμεῖς is the subject of the copulative verb ἐστέ all the way at the end of the sentence. It points specifically to Gentiles to affirm they are indeed connected to Sarah. The nom. noun ἀδελφοί acts as a voc.[33] Neither the pronoun nor the direct address are required here, given the clarity of the context and the verb ἐστέ, so these help the reader transition from illustration to application.[34] The prepositional phrase κατὰ Ἰσαάκ indicates the standard or mode by which the assertion is true.[35] The phrase ἐπαγγελίας τέκνα shows inverted word order for emphasis. The gen. ἐπαγγελίας is attributive but in a loose sense. The force of the construction comes more from the idiom "sons of X" where X describes the referent of "sons" in some metaphorical manner, the force of which is drawn exactly from the context; τέκνα is simply a synonymous use.[36]

33. For an interpretation that sees this nom. acting as nom., see T. W. Martin, "The Brother Body: Addressing and Describing the Galatians and the Agitators as Adelphoi," *BR* 47 (2002): 5–18.

34. See S. E. Runge, *Discourse Grammar of the Greek New Testament: A Practical Introduction for Teaching and Exegesis* (Peabody, MA: Hendrickson, 2010), 120, who says, "The form of address and what traditionally is called a 'contrastive pronoun' mark a discontinuity in the text to help the reader make the transition from the illustration to the point associated with it."

35. See Robertson, *Grammar*, 1379, with reference to p. 609.

36. See MHT, 2:441; MHT, 3:207–8; Zerwick, *Biblical Greek*, 16.

The noun τέκνα is the predicate nom., that which the Gentiles in fact are. As a counter move against his opponents, Paul claims the role of Isaac for his Gentile converts, taking it from those who would apply it only to those who are Law-observant (Hays, 305).

4:29 ἀλλ' ὥσπερ τότε ὁ κατὰ σάρκα γεννηθεὶς ἐδίωκε τὸν κατὰ πνεῦμα, οὕτως καὶ νῦν. Paul extends the analogy beyond the realm of the theological into application. Here he provides a strong contrast with the positive statement about the Galatians in v. 28. Despite the positive truth of the statement about their similarity to Isaac, their present experience is negative in that they are persecuted for their faith in Paul's gospel. Here Paul gives the Galatians a path for action against those who are standing against them. The word ὥσπερ marks the protasis of a comparison; the related clause is the state in the past to which Paul compares his readers. The apodosis begins with οὕτως, marking the present situation in the comparison. The particle πότε marks the earlier timeframe of the analogy, that is, the prior time frame of the biblical narrative. The phrase ὁ κατὰ σάρκα γεννηθείς refers backwards in Paul's discourse to the son born to Abraham according to flesh, Ishmael, who in the present time corresponds to Paul's opponents. The verb ἐδίωκεν implies some duration to the persecution that Isaac experienced at the hands of Ishmael, and in turn implies that the Galatians had been experiencing a similar, extended time of persecution. Isaac is not here identified by name, but rather by a similar phrase to that which identified Ishmael, τὸν κατὰ πνεῦμα. The nature of the persecution Isaac experienced is not explicitly mentioned. The OT narrative is rather terse in this regard. During a feast to celebrate the weaning of Isaac, Sarah saw Ishmael laughing (Gen 21:8–9). Though the text does not say this, the implication is that he was mocking Isaac in some fashion (see the footnote in the ESV on 21:9). At this time he would have been around seventeen years old, and mocking may very well have been his reaction to the celebration for the specially favored child. Paul may have been relying upon later traditions that made this mocking explicit or perhaps upon the larger history of the relations between the descendants of the two brothers (Lightfoot, 184; Betz, 250n116; Bruce, 223–24; Longenecker, 217; Moo, 310).[37] Regardless of the source of the clarification, Paul emphasizes the negative attitude Ishmael had, identifying it as persecution. The apodosis that concludes the analogy places emphasis on the present time. He does not imply in any sense that mockery is what the Galatians were experiencing at the hand of the opponents. Instead, they are persecuted by being pressured to

37. For texts, see SB 3:575–76. Note that Josephus, *Ant.* 1.215, assumes that Sarah took action because of fear that Ishmael might harm Isaac after Abraham's passing: "but when she herself gave birth to Isaac, she held it wrong that her boy should be brought up with Ishmael, who was the elder child and might do him an injury after their father was dead." Josephus, *Jewish Antiquities*, vol. 1, *Books 1–3*, trans. H. S. J. Thackeray, LCL 242 (Cambridge, MA: Harvard University Press, 1930), 107.

draw away from the gospel Paul had set out for them with a looming threat of exclusion from fellowship (Burton, 266; Witherington, 338; de Boer, 307).

4:30 ἀλλὰ τί λέγει ἡ γραφή; Paul goes to the Scripture both to explain the negative situation and the proper response. The immediate implication of the contrastive conj. is that the negative situation—the "persecution" of the Galatians by the opponents—will not endure. Their proper response to the persecution will made the situation different. The neut. interrogative pronoun τί asks "What?" It seeks the content of the scriptural proclamation, identified through the subject ἡ γραφή. The verb λέγει is a perfective pres.,[38] very important hermeneutically. By using the pres. tense and not the pf. as before, Paul identifies the immediate value of the Scripture for the present situation. The Scripture itself, in keeping with the analogy, describes how the Galatians themselves should respond to their situation.

Ἔκβαλε τὴν παιδίσκην καὶ τὸν υἱὸν αὐτῆς· οὐ γὰρ μὴ κληρονομήσει ὁ υἱὸς τῆς παιδίσκης μετὰ τοῦ υἱοῦ τῆς ἐλευθέρας. This citation from Gen 21:10, taken directly from the LXX text with only slight modification to fit the present context, is in two parts: command and explanation. Within the context of the Genesis narrative, this is Sarah's response to Ishmael's mocking of Isaac. It is a command she gave to Abraham. Paul uses it as a scriptural imperative that the Galatians are to follow. Again, analogy is in play: Just as Abraham was to cast out Ishmael for his persecution of Isaac, the Galatians are to cast out the opponents for their persecution of those who exercise faith in Jesus apart from the Law. The command proper is rather simple: the aor. impv. ἔκβαλε with two direct objects, τὴν παιδίσκην and τὸν υἱὸν αὐτῆς. The explanation is a bit more involved. The conj. γάρ identifies this clause as the grounds for the command. Emphatic negation occurs here with οὐ μή with the fut. indic. (as opposed to aor. subjunctive) to indicate either a denial or a prohibition.[39] The best logical relationship sees this as a prohibition, and the earlier command is the way the prohibition will be carried out. The noun phrase ὁ υἱός is the subject of the verb with the gen. τῆς παιδίσκης indicating relationship. The prepositional phrase μετὰ τοῦ υἱοῦ τῆς ἐλευθέρας ultimately disassociates the son of the slave woman from the son of the free. This phrase is modified somewhat from the original wording in the MT and LXX. Paul changes it away from the 1 sg. poss. of the original to fit the present context, ultimately making the expression generic. It is not accidental that this verse uses the verb κληρονομέω. Paul likely chose the verse in part because it used the verb cognate to the noun κληρονομία that he used before in Gal 3:18. The concept of inheritance is important to his prior argument, where he emphasized strongly that inheritance comes only through the promises God gave

38. So Wallace, *Greek Grammar*, 533.

39. For denial see MHT, 3:96. For prohibition see Robertson, *Grammar*, 942; MHT, 1:177.

to Abraham, not the Law that came later. Here he is able to emphasize that same point again through the vehicle of the Genesis narrative.

The remaining question is whether Paul intends the Galatians to take this as a command directed to them. That is entirely feasible, given the analogy the text makes to the present time. The difficulty with this interpretation is the final conclusion that follows the citation. After the Scripture citation, Paul concludes the entire paragraph with a restatement of the Galatians' position as the proper sons of the free woman. He lands on a theological position, not a practical one. In light of the ending, the citation more likely serves as a reminder of the position of the opponents outside the true family of God. It does not appear to be a true command as such, although one can imagine Paul not being upset at the prospect of the Galatians acting upon it. The power is in the reversal: According to the Scripture that the opponents had been using against Paul, the opponents themselves are the ones who are to be cast out (de Boer, 307).

4:31 διό, ἀδελφοί, οὐκ ἐσμὲν παιδίσκης τέκνα ἀλλὰ τῆς ἐλευθέρας. Paul now closes the loop on his argument and reasserts the final conclusion about the nature of the Galatians' relationship to God as his true children. The statement here is similar in content and function to his previous statement in 4:28; this verse reasserts that argument with slightly different language. The assertion here involves both a negative and a positive. The negative denies any identification of the Galatians with the children of the slave woman. The main verb ἐσμέν is 1 pl., which is significant, as with it Paul brings Jews and Gentiles together into the same negative affirmation.[40] Interestingly Paul does not use the article with παιδίσκης; this makes it qualitative, broadening it to refer to any form of religion that leads to slavery (Lightfoot, 185; Burton, 267). The conj. ἀλλά contrasts the negated relationship with the true one. The article with ἐλευθέρας is specific, referring to the free woman, identified in the analogy as Sarah and the new Jerusalem, that is, the church established by Paul's Law-free gospel. Paul's closing words affirm, encourage, and strengthen the Galatians. Without doubt the Galatians trace their connection to Abraham and thus to God properly through Sarah and her free children, not through Hagar and her enslaved ones.

The burden of the major argument in 3:6–4:7 is to show that the Galatians, by virtue of the faith they exercise toward Jesus Christ, whom Paul proclaimed to them, are related to Abraham. They are without doubt his children and thus within the family of God. Subsequent to this section, Paul tightens that argument even further. It is not sufficient only to be related to Abraham, as Paul's opponents likely proclaimed. One has to be related to Abraham in the proper way. The extended analogy Paul makes in this paragraph drives that point home. The Scripture itself testifies that Abraham had two sons. Ishmael, born through normal human means, was not party to the

40. This is different from the prior statement in 4:28, which was 2 pl.

promises God had made. Indeed, he was eventually cast out and prohibited from ever being an heir. The son who was to receive the blessings promised to Abraham was Isaac. It was he that was born through the promise, and it is he that the Galatians emulate with their faith. This analogy proves that even though the opponents on the one hand and Paul on the other can both claim a legitimate connection to Abraham, it is only those who connect to Abraham through the promise who will be heirs, and that promise is realized only through faith in Jesus Christ. Paul holds together Hagar, Ishmael, the Sinai covenant, the earthly Jerusalem, and her children under the concept of bondage, whereas he sees a straight line through Sarah, Isaac, the covenant of faith, the Jerusalem above, and believers, all joined together by freedom (Fung, 207, 209).

Theological Comments

Throughout the book of Galatians Paul has a singular, pastoral purpose: to restore the Galatians to the gospel he had originally preached to them. He fulfills this purpose through a variety of means, though, and this particular paragraph stands out to contemporary readers as one of the most unusual because of his stated use of allegory in his reading the OT. As the exegesis above shows, though, this "allegory" on Paul's part is not allegory as much as it is analogy. Paul does not interpret the details of the Genesis narrative under consideration apart from the clear teaching of the narrative itself. Rather, the details Paul identifies are in complete agreement with the content, meaning, and intent of the narrative. Thus Paul's interpretation of Scripture here does not construe a deeper or hidden meaning but rather part of the literal sense.

The key point emphasized with this interpretation cannot be understated or underestimated for Paul's argument: The Law itself, through the narrative of the birth of Abraham's sons, testifies that membership in the family of Abraham—in the very people of God—comes only through promise, not through the Law. One thing Paul and his opponents would apparently agree on is that membership in God's people is secured through a connection to Abraham. Paul's entire point is that the Genesis narrative clearly shows that Abraham had two sons, only one of whom was born by means of the promise. Thus the claim of the opponents to be Abraham's sons through the Law is invalidated on the claim of the Law itself. Paul had shown earlier that the promise had priority over a physical, genetic connection to Abraham, thus Gentiles through faith could enter the family of God. Now he corrects the misunderstanding that Gentiles have to remain faithful to the Law. This paragraph shows that promise has priority over the Law; obedience to Law cannot be enforced as a standard for entrance into or maintenance of that relationship for Gentiles.

Paul extends this argument even further past the bounds of Torah through a citation from the prophet Isaiah. In its original context, the citation Paul uses was a promise to Jerusalem regarding her restoration from exile. Read in the dual light of the Genesis narrative and the fulfillment of the promise in Christ, Paul sees this promise to Jerusalem as analogous to the promise God gave about Sarah bearing children. Thus the promise is the means by which God would graciously grant Sarah to bear children, that same promise meant that Jerusalem would not be left destitute, and that promise is currently enacted in the inclusion of the Gentiles in God's family through faith in Christ. This alignment of a prophet with the original Genesis narrative shows that a key theme of the OT is the fulfillment of the Abrahamic promise. Paul reads the entire OT in light of that promise and shows that his opponents in reading the Law strictly have missed what the Law itself confessed about its ultimate role in fulfilling those promises.

Application and Devotional Implications

Application of Gal 4:21–31 involves both an interpretive stance and a practical action. Although many contemporary readers of Galatians are uncomfortable with the concept of allegory, Paul uses it to tremendous effect to drive home the primacy of promise in God's plan to bless Abraham and the role of faith in the fulfillment of those promises. It is important to note that Paul does not interpret the Genesis narrative in a vacuum, nor is his use of allegory, so to speak, without reference to the plain sense of the text. A full understanding of what Paul does actually reinforces the literal sense of the text, working in tandem with it instead of contrary to it or without regard to it. Paul's interpretive anchors are two: God's promises to Abraham and the fulfillment of those promises in Christ. The first came from the literal sense of the text itself, and the second came from his experience on the Damascus Road. Paul read the entire OT through the lens of each of these anchor points. Our responsibility in interpretation is to understand Paul's argument and interpret the Scripture similarly.

In citing the Genesis narrative, Paul cites the command from Sarah to "cast out the slave woman and her son" on the grounds that they are prohibited from even being heirs along with Isaac, the son of the promise. Given the social dynamics of the Galatian situation, it is not hard to see Paul using this citation as a condemnation of his opponents who preached Law observance. As the exegesis above indicates, it is difficult to tell whether Paul intended this as a command for the Galatians to follow. At the very least, though, this forces contemporary believers to recognize both the practical and eschatological disconnection between those who hold to Law observance and those who preach the promise. Those who hold to Law observance for present inclusion in the family of God are not themselves part of the family of God and should not have fellowship with those who are. Those who hold to Law observance for present inclusion in the family of God will not inherit the future blessings coming through the promise. It is likely that many contemporary evangelical churches would not have a problem with these statements on their face, but as people who routinely value performance over grace, we must be vigilant to teach the priority of the promise over the Law and live out that priority in every way we can.

Additional Exegetical Comments

4:21–31 S. Elliott has emphasized the Anatolian religious context as a way to understand this passage, and indeed the entirety of the book of Galatians.[41] She argues that the logical links of Paul's comparison rest in the Anatolian Mountain Mother goddesses whose functionaries were self-castrated. I appreciate her attempt to apply the religious context of the audience to exegesis of Paul's enigmatic logic, but at present I remain unconvinced that these connections were paramount in Paul's mind.

4:24 Betz, 239, refers to what Paul does with the Genesis passage as a mixture of allegory and typology. According to Betz, allegory takes concrete matters from Scripture as the appearance of deeper truths that the method brings to light, while typology interprets historical matters as prototypes of present events, connecting them through fulfillment, repetition, or completion within a framework of salvation history. I can accept typology here as a repetition of a historical situation but not necessarily as a fulfillment or completion.

4:24 D. Hunn examines Paul's use of the Genesis narrative in light of the primary point of correspondence he intends to make.[42] She helpfully notes that the issue is not a dichotomy of Jew versus Gentile. Rather, Paul distinguishes between covenants of Law and promise. The problem is that Jew and Gentile could become party to each covenant, and some of Paul's readers (and certainly his opponents) believe they need each. Thus he does not invert the covenants through his allegory, but rather separates them. He shows a correspondence of destiny: An individual cannot be party to both because the consequences for the original sons also apply to the counterparts.

4:25–26 In the LXX, as in the NT, there are two spellings for the name Jerusalem. Ιερουσαλημ is the much more common one, occurring hundreds of times, while Ἱεροσόλυμα is much rarer, occurring dozens of times. Longenecker, 33–34, states that the former has sacred connotations and the latter profane, but the relatively even distribution of the terms within the NT would argue against that thesis. Murphy-O'Connor makes a more feasible

41. S. Elliott, "Choose Your Mother, Choose Your Master: Galatians 4:21–5:1 in the Shadow of the Anatolian Mother of the Gods," *JBL* 118 (1999): 661–83; S. Elliott, *Cutting Too Close for Comfort: Paul's Letter to the Galatians in Its Anatolian Cultic Context*, LNTS 248 (London: T&T Clark, 2003).

42. D. Hunn, "The Hagar-Sarah Allegory: Two Covenants, Two Destinies," *Bib* 100 (2019): 117–34.

argument that Paul's normal usage was the Semitic Ἰερουσαλήμ; he shifted to the Greek Ἱεροσόλυμα when countering his opponents' use of that term, which they used with the Galatians as the more comprehensible spelling for Greek speakers.[43] This is a helpful explanation, but it changes nothing with regard to reference or nuance, thus nothing should be made of the fact that Paul uses one spelling here and another in the rest of the book.

Selected Bibliography

Hunn, D. "The Hagar-Sarah Allegory: Two Covenants, Two Destinies." *Bib* 100 (2019): 117–34.

Josephus. *Jewish Antiquities.* Vol. 1, *Books 1–3*. Trans. H. S. J. Thackeray. LCL 242. Cambridge, MA: Harvard University Press, 1930.

Neusner, J., A. J. Avery-Peck, and W. S. Green, eds. *The Encyclopaedia of Judaism.* 4 vols. Leiden: Brill, 2005.

Son, K. *Zion Symbolism in Hebrews: Hebrews 12:18–24 as a Hermeneutical Key to the Epistle.* Paternoster Biblical Monographs. Milton Keynes: Paternoster, 2005.

43. J. Murphy-O'Connor, "ΙΕΡΟΣΟΛΥΜΑ/ΙΕΡΟΥΣΑΛΗΜ in Galatians," *ZNW* 90 (1999): 280–81.

A Proclamation of Freedom (5:1–6)

Textual Notes

5:1 The textual variation at this point in the text is considerable, but the reading that best explains the rise of the others is the verse as it appears in NA[28]. All the variation can be explained as an attempt to soften this reading, marked by asyndeton and a somewhat abrupt introduction of imperatives.[1] The majority of manuscripts read Τῇ ἐλευθερίᾳ οὖν ᾗ Χριστὸς ἡμᾶς ἠλευθέρωσεν στήκετε, "Therefore stand firm in the freedom for which Christ freed us." Introducing the relative pronoun and moving the conj. forward makes for a much smoother transition into this new paragraph. On that basis alone the NA[28] reading should be preferred, but external evidence is also on the side of the NA[28] reading, as it is supported by the exceptional witnesses א* A B D* 33.

Translation

1 Christ truly set us free![2] So stand firm and do not be subject again to a
yoke of slavery. **2** Look—I, Paul, say to you that if you submit yourselves to
circumcision,[3] Christ will not help you in any way. **3** And I testify again to

1. So B. M. Metzger, *A Textual Commentary on the Greek New Testament* (New York: United Bible Societies, 1994), 528. Arguing the contrary position, Lightfoot, 202, says, "The reading τῇ ἐλευθερίᾳ without ᾗ is so difficult as to be almost unintelligible. At a certain point Bengel's rule, 'proclivi scriptioni praestat ardua,' attains its maximum value; beyond this point it ceases to apply. And in the present instance it is difficult to give an interpretation to the words which is not either meaningless or ungrammatical."

2. This is similar to the NLT: "So Christ has truly set us free." The more common translation is formal, likely treating the dat. τῇ ἐλευθερίᾳ as a dat. of destination: "For freedom Christ has set us free" (NET, ESV, NRSV; see similarly CSB, NASB, NIV).

3. The verb περιτέμνησθε could be midd. or pass., and each voice could be understood to have different nuances. This leads to some variation in the way this phrase is translated: "if you let yourselves be circumcised" (NET), "if you get yourselves circumcised" (CSB), "if you accept circumcision" (ESV), "if you let yourselves

every man who submits to circumcision that he is obligated to do the whole Law. **4** You are estranged from Christ,[4] you who are justified by the Law; you have fallen from grace! **5** For we eagerly await by the Spirit [and] by faith the hope of righteousness.[5] **6** For in Christ Jesus neither circumcision nor uncircumcision accomplishes anything, but faith energized through love does.

Commentary

Paul is always fond of building his practical, ethical commands upon the foundation of his theological arguments. Such is the case here, although the theological framework of his thought never remains simply foundational. In many places, as here, Paul's theological understanding is as practical for his readers as any specific command to action. In this section Paul grounds his exhortation for the Galatians not to take on the requirements of the Law upon the work of Christ, the intended goal of that work, and the future hope those who have faith in him receive. Paul's particular emphasis on freedom for those who have faith in Christ indeed summarizes the essential argument of the whole book (so Burton, 270; Betz, 255; Longenecker, 223). He draws a contrast with those who seek justification in the Law, which separates them from Christ and only leads to condemnation. By direct command and by negative example, Paul continues on his constant trek to see the Galatians return to his gospel and turn away from those who would require them to abide by the Law.

The theological juxtaposition in this paragraph between Paul and the Galatians on the one hand and his opponents on the other is quite stark: Paul's opponents, and perhaps some of the Galatians who had been swayed by them—"you who are trying to be justified by the Law"—have removed themselves from the only one who is able to justify them and to make them righteous. They have fallen away in the worst sense of the term. This provides a very practical exhortation to the Galatians not to submit to the yoke that these people themselves wear and attempt to place upon others. Instead, the

---

be circumcised" (NRSV, NIV), "if you receive circumcision" (NASB), "if you become circumcised" (NKJV). The same issue pertains as well in v. 3 with the ptc. περιτεμνομένῳ.

4. Compare the stronger although not incorrect translations in ESV, NASB "You are severed from Christ"; NRSV "You ... have cut yourselves off from Christ"; NLT "you have been cut off from Christ!"

5. I have included the conj. "and" in the translation to clarify that both πνεύματι and ἐκ πίστεως modify the verb ἀπεκδεχόμεθα. This is similar in sense to several translations; compare NET "For through the Spirit, by faith, we wait expectantly for the hope of righteousness." The NKJV interprets the phrase ἐκ πίστεως as modifying the noun δικαιοσύνης: "For we through the Spirit eagerly wait for the hope of righteousness by faith."

Galatians are to remain in freedom, an important aspect of Christ's work and, based upon the prior argument in the analogy of Gal 4:21–31, a fundamental means for God's outpouring of the promise to Abraham.

5:1 τῇ ἐλευθερίᾳ ἡμᾶς Χριστὸς ἠλευθέρωσεν. Paul begins his new approach in this paragraph with a rather abrupt, fairly concise statement: "For freedom Christ freed us." Marked by asyndeton, this logically grounds the following impvs. The dat. noun τῇ ἐλευθερίᾳ has been brought forward in the sentence to a position of prominence. This left-dislocation provides a frame of reference for understanding the following commands.[6] Despite its emphasis in the word order, this noun is somewhat ambiguous in its meaning. One option is to take τῇ ἐλευθερίᾳ as a dat. of destination; the translation "for freedom" would imply this nuance (NET, ESV, NRSV, NIV, CSB).[7] On this construal freedom is the destination, goal, or purpose for the action of the main verb. The problem with this interpretation is that the dat. of destination occurs only with intransitive verbs,[8] which is not the case with the verb ἐλευθερόω, and the prep. εἰς would have been better suited for that nuance (Burton, 271). Another reasonable interpretation is to see this as a cognate dat.[9] This use of a dat. noun cognate to the verb is a means to intensify the action of the main verb. This is possibly a Semitism, equivalent to a Hebrew inf. abs. of the same root as the main verb,[10] which intensifies the meaning of the main verb.[11] If that nuance is present here, the dat. would double down on the meaning of the main verb: "Christ has completely set you free!" This fits logically with the following admonition to avoid at all costs becoming enslaved again, as that would run contrary to the finished work of Christ. The latter interpretation is preferred because of the word order, which matches the word order of the common Hebrew construction, and because of its internal logic. Thus this statement is about the finality and completeness of the action that Christ undertook to free the Galatians. After the dat. noun τῇ ἐλευθερίᾳ, the kernel of the sentence follows. The pronoun ἡμᾶς is the dir. obj., brought forward to emphasize both Jew and Gentile in keeping with the final note of chapter 4. The 1 pl. pronoun is not without rhetorical effect.

---

6. See S. E. Runge, *Discourse Grammar of the Greek New Testament: A Practical Introduction for Teaching and Exegesis* (Peabody, MA: Hendrickson, 2010), 277.

7. See BDAG, 317: "τῇ ἐλευθερίᾳ *for freedom* (fr. the Mosaic law, w. implication of God as patron)."

8. D. B. Wallace, *Greek Grammar Beyond the Basics: An Exegetical Syntax of the New Testament* (Grand Rapids: Zondervan, 1996), 147.

9. See Wallace, *Greek Grammar*, 168–69, for discussion of this nuance.

10. MHT, 3:241–42.

11. See B. K. Waltke and M. O'Connor, *An Introduction to Biblical Hebrew Syntax* (Winona Lake, IN: Eisenbrauns, 1990), 584. The classic example of this construction is Gen 2:17. Describing the result of disobedience regarding the tree, God says מוֹת תָּמוּת, "dying you will die"; more properly, "You will surely die!"

By using an "inclusive" we, Paul again identifies himself and the Galatians as members of the same group. Using that tie strengthens the foundation for the exhortation to follow.

The verb ἠλευθέρωσεν is aor. tense and in context refers to a past action. It means generally "to set free," and it is used in a variety of contexts—political, financial, or even personal[12]—and with a number of different objects. Two interpretive issues present themselves: to what action Paul refers and from what believers have been freed. The first is fairly easy to explain: With the verb ἠλευθέρωσεν Paul refers to Jesus's crucifixion and resurrection; that event is the decisive moment of spiritual liberation for those, like Paul and the Galatians, who exercise faith in Christ for justification. The latter issue is more difficult to solve. Compared to Paul's use of this same verb in Romans, which specifies from what the believer has been freed (namely, sin; see Rom 6:18, 22), the usage of ἐλευθερόω in Gal 5:1 is somewhat open ended. Within Galatians there is not much to go on to specify to what realm this freedom pertains. On the one hand, freedom from the Mosaic Law is certainly implied given the broader context of the book's argument, but this does not exhaust the meaning here. When Paul preached to the Galatians originally, they were not following the Law, but rather local Anatolian religion. By omitting the obj. of the verb, Paul makes the statement applicable to them from either side of their conversion. Christ set them free equally from the practice of the Law, but also from the bondage of their former religion. Christ's ministry to the Galatians was not an addition to the Law; rather, it replaced the Law, and as such shows that neither Law nor former religion are necessary any more.

στήκετε οὖν καὶ μὴ πάλιν ζυγῷ δουλείας ἐνέχεσθε. This clause introduces two commands addressed directly to the Galatians, and in a sense it encapsulates Paul's purposes for the entire book. These are not the first imperatives within the book (see 4:12 for another important ethical exhortation), but these mark a turning point in terms of frequency. The verb στήκετε occurs elsewhere in Paul's exhortations (1 Cor 16:13; Phil 1:27; 4:1; 1 Thess 3:8; 2 Thess 2:15). Here it is a pres. impv., which in this context implies a customary, continual action (so also Lenski, 251). It is possible that this has an ingressive-progressive nuance, by which Paul would mean "begin standing firm and continue to do so." However, the general, foundational statement that preceded about Christ's work among the Galatians leads to the conclusion that this is a more general statement as well.[13] The conj. οὖν is inferential; this action of standing firm is the logical outcome from the freedom Christ brought. The verb στήκω can mean "stand" in a literal sense (see, e.g., Mark 11:25), but the meaning here is figurative: "to be firmly committed in conviction or belief,"[14] "stand firm," "remain committed." The implication is that the

---

12. See Herodotus 5.62; 6.59; and Sophocles, *Oedipus* 706.

13. See Wallace, *Greek Grammar*, 721–22, for a discussion about these nuances of the pres. impv.

14. BDAG, 944.

Galatians are sorely tempted to move from their commitment to freedom in Christ. Paul's command addresses their resolve, exhorting them to remain as they are, unencumbered by the Law. The second impv. ἐνέχεσθε comes at the end of its clause. It also is a pres. impv. and shares the customary nuance of the prior command. The verb ἐνέχω in the pass. voice means "to be entangled or burdened down." This meaning can be literal: Xenophon, *Anabasis* 7.4.17, speaks of Thracian soldiers who while attempting to jump over defensive spikes got their shields entangled in them. In the present context, because of the collocation with ζυγῷ δουλείας, "yoke of slavery," the verb ἐνέχω should be understood to have the figurative meaning "to be weighed down, burdened." The particle μή makes the command a prohibition, while πάλιν positions this as a prohibition against reverting to a prior state. The implication is that the Galatians were in slavery before; Paul is prohibiting them from entering that state again. That under which one is burdened occurs in the dat., in this case ζυγῷ δουλείας. The lack of an article makes this general, referring to any burden that enslaves (Burton, 271; Lenski, 252), appropriate for the Galatians who had left the burden of their pagan religion behind but were in danger of taking on a different one, the burden of Law observance. In this phrase the gen. δουλείας is apposition, that is, "the yoke that is slavery." The image of a yoke was used regularly to refer to the religious requirements and obligations of the Torah. Within Jewish contexts this was viewed positively (2 Bar. 41:3; *m. Ber.* 2.2; *m. 'Abot* 3:5).[15] Jesus inverted the image and used it positively to refer to himself (Matt 11:29–30). Peter referred to the Law as a yoke in his speech at the Jerusalem Council with a negative emphasis upon Israel's inability to bear it (Acts 15:10). This background imagery reinforces what is clear from the context: The image of the yoke refers to the burden of obedience to the Law, which for the Galatians would be tantamount to slavery.

This verse in a sense encapsulates the entirety of Paul's argument, expressing his understanding of Christ, the Law, and an individual's relationship to each clearly. The Galatians were in slavery before to false gods, and now they are in danger of becoming enslaved to the Law. Christ freed them from the state of slavery. Because of this changed situation, they are never to go back to what they were before, no matter who the master would be. To do so would impugn and dishonor what Christ had done for them.

5:2 Ἴδε ἐγὼ Παῦλος λέγω ὑμῖν ὅτι ἐὰν περιτέμνησθε, Χριστὸς ὑμᾶς οὐδὲν ὠφελήσει. Paul now supports his commands to the Galatians with a statement about the complete lack of spiritual value circumcision now holds. This verse begins with a rather involved metacomment designed to grab the attention of the Galatians, reminding them of Paul's authority as an apostle. The particle ἴδε in and of itself garners attention, but Paul then identifies himself in an explicit way, using both the personal pronoun ἐγώ and his own name Παῦλος in apposition, neither of which is required by the syntax. Paul rarely identifies

15. Similarly Sir 51:26 refers to taking on Wisdom's yoke.

himself by name outside of letter openings (see 2 Cor 10:1; Gal 5:2; Eph 3:1; Col 1:23; 1 Thess 2:18; Phlm 1:19). Doing so marks a solemn tone and hearkens back to the very first verse of the epistle where Paul identifies himself by name as an apostle—Παῦλος ἀπόστολος (1:1)—reemphasizing that same authority. The statement λέγω ὑμῖν takes on the nuance of a pronouncement, perhaps even with legal overtones (see Dunn, 263), and the ὅτι then marks out the content of the pronouncement Paul makes.

The pronouncement Paul makes is a third class condition, marked by ἐάν plus a subjunctive in the protasis.[16] The protasis is rather simple with only the particle ἐάν and the subjunctive verb περιτέμνησθε, and the apodosis is a brief but powerful statement of the effect that will follow. Two aspects of the conditional statement as a whole are important to examine: the force of the conditional statement as a third class condition and the relation of the protasis (the "if" clause) to the apodosis (the "then" clause). Regarding the force of the conditional statement, the third class condition as a whole is capable of a variety of nuances. "The third class condition encompasses a broad range of potentialities in Koine Greek. It depicts what is likely to occur in the future, what could possibly occur, or even what is only hypothetical and will not occur."[17] Thus the content and context must come into play to discern the nuance more carefully. In light of the entire situation Paul addresses in the book, here he describes something in the protasis that is likely to occur, hence such strong words in his attempt to avert it. The Galatians are on the cusp of fully embracing on the Law, in this particular instance through accepting the rite of circumcision. The Galatians are about to go under the knife, literally and figuratively, and Paul objects strenuously in order to stop the procedure. So with many commentators I argue that the Galatians had not yet accepted circumcision at this point; the issue was pending, but they were trending positively toward it. Regarding the relation of the protasis to the apodosis, the better construal is cause-effect given the logical connection of a potential action (acceptance of circumcision) and consequences (Christ offering no help) in the context.

This verb περιτέμνησθε is pres. tense, which appears odd for the act of circumcision; one might expect the aor. here as more natural, as in Gal 2:3 when Paul discusses Titus's lack of circumcision. Likely Paul intends circumcision here to represent not simply that act alone but all it would imply, that is, complete submission to the Law. It was the final, decisive act on the path back to Judaism (Betz, 258; Matera, 189; Dunn, 264). It was also an act that was broad in scope. We tend to think of it as applying to men only, but it would involve churches that would adopt it as the key mark of their identity, implicating women, mothers, and families in the practice (de Boer, 311–12). So in a sense submission to circumcision as a representative act would

16. This is also the sign of the fifth class condition, but that requires a pres. indic. in the apodosis, and here there is a fut. indic.

17. Wallace, *Greek Grammar*, 696.

go far beyond the simple physical alteration of a single male individual. In that way the pres. tense fits well. The verb is either midd. voice ("if you submit yourselves to circumcision") or pass. ("if you become circumcised"); the former is preferred given the emphasis is on both the individual and community presenting themselves to the act.[18] There is little difference in meaning between the two voices here (Schreiner, 313), as the mental state of the Galatians would be the same in each.

The apodosis addresses the effect that would come from circumcision: "Christ will not help you in any way." The verb ὠφελέω means "to help, aid, benefit," but the contours of its usage are rather broad. It is found in both the act. and pass. voice, and it is used absolutely, impersonally, or with a personal subject and obj., as here in Gal 5:2. In this instance the sense is that the subject helps or aids the entity in the acc. case. A helpful parallel is found in 1 Cor 14:6, where Paul states the following:

> ἐὰν ἔλθω πρὸς ὑμᾶς γλώσσαις λαλῶν, τί ὑμᾶς ὠφελήσω, ἐὰν μὴ ὑμῖν λαλήσω ἢ ἐν ἀποκαλύψει ἢ ἐν γνώσει ἢ ἐν προφητείᾳ ἢ [ἐν] διδαχῇ;
>
> If I come to you speaking in tongues, in what way will I help you, unless I speak to you with a revelation or knowledge or prophecy or teaching?

The parallel shows that the subject actively seeks to help the object. The same nuance is present in Gal 5:2: "If you are circumcised, Christ will help you in no way." Christ actively seeks to aid and help the Galatians, but submitting to circumcision removes them from the sphere of his beneficence. It is not as if Christ is simply a circumstance or tool of which the Galatians do not avail themselves. Rather, he acts actively to help them, and circumcision negates those actions. "Christ will provide unlimited help to those who place their undivided trust in him, but no help at all to those who bypass his saving work and think to become acceptable to God by circumcision or other legal observances" (Bruce, 229). Paul casts his statement absolutely because of the totalizing power of the Law: Everything it touches becomes beholden to it to the exclusion of everything else, even the Lord Jesus Christ. For this reason the two cannot coexist in any way within the faith commitments or allegiances of an individual or community.

5:3 μαρτύρομαι δὲ πάλιν παντὶ ἀνθρώπῳ περιτεμνομένῳ. Paul begins this sentence with another link to his implicit claim for apostolic authority expressed in the prior verse. The verb μαρτύρομαι is a pres. indic. that, when used without an obj., means "to affirm someth. with solemnity" (similarly Burton,

18. See A. T. Robertson, *A Grammar of the Greek New Testament in the Light of Historical Research* (Nashville: Broadman, 1934), 816. MHT, 1:162, argues that often there is not a hard and fast distinction between the midd. and pass. voice in this regard.

274).[19] The adv. πάλιν, which Paul already used in 5:1, emphasizes that the teaching of this verse has been mentioned to the Galatians before. Exactly when this was is a matter of debate, relating somewhat to the question of when Paul visited Galatia. For example, Burton, 274, argues that it cannot refer to 5:2 or anything else prior in the book because of the different content, so it refers to something Paul said to the Galatians between his original preaching and this letter. More specifically, Lenski, 255, argues that this references Paul's visit to Galatia after the pronouncement of Acts 15 when he gave them the good news of the affirmation of his Law-free gospel. Matera, 181, argues that this is a reference to 1:9–10 due to similar content. These arguments have some merit, but the simplest solution, adopted by Bruce, 229, and Soards and Pursiful, 248, is that πάλιν implies that v. 3 is a reiteration of what Paul just said in v. 2. With this repetition in vv. 2 and 3 Paul makes perfectly clear to the Galatians where he stands on these matters and what the result will be for them if they follow through with their defection. The dat. phrase παντὶ ἀνθρώπῳ περιτεμνομένῳ identifies to whom Paul speaks in this solemn way. Paul here is not speaking to all the Galatians as he did before but to a particular class of individuals among them, namely, the men who are contemplating submission to the act of circumcision (Burton, 275; Martyn, 470). The adj. παντί here with ἀνθρώπῳ in the sg. focuses generically upon the individual, that is, every individual man who fits this description. The ptc. is pres. midd. just as the verb περιτέμνησθε is in the previous verse, invoking both the enduring nature of the commitment to the Law in view (de Boer, 313) and the permissive attitude toward circumcision (Lightfoot, 204). Paul likely uses this phrase not because he has specific knowledge that some from among the Galatians have submitted to circumcision. Rather, it functions as a rhetorical device to get the attention of those who are considering it.

ὅτι ὀφειλέτης ἐστὶν ὅλον τὸν νόμον ποιῆσαι. The ὅτι marks the dir. obj. of μαρτύρομαι, the content of which Paul testifies. As indicated in the prior phrase, the content of Paul's testimony is directed toward "every man who submits to circumcision." Thus the verb ἐστίν in the ὅτι clause has as its implied subject that individual, namely, the one who submits to circumcision. The predication about this individual is that he is now ὀφειλέτης, a person under obligation, and that to which he is obligated is indicated by the inf. phrase ὅλον τὸν νόμον ποιῆσαι, "to do the whole Law."[20] There is an important play on words here: The benefit conveyed by Christ (ὠφελήσει, v. 2) is now replaced with being a debtor (ὀφειλέτης, v. 3; Dunn, 265; de Boer, 312). The circumcised man is now obligated to keep the whole Law. One cannot commit simply and only to circumcision. Taking on that requirement of the Law then obligates that person to obey the entirety of the Law because

19. BDAG, 619.

20. See BDAG, 742. Occasionally the inf. occurs with nouns cognate to verbs that take an inf. as obj.; see E. D. W. Burton, *Syntax of the Moods and Tenses in New Testament Greek* (1900; repr., Grand Rapids: Kregel, 2000), 152.

circumcision itself is a sign of acceptance of the Mosaic covenant and all it entails (de Boer, 313). In light of mankind's inability to keep the Law (see 3:10–14), this way is a dead end.

The Law obedience Paul describes is the exact opposite of what Christ designed for the believer. Becoming an ὀφειλέτης is diametrically opposed to living in ἐλευθερία. The weight of Paul's argument falls on what the individual would now be obligated to do: ὅλον τὸν νόμον, "the whole Law." Paul implies that this burden is impossible to fill because of the Law's totalizing force.[21] Hays, 312, echoes my sentiment here when he states the Law is a "total way of life." One could not fulfill the Law simply by submitting to circumcision; one had to submit to all of the Law, and in so doing would take on a burden that never failed to condemn. It is possible that Paul's opponents might have advocated only for circumcision, not the entire Law (so Burton, 274; Bruce, 229), so Paul could be responding to a more limited ask on the part of the opponents. But this would make Paul even more in the right: A more limited ask betrays either the opponents' misunderstanding about how the Law actually functions or their dishonesty in presenting the issue to the Galatians. No matter how the opponents presented the issue to the Galatians, Paul spells out the real consequences of this seemingly small step (George, 358). Paul knew the theological ramifications of the act better than his opponents did and did not hesitate to explain them.

5:4 κατηργήθητε ἀπὸ Χριστοῦ, οἵτινες ἐν νόμῳ δικαιοῦσθε, τῆς χάριτος ἐξεπέσατε. The solemnity and severity of Paul's argument attains its zenith in this sentence. Marked by asyndeton like a number of sentences in this emotional paragraph, it contains two different phrases that describe the result of dependence upon the Law. Sandwiched in between the two statements is a short phrase that identifies Paul's intended audience for this specific utterance: οἵτινες ἐν νόμῳ δικαιοῦσθε. It is important to examine this first, as it sets the context for understanding Paul's argument here. The pronoun οἵτινες identifies all who do the associated action; coupled with the 2 pl. verbs, a translation of "you who (do such-and-such)" is appropriate. The phrase ἐν νόμῳ modifies the verb δικαιοῦσθε, indicating the means by which the action of the verb is accomplished.[22] This prepositional phrase occurred earlier in Gal 3:11 with a similar meaning. The verb δικαιοῦσθε is a pres. indic., focusing on the current status of the action. This verb portrays a present reality, but this must be taken with a grain of salt within Paul's entire argument, as he argued earlier that there is indeed no justification in the Law. This verb could be conative ("you who are seeking to be justified by the Law"; see

---

21. Given the historical trouble theologians have had reconciling James and Paul, it is ironic that Paul finds support from Jas 2:10 on this point.

22. See BDF, §195(1).

Lenski, 257; Bruce, 231; Longenecker, 228; Martyn, 471; de Boer, 314),[23] or gnomic,[24] but neither fits well with the aor. tense of the surrounding verbs. A better option is to see Paul speaking ironically, even sarcastically. From the standpoint of the individuals in view, "you who are justified by the Law," the action is real and in progress; they are achieving justification through the Law! So it may be that Paul's utterance here in v. 4 is directed toward those who are presently "justified by the Law," which would be a different group than those in v. 3 who were considering submission to circumcision. Paul could refer to his opponents, who were at the logical end point of what the Galatians were themselves considering. But certainly Paul has in mind those who are still at a point of decision, and he seeks to sway them. By affirming as true something that he has already declared as false, Paul rhetorically pulls those on the fence toward his side. He forces them to recognize that that the spiritual situation they desire through Law observance would actually be the exact opposite of what they expect.

On either side of this phrase are statements about those who are "justified by the Law." The first is κατηργήθητε ἀπὸ Χριστοῦ, the second τῆς χάριτος ἐξεπέσατε. Each clause is constructed similarly: an aor. verb modified by something that indicates separation.[25] The verbs are each 2 pl. Paul no longer speaks in the 3 sg. about the individual man who considers circumcision; he turns to address directly and dramatically those who have cast their lot in with the Law. The verb καταργέω here is used quite vividly. It has a wide range of meanings that cluster around the dual notions of hindering or abolishing. Some of the uses are in positive contexts. For example, Paul used the verb earlier in Gal 3:17 to deny that the Law could ever nullify the promise God gave to Abraham. Many times the verb is negative, however, used in the context of divine judgment (see Rom 6:6; 1 Cor 1:28; 2:6; 6:13; 15:24, 26; 2 Thess 2:8; 2 Tim 1:10; Heb 2:14). It is this latter nuance that informs the present passage. In this context with a person as the object of separation, the sense "estranged" fits nicely.[26] The prepositional phrase ἀπὸ Χριστοῦ indicates from whom those who seek justification in the Law are estranged. This must be taken at face value: Those who seek justification in the Law have been estranged from Christ—the one whom God raised from the dead, the one who gave himself for their sins, the one who will rescue them from this present evil age, the one who is the only means for justification. Christ is the one through whom God works for salvation. Estrangement from him

23. So BDF, §319; Robertson, *Grammar*, 880; Burton, *Syntax*, 8; Wallace, *Greek Grammar*, 535; MHT, 3:63.

24. MHT, 3:73.

25. On the force of ἀπό here, see BDF, §211. G. B. Winer, *A Treatise on the Grammar of New Testament Greek, Regarded as a Sure Basis for New Testament Exegesis* (Edinburgh: Clark, 1882), 531, argues that the gen. following ἐκπίπτω indicates that this expression is figurative.

26. See BDAG, 526.

means separation from the one and only salvation, with a sure result of condemnation. There is no possibility for any dual attachment, on the one hand to Christ and on the other to the Law or anything else (Martyn, 471). The phrase τῆς χάριτος ἐξεπέσατε parallels this affirmation and describes this judgment in a slightly different way, explaining it further (Fung, 223). The verb ἐκπίπτω means "to fall," here in the sense of losing status or possession.[27] The referent for the noun τῆς χάριτος is not "grace" generally in the sense of the gracious nature of God's character but that grace that is specifically found in Christ's death and resurrection as it is proclaimed in Paul's apostolic ministry (see Gal 1:6, 15; 2:9, 21). Those who seek to be justified by the Law have fallen away from the only means of salvation available to them through the apostle who proclaimed it.

The verbs here are aor. indic. and as such present some interpretive difficulties. This could reference a true past act, in that the moment of decision to trust circumcision and the Law is the same moment when the person is estranged from Christ. This would fit with the identification of "you who are justified by the Law" as Paul's opponents; they made a choice in the past to trust the Law for justification, and that marked the moment they were cut off from Christ. Given Paul's purpose in the book as a whole to persuade the Galatians against this action, it is possible Paul is speaking dramatically, using a past tense to express a future idea (Bruce, 231; Matera, 182; Witherington, 369).[28] This would be a vivid depiction of a future, eschatological event as a past reality, emphasizing its certain outcome. This is supported by the emphasis on the believer's future expectation Paul makes in v. 5. Zerwick's discussion of this verse argues for the proleptic nature of these verbs but on the grounds that the relative clause has a conditional sense.[29] The conditional nuance for the relative clause is supported by the generalizing nature of ὅστις,[30] but this is mitigated by the order of the clauses and the asyndeton of the phrase. A more appropriate reason for accepting an eschatological interpretation here is the close connection of v. 5 to v. 4 (note the explanatory γάρ). Some have even argued that these verbs are gnomic aorists (so Lenski, 257; Schreiner, 314, who compares v. 2). The proleptic interpretation is most fitting to the context, but it also fits within his sarcastic tone for a rhetorical purpose. Paul makes what appears to be a definitive statement about the future judgment of those who trust in the Law; this serves to warn the Galatians away from that path.

---

27. BDAG, 308.

28. See Wallace, *Greek Grammar*, 563–64, for a discussion of this use of aor. tense, which he terms proleptic.

29. M. Zerwick, *Biblical Greek: Illustrated By Examples*, trans. J. Smith, Scripta Pontificii Instituti Biblici 114 (Rome: Pontifical Biblical Institute, 1963), 85.

30. See Wallace, *Greek Grammar*, 343–45; Robertson, *Grammar*, 960.

5:5 ἡμεῖς γὰρ πνεύματι ἐκ πίστεως ἐλπίδα δικαιοσύνης ἀπεκδεχόμεθα. At this point Paul grounds his argument about the future of those who trust in the Law with compressed, concise arguments about those who have faith in Christ alone. Betz, 262, somewhat overstating the case but not by much, states that this is "a series of dogmatic formulaic expressions, which functions as abbreviations of dogmatic statements" (similarly Soards and Pursiful, 250). Paul certainly gives us a lot to unpack. In context the condemnation of those who seek justification in the Law is contrasted to the confident hope of righteousness for those who are of faith. Even so, there is a sense in which this verse, as others in this section, highlights the argument Paul has been making since 3:1, and it also looks forward to the full discussion of the Spirit to follow (de Boer, 315). The pronoun ἡμεῖς comes first in the sentence, which would be the expected word order, but the contrast with the second-person utterance in the prior verse is striking. The question for interpretation is whether this "we" is inclusive or exclusive. In the context Paul juxtaposes "you who are justified by the Law" (v. 4) with "we" who are "by faith." So likely Paul intends this to be an exclusive "we": On the one hand is Paul and those who are ἐκ πίστεως, whoever they might be, and on the other are those whom he just addressed, who are ἐν νόμῳ, whoever they might be. In this key encouragement Paul shows that he has not given up on any of the Galatians (Lenski, 258). By use of "we" he continues to invite them to return to his gospel.

The dat. noun πνεύματι presents two problems for interpretation, the sense of the dat. case and the referent of the noun. Regarding the case, this noun could be a dat. of sphere, describing the realm in which Paul and those by faith wait, but a more fitting option is dat. of means or instrument, "by the Spirit," describing the means by which they wait.[31] Concerning the referent, this is better construed as a reference to the Holy Spirit (Dunn, 269) than the human spirit (Lenski, 259). This statement as a whole hearkens to Paul's prior emphasis on the importance of the Spirit for essential proof about the spiritual life of the Galatians: The Galatians had indeed received the Spirit through faith (3:1–5), the Spirit is the blessing of Abraham for them (3:14), and the Spirit testifies to their relationship as sons of God (4:6). Paul adds to the important work of the Spirit here by focusing on the Spirit's enablement for believers to properly await their future hope.[32] The prepositional phrase ἐκ πίστεως retains the same meaning as before, that of grounds or means: "on the basis of faith." Paul places it directly after the dat. noun πνεύματι, indicating that πνεύματι ἐκ πίστεως should be understood as a unit, referring to the Spirit received because of faith in Christ (see de Boer, 316–17).

---

31. So MHT, 3:240; Wallace, *Greek Grammar*, 166n77.

32. This is a similar argument to that which Paul makes about the Holy Spirit being the ἀρραβών, the "pledge" or "down payment" for the believer's future redemption in 2 Cor 1:22; 5:5; Eph 1:14.

The final phrase of the verse consists of the dir. obj. then the main verb; we attain better understanding when we address them in reverse order. The verb ἀπεκδεχόμεθα describes the present expectation possessed by those of faith. The midd. voice here is appropriate for this verb, describing the full emotional involvement of the subject in the action. The verb ἀπεκδέχομαι focuses on the confident, future expectation believers have for salvation to be fully extended to them by God through Christ. It embodies the positive outlook believers have toward their eschatology. Although this is the only place ἀπεκδέχομαι occurs in Galatians, Paul uses it elsewhere to refer to future eschatological fulfillment of salvation for believers (see Rom 8:19, 23, 25; 1 Cor 1:7; Phil 3:20). The noun ἐλπίδα is that for which Paul and the Galatians wait. It is modified by the gen. noun δικαιοσύνης, which creates some complexity for how this should be construed. Given the eschatological nuance that ἐλπίς can have in Paul (see Rom 8:24; 12:12; 15:13; Eph 2:12), apposition is preferred with its attendant focus on the future reality (so also Martyn, 472; Schreiner, 316): "the hope, that is, righteousness." This causes δικαιοσύνη to shade almost entirely into its forensic sense (so also Schreiner, 316; *contra* Burton, 278) because it would thus refer to future justification, the declaration by God of the believer's righteous state. Lenski, 259–60, states it with traditional language, but he states it well:

> Now our righteousness is due to the secret verdict pronounced by God in heaven the moment we believe. Our assurance of that secret verdict is the Word of Scripture which we must believe. We await the great hope when, on judgment day, the heavenly Judge will pronounce that verdict face to face with us before the whole universe. Then our great hope of righteousness will be consummated.

Taken with the prior verse, the comparison Paul makes has its full effect: The future condemnation of those who seek justification in the Law is absolutely certain (it can be spoken of in the past tense!) because those who have faith in Christ by means of the Spirit have the confident expectation from their righteous status with God that in the future they will be fully saved and finally vindicated.

5:6 ἐν γὰρ Χριστῷ Ἰησοῦ οὔτε περιτομή τι ἰσχύει οὔτε ἀκροβυστία. In short order Paul offers another tightly worded theological assertion. Logically v. 6 provides the grounds for the two previous sentences in vv. 4–5, which hang together as a unit, the first expressing the terrible end of those who rely on the Law, the second the blessed hope for those who rely on faith. The content of the present verse actually covers both groups to which Paul has recently referred. The nouns περιτομή and ἀκροβυστία would correspond to οἵτινες ἐν νόμῳ δικαιοῦσθε in v. 4 and its attendant emphasis on circumcision as a sign of obedience to the Mosaic covenant, while πίστις δι' ἀγάπης ἐνεργουμένη would correspond to ἡμεῖς ἐκ πίστεως in v. 5, describing their altogether new manner of life. The prepositional phrase ἐν Χριστῷ Ἰησοῦ indicates sphere, that is, the location in which the assertion is true. This tightly encapsulates much of what he has said before, the "in Christ" formula standing in for the larger conception of being a member of God's people, justified through faith in Christ. Paul argued with similar language and concepts before in 3:28.

Paul uses the correlative repetition of οὔτε to deny the efficacy of two separate entities, which in this instance are religious opposites: περιτομή and ἀκροβυστια. Within this context each is multivalent. The initial reference would be the physical status of circumcision and uncircumcision, but this has a broader reference to those ethnic groups characterized by that physical state, namely, Jews and Gentiles. The assertion thus ends up being quite broad: Neither circumcision nor uncircumcision, neither the ethnic status of Jew nor Gentile amount to anything. The verb ἰσχύω here means "to have meaning, be valid, be in force."[33] The pronoun τι is most likely an acc. of reference: "Neither circumcision nor uncircumcision are valid with reference to anything." This statement removes any human status or activity as grounding for the prior eschatological proclamations, and as such is a powerful argument within Paul's arsenal to vacate the arguments of the opponents, who were indeed arguing the value of circumcision and Jewish ethnicity. Paul repudiates fully any physical, ethnic requirement to join the people of God (Burton, 280–81). In Christ circumcision and uncircumcision no longer matter (de Boer, 318). It is important to note that Paul does not invert the argument of his opponents, elevating uncircumcision over circumcision. Rather, he correctly vacates either as having any value in Christ.

ἀλλὰ πίστις δι' ἀγάπης ἐνεργουμένη. The conj. ἀλλά contrasts the ineffectiveness of circumcision and uncircumcision with what is in fact valid. The noun πίστις is the subject of the elided verb ἰσχύει, implied due to the parallelism with the prior half of the sentence. The prepositional phrase δι' ἀγάπης modifies what follows, describing the means by which the action of working is accomplished.[34] What is unclear is whether this refers to the believer's love or God's love. The other occurrences of ἀγάπη in Galatians do not provide clear support for either. This is the first of three times Paul mentions ἀγάπη in the book. The occurrence of the noun in 5:13 in the phrase διὰ τῆς ἀγάπης δουλεύετε ἀλλήλοις is likely anaphoric, referring back to this instance. The context there of serving one another could very well mean love toward other believers here, but this context does not require that meaning. It would be just as logical to argue that the love of God motivates proper service toward others within the believer's freedom. The third occurrence in 5:22, within the list of the fruit of the Spirit, most likely refers to human love given the emphasis on the behaviors that the Spirit generates, but the fruit's genesis with the Spirit means that divine love is never out of sight. The use of the verb ἐνεργέω could help answer the question of which love is in view. The other occurrences of ἐνεργέω in Galatians refer without doubt to

33. BDAG, 484.

34. Robertson, *Grammar*, 583, argues that here means and manner are both in view.

God's work: Gal 2:8 refers to God working equally through Peter and Paul in their respective apostleships, and Gal 3:5 speaks of God working miracles among the Galatians. Pauline usage elsewhere is not completely uniform, but more often than not it refers to God's activity.[35] It is most likely, then, that the ptc. ἐνεργουμένη refers to God's activity (the voice of the ptc. would be pass. in this instance, *contra* most commentators) which energizes and works through faith. This would then mean that ἀγάπη here is God's love, perhaps even more specifically the love of Christ evidenced in his self-sacrifice on the cross (see Gal 2:20), which in turns engenders and works through faith in the individual. The contrast with dependence upon the Law is clear: What matters instead is faith, and faith is energized and actualized through God's love in Christ.

This last phrase of the verse bears an importance inversely proportional to its brevity. The fundamental structure of the spiritual fabric of the universe has changed. Ethnicity—more specifically, association or non-association with Israel—is of no consequence. Circumcision—more specifically, the physical state that marked complete obedience to the Law—or the lack thereof has no value. Instead, what is effective and has value is a response of faith, which finds its genesis in the work of God in the individual through the means of Christ's self-sacrifice on the cross for sin.

Theological Comments

As with other parts of the letter, this short paragraph forms a tight link between what precedes and what follows. It is well known that the letter generally divides into three sections of two chapters each. Following Barrett, George, 350, identifies these sections simply as history, theology, and ethics.[36] Although Martin Dibelius is well known for his argument that NT paraenesis is largely stock material without detailed connection to the setting in which it is found,[37] it is difficult to make that argument here. As with much of Pauline theology, the ethical imperative directed to the Galatians finds its grounding in the theological indicative of what God has done through Christ for the Galatians. Paul states that directly in the succinct first verse of the paragraph; the conj. οὖν carries full logical and rhetorical weight here.

---

35. For places that refer to something other than God's activity, see Rom 7:5 (sin); 2 Cor 1:6 (sufferings); 2 Cor 4:12 (death and life); Eph 2:2 (Satan); 2 Thess 2:7 (power of lawlessness). These exceptions prove the rule here because each pictures something else working upon the individual in view.

36. C. K. Barrett, *Freedom and Obligation: A Study of the Epistle to the Galatians* (Philadelphia: Westminster, 1985), 3.

37. See M. Dibelius, *James*, trans. M. A. WIlliams, Hermeneia (Philadelphia: Fortress, 1975), 2–3.

What is important to catch here is Paul's continued call upon the Galatians. He does not assume that he has won the day and the Galatians are now on his side again such that he can turn to address how they should behave. Rather, this ethical exhortation becomes another facet of his overall strategy to bring the Galatians back to his fold. It is a truism that belief engenders behavior, and in a very real sense Paul spends the central two chapters of Galatians addressing that reality. But it is also true that behavior engenders belief. Thus Paul turns his attention to the behavior of the Galatians, proclaiming a vision of how they should live as those who have faith in Christ as a means to help them return to and strengthen that faith. This helps explain the purpose of the warnings here with their sharp dichotomies: Warnings are a means by which God preserves a believer's faith; salvation is secure, but God uses these as a means to make it secure (Schreiner, 318–20).

The ethical command in this section is short and sweet: "So stand firm and do not be subject again to a yoke of slavery." This is a call to live according to what Christ had accomplished in them. Christ through his sacrifice had freed the Galatians from their prior slavery to demonic forces. Paul intends them to remain in that freedom instead of turning to the Law. What is not specified until later is the contour and shape of that freedom. Paul in no way intends this to be a license for whatever behavior is desired. Instead, as he specifies later in 5:13, the freedom that Christ won serves as a means to build the people of God promised to Abraham. As is commonly said on this point, humans are always in servitude to something; Paul intends here that the Galatians be slaves of Christ, which allows them to be truly free to love one another. The final line of the paragraph emphasizes this point: Their faith will be worked on and worked out through the love of Christ for them.

Application and Devotional Implications

It is often difficult to express concisely the full scope of the Christian life because the biblical expressions of what that life entails are wonderfully pluriform. Even within Paul—a single author!—there are a multitude of portrayals of what God accomplished in Christ for the believer and how the believer should respond. In this short paragraph Paul draws together three threads and weaves them into a strong affirmation of how life with God and Christ is to be lived: The freedom Christ secured in the past for the believer engenders confident hope for the future empowered by faith in Christ in the present.

Paul begins this short paragraph emphasizing freedom. Christ in his death and resurrection completely freed the believer. There is no doubt in Paul's mind that this freedom was truly and finally accomplished. The life of the believer is positionally free, and thus we have a responsibility to guard and maintain that freedom. This is why Paul is so adamant against the Galatians going back to the Law; that would be tantamount to reentering slavery, and it would impugn Christ's work on the cross. Believers are responsible to live out this freedom individually and corporately, so we must avoid any form of slavery. Religious requirements outside of faith alone for acceptance into God's people are anathema. Addictions to substances or experiences that wrest control of the believer away from the Spirit-guided self must be defeated. Freedom is the hallmark of how God promised, how Abraham received the promise, and how all are now incorporated into the promise. Thus freedom must mark everything the believer does: how she acts, how he lives.

A centerpiece of Paul's argument in this chapter is the hope believers have for the future, which contrasts mightily with the sure condemnation those who depend upon the Law can expect. This is not an ambiguous hope that "everything will work out in the end." Rather, this is a specific hope, born out of OT promise and prediction, that God will one day intervene to set things right in the world. And when he does, those who have faith in Christ—those who are righteous in the present time—can expect to be vindicated and glorified with him. This confident expectation for the future of the believer creates a powerful ethical mandate in the present. Many passages in the biblical text connect proper living in the present with our future expectation. When God finally intervenes and Christ returns, as his followers we want to be found living in a way that would please him. So we must not only train our eyes on the future; we must also reflect on how that changes our present.

The freedom that Christ accomplished and the future that believers expect form natural bookends around the faith that Paul preaches, to which he calls the Galatians. The freedom that Christ accomplished in the past is appropriated to the believer through faith in Christ; it is not found by retreating into the Law. The work Christ accomplished on the cross and in his resurrection is realized only when the individual expresses faith in him. The confident hope the believer has for the future is empowered by faith. The present moment holds little proof of the future vindication, so faith is required to see beyond to the final action of God and to make changes in the present to live in accordance with that future. As Paul has argued before in this book, faith is central. It is the pivot point on which the spiritual life rests, and believers should nurture and express it in all facets of their existence.

Additional Exegetical Comments

5:1 F. F. Bruce makes a strong biblical-theological argument for the scope of the freedom the believer now enjoys.[38] The believer is free from the Law, which is most clearly supported from the immediate context. The believer is also free from the στοιχεῖα, supported by the wider argument of chapter

38. F. F. Bruce, " 'Called to Freedom': A Study in Galatians," in *New Testament Age: Essays in Honor of Bo Reicke,* ed. W. C. Weinrich (Macon, GA: Mercer University, 1984), 61–71.

4. The believer is also free from apostolic dictation to be devoted to Christ's gospel only; based upon Paul's curses in 1:8–9, the apostle is only the messenger of Christ when he accurately conveys Christ's gospel. Finally, the believer is free from discrimination, which is supported by the broad message of how the Gentiles are now in the church only because of their faith.

5:2–4 D. H. Fletcher offers a helpful analysis of this passage from the context of the New Perspective on Paul and its emphasis on Jewish identity markers in the context of covenant nomism.[39] The opponents are calling on Gentiles to take up Jewish identity markers in order to be genuine children of Abraham, but this is counter to redemptive history. The Messiah has come and inaugurated a new era of faith and life empowered by the Spirit. Any movement back to the Law is "retrograde redemptive-historical motion."[40]

5:2–4 M. A. Shanks understands these verses in a very specific way: Paul directed them to Gentile men who had already sided with the opponents and were seeking justification through the Law. They had made a profession of sorts, but it was not genuine because they were devoted to a counterfeit gospel, had become opponents of Paul's true gospel, and were not true believers. Consequently Paul referred to them as "false brethren" (2:4).[41]

5:4 George, 360, presents a legitimate way to construe this passage that properly avoids seeing it as speaking about an individual loss of salvation: "Contrary to the Arminian interpretation of this text, Paul did not here contemplate the forfeiture of salvation by a truly regenerated believer. He was writing to Christian churches that were founded on the doctrines of grace but that were in danger of forsaking that sound doctrinal bedrock for a theology that can only lead to ruin." Thus this is a community exhortation, not an individual one.

5:5–6 D. Hunn uses evidence from these verses to support an obj. gen. reading for πίστις Χριστοῦ in Galatians.[42] Her argument is twofold: In this paragraph Paul picks up again the contrast between πίστις and νόμος he developed in chapters 2–3 such that πίστις here is shorthand for πίστις Χριστοῦ there, and πίστις here refers to human faith because it works through human love. This construal supports the obj. gen. reading. I agree with her that the faith Paul mentions here refers to the prior concept; ἐκ πίστεως functions as a shorthand in Paul almost everywhere it occurs, and the prior fuller mentions are the

39. D. H. Fletcher, "Retrograde Redemptive History: The Law in Galatians 5:2–4," *RestQ* 58 (2016): 23–38.
40. Fletcher, "Retrograde Redemptive History," 38.
41. M. A. Shanks, "Galatians 5:2–4 in Light of the Doctrine of Justification," *BSac* 169 (2012): 188–202.
42. D. Hunn, "Πίστις in Galatians 5.5–6: Neglected Evidence for 'Faith in Christ,'" *NTS* 62 (2016): 477–83.

anchor point. However, I do not hold that ἀγάπη here refers to human love, so I cannot support her argument in its entirety.

Selected Bibliography

Barrett, C. K. *Freedom and Obligation: A Study of the Epistle to the Galatians.* Philadelphia: Westminster, 1985.

Bruce, F. F. " 'Called to Freedom': A Study in Galatians." In *New Testament Age: Essays in Honor of Bo Reicke*, ed. W. C. Weinrich, 61–71. Macon, GA: Mercer University, 1984.

Dibelius, M. *James*. Trans. M. A. WIlliams. Rev. by Heinrich Greeven. Hermeneia. Philadelphia: Fortress, 1975.

Fletcher, D. H. "Retrograde Redemptive History: The Law in Galatians 5:2–4." *RestQ* 58 (2016): 23–38.

Hunn, D. "Πίστις in Galatians 5.5–6: Neglected Evidence for 'Faith in Christ.'" *NTS* 62 (2016): 477–83.

Shanks, M. A. "Galatians 5:2–4 in Light of the Doctrine of Justification." *BSac* 169 (2012): 188–202.

The Power of Paul's Persuasion (5:7–12)

Textual Notes

5:7 A few ancient and very important manuscripts (א* A B) lack the article before ἀληθείᾳ in this verse. The absence of the article would give this noun a generic sense: "Who hindered you such that you do not obey truth?" The presence of the article would be anaphoric, contextually connecting this occurrence of ἀληθείᾳ with "the truth of the gospel" in 2:5, 14. On internal grounds the articular reading is preferred. The word ἀληθείᾳ is articular in the prior two occurrences in Galatians, and a specific statement with ultimate reference to the "truth of the gospel" rather than truth generally fits Paul's arguments better, as he is tightly focused on the former in this book. This is not an open and shut case, though, because the longer reading could readily be a clarifying addition.[1] In addition, the manuscripts that lack the article are some of the strongest manuscripts we possess. Ultimately, though, the articular reading is to be preferred: The strength of the evidence that does support the inclusion of the article cannot readily be brushed aside (there is wide geographical distribution of the reading, plus support from important manuscripts) and the internal arguments for it are indeed significant. The brackets around the word in NA[28], indicating the difficulty of the decision, are certainly well earned.

5:9 There is a variant reading here that is fascinating not only for its sense but for its hermeneutic. The reading of the vast majority of manuscripts here is μικρὰ ζύμη ὅλον τὸ φύραμα ζυμοῖ, "A little leaven ferments the whole batch of dough." The Western text and two church fathers (D* lat, Marcion [according to Epiphanius], Lucifer) instead read μικρὰ ζύμη ὅλον τὸ φύραμα δολοῖ, "A little leaven adulterates the whole batch of dough."[2] On both internal and external grounds the former reading is to be preferred. It is internally coherent, and Western readings by themselves cannot often claim originality. The hermeneutic of the reading, however, deserves attention as a clarification of the sense of the original. The original reading ζυμοῖ uses the literal meaning

1. So argued by Burton, 282.

2. See also 1 Cor 5:6, where D makes the same change.

of the verb in a figurative way: The action of yeast rising throughout a batch of dough serves to illustrate the extensive reach of the corrupting teaching against which Paul rails. The reading of the Western text exchanges that figure for the verb δολοῖ, making the implicit meaning of the figure explicit and literal. A reference to adulteration refers directly to the effect of the false teaching upon the Galatians. The short of it is that the variation is an explanation, not just a variation, and a correct one at that.

Translation

7 You were running so well! Who hindered you such that you do not obey
the truth?[3] **8** This persuasion is not from the one who called you. **9** A little
yeast makes the whole batch of dough rise.[4] **10** I am convinced for you in
the Lord that you will think nothing else, but the one who confuses you,
whoever that may be, will bear his judgment. **11** Now I, brothers and sisters,[5]
if I still preach circumcision, why am I still persecuted? The offense[6] of the
cross would thus be removed. **12** I wish those who trouble you would even
mutilate themselves![7]

Commentary

Because of the emotion on display in this letter, Paul's train of thought is not as precise as we might like. There are times both within the flow of individual paragraphs and within the broader arrangement of thought that disjunction seems the best explanation. Paul's meaning is never lost, however, because disjunctions that shock the readers are part and parcel of Paul's argument. They serve well his desire to motivate the Galatians to different beliefs and behavior than what they exhibit currently. The present paragraph is just such a disjunction. This is the emotional zenith of the letter, and thus disjunction and emotion present themselves in numerous ways throughout. The overall

3. The NIV has a more formal translation ("Who cut in on you?") instead of a more functional one like most English translations.

4. I have followed the NET here with a functional translation. Other translations are more formal, e.g., CSB "A little leaven leavens the whole batch of dough."

5. Here I follow recent scholarship that sees the pl. ἀδελφοί as referring to all members of the group regardless of sex; see BDAG, 18.

6. NASB retains the traditional translation "stumbling block."

7. Paul's language here makes for difficult translation, as he speaks rather periphrastically: "I wish those who trouble you would even cut off!" Translations vary in their specificity: "I wish those agitators would go so far as to castrate themselves!" (NET; cf. NRSV); "I wish those who unsettle you would emasculate themselves!" (ESV; cf. NIV); "I wish that those who are troubling you would even mutilate themselves" (NASB; cf. CSB, NLT).

flow of the argument shows this paragraph to be "a personal parenthesis" (George, 363). Paul wants to transition to a new section in which ethics and behavior are front and center (see 5:1, 13), but before he begins the full discussion of how his gospel should affect the behavior of the Galatians, he rails once more at the incongruity of their turn toward the Law and the dire straits of those who are influencing them in that direction. Indeed, in a vein similar to the judgment he called down upon the opponents in 1:8–9, here he wishes that they would mutilate themselves, thus cutting them off completely from what they regard to be their salvation. But the emotion shows as well in Paul's grammar and syntax. This section lacks conjunctions and particles, making it into a series of short, staccato sentences (Longenecker, 230; Dunn, 273; Moo, 332). These are signs that Paul's emotions are running high, and what he writes should be interpreted in that light.

In the letter Paul's attention is most usually on the Galatians, and properly so, as his goal is to motivate them away from the Law-observant stance they were adopting under the influence of the opponents. On occasion, however, Paul's attention falls on the opponents. He never addresses them directly (save perhaps in Gal 5:4, but this would also include Galatian believers who had fully given themselves over to the opponents' teaching), but here he takes them head-on in the most direct attack in the epistle.[8] This paragraph is the culmination of his feelings about the opponents, and as he makes clear in 5:12, his wish for them, given the difficulty they caused among those who accepted Paul's gospel, is for self-mutilation, which is tantamount to self-destruction. As such, this paragraph serves as an implicit encouragement to the Galatians to resist them and their teaching (Schreiner, 321).

5:7 Paul begins this paragraph with an utterance about the past state of the Galatians. This comment was brought on by the closing remark of v. 6: The only thing that matters is "faith energized through love." This made Paul remember previously when the Galatians had indeed been motivated by that faith, not a desire to become circumcised. Thus he reminisces about their prior devotion, seeking to find those who were responsible for the change as a rhetorical means to make the Galatians face their disobedience. This in turns puts his attention on the opponents in this paragraph. He does not address them directly, but they are the subject of this discourse, and Paul may have even have stated these things knowing that the opponents would have been in the midst of the Galatian churches when the letter was read aloud. So grammatically Paul addresses the Galatians with reference to the opponents, but rhetorically the opponents are in his sights.

Ἐτρέχετε καλῶς. The verb τρέχω means "to run" or "make progress," and it is a frequent Pauline image.[9] Paul uses this metaphor for his own ministry

---

8. He discusses them again in 6:12–13, where his intention is to summarize the situation, given the function of 6:11–18 as a synopsis of the book.

9. BDAG, 1015.

earlier in the book (Gal 2:2; cf. Phil 2:16) and elsewhere for obedient living as a believer (1 Cor 9:24, 26). Here it is a metaphor for the Galatians' proper response to Paul's preaching of the gospel, and perhaps even their growth in Christ engendered by that response. The verb ἐτρέχετε is impf., indicating a progressive action in the past. This partly explains Paul's emotions here: The Galatians had indeed followed Paul's gospel beyond their moment of conversion, perhaps even for quite a while (Dunn, 273). That they would turn away now was disheartening.[10] The adv. καλῶς describes the manner in which the Galatians were running. Before the difficulties in Galatia, the Galatians were running well; they were responding properly to Paul's gospel. Something had changed, and Paul turns to address the source of that change head-on.

τίς ὑμᾶς ἐνέκοψεν τῇ ἀληθείᾳ μὴ πείθεσθαι; Paul does not address the change in the Galatians' stance toward him and his gospel as a matter of either doctrine or belief. Rather, he addresses the source as a person. This issue is intensely personal for Paul, and the doctrine espoused cannot be divorced from the persons who were its source. This question boldly asks about the identity of those who hindered the Galatians from continuing in their dedication to the gospel. If this is a rhetorical question, which is likely, its use would not necessarily imply that Paul did not know his opponents or who was presently preaching to the Galatians. Paul instead wants to highlight them among the Galatians in contrast to himself. To extend the metaphor, Paul had started the Galatians on this race. He had preached Christ to them and started them running after him. Someone had hindered them on this road, and Paul wants their identity among the Galatians to be fully exposed so the contrast between them is clearly evident. The main verb ἐνέκοψεν means "to make progress slow or difficult."[11] This fits quite naturally with the image of running from the first clause. The aor. indic. naturally implies a past action, especially in conj. with the impf. verb of the prior clause. The Galatians had been running well and then someone hindered them. The verb fits the metaphor of running a race, as it suggests one runner pushing in front of or tripping another (Longenecker, 230; Dunn, 274). The inf. phrase τῇ ἀληθείᾳ μὴ πείθεσθαι indicates the result of the action of the main verb:

10. This is supported by the interpretation of οὕτως ταχέως as referring to the speed with which the Galatians turned, not the brevity of the interval between their conversion and defection.

11. BDAG, 274. G. Stählin, "ἐγκοπή, ἐγκόπτω," *TDNT*, 3:855, states that this verb takes this meaning "from the military practice of making slits in the street to hold up a pursuing enemy." This would fit from the etymology of the word: ἐν + κόπτω, "in" + "cut." The etymology of the word is clear enough that Hays, 315, argues for a double entendre here: "The Missionaries have 'cut in' on them by demanding to cut the flesh of their foreskins."

"Who hindered you with the result that you do not obey the truth?"[12] The pres. tense of the inf. is progressive; the pass. voice focuses on the complete persuasion of the subject.[13] The dat. noun τῇ ἀληθείᾳ indicates the thing followed or obeyed. Here it is not truth generally that is in view. Rather, the article is anaphoric, referring back to the longer phrases ἡ ἀλήθεια τοῦ εὐαγγελίου (Gal 2:5) and τὴν ἀλήθειαν τοῦ εὐαγγελίου (Gal 2:14). The arrangement of the tenses in this question powerfully demonstrates the change that took place in the lives of the Galatians: They were running well in the past, but someone hindered them in the past at a specific point with the result that now they do not presently obey the truth.

The πείθω word group takes on heightened importance in this paragraph.[14] The verb has a broad semantic domain, ranging from convincing or persuading with a mental result ("believe"), to convincing so that trust and confidence is the result ("trust"), to the action that flows from belief and trust ("obey").[15] In this verse the negated inf. μὴ πείθεσθαι describes the current behavior of the Galatians. Paul references their prior mode of life as a whole with the verb ἐτρέχετε; with the inf. he does the same thing with added emphasis upon the belief and trust that underlies their behavior (similarly Moo, 333). The related noun πεισμονή occurs in v. 8 and describes similarly their persuasion to the resultant behavior as a single idea. Then Paul uses the pf. verb πέποιθα in v. 10 to describe his own conviction about the Galatians. In essence Paul says that the Galatians had been improperly persuaded to a new course of action, yet he himself is persuaded that they will eventually return to his way of thinking. This highlights the important goal in the ancient world of persuading others. The entire goal of the rhetorical enterprise was to convince others with appropriate arguments. Paul had originally persuaded the Galatians, but someone came along later and persuaded them differently. Paul now seeks to reverse that damage by persuading them again to his way of thinking.

5:8 ἡ πεισμονὴ οὐκ ἐκ τοῦ καλοῦντος ὑμᾶς. Paul affirms the reality of the Galatians' current state of conviction about circumcision, condemning both the Galatians and the ones who persuaded them. The function of this

---

12. D. B. Wallace, *Greek Grammar Beyond the Basics: An Exegetical Syntax of the New Testament* (Grand Rapids: Zondervan, 1996), 109, implies that the inf. is a gen. of separation, but lacking the article this is a difficult determination. See as well Wallace, *Greek Grammar*, 664, where he give this as an example of the inf. of result.

13. See BDAG, 792, where the pass. voice is identified with the meaning "obey, follow." This implies that the subject has been completely persuaded. See also Wallace, *Greek Grammar*, 416.

14. Paul had used the verb πείθω before in Gal 1:10 to refer to his own acts of persuasion. They were directed to men, not God, because God is already convinced of the rightness of Paul's preaching and actions.

15. BDAG, 791–92.

utterance, however, is not simply to condemn. Paul maintains his goal of effecting a return to his gospel by emphasizing the divine action of God in continuing to call the Galatians. The noun πεισμονή is cognate to the verb πείθω, which occurs in the prior verse as an inf. The action referred to by the noun could be active or passive. If active, it points to the act of persuasion and would refer to the opponents. If passive, it points to the state of being persuaded and would refer to the Galatians. The latter is simpler, given Paul's reference to the Galatians in the prior verse (Lightfoot, 206), but the former aligns well with the active calling of God (Fung, 236). Both make sense in the context (de Boer, 320), however, and it is not unreasonable in this instance to think Paul had both in mind: The Galatians were persuaded to a different view only because the opponents had actively persuaded them. The article with πεισμονή is anaphoric (Burton, 282; Moo, 333), pointing back to the effect wrought in the Galatians by the opponents mentioned in the prior verse. A translation that brings out this understanding is "this persuasion" (so NET "This persuasion"; cf. NRSV "Such persuasion"; NIV "That kind of persuasion"). The verbal link between πείθεσθαι and πεισμονή is difficult to bring out in English, but it would have been clear to Paul's audience. The emphasis falls on what Paul asserts regarding the source of this persuasion: It is "not from the one who calls you." The phrase ἐκ τοῦ καλοῦντας ὑμᾶς hearkens back to the phrase ἀπὸ τοῦ καλέσαντος ὑμᾶς in Gal 1:6. There the phrase referred to God the Father's action of calling the Galatians to himself through the preaching of the gospel of Christ to the Galatians by Paul; the aor. tense pointed to the past action of Paul's proclamation. Here the ptc. is pres. tense, showing that God continues to call to the Galatians in the present time (*contra* commentators who argue that the pres. tense is used to refer to God's person rather than his action; see Lightfoot, 206; Dunn, 275). Even though the Galatians had turned from Paul's gospel and ultimately from God himself, God continues to call them to return to him, to turn away from the preaching of Paul's opponents (similarly de Boer, 320–21; Soards and Pursiful, 255). This is both a powerful statement on the one hand about God's unfailing love and devotion to those whom he calls and on the other hand to his working through Paul in the present moment to bring the Galatians back to himself. In essence, Paul pronounces judgment again upon the opponents (Schreiner, 324). Neither their passion nor their success in Galatia automatically means they are on God's side.

5:9 μικρὰ ζύμη ὅλον τὸ φύραμα ζυμοῖ. With this short, gnomic statement Paul describes in no uncertain terms the danger in which the Galatians find themselves. The statement itself is not difficult to understand: It is a pithy proverb about how yeast leavens a whole batch of dough. Burton, 283, argues that the main verb ζυμοῖ is progressive, pointing to progress made among the Galatians by the opponents, but a simpler solution given the content is to see it as gnomic. The point of the image is twofold. First, yeast itself was a common symbol for something evil or pernicious (Lightfoot, 206;

Longenecker, 231; Dunn, 275; Soards and Pursiful, 256).[16] Thus Paul warns the Galatians against something evil in their midst. Second, there is a powerful contrast between the adjectives μικρά and ὅλον with an emphasis on an unpredictable, outsized effect. Even though the amount of yeast used in baking is small, it thoroughly affects everything it touches. It is unclear whether Paul intends for this image to refer to the teaching of the opponents or to the opponents themselves. The latter could be preferred based on the parallel with 1 Cor 5:6 (Lightfoot, 206) and the personal focus of the paragraph (Moo, 334), while the former could be preferred based on Paul's desire to keep his gospel pure (Dunn, 276).[17] A reference to the teaching is also in keeping with the metaphor itself: It is more feasible that Paul would have described the teaching of circumcision as small in influence but huge in result given his emphasis elsewhere on the attendant requirement of Law observance it would bring. The opponents themselves were likely regarded as influential and would not fit this image. So with this timeless expression Paul expresses the danger of the teaching the Galatians had embraced. He wants to keep the Galatians from compartmentalizing or minimizing the teaching of the opponents. Presumably the Galatians could have thought, or been taught, that this teaching did not affect in any substantial way their standing before God. It was only the single, simple matter of behavior or covenant sign that needed to be obeyed but did not substantially change their relationship to Abraham, Christ, or God. Paul refuses to allow anything like that line of thinking. The "small" matter of obedience to circumcision would have a deleterious effect on everything, and thus this teaching, however, small or insignificant on the surface, must be decidedly rejected. Although Paul does not state this, surely he must have in mind the way the Jews in Antioch and even Barnabas were persuaded away from the truth because of Peter's behavior (see Gal 2:13). This would have been a real, painful memory of the infectious nature of the opponents' teaching. Paul wanted to warn the Galatians away from that terrible effect in no uncertain terms.

5:10 ἐγὼ πέποιθα εἰς ὑμᾶς ἐν κυρίῳ ὅτι. Paul never once settled to leave the Galatians in condemnation, to languish in their state of disobedience. His entire argument seeks to motivate them to return to where they were, accepting his gospel and relying upon faith alone for membership in the family of Abraham. The verse, on the heels of a stinging statement about the danger of the teaching they had potentially accepted, acts like a helping hand to lift the Galatians back to solid ground. The utterance consists of a metacomment

16. *Contra* Moo, 334, who argues that the aphorism itself is neutral, but Paul uses it to refer to something evil.

17. In the parallel of 1 Cor 5:6 Paul refers to the sexual sin of an individual whom the church had left unpunished. His point is essentially the same: Sin left unchecked will thoroughly infect the church, which is contrary to its nature as the body of Christ, our Passover lamb.

followed by the content about which Paul is convinced. The metacomment itself expresses Paul's confidence in the Galatians' ultimate return, which contrasts with the negative persuasion of the Galatians by the unnamed opponents mentioned in 5:7–8. In the metacomment Paul uses the personal pronoun ἐγώ to identify himself emphatically (Lightfoot, 206), even though that was not technically required either by syntax or context. In this epistle any 1 sg. verb would clearly refer to Paul. Thus this use of the pronoun is a further emphasis upon himself as a source of authority for the Galatians. The verb πέποιθα hearkens back to the cognate words earlier in this paragraph. This form is a pf. indic. with present force (so also Lenski, 267); the emphasis is on Paul's present state of being convinced.[18] The prep. εἰς functions to indicate a point of reference for the verb.[19] Thus Paul indicates that he is convinced with regard to the Galatians, but the source of his confidence is elsewhere. The prepositional phrase ἐν κυρίῳ indicates sphere and thus the basis for Paul's confidence (Soards and Pursiful, 256): "In the Lord"—that is, in Christ (Burton, 285)—is the realm in which Paul is convinced. This makes his statement of confidence a proclamation of faith in the power of Christ to keep those who are his. The ὅτι concludes the metacomment, pointing forward to the facts of which Paul is convinced.

οὐδὲν ἄλλο φρονήσετε. This phrase is the first fact of which Paul is convinced. It is a predictive statement, implying that ultimately the Galatians will return to a proper way of thinking. This confidence flows naturally from Paul's confidence in Christ that he expressed in the preceding metacomment. Exactly what this thinking is in context is unclear. It could refer to the statements Paul makes in the immediate context regarding the improper persuasion of the opponents, but it could also refer to the global point about their attitude toward Paul's gospel. The former is simpler given the emphasis Paul makes about the opponents here, but their ultimate stance toward the gospel is certainly in view, too. It is hard to unravel the persuasion of the opponents from the Galatians' changed attitude toward the gospel. In any case, Paul is confident that in the Lord the Galatians will ultimately agree with him, and not the opponents, about his gospel. As Bruce, 235, states, Paul understands the logic of the gospel: If the Galatians have truly believed it, they will ultimately think as he does about it. Even more so, Paul was convinced of the transforming power of Christ's life through the gospel (2:19–20). If the Galatians have experienced it, and they have as the work of the Spirit in their midst proves (3:1–5), then Christ will have his ultimate effect in them by keeping them secure (see also George, 366).

ὁ δὲ ταράσσων ὑμᾶς βαστάσει τὸ κρίμα, ὅστις ἐὰν ᾖ. This sentence is the second fact of which Paul is convinced. The subst. ptc. ὁ ταράσσων hearkens

18. See Wallace, *Greek Grammar*, 579–80, for discussion of this use of the pf.

19. See BDAG, 291, for this use. Robertson, *Grammar*, 540, argues that the prepositional phrase εἰς ὑμᾶς here indicates the dir. obj., which is another legitimate construal.

back to the prior use of the verb in Gal 1:7, where those who disturb the Galatians were also "the ones who want to distort the gospel of Christ." The pl. use there confirms that the sg. here is generic (Bruce, 235–36). Paul identifies the opponents here by their effect on the Galatians vis-à-vis his gospel, which was in no way good. The verb βαστάσει is fut., parallel to φρονήσετε, and expresses the second fact Paul is confident will occur in the future. The verb βαστάζω generally means to bear or carry. In this instance, because of the dir. obj. κρίμα, an abstract noun, the idea of carrying would be figurative. This is the only occurrence of τὸ κρίμα in the book, although the concept of judgment occurs earlier in 1:8–9 through the use of ἀνάθεμα, and Paul regularly implies that he himself has rendered judgment upon the opponents. Together the verb βαστάσει and the obj. κρίμα imply the certainty of judgment upon those who trouble the Galatians.[20] Whether this judgment is immediate or eschatological is unclear. The presence of the article would favor the latter interpretation (Longenecker, 232), as would Paul's stark statements in 1:8–9. Paul makes clear in no uncertain terms the danger the opponents are in. What follows is an indefinite relative clause, ὅστις ἐὰν ᾖ, reinforcing the generic nature of ὁ ταράσσων. The combination of ὅστις and ἐάν makes the statement quite indefinite.[21] The sense is "whoever it may be."[22] This phrase could be a rhetorical move on Paul's part. He refuses to acknowledge the identity of the opponents in a bid to reduce their influence over the Galatians (so also Longenecker, 232).

5:11 This verse marks a difficult parenthesis in Paul's argument in this paragraph. If this sentence were absent, Paul's statement about the certainty of future judgment for the agitators would lead naturally into Paul's wish that they would mutilate themselves in v. 12. Instead, Paul inserts a short argument about circumcision, persecution, and the offense of the cross, difficult not only for the way it fits into the present argument but also for the implied logic of its parts. It is generally agreed by most commentators that Paul here reacts against something the opponents have said about him to the Galatians, but what exactly they said is open to debate. The most logical option within the history of discussion is that the opponents challenged Paul with reference to some inconsistency on his part relative to preaching circumcision. Everyone knew that Paul had been an ardent, pious Pharisee before his conversion; the question is his present approach to circumcision in light of his past. Thus the critique could relate to Paul's general acceptance of Jewish believers maintaining a Jewish lifestyle or his own personal conduct as a Jew (Longenecker, 232), or even the validity of preaching the gospel among the Jews at all (de Boer, 323). If Paul wrote to the Galatians

20. See BDAG, 171, which states that βαστάζω with κρίμα means "must pay the penalty."
21. See BDAG, 729.
22. BDF, §303.

after the events of Acts 16:3, when he had Timothy circumcised, this charge of inconsistency would be quite potent (Rapa, 623; Bruce, 236). Even if Paul wrote Galatians before Acts 16:3, it could indicate his normal practice with regard to Jewish Christians (Schreiner, 326; Moo, 336), which could have been widely known. In any case, the tenor of the statement makes clear that Paul accepts nothing of the sort. As he has just said in the first part of this chapter, neither circumcision nor uncircumcision is anything. Where he may have acted in liberty, the opponents are making a requirement (Lenski, 268–69; Fung, 240). He uses his own personal history of persecution for the cross to affirm his constancy on this matter.

ἐγὼ δέ, ἀδελφοί, εἰ περιτομὴν ἔτι κηρύσσω, τί ἔτι διώκομαι; The subject matter changes from that for which Paul is confident in the future to a rhetorical question about the source of Paul's persecution. This statement is a condition with the protasis contained within the apodosis. Paul again uses the pronoun ἐγώ and the noun ἀδελφοί, a nom. for voc., to identify and emphasize himself and his readers as a coherent group, distinct from the opponents. Paul begins the protasis of the conditional sentence with the particle εἰ, marking this as a first class condition, essentially assumed true for the sake of the argument.[23] The adv. ἔτι implies a temporal continuation of the action of the verb, perhaps beyond what was expected. In other words, the "if" clause posits that some aspect of his prior favor toward circumcision has carried over into his present ministry. Paul used the verb κηρύσσω previously in 2:2 within the specific context of his proclamation to the Gentiles; that audience would be implied here as well. Thus the sense of the protasis is "If I am still preaching [at present] circumcision [to you Gentiles]." The apodosis is short and succinct. The pronoun τί here means "why?" asking for the grounds for the present circumstance. The adv. ἔτι modifies the verb διώκομαι, here emphasizing a logical inference.[24] The verb διώκομαι is either progressive or customary, implying the action of persecution occurs in the present time; the pass. voice shows Paul to be the recipient of the persecution. Thus the sense of the apodosis is "then why am I being persecuted [at present]?" It is difficult to tell whether the persecution in view is actual physical violence against Paul or whether it is resistance to his gospel (de Boer, 323),

---

23. BDF, §372(3), argues that here εἰ has encroached upon the domain of ἐάν for the sake of "vivid presentation," presumably expecting instead a third class condition on the grounds that Paul would want to distance himself even more noticeably from the idea of preaching circumcision. A possible implication of the first class condition, here with the adv. ἔτι, is that Paul did indeed once preach circumcision in the same way as his opponents. Paul never describes his former life in this fashion, and thus this must be taken not as a necessary implication of the grammatical construction. It is correct that the εἰ does make for vivid presentation, but one need not argue that Paul's ultimate intention is an unreal condition.

24. BDAG, 400.

but without doubt the Galatians would have understood and this statement would have had its effect upon them.

The force of the protasis in a first class condition is assumed true for the sake of argument.[25] The sense of the statement can be expanded as follows: "If I am still preaching circumcision—and let's assume that I am indeed doing that—then why am I persecuted now?" Implied underneath this condition is the warrant for the question: Those who preach circumcision are not persecuted. The conclusion that Paul wants his readers to make is that he is in fact not preaching circumcision, the warrant for which is that Paul is presently persecuted. The relation of protasis to apodosis here is evidence-inference,[26] but in this instance it implicitly contrasts a hypothetical with the actual present circumstance. The hypothetical is that Paul still preaches circumcision. If that were so, then there would be no grounds for his present circumstance of persecution. This implies that Paul sees a different grounds for his present circumstance, which then leads to the conclusion of this sentence.

ἄρα κατήργηται τὸ σκάνδαλον τοῦ σταυροῦ. The conj. *ἄρα* positions this as a logical inference from the prior conditional sentence. Here the logical deduction proceeds from the hypothetical implication of the prior sentence: If Paul were preaching circumcision, then his persecution would be removed. The conj. *ἄρα* links the hypothetical removal of persecution to a hypothetical negation of the scandal of the cross, which Paul immediately and completely rejects as untenable. Paul implicitly ties his present state of being persecuted to the offense of the cross that arises through his preaching of the gospel. The verb *κατήργηται* is pf., focusing on the present results of this hypothetical situation. This noun *σκάνδαλον* and the related verb *σκανδαλίζω* do not occur outside Jewish or Christian authors.[27] The noun can mean a literal trap or snare, and this is extended figuratively to mean a temptation or offense.[28] Paul uses it here to refer to the source of the persecution that he endures for his preaching of the gospel: It is the offense that his message of a crucified Messiah causes. Within the context of Galatians "the offense of the cross" points to the natural Jewish reaction to recoil both from crucifixion of the Messiah as under a curse and from any message that negates adherence to the Law (see Betz, 270; Oakes, 165), in other words, a reliance not upon any personal action but only on grace and faith (Moo, 337). The sense of this statement in conj. with the prior would be as follows: "In light of this hypothetical removal of persecution, which would come if I indeed preach circumcision, the inference is that the offense of the cross would be removed." Since Paul is indeed persecuted, the Galatians can infer that he is not preaching circumcision, and thus the scandal of the cross is affirmed in Paul's life and ministry in stark contrast to the opponents.

25. Wallace, *Greek Grammar*, 690.

26. See Wallace, *Greek Grammar*, 682–84, for discussion.

27. *NIDNTTE*, 4:296.

28. See LSJ, 1604; MGS, 1920; LEH, 2:427; BDAG, 926.

5:12 ὄφελον καὶ ἀποκόψονται οἱ ἀναστατοῦντες ὑμᾶς. The asyndeton of this sentence marks its emotion. With this sentence Paul expresses a strong wish regarding his opponents, effectively pronouncing judgment on them all over again. Although ὄφελον originally derived from the verb ὀφείλω, "I owe, I am obligated," in the NT it is essentially a fixed form used to express a wish. Whether this introduces an attainable or unattainable wish is open to debate. BDAG argues that ὄφελον is "a fixed form, functioning as a particle to introduce unattainable wishes."[29] BDF argues differently that the wish is indeed attainable.[30] In this instance, the attainability of the wish does not change the essential force of the construction, which serves primarily to express Paul's final thoughts on those who are troubling the Galatians. The conj. *καί* functions intensively and could be translated as "even." The fut. tense verb is an anomaly—a secondary tense is the norm—and indicates either present or future time. The midd. tense of the verb could be causative,[31] but Paul much more likely intends this to be a dir. midd: "Would that they castrate themselves!"[32] The subst. ptc. οἱ ἀναστατοῦντες is the subject of the verb and has its own dir. obj. in ὑμᾶς. The pres. tense of the ptc. points to the action of the opponents in the present time in the midst of the Galatians.

Paul uses the verb ἀποκόπτω in Gal 5:12 to describe what he wishes those who are troubling the Galatians would do to themselves. Without doubt this is strong language, expressing something that strikes the contemporary reader as revolting: "I wish those agitators would go so far as to cut off their own genitals!" This emotional utterance expresses Paul's frustration in no uncertain terms. To put it bluntly, why stop with just the foreskin? If cutting off a part of the body is what God wants, go all the way and cut off the entire body part! Beneath the emotion, however, is subtle rhetoric on Paul's part; it is in a sense a valid *reductio ad absurdum* because it shows self-mutilation to be the logical end result of allowing circumcision to be the entrée into God's people.[33] The problem here is not in the self-mutilation itself, which is abhorrent, but the spiritual result it brings. The word ἀποκόπτω is the same one used in the Septuagint to describe particular men who were prohibited from entering the assembly because of injury or harm to their sexual organs: "A eunuch or man with severed genitals may not enter the assembly of the Lord" (Deut 23:2 LXX [23:1 ET]). Two groups are described here, the first

---

29. BDAG, 743. See also Zerwick, *Biblical Greek*, 123, who says it indicates "a desire possible of attainment but not seriously entertained." Cf. MHT, 1:201.

30. See BDF, §384, which says, "ὄφελον (s. §359(1)) is used with the future indicative for an attainable wish: G 5:12 ὄφελον καὶ ἀποκόψονται (-ψωνται 𝔓[46]DEFG) οἱ ἀναστατοῦντες ὑμᾶς 'would that they would go ahead and castrate themselves.' " Cf. Burton, *Syntax*, 13.

31. So BDF, §317; Robertson, *Grammar*, 809; Wallace, *Greek Grammar*, 424.

32. So Zerwick, *Biblical Greek*, 75.

33. Dunn, 284, also views this as a *reductio ad absurdum*, but he sees the additional cutting as accidental, while I see Paul's point as satirical.

with the noun θλαδίας, "eunuch," and the second with ἀποκεκομμένος, a pf. ptc. from ἀποκόπτω. With this word linkage, Paul makes his point: Requiring circumcision in obedience to the Law is a self-defeating proposition. It leads only to self-mutilation, which restricts one from fulfilling the Law. Circumcision is ultimately a dead end. Those who emphasize circumcision for the Galatians essentially ensure that the Galatians will never be able to fulfill the Law! It is only faith in Christ that leads to fulfillment and freedom; anything else is ultimately self-destructive. For that reason the message of circumcision preached by those who trouble the Galatians should be rejected.

This paragraph is the last one in which Paul references his opponents in any way until the epilogue in 6:11–18. The strong language here shows in no uncertain terms Paul's assessment of the opponents. They are condemned in his sight for several reasons: They hindered the Galatians from properly following Paul's preaching of the gospel of Christ. Their teaching is infectious, extensively affecting both the individual and the congregation. They have a sure punishment coming from the Lord. Their doctrine ultimately is self-defeating. Paul in no way wants to join in their preaching, even though it would mean that the persecution he experiences would lessen. The cost would be too great because it would remove the offense of the cross, which is the very nature of the gospel message. Thus Paul speaks starkly against the opponents, expressing their certain state as judged by God.

Theological Comments

In the book of Galatians Paul freely condemns those who work counter to his purposes. The basis for this judgment is always his calling by God to preach Christ to the Gentiles. His opponents hinder that mission by perverting the gospel at its root; consequently they stand condemned in Paul's eyes. Paul's condemnation of the opponents never arises from personal animus. Paul quickly puts aside his own aspirations and goals, making them subservient to God's. His condemnation of the opponents is always apostolic: It flows out of his role as an apostle appointed by God. Those who oppose him ultimately oppose God, which is the ultimate issue. Their opposition to Paul is the presenting issue; their opposition to God is the foundational issue. In this passage the central data relative to this argument is found in Gal 5:8: "This persuasion is not from the one who calls you." Here Paul offers a summary assessment about the teaching of his opponents: They have convinced the Galatians contrary to God's will. God himself calls the Galatians to return to him through Paul's pleading; the opponents have thwarted that. Thus Paul condemns them because they work counter to God's purposes as revealed in Paul.

When Paul speaks of his own stance vis-à-vis the opponents by discussing his present persecution, he ultimately lands on his commitment to the message of the crucified Messiah, a commitment he will maintain at all costs. He uses the intriguing phrase τὸ σκάνδαλον τοῦ σταυροῦ to encapsulate that idea. As discussed in the commentary, the Greek word *σκάνδαλον* means a trap, an enticement to sin. Paul's wording gets to the fundamental nature of the cross, which as a figure refers to the fact that the one now proclaimed as Messiah was crucified there. The cross assaults the sensibilities; it cannot be understood rationally. Without faith those who contemplate it reject it, falling into error. The crucifixion of the Messiah is a contradiction in terms, and as such it provokes offense and stumbling. Essentially Paul here reflects on the effect his preaching of Christ crucified has upon those Jewish Christians who still proclaim circumcision. A comparison to 1 Cor 1:23 is significant, as there Paul addresses the contrary reception the cross receives among Jews and Gentiles: "we preach about a crucified Christ, a stumbling block to Jews and foolishness to Gentiles" (NET).[34] Within the present context in Galatians, Paul focuses only on the Jewish side of the equation, which fits well with his overall purpose to show that the Gentiles are included now within God's family on equal footing with Jews. This provides as well an appropriate context for his argument against adopting a pro-circumcision stance. If he were to do that and thus remove the offense to the Jews, then the offense of the cross would disappear. Thus "the offense of the cross" is such explicitly because it no longer requires circumcision, that is, that which marks Jews *qua* Jews.

Application and Devotional Implications

A common theme within the NT and other early Christian literature is the danger of false teaching. Paul was not the only one to face this issue in ministry or to address it in writing, although some of his writings on this topic are the most well known. In the Olivet Discourse Jesus warned of false Christs and false prophets (Matt 24:24; Mark 13:21). Peter devotes the entirety of the second chapter in his second letter to the character, teaching, and future judgment of the false teachers who will arise in the church. This material in 2 Peter is mirrored in Jude, where the entire central argument of the epistle is against these false teachers. Polycarp warns his readers against false teaching (Pol. *Phil.* 7:2), and the entirety of Did. 11 is a warning against false teachers with instruction on how to identify them. It is a common theme in early Christian literature that believers recognize and refute false teaching and teachers. Paul deals with that reality head-on in the book of Galatians, and the paragraph in Gal 5:7–12 contains his most pointed, confrontational words on this matter.

From this admonition against false teachers come two applications for the believer. The first application requires alignment of behavior and doctrine. The believer must seek both to believe and behave in accordance with the truth. The falsity of the teaching against which the early church wrote is not limited to doctrinal matters; it is often a matter of behavior. In

34. While *σκάνδαλον* is applied to Jews, the different term *μωρία* is applied to Gentiles.

a practical way, this is the situation Paul faced. Likely he and his opponents would agree that Jesus is the Messiah, that he was crucified and rose again on the third day. The difference was that their behavior—dependence upon and promotion of circumcision specifically and the Law more generally—was in conflict with that doctrine. The believer who seeks to follow Christ in all things must analyze his behavior as closely as he examines his doctrine. Did. 11:10 speaks to this well: "But any prophet teaching the truth, if he does not do what he teaches, he is a false prophet." One can teach the truth, but still be false if behavior does not match.

The second application arises from a proper understanding of the function of Paul's language. In this paragraph Paul speaks as an apostle appointed by God, called directly by him to share the gospel of Christ among the Gentiles. His words come not only from his heart but from his office. As such, Paul's words carry great weight. But we cannot directly imitate Paul's stance or take up his apostolic mantle to pass judgment on false teachers. In applying this passage, we do not share Paul's office. Rather, we imitate the role of the Galatians. Our responsibility is to hear Paul's words in Scripture and measure teaching against them. We cannot know directly as Paul did, without intermediary, that false teaching "is not from the one who calls you" (Gal 5:8). We only know this by careful examination and understanding of the Scripture that God has given us. Our responsibility is to measure teaching against the standard of the biblical text and by so doing discern that which is true and that which is false, embracing the former and rejecting the latter. Paul states this idea himself more fully in 2 Tim 2:24–26:

> And the Lord's slave must not engage in heated disputes but be kind toward all, an apt teacher, patient, correcting opponents with gentleness. Perhaps God will grant them repentance and then knowledge of the truth and they will come to their senses and escape the devil's trap where they are held captive to do his will.

Additional Exegetical Comments

5:12 George, 372, regards this as a reference to Deut 23:2 (23:1 ET) on the basis of the phrase ἐκκλησίαν κυρίου used there. This connection would certainly be possible given Paul's use of τὴν ἐκκλησίαν τοῦ θεοῦ in Gal 1:13, but the verbal link with the forms of ἀποκόπτω and the content are much more likely to be how Paul makes the connection.

5:12 Many commentators see a reference here to the cult of Cybele, whose priests would castrate themselves (see, e.g., Lightfoot, 207; Burton, 289; Lenski, 272; Martyn, 478; de Boer, 325; Soards and Pursiful, 262).[35] This is

35. See also J. R. Edwards, "Galatians 5:12: Circumcision, the Mother Goddess, and the Scandal of the Cross," *NovT* 53 (2011): 319–37.

certainly possible given the background of the cult to the Galatians' experience, but the language does not require it. Indeed, everything Paul says can be explained entirely within a Jewish or Jewish-Christian context, which is how Paul has argued throughout the letter. Like Bruce, 238, and Fung, 242, I see no need to posit an allusion to this cult as the passage is perfectly clear (and simpler) without it.

Selected Bibliography

Edwards, J. R. "Galatians 5:12: Circumcision, the Mother Goddess, and the Scandal of the Cross." *NovT* 53 (2011): 319–37.

Freedom in Christ, Lived by the Spirit (5:13–26)

Textual Notes

5:14 The majority of manuscripts (D F G K L P Ψ 0122 630 1505 1881 2464 𝔐 latt) here read the pres. tense verb πληροῦται: "For the whole law is fulfilled by one saying." This variant is solidly Western and Byzantine, which does give it an ancient pedigree. There is strong Alexandrian evidence, however, for the pf. tense verb πεπλήρωται (𝔓[46] ℵ A B C 062[vid] 0254 0278 33 81 104 326 1175 1241 1739 co; Mcion[E]). The pf. tense can be preferred on the basis of the Alexandrian testimony alone, but it is also supported by Paul's implicit argument here that the work of the Spirit in the life of the believer (past action) has fulfilled the intent of the Law (present result), and thus the Law stands fulfilled presently. One manuscript reads an entirely different verb but with a similar sense: The minuscule 365 reads ἀνακεφαλαιοῦται, "For the whole law is summarized by one saying." This reading has no standing to be considered original, but it is an appropriate clarification of the meaning of πεπλήρωται in context and thus implicitly supports that reading.

5:17 The manuscript tradition shows variation at this point in the text regarding the conj. that joins the short sentence ταῦτα ἀλλήλοις ἀντίκειται to the previous statements about the contrary desires of the Spirit and flesh. A minority of manuscripts read γάρ here (𝔓[46] ℵ* B D* F G 33 lat) while the majority read δέ (ℵ[2] A C D[2] K L P Ψ 0122 0278 81 104 365 630 1175 1241 1505 1739 1881 2464 𝔐 sy[h]). The difference between the conjunctions is one of basis versus clarification: The conj. γάρ establishes the opposition between the Spirit and the flesh as the basis for their contrary desires. The conj. δέ simply connects the ideas, presenting the opposition between the Spirit and the flesh as a further description of their contrary desires. The γάρ is preferred on external grounds because it is a solidly Alexandrian and Western reading. It is preferred on internal grounds because of the better logical flow it creates in this verse and the likelihood that scribes changed γάρ to δέ under the influence of the δέ in the preceding clause.

5:19 The majority of manuscripts insert μοιχεία or μοιχεῖαι ("adultery/adulteries") as the first item in the vice list, likely under the influence of Matt 15:19

and Mark 7:21–22. In these Gospel passages Jesus details defiling activities that come from the heart. The list in the Matthean passage places μοιχεῖαι immediately before πορνεῖαι with no variants listed in NA[28]. The NA[28] text of the Markan passage has μοιχεῖαι following a few words after πορνεῖαι, but there is a great deal of variation that places μοιχεῖαι immediately in front of πορνεῖαι. The textual tradition testifies to an impulse on the part of scribes to align the vice lists with the Matthean version, likely due to the primary influence of that Gospel in the early church. On that basis the inclusion of μοιχεία/μοιχεῖαι in Gal 5:19 can be rejected as a secondary scribal alteration. This decision is confirmed by the solid manuscript evidence for the shorter reading (א* A B C P 33 81 1175 1241 1739[txt] 1881 2464 ar vg sy[p] co Clement).

5:21 The majority of manuscripts, many of them exceptional witnesses, add the noun φόνοι, "murders," here after φθόνοι, "jealousies" (A C D F G K L P Ψ 0122 0278 104 365 630 1175 1241 1505 1739 1881 2464 𝔐 lat sy[(p)] bo Cyprian). The reading that lacks the word has exceptional support from the Alexandrian text type (𝔓[46] א B 33 81 323 945 vg[mss] sa Clement Ambrosiaster). Based solely on external evidence, the decision is difficult. The longer reading has wide geographic distribution plus genealogical solidarity within the Western and Byzantine text, but its oldest Alexandrian witnesses are A and C, which are secondary Alexandrian. The shorter reading is solidly Alexandrian with the important manuscripts 𝔓[46] א B on its side. So the answer to this textual problem is found in internal evidence. The similar spelling of φθόνοι and φόνοι makes a variant reading here understandable. It is possible the word could have been removed accidentally because of homoioteleuton, but the more likely explanation is that a scribe added the term under the influence of Rom 1:29 where φόνου immediately follows φθόνου.[1] So in this instance the shorter reading is to be preferred because φόνοι is more likely an intentional addition by a scribe due to harmonization; once added, it would have understandably become the majority reading.

5:24 The NA[28] text here reads τοῦ Χριστοῦ ['Ιησοῦ]. The brackets around 'Ιησοῦ indicate that there is considerable doubt as to whether this word is original. This is an interesting textual problem because the longer reading in this instance has exceptional Alexandrian support (א A B C P Ψ 0122¹ 0278 33 104* 1175 1241 1739 1881 *l*249 co) while the shorter reading is Western and Byzantine (𝔓[46] D F G K L 0122*.² 81 104[c] 365 630 1505 2464 𝔐 latt sy). One might prefer the shorter reading on the grounds that scribes would naturally fill out τοῦ Χριστοῦ here, but doing so creates an unusual expression, as the

1. Lightfoot, 212, argues differently for the longer reading: "The fact however of the same alliteration occurring in another epistle written about the same time is rather in its favour, and the omission in some texts may be due to the carelessness of a copyist transcribing words so closely resembling each other."

phrase τοῦ Χριστοῦ Ἰησοῦ is found elsewhere only in Eph 3:1.[2] The support of $\mathfrak{P}^{46}$ for the shorter reading is important, but it cannot outweigh the otherwise solid Alexandrian support for the longer reading. The best historical reconstruction is that the longer reading is original and then Ἰησοῦ was dropped from the text accidentally because of homoioteleuton.

Translation

13 For you were called to freedom, brothers and sisters![3] Only we do not
have this freedom as an opportunity for the flesh. Instead, through his love
serve one another. **14** For the whole Law has been fulfilled in the one saying:[4]
"Love your neighbor as yourself." **15** But if you continually bite and devour
one another, be careful that you aren't destroyed by each other! **16** Now I
say, walk[5] by the Spirit and you will never accomplish the desire of the flesh.
17 For the flesh has desires contrary to the Spirit and the Spirit contrary to
the flesh[6] because these oppose each other with the result that you do not
do what you want. **18** And if you are led by the Spirit, you are not under the
Law. **19** And the works of the flesh are evident, such as sexual immorality,
corruption, self-abandonment, **20** idolatry, witchcraft, enmity, strife, jealousy,
rage, selfishness, dissension, factions, **21** envy, drunkenness, partying, and
things similar to these, about which I tell you in advance, just as I said before,
that those who do such things will not inherit the kingdom of God! **22** But
the fruit of the Spirit is love, joy, peace, patience, kindness, generosity, faith,
23 humility, self-control. The Law is not against such things,[7] **24** and those
who belong to Christ Jesus crucified the flesh with its interests and desires.

---

2. B. M. Metzger, *A Textual Commentary on the Greek New Testament* (New York: United Bible Societies, 1994), 529.
3. Here I follow recent scholarship that sees the pl. ἀδελφοί as referring to all members of the group regardless of sex; see BDAG, 18.
4. Some English translations treat the verb πεπλήρωται with a slightly different nuance: "For the whole law can be summed up" (NET, NLT; cf. NRSV).
5. Some translations use the more functional word "live" (NET, NRSV). Compare the more dynamic NLT "let the Holy Spirit guide your lives."
6. Paul's language here is both crisp and unusual, which allows for some variation in translation. Some examples: "For the flesh desires what is against the Spirit, and the Spirit desires what is against the flesh" (CSB); "For the desires of the flesh are against the Spirit, and the desires of the Spirit are against the flesh" (ESV); "For the flesh sets its desire against the Spirit, and the Spirit against the flesh" (NASB).
7. The more traditional translation implies a more general idea: "Against such things there is no law" (NET, ESV, NASB, NIV; cf. NRSV, NKJV)

25 If we live by the Spirit, we must also live in conformity to the Spirit.[8]
26 Do not be conceited with the result that you challenge each other and are jealous of each other.

Commentary

Having already hinted at his ethical exhortation about living in freedom because of the work of Christ on behalf of the Galatians (5:1), Paul now approaches this topic head-on with concentrated discussion about how the Galatians should properly live together in community as the family of Abraham. The exhortation is focused on two opposite poles: On the one hand is the flesh and its negative, life-stealing effects when it is in control. On the other hand is the Spirit and its positive, life-giving changes when it is the standard and guide for existence. Because the Spirit is the blessing of Abraham given to those who are now part of his family, the Spirit is the means by which that family lives. Paul's exhortations motivate the Galatians to live by that standard, not the standard of Torah observance, and thus fulfill the blessing God intended for them. A key idea in this section is the Spirit as the means or instrument for living; Paul uses the dat. noun πνεύματι in key ways to emphasize this idea. Four phrases show this emphasis: "walk by the Spirit" (5:16), "if you are led by the Spirit" (5:18), "if we live by the Spirit" and "let us live in conformity with the Spirit" (both in 5:25). Here the blessing of the Spirit given to believers through Abraham manifests itself through the work of the Spirit in producing a life in conformity with God's character and design.

The most well-known feature of this passage are the lists Paul uses to drive home the disparity between living by the flesh or by the Spirit. In the course of his argument, Paul enumerates several "works of the flesh" (vv. 19–21) and the multiform "fruit of the Spirit" (vv. 22–23). These are well understood within the genre of vice and virtue lists that were common in Greco-Roman literature (Longenecker, 249–51). Similarity to other Pauline texts implies that this "vice list" was a fundamental part of his thinking (de Boer, 358; Oakes, 175). But understanding these lists simply as a Pauline example of a common genre does not do justice to the argument Paul makes.[9] The matter is not simply about the individual choosing the Spirit over the flesh

---

8. The latter clause of this verse is variously translated: "let us also behave in accordance with the Spirit" (NET); "let us also keep in step with the Spirit" (CSB, ESV; cf. NIV); "let us also be guided by the Spirit" (NRSV); "let us also walk by the Spirit" (NASB; cf. NKJV).

9. See Martyn, 484, who agrees with this assessment but for different reasons, namely, Paul views the flesh and the Spirit through an apocalyptic lens. His viewpoint here is defensible, but I believe Paul has set up his argument in a fundamentally different way.

as a means of existence, as if the choice was an ethical abstraction without regard for any of Paul's prior argument regarding the Law. Indeed, the final verse of this section points back to the specific problem of the conflict within the Galatian churches brought about by the opponents' teaching (George, 389). Paul makes a deeper argument, more pressing and fundamental for his overall purpose of motivating the Galatians to return to his gospel. In these ethical exhortations Paul equates following the Law in the present time with fulfilling the desires of the flesh. This is a shocking connection, but it is not primarily an argument about the derelict nature of the Law. Rather, it is an argument about the innate ability of the flesh to pervert that which God intended as good, that which God had used for his good purposes at the appropriate time. In the present time, after the advent of the Messiah through whom the promise of the Spirit has been extended to all, following the Law is not a means of fulfilling God's purposes. Instead, the flesh has co-opted it as a means of fulfilling its own desires. As such, obedience to the Law is entirely contrary to the work of the Spirit because it plays right into the desires of the flesh.

Thus Paul has in this paragraph a practical and ethical goal, but also a theological one. He wants the Galatians to understand that it is only by the Spirit, in the freedom to which God called them, that they will fully develop into the people God intends them to be, part of the worldwide family of Abraham based in faith. Moving toward the Law in essence moves them toward the flesh and the sinful works it now engenders, and at the same time moves them away from the present blessing of the Spirit. This is both a theological and practical exhortation for them to return to Paul's gospel. It provides a theological basis for the life of the believer, a life governed by Spirit and not by Law (Moo, 339–40). On this basis, I see little grounds for the dual-front hypothesis, which argues that here Paul addresses libertinism within the churches (similarly Schreiner, 331; for this view see Betz, 8–9; Rapa, 624; George, 375; and others). It may be that Paul is responding to an argument that only a version of the gospel with Law observance is capable of restraining sin (Moo, 341). Even if that is the occasion for this argument, Paul's underlying argument remains unchanged. "The solution to moral disorder is not the law but the Spirit" (Schreiner, 331; similarly Bruce, 239).

5:13 Ὑμεῖς γὰρ ἐπ' ἐλευθερίᾳ ἐκλήθητε, ἀδελφοί. This sentence as a whole is a recapitulation of the theme begun in 5:1 but with some variation and expansion. The similar wording between 5:1 and 5:13 implies that Paul is now getting back on track, so to speak, having digressed somewhat due to his emotional reaction against the opponents.[10] The *γάρ* here is not explanatory but more simply continuative or resumptive (see Longenecker, 238–39;

10. Extensive digressions like this are not unheard of in Paul. See another at Eph 3:1 which is resumed in Eph 3:14.

Soards and Pursiful, 272; *contra* Lenski, 273).[11] The pronoun ὑμεῖς refers to the Galatians, but this does not imply any distinction between Gentiles and Jewish Christians because the 1 pl. pronoun is used in 5:1, the original presentation of this restatement.[12] More likely it distinguishes the Galatians from the opponents (Matera, 192). The prepositional phrase ἐπ' ἐλευθερίᾳ denotes the purpose or goal of the main verb ἐκλήθητε (so also Longenecker, 239; Schreiner, 333; Bruce, 240).[13] This use provides a nice contrast to the emphatic nature of the modifier in the original statement of 5:1,[14] the current phrasing complementing the previous. The main verb ἐκλήθητε is aor. pass., pointing back to a particular past event, namely, the initial calling of the Galatians by God through Paul's preaching of the gospel. The nom. for voc. ἀδελφοί identifies the Galatians vis-à-vis their relationship to Paul in a positive way.[15] Despite the difficulties of their present situation, Paul regards them positively as siblings within the family of Abraham. In a nutshell, his exhortation is simply for them to behave as the family members they are in reality.

Previously in the letter Paul has mentioned freedom in suggestive ways without defining any ethical content. He mentions believers' freedom in Christ Jesus being spied upon by the opponents (2:4). He mentions that in

---

11. See M. Zerwick, *Biblical Greek: Illustrated By Examples*, trans. J. Smith, Scripta Pontificii Instituti Biblici 114 (Rome: Pontifical Biblical Institute, 1963), 159, who suggests that here γάρ may be equal to δέ with no causal sense intended, owing in part to the sense of the textual variation here. The conj. δέ would thus be a "«correction» for a γάρ whose causal sense is not apparent." See S. E. Runge, *Discourse Grammar of the Greek New Testament: A Practical Introduction for Teaching and Exegesis* (Peabody, MA: Hendrickson, 2010), 54, who argues that the γάρ here strengthens the previous section of Gal 5:1–12 instead of developing the argument with new information.

12. This is *prima facie* evidence that the distinctions between "we" and "you" in the book have to be examined on a case-by-case basis. Runge, *Discourse Grammar*, 212, identifies the 2 pl. pronoun in 5:13 as a topical frame that highlights for the reader a new section of the discourse.

13. See BDAG, 366, which says, "marker of object or purpose, with dat. In ref. to someth. … καλεῖν τινα ἐ. Τινι call someone for someth. Gal 5:13." See also BDAG, 316, which says, "ἐπ' ἐλευθερίᾳ καλεῖσθαι be called for freedom (=to be free…) Gal 5:13a." In addition see BDF, §235(4); Zerwick, *Biblical Greek*, 43; A. T. Robertson, *A Grammar of the Greek New Testament in the Light of Historical Research* (Nashville: Broadman, 1934), 605; G. B. Winer, *A Treatise on the Grammar of New Testament Greek, Regarded as a Sure Basis for New Testament Exegesis* (Edinburgh: Clark, 1882), 492.

14. The dat. noun τῇ ἐλευθερίᾳ in 5:1 is a cognate dat., intensifying the force of the main verb ἠλευθέρωσεν.

15. For an interpretation that sees this as nom. acting as nom., see T. W. Martin, "The Brother Body: Addressing and Describing the Galatians and the Agitators as Adelphoi," *BR* 47 (2002): 5–18.

Christ the social boundary between free and slave breaks down (3:28). In his extended analogy of the Abraham-Sarah-Hagar story he describes Sarah as a free woman and as such the most appropriate person through whom the fulfillment of God's promise to Abraham regarding an heir should come (4:22, 23, 30, 31). Paul extends the analogy by connecting the heavenly Jerusalem to Sarah in that it is free, too (4:26). In this ethical section he describes much more carefully what that freedom entails. In 5:1 the freedom Christ gained for the Galatians was the basis for his admonition not to slip back under the Law, graphically depicted there as ζυγῷ δουλείας, "a yoke of slavery." This prior mention of freedom looks backwards in contrast to that which enslaves. In 5:13 Paul looks forward in fulfillment to new actions to be undertaken in light of this freedom, defined entirely within the context of loving service to others in the community.

μόνον μὴ τὴν ἐλευθερίαν εἰς ἀφορμὴν τῇ σαρκί. Paul uses this phrase to clarify the meaning of the first, identifying negatively that to which the Galatians have not been freed. The balance of the paragraph shows the dangerous results when the individual is given free rein to indulge their natural impulses under the power of the flesh. Paul foreshadows that discussion, well known by its "works of the flesh," with this clarification. This phrase is a rather free ellipsis, requiring both subject and verb to be supplied.[16] Likely the indicative ἔχετε has been elided with an implied contrast: "[but we have] this freedom only not as an opportunity for the flesh."[17] The word μόνον is the neut. form of μόνος used adverbially as a form of limitation.[18] Paul uses it as a clarification to prevent misunderstanding (Schreiner, 333). The μή serves its normal purpose of negation. Presuming that a verb should be supplied in this sentence, the acc. noun τὴν ἐλευθερίαν would be the dir. obj.[19] The article with ἐλευθερίαν is anaphoric, referring to ἐλευθερίᾳ in the prior clause (so also Burton, 292; Witherington, 376, who also sees it referring to 5:1; Moo, 343; Soards and Pursiful, 273). The prepositional phrase εἰς ἀφορμήν indicates the goal or purpose of the freedom. The word ἀφορμή in military contexts meant "a base of operations"; here by extension it means "occasion" or "opportunity."[20] The dat. noun τῇ σαρκί is a dat. of reference, delimiting the particular opportunity in mind.[21] The believer in Abraham's family is free, but that freedom was gained not so the individual could now take an

16. Robertson, *Grammar*, 1202.
17. So BDF, §481. *Contra* de Boer, 335, who argues that a form of τρέπω ("I turn") should be supplied.
18. BDAG, 659.
19. Another construal is to see it is an acc. of reference, providing a frame of reference for this qualification and clarification.
20. LSJ, 292; MGS, 359; BDAG, 158. Martyn, 485, and de Boer, 335, favor the military connotations.
21. The use of the noun ἀφορμή in Rom 7:8, 11, with reference to ἁμαρτία is an intriguing theological development.

opportunity to indulge the flesh, or by extension, so that the flesh could take it as an opportunity to build its works.

There is no doubt that σάρξ is a key concept for Paul, both within his writings as a whole and specifically within Galatians. He uses the term eighteen times in sixteen verses in this book, concentrated largely in this paragraph but also spread throughout. The usual take on Paul's use of the term is that it ranges from neutral, referencing the physical body or the life lived in the body, to negative, referencing the sinful desires of the human person that are localized in the flesh. The neutral uses are illustrated well with Gal 1:16; 2:20. The negative uses are illustrated by practically all the occurrences in the present paragraph, most notably 5:19 which highlights the "works of the flesh." This interpretive take can be illustrated with BDAG's elaboration along these lines: "In Paul's thought esp., all parts of the body constitute a totality known as σ. or flesh, which is dominated by sin to such a degree that wherever flesh is, all forms of sin are likew. present, and no good thing can live in the σάρξ."[22] When wrestling with Paul's argument in this paragraph, however, his use of σάρξ is not as clear-cut as one might think. Paul's goal in this paragraph is to set up flesh as contrary to the Spirit; as such this *develops* the idea of "flesh," moving it into a realm where it did not yet make a theological claim. The Galatians would have likely understood "flesh" in the neutral sense, and the purpose of Paul's argument is to make them realize that it is in fact not neutral. Take v. 17, for example; this opposition appears to prove that σάρξ in this instance embodies the sinful tendencies of the human person. The problem with this view is simply that if Paul has to explain this to the Galatians as explicitly as he does, the word itself must not have held that denotation (or connotation) normally. The Galatians needed to understand something new about the flesh that they had not known before. Paul graphically explains it by illuminating the native opposition between the flesh and the Spirit and by illustrating without any doubt where following the flesh leads. This distinction is important for understanding his argument as a whole: The Galatians were tempted to submit to circumcision, something done in their flesh. They needed to realize that emphasizing the flesh in this way was counter to the work of the Spirit, something they did not know before. Paul helps them realize that their bodies, and more broadly their human persons and personalities, if given the opportunity, will act contrary to the Spirit whom God has given to them in line with the blessings of Abraham. This at the same time deepens the lexical connotations of σάρξ and the theology of sin, neither of which were understood previously simply based on the meaning of σάρξ. To put it another way, after the Galatians read this passage they would not say, "Yes, we knew all along how bad the flesh was." Instead, they would say, "We never knew our flesh could lead to such problems."

---

22. BDAG, 915.

ἀλλὰ διὰ τῆς ἀγάπης δουλεύετε ἀλλήλοις. Paul utters this positive command as a foil to the previous negative statement. The command given here is the essential opposite of giving the flesh opportunity: Instead of believers' freedom in Christ leading to focus on the self, it instead leads to sacrificial service for others. The prepositional phrase διὰ τῆς ἀγάπης expresses the means by which the action of the main verb, the service to others, is carried out. It is more than simply instrument or means, though; instead the prep. marks "the conditioning cause" that makes service toward others possible (Burton, 293; Longenecker, 241). Moo, 345, regards it as both reason and manner. This is an expression with quite a full sense. The referent of ἀγάπης in this phrase cannot be divorced from a similar use of the word in 5:6. There Paul states that the only thing that matters is πίστις δι' ἀγάπης ἐνεργουμένη, "faith that is energized through love," with love referring to God's love toward humanity.[23] The current phrase refers back to this one; the article with ἀγάπης is anaphoric (so also Burton, 293; Longenecker, 242).[24] Thus the divine love mentioned there is also in view here. The same love that God has toward humanity grounds and characterizes the believer's service toward others. The main verb δουλεύω means "to be a slave to" or "serve as a slave."[25] It is somewhat surprising that Paul enjoins slavery here. Both Dunn, 288, and Witherington, 378, argue this has a certain shock value given that slavery was the antithesis of freedom in Greek thought. Previously Paul had spoken strongly against slavery as a mode of existence (4:1–7, 8–9, 24–25; 5:1). Now in this context he encourages the Galatians to "be enslaved to" one another, the dat. pronoun ἀλλήλοις identifying those to whom the individual is enslaved. The resolution to this supposed contradiction in Paul's argument lies in the qualifications. He was not a champion of the individual's free will or self-determination at all costs and in all contexts. Rather, Paul saw slavery as good when one serves the proper person. Most notably Paul even described himself as Christ's slave (Gal 1:10).[26] This provides a proper context for understanding this present command: In the new family of Abraham that Jesus enabled through his death and resurrection, servitude toward others in Christ is not demeaning, nor does it negate God's purposes for the individual. Instead, it allows the self to be fully human, living for the other within the purposes of God. The power of this slavery within the family of God is its reciprocal nature as evidenced by the pronoun ἀλλήλοις. This pronoun routinely emphasizes the

---

23. See previous discussion on Gal 5:6.

24. *Contra* D. B. Wallace, *Greek Grammar Beyond the Basics: An Exegetical Syntax of the New Testament* (Grand Rapids: Zondervan, 1996), 227, who classifies this article more simply as an article with an abstract noun.

25. BDAG, 259. Compare the verb "serve" in most English translations with the NRSV "become slaves to one another."

26. See also Rom 1:1; Phil 1:1; Titus 1:1. Non-Pauline uses are in Jas 1:1; 2 Pet 1:1; Jude 1.

mutual relations involved in the accompanying assertion.[27] Paul envisions the Galatians serving each other mutually and equally, not hierarchically (so also Hays, 321–22). Believers enslaved to other believers within the body is perfectly in keeping with the freedom Christ gained. As Lightfoot, 208, summarizes well, Paul's argument is that believers temper liberty with love to avoid license.

5:14 ὁ γὰρ πᾶς νόμος ἐν ἑνὶ λόγῳ πεπλήρωται, ἐν τῷ· Ἀγαπήσεις τὸν πλησίον σου ὡς σεαυτόν. The conj. γάρ marks this statement as an explanation of the ethical command to serve one another in the prior verse. This verse provides as well a biblical-theological basis for Paul's broader argument that the Galatians need not obey the Law: Properly understood, the Law's commands fulfill the purpose of the Law, and the Galatians' service toward one another within their new Abrahamic family is part and parcel of that fulfillment. In a sense the Galatians' desire to fulfill the Law is not wrong; if it were, Paul could not speak of the Law's fulfillment relative to their current situation. Rather, the concern is the mode by which that fulfillment comes. Fulfillment of the Law through slavish obedience to circumcision is a dead end because it focuses on the flesh and has the individual as its only context and limit. Fulfillment through loving service toward others in the family of Abraham is the way forward because this focuses on the new family God has created in Christ.

The subject of the sentence is ὁ πᾶς νόμος. This first attributive construction emphasizes the noun as a whole in contrast to the individual parts (Lightfoot, 208),[28] but it does so without losing sight of those individual parts.[29] This is important given the contrast with the number εἷς in the phrase ἐν ἑνὶ λόγῳ.[30] The prepositional phrase ἐν ἑνὶ λόγῳ shows that the Law has been fulfilled in a single precept. The noun λόγος here carries a broader meaning of "statement" or "saying." The verb πεπλήρωται is significant on account of the lexeme and the tense. This is the only place Paul uses the verb πληρόω in the epistle. Here it means "to bring to completion that which was already begun, complete, finish"; the sense is that the Law finds its full and complete expression in the one saying.[31] The tense is important because the pf. emphasizes a present state from a past action. This emphasis dovetails nicely with Paul's arguments previously that the Law in essence has

---

27. Robertson, *Grammar*, 692; S. E. Porter, *Idioms of the Greek New Testament* (Sheffield: Sheffield Academic Press, 1995), 132.

28. BDAG, 784; BDF, §275(7); Robertson, *Grammar*, 773. Compare Zerwick, *Biblical Greek*, 61: "ὁ πᾶς νόμος «the law in its entirety» Gal 5:14."

29. *Contra* Burton, 296, who argues that the first attributive position emphasizes totality without reference to the parts.

30. See J. W. Johnston, *The Use of* Πᾶς *in the New Testament*, SBG 11 (Peter Lang, 2004), 164, who says, "The multiple precepts of the Mosaic Law stand in contrast to their fulfillment in one command."

31. BDAG, 828.

its own sunset clause, that is, the Law itself shows that it was never meant to last forever.[32] Rather, it pointed to its own fulfillment in the future, and the advent of the Messiah has finalized that fulfillment, which now stands complete. The prepositional phrase ἐν τῷ refers back to the ἑνὶ λόγῳ. The dat. sg. article here makes the following citation into a substantive, identifying it as the "one statement" in view.[33]

The citation that follows is from Lev 19:18 and matches the LXX exactly: "Love your neighbor as yourself." The neighbor in the original context of the passage was a fellow Israelite (Burton, 296; Witherington, 384), but the referent in Paul's context is a fellow believer.[34] Paul's argumentation about the Law's fulfillment in this OT passage is not original. This passage is in Jesus's teaching (Dunn, 291; Moo, 346) where he likewise presents this verse as a fulfillment or summation of the entire Torah.[35] This tendency to summarize the Law occurs even in Jewish literature (Bruce, 241; Dunn, 289); the logic was to identify commands that were particularly important, from which other commands could be deduced (Moo, 349–50). Paul shows both that he is a logical thinker and that he understands how to properly interpret the Torah. The Law *qua* the Law no longer applies to the Galatians as a body of law because it has been fulfilled in this command to love one's neighbor, which is now realized in Christ through loving service for one another in Abraham's family.

An essential interpretive question is how this verse relates to what Paul said earlier in the chapter. In v. 3 he stated μαρτύρομαι δὲ πάλιν παντὶ ἀνθρώπῳ περιτεμνομένῳ ὅτι ὀφειλέτης ἐστὶν ὅλον τὸν νόμον ποιῆσαι, "And I testify again to every man who submits to circumcision that he is obligated to do the whole Law." Paul addresses the Law in each place but with complementary approaches. In v. 3 his approach is negative; he addresses the unavoidable failure of those who attempt to obey the Law through circumcision. Here his approach is positive; he addresses the fulfillment of the Law in Christ through loving service to others in the body. He essentially addresses different lifestyles that embody different attitudes and approaches to the Law (Dunn, 289–90). In addition, the key verbs used in each place show that his assertions, though not identical, are congruent. The key word in v. 3 is ποιῆσαι, "to do." Paul's underlying argument is that the Law cannot be "done" completely or appropriately in any sense of the term. That statement refers back to his entire argument in 3:10–13 about humanity's inability to do the Law. Here he uses a different word, the term πεπλήρωται, "fulfilled." This is a different conception that speaks to accomplishment of purpose and design. The Law cannot be done, but it certainly can be fulfilled, that is, its purposes can be

32. See my comments on Gal 4:20.

33. See BDF, §267(1); MHT, 3:182.

34. Garlington 2007, 324, argues that Paul expands the range of the word πλησίον, but more exactly he maintains the same sense while replacing the referent.

35. See Matt 19:19; 22:39; Mark 12:31, 33; Luke 10:27. Compare as well Jas 2:8.

accomplished in Christ as the Spirit guides the body to love one another.[36] Soards and Pursiful, 277, state it well: "The Law, spoken of in the present tense active voice (5:3), is an entity capable of enslaving those who would pursue its observance (3:12). But the Law spoken of in the perfect tense passive voice as made complete by Christ himself (3:13, 14, 22, 26, 29; 4:4–7) is liberating (5:14) and community building." Treating the Law as a present requirement unleashes its enslaving power. Treating it as a corpus fulfilled in Christ liberates the believer to a life of love that affirms that fulfillment.

5:15 εἰ δὲ ἀλλήλους δάκνετε καὶ κατεσθίετε, βλέπετε μὴ ὑπ' ἀλλήλων ἀναλωθῆτε. The conj. δέ links this conditional sentence with the previous discussion of the OT citation, but the exact relation of the statements is unclear. Paul has not given any prior indication in the epistle that the Galatians suffered from internal strife. Likely this statement about internal attacks is just a logical opposite to "loving your neighbor as yourself." The opposite of loving service to one another would be intramural attacks with mutually assured self-destruction (similarly de Boer, 351). A key to this understanding is the first class condition, which assumes the truth of the hypothesis in order to advance the logic of the argument. This cannot be taken as an implicit assertion that the Galatians are indeed involved in intramural strife. They *may* be, but the condition cannot be used as proof for that (similarly de Boer, 351; *contra* Martyn, 491; Soards and Pursiful, 278). Paul is simply stating the condition without any assertion as to likelihood of fulfillment. The verb δάκνω means "to bite," and the verb κατεσθίω means "to devour."[37] The related meanings could mark this as a hendiadys: "Bite and devour" would mean "viciously consume" or something similar. The words are used metaphorically to reference personal attacks and interpersonal strife.[38] The apodosis of the conditional sentence—βλέπετε μή plus the aor. subjunctive—conveys the idea of being careful to avoid the stated negative outcome. The verb ἀναλωθῆτε is the aor. pass. subjunctive of ἀναλίσκω, which means "to destroy or

---

36. Matera, 197, appropriately notes that Paul employs a similar "do" versus "fulfill" contrast in Rom 2:25; 8:3–4. For a further explanation of the difference between ποιέω and πληρόω, see S. Westerholm, "On Fulfilling the Whole Law (Gal 5:14)," *SEÅ* 51–52 (1986): 234–36.

37. BDF, §318(5), gives κατεσθίω as an example of a verb for which the prefixed prep. affects the aspect of the verb by emphasizing perfected action: "the action is conceived as having reached its consummation (aorist, e.g. κατέφαγον 'devoured' Mt 13:4) or as continuing to its completion or as repeatedly achieved (present stem, e.g. κατεσθίειν G 5:15, Mk 12:40)."

38. BDAG, 211, when discussing the verb δάκνω, lists Gal 5:15 under the figurative meaning "harm," but that removes the power of the metaphor. See as well BDAG, 532, under the entry for κατεσθίω: "to engage in spiteful partisan strife: betw. δάκνω and ἀναλίσκω (q.v.), someth. like *tear to pieces* Gal 5:15." See Moo, 349, for an even-handed analysis of the imagery used here.

consume entirely,"[39] a perfect complement to the verbs in the protasis. The prepositional phrase ὑπ' ἀλλήλων indicates the agent of this pass. main verb, emphasizing the mutual nature of the inflicted harm.

The main difficulty with this sentence is its abrupt introduction of a very negative situation. Indeed, the structure of the sentence implies some resignation on the part of Paul to interpersonal strife within the Galatian communities. Assuming the reality of the strife referenced in the protasis, Paul's only warning in the apodosis is to not carry the strife to an extreme end! The best solution is to regard Paul's statement here as sarcastic (similarly Longenecker, 244; Rapa, 626): "I've just told you that to fulfill the Law you should love your neighbor as yourself. So if you do go about biting and eating each other, just show enough love so that you don't totally destroy one another!" This sarcasm highlights the natural end result of anyone giving the flesh an opportunity while within the body of Christ: It can ultimately make the body self-destruct. The sarcasm reinforces the original command to lovingly serve one another by showing the extreme danger when that command is not followed.

5:16 Λέγω δέ, πνεύματι περιπατεῖτε καὶ ἐπιθυμίαν σαρκὸς οὐ μὴ τελέσητε. Paul continues his discussion of proper behavior that fulfills the Law by expanding upon the command to lovingly serve each other in v. 13 with the means by which that command can be fulfilled. This verse comprises two short sentences that ultimately take on a conditional nuance. The essential structure is impv. plus καί plus a fut. indic.[40] In this particular example the fut. indic. is replaced by emphatic negation with the aor. subjunctive.[41] The end result for the meaning of the text is that the impv. has a conditional nuance while retaining at the same time the impv. force (so also Burton, 297).[42] The force of this utterance would thus be, "If you walk by the Spirit—and you must do that!—then you will never fulfill the desire of the flesh."

The conj. δέ continues to develop the argument from the previous verse. It is slightly contrastive in light of the sarcastic warning in v. 15 that precedes it. Paul introduces this affirmation with the verb λέγω. Here λέγω has two functions: It adds emphasis to what follows (Burton, 297; Matera, 199; Witherington, 393), and it highlights Paul's authority to demand proper behavior within the community. The pres. impv. περιπατεῖτε is modified by the simple dat. πνεύματι. This simple command to "walk by the Spirit" becomes the central theme for the paragraph. The verb περιπατέω literally

39. BDAG, 67.
40. For other examples of this construction in the NT, see Matt 7:7; Mark 11:29; Luke 10:28; John 1:39; Rom 13:3.
41. The same meaning is in play because emphatic negation is semantically equivalent to the fut. indic. See Wallace, *Greek Grammar*, 490.
42. See Wallace, *Greek Grammar*, 489–92, for discussion on the conditional impv.

means "to walk," but Paul often uses it figuratively to refer to conduct of life.[43] This could be a rhetorical move on Paul's part: Language from the OT that implies moral obligation could persuade those attracted by Law observance (Dunn, 295; Witherington, 393). The pres. impv. here has the simple force of "continue to do this action"; this is a general precept, meant to be followed at all times. The emphasis of the first miniature sentence falls squarely on the dat. modifier πνεύματι, brought forward before the verb for emphasis. The dat. case here indicates means or instrument, explaining how the action of the main verb is to be carried out, but this is to be understood in the fullest sense possible.[44] The Spirit is the means for proper living in that he enables daily actions but also gives guidance and shape to the whole of life. Moo, 353n2, helpfully notes that the verb περιπατέω in Paul occurs with a number of prepositions and objects, thus giving the dat. phrase here a broad sense.[45] The role of the Spirit as an enabler of proper behavior, behavior that ultimately fulfills the Law, is theologically significant given the role of the Spirit previously in Paul's argument. Paul hints at what will ultimately become a robust pneumatology: The Spirit is the blessing promised by God to Abraham, so it is the eschatological end point of the promises. But the Spirit is not an end unto itself because the Spirit in turn motivates the behavior within Abraham's family that fulfills the Law's requirements, behavior that ultimately receives God's approbation.

The second part of the verse begins with the acc. dir. obj. ἐπιθυμίαν, brought forward for emphasis to contrast with πνεύματι. Without context the noun ἐπιθυμία simply means "desire or longing"; it is used with neutral and even positive objects on occasion.[46] It does appear frequently with negative objects, but that does not mean that on its own ἐπιθυμία means a sinful desire or craving.[47] The beneficent or harmful nature of the desire is determined by the context. Interestingly, in this first occurrence of the term in Galatians Paul uses the sg. while the subsequent use in 5:24 is pl. This would imply that with the sg. Paul has a particular desire in mind, not all the multifarious desires the flesh can manifest. Here the noun ἐπιθυμίαν is modified by the poss. gen. σαρκός. As argued above, an appropriate meaning for σάρξ within Paul's argument at this point would be intrinsically neutral.

---

43. See among many others Rom 6:4; 1 Cor 3:3; 2 Cor 5:7; Eph 2:2; Phil 3:17; Col 1:10; 1 Thess 2:12. Cf. LSJ, 1382; MGS, 1637; BDAG, 803.

44. So MHT, 3:240. BDF, §198(5), categorizes this as an associative dat., "used more loosely to designate accompanying circumstances and manner." See Wallace, *Greek Grammar*, 165–66, for a discussion of why this cannot be a dat. of agency. Winer, *Grammar*, 274, takes this as a figurative use of the dat. of place, which is essentially equal to sphere.

45. See Soards and Pursiful, 281, who argue that it is reasonable to see multiple senses of the dat. occurring at once.

46. See BDAG, 372.

47. Cf. the KJV translation "lust," which as an English verb has a negative denotation.

Paul's point is to bring new information, showing that the flesh on its own does not lead to anything good. This becomes a theological linchpin for Paul in this section. The natural human condition regards the "desire of the flesh" as neutral or even positive. Paul's point is to show that this desire to do something in the flesh is actually harmful and contrary to God's purposes.

A final issue to discuss about this phrase concerns the nature of the gen. case used. The default understanding of most commentators is that *σαρκός* is a subj. gen. (so, e.g., Moo, 353), that is, the flesh is performing the action of the verbal noun *ἐπιθυμία*. This could be translated as "Walk by the Spirit and you will not do what the flesh desires" (cf. NLT). This leads to numerous discussions in the commentary literature about the Jewish teaching of the evil impulse (see, e.g., Martyn, 492; Hays, 325–26; Moo, 353; Soards and Pursiful, 282). A different understanding of the gen. is possible here, though, and perhaps even preferred given Paul's prior use of *σάρξ* in the text to refer to the physical body. This gen. could very well be obj., that is, the flesh is the object of the desire. If so, the phrase "desire *for* the flesh" would be a grammatically picturesque way to refer to the Galatians' desire for circumcision. This latter construal makes a great deal of sense because it places the topic of discussion back where it has been all along, namely, the Galatians' desire to turn back to following the Law through the specific action of circumcision. Confirmation for this view is found in the restatement of the central idea of the paragraph later in v. 18: "If you are led by the Spirit, you are not under the Law." Paul's point is not primarily to show how people are intrinsically bad and sinful in their flesh, although that is a logical deduction of his argument. Rather, he desires to show how the practice of the Law is centered on the flesh, not on the Spirit, which is counter to what God has done in the Galatians through their faith in Christ.

The construction *οὐ μή* plus the aor. subjunctive that finishes the verse indicates emphatic negation. It is emphatic because it negates not only the reality of something but the very possibility of something.[48] So Paul denies even the possibility of fulfilling the desire of the flesh when walking by the Spirit. The verb τελέω in this context means to perform or accomplish.[49] The normal force of the aor. tense of this verb in the NT is consummative, that is, the verb describes an action that is brought to its logical completion, but here a continuous aspect is possible.[50] Paul's assertion is that if the Galatians live by the means of the Spirit that God has graciously given to them through their faith in Christ, they will not fall under the sway of circumcision or Law obedience any more.

5:17 *ἡ γὰρ σὰρξ ἐπιθυμεῖ κατὰ τοῦ πνεύματος, τὸ δὲ πνεῦμα κατὰ τῆς σαρκός.* The implicit promise within the conditional statement of the prior verse is

48. Wallace, *Greek Grammar*, 468.

49. BDAG, 997–98.

50. MHT, 1:118. Robertson, *Grammar*, 834, simply describes this as constative.

now grounded upon the innately different desires of the flesh and the Spirit. Here Paul presents the flesh and Spirit in stark contrast, but his discussion is not about humanity's sinful nature as much as it is about the different modes of existence the Spirit and the flesh each offer. The conj. *γάρ* links this statement to the previous as an explanation; it serves as proof of v. 16 (Burton, 300). The noun *ἡ σάρξ* is the nom. subject of the first clause. All the articles in this sentence are anaphoric (so also Lenski, 282), pointing back to the occurrences of these words in the prior verse, providing strong continuity and focus on "flesh" and "Spirit" as opposite powers, not general principles. The main verb ἐπιθυμεῖ is pres. indic., here with a gnomic force. Paul presents a generalization that is true at all times. The verb ἐπιθυμέω, "desires," refers to the interests and intentions of the flesh in the first clause and the Spirit in the second. As with the use of ἐπιθυμία in v. 16, the use of ἐπιθυμέω here does not imply anything intrinsically bad. If that were the case, then Paul's predications about the Spirit with this verb would make no sense.[51] Rather, Paul's point is more foundational and essential: The desires and longings of the flesh—flesh here best understood as the body, ultimately representative of the human person and personality—are simply contrary to those of the Spirit (similarly Fung, 249). The use of the prep. *κατά* describes the contrary position or state of mind between *σάρξ* and *πνεῦμα*. The use of *κατά* after ἐπιθυμέω is unusual to say the least; Paul's meaning is clarified by Polycarp, *Phil.* 5:3, who says, *πᾶσα ἐπιθυμία κατὰ τοῦ πνεύματος στρατεύεται*, "Every desire wars against the Spirit" (Martyn, 493; de Boer, 353). Paul's point is a novel one in his context: The natural desires of the human person, which most people would arguably think of as neutral or even good, run counter to the undeniable, real good of the Spirit given by God. They are in constant conflict.

ταῦτα γὰρ ἀλλήλοις ἀντίκειται, ἵνα μὴ ἃ ἐὰν θέλητε ταῦτα ποιῆτε. The conj. *γάρ* links this statement to the previous as an explanation. This evidence proves the prior assertion about the conflicting desires of the flesh and Spirit. The contrary desires of the flesh and Spirit are deduced from their inherent opposition, attested by the personal experience of the Galatians. The pronoun *ταῦτα* conceptualizes both *σάρξ* and *πνεῦμα*, grouping them together for the purposes of the argument. They are also referred to mutually by the distributive pronoun *ἀλλήλοις*. The verb *ἀντίκειται* is pres. indic. as was ἐπιθυμεῖ previously, again indicating a general, universal action. The verb *ἀντίκειμαι* can have a somewhat neutral meaning of "to be opposite, opposed," but it can also take on a stronger meaning of "resist" or "be adverse."[52] The latter meaning is more appropriate here on the basis of the emphatic language Paul uses. The prep. *κατά* makes this opposition outright, and the inherent conflict of the following *ἵνα* clause confirms this. That *ἵνα* clause is logically the

51. *Contra* Lightfoot, 210, who argues some verb other than ἐπιθυμέω is implied since that is not applicable to the Spirit.

52. LSJ, 156; MGS, 199.

result of the opposition.[53] Its structure is somewhat complex. The particle μή negates the main verb of the clause, in this case the pres. subjunctive ποιῆτε, which describes an ongoing action or state of affairs: "with the result that ... you do not regularly do." The relative clause ἃ ἐὰν θέλητε, a pendant acc.,[54] is the dir. obj. of ποιῆτε. The force of ἐάν makes the relative clause indefinite: "you do not regularly do ... whatever you want." In this construction ταῦτα resumes the prior relative clause: "with the result that, whatever you might want, these things you do not regularly do."[55] A more idiomatic English translation would be "with the result that you do not do what you want."[56]

A great deal of ink has been spilt on the difficulties of this verse. A proper understanding is attained when we recognize that Paul speaks to the particular situation of the Galatians, not generally about the spiritual life. The opponents had ignited in them a desire to fulfill that which the Law required. Well and good! But the means by which the opponents argued that fulfillment was attained, namely, the modification of the flesh through obedience to the Law (that is, "doing the Law") only ignited the power of the flesh within them, which in reality short-circuited the Law's fulfillment. This echoes Paul's arguments from 3:10–13: No one will ever do the Law completely such that they can escape its curse. Thus the Galatians were presently caught between the flesh and the Spirit: They wanted to fulfill the desires of the flesh while enjoying the blessing of the Spirit, a position that could not be maintained because of the flesh's and Spirit's contrary desires. Paul's argument serves to push them away from the flesh to the Spirit, the only means for fulfilling the Law through mutual, loving service to one another in Christ. This verse thus explains Paul's foundational statement in v. 16: "Walk by the Spirit and you will never accomplish the desire of the flesh." In a sense Paul pictures both the struggle and the victory of the Galatian believers: The pull of the flesh is real, so they must cooperate with the Spirit. When they do, the desires they have for the flesh will be opposed victoriously by the Spirit. The theological ramifications of this argument are clear: Any effort to begin or maintain membership in God's family through actions of the self, without guidance from and dependence upon the Spirit in Christ, will fail because of the power of the flesh. As believers depend on the Spirit, the self-oriented desires they do have will be overcome by his power.

5:18 εἰ δὲ πνεύματι ἄγεσθε, οὐκ ἐστὲ ὑπὸ νόμον. The logical connection of this sentence with what precedes is fuzzy. The δέ links this conditional statement

53. So Wallace, *Greek Grammar*, 473; Lightfoot, 210; Lenski, 282; Martyn, 494; de Boer, 355; Fung, 250; Matera, 199. Those who favor purpose include Burton, *Syntax*, 94; Longenecker, 246; Dunn, 299; Witherington, 394–95; Schreiner, 344.

54. So Wallace, *Greek Grammar*, 198.

55. See Robertson, *Grammar*, 698.

56. Compare "so that you don't do what you want" (CSB); "so that you cannot do what you want" (NET).

to the preceding as a development, but the nature of that development is unclear. On the surface, this verse appears to augment what Paul stated in 5:16 by making the conditional idea explicit. The initial clauses are indeed similar: Both use the dat. πνεύματι to indicate means, and the verbs περιπατεῖτε and ἄγεσθε both address the conduct of the Galatians. The latter clauses also show conceptual similarity: Assuming that ἐπιθυμίαν σαρκός refers to the Galatians' desire for circumcision as argued above, this would parallel nicely with ὑπὸ νόμον. The words and phrases are different enough, however, that the verses each convey different meanings, or at least different nuances. So the conj. δέ here has the force of development and addition, restating and recasting the idea of v. 16 after the short parenthesis of v. 17 (*contra* Longenecker, 246, who argues the conj. is simply connective here). Paul here resolves the problem of v. 17 (Dunn, 300; Schreiner, 345), which itself arose out of the thought of v. 16, to properly guide the Galatians to be led by the Spirit.

This verse is a first class condition, which expresses a simple condition that posits evidence-inference. If the evidence given in the protasis is true, then the reality of the apodosis can be inferred. The main verb ἄγεσθε as a pres. indic. implies a continuous, progressive action, paralleling the tense of περιπατεῖτε in v. 16. The verb ἄγω can be used with a literal sense of "lead, bring." The current use refers to spiritual guidance in the sense of "lead, guide, direct."[57] The dat. noun πνεύματι has the same force as in v. 16, that of means or instrument.[58] To be led by the Spirit means to be guided by his will and desires. Longenecker, 246, argues that the pass. verb ἄγεσθε is "practically synonymous" with περιπατεῖτε. In a sense that is true, but the pass. voice emphasizes personally yielding to the work of the Spirit rather than the willing, decisive action implied in περιπατεῖτε (see also Matera, 207). Between v. 16 and here Paul provides an appropriate balance: "Those who wish to walk by the Spirit have to be led by the Spirit; those who wish to be led by the Spirit have the responsibility to conduct themselves accordingly" (Dunn, 300).

The apodosis presents the inference that can be drawn from the evidence of being led by the Spirit. It is a simple statement of status and existence. The life led by the Spirit replaces life under the Law. The emphasis falls on the prepositional phrase ὑπὸ νόμον, used significantly in the theological section of the book (Gal 3:23; 4:4, 5, 21). Through the work of the Spirit, "under the Law" is a place the believer lives no longer. Indeed, the Spirit has replaced the Law in the believer's life. Moving back to the Law in any way as a mode or means of existence negates the work of the Spirit, replacing freedom in Christ to God with bondage to the Law.

5:19 φανερὰ δέ ἐστιν τὰ ἔργα τῆς σαρκός, ἅτινά ἐστιν πορνεία, ἀκαθαρσία, ἀσέλγεια. Paul had stated in brief previously that the flesh and Spirit were opposed

57. BDAG, 16.

58. So MHT, 3:240.

to one another. By juxtaposing the "works of the flesh" with the "fruit of the Spirit" as he continues the paragraph Paul develops this opposition considerably. A slight turn of phrase shows how in Paul's thinking Law and flesh have converged. Prior occurrences of the word ἔργον in the book had been pl. followed by the gen. noun νόμου (Gal 2:16 [3x]; 3:2, 5, 10). The use of the pl. ἔργα here would create the expectation of an allusion to those prior instances with νόμου. Instead, Paul changes the game by using the gen. τῆς σαρκός. This replacement, along with his juxtaposition of the flesh and the Law in his parallel statements in vv. 16 and 18, confirm Paul's meaning: Desire for the Law in the present moment is actually desire for the flesh, and as he is about to explain, accommodating the flesh will have terrible consequences, giving it a power that will lead to the exact opposite of what the Galatians hoped to attain through obedience to the Law. Their goal in accepting circumcision is to confirm their acceptance by God, but the actual result would be manifestation in their flesh of works hated by God. Paul does not rehearse what they already know. Instead, he warns them about what will develop out of their inappropriate desire to do something in their flesh.

The adj. φανερά is a predicate nom. that Paul uses to describe "the works of the flesh." The term means "visible, evident."[59] Paul does not proffer this as a self-evident, logical assertion based on the nature of the flesh, a common understanding of this passage. Paul's point is instead phenomenological and then theological: These negative behaviors are clearly manifested within human behavior, and Paul identifies them as "the works of the flesh." That identification is a novel theological development especially in light of Paul's juxtaposition of the flesh vis-à-vis the Law. In the phrase τὰ ἔργα τῆς σαρκός the gen. τῆς σαρκός identifies the root of the problem. It is either a gen. of source (Schreiner, 346), "works that arise from the flesh," or a subj. gen., "works that the flesh does." The indefinite relative pronoun ἅτινα refers back to τὰ ἔργα τῆς σαρκός and identifies the elements in the following list as belonging to that class of entities, but they do not exhaust it (so also Lightfoot, 210).[60] Thus the list that follows contains flagrant examples of what the flesh accomplishes, but these are not the only ones.

Paul begins this list with a word common to vice lists that refers to sexual sin.[61] Throughout Greek literature πορνεία describes sexual activity in a negative sense. This word can refer to specific forms of sexual sin—prostitution

---

59. BDAG, 1047.

60. See BDAG, 730, which states that ὅστις can "emphasize a characteristic quality, by which a preceding statement is to be confirmed."

61. I am not inclined to think that Paul listed this first because it was the worst, but given human sexuality and the prevalence of sexual immorality across times and cultures, perhaps he listed it first because of its commonality and ubiquity. It is truly manifest and apparent as a work of the flesh in all times and places. For Pauline usage in another vice list, see Col 3:5. For extrabiblical examples, see Did. 5:1; Herm. Mand. VIII, 3.

or fornication, even prohibited degrees of marriage[62]—but Pauline usage is more general, referring to any kind of illegitimate sexual activity outside the marriage relationship.[63] The LXX and the NT have certain negative nuances not found in broader extrabiblical literature, such as metaphorical uses to describe spiritual unfaithfulness toward God. In much of the book of Hosea, for example, πορνεία literally describes sexual immorality, but the whole book functions as a broad metaphor for Israel's covenant unfaithfulness. The usage of the term in the book of Revelation is similar, as there it is powerfully applied to spiritual unfaithfulness and unbelief, especially so in the image of the great harlot in Rev 17–18. Thus this word is especially apropos to begin the list of works that the flesh produces. Attending to the flesh will lead to sexual immorality, which at its root shows a lack of immediate faithfulness to the marriage partner and ultimately a lack of fidelity to God.

The word ἀκαθαρσία appears in non-biblical Greek literature to describe a bodily ailment, either the infection of a wound or an impurity in the bloodstream, but also to refer to moral depravity.[64] The word was taken up in the LXX to translate the concept of ceremonial uncleanness, occurring twenty-three times in Leviticus alone. While this ceremonial uncleanness was occasionally a disease or bodily emission, the primary emphasis in Leviticus is on ceremonial uncleanness and its spiritual effects. In the NT the term only occurs outside of Paul once, but that usage is illustrative. In Matt 23:27 Jesus spoke against his opponents: "Woe to you, experts in the law and you Pharisees, hypocrites! You are like whitewashed tombs that look beautiful on the outside but inside are full of the bones of the dead and of everything unclean (καὶ πάσης ἀκαθαρσίας)." This usage shows well the metaphorical use: The vehicle is the dead human remains inside the tomb, and the tenor is the horrid spiritual state of the individual. This image would be especially potent in a Jewish context where contact with a corpse created ceremonial uncleanness. The other nine uses of the term in the NT are Pauline. Paul uses the term generally (Rom 6:19; Eph 4:19; 1 Thess 2:3), but he also uses the term in contexts discussing sexual sin (Rom 1:24; 1 Thess 4:7) and in close connection to πορνεία (2 Cor 12:21; Eph 5:3; Col 3:5; here). Paul's point of including ἀκαθαρσία here on the heels of πορνεία is to expand on the realm of sexual sin that is produced by the flesh. Not only do improper sexual deeds (πορνεία) spring from the power of the flesh, anything improper in the sexual realm leads to spiritual defilement (ἀκαθαρσία)—even thoughts, attitudes, and feelings, these too showing the power of the flesh.

The word ἀσέλγεια—translated variously as "depravity" (NET), "licentiousness" (NRSV), "debauchery" (NIV), "promiscuity" (CSB), and "sensuality" (ESV)—refers to a lack of self-control that leads to conduct that

62. BDAG, 854.

63. *NIDNTTE*, 4:115.

64. LSJ, 46; MGS, 62.

violates social norms.[65] It does not always refer to sexual behavior. For example, Aristotle, *Politics* 5.1304b.22, argues that in democracies demagogues are often overthrown due to this quality. However, in Classical Greek and in the LXX ἀσέλγεια very often describes sexual behavior that deviates widely from acceptable standards. For example, in Wis 14:26 when decrying idolatry, the author lists ἀσέλγεια together with other sexual sins. Both general and specific uses are found in the NT. Jesus warns in Mark 7:22 against ἀσέλγεια because it proceeds from the darkness of the human heart. His grouping of the word in the list could imply sexual sin, but more likely he speaks generally about personal excess. Jude 4 warns that false teachers turn God's grace into ἀσέλγεια, the freedom to pursue personal desires to an extreme. Other uses are more specifically focused on sexual sin. Second Peter 2:7 summarizes the sexually deviant conduct of the men of Sodom with this word. Paul uses the term similarly to these other NT uses. His use in Eph 4:19 could be more general, but his uses in Rom 13:13 and 2 Cor 12:21 clearly reference sexual sin. In Gal 5:19 because of the emphasis on sexual sin that precedes this word, likely Paul intends that nuance here. The term conveys that the works of the flesh include not only that which is demarcated as outside of God's ideal sexual ethic for humanity (as intimated by other terms in the list), but they also include the abandonment of the self to pursue the farthest boundaries of sexual deviancy with greediness and excitement. The same pull of the flesh that tempts the believer to transgress sexual boundaries with small steps tempts him to cross those boundaries with leaps and bounds as well.

5:20 The term εἰδωλολατρία, "idolatry," appears only in the NT and early Christian literature with reference to the worship of images.[66] Based on Paul's usage in Col 3:5, where πλεονεξία, "greediness," is equated with εἰδωλολατρία, the latter can be understood as the quintessence of sinfulness. Sin is essentially idolatry in that, whether consciously or not, it worships something other than the one true God. Paul's use here would be directed powerfully at the Galatians. Likely both Paul and the opponents in their preaching had spoken against the native idolatry of the Galatians. By including this term in the vice list Paul implicitly compares dependence upon circumcision with worship of false gods. Desiring the former is essentially idolatry.

In the classical period the term φαρμακεία was used to describe harsh medicines that caused people to purge (see, e.g., Hippocrates, *Aphorisms* 2.36). In the LXX φαρμακεία refers to magic or sorcery, routinely considered immoral and contrary to the ways of God. In the Koine period as in the classical, φαρμακεία referred to medications; the word could even be used for an abortifacient (see Soranus 1.59). During this period the term took on the additional meaning of "poisoning," possibly due to the harmful connotations attached to magic in the ancient world. People would concoct medications

65. BDAG, 141.

66. See 1 Cor 10:14; here; Col 3:5; 1 Pet 4:3; Did. 3:4; 5:1.

(i.e., poisons) that would bring about such great harm to others that the damage appeared to have occurred magically. In the NT, φαρμακεία is used similarly as in the LXX to describe magic or sorcery. While medicine as the specific referent may not be in view in the New Testament, the principle of harming another person certainly is, hence the inclusion of the term in this list that focuses on harmful, damaging ways people relate under the power of the flesh.[67]

The word ἔχθρα has a long history, occurring consistently throughout the classical and Koine periods. It is refers to a hostile feeling toward another, usually translated as "enmity" or "hatred." The pl. includes hostile feelings and the actions that arise from them.[68] The sense could be passive, describing someone who receives hate ("hated"), or active, describing a feeling directed toward someone ("hating" or "hostile").[69] The word can describe personal animosity between individuals (Luke 23:12) or groups (Eph 2:15). Paul uses it here to refer to intense personal discord that can arise among individuals, even within a Christian context. The flesh creates animosity and disrupts relationships within the church on a very personal level.[70]

The word ἔρις means "discord" or "strife," pointing to a social manifestation of some kind of rivalry.[71] Although Paul does not signal any particular connection with the previous word, they are logically and internally connected as cause and result. Paul mentions ἔρις a number of times in his vice lists, such that it almost appears to be a fixed element.[72] Even so, this must be taken seriously as a work of the flesh and not disregarded as a stereotypical mention. Any division within the body of Christ not met with a Spirit-guided response will become rancorous, harming the fellowship.

The word ζῆλος refers to intense feeling and emotional attachment to something. Appropriate senses would be "zeal" or "ardor."[73] The meaning itself is largely neutral. Both in the LXX and the NT whether this zeal is positive or negative is determined by the context.[74] Paul himself uses the term positively on occasion (e.g., 2 Cor 7:7, 11). But here, as in Rom 13:13 and

---

67. From this term one should not argue that Paul would think medications themselves to be sinful. Rather, the use of magic or sorcery to bring about harm to others is a sinful work of the flesh. The intent of the heart is primarily in view, not the specific instrument of action.

68. BDAG, 419.

69. *NIDNTTE*, 2:344.

70. *EDNT*, 2:94, appears to classify the occurrence here as hostility toward God, but that is unlikely given the interpersonal nature of so many of the works of the flesh.

71. BDAG, 392.

72. *EDNT*, 2:53.

73. BDAG, 427.

74. For a positive connotation in the LXX see Ps 68:10, which speaks of zeal for the house of God. For a negative connotation see Job 5:2, which refers to jealousy that leads to death.

2 Cor 12:20, the context is a vice list and as such the term has to be interpreted negatively. It refers to an intense, negative feeling of desire, that is, "jealousy." As with the previous words ἔχθραι and ἔρις Paul simply juxtaposes ζῆλος to the preceding two words, but the inner connection they share is clear. When animosity creates dissensions, people takes sides, creating jealousy among those who should instead desire the best for each other. Paul here speaks of the emotions and results of interpersonal discord and conflict, all of which will arise among believers who give place to the flesh.

In the classical period, θυμός meant "soul" or "spirit," referring to the center of life and thought, and then by extension the emotional evidence of that, that is, "feeling, passion, desire."[75] It is the place whence courage, willpower, desire, anger, and other strong feelings arise (see, e.g., Plato, *Cratylus* 419e.1). In the LXX the term carries a variety of senses: "sorrow" in Eccl 7:4; "will" or "desire" in 4 Kgdms 24:3; "anger" in Prov 20:2. This last meaning is especially appropriate when θυμός is used to denote God's response to sin (see, e.g., Lev 26:24). The NT use of the term emphasizes the meaning "anger." In eight of the eighteen occurrences of θυμός in the NT, it relates to the concept of God's wrath or indignation against sin (Rom 2:8; Rev 14:10, 14:19, 15:1, 15:7, 16:1, 16:19, 19:15). However, it is also used to describe anger of other persons: the devil (Rev 12:12), an earthly king (Heb 11:27), or even of members of the believing community (Eph 4:31). When it is used in vice lists such as here and 2 Cor 12:20, it speaks of an individual's "anger" or "temper." Given that anger manifests itself in outbursts that harm relationships and that Paul has just used words that relate to negative states of relationships, "outbursts of anger" may be the best translation in this context.[76]

In all of classical Greek literature available in TLG, the term ἐριθεία is used only twice. In both instances it occurs in Aristotle and means "self-seeking pursuit of political office by unfair means."[77] The word does not occur even once in the LXX. In the Koine era, related forms of the word were used to mean "party spirit" with implications of strife (see *SIG* 177.45). The term occurs seven times in the NT, twice in James and five times in Paul, but it nowhere receives an extended treatment. Because of this its meaning in the NT is unclear, but "selfishness, selfish ambition" is most likely.[78] In the case of this list, Paul previously included ἔρις with the meaning of "discord" or "strife." The meaning of "selfish ambition" for ἐριθεία would add nuance not mentioned previously: Self-interest and self-seeking ambition—undoubtedly to the neglect or detriment of others—is a work grounded in the flesh.

75. LSJ, 810; MGS, 954–55.

76. BDAG, 461.

77. BDAG, 392. See his *Politica*, 5.1302b.5 and 5.1303a.15–17.

78. BDAG, 392; J. H. Moulton and G. Milligan, *Vocabulary of the Greek Testament* (Peabody, MA: Hendrickson, 1997), 254.

The somewhat uncommon word διχοστασία has the undisputed meaning of "dissension, discord."[79] It occurs only one other time in the NT in Rom 16:17 in a warning against those who would create division in the church. This term describes the state resulting from the previously mentioned emotions and attitudes that divide and dissolve relationships in the church. No matter how it arrives in the body, dissension should be regarded as unhealthy and sinful since it arises from the power of the flesh.

The word αἵρεσις means "party" or "sect."[80] It occurs nine times in the NT, six of which are in Acts with clear reference to parties or sects within Judaism: either the Sadducees (Acts 5:17), the Pharisees (Acts 15:5; 26:5), or Christians (Acts 24:5, 14; 28:22), which Judaism initially regarded as a sect. Paul's other usage occurs in 1 Cor 11. In v. 18 he acknowledges the reality of σχίσματα ("divisions") in the Corinthian church at the partaking of the Lord's supper, and in v. 19 he sarcastically argues that different αἱρέσεις ("parties") are needed in the church to show who actually behaves properly. The sense of "party" or "faction" is readily apparent here in Galatians, following on the heels of "dissensions." Where divisions exist, parties coalesce, contrary to the Spirit's desire for the church.

5:21 As Paul continues his tour of relationship drama created by the flesh, he stops with the noun φθόνος, which means "envy, jealousy."[81] The word occurs nine times in the NT, notably in other vice lists (see Rom 1:29; 1 Tim 6:4; cf. Titus 3:3; 1 Pet 2:1).[82] It makes logical sense to include this word after αἵρεσις: Where parties coalesce, jealousy arises, this too is a work of the flesh.

The two final words in Paul's enumeration of the works of the flesh can be treated together. The word μέθη in the classical period meant "heavy drinking," "strong drink," and "drunkenness."[83] In the NT only the latter meaning occurs with this word.[84] Other occurrences of the term in the NT are collocated with related nouns: In Luke 21:34 it is paired with κραιπάλη, which refers to excessive drinking, and in Rom 13:13 it is paired with κῶμος, as here, which means "excessive feasting, carousing, revelry."[85] So Paul means drunkenness arising from excessive drinking, which serves as an indictment of both the inebriated state and the desire that seeks it out. The word κῶμος pairs naturally with the prior word, as feasting and drinking naturally go together. Just as Paul condemns excessive drinking that leads to

---

79. LSJ, 439; MGS, 541; BDAG, 252; *EDNT*, 1:337.

80. BDAG, 27.

81. BDAG, 1054.

82. For other occurrences not in vice lists, see Matt 27:18; Mark 15:10; Phil 1:15; Jas 4:5.

83. LSJ, 1090; MGS, 1295.

84. BDAG, 625.

85. BDAG, 580.

drunkenness, he condemns excessive eating with its emphasis on sensuality and engorgement.

καὶ τὰ ὅμοια τούτοις. Paul terminates his list of the works of the flesh with a phrase that indicates that other behaviors can be included in the category. The phrase τὰ ὅμοια τούτοις consists of the neut. pl. article plus the corresponding form of the adj. ὅμοιος, which means "similar, of like nature." The article turns the adj. into a substantive: "similar things." The dat. pronoun τούτοις indicates the things to which the comparison is made, referring back to all the things in the list: "things similar to these." This phrase reinforces the function of the indefinite relative pronoun in v. 19 to identify these items as representative manifestations of the "works of the flesh," not as a full enumeration of the category. Thus this list of "works of the flesh" is not exhaustive but representative. Wisdom can identify modern behaviors and attitudes unknown to Paul but common to current experience, like addictions or the exaltation of self on social media, as being grounded in the flesh just as these particular things Paul mentioned are.

ἃ προλέγω ὑμῖν, καθὼς προεῖπον ὅτι οἱ τὰ τοιαῦτα πράσσοντες βασιλείαν θεοῦ οὐ κληρονομήσουσιν. Paul steps beyond enumerating the list of "works of the flesh" to offer an apostolic judgment upon them. The neut. pl. pronoun ἅ points back to the entire list, essentially meaning "these things I just mentioned." As an acc., it is an acc. of reference relative to the verb προλέγω.[86] The verb προλέγω means "to tell in advance," but given the content of the ὅτι clause that follows the sense can readily be "to warn" (see Longenecker, 258; NET). Paul uses it here in the pres. tense and then joined with καθώς in the aor.: "I warn you now, just as I warned you before." The implication of these two tenses is that Paul warned the Galatians similarly in his original preaching to them during his missionary visits, just as he does now, but obviously the current context contains additional explanation that he did not elucidate before. This metacomment highlights the importance of the warning Paul gave, which he is going to mention again.

The ptc. phrase οἱ τὰ τοιαῦτα πράσσοντες is the subject of the content clause that constitutes Paul's warning. Paul pronounces a broad judgment upon anyone who does these things, these "works of the flesh." The dir. obj. τὰ τοιαῦτα is the adj. τοιοῦτος made into a substantive: "such things," again referring back to the entirety of the list of "the works of the flesh." The idea of the ptc. phrase is thus "those who do such things as I have enumerated here." The phrase βασιλείαν θεοῦ is the dir. obj. of the fut. verb κληρονομήσουσιν. With the negation οὐ the verb is a prediction of something that will not occur. Those who do things like those that Paul enumerated will not inherit

86. *Contra* BDF, §476(3), and MHT, 3:325, which argue that this relative pronoun is an example of prolepsis in that it points forward to the ὅτι clause (similarly Longenecker, 258). Describing the relative pronoun thusly does not explain well the pl. number of the pronoun nor the deictic force of τοιαῦτα. Taken together these both create a conceptual tie back to the list just enumerated.

the kingdom of God. With this statement Paul has invoked his apostolic authority to pronounce judgment upon those who practice such things and by implication upon those who have succumbed to the pull of circumcision.

The idea of inheritance is critical, as it restates an important theme found in the central section of the book (Gal 3:18, 29; 4:1, 7, 30). Here "inherit the kingdom of God" cannot be understood apart from the idea of inheritance related to Abraham. Even though the phrase "kingdom of God" is new to Paul's argument in Galatians, it is not new conceptually. Within Paul's argument there is an equivalence: The inheritance of Abraham and the kingdom of God are the same thing. Because the manifestation of the works of the flesh would mean that an individual is not guided by the Spirit and thus has not accepted the rule of God in Christ over them (Fung, 261–62), Paul can affirm that those who manifest those works are not part of God's family and will not receive the eschatological blessings promised to Abraham. This does not mean that perfection must be attained in order to be saved. Rather, it means that a consistent preoccupation with the "works of the flesh" means a person is not being led by the Spirit (Moo, 363), which casts doubt upon any profession of allegiance to Christ. Paul intends his warning to be fully felt by his audience so that the Galatians might return to his gospel.[87]

5:22 *Ὁ δὲ καρπὸς τοῦ πνεύματός ἐστιν ἀγάπη χαρὰ εἰρήνη, μακροθυμία χρηστότης ἀγαθωσύνη, πίστις.* Paul now turns to the opposite side of the flesh/Spirit equation to detail the positive outcomes of the Spirit in the life of the individual who has faith in Christ. This argument rests on the assertion Paul made in v. 17 about the nature of flesh and Spirit. They desire different things because they are antithetical to one another. The two lists enumerating the "works of the flesh" and the "fruit of the Spirit" should be conceived of similarly as organic outcomes: As the Galatians submit to one or the other, the differing outcomes will be produced. This is especially so given the figurative use of the word "fruit," which is well suited to indicate the result of a life's direction (see Dunn, 308). The singular subject *ὁ καρπός* is modified by the gen. *τοῦ πνεύματος*, which like *τῆς σαρκός* previously is subj. or source. There is a singular fruit produced by the Spirit—a singular outcome in the life of the individual who walks by the Spirit (v. 16) and who is led by the Spirit (v. 18)—that manifests all these qualities. This contrasts with the works of the flesh, which were chaotic (similarly Betz, 286). Any of the works of the flesh Paul mentioned—or anything like them—can be produced in the life of someone who favors the flesh. There is no singular way to be wrong in

87. For a helpful overview of interpretations that relate these vices to inheriting the kingdom, see R. López, "Views on Paul's Vice Lists and Inheriting the Kingdom," *BSac* 168 (2011): 81–97; R. López, "Paul's Vice List in Galatians 5:19–21," *BSac* 169 (2012): 48–67. For a broader discussion of kingdom in Paul, see K. P. Donfried, "The Kingdom of God in Paul," in *The Kingdom of God in 20th-Century Interpretation,* ed. W. L. Willis (Peabody: Hendrickson, 1987), 175–90.

this instance. In contrast, the fruit of the Spirit is singular. All these elements will mark those who submit to the Spirit, so only one multifaceted outcome is in view.[88]

The first quality that Paul mentions as a fruit of the Spirit is *ἀγάπη*. The two prior occurrences of the term in the book refer to God's love (Gal 5:6, 13), while this reference refers to love exercised by the believer. The works of the flesh were disruptions in personal relationships caused by attention to the flesh, so this love should readily be construed as the inverse, that is, proper attitude and attention toward others that restores and rejuvenates relationships within the body. Love as first in the list marks it in some way as all-encompassing (Dunn, 309), flowing from God to the believer and then outward to others. While it is uncertain whether Paul maintains a logical order of qualities here, love could easily be considered the sum total and outworking of all the other characteristics mentioned afterwards because of its all-encompassing nature. Luther, 280, stated it well: "It would have been enough to have said love and no more, for love extends to all the fruit of the Spirit."

The word *χαρά* signifies an experience of gladness, routinely translated as "joy."[89] Paul does not use the word anywhere else in this epistle, but it occurs frequently in his writings (twenty-one times total). In contrast with the negative feelings toward others that the flesh engenders, the Spirit creates gladness centered in Christ that flows outward to others.

Paul used the word *εἰρήνη*, "peace," previously in the letter introduction (Gal 1:3) with a specific theological nuance: a state of well-being sourced in God and his activity on behalf of the believer. That theological nuance is certainly in the background here, as these qualities are the fruit of the Spirit guiding and leading the believer, but the more immediate sense is the presence of accord or harmony between two parties. Especially in contrast to the dissension and discord caused in the body by the works of the flesh, the peace and agreement brought by the Spirit is a powerful testimony of his work among believers.

The word *μακροθυμία* means "patience," the attitude of tranquility while waiting, but also "forbearance," the ability to bear with difficult circumstances and duress.[90] Paul uses the word the most of its NT occurrences (ten times out of fourteen times total), incorporating it regularly into his practical exhortations.[91] This contrasts significantly with the works of the flesh, all of which could arguably spring from impatience with another in some aspect of a relationship, especially given his use of θυμός ("outburst of anger"). In a sense *μακρουθμία* serves as an antonym for that word in the prior list.

---

88. As a pastor from my youth would say, "There are a thousand ways to be crooked, but only one way to be straight."

89. BDAG, 1077.

90. BDAG, 612.

91. *NIDNTTE*, 3:212.

The word *χρηστότης* is beautiful, signifying "the quality of being helpful or beneficial," very appropriately translated as "goodness, kindness, generosity."[92] Paul is the only NT author to use this word (ten times total), and often it refers to God's kindness toward humanity (see Rom 2:4; 11:22; Eph 2:7; Titus 3:4). It occurs only here in Galatians, referring to an attitude toward others that seeks their good and benefit. It is an essential characteristic of love and a chief manifestation of the Spirit's work in the life of a believer.[93]

Similar to the preceding word, the noun *ἀγαθωσύνη* means "goodness." But in contrast to the previous word, which focuses more on the actions that flow from the attitude, this word focuses on the innate, moral quality that seeks the good of others.[94] With these two words, then, Paul shows that the Spirit affects both attitude and action. The word *ἀγαθωσύνη* is rare in the NT, occurring only in Paul (Rom 15:14; here; Eph 5:9; 2 Thess 1:11). The use in Eph 5:9 provides a suggestive parallel with the current verse, showing that goodness is the natural outworking of salvation in the life of the believer.

The noun *πίστις* is certainly common in Paul (142 times total) and even in this epistle, occurring eighteen times before this verse. Understanding the meaning here requires that we take careful note of the context. Almost every use of the noun in the book refers to the response of trust on the part of the individual to the person of Christ revealed by God in the historical event of his death and resurrection.[95] Claiming that nuance here, however, would put the cart before the horse since this verse speaks of the fruit that the Spirit, graciously given to the believer because of the response of trust, creates in character and action. Much more likely is the meaning "faithfulness," that is, the quality of character that evokes confidence and trust.[96] This would be especially appropriate given the prior emphasis in the works of the flesh on discordant human relationships. In stark contrast to the flesh, the Spirit creates relationships in which each party can be trusted to desire the good of the other.

5:23 *πραΰτης ἐγκράτεια· κατὰ τῶν τοιούτων οὐκ ἔστιν νόμος.* The first two words of this verse are the final elements of the positive list detailing the fruit of the Spirit. The word *πραΰτης* signifies "the quality of not being overly impressed by a sense of one's self-importance."[97] It is most often translated as "gentleness" (so NIV, CSB, ESV, NET, and many other English translations), which reflects the outward manifestation of character, but "humility" would also be appropriate, stressing the inner character itself. As with other words in this

---

92. BDAG, 1090.
93. *NIDNTTE*, 4:687.
94. BDAG, 4.
95. See the excursus "Paul's Use of the πιστ- Word Group in Galatians" following the commentary on 2:15–21.
96. BDAG, 818.
97. BDAG, 861.

list describing the fruit of the Spirit, this word has its full impact when seen in contrast to the works of the flesh. The flesh focuses on the individual, causing pride and strife at every turn. The Spirit through gentleness focuses on the other, creating harmony and unity in all aspects of personal relationships.

The final word of the list, ἐγκράτεια, refers to self-control.[98] This is the quality of character that restrains the sinful impulses of the individual, enabling the life of Christ to shine forth and personal relationships to be improved. The word is not common in the NT, occurring only twice otherwise, but it is foundational to the ethical life of the believer. In Acts 24:25 Paul speaks of this quality to Felix, along with righteousness and the coming judgment as a summation of "faith in Christ Jesus." In 2 Pet 1:6 this quality is presented as part of the process of sanctification intended for all believers. Paul in this verse perhaps uses it in direct contrast to ἀσέλγεια in the prior list but with connotations other than sexual. It refers to all aspects of human life—emotional, mental, physical—and implies a quality of life marked by circumspection and moderation that enables unity of the body to be paramount.

The sentence that concludes this list is marked by asyndeton. It begins with the prepositional phrase κατὰ τῶν τοιούτων. The pronoun τοιούτων in this prepositional phrase connects this sentence to the list. It shows that the entire list is in view, but is also suggests that these virtues may also be representative of other godly qualities that the Spirit produces in the believer (see Fung, 273). The sense of κατά with the gen. is similar to the sense used before in Gal 3:21 and 5:17, that of opposition, being against. The primary difficulty for interpretation is the anarthrous occurrence of νόμος. Normally in Galatians νόμος has the article unless it is in a prepositional phrase or has some other grammatical feature to lend definiteness.[99] Similar anarthrous occurrences of νόμος are in 2:19; 3:17; 6:13. Each of these can be defended as "the Law" based on the context. So an anarthrous νόμος does not automatically mean "law" as a principle or general idea as opposed to the one Law (*contra* Longenecker, 263). In Galatians νόμος regularly takes on the technical meaning of "Torah" and need not be articular to be identified as such. So Paul's assertion here is that the Law, that is, that to which the Galatians were tempted to submit in their particular situation, has no strictures against the fruit of the Spirit. Indeed, by exhibiting this fruit the Galatians would in fact be obedient to the Law and fulfill it. In this construal Paul sees the Law as a restrainer of sin, also what his opponents were likely preaching. The Law is not needed to restrain a Spirit-filled believer because they produce a life of Spirit character, a character that is not prohibited by the Law in any way (similarly Lightfoot, 213). Thus this argument echoes what Paul implied earlier regarding Lev 19:18. The fulfillment of the Law is not found in circumcision but in living by

98. BDAG, 274.

99. See Wallace, *Greek Grammar*, 245–54, for a discussion of ways in which nouns can be definite without the article.

means of the Spirit. The Spirit enables fulfillment of the Law's requirement, rendering the Law complete in the present time with nothing left in it to obey (see also de Boer, 366).

5:24 οἱ δὲ τοῦ Χριστοῦ Ἰησοῦ τὴν σάρκα ἐσταύρωσαν σὺν τοῖς παθήμασιν καὶ ταῖς ἐπιθυμίαις. The conj. δέ links this statement about the crucifixion of the flesh to the statement of the Law not being against the fruit of the Spirit, binding them together as a conceptual unit. This binding is highlighted by the asyndeton that occurs before the first phrase in v. 23 and the asyndeton that follows at the beginning of v. 25. Thus these two statements taken together should be understood as a theological response to the enumeration of the works of the flesh and the fruit of the Spirit. There is even a logical chiasm here:

> the works of the flesh [enumerated]
> the fruit of the Spirit [enumerated]
> The Law is not against the fruit of the Spirit.
> Those who belong to Christ have crucified the flesh.

Paul's intention is to show that those who are in Christ, those who have received the blessing of the Spirit, are able to live in accord with the Spirit because of their co-crucifixion with Christ. They can thus resist the pull of both the flesh and the Law.

The subject of the sentence is the phrase οἱ τοῦ Χριστοῦ Ἰησοῦ. This is the poss. gen. used substantivally: "those who belong to Christ Jesus."[100] A similarly important use is found in 3:29, where Paul defines what it means to "belong to Christ": Those who belong to Christ are the promised seed of Abraham, those who will be heirs according to the promise given to him. This linguistic and conceptual connection shows that Paul has not left behind his central exegetical, theological argument for more general, spiritual territory. He attends to the same concepts as explained previously and simply argues that they lead to practical, Spirit-led behavior. His assertion is that the people in view have crucified the flesh. Paul's use of σταυρόω here hearkens back to his use of συσταυρόω with reference to his co-crucifixion with Christ (see Gal 2:19–20). Each ultimately refers to the same event and the same theological reality, that is, Christ's historical crucifixion and the believer's participation in it through faith (Bruce, 256). There Paul speaks of the co-crucifixion with regard to its positive effects: The life he now lives is empowered by the life of Christ in him. Here he speaks of the crucifixion of the flesh and the nullification of its negative power over the individual. This argument lines up with his current concern for the Galatians: Being in Christ means that they have fundamentally transformed their stance toward circumcision and by extension the Law. They need not live under the sway of either any longer.

---

100. Robertson, *Grammar*, 767, implies that a noun like μαθηταί should be supplied here, but that obscures the connection to the prior verse.

The prepositional phrase that follows the main verb has two objects: σὺν τοῖς παθήμασιν καὶ ταῖς ἐπιθυμίαις. The prep. σύν invokes association and fills out the idea of the flesh here. The flesh is not neutral after all, as some of the Galatians might have thought, but rather has its own desires and tendencies, the two words emphasizing the flesh with its passive and active sides (Lightfoot, 213). In the believer's co-crucifixion with Christ, these desires and intentions of the flesh have themselves been crucified. The two nouns παθήμασιν and ἐπιθυμίαις could be taken as a hendiadys meaning "passionate/powerful desires," but this is unlikely given the repetition of the article before each. These articles function as poss. pronouns, referring back to σάρκα and identifying these as its possessions (Burton, 320).

5:25 εἰ ζῶμεν πνεύματι, πνεύματι καὶ στοιχῶμεν. This continuation of Paul's argument is marked by asyndeton.[101] The content develops the co-crucifixion theme Paul mentioned in the previous verse. The original statement of this idea in 2:19–20 referenced co-crucifixion with Christ and then living through the power of Christ; the Spirit was not mentioned there. Paul's present argument augments this theme with his mention of crucifixion of the flesh in v. 24, then living by the means of the Spirit in v. 25. The verb ζάω is used as an ethical synonym to περιπατέω (de Boer, 370). The dat. noun πνεύματι as before indicates means or instrument. The protasis echoes the similar statements Paul made in v. 16 and 18 concerning living in submission to the Spirit's guidance. The apodosis contains the hortatory subjunctive στοιχῶμεν, intensified by the particle καί, which here has adjunctive force, "also." The verb στοιχέω should not be taken simply as a synonym for περιπατέω. That would render Paul's argument tautologous and be out of step with the wider sense of the term.[102] The verb means "to be in agreement with, to be in step with," and that sense fits here perfectly.[103] It reflects both the internal attitude and the external actions that arise thence. The dat. πνεύματι in the apodosis marks the entity to which the subject of the verb στοιχῶμεν conforms.[104] Conformity to the Spirit is a heightened requirement that goes beyond simply living by the Spirit. A life of obedience to the Spirit is expected of believers, but the entire character of a believer's life should conform to the Spirit's character of life.

This brings up the question of referent for the apodosis, and the most natural sense is in line with everything Paul has argued up to this point in the letter. "Living in conformity with the Spirit" is synonymous with remaining faithful to Paul's gospel by refusing circumcision or any other type of Law

---

101. Both the weak transition and content lead some commentators (e.g., Martyn, 541; Moo, 370) to see the beginning of a new section that runs until 6:10.

102. Pun intended.

103. G. Delling, "στοιχέω et al.," *TDNT*, 7:667–69.

104. So BDAG, 946; *contra* Wallace, *Greek Grammar*, 166, who implies that this is a dat. of means.

observance. The logic runs thusly: Up to this point Paul has endeavored to show that the reception of the Spirit is God's way of blessing the Gentiles, and he is also the means by which the Gentiles will fulfill what God requires of them. Their faith in Christ means that they have received the Spirit, that they are indeed "living by the Spirit." This is the protasis of the conditional sentence. The apodosis wrestles with their current choice, namely, whether to submit to circumcision. "Conforming to the Spirit" in the Galatians' experience means refusing circumcision and committing instead to Paul's gospel anew by which the Gentiles have been included in Abraham's family based only on faith in Jesus, without any other requirement. Thus this verse presents in a compact, balanced way the indicative and the imperative of the gospel (Longenecker, 266; Moo, 373). This verse affirms that the Galatians are indeed properly related to God; they have been given the Spirit because of their faith in Christ. This verse also requires that in light of that reality they continue to live in line with the Spirit's work in them, apart from any submission to the Law.

5:26 μὴ γινώμεθα κενόδοξοι, ἀλλήλους προκαλούμενοι, ἀλλήλοις φθονοῦντες. This verse applies the potentially ambiguous hortatory command in the prior verse. In essence, those living by the Spirit, that is, all the Galatians who have faith in Christ, should conform to the Spirit by refusing circumcision. Very likely the agitators had created strife among the Galatians through their preaching of circumcision. As some were swayed to accept that point of view, strife and discord would spring up within the Christian communities as different factions fought over the issue. The exhortation in this verse intends to halt any discord over the issue of Law observance. The strife created by insistence on Law observance testifies to its wrongheadedness. Paul's admonition against the intense division shows that its root is problematic.

This verse begins with a hortatory subjunctive as in the previous verse, but this time in the form of a prohibition: μὴ γινώμεθα. This could mean either "let us not be," with an implication that the Galatians were already marked by the negative characteristics described here, or "let us not become," with the implication that Paul is attempting to forestall any progression in the wrong direction. Although there is no textual evidence otherwise that the Galatians were experiencing internal strife over circumcision,[105] it stands to reason that they were indeed experiencing some given the entire freight of the letter. Paul would not issue the command unless the problem were real or at the least very probable. The weight of this prohibition rests on the adj. κενόδοξοι, which means "conceited" or "boastful."[106] Paul's use of the word implies that some of the Galatians had become conceited about their spiritual state toward others. Paul wants that self-exaltation to stop. It does not comport with a proper understanding of God's gracious work through Christ

---

105. See the discussion about the first class condition in v. 15.

106. BDAG, 539.

by the Spirit, nor does it exemplify loving service toward others as prescribed in v. 13. The balance of the verse contains two ptcs., each of which functions as a ptc. of result. They could be means (so Moo, 373), but the internal logic of the admonition is that conceit on the part of individuals results in strife within the community. The verb προκαλέω means "to provoke or challenge someone," and the verb φθονέω means "to envy or be jealous of someone."[107] The pronoun ἀλλήλων is used as the dir. obj. of each ptc. in the acc. and dat. case respectively.[108] This verse forms an *inclusio* of sorts with v. 13, but through an antithetical idea, not a synonymous one. Conceited self-attention that results in interpersonal challenges and envy is diametrically opposed to what living by means of the Spirit will accomplish in the Christian community. This serves both as appropriate paraenesis given Paul's theological argument, but it also indicts the opponents whose preaching has created division, not caring community.

In this poignant section of the letter, Paul drives home his admonition to the Galatians to live free from the Law in accordance with his gospel. His desire has not changed at all from the personal and theological sections of the letter: He wants to motivate the Galatians to reject the opponents and their arguments for Law observance by rejecting the pull of circumcision and by renewing their commitment to Paul's gospel. The dress of the motivation in this section, however, is ethical and behavioral, as Paul addresses specific issues relative to how the Galatian communities live. The short of Paul's argument is a logical one based on his understanding of the work of the Spirit: The Spirit working in the Galatians is proof that they are rightly related to God. Thus they should reject Law observance and instead live in conformity with the Spirit through loving service toward others manifested through Spirit-generated behaviors that preserve and nurture proper community.

Theological Comments

In a very legitimate sense, the most important issue in this paragraph is not practical but theological: How does Paul understand the relationship between the flesh and the Spirit? Are these concepts to be understood generally, such that this paragraph is best construed as broad teaching about how best to live the Christian life? Or are these ideas specifically tied to the context, such that they have a particular referent given Paul's argument about the Law and his gospel? I believe the latter is the best way to take these and ultimately leads to a richer understanding of Paul's hamartiology and pneumatology than otherwise understood.

107. See BDAG, 1054.

108. Concerning the dat. Case with φθονοῦντες, Robertson, *Grammar*, 541, agrees that ἀλλήλοις is a dir. obj., but Winer, *Grammar*, 261, argues for a dat. of reference.

The overarching purpose of Paul's writing to the Galatians is to encourage them, to motivate them—indeed, to command them in the strongest way possible—to remain faithful to his gospel. The gospel he preached to them displayed the power of the crucified Christ to include all people, Jews and Gentiles alike, in Abraham's family on the basis of faith alone. The agitators had come to the Galatian churches after Paul left. They were preaching a gospel of circumcision and thereby undermining Paul's message. Everything Paul has written in this letter is designed to undo this damage, and this paragraph with its attendant emphasis upon flesh and Spirit is no exception.

The concept of flesh to Paul, in this context, is very physical, more concrete than metaphorical. Circumcision was an action done to the flesh on the most intimate of levels. The removal of the foreskin from the male genitals was a deeply physical, embodied act with a powerful affect upon the human person, both psychologically and spiritually, especially for adults. First and foremost, at this juncture flesh for Paul was not fundamentally the human personality broadly conceived of as a sinful entity. That would put the cart before the horse in Paul's thinking. Rather, flesh was the actual human body, which served as a representative or gateway to the personality. Paul's theological development here does not build upon the idea of the human body as a source of sinfulness. Instead, he establishes that linkage in real time. This is what makes circumcision so dangerous in Paul's mind. It is an emphasis upon the human body that elevates the physical over the spiritual. That emphasis opens the door for all other kinds of abuses that the flesh establishes. This is the prototype for Paul's argument that the flesh is an agent for sin and as such uses every opportunity to wreak havoc upon the human person and create bondage. In this very paragraph we see Paul's theological development on both anthropology and hamartiology.

The Spirit also requires particular definition here. One could readily assume that the flesh as the sinful part of human nature is juxtaposed with the spirit as the part that is sensitive to God's leading and able to live in light of redemption. This construal, however, ignores the context of Paul's theological argumentation. The Spirit in the central exegetical portion of the book is always God's Spirit, the Holy Spirit, who has been given to those who believe in Jesus. This Spirit is the proof that Paul's gospel was ordained by God and that God was at work in the midst of the Galatians by means of that gospel. Paul does not change that identification here. He speaks directly of the Holy Spirit and identifies him not only as the blessed gift originally promised to Abraham but as the divine means by which this new family of Abraham will live together in a way which pleases the Lord.

It is this juxtaposition within the context of the presenting problem of the book that gives Paul's ethical argument such theological force. The opponents were calling the Galatians to submit to circumcision in supposed obedience to the Law. Instead, what they were offering the Galatians was an insidious means for the flesh to gain control of them, and control them it would if given the chance. If they allowed this desire for their flesh to accomplish its work, the results would be catastrophic. The enumeration of the works of the flesh is not a warning of what to avoid. It instead is a warning of what would undoubtedly occur if they submitted to the flesh by accepting circumcision. The end result would be eschatological judgment. In contrast, the Galatians needed to live by the Spirit, to be led by the Spirit. The outcome of that submission would be a fruit pleasing to God, in accordance with his character, which ultimately fulfills the purpose of the Law. Paradoxically, the only way for the Galatians to guarantee the fulfillment of the Law within their experience, and thus honor God, would be to ignore its mandate to emphasize the flesh. The Spirit, promised in fulfillment of the Law's teachings and intent, provided the only means in the present time to accomplish the goal of fulfilling the Law.

Spirit and flesh in this paragraph are thus neither general or ephemeral. Rather, they are specific and concrete entities that together serve as the point of stasis in the conflict Paul has with his opponents. Paul's theological understanding of each entity leads to concrete, real exhortations, all designed to show the dead end of Law observance and the rich reward of the gospel he had preached, which the Galatians had in fact believed.

Application and Devotional Implications

This paragraph is replete with exhortations that have immediate application to the life of the believer. Paul's theological argument has developed into a practical vision of loving service toward each other in the community through the guidance of the Spirit God has gifted through faith in Christ. This vision grants the means by which the nascent community can ultimately develop into the worldwide family of Abraham that God intends. Here I want to highlight three key aspects of that practical vision.

At the very beginning of the paragraph, Paul makes a clear, direct command: διὰ τῆς ἀγάπης δουλεύετε ἀλλήλοις, "through love serve each other." As argued above in the commentary, the love Paul has in view is not human love from within but God's divine love affecting the believer from without. This command envisions an individual motivated by the love of God to serve others in the community. This presents an immediate challenge to all believers as they consider their relationships to others within the body of Christ. Are our actions toward others motivated by the love God has shown, or are they in some way self-serving? Do we strive through his love to meet the needs of others, or do we serve only ourselves? There is freedom here to serve creatively, as Paul does not enumerate of what that service consists, but he is quite concerned about its source and its character. Believers must constantly measure their attitudes and actions toward against the holy standard of God's love for us.

In the middle of the paragraph Paul gives two commands, meant to be understood somewhat in parallel. In v. 16 he gives a command that directly contrasts the guiding roles of Spirit and flesh: πνεύματι περιπατεῖτε καὶ ἐπιθυμίαν σαρκὸς οὐ μὴ τελέσητε, "walk by the Spirit and you will not fulfill the desire of the flesh." In v. 18 he restates this idea as a conditional sentence: εἰ δὲ πνεύματι ἄγεσθε, οὐκ ἐστὲ ὑπὸ νόμον, "and if you are led by the Spirit, you are not under Law." The Spirit here is presented as the means by which the believer lives properly, in obedience to God with a desire to please him. But all too often we misunderstand or misappropriate the Spirit. In my Protestant, evangelical, Bible church tradition, the Spirit is often an unwelcome guest to our weekly gathering: We know he's there but we'd rather he not say or do much.[109] In charismatic congregations, the Spirit is welcome, but he's always expected to be the life of the party. It's either go big or go home! In between the extremes we must recognize on the one hand the Spirit's constant presence and on the other hand his divine authority. The Spirit is the blessing God promised, which is now given to those who believe in Christ. He is meant to be near, tangible, and powerful in the lives of believers. At the same time, it is his will that guides us, not the other way around. We must submit to his leading and authority and mode of working, even if we might prefer something other. The leading of the Spirit is in contrast to the flesh. Here Paul has in mind the very physical act of circumcision. Paul does not want the Galatians to submit to the desires centered on their physical body rather than the desires of the Spirit. This would simply open the door for the flesh to run roughshod over us, doing with us whatever it desires. This leads to an important theological principle, well understood from this passage and many others: Our natural human impulses are not necessarily godly ones.[110] Just as the Galatians' desire for the flesh was not God's will for them, nor would it lead to holiness, our natural desires are not necessarily holy in and of themselves.

---

109. Early during my seminary education I was privileged to read an article that helped me immensely as a cessationist to wrestle with my attitude toward the Spirit: D. B. Wallace, "Who's Afraid of the Holy Spirit? The Uneasy Conscience of a Noncharismatic Evangelical," *CT* 38 (1994): 34–38.

110. This is a central theological argument against the current trend in much secular and even church culture that rationalizes and justifies many behaviors, most notably homosexuality and same-sex marriage, by lauding the natural desires of the individual as God-given and God-sanctioned. This narcissistic inversion flies in the face of our fullest understanding of the sinful human person. We are continually bent toward sin. No human behavior should be categorically accepted as good without warrant from God's revealed Word. Paul makes this point specifically about sexuality when he uses the words πορνεία, ἀκαθαρσία, and ἀσέλγεια to identify the works of the flesh in 5:19. They cover the gamut of our sexuality, including external behaviors and internal attitudes, actions, and feelings. Anything sexual outside the union of one man to one woman in marriage is a work of the flesh and not God's will. At the same time, we have to recognize that sex is not the only problem in view; the problem of the flesh is much bigger than sex alone (Hays, 330).

Wrestling with this paragraph brings great conviction. What believer can say that he has truly submitted to the leading of the Spirit in all matters? Can we truly say that our actions toward others are only motivated by God's love with their best interests in mind? Have we followed our flesh when we should have been guided by the Spirit? Even though we fail miserably, God continues to work through his Spirit, enabling us to lovingly serve others in community so that our family of Abraham might be encouraged and edified. Let us be thankful and worship him for his gracious patience!

Additional Exegetical Comments

13 It's worth repeating F. F. Bruce's strong biblical-theological argument for the scope of the freedom the believer now enjoys.[111] The believer is free from the Law, which is most clearly supported from the immediate context. The believer is also free from the στοιχεῖα, supported by the wider argument of chapter 4. The believer is also free from apostolic dictation to be devoted only to Christ's gospel; based upon Paul's curses in 1:8–9, the apostle is only the messenger of Christ when he accurately conveys Christ's gospel. Finally, the believer is free from discrimination, which is supported by the broad message of how the Gentiles are now in the church only because of their faith.

5:13 Regarding the pass. voice of ἐκλήθητε, Soards and Pursiful, 272, make an important theological point. Paul's wording in 5:13 echoes his statement in 5:1, but in the prior verse Christ was the actor, while in 5:13 the assumed actor who called the Galatians to salvation was God. Thus both Christ and God are involved in calling the Galatians to freedom from what had previously enslaved them. This is not something Paul highlights in his argument, but it is an appropriately theological entailment.

5:14 My interpretation of this verse focuses on the fulfillment of the Law enabled by the Spirit in the present Christian community. The Law *qua* the Law no longer applies to believers as a body of law because it has been fulfilled in the one command to love neighbor as self, which is now realized in Christ through loving service for one another in Abraham's family. A similar interpretation but with a slightly different focus on the point of fulfillment argues that Christ brought the Law to completion himself by loving his neighbor, and so, taking the Law in hand, he now properly provides it to the church as a fulfilled Law that makes no current requirement (Martyn, 490; so also Moo, 347–48).

---

111. F. F. Bruce, "'Called to Freedom': A Study in Galatians," in *New Testament Age: Essays in Honor of Bo Reicke,* ed. W. C. Weinrich (Macon, GA: Mercer University, 1984), 61–71.

5:14 Hays, 322, makes a strong argument here that "the Law has undergone a hermeneutical transformation, so that it now becomes a witness to the gospel." Essentially Paul reads the Law anew through the lens of Christ and the cross so that he understands it altogether differently from the way he did before when he read it as a Pharisee. In essence I think Hays is right, but I would add two qualifiers. First, it is not the Law that has undergone a hermeneutical transformation, but Paul himself as he understands the full scope of what God is fulfilling about the Law in Christ. Second, that fulfillment was always there had Paul had eyes to see it and the further revelation to connect it. Jesus himself demonstrated this hermeneutical acuity on the road to Emmaus (Luke 24:27). So Paul's reading may in one sense be new, but it is not novel. It was actually there, latent and implicit, all the time.

5:17 J. J. Kilgallen here argues that the best construal of this verse sees the center two clauses as a parenthesis:

> For the flesh strives against the spirit
> (but the spirit strives against the flesh,
> for these [two] are opposed to each other)
> in order that (with the result that) the things you want to do,
> these you do not do.[112]

In this arrangement, the believer not doing what he desires is directly related to the flesh's influence; it does not arise intrinsically from the "reciprocal struggle of flesh and spirit." The benefit of this view is how it cuts the Gordian Knot of this verse's interpretation, but it cannot be accepted wholesale because the way Paul strings together the conjunctions here could argue against it. Further study of the syntax of Pauline parentheses would illuminate this question.

5:19 E. Miller makes an argument that Paul uses *ἀκαθαρσία* as an oblique reference to homosexual sexual activity.[113] Although his argument is suggestive in light of Pauline word usage and collocations, it cannot be clearly established by extrabiblical usage. This interpretation is not required, however, to support the interpretation that Paul includes homosexual sexual activity as one of many referents when he refers to works of the flesh that manifest in illicit sexual behavior.

5:23 R. A. Campbell argues that the clause *κατὰ τῶν τοιούτων οὐκ ἔστιν νόμος* is best understood as referring to people, taking *τῶν τοιούτων* as masc., and serves to balance the admonition at the end of the vice list in v. 21.[114]

---

112. J. J. Kilgallen, "The Strivings of the Flesh. (Galatians 5,17)," *Bib* 80 (1999): 113–14.
113. E. L. Miller, "More Pauline References to Homosexuality?," *EvQ* 77 (2005): 129–34.
114. R. A. Campbell, " 'Against Such Things There is No Law'? Galatians 5:23*b* Again," *ExpTim* 107 (1996): 271–72.

Understanding it this way makes the clause holistic in force, reemphasizing the life given by the Spirit to believers. Against this view is the previous use of τοιοῦτος in v. 19 with clear reference to the list of vices, which would mean that in v. 23 it would logically have a neut. reference, too.

Selected Bibliography

Campbell, R. A. " 'Against Such Things There is No Law'? Galatians 5:23*b* Again." *ExpTim* 107 (1996): 271–72.

Donfried, K. P. "The Kingdom of God in Paul." In *The Kingdom of God in 20th-Century Interpretation*, ed. W. L. Willis, 175–90. Peabody: Hendrickson, 1987.

Johnston, J. W. *The Use of* Πᾶς *in the New Testament*. SBG 11. Peter Lang, 2004.

Kilgallen, J. J. "The Strivings of the Flesh. (Galatians 5,17)." *Bib* 80 (1999): 113–14.

López, R. "Views on Paul's Vice Lists and Inheriting the Kingdom." *BSac* 168 (2011): 81–97.

———. "Paul's Vice List in Galatians 5:19–21." *BSac* 169 (2012): 48–67.

Miller, E. L. "More Pauline References to Homosexuality?" *EvQ* 77 (2005): 129–34.

Westerholm, S. "On Fulfilling the Whole Law (Gal 5:14)." *SEÅ* 51–52 (1986): 229–37.

Manifestations of the Spirit (Part 1) (6:1–5)

Textual Notes

6:1 The reading of NA[28] states generically ἐὰν καὶ προλημφθῇ ἄνθρωπος ἔν τινι παραπτώματι, "even if a man is overtaken in some transgression." The textual variation at this point provides clarity as to which man is in view. Some witnesses add the prepositional phrase ἐξ ὑμῶν after ἄνθρωπος (Ψ 0278 1175 2464 sy[h] sa); a few others replace ἄνθρωπος with the phrase τις ἐξ ὑμῶν. Both these clarifications can be understood as scribal alterations, meant to avoid confusion in the application of this text by making explicit whom Paul had in view. The prepositional phrase ἐξ ὑμῶν in each variant specifies that the individual in view comes from the Galatian churches, so each clarification specifies that the guidance and care envisioned takes place *within* the Christian community.

6:2 There is some textual uncertainty surrounding the main verb in the second clause of 6:2. The majority of witnesses, many quite important, read the aor. impv. ἀναπληρώσατε (א A C D K L P Ψ 0122 33 81 104 365 630 1175 1241 1505 1739 1881 2464 𝔐). This would make the second clause a command, similar to the first: "Bear each other's burdens and thus fulfill the law of Christ." The manuscript 𝔓[46] reads ἀποπληρώσετε, the fut. indic. of ἀποπληρόω, meaning "fill up, satisfy, accomplish."[1] This would be translated as "Bear each other's burdens and thus you will satisfy the law of Christ." NA[28] reads ἀναπληρώσετε, the fut. indic. of ἀναπληρόω, supported by several ancient witnesses (B F G 323 latt): "Bear each other's burdens and thus you will fulfill the law of Christ."

Considering external evidence, the reading of 𝔓[46] can be dismissed since it is a singular reading, but it does give early support to the fut. tense as original and consequently could be viewed as confirmation of the fut. form ἀναπληρώσετε. The manuscript support for the aor. impv. is quite strong; without the confirming witness of 𝔓[46] it would certainly be stronger evidence than that for the reading of the text.

1. LSJ, 213; MGS, 264.

Considering the internal evidence involves questions of context and grammar. Considering the immediate context leads to a preference for the fut. indic.; scribes would be much more likely to change the fut. indic. to the aor. impv. under the influence of the preceding impv. verbs.[2] However, this preference is mitigated by the question of the grammar. The passage under consideration has an impv. followed by καὶ οὕτως and another verb. At issue is whether the second verb is indic. or impv. The only clear parallel in the Pauline corpus is 1 Cor 11:28: δοκιμαζέτω δὲ ἄνθρωπος ἑαυτὸν καὶ οὕτως ἐκ τοῦ ἄρτου ἐσθιέτω καὶ ἐκ τοῦ ποτηρίου πινέτω. The verbs following οὕτως in this instance are imperatives.[3] This would lead to the acceptance of the aor. impv. on the basis of authorial usage elsewhere.

This is a difficult problem to solve because neither the external nor internal evidence points decisively in a particular direction.[4] Given the strength of the manuscript evidence in favor of the aor. impv. and the grammatical parallel in 1 Cor 11:28, my preference is to see the aor. impv. as more likely original. The difference in meaning between that and the reading of NA[28] is not large. It simply strengthens the emphasis upon fulfilling the law of Christ as a command, not simply as a result. The logical means of doing this is still bearing one another's burdens. The force of οὕτως does not change in this construal.

6:4 𝔓[46] B and some versions omit the word ἕκαστος. This omission creates a stronger link between this verse and the previous one. The subject of δοκιμαζέτω would become the person highlighted in v. 3, that is, the one who thinks he is something when he is nothing. There is an inherent logic to this reading, as it ties vv. 3–4 together, addressing an individual who exhibits pride and the appropriate penitent response. The difficulty with this shorter reading is the sheer preponderance of manuscript evidence for the inclusion of the word; every other witness supports inclusion. Likely the word was omitted from these few witnesses on the grounds that the first repetition of ἕκαστος in this paragraph was redundant.

---

2. B. M. Metzger, *A Textual Commentary on the Greek New Testament* (New York: United Bible Societies, 1994), 530.

3. To find this parallel I searched for an impv. followed by καὶ οὕτως followed by either an indic. or impv. verb; the only ordering restriction was no intervening word between καί and οὕτως. Other verses that were found by this search were 1 Cor 7:17; Jas 2:12. Each can be excluded as a true parallel because the leading verb in both places is itself preceded by οὕτως, which marks it as a conclusion in and of itself, not as grounds or basis as in the current passage.

4. This is reflected in the C rating given to the preference for the fut. Indic. by the editors of UBS[5].

Translation

1 Brothers and sisters,[5] even if a man is overtaken by some transgression,[6] you who are spiritual restore such a person with a gentle spirit, watching out for yourself lest you are also tempted. **2** Bear each other's burdens and thus you will fulfill the law of Christ. **3** For if someone thinks himself to be something special when he is nothing, he deceives himself. **4** And each one should examine his own work, and then he will have a reason to boast about himself alone and not about another. **5** For each one must bear his own burden.

Commentary

Even though Galatians 6:1–5 is set apart as a paragraph unto itself in NA[28] and UBS[5], it has a strong thematic connection to the prior material in 5:13–26. There Paul sets forth the ideal of the individual living through the power of the Spirit in community in such a way that each person serves one another. He sets out a lofty, theological goal of a community guided by the Spirit such that the flesh has neither room nor opportunity to control behavior. But in Paul's mind theology always enjoins a particular practice; the indicative of the faith always leads to the imperative, the doctrinal to the ethical. Such is the case here as Paul discusses practical ways the community should "walk by the Spirit" and "keep in step with the Spirit" (see Bruce, 259; George, 408; Witherington, 417; Rapa, 632) both as individuals and as a corporate body (de Boer, 375).[7]

The link to the previous section is strong because of the subject matter of v. 26, the last verse of the prior section. In that verse Paul instructed the Galatians to avoid conceit, which would lead to interpersonal challenges and jealousy. Then in v. 1 of the current chapter Paul addresses the reality of sin in the community and how it should be addressed with an attitude of meekness and a response of self-examination. This connection is strong enough that some commentators argue that chapter 6 should actually begin with 5:25 (Martyn, 541; de Boer, 368) or 5:26 (Lenski, 296). Against this is the change of topic Paul effects in 6:1, speaking directly to churches on how to respond to sinful behavior. The language of 6:1 certainly could include the conceit expressed in 5:26, but it is also general enough to include much more. So I would argue that in 6:1 Paul moves to a new topic and starts a new

5. Here I follow recent scholarship that sees the pl. ἀδελφοί as referring to all members of the group regardless of sex; see BDAG, 18.

6. Many translations ignore the καί in this clause, which weakens the sense somewhat: "if a person is discovered in some sin" (NET); "if anyone is caught in any transgression" (ESV); "if someone is caught in a sin" (NIV).

7. J. M. G. Barclay, *Obeying the Truth: A Study of Paul's Ethics in Galatians*, SNTW (Edinburg: T&T Clark, 1988), 149–50.

section. Paul is concerned in this paragraph not only with the restoration of those who have sinned but also with the way this restoration is carried out. This paragraph addresses the attitude of those who restore another, the key element that sets the mode of restoration.[8] Paul continues his call to be led by the Spirit but does so within the practical framework of personal self-attention and how that properly serves to restore brothers and sisters who have sinned. Paul speaks as a realist: He is "mindful of the danger that not all those who purpose to live by the Spirit will always live thus" (Burton, 325), so he speaks to address that practical reality.

Although Paul does not speak of spiritual gifts or ecclesiology here, it is quite appropriate to consider this passage within the context of those topics. The framework is pastoral care (pastoral with a lower-case "p") as individuals within the community of the redeemed care for those within their midst who have sinned and need restoration. Paul speaks both to individual giftedness and responsibility within the act of restoration and the wider context of restoration taking place within the local body. The tone is both tender, as Paul envisions members dutifully and gently caring for one another in times of spiritual need, and hopeful, as Paul describes further means by which the Spirit's work will be manifest in the community. In many ways, this pastoral care is a picture of his gospel because it flows naturally from the Spirit among the believers, and as such serves as the truth opposed to the counterfeit community promoted by his opponents.

6:1 *Ἀδελφοί, ἐὰν καὶ προλημφθῇ ἄνθρωπος ἔν τινι παραπτώματι, ὑμεῖς οἱ πνευματικοὶ καταρτίζετε τὸν τοιοῦτον ἐν πνεύματι πραΰτητος, σκοπῶν σεαυτόν, μὴ καὶ σὺ πειρασθῇς.* In this verse Paul turns to the problem of sin in the community, finding the solution in interpersonal interaction that brings restoration. This kind of community self-care was not unheard of in Jewish contexts. Hays, 332, identifies 1QS 5:24–6:1 as a helpful parallel, but more helpfully he points to Lev 19:17 as the root of Paul's admonition: "You must not hate your brother in your heart. You must surely reprove your fellow citizen so that you do not incur sin on account of him" (NET). Given that Paul makes much of Lev 19:18 earlier in the book, the possible connection to Lev 19:17 is significant. In any case, reproving sin in the community has Jewish antecedents, and here Paul applies the same concept to the early Christian communities.

The entirety of this verse is a third class condition. As such, it presents a situation that is probable, not necessarily real in the present time, but likely to see fulfillment at some point in the future. The word *καί*, used here adverbially with two functions, helps elucidate the import of the sentence as a whole. First, acting intensively to modify the whole clause (so Burton, 326),

8. I find it interesting that Paul addresses the attitude of those who restore rather than that of those who need to be restored. On this basis, perhaps in the process of restoration we ought to call more loudly for humility on the part of church leadership rather than remorse on the part of the sinner.

it indicates that Paul considered the fulfillment of the apodosis as an extreme case. Thus it is best not to construe this as a condition that is likely to occur but rather as a possibility.[9] This is in keeping with the normal function of the third class condition. Second, it highlights this material as a thematic addition, providing a link back to the end of chapter 5:

> Thematic addition at the beginning of v. 1 constrains the reader to search for an intended parallel in the preceding context. Chapter 5 closed by highlighting the strategies for avoiding sin. Chapter 6 opens with what to do if you do not avoid sin and even are caught in it. The additive here provides a link back to the previous chapter, even though it begins a new pericope. The parallel is between the actions of avoiding sin/the flesh and being caught in sin.[10]

The relationship between the protasis and the apodosis in this conditional sentence is best understood as cause-effect: If the condition of the protasis is fulfilled—someone is overtaken in some sin—then the response in the apodosis is effected—those who are spiritual restore that individual, albeit with proper attention to themselves as well. Thus the sentence as a whole prepares the Galatian communities to respond to the possible instance that someone in their midst will be overtaken in sin and need restoration.

Paul begins the protasis with ἀδελφοί, which directly addresses the Galatians with the nom. used as the voc. This strikes a tone of community and connection between Paul and his readers, which is important to his overarching goal of restoring the Galatians to his gospel. The protasis is formed by ἐάν plus the aor. pass. subjunctive προλημφθῇ. The verb προλαμβάνω in this context means "overtake" with decidedly negative implications.[11] The verb vividly portrays the individual being surprised, caught, or overtaken by a transgression. It conveys a strong mental image of capture and lack of control. Based upon the vivid parallel in T. Jud. 2:5, one could even see a strong element of personification.[12] Paul might intend to emphasize the inadvertent nature of the transgression such that intentional sin is not in view.[13] Given the rather general tone of the passage, however, and lacking any clarification of that sort, it is better to understand this passage as describing any sinful stumble, whether intentional or not. Given the emphasis on the

---

9. So E. D. W. Burton, *Syntax of the Moods and Tenses in New Testament Greek* (1900; repr., Grand Rapids: Kregel, 2000), 115. See also A. T. Robertson, *A Grammar of the Greek New Testament in the Light of Historical Research* (Nashville: Broadman, 1934), 1026–27, for discussion of εἰ καί where he also discusses parallels with ἐὰν καί.

10. S. E. Runge, *Discourse Grammar of the Greek New Testament: A Practical Introduction for Teaching and Exegesis* (Peabody, MA: Hendrickson, 2010), 344.

11. BDAG, 872.

12. For a similar parallel see POxy 9288. For a less vivid parallel see Wis 17:16 (17 in the ET).

13. So G. Delling, "προλαμβάνω," *TDNT*, 4:14–15.

egregious nature of the transgression, the force of καί becomes all the more important. Here it is used intensively:[14] "*Even* if a man is overcome by some transgression." Normally this verse is understood as a call to the exercise of spiritual discipline and restoration generally. It is certainly that, but it is more appropriately an encouragement to exercise spiritual discipline even in the most difficult of cases. Thus there is an implicit lesser-to-greater argument: If restoration is practiced for small transgressions, which is implied, restoration should be practiced for egregious infractions, which is stated explicitly. The noun ἄνθρωπος is used here generically, almost as a substitute for τις (which does in fact show up in v. 3). The prep. ἐν carries the idea of means or instrument, explaining how the action of the main verb is accomplished. The noun παράπτωμα means "a violation of moral standards," usually translated as "sin" or "transgression."[15] It is possible based on the prior context of the book that Paul had something specific in mind: the vices from 5:19–21 (so Betz, 296; Dunn, 319), personal vanity in light of 5:26, or embracing the Law in light of his entire argument. The lack of specificity in his wording, however, does not allow for precision of referent in this instance, especially since in this section Paul looks generally to the practical manifestation of the Spirit in the life of the community. The use of τινι serves to generalize the idea even further: "in some [unspecified] transgression." Paul uses general language here to make his point as broad as possible: His concern is not the nature of the sin, but rather the fact, or perhaps the extent, of it. The construction with the pass. verb puts the emphasis on sin as the power controlling the individual in view. This aligns with Paul's discussion elsewhere in the book about sin (see Gal 2:17; 3:22).

The apodosis of the conditional sentence commands a particular group of people to restore in a particular way the individual overtaken by some sin. Paul identifies these individuals, those who should act in response to the sinning individual, with the emphatic phrase ὑμεῖς οἱ πνευματικοί, "you who are spiritual." The word πνευματικός is an adj. derived from the noun πνεῦμα. It means rather simply "pertaining to πνεῦμα" with the referent of πνεῦμα defined by the context. Taken broadly, πνεῦμα can refer to air, wind, breath, or spirit. Where "spirit" is in view, the referent could be either the human spirit (or personality), the divine Spirit, that is, the Holy Spirit, or more mundanely "spiritual" as opposed to "physical." So the meaning of the adj. πνευματικός in any instance is defined by the context, which controls which referent of πνεῦμα would be in view. In the present passage under consideration, both the Holy Spirit and the human spirit are in the context, but the former is much more in the foreground. In the prior context Paul argued clearly and decisively for the Galatians to align their attitudes and actions with the Spirit whom God has given to them through their faith in Christ. Every occurrence of πνεῦμα in 5:13–26 and indeed in all prior material

14. See BDAG, 495–96.
15. BDAG, 770.

refers to the Holy Spirit. This would argue that πνευματικός here should also reference the Holy Spirit. In the following context of the verse, however, Paul refers to πνεύματι πραΰτητος, which likely refers to the human spirit given the meaning of the gen. modifier. In this instance ὑμεῖς οἱ πνευματικοί would mean those who are guided by their spirit as opposed to their flesh. This is problematic, though, as Paul does not speak of the human spirit as the standard for living at any point; indeed, his prior admonitions in 5:13–26 give that role to the Holy Spirit. The weight of the prior context leads most naturally to understanding ὑμεῖς οἱ πνευματικοί as those who show evidence of living in accordance with the Spirit: They walk by him, they are led by him, they show his fruit, etc. (Lenski, 298; Burton, 327). A variation of this view sees the references as all believers, as all are characterized by the Spirit as Paul has consistently argued up to this point in the book (so Betz, 297; Longenecker, 273; Hays, 332; Rapa, 633; Schreiner, 358; de Boer, 374). This would either be in contradistinction to the opponents Paul faced in Galatia or used as a subtle exhortation for the community to live up to its nature. I am swayed by the prior context and the inherent logic of the more restricted referent: Paul, ever the realist, acknowledges that in the imperfect communities there would be those individuals who were more mature than others in their living by the Spirit, and these mature individuals have the authority and responsibility to carry out the action of the impv. καταρτίζετε. As Dunn, 320, notes, "The test of spirituality indicated is one involving delicate personal relationships, where the spirituality is marked by the character of the objective and means: to restore the erring fellow member to his former condition and mend the injured relationships."

The verb καταρτίζω generally means "to put in order" or "adjust."[16] This can refer to the initial creation or use of an object, with the sense "prepare, outfit," or to subsequent use with an implication of damage or loss, "restore, mend."[17] The latter is in view here given the context of recovery from sin through proper spiritual care. The word can be used to mean "restore" in a very literal sense (see Matt 4:21; Mark 1:19). In this passage Paul uses the term metaphorically to describe the process of restoration from sin. The exact nature of this restoration is not spelled out, but the idea of control or capture in the verb προλαμβάνω helps define it: Proper restoration moves the individual out from the control of the transgression back under the control and guidance of the Spirit, fully functioning again as a member of the community in step with the Spirit. The dir. obj. of the verb is identified by the phrase τὸν τοιοῦτον, "such a person"; the pronoun τοιοῦτος refers back to the person overtaken by sin mentioned in the protasis. The referent of the phrase ἐν πνεύματι πραΰτητος is the human spirit; the noun πραΰτητος acts as an attributive gen.: "a meek/gentle spirit."[18] The word πραΰτης indicates a

16. LSJ, 910.

17. MGS, 1077; BDAG, 525.

18. So Wallace, *Greek Grammar*, 88.

demeanor marked by gentleness born out of a humble sense of self.[19] It is very important to note that πραΰτης is a fruit of the Spirit (Dunn, 321; de Boer, 373).[20] This reinforces the interpretation that ὑμεῖς οἱ πνευματικοί references those mature individuals who manifest gentleness, a key characteristic for properly restoring others from sin.

The concluding clause of the apodosis qualifies temporally the action of the main verb. The verb σκοπέω means "to pay careful attention to something."[21] The reflexive pronoun σεαυτόν is the dir. obj. of the ptc. The switch to 2 sg. conveys that the individuals involved in restoration of a sinning believer must be careful before the Lord regarding their own spiritual state during the process. Those who restore others must throughout that process give careful attention to themselves. The construction μή plus subjunctive indicates a negative purpose, that is, one action is undertaken preventatively that something else not occur. The verb πειράζω means "tempt" to improper, sinful behavior.[22] The nature of the sin to which one might be tempted is unclear. The force of καί here is "also," implying that the temptation could be similar in nature to that which affected the individual previously, but given Paul's admonitions against conceit and arrogance in 5:26 and 6:3, a very reasonable construal would see the sin as arrogance toward the one being restored (Betz, 298; Matera, 214; Schreiner, 358; Moo, 375; Soards and Pursiful, 308). Taken as a whole Paul's language lacks the specificity to make either option certain. Paul speaks generally, and as such his language should be interpreted broadly, making a broad point of application: Those who restore others from sinning may be tempted in any number of ways, so they must diligently guard against any sin that tempts them during the process. Not to be missed in this verse is Paul's budding hamartiology: Implied in Paul's language is the dangerous, infectious nature of sin. Sin attacks both the transgressor and the one who restores in unexpected ways (Schreiner, 357). The verb in the protasis and the qualification of the main verb in the apodosis warn all those involved concerning the danger of sin and the need for gentle, effective correction by the Spirit-led community.

6:2 ἀλλήλων τὰ βάρη βαστάζετε καὶ οὕτως ἀναπληρώσετε τὸν νόμον τοῦ Χριστοῦ. Paul continues his discussion concerning restoration of a sinning believer, which itself is a practical continuation of how to live by the Spirit, with another pl. command directed toward the spiritually mature to whom he spoke in the previous sentence. The asyndeton that marks this sentence conveys the gravity of the discussion. This sentence comprises two shorter sentences joined by καί. The syntax of an impv. plus καί οὕτως plus fut. indic.

---

19. BDAG, 861.

20. One important note for a biblical theology of this concept is that the cognate adj. πραΰς is applied to Jesus himself (Matt 11:29).

21. BDAG, 931.

22. BDAG, 793.

marks the impv. as conditional and the fut. indic. the result of proper fulfillment of the commanded action. The adv. οὕτως clarifies the force of the fut. indic., indicating the basis for its fulfillment.

The first part of the verse contains the imperative: "Bear each other's burdens." The reciprocal pronoun ἀλλήλων indicates possession relative to τὰ βάρη. This is the final occurrence of this reciprocal pronoun in the book; the prior uses are all in 5:13–26, marking this paragraph as tightly related to that paraenesis. The noun τὰ βάρη means "burden,"[23] here used metaphorically. The main verb βαστάζετε means "carry, bear."[24] It is a conditional impv., but it does not lose its force as a command.[25] The sense is, "If you bear one another's burdens—and you should do this!—then in this way you will fulfill the law of Christ." Paul shifts back to the pl. with this command, reorienting his discussion to the pl. group identified as the spiritually mature individuals in the prior verse. Given the subject matter of v. 1, Paul could intend the burden to be the sin referenced in the prior verse. However, the metaphorical nature of the language more likely refers to anything that impedes a life led by the Spirit, whether that is something as egregious as sin or something innocuous, like difficulties generically (similarly Moo, 376; *contra* Burton, 329, who argues that the referent is indeed the sin of the prior verse but draws out a general principle for application). As Schreiner, 358, argues, believers have lots of burdens that are not themselves sin. Thus Paul commands pastoral care in a variety of circumstances by helping one another with all the difficulties and vicissitudes of life. This interpretation would fit well with parallels to bearing burdens in friendship contexts (Betz, 299) and within Paul's own writings in Rom 15:1–2 (Hays, 332–33).

The adv. οὕτως begins the second clause, clarifying that the first clause of v. 2 is the means by which the second clause will be realized. The second sentence is unadorned: "in this way you will fulfill the law of Christ." The fut. tense verb ἀναπληρώσετε within the larger clausal structure indicates the result of bearing one another's burdens. The verb ἀναπληρόω here means "fulfill," just as the simpler form πληρόω would.[26] However, the prefixed prep. ἀνά stresses the sense of completeness (Lightfoot, 216; Matera, 214; similarly Longenecker, 275; *contra* Moo, 376). The phrase τὸν νόμον τοῦ Χριστοῦ is the dir. obj. of the main verb, that is, that which is fulfilled. As such, it is the specific goal of the command to bear one another's burdens, but it also is the outcome of restoring believers who have sinned to a life in step with the Spirit.

Paul does not define the phrase τὸν νόμον τοῦ Χριστοῦ, so the reader is left to infer the referent from the context. The only parallel to this concept elsewhere in his writings is the statement in 1 Cor 9:21 that he is ἔννομος

---

23. BDAG, 167.

24. BDAG, 171.

25. So Wallace, *Greek Grammar*, 490.

26. BDAG, 70, 827–28.

Χριστοῦ, "subject to the Law of Christ." The closest parallel outside his writings occurs in Luke 2:23, 24, 39, where the author speaks of the "the Law of the Lord" with reference to the Torah.[27] Many commentators argue that with this phrase Paul refers to Jesus's own ethical teaching. In brief, Paul thought of the love command from Lev 19:18 just as Jesus did, so "the Law of Christ" would refer to Jesus's ethical teaching to love one another as a proper summation and fulfillment of the Law (Burton, 329; Bruce, 242, 261; Fung, 288; Dunn, 322–24). Others argue that "the law of Christ"[28] points to Christ's act of self-sacrifice on the cross, an act of love that believers are to emulate as a new standard of behavior (Schreiner, 360; Oakes, 180). Similar to this is the view that in his loving act of self-sacrifice on the cross, Christ fulfilled the Law and made it his own; believers do the same as they imitate Christ and love one another (Martyn, 547; Soards and Pursiful, 311). The best context for understanding the referent of the phrase is the entire salvation-historical argument that Paul has laid out within Galatians. Paul seeks to motivate the Galatians to return back to his gospel by rejecting the Law-observant requirements of his opponents. The essence of his motivation is what God has done in Christ for the Galatians: Through their faith in Christ, God has brought them into Abraham's family, making them heirs of his promise, and God has given them the Spirit, the blessing that was originally promised to Abraham and his descendants. The Galatians along with believing Jews are now part of God's family, a new community in which each believer in Christ is free from the Law to be enslaved to one other for mutual encouragement and edification in the Spirit. In this new dispensation there is no Law any more, nor is there any written code that controls the behavior of the individual vis-à-vis God or the other. Rather, each individual seeks to be led by the Spirit in service to one another. Within this framework "the law of Christ" refers not to a written code but to the obligation of each believer in Christ to be led by the Spirit for the benefit of the other within the community. The Galatians were tempted by the Law of Moses; submitting to it would only lead to perdition of the self and the community. Paul proffers instead the law of Christ, that is, the rule of the Spirit within them; submitting to this law will lead to a fuller manifestation of the Spirit to the benefit of all within the community of faith.[29] Thus "law" is a play on words, designed to undercut the argument of the opponents; there is indeed a requirement expressed, but it is not from Torah. The requirement is to fulfill the intention of the new community created by God in Christ through the Spirit. As Longenecker, 275, states it (and as reiterated by Moo, 376–78), the law of Christ involves

27. The exact wording is ἐν νόμῳ κυρίου in Luke 2:23, ἐν τῷ νόμῳ κυρίου in v. 24, and τὸν νόμον κυρίου in v. 39.

28. Note here I have chosen the lower-case "law" to clarify that this interpretation does not refer to the Torah.

29. For a very similar argument, see M. Winger, "The Law of Christ," *NTS* 46 (2000): 537–46.

principles stemming from Paul's gospel applied by the Holy Spirit in love. These principles often parallel the example and teachings of Jesus, but they are not literarily or substantively based upon them.

6:3 εἰ γὰρ δοκεῖ τις εἶναί τι μηδὲν ὤν, φρεναπατᾷ ἑαυτόν. The conj. γάρ marks this short conditional sentence as the logical basis for what was argued previously, likely all of vv. 1–2 because of the asyndeton at the beginning of the latter verse (*contra* Lightfoot, 216, and Hays, 334, who argue that the proper connection is to 6:1). So generally speaking, a proper assessment of personal value and worth on the part of the individual vis-à-vis others within the community grounds proper pastoral care within the body of Christ. This verse circles back around to further define the individuals Paul identifies in v. 1, ὑμεῖς οἱ πνευματικοί, albeit in a negative way by picturing those who would not be qualified as πνευματικός. The conditional sentence is a first class condition, indicating the assumption of the truth of the protasis in order to advance the argument toward the apodosis. This particular condition is evidence-inference: The apodosis is an inference drawn about the character of the individual who fulfills the protasis.

The protasis contains the pres. indic. δοκεῖ as the main verb, which Paul has used previously in the book with reference to the perception or reputation of the Jerusalem apostles (see Gal 2:2, 6, 9). A similar idea is in play here. The subject is the indefinite pronoun τις, the inf. εἶναι is indir. discourse to the main verb, and the neut. pronoun τι is a predicate nom., functioning as the assertion about the self. The sense is regarding oneself as "something special."[30] The lack of concord here in gender shows that the subject is conceived of abstractly as a class.[31] The exact referent of the phrase is hard to pin down. Because of the similar language used previously in Gal 2, it is possible that Paul is referring again albeit obliquely to the Jerusalem apostles. If so, Paul would be chiding those who take on a similar authority to govern the lives of the Galatians when they have no right or standing before God to do so. It could be a sideways reference to the opponents who had taken on a place of prominence among the Galatians. Martyn, 214, argues that context indicates that "thinking one is something" relates to pride after restoring a believer or "a sense of immunity from a similar failure in one's own life." The best option, however, given the general, metaphorical nature of the entire passage, is to take this as a reference to anyone who has an opinion of themselves elevated beyond what is warranted or appropriate within the community. The short phrase μηδὲν ὤν provides the real assessment of the individual. The ptc. ὤν

---

30. See BDF, §301(1), which says, "thus εἶναί τι 'something special' G 2:6 (exactly like δοκούντων εἶναί τι Plato, Gorg. 472 A), 6:3."

31. See BDF, §131, which says, "When the predicate stands for the subject conceived as a class and in the abstract, not as an individual instance or example, then classical usage puts the adjectival predicate in the neuter sing., even with subjects of another gender." See also MHT, 3:311.

is either temporal ("while he is nothing") or concessive ("even though he is nothing").[32] Lightfoot, 216, rightly states, " 'being nothing,' i.e. 'seeing that he is nothing,' not 'if he is nothing,' for the very fact of his thinking highly of himself condemns him." The pronoun *μηδέν* is a predicate nom. of the copulative verb, just as *τι* is. Taken as a whole the protasis indicates discord between the self-conception and the reality: "If someone considers [himself/herself] to be something, even though he/she is nothing."

The apodosis, also short and pithy, indicates the inference to be made about this individual with improper self-assessment, namely, he deceives himself. The tone of Paul's comment is less observation and more condemnation. He does not approve of individuals in this situation and seeks to help them understand their proper place, moving from pride to *πνευματικός*. In the present context, it is clear that Paul believes conceit makes an individual unwilling to bear another's burden (Longenecker, 276; Rapa, 634) and unwilling to gently restore them from sin. It also makes one unwilling to receive help when burdened or sinning (Lenski, 300). The antidote is humility and utter dependence on God's grace in Christ through the Spirit.

6:4 *τὸ δὲ ἔργον ἑαυτοῦ δοκιμαζέτω ἕκαστος, καὶ τότε εἰς ἑαυτὸν μόνον τὸ καύχημα ἕξει καὶ οὐκ εἰς τὸν ἕτερον.* Taken as a whole this verse gives a command and result similar to that found in v. 2. On the same basis as before, the impv. verb in the first clause can be construed as conditional, although still retaining the force of the command, and the fut. verb of the second clause can be construed as a predictive fut. that indicates a result of the command. The force could be translated in this way: "And if each person examines his own work—and you should do this!—then he will have a reason to boast about himself alone and not about another." This verse continues to explore the proper attitude the individual has toward the self as grounds for the commands to restore one another from sin and to bear one another's burdens resulting in the fulfillment of the law of Christ. More specifically, this verse provides the antidote for the self-deceit of the prior verse (so also Soards and Pursiful, 312).

In the first part of the verse, emphasis falls on the distributive pronoun *ἕκαστος* which points to every member of the Galatian congregations; thus this command has a universal, iterative application among Paul's readers. In this context, following the assertion about potential self-deception, the verb *δοκιμάζω* means "test" or "examine."[33] Paul enjoins appropriate self-reflection relative to one's standing among others within the community. The reflexive pronoun *ἑαυτοῦ* indicates possession, referring to the same individual as *ἕκαστος*. The nature of this work in view is not specified in the context. Previous occurrences of *ἔργον* in the book were either joined to *νόμος* (Gal 2:16; 3:2, 5, 10) or *σάρξ* (5:19); the word's connotation was decidedly negative. Here the

32. Cf. Robertson, *Grammar*, 1127, who says, "It is hard to tell how to classify a participle like that in Gal. 6:3, *μηδὲν ὤν*. It makes sense as temporal, causal or modal."
33. BDAG, 255.

connotation is neutral; the meaning should be construed generally perhaps as "output" or even "conduct" (Moo, 379).[34] Paul's ultimate goal is to move all the Galatians into the category of ὑμεῖς οἱ πνευματικοί. This universal admonition helps accomplish that goal as each one examines her life against the standard of the Spirit.

The latter clause of the verse indicates the result of the commanded self-examination. The subject of this clause is not specified; the ἕκαστος of the prior clause is assumed given the 3 sg. verb. The main verb ἕξει has τὸ καύχημα as its dir. obj.; "a reason for boasting" is what will be gained through proper self-examination vis-à-vis another. The noun καύχημα is challenging to understand given the different options for the word itself within the Greek language but more specifically given the negative connotations that were often associated with it. Within Greek and Jewish literature καύχημα and related words were associated with both extremes: on the one hand with legitimate pride and self-respect, on the other with personal arrogance and bragging.[35] Paul's use of the word group shows similar breadth. The prior emphasis upon the work of the Spirit in 5:13–26 makes the best meaning in context for καύχημα "a reason or basis for boasting," and the connotation is proper self-understanding with the broader framework of the Spirit's work. The prepositional phrases specify the reference point for the boast. Paul sets up a contrast here: εἰς ἑαυτὸν μόνον versus εἰς τὸν ἕτερον. This is a subtle challenge to Paul's opponents: Paul frames proper boasting as relative to a humble stance concerning the self toward the community of faith. This contrasts deeply with the opponents who were taking a prideful stance concerning the behavior of others within the community, specifically with regard to circumcision.

6:5 ἕκαστος γὰρ τὸ ἴδιον φορτίον βαστάσει. The conj. γάρ links this to the previous as an explanation. The requirement for proper self-examination leading to proper boasting relative to the self is grounded in the individual's responsibility to properly bear his own responsibilities. The distributive pronoun ἕκαστος appears here again, reemphasizing the universal application of this command to Paul's readers. The main verb βαστάσει is an impv. fut. in keeping with the other explicit imperatives in the context. The fut. here could be eschatological (Matera, 215; George, 418; Hays, 335; Schreiner, 362; Moo, 381), but the immediate context points to the daily lives of the Galatians and the gnomic force of this statement would make this more a maxim than an eschatological prediction (see Burton, 334; Betz, 304). The noun phrase τὸ ἴδιον φορτίον is the dir. obj. of the main verb. The pronoun ἴδιον stresses personal ownership and responsibility. This repeats the idea of bearing burdens in v. 2, but instead of emphasizing the shared nature of

---

34. This is supported by BDAG, 390; see the definitions "1. that which displays itself in activity of any kind" and "2. that which one does as regular activity."

35. *NIDNTTE*, 2:651–52.

some burdens, this verse emphasizes the personal responsibility each believer has to live properly before the Lord. The major exegetical challenges are the explicit difference between the commands in v. 2 and here and the difference in meaning between the words βάρος and φορτίον, each of which can reasonably be translated as "burden." On the face of it, Paul appears to traffic in a paradox, which he is wont to do on occasion (Lightfoot, 217; see Phil 2:12–13; 2 Cor 12:10). One way around this contradiction is to appeal to subtle differences in the meaning between βάρος and φορτίον (Lightfoot, 217), but this subtlety controverts Paul's intended meaning, especially in light of the command for mutual help in v. 2.[36] It is best to argue that the paradox is intentional because Paul presents complementary truths (Dunn, 326; Hays, 335; Soards and Pursiful, 313): At the same time, believers are personally responsible before the Lord regarding their conduct but are also responsible to care for others within the community when they are burdened, whether with sin or something else. "It is the man who knows he has a burden of his own that is willing to bear his fellow's burden" (Burton, 334).

Paul's admonitions in this short paragraph begin with restoration of others and end with proper self-reflection and responsibility. His eye is both on the community and the individuals that compose it. His attention is on the community when he speaks of restoration of a sinning brother through the tender care of those who are living under the control of the Spirit. His attention turns to the individual when he speaks of proper self-assessment and responsibility before the Lord. The important logical connection between them is grounds and basis. It is when individuals are properly assessing their conformity to the Spirit that they are in a position to carefully and gently restore others in need. This starts a gracious circle as those who are aware of their own need before the Lord tenderly care for others who exhibit similar need.

Theological Comments

In this short yet powerful paragraph Paul intertwines two related theological concepts: that which could reasonably be called a theology of humility, or perhaps more broadly a theology of the self, and the more properly defined *topos* of ecclesiology. These are worthy topics within themselves, but Paul does not view them in isolation from one another. Indeed, his essential contribution is how the first, the theology of humility, is foundational for the second, the theology of the church.

Throughout his writings Paul is very quick to command a proper attitude toward the self. He does this first and foremost relative to his own

36. See discussion of this facet and others related to the problem in *NIDNTTE*, 1:470–71, and M. Silva, *Interpreting Galatians: Explorations in Exegetical Method* (Grand Rapids: Baker, 2001), 56–57.

person. Within the context of his apostleship Paul acknowledges his lowly status because of his prior persecution of the church (1 Cor 15:9; cf. Eph 3:8), something no other apostle could lay claim to. His ministry in no way exalted himself but focused solely on Christ (1 Cor 2:1–5). Paul ultimately saw no cause for boasting in his own person. Rather, the only source of boasting was in the cross on which Christ was crucified (Gal 6:14). Parallel to this attitude toward himself, Paul commanded that others have a humble sense of self. The classic expression of this comes in Phil 2:1–11, as Paul commands personal humility and high regard for others, lifting Christ up as the epitome of this humble attitude. Even though the kenosis in vv. 5–11 is highly regarded for its Christology, within the context of Paul's argument it serves instead as a model of humility. Paul's comments within Gal 6:1–5 directed toward the self are the first of many he ultimately makes on this matter. Essentially Paul commands a proper sense of the self vis-à-vis others within the community. Individuals must not think more of themselves than is proper (6:3). Each person must examine carefully his own conduct (6:4), measuring it against the standard of the Spirit. And each individual must properly handle his own areas of responsibility (6:5). In so doing the individual will be rightly related both to God and to his brother or sister in community.

Paul's theology of humility is not important simply for the self, however; it also serves as the foundation for his nascent ecclesiology. It is perhaps an overstatement to argue that Paul discusses ecclesiology in this section, but there is an important emphasis on individuals helping one another within the church to live in accordance with the Spirit. Since Paul's admonitions are designed to benefit the entire body, then ecclesiology is a good fit. The emphasis in this section is what might in contemporary parlance be termed church discipline. Paul describes how believers who are overtaken in sin can be restored to fellowship with one another and with the Lord. The foundation for this is a proper theology of the self: Those who properly understand their own need before the Lord, those who seek to be led by the Spirit, are properly positioned to restore others when necessary in their spiritual walk. This should be done with a gentle attitude and careful concern for the self so that sin does not multiply. Paul's vision of restoration involves those who humbly walk with the Spirit restoring with gentle care those who have sinned. In this way the body as a whole will be enabled to fulfill its mandate to live by the Spirit and not by the flesh.

Application and Devotional Implications

This section of Paul's epistle is imminently practical, as it deals with two certainties within human experience: self-centered pride and sinful behavior. In fact, this paragraph could be considered a primer on proper pastoral care of those two issues. Paul initially describes an individual who is entrapped by sin, controlled by it, and at its mercy like the prey caught by the hunter. Paul's concern is that the *de facto* spiritual leaders of the community restore that individual. These individuals are not identified by titles but by humble character. This humility on the part of those "who are spiritual" enables the process of restoration to move forward while inhibiting the multiplication of sin. This leads very naturally to two salient applications: the need for proper self-reflection on the part of the individual and the requirement for gentle restoration for those who sin.

The latter half of this paragraph focuses squarely on the proper attitude individuals should have toward themselves within the community of faith. Paul does not mention it with specific words, but he speaks squarely against personal pride and self-aggrandizement, one of the most common manifestations of sinfulness. His antidote is threefold. First, individuals must be honest with themselves about their status within the Christian community. In v. 3 Paul points out that individuals who have an inflated sense of worth deceive themselves. This deception most normally comes when we give credit to ourselves rather than to God for benefits or blessings we attain. Each believer must remember that "every good and perfect gift is from above" (Jas 1:17 ESV). As such, the sum total of our physical and spiritual life is a gracious gift from God. Our proper response is never to exalt the self but simply to graciously give thanks to God for his gifts and enablement. Second, each person must evaluate their conduct against the standard of the Spirit. In v. 4 Paul's antidote to self-aggrandizement is proper self-evaluation. Believers should appropriately evaluate themselves against the standard of the Spirit as a proper way to enable reflection and repentance for sinful behavior. Third, each person must recognize his own responsibility before God. In v. 5 Paul reminds the Galatians that each person will bear his own burden. Each person is responsible before God to live in accordance with the Spirit. That responsibility can never be offloaded to another.

The first half of the paragraph focuses squarely on the fact and manner of restoration from sin. An unfortunate consequence of the Fall is that people sin; sinful behavior is a normal part of the human experience until Christ returns. As a community of people who have been redeemed from sin but not yet fully delivered from it, the church has the God-given role of standing in the gap for those within its midst. When anyone sins, the church plays a powerful role in enabling and enacting restoration, a function of the full redemption for sin secured by Christ. Thus each church must be about the business of "church discipline," that is, of restoration of individual members from sinful behavior. This can take on many forms. The most direct would be handling the sin of individual members through a process of identification, rebuke, and restoration. But this can also be more general and diffuse, such as sponsoring recovery groups for those who struggle with addiction. The big point is that the church cannot turn a blind eye to sinful behavior. She has the responsibility and the right to address it and ameliorate it. Paired with the fact of restoration is the manner: Paul requires that restoration from sin be accomplished "with a spirit of meekness," that is, with a gentle and caring manner. This shows why the theology of humility that Paul espouses in the latter half of the paragraph is so important. Only those who are fully cognizant of their own sinfulness, those who humbly recognize their own need for the Savior, can properly care for others. Paul does not explain how the restoration should be effected; that would be determined by the individual circumstances of each case. But the manner of the restoration should be gentle and meek, on the one hand acknowledging the gravity of sinful behavior and on the other hand recognizing that all believers stand in need of Christ's salvation. In this way those who are spiritual will restore others while at the same time exercising careful attention to themselves lest they also be tempted and sin multiply.

Additional Exegetical Comments

6:1 When discussing the referent of *παράπτωμα*, Martyn, 546, makes a very salient point: It is a legitimate question how the Galatians will identify transgressions now that Paul has abrogated the Law. The answer comes from the larger flow of Paul's argument. First, Paul has enumerated works of the flesh that could legitimately be in view. Second, he now discusses things that destroy community. Both of these are clearly not the work of the Spirit and should be subject to discipline and restoration.

Selected Bibliography

Barclay, J. M. G. *Obeying the Truth: A Study of Paul's Ethics in Galatians*. SNTW. Edinburg: T&T Clark, 1988.

Winger, M. "The Law of Christ." *NTS* 46 (2000): 537–46.

Manifestations of the Spirit (Part 2) (6:6–10)

Textual Notes

6:7 The NA[28] text reads the sg. pronoun in each part of the clause: ὃ γὰρ ἐὰν σπείρῃ ἄνθρωπος, τοῦτο καὶ θερίσει, "for whatever a man sows, that also will he reap." Some manuscripts change these pronouns to the pl. 𝔓[46], the Vulgate, and part of the old Latin witness read "for whatever things a man sows, these also will he reap." (Interestingly D* F G read the sg. pronoun in the first clause and the pl. in the second.) Although the plural pronouns produce an interesting reading, the manuscript evidence that supports it is not enough to be convincing, nor is there any significant change in the sense.

6:9 At this point in the text there is substantial variation in the manuscript tradition, but it all circulates around synonyms and similar grammatical forms with the result that the meaning of the text is hardly affected. The lexemes involved are ἐκκακέω, "I lose heart"; ἐκλύω, "I become weary, give out"; and ἐγκακέω, "I become discouraged, lose heart." These are close enough in meaning, whether taken literally or figuratively, that the sense of the passage is unchanged no matter the verb in view. The grammatical forms involved are ἐκκακῶμεν, a pres. subjunctive; ἐκκακήσωμεν, an aor. subjunctive; ἐκλυθῶμεν, an aor. pass. subjunctive (but with active sense); and ἐγκακῶμεν, a pres. subjunctive. These all act as hortatory, enjoining action on the part of the group addressed, with only subtle differences in emphasis depending upon the tense. All things considered, the reading ἐγκακῶμεν of NA[28] should be considered the most likely to be original. It is found in excellent manuscripts (א A B D* 33 81 326), and the verb ἐγκακέω has parallels within the Pauline literature while the other verbs do not. Within the NT the verb ἐκκακέω occurs only in variant readings. The verb ἐκλύω occurs five times, once later in the verse but no other times within Paul. In contrast, the verb ἐγκακέω occurs five times outside of the verse under present consideration, four of which are in Pauline texts.

6:10 The NA[28] text reads the indic. verb ἔχομεν while a few important manuscripts read the subjunctive ἔχωμεν.[1] The subjunctive has strong witnesses on

1. At first blush this might appear to be a thorny problem very similar in contour to the famous one in Rom 5:1, but here the evidence is decidedly on the side of the

its side (א B* 6 33 104 326 614), but this is evenly matched by the extensive support across all text types for the indic. reading. The indic. fits the context better; for the subjunctive to make the best sense the phrase would need to include ἄν or ἐάν.[2] On both internal and external evidence the indic. can be considered more likely original. Likely the subjunctive arose due to confusion of vowel sounds at some point in the transmission process.

6:10 The variation at this point in the text centers around different forms of the same verb: ἐργαζόμεθα, a pres. indic. (supported by A B² L P 6 104 1175 1881 *pm*), ἐργασώμεθα, an aor. subjunctive (supported by 𝔓⁴⁶ K 1505 2464); and ἐσγαζώμεθα, a pres. subjunctive (supported by א B* C D F G Ψ 33 81 365 630 1241 1739 *pm* lat). Given the emphasis on exhortation in this section in the book, a subjunctive form is to be considered as more likely original than the indic. Between the two subjunctive forms, the pres. subjunctive is to be preferred because of the strength of its attestation. It has several important witnesses on its side, and the reading is strongly Alexandrian and Western. Similarly to the textual problem earlier in the verse, the variants likely arose due to confusion of letter sounds at some point in the process of transmission.

Translation

6 The one who is taught the word must share all good things[3] with the one who teaches. **7** Do not be deceived: God cannot be mocked![4] For whatever someone sows, that they also reap, **8** because the one who sows to his own flesh from his flesh will reap destruction and the one who sows to the Spirit from the Spirit will reap eternal life.[5] **9** And do not grow weary while doing this good thing,[6] for we will reap at the proper time if we do not give out. **10** Therefore as we have opportunity, we must do good to all people, and especially to members of the faith family.

---

indic. There the evidence is more evenly divided, making that problem much more difficult to solve.

2. See BDAG, 1106.

3. The translation "share in all good things" (NRSV, NKJV) is more formal but misconstrues the sense ever so slightly.

4. Compare the more functional translation "God will not be made a fool" (NET).

5. The NRSV translates these generic subst. ptcs. as conditional clauses: "If you sow to your own flesh … but if you sow to the Spirit."

6. I have translated so the connection to v. 8 is clear; compare the more general "So we must not grow weary in doing good" (NET and most other English translations).

Commentary

Paul is never one to shy away from very practical, concrete instruction, but that instruction is never divorced from spiritual or theological reality. As is commonly said, for Paul the imperative of the faith rests on the indicative, and such is the case here. Paul gives concrete admonitions to the Galatian believers regarding how they are to support those among them who teach the word, how they are to persevere in doing good, and how they are to do good to all people. These admonitions, even though they are cast somewhat generally, provide a concrete course of action for the Galatian believers as they consider more carefully how to live by the Spirit. These admonitions do not occur in a vacuum, though; they are founded on a truth that for Paul amounts to a foundation for understanding how God acts in the world. Using the agricultural actions of sowing and reaping as a metaphor, Paul establishes a principle the Galatians are to understand relative to the flesh and the Spirit: Those who sow to their flesh reap only corruption, while those who sow to the Spirit reap eternal life. God as the sovereign Creator cannot be outwitted in this regard. The spiritual results of sowing are just as sure as agricultural ones. Implicitly Paul seeks to motivate his readers to sow to the Spirit rather than to the flesh, that is, to follow his gospel and its promise of the Spirit's work instead of the gospel of the opponents and its focus upon circumcision in the flesh. Even though this paragraph is more properly paraenesis, Paul's overarching goal has not changed: He wants the Galatians to remain faithful to his Law-free gospel, and the promise of reaping eternal life in the future is as strong a motivation in this regard as his previous arguments.

Much in this paragraph is stated quite generally. Taken on their own, without reference to the prior context, the admonitions fall to the level of platitudes devoid of specific content. This is not Paul's intention, however. The whole context of the book, in which Paul seeks to motivate the Galatians to remain faithful to his gospel instead of submitting to circumcision, comes to bear on defining the content here. The immediate context of the role of the Spirit in guiding the life of the individual, written about at the end of chapter 5, works in concert with Paul's broader goal to provide appropriate specificity to his argument. Thus sowing to the flesh is not a generic activity but specifically circumcision; sowing to the Spirit is not any activity but rather following Paul's gospel, which appropriately understands the role of the Spirit. There are certainly more general applications of these ideas, as v. 10 itself proves, but the immediate context into which Paul writes has not changed. This defines the content as centered on manifestations of the Spirit's guidance among the Galatians.

6:6 Κοινωνείτω δὲ ὁ *κατηχούμενος* τὸν *λόγον* τῷ *κατηχοῦντι* ἐν *πᾶσιν* ἀγαθοῖς. Paul begins this short paragraph with an idea that he has not yet referenced in the epistle, that of sharing in a concrete way within the community of faith.[7] Although it introduces its own specific ideas, this paragraph continues the general theme of the previous one, which addressed specific behavior guided by the Spirit vis-à-vis the community. The command that begins this paragraph is κοινωνείτω, a 3 sg. impv. This is the only place Paul uses this word in Galatians, but it shows up elsewhere in his writings with somewhat the same force (e.g., Rom 12:13). The verb κοινωνέω means "to share" and in the context means a very concrete action of sharing something with another person.[8] The subject of the command is the subst. ptc. phrase ὁ κατηχούμενος τὸν λόγον. The ptc. is the pres. pass. form of the verb κατηχέω, which in this context means "teach" or "instruct."[9] Thus Paul's command is given to "the one who is taught the word." The remaining phrases in the sentence clarify the extent of the command κοινωνείτω. The phrase τὸν λόγον τῷ κατηχοῦντι identifies the person with whom the one who is taught shares: "the one who teaches the word." The prepositional phrase ἐν πᾶσιν ἀγαθοῖς indicates what is shared; it is the equivalent of a partitive idea.[10] The collocation of πᾶς and ἀγαθός without the article makes the idea very general; it should not be construed as indicating a totality of number but more the extent of essence.[11] Elsewhere the phrase "good things" refers to things necessary for life (Schreiner, 368). The use of τὸ ἀγαθόν in 6:10 would point to specific material aid here (Witherington, 430). Thus Paul intends not just financial support but other material support as the teachers have need.

Grammatically the sentence is easy to grasp. Much more challenging is the situation it describes in reality, given the nature of the command, its implication for the life of the Galatian churches vis-à-vis the discussion of early catholicism, and the overall import of this phrase for understanding the life of the early church. This hinges on two key elements: the meaning of the verb κατηχέω and the referent of the word λόγος. The verb κατηχέω generally means "to inform, report" but in important uses within the NT it takes on the meaning of "instruct, teach." The general meaning does not imply any

---

7. This command forms something of a conceptual *inclusio* with the last verse of the paragraph in which Paul commands the Galatians to do good to all people.

8. BDAG, 552. The related noun κοινωνία takes on great significance in Paul's writings, referring to the intensely theological concept of fellowship in Christ (see *NIDNTTE*, 2:711–12; cf. Gal 2:9), and this verb can take on some of that nuance (cf., e.g., Rom 15:27). In this verse, however, the verb does not carry that theological significance; it simply references the act of sharing. The context is within the body of believers, but that nuance is explicitly stated and does not come from the verb itself. See Paul's similar use in Phil 4:15.

9. BDAG, 534.

10. See BDF, §169, which says that the classical idiom of the partitive gen. with verbs meaning "to take from, to eat of" has been replaced to a large extent in the NT by prepositional phrases or other cases.

11. See MHT, 3:200.

particular content; it simply refers to passing information along.[12] This general use is found in the NT (see Acts 21:21, 24), but the majority of the NT uses of the verb refer specifically to instruction or teaching. In the current verse the two uses of the term refer to instruction within the context of the Galatian churches; the thing specifically taught is τὸν λόγον. The only other place where Paul mentions λόγος in the book is 5:14, which refers to a specific saying from the Law fulfilled in the current Christological moment. The context here points to something much broader. In contemporary Christian parlance "the word" can refer to the Scriptures, that is, the entirety of the written revelation given by God to man. It is tempting to see that nuance here, but there is nothing in the balance of the letter that would indicate that is in view. Much more likely "the word" refers to the apostolic gospel that Paul had proclaimed to the Galatian congregations, with emphasis on the broad proclamation about Christ and his work on the cross and in his resurrection (similarly Burton, 337; Dunn, 327).[13] The implication of these nuances is that there was a full-time teaching office within the Galatian congregations (Dunn, 328).[14] It may have been a *de facto* office because Paul focuses on the faithful teaching function as opposed to the name of the office (Schreiner, 367). The one who held this office would pass on Paul's apostolic preaching and very likely work out its implications and applications for the life of the community. It is not possible to tell whether each individual church had this office, or whether the office might have been itinerant among the churches, or whether the injunction was necessary because the opponents had drawn support away from these faithful, local teachers (George, 420; Martyn, 552; de Boer, 385–86). In any case, Paul clearly marks out a responsibility for the one who is taught the word to support the one who teaches the gospel faithfully, a fitting recompense for sharing words of life with the congregation.

6:7 μὴ πλανᾶσθε, θεὸς οὐ μυκτηρίζεται. The sense of this individual phrase is clear enough. Paul admonishes the Galatians against being misled about whether one is able to mock God. The difficulty is understanding the meaning in light of the context because of the asyndeton. Does Paul intend this to be a general statement about mankind's dealings with God, or does he have a specific referent in mind? The best understanding is attained by linking this phrase more closely to what follows instead of what precedes. Considering that, Paul points with this phrase to God's sovereign ordering of salvation history and the emphasis in the present dispensation upon the Spirit and not the flesh. Likely Paul has used as a mental hinge the concept of λόγος as his apostolic proclamation that was being taught in the churches. He moves from the very real responsibility of supporting those who teach the gospel to the more global ramifications of not following that teaching. This

12. A helpful example is found in Josephus, *Life* 366.

13. *NIDNTTE*, 3:163. Compare 1 Thess 1:6, where Paul uses "the word" without adjunct as here to refer to his apostolic preaching of Christ.

14. *NIDNTTE*, 2:648.

sentence thus becomes a microcosm of his entire argument in the book: The Galatians should not be deceived by the opponents regarding the truth of Paul's gospel because doing so would bring them into conflict with God's sovereign ordering of salvation history.

The phrase μὴ πλανᾶσθε taken as a whole is a metacomment that attracts significant attention to the truth that follows (Moo, 384).[15] The construction μή plus pres. impv. indicates a general precept.[16] This is reinforced by the gnomic nature of the language that follows in the remainder of this verse and the next. The sense of the verb πλανάω is "mislead" or "deceive."[17] The voice of this impv. is either midd. or pass., and given Paul's emphasis in this paragraph and the preceding one on the practical outworking of the Spirit in the lives of the Galatians, the midd. voice would make more sense.[18] Paul addresses the way the Galatians themselves are thinking regarding their relationship to God. The asyndeton of the next clause marks it as emotionally solemn and intense. The verb μυκτηρίζεται means "to turn up the nose at" or "treat with contempt."[19] The pass. voice indicates that God as subject receives the contempt or disdain. Absent from the context is explicit mention of who does the action, but Paul most likely has in mind the Galatians themselves. This sentence could be transformed to make the sense more direct: "You Galatians simply cannot mock God." This sentence serves as a theological reminder of the sovereignty of God in the progress of salvation history and a reminder that the Galatians must return to Paul's gospel or face the consequences. The two other uses of this impv. in Paul (1 Cor 6:9; 15:33) have a clear eschatological focus, and that nuance fits here as well (Schreiner, 368).

ὃ γὰρ ἐὰν σπείρῃ ἄνθρωπος, τοῦτο καὶ θερίσει. Linked to the previous by the conj. γάρ, this sentence explains why the Galatians cannot mock God. The reason they cannot accept circumcision and obedience to the Law that that entails and still expect to receive the eschatological blessing of salvation is because of the divinely ordered link between an action and its consequence.

---

15. S. E. Runge, *Discourse Grammar of the Greek New Testament: A Practical Introduction for Teaching and Exegesis* (Peabody, MA: Hendrickson, 2010), 101. See also pp. 111–12 for his discussion of the exact same phrase in Jas 1:16–17.

16. See D. B. Wallace, *Greek Grammar Beyond the Basics: An Exegetical Syntax of the New Testament* (Grand Rapids: Zondervan, 1996), 724–25, for an overview of the force of the pres. impv. in prohibitions.

17. BDAG, 821–22.

18. This is also implied by the wording of BDAG, 822, but not clearly stated, given that this section discusses uses of the pass. voice.

19. BDAG, 660. The first is a rather literal translation of μυκτήρ, "nostril," but the linguistic association of the nose with contempt or sneering has ancient roots in Greek and finds parallel in many cultures and languages.

Clearly a maxim with gnomic force,[20] this sentence emphasizes the inescapable consequence of turning away from Paul's gospel through the agricultural image of sowing and reaping with the verbs σπείρω and θερίζω.[21] This sentence begins with an indefinite relative clause that acts as a pendant nom., focusing the reader's attention on the initial action. The relative pronoun ὅ with ἐάν marks the dir. obj. of the clause as indefinite: "whatever." The subject is the noun ἄνθρωπος used here generically, practically as a substitute for the indefinite pronoun τις. The subjunctive verb σπείρῃ is in keeping with the indefinite nature of the clause: "whatever a man sows." The relative clause is resumed in the sentence proper by the demonstrative pronoun τοῦτο, the dir. obj. of the verb θερίσει. The continuity between what is sown and what is reaped is emphasized by the particle καί, here acting adverbially with an adjunctive force: "this he also will reap."

6:8 ὅτι ὁ σπείρων εἰς τὴν σάρκα ἑαυτοῦ ἐκ τῆς σαρκὸς θερίσει φθοράν, ὁ δὲ σπείρων εἰς τὸ πνεῦμα ἐκ τοῦ πνεύματος θερίσει ζωὴν αἰώνιον. This verse presents a contrast between the flesh and the Spirit similar to what Paul stated previously in Gal 5:17 and then enumerated further with his discussion of the works of the flesh and the fruit of the Spirit. The ὅτι here is explanatory (Schreiner, 368; Moo, 385), elucidating the prior statement in v. 7 about the certain connection between what is sown and what is reaped. That gnomic, general statement is supported by the specific, inevitable result of sowing to the flesh or sowing to the Spirit.

This statement is constructed with two parallel sentences; the contrasted ideas are "his own flesh/the Spirit," "the flesh/the Spirit," and "corruption/eternal life." The subst. ptc. ὁ σπείρων is the subject in each instance, and in each half it is modified by a prepositional phrase. The first half speaks of one who sows εἰς τὴν σάρκα ἑαυτοῦ, "to his own flesh." Within the metaphor of sowing and reaping, the prep. εἰς identifies the "field" in which one sows.[22] The seed has fallen out of view in the metaphor, implying that the particulars of the action are unimportant. What is critical is the overall framework of the individual's actions, whether he seeks to favor the flesh or the Spirit (similarly Lenski, 306; Moo, 386). The dynamic translation "he who seeks to get a return from [his flesh/the Spirit]" captures the force of the metaphor well. The referent of σάρξ in the book has consistently been the physical body as the locus of attention for the opponents. Given the emphasis upon circumcision prevalent in the book, this association is appropriate to maintain here. The reflexive pronoun ἑαυτοῦ makes σάρξ in this context quite

20. The imagery of sowing and reaping is common in ancient literature (Betz, 307). For representative examples, see T. Levi 13:6; 2 En. 42:11; Philo, *Confusion* 21; *Names* 268.

21. Paul uses these verbs frequently, most notably to discuss the resurrection (1 Cor 15) and giving (2 Cor 9).

22. BDAG, 936.

personal and physical (similarly Burton, 341; *contra* de Boer, 388; Moo, 385–86). Sowing to the flesh means putting confidence in circumcision (Matera, 216; Hays, 336). The prepositional phrase appropriately switches to ἐκ τῆς σαρκός when reaping is in view. The noun φθοράν is that which is reaped. It is very graphic, referring to physical decay and destruction.[23] The parallelism makes clear, though, that Paul uses the term metaphorically for spiritual realities (Lightfoot, 219; Moo, 386). One cannot read this phrase without thinking about the works of the flesh mentioned in 5:19–21. This statement generically restates the same idea: Emphasizing the flesh inevitably leads to corrupt behavior. The image is meant to shock: Under the influence of the opponents the Galatians would never have thought such a negative result could come from circumcision, but Paul sets them straight on the results they can expect. The second sentence of the verse focuses on blessing received in return for submitting to the Spirit. The prepositional phrase that modifies ὁ σπείρων here is εἰς τὸ πνεῦμα, "to the Spirit." The reflexive pronoun, present before to make σάρξ personal, is absent; thus πνεῦμα here cannot mean the human spirit (so also Dunn, 330). The greater context, specifically the parallels with 5:17, clarify the referent here as the Holy Spirit.[24] As in the first half of the verse, the prepositional phrase ἐκ τοῦ πνεύματος indicates from where the reaping is done. This passage speaks of the enduring care of the Spirit over the believer. The believer who seeks to be guided by the Spirit will in return receive eschatological blessings from him.

The phrase ζωὴν αἰώνιον is the dir. obj. of θερίσει. It is that which will be reaped in the future. This phrase is well known for its frequent use throughout the NT.[25] Paul himself uses the phrase regularly (4x in Romans, 2x in 1 Timothy, 2x in Titus), but this is the only place in Galatians. Given the sg. here and the likely order of Galatians as the earliest Pauline epistle, it is worth taking a closer look within the context to determine what Paul intended with the phrase. Neither the adj. αἰώνιος nor the noun ζωή occur elsewhere in Galatians, but cognate words do. The noun αἰών occurs in Gal 1:4–5, with present and future reference. Paul speaks of believers' rescue from ἐκ τοῦ αἰῶνος τοῦ ἐνεστῶτος πονηροῦ, "this present evil age," on the one hand, and on the other hand he speaks of glory to God εἰς τοὺς αἰῶνας τῶν αἰώνων, "to the ages of the ages," a future-looking reference. The adj. αἰώνιος

---

23. BDAG, 1054–55. Plutarch, *Art.* 16.6, has a vivid use of the word, describing the physical decay of a body through a rather brutal form of torture.

24. Most every occurrence of πνεῦμα in the book references the Holy Spirit. The lone passage that does not (6:1) has a gen. modifier to signify the human spirit is in view.

25. The phrase occurs forty-three times in the NT, almost always as ζωή αἰώνιος, the fourth attributive position (see Wallace, *Greek Grammar*, 310–11). First attributive position is found in John 17:3; Acts 13:46; 1 Tim 6:12. Second attributive position is found in 1 John 1:2; 2:25. See 1 John 5:13 for the unusual instance of the indic. verb separating the noun and adj.: Ταῦτα ἔγραψα ὑμῖν, ἵνα εἰδῆτε ὅτι ζωὴν ἔχετε αἰώνιον.

shows similar flexibility in its temporal reference among its NT uses.[26] It is fair to argue that in addition to the temporal reference of its root, the word takes on a sense of quality, "without end." The adj. invokes the same eschatological context that *αἰών* does in the introduction to the book: God is at work within the present age to secure believers' place in the next. Related to the noun *ζωή* is the verb *ζάω*, which Paul uses frequently within the book. One use is mundane (Gal 2:14), but the remaining uses are pregnant with theological meaning. Within the theological crux of the book Paul speaks of living to God (2:19) and of living his present life through faith in Christ (2:20). In 3:11–12 Paul cites Hab 2:4 and Lev 18:5, both of which use *ζάω* significantly. Lastly, Paul speaks in 5:25 of living by the Spirit, perhaps the key reference for understanding the present context given his focus on the Spirit. Life within Galatians is not simply being alive. Rather, it is living to God by faith in Christ through the means of the Spirit. Paul's argument in the present paragraph focuses directly upon the role of the Spirit in that process. A believer sowing to the Spirit—in context defined as acceptance of and obedience to Paul's gospel that properly understands the role of the Spirit in the present time—receives in return from the Spirit the blessing of a life with God in Christ that spans the gap between the present age and the age to come.

6:9 *τὸ δὲ καλὸν ποιοῦντες μὴ ἐγκακῶμεν*. Continuing the prior argument by marking this clause with *δέ*, Paul directly addresses the discouragement believers experience as they try to sow to the Spirit. Specifically, the Galatians were in the midst of a difficult situation with the opponents. Likely they were discouraged by their own efforts and consequently much more likely to give in to the opponents' demands. Paul's encouragement strengthens them so they can stay the course. Generally, this verse has broad reference to believers in their efforts to remain faithful to the gospel in the midst of a world that pulls them from it at every turn. The prior context defines the first concept of this sentence, *τὸ καλόν*. The adj. *καλός* regularly means "good" or "useful."[27] The article serves to make the adj. a substantive, but it also clarifies it in the context by acting anaphorically, pointing backwards to what is in fact "the good."[28] Both based on the prior context and the connection made by the conj. *δέ*, "the good thing" Paul has in view is sowing to the Spirit, which in the larger context of the book is the Galatians' return to and continued adherence to Paul's gospel. The term *τὸ καλόν* is the obj. of the temporal ptc. *ποιοῦντες*, which in turn modifies the main verb of the clause, *μὴ ἐγκακῶμεν*. This hortatory subjunctive commands action on the part of both Paul and

26. Although normally interpreted as having future reference, it can also have a past reference. See BDAG, 33, who cite Rom 16:25; 2 Tim 1:9; Titus 1:2.

27. BDAG, 504.

28. MHT, 3:182, argues that the article here either identifies a quotation or marks *τὸ καλόν* as generic. Neither of these makes good contextual sense.

the Galatian believers. This is an inclusive "we" in which Paul views himself and the Galatian believers together as a community. The verb ἐγκακέω means "lose enthusiasm" or "be discouraged."[29] The negation makes this a prohibition, and the pres. tense positions this as a general precept. Paul's command serves to encourage the Galatians to remain faithful continually as they recommit to Paul's gospel.

καιρῷ γὰρ ἰδίῳ θερίσομεν μὴ ἐκλυόμενοι. Paul grounds his admonition to faithfulness in a promise. The conj. γάρ marks this clause as the basis or grounds for the previous hortatory subj. This is the reason believers should not grow weary while sowing to the Spirit. The main verb of this clause is the fut. tense θερίσομεν. This predictive fut. serves as a promise to believers that they will indeed reap if they do not give up. The prior verse provides context for this one: The Spirit himself is the essential agent for fulfillment of this promise, and ζωὴν αἰώνιον should be understood as the implied dir. obj. The phrase καιρῷ ἰδίῳ is idiomatic, meaning "in due time."[30] This temporal note emphasizes the certainty of the fulfillment. The negated ptc. ἐκλυόμενοι is synonymous to ἐγκακῶμεν in the prior line. The verb there referred to an emotional state; this refers to the physical, although a figurative use here is likely. Paul simply varies his language for a more interesting style. The ptc. here is conditional; it expresses a condition that must be fulfilled for the main verb to be true.[31] Thus Paul reemphasizes the need to remain strong and faithful while sowing to the Spirit. Fulfillment of that condition will enable fulfillment of the promise to reap eternal life from the Spirit.

6:10 ἄρα οὖν ὡς καιρὸν ἔχομεν, ἐργαζώμεθα τὸ ἀγαθὸν πρὸς πάντας. Paul continues his exhortation to the Galatian believers with another hortatory subjunctive positioned as a general precept. He moves from the specific content of sowing to the Spirit, that is, remaining committed to his gospel, to the general content of good actions toward all people. The final admonition of the paragraph is connected to the previous by the combined conj. ἄρα οὖν. The first word of the pair expresses the inference from what precedes, and the

---

29. BDAG, 272.

30. BDAG, 498. See Wallace, *Greek Grammar*, 157, who argues that the dat. restricts this to a point in time: "at the proper moment."

31. So Wallace, *Greek Grammar*, 633; A. T. Robertson, *A Grammar of the Greek New Testament in the Light of Historical Research* (Nashville: Broadman, 1934), 1022–23, but see also p. 1129 where he allows for ambiguity; E. D. W. Burton, *Syntax of the Moods and Tenses in New Testament Greek* (1900; repr., Grand Rapids: Kregel, 2000), 169; G. B. Winer, *A Treatise on the Grammar of New Testament Greek, Regarded as a Sure Basis for New Testament Exegesis* (Edinburgh: Clark, 1882), 607. *Contra* MHT, 3:285, and M. Zerwick, *Biblical Greek: Illustrated By Examples*, trans. J. Smith, Scripta Pontificii Instituti Biblici 114 (Rome: Pontifical Biblical Institute, 1963), 148, who allow for a simple affirmation here.

latter expresses the transition to this idea.[32] These conjunctions prove there is indeed a flow and argument to this section; the paragraph should not be interpreted as disjointed commands (Witherington, 434). The particle ὡς here acts as a temporal conj.; paired with the pres. tense ἔχομεν, it focuses on duration or extent of time: "as long as, while we have time."[33] The noun καιρός normally means "time," but here it has the nuance of "appropriate, favorable time" and could reasonably be translated "opportunity."[34] Paul's emphasis is on continued action whenever the opportunity avails itself. The verb ἐργαζώμεθα, another hortatory subjunctive, is the central affirmation. The verb means "to do, accomplish" and commands action. The dir. obj. of the verb, that which is to be done or accomplished, that to which the action must lead, is τὸ ἀγαθόν. Just like τὸ καλόν at the beginning of v. 9, this is the adj. ἀγαθός made into a substantive by virtue of the article. The words καλός and ἀγαθός are synonymous (so also Moo, 388), but there is a strong disjunction between vv. 9 and 10. It is best to understand "the good" in this verse as different from "the good" in the prior verse. There it was specific; here it is general. In context τὸ ἀγαθόν refers generally to good actions that can be done to and for another person. Seen within the context of the final phrase, πάντας here refers truly to all people, both within and without the community of faith.

μάλιστα δὲ πρὸς τοὺς οἰκείους τῆς πίστεως. The final phrase with the adv. μάλιστα clarifies that those within the family of faith should receive special focus as recipients of good. The adj. οἰκείους is used as a substantive to refer to those within a household or family. The gen. noun τῆς πίστεως, because of the meaning of οἰκεῖος, acts as a partitive gen. It is the "household" of which the members are a part. The noun οἰκεῖος is rare for Paul; he uses it only here, Eph 2:19, and 1 Tim 5:8. The use in Eph 2:19 has similar contours to the present text. There Paul describes the Ephesians as οἰκεῖοι τοῦ θεοῦ, "members of the household of God." The referent is spiritual relationship.[35] This imagery finds its roots in the OT as the people of Israel were often referred to as a "house." Paul applies something that would be true of Jews particularly and changes the referent to the church, inclusive of Jews and Gentiles, to reemphasize that the new organism is constituted by faith and faith alone (Dunn, 333; Garlington 2007, 375)

Within this short paragraph Paul commands a number of actions, all of which derive from the power of the gospel he preached to the Galatians. They are to support those who teach them the gospel and its implications, showing respect both to the teachers and then by extension to Paul who originally preached to them and to God who ordained them. The Galatians

32. BDAG, 127.

33. BDAG, 1105–6.

34. BDAG, 497; so most English translations.

35. The use in 1 Tim 5:8 is used concretely to identify those who are related within a family.

are to remain faithful in sowing to the Spirit, showing their belief in Paul's gospel over time in view of an eternal reward through the ministry of the Spirit. And they are to do good to all people, showing that the gospel is not theirs to hoard but theirs to announce as it lays claim to the world through the power of the crucified Lord. Paul's understanding of the gospel was deeply theological, but it was also soundly ethical. His commands rest upon a sure foundation that bears fruit in the present daily experience of those who adhere to it.

Theological Comments

Within this paragraph of Galatians are two important biblical and theological concepts. One is implicit, the other explicit; one speaks of an important function of the church, the other an important reality of spiritual existence that all believers must recognize, especially in light of the pull of the flesh.

The implicit concept found here is the important role of teaching the word within the Christian community. As mentioned in the commentary, Paul's admonition in Gal 6:6 implies that there was a full-time teaching role within the local Galatian congregations. Even if I am wrong about this implication, Paul at a minimum enjoins support of those who do teach in some capacity, most likely so that they can continue in this teaching ministry without difficulty. This evidence is in concert with other passages in the NT that discuss a teaching ministry within the church, but this has the distinction of being perhaps some of the earliest evidence, which runs counter to some of the current scholarly narrative of how the early church developed. The NT as a whole gives consistent witness that the early church regularly taught the gospel within its community. The first churches were built around "the word" and considered instruction in it very important (Dunn, 328). Paul gives his own evidence on this matter both with explicit statements (see, e.g., 1 Cor 15:3) and implications stemming from his use of pre-formed tradition (see Phil 2:6–11). Other books show a similar emphasis on teaching. The book of Matthew does this with its arrangement of teaching material into five distinct blocks and with the explicit statement at the end of the book (see Matt 28:18–20). Similarly the book of James explicitly mentions the teaching role (see Jas 3:1) but also implies it through the arrangement of its material as a compendium of teaching material. The early church thus regarded its teaching role as central to its ministry and mission, as it on a broad scale advanced the gospel of the Lord and on a more focused scale ensured consistency of behavior and belief among those within the community.

The explicit concept found here is the eschatological contrast between the flesh and the Spirit. As stated above in the commentary, this passage presents a powerful contrast between the flesh and the Spirit. The flesh without fail leads to corruption and judgment, but the Spirit without doubt leads to eternal life and blessing. What is important to note is Paul's eschatological viewpoint regarding both. Although he specifically mentions the adj.

αἰώνιος only in conjunction with life related to the Spirit, the implication is that the corruption experienced through the flesh has the same parameters. Indeed, he makes this explicit in the prior paragraph (see Gal 5:21). So Paul is not simply speaking morally or ethically. Rather, he speaks eschatologically, even apocalyptically, as he endeavors to help the Galatians understand the implications of the matters he places before them.

Application and Devotional Implications

Paul speaks directly to the Galatian believers in this paragraph of Scripture, commanding some tangible behaviors from them in light of the gospel more broadly and the power of the Spirit more specifically. These behaviors involve supporting, sowing, staying faithful, and doing good. They find direct application in the life of the church today as we seek to remain faithful to the gospel Paul preached, in light of the power of the Spirit, just as the Galatians did.

First, support those who teach in the local church. Paul starts this paragraph with a very clear admonition to support those who teach the word. Although not stated explicitly, this command is based on their role in defending and advancing the gospel Paul preached. In the contemporary church, there are a variety of ministry roles that could fit under the broad category of one who teaches the word. Certainly pastors and elders who preach and teach regularly on Sundays would be included, but this would also include many lay teachers who serve every Sunday teaching classes of all ages. The responsibility in this command falls on those who are taught: They must share "in all good things" with their teachers. This is a broad command that almost knows no bounds. Many churches pay their pastors, but a salary for those who are full time is not sufficient to meet Paul's demands. Those who are taught must regularly show tangible signs of support to those who teach. There are many ways this could be accomplished. Gifts at various points throughout the year are appropriate, as are acts of kindness that meet needs in the teachers' lives. But there are other kinds of support that should be offered regularly, such as mental or emotional help. Having personally received them, I can testify that even notes of thanks and encouragement provide important support in my teaching task. Paul chose the words "in all good things" intentionally so as not to restrict the kind of support teachers could receive from those whom they teach. Churches should creatively meet the needs of their teachers in whatever way is appropriate to their situation.

Second, sow to the Spirit. Paul does not specifically state this as a command, but there is no other takeaway from his statement in vv. 7–8 concerning God's sure return for what people sow. Each believer must endeavor to sow to the Spirit, not to the flesh. This command is defined most readily by the larger context of the book in which Paul defines the present ministry of the Spirit relative to his gospel. Thus the most specific application in context is sowing to the Spirit by remaining faithful to the gospel Paul preached. Defend the gospel's content and implications, just as Paul did before the Galatians. Proclaim the gospel clearly and convincingly both to those who need to hear and to those who stray from it. A more general application is sowing to the Spirit by submitting to his leading daily. This is driven largely by the preceding context, in which Paul guides the Galatians to be led by the Spirit. For the church today, this means we must become aware of the ministry of the Spirit. We should seek his leading on a daily basis and live by his rule and standard.

Third, remain faithful to the gospel Paul preached. In this paragraph there is tremendous encouragement in Paul's admonitions not to grow weary. These are based on the promise that a time of reaping will come after the difficulty of sowing. This promise gives believers the encouragement to continue in the task. In context "the good" is defined as "sowing to the Spirit," which is directly connected to remaining faithful to the gospel Paul preached. Thus believers should remain faithful to the gospel Paul preached because eternal life will be the result. This command is one of evangelism and discipleship as believers are faithful to Paul's gospel relative to those outside the community of faith and to those within as they seek to live out the implications of the gospel as brothers and sisters in Christ.

Fourth, do good to all people. The unfortunate problem with this admonition is its generality. Paul clearly calls upon believers to "do good to all people," but what that is exactly is left undefined. When considered as a whole, within the context of the book's argument, both general and specific applications are appropriate: General good toward others creates an avenue for evangelism, and specific good enables the gospel to be believed and lived. A major implication of the pronoun "all" is that this attention, this action of accomplishing good, should fall on those outside the community of faith. As believers live their lives, day in and day out, those outside the church should directly benefit from their behavior. Believers should seek to do good to those who do not know Christ. As stated above, this good is undefined, so believers must use the contingencies of their own situation to guide them as to the most appropriate actions in each instance. But without doubt these actions of "good" should benefit those who receive them and open the door for reception of the gospel. Paul goes further, though, and defines a specific group for attention: Most especially, those within community of faith should be recipients of our actions. This emphasis is born out of the organic relationship between believers. They are all within Abraham's family of faith. As the locus of God's attention in the present time, the church as the present manifestation of Abraham's family should exhibit the love and concern of God himself. As we care for others within the community of faith and do good to them, we live out what God intended for this family he created.

Additional Exegetical Comments

6:7 Witherington, 431, notes that in the other places where Paul uses this image of sowing and reaping (1 Cor 9:10–11; 2 Cor 9:6) it refers to finances; he believes this probably derives from Prov 22:7–9. Moo, 385, is more on the mark, however: Despite the similarity to 2 Cor 9:6, this image in Gal 6:7 is not a reference to finances because of the clear connection to v. 8, which is about proper behavior in light of coming judgment. Thus the stronger connection of this verse to what follows rather than what precedes is determinative for meaning.

Selected Bibliography

Davis, B. S. "Severianus of Gabala and Galatians 6:6–10." *CBQ* 69 (2007): 292–301.
Snyman, A. H. "Modes of Persuasion in Galatians 6:7–10." *Neot* 26 (1992): 475–84.

Conclusion of the Letter (6:11–18)

Textual Notes

6:13 At this point in the text an important variant occurs. The NA[28] text reads περιτεμνόμενοι, a pres. ptc., while many manuscripts have the variant περιτετμημένοι, a pf. ptc. The difference in meaning relates to the timing of circumcision: The pf. tense would refer to those who have been circumcised in the past with results that continue (obviously!) into the present time, the most likely referent being Paul's opponents. The pres. tense would refer to those who are currently counted among the circumcision, which could also include members of the Galatian congregations who had undergone circumcision. The external evidence for this problem is divided fairly evenly. The variant is supported by important Alexandrian manuscripts (𝔓[46] B 1175), as is the variant (ℵ A C 33 81 104 1739). Each has the support of a great many of the later Byzantine witnesses as well. This problem is likely solved on the basis of internal evidence. Of the six times the verb περιτέμνω is used in Galatians, five are pres. tense, of which one is an undisputed pres. ptc. in Gal 5:3. For Paul to switch to the pf. tense here in only one instance is unlikely. In addition, Paul is dealing with a current situation arising from claims regarding the necessity of circumcision by the opponents, who themselves were also circumcised. This variation is likely a scribal error to establish clarity with respect to who is in view. More likely the pres. ptc. is the original reading.

6:15 This verse shows interesting textual variation due to fairly close linguistic parallels with Gal 5:6. Of interest is how the parallel wording affects the textual variation and how this conclusion to the book parallels prior material. In essence there are two textual problems here. The first concerns whether ἐν Χριστῷ Ἰησοῦ should be included at the beginning of the verse: NA[28] lacks the phrase, while the variant includes it. The second concerns whether the text should read ἐστιν or ἰσχύει as the main verb.[1]

In terms of internal evidence, the parallel to 5:6 is telling and perhaps even decisive. Each of the variant readings is lifted directly from Gal 5:6.

1. This latter problem has little bearing on the meaning of the text. In both cases, Paul is stating that neither circumcision nor its lack has any spiritual significance.

Here are the two texts rearranged to highlight the similarity, the latter with changed word order for emphasis:

> 5:6 ἐν γὰρ Χριστῷ Ἰησοῦ
> οὔτε περιτομή τι ἰσχύει οὔτε ἀκροβυστία
> ἀλλὰ πίστις δι' ἀγάπης ἐνεργουμένη.
>
> 6:15 γὰρ
> οὔτε περιτομή τί ἐστιν οὔτε ἀκροβυστία
> ἀλλὰ καινὴ κτίσις

Given this parallel, it is reasonable to argue that in each instance scribes changed 6:15 under the influence of the similar language in 5:6. It is unlikely that scribes would remove the variations if they were originally present. The external evidence points in this direction as well. The reading that includes the prepositional phrase ἐν Χριστῷ Ἰησοῦ has excellent support from exceptional manuscripts across all text types, but the text reading is supported by the best Alexandrian witnesses (𝔓[46] B 33 1739). The situation with the second reading is similar: The text reading has excellent primary Alexandrian support (𝔓[46] ℵ B 1739) plus the support of D, while the variant is supported by some secondary Alexandrian witnesses and the Western and Byzantine text types. On the basis of both internal and external evidence, it is more likely that the text reading in each instance is correct.

6:17 There is a surprising amount of variation at this point in the text. Instead of Ἰησοῦ, the reading of NA[28], the manuscript tradition has Χριστοῦ, κυρίου Ἰησοῦ, and κυρίου ἡμῶν Ἰησοῦ Χριστοῦ.[2] In one sense the meaning of the text is unchanged, as the referent is the same for each reading, but the different nuances of each phrasing are important, especially given the subject matter Paul discusses at this point. Because of the multiplicity of textual variants, the external evidence is quite diverse. Far and away, though, the oldest and best evidence is on the side of Ἰησοῦ (𝔓[46] A B C*), which points to it as more likely original. This reading is also supported when the genesis of each variation is reconstructed. Likely Ἰησοῦ was the original text to which scribes added over time: κυρίου Ἰησου first, and then κυρίου ἡμῶν Ἰησοῦ Χριστοῦ later. The reading Χριστοῦ could be an independent alteration to include a more magisterial title for the Lord. Given the collocation with τὰ στίγματα, Ἰησοῦ could be considered the harder reading. This would be an emphasis on the historical Jesus that is rare in Paul's letters. One should not discount the influence of the following verse in any reconstruction, which reads τοῦ κυρίου ἡμῶν Ἰησοῦ Χριστοῦ. Scribes may have been influenced by that wording to replace the shorter reading Ἰησοῦ in v. 17. All things considered, Ἰησοῦ stands as the reading most likely to be original.

---

2. These variants themselves show variation, as the pronoun ἡμῶν is replaced by the 1 sg. pronoun (1739) and sometimes omitted (ℵ D[1]).

Translation

11 See how I have written to you with such big letters with my own hand! **12** Those who want to make a good showing in the flesh,[3] these compel you to be circumcised only so that they will not be persecuted with regard to the cross of Christ. **13** For these who are circumcised do not themselves obey the Law, but they want you to be circumcised so that they might boast in your flesh. **14** But as for me, may I never boast[4] except in the cross of our Lord, Jesus Christ, through whom the world was crucified to me and I to the world. **15** For neither circumcision nor uncircumcision count for anything,[5] but new creation is what matters! **16** And those who act in accordance with this rule, peace and mercy upon them and upon the Israel of God.[6] **17** From this point on let no one cause me trouble, for I bear on my body the marks of Jesus. **18** The grace of our Lord Jesus Christ be with your spirit, brothers and sisters.[7] Amen.

Commentary

In this final section of the letter, Paul takes the pen from his amanuensis, adding the final colophon in his own hand to grant authority and approval to what had been written, but also to summarize and restate his central arguments (Lightfoot, 220; Burton, 347; Dunn, 334; Schreiner, 376; Soards and Pursiful, 320).[8] This concluding paragraph becomes a lens through which

---

3. Compare the more dynamic rendering "a good showing in external matters" (NET).

4. Some translations handle the phrase μὴ γένοιτο differently: "far be it from me to boast" (ESV); "God forbid that I should boast" (NKJV).

5. Compare these other translations for different wording but similar sense: "both circumcision and uncircumcision mean nothing" (CSB); "in Christ Jesus neither circumcision nor uncircumcision avails anything" (NKJV); "Neither circumcision nor uncircumcision means anything" (NIV).

6. Different translations reflect different decisions about the exegetical issues in this verse. Even the placement of the comma is significant. See, for example, the following: "And all who will behave in accordance with this rule, peace and mercy be on them, and on the Israel of God" (NET); "May peace come to all those who follow this standard, and mercy even to the Israel of God!" (CSB); "Peace and mercy to all who follow this rule—to the Israel of God" (NIV).

7. Here I follow recent scholarship that sees the pl. ἀδελφοί as referring to all members of the group regardless of sex; see BDAG, 18.

8. For a fascinating look at letter writing in the ancient world, see G. J. Bahr, "Paul and Letter Writing in the First Century," *CBQ* 28 (1966): 465–77. For specific discussion of Pauline subscriptions, see G. J. Bahr, "Subscriptions in the Pauline Letters," *JBL* 87 (1968): 27–41. However, his generic conclusion in the first article and his specific conclusions in the second about what can be attributed to Paul originally

to view the whole (Betz, 313). Normally letter subscriptions are polite and wish the recipients well. Paul dispenses with the niceties here because the situation is urgent (Moo, 390), perhaps even reflecting a strained relationship between Paul and the Galatians (Matera, 228; Hays, 341).

There are several explicit lexical connections between this section and what Paul wrote previously. The idea of circumcision, mentioned explicitly in 2:3 and 5:2–3, gets explicit mention here in 6:12–13. Indeed, here Paul uses almost the same phrasing as that used in 2:3: οὗτοι ἀναγκάζουσιν ὑμᾶς περιτέμνεσθαι here versus ἠναγκάσθη περιτμηθῆναι previously. In 5:11 Paul had mentioned τὸ σκάνδαλον τοῦ σταυροῦ with reference to persecution he received; here he mentions τῷ σταυρῷ τοῦ Χριστοῦ with reference to persecution the agitators want to avoid. Paul had previously mentioned his co-crucifixion with Christ in 2:19–20; now he mentions his crucifixion to the world in 6:14. The wording of 5:6 and 6:15 is very similar: Both pair περιτομή and ἀκροβυστία, comparing them to what truly matters. The verb στοιχέω is used similarly in 5:25 and 6:16, both focusing on living according to a particular standard.

The thematic connections are also prominent. Here Paul faces head-on his opponents who were compelling the Galatians to be circumcised, taking these agitators to task for their hypocrisy relative to the Law. This reflects the central argument Paul has made about the Law throughout the book: A proper understanding of the Law relative to God's promises to Abraham does not lead to the opponents' position. Circumcision is no longer required in order to be in Abraham's family. Rather, a proper understanding of the Law leads to faith in the Messiah, in whom membership in Abraham's family is found. Paul chides the opponents for focusing on the flesh as if that were still (or ever!) the locus of God's attention. This reflects the consistent warnings about the flesh Paul makes in the ethical portion of the book and his attendant emphasis on the work of the Spirit within the community. His call to conformity in 6:16 echoes his constant call for the Galatians to return to his gospel. His mention of the marks of Jesus on his body, presumably a reference to scars he received due to persecution during his apostolic ministry, points to his authority as an apostle, a central theme of the biographical portion of the book.

All these connections, both lexical and thematic, make this final section an important interpretive key for the book. Paul restates themes and reemphasizes points in his final effort to motivate the Galatians to stay faithful to the gospel he preached to them. This allows for mutual reinterpretation as the book is read in light of this paragraph and as this paragraph is read in light of the book.

---

within the Pauline corpus should be rejected. While it is possible that the particular wording of his letters may be from the mind of another writer, it is inconceivable that Paul would not be the originator of the theological and logical substance of his letters.

This final section of the book contains the central paragraph of vv. 12–16, which encapsulates Paul's central argument against the opponents. This is bracketed on either side with statements that highlight Paul's apostolic authority in vv. 11 and 17. Verse 18 concludes the letter as a whole with an appropriate benediction.

6:11 Ἴδετε πηλίκοις ὑμῖν γράμμασιν ἔγραψα τῇ ἐμῇ χειρί. At this point in the letter, Paul presumably takes the pen from his amanuensis to write the final section of the letter himself.[9] He does this elsewhere explicitly in 1 Cor 16:21; Col 4:18; 2 Thess 3:17; Phlm 19.[10] This action granted approval to what the amanuensis had written, authenticating the material as it were, but it also subtly emphasized Paul's apostolic authority. Throughout the book Paul has had as a constant theme his role as an apostle. To mention his own handwriting would implicitly point to himself in that role one more time. Throughout the letter Paul never loses sight of his desire to motivate the Galatians to return to his gospel; this is one more example of that consistent encouragement. Paul uses Ἴδετε, a 2 pl. impv., to command the attention of his readers. The emphasis on physical sight is paramount, perhaps even implying that the reader would hold the document up within the congregations for the audience to see (Witherington, 440–41).[11] The balance of the verse is what Paul wants his readers to see, that is, how he has written to them with such large letters. The main verb of the clause is ἔγραψα, an epistolary aor. (so most commentators).[12] The dat. pl. noun γράμμασιν, modified by the correlative pronoun πηλίκοις, is a dat. of material, showing what Paul

9. For a classic study on this matter, see R. N. Longenecker, "Ancient Amanuenses and the Pauline Epistles," in *New Dimensions in New Testament Study,* ed. R. N. Longenecker and M. C. Tenney (Grand Rapids: Zondervan, 1974), 281–97. For a more recent study that addresses Galatians specifically and draws some defensible conclusions, see S. Reece, *Paul's Large Letters,* LNTS 561 (New York: Bloomsbury T&T Clark, 2016). For an argument that Paul did not use an amanuensis for Galatians, see deSilva, 502–4.

10. It is unclear if the phrase ἐν πάσῃ ἐπιστολῇ in 2 Thess 3:17 refers to the Thessalonian correspondence only or to all of Paul's letters.

11. Note that BDAG, 279, includes Gal 6:11 under definition 1.c, referencing the physical sense of sight, as opposed to the other entries, which refer to mental perception or understanding.

12. So also D. B. Wallace, *Greek Grammar Beyond the Basics: An Exegetical Syntax of the New Testament* (Grand Rapids: Zondervan, 1996), 563. See A. T. Robertson, *A Grammar of the Greek New Testament in the Light of Historical Research* (Nashville: Broadman, 1934), 846, who argues this is especially so here if Paul refers to the final paragraph of the epistle.

used to write the epistle.[13] Here πηλίκοις serves to mark the statement as an interjection.[14] The pronoun ὑμῖν is an indir. obj., identifying the readers as the recipients of the letter. The phrase τῇ ἐμῇ χειρί functions as a dat. of means. The use of ἐμός is emphatic, as Paul stresses his own role in the physical process of writing the letter. The reason or purpose for the size of Paul's letters is hard to ascertain. Conjectures about the reason Paul would write with large letters abound (e.g., hand injury, poor eyesight, clumsy style). In other places when he references his own writing, he makes no comment about the size of his handwriting, which minimizes the possibility of some sort of physical problem. Given the information we have, the best conclusion is that Paul wrote in large letters to emphasize this conclusion to the letter (so Betz, 314; Bruce, 268; Longenecker, 290; Dunn, 335; Martyn, 560; Hays, 342; de Boer, 395).[15] By starting this subscription in such a way, Paul develops further respect for his authority and tightens the bond between himself and his readers.

6:12 ὅσοι θέλουσιν εὐπροσοπῆσαι ἐν σαρκί, οὗτοι ἀναγκάζουσιν ὑμᾶς περιτέμνεσθαι. With this statement Paul begins the final review of his argument in the letter. The paragraph contained in vv. 12–16 summarizes and elucidates what was written before by the amanuensis. The clause that begins this verse refers emphatically to the individuals Paul has in mind, namely, his opponents. Here he lays bare their true intentions so that he can discredit them in the eyes of the Galatians. The pronoun ὅσοι is the subject of the clause; here it functions almost as an indefinite relative pronoun. The main verb θέλουσιν is modified by the complementary inf. εὐπροσοπῆσαι, which means "make a good showing."[16] The verb εὐπροσωπέω is not at all common in Greek literature. This is the only occurrence of it in the NT, and a search of the TLG database only found 27 occurrences, many of them citations of this passage.[17] The meaning of the verb is similar to the related adj. εὐπρόσωπος, which means

13. See Wallace, *Greek Grammar*, 169–70, for discussion on the dat. of material. BDAG, 811, classifies πηλίκος as a correlative pronoun, but see Robertson, *Grammar*, 291–92, and H. W. Smyth, *A Greek Grammar for Schools and Colleges* (Cambridge: Harvard University Press, 1956), 98, who classify this as an interrogative. Burton, 348, argues conclusively that this phrase cannot refer to the length of the letter.

14. Robertson, *Grammar*, 159; MHT, 3:50.

15. Keener, 562–63, argues that Paul drew attention to his script, different from the scribe's, so the Galatians would recognize his effort, thus emphasizing his words. In essence, this means he did so for emphasis but with an intermediate means.

16. BDAG, 411.

17. LSJ, 728, and J. H. Moulton and G. Milligan, *Vocabulary of the Greek Testament* (Peabody, MA: Hendrickson, 1997), 264, each point to a lone papyrus from the second century BC that contains this verb. P. Tebt. I. 19:12 (dated 114 B.C., 200 years before Paul wrote Galatians) reads ὅπως εὐπροσωπῶμεν, "that we may make a good show."

"fair of face" or "beautiful."[18] The verb takes on a causative nuance but with a figurative meaning: "to look good." The emphasis is not on the physical appearance as such but on the positive assessment made by others, involving honor and reputation. By using this verb Paul indicts the opponents for their intention to please people. This is in direct contrast to his own attitude that is to please God at all costs (see 1:10). The prepositional phrase *ἐν σαρκί* indicates a very literal location, given the prominence of circumcision throughout the book generally and in this paragraph specifically. Some commentators (e.g., Burton, 350–51; Moo, 392) argue that Paul does intend a theological nuance here, but as I have argued previously, Paul's anthropology is not that developed yet. Here he intends the physical body, the flesh, which has the attention of his opponents. The clause that begins the sentence serves to identify the subjects Paul has in mind more clearly than the demonstrative pronoun *οὗτοι* can alone. On the level of the entire discourse, this is a new identification of the opponents that highlights their motives among the Galatians. The sentence proper begins with the demonstrative pronoun *οὗτοι*, acting as the subject of the independent clause. It points to the same referent as the prior clause, that is, the opponents. The verb *ἀναγκάζουσιν* is followed by *ὑμᾶς*, indicating who the opponents are attempting to compel, and *περιτέμνεσθαι*, indicating what the opponents are compelling the Galatians to do. As a whole the construction is conative (so Bruce, 268; Martyn, 560; Moo, 393), because of both the pres. tense and the meaning of the main verb. The opponents are compelling the Galatians to be circumcised, but Paul makes no comment as to their success.[19] The verb *ἀναγκάζω* shows up twice before in Gal 2:3, 14; both those uses are theologically significant. The former relates directly to the current wording because of the similar collocation of *ἀνακάζω* and *περιτέμνω*. This linguistic similarity between the two verses indicates some connection between the two situations. Perhaps Paul means to imply that some of the same people were involved. It is entirely feasible that some of the people lurking in the background of Paul's Jerusalem meeting (see Gal 2:4–5) came out of the woodwork, making the trip to Anatolia specifically to influence the Galatians.

μόνον ἵνα τῷ σταυρῷ τοῦ Χριστοῦ μὴ διώκωνται. This final clause provides a clarification for the motive of the prior one. The opponents compel the Galatians to be circumcised for this negative purpose. The word *μόνον* here acts adverbially with *ἵνα* to introduce a dependent purpose clause. It provides a specific point of focus: "solely in order that."[20] As a whole the purpose is negative as the main verb *διώκωνται* is negated by *μή*. The opponents

---

18. LSJ, 728; MGS, 862.

19. Burton, 351, argues this specifically: "There is some reason to believe that expressions of compulsion, consisting of a verb and a dependent infinitive are thought of as constituting a unit, and as being as a whole either conative or resultative. ... The present and imperfect of *ἀναγκάζω* are conative and are followed by a present infinitive."

20. BDAG, 659.

urged circumcision in order to avoid their own persecution. Thus Paul calls into question their motives for preaching to the Galatians (Lightfoot, 222; Burton, 349; Hays, 342). The verb διώκω occurs previously in Galatians to reference Paul's preconversion persecution of the church (1:13, 23), the treatment of Isaac by Ishmael (4:29), and Paul's own persecution because of his preaching of the gospel (5:11). Paul has not previously mentioned or implied that the opponents themselves were being persecuted. There are no contextual clues to identify any details about this situation; any discussion of the historical context has to be divined from other factors. What can be said is that the opponents were preaching circumcision because the lack of preaching circumcision brought persecution. By implication then the persecution came because preaching Christ and his cross alone as sufficient for inclusion with Abraham brought offense (Dunn, 337; Moo, 394). Whether this offense came from non-believing Jews (so Longenecker, 291) or Jewish Christians who advocated strongly for circumcision (so Betz, 316; de Boer, 398) is impossible to tell.[21]

Paul's mention of the cross of Christ is an important conceptual element within his argument. Taking its function broadly construed, the noun *σταυρός* should be understood as a metonymy that stands in for the gospel Paul preached (so also Burton, 350). His central message was about the crucified and risen Christ. Mention of the cross served as a compact means to reference the entirety of his message. He had mentioned the cross before in 5:11 within the context of his own persecution, implying that his gospel message caused offense to some who in turn persecuted him. Preaching circumcision instead of the cross would remove the problem and make the persecution cease. Paul also mentions the related concept of crucifixion through the verb *σταυρόω* and related forms. He speaks of his co-crucifixion with Christ (2:19), his public description of Christ as crucified in his gospel preaching (3:1), and the crucifixion of the flesh for those who are in Christ (5:24). The concepts of cross and crucifixion are the means by which Paul explains both the content and implications of his gospel. This message brought persecution in some form or fashion to the early believers. The opponents had decided to press for circumcision in order that they themselves would not be subject to those difficulties.

6:13 *οὐδὲ γὰρ οἱ περιτεμνόμενοι αὐτοὶ νόμον φυλάσσουσιν*. This sentence explains further the negative purpose clause at the end of v. 12 by recasting it. The word *οὐδέ* often acts as a conj., but here it simply emphasizes; the best translation

21. For a cogent argument for persecution from non-believing Jews, see R. Jewett, "The Agitators and the Galatian Congregation," *NTS* 17 (1971): 198–212. Matera, 230, argues against Jewett's thesis considering the distance involved from Jerusalem to Galatia. Martyn, 562, argues for a middle way: Persecution came from "the False Brothers and their cohorts in the circumcision party, persons now possessing considerable power in the church of Jerusalem."

in context would be "not even."[22] With it Paul emphasizes the inconsistency of the opponents vis-à-vis their own circumcision and their motives for preaching circumcision. The subst. ptc. οἱ περιτεμνόμενοι from the verb περιτέμνω acts as the subject of the sentence. It has the same reference as the pendant nom. in the prior verse. Even though it is possible some within the Galatian congregations had been circumcised, Paul's attention is squarely on the opponents. Referring to them as "those who are circumcised" is a concise way to identify them by ethnicity, by practice, and by preaching. Likely the ptc. is pass. voice, as opposed to the midd. that was used previously in 5:2–3 to refer to the Galatians themselves becoming circumcised. The pronoun αὐτοί is used intensively to further emphasize the subject and their inconsistency of behavior: "For not even the circumcised themselves keep the Law." The verb φυλάσσω is a synonym to τηρέω, which is about twice as common in the NT. Both mean "keep, guard, observe," and frequently have a commandment or regulation as their obj.[23] The noun νόμον here points to the Torah. Paul's point is an indictment: Despite their adherence to circumcision, the opponents have themselves failed to live up to the Law's requirements. They have failed to understand the Law on its own terms and presently advocate for circumcision in opposition to the Law's true intent, which Paul has explained at length in the theological section of the letter (so also Longenecker, 293; Moo, 394–95).

ἀλλὰ θέλουσιν ὑμᾶς περιτέμνεσθαι ἵνα ἐν τῇ ὑμετέρᾳ σαρκὶ καυχήσωνται. The conj. ἀλλά is a strong adversative. It contrasts the inconsistency of the opponents with their true goal and purpose. Paul sets up the grammatical contrast to communicate the irony and hypocrisy of their position. The clause θέλουσιν ὑμᾶς περιτέμνεσθαι restates similarly what Paul said about the opponents in v. 12: Their desire is that the Galatians submit to circumcision. The conj. ἵνα as in v. 12 indicates the purpose for this insistence. This purpose clause is stated positively while the prior one is stated negatively. The subjunctive verb καυχήσωνται is that for which the agitators aim. They compel circumcision so that they might boast. The prepositional phrase ἐν τῇ ὑμετέρᾳ σαρκί shows the person or thing that is the source of the boasting or pride. The noun σάρξ here would be a metonymy for circumcision. The poss. pronoun ὑμετέρᾳ retains a focus upon the Galatians as the locus of the opponents' attention.

There is an implicit connection between all the assertions Paul has made about the opponents. At root they wish to have a particular reputation before an unspecified group of people. The means to do this is to compel the Galatians to be circumcised. Their purpose is to boast about the Galatians' circumcision, which would in turn remove the persecution they face for the gospel. The presenting issue is their preaching of circumcision to the Galatians, but Paul draws back the curtain to expose their intentions

22. BDAG, 735.

23. BDAG, 1068.

behind the proclamation. In so doing, Paul discredits them by showing their motives to be self-serving and not ultimately from a pure intention to fulfill the Law. This serves further to motivate the Galatians to turn away from the opponents and their preaching of circumcision and return to his gospel.

6:14 ἐμοὶ δὲ μὴ γένοιτο καυχᾶσθαι εἰ μὴ ἐν τῷ σταυρῷ τοῦ κυρίου ἡμῶν Ἰησοῦ Χριστοῦ. Here Paul shifts to a different emphasis. He has first focused on discrediting the opponents by exposing their true motives. Now he focuses upon what the believer's proper focus should be: the cross of Christ and the new creation that it inaugurated. Paul speaks of himself and his attitude toward the cross as paradigmatic, which parallels his discussion of co-crucifixion in Gal 2:19–20. This short discussion parallels the former discussion but also expands on it by referencing the believer's relationship with the world, which the cross has nullified.

With the conj. δέ, adversative in this context (so also Moo, 395), Paul turns his attention to his own attitude about circumcision and the Galatians. The pronoun ἐμοὶ is an ethical dat. that lays strong emphasis on Paul's feelings and point of view (so also Lenski, 318). It creates a strong contrast between his own attitude, centered entirely on the cross, and the attitude of the opponents, centered upon themselves. The phrase μὴ γένοιτο is a well-known negative expression in the optative. Paul uses it most frequently to express his unequivocal opposition to a stated premise, but here the optative functions as a wish.[24] Technically the inf. is the subject of the optative expression: "May boasting never be [may it never exist] with reference to me." Paul then qualifies this statement with the phrase εἰ μὴ; what follows is the exception to his prohibition about boasting. This exception is expressed entirely as a prepositional phrase with ἐν that indicates the person or thing in which someone boasts, that is, the basis of pride or boasting. Paul again references the cross and identifies it emphatically with the extended gen. phrase τοῦ κυρίου ἡμῶν Ἰησοῦ Χριστοῦ. In this epistle Paul identifies Jesus in such an extensive way only here, in the benediction proper (6:18) and the introduction (1:3). This implies gravity and solemnity on his part with reference to this concept of the cross of Christ. Similarly to the prior use in v. 12, the noun σταυρός stands for the gospel about Jesus, for which his crucifixion forms a central affirmation.

This statement to contemporary Christians sounds warm and comforting, but we must not forget the shock and disgust that this statement would have caused in the ancient world. Because the cross was an instrument of torture and death, "the most ignoble of all objects" (Bruce, 271), boasting in it would seem extremely strange (Moo, 395).[25] In contemporary times it would be analogous to venerating the electric chair or a noose as a symbol

---

24. Prior occurrences of the phrase in Galatians occur at 2:17 and 3:21.

25. For a classic study in this regard, see M. Hengel, *Crucifixion in the Ancient World and the Folly of the Message of the Cross*, trans. J. Bowden (Philadelphia: Fortress, 1977).

of religious devotion (Longenecker, 294). But for Paul and for the contemporary Christian, the cross was the fulcrum of faith, and in it one may boast, knowing that there salvation was secured.

δι᾽ οὗ ἐμοὶ κόσμος ἐσταύρωται κἀγὼ κόσμῳ. This relative clause serves to further describe Jesus, but it also serves to expand the concept of the cross from the prior line, referencing in a compact way Paul's co-crucifixion with Jesus (see 2:19). He now includes the nullification through crucifixion of the world's power and influence over the believer. The prep. διά which begins the clause indicates the means by which the action of the main verb ἐσταύρωται is accomplished. The relative pronoun has as its antecedent τῷ σταυρῷ in the prior line. Some commentators argue the antecedent of the relative pronoun is Christ (e.g., Dunn, 341), but the more logical phrasing would have been ἐν ᾧ or σὺν ᾧ if Christ were the referent (Lightfoot, 223). The two short sentences following the introductory prepositional phrase have the same essential structure: subject plus form of σταυρόω plus ethical dat. Paul states that the world has been crucified to him and he has been crucified to the world. The noun κόσμος is anarthrous by virtue of being monadic.[26] The only other use of this word in Galatians occurs in 4:3, where Paul mentions τὰ στοιχεῖα τοῦ κόσμου, but a conceptual parallel is found in 1:4 when Paul speaks of Christ rescuing believers from τοῦ αἰῶνος τοῦ ἐνεστῶτος πονηροῦ. In this context the world refers to that present sinful realm, opposed to God in all things, that will soon pass away (similarly Moo, 396). Indeed, the cross in which Paul boasts is the means by which that passing is accomplished, "the transformative event that ended the old order of things" (Hays, 344). The verb ἐσταύρωται is a pf. pass. Both the tense and voice have significance in the context. The pf. tense indicates that a completed action has ongoing results. As with the prior use of the verb συσταυρόω 2:19, the pf. here points back to a definitive event that has present consequences. In context this would be the moment of conversion when the co-crucifixion occurs. The pass. voice shows that each subject was acted upon by an agent through the means of the cross. Context would point either to God or Christ as the ultimate agent of this action. With these statements Paul expresses his own utter and complete change of viewpoint with reference to the world as a result of the cross, and the complete lack of power the world now exercises over him as a result. This implicitly invites the Galatians to join him in this stance against the world by reaffirming their association with his gospel.

6:15 οὔτε γὰρ περιτομή τί ἐστιν οὔτε ἀκροβυστία, ἀλλὰ καινὴ κτίσις. This verse is linked to the previous material by γάρ, serving as the grounds for Paul's prior statements. Most likely this sentence reaches back to the first assertion of v. 14, expressing the grounds for Paul's confidence only in the cross. Martyn, 565, correctly notes that the γάρ is critical, for it carries over "the cosmic and therefore the absolute dimensions of v 14" (similarly Soards and Pursiful,

26. Robertson, *Grammar*, 796.

327). Each word in the correlative pair οὔτε ... οὔτε introduces a nom. subject that is negated or denied as having any value for the life of the believer at present. The nouns περιτομή and ἀκροβυστία are the subjects, referencing respectively the status of being circumcised on the one hand and the status of being uncircumcised on the other. The indefinite pronoun τι acts as a predicate nom.[27] The sense of the neut. sg. is "anything" with the connotation of having value or worth.[28] The resultant sense is clear: "For neither circumcision nor circumcision are anything" or more dynamically, "Neither circumcision nor uncircumcision have any value." Most important to note is that Paul does not limit the statement to circumcision only, which would be logical, even expected, given the emphasis on that practice throughout much of the book. By mentioning both circumcision and uncircumcision Paul avoids a terrible error: Mentioning circumcision alone might have allowed his readers to infer that uncircumcision was now more valuable than circumcision, with the logical deduction that Jews were no longer valued in God's sight and that God's emphasis in salvation history had shifted to the Gentiles. This would lead to a thoroughgoing supercessionism, which Paul summarily and unequivocally rejects. The inclusion of uncircumcision here along with circumcision makes perfect sense given Paul's arguments throughout the book concerning the present roles of flesh and the Spirit. Stated generally, the physical state of the body makes no difference anymore. More specifically, the condition of the foreskin is no longer any measure of one's relationship to God. It can be removed through circumcision or left intact. The fulfillment in Christ of the promises God gave to Abraham means that the physical sign of the covenant simply makes no difference any more. Here Paul states succinctly what he argued before in 3:28: All differences that matter to the world have now fallen away in Christ (Moo, 397).

What matters instead is indicated in the latter half of the verse. ἀλλά as a strong adversative conj. sets up a contrast between περιτομή and ἀκροβυστία, things that no longer matter, and καινὴ κτίσις, that which truly matters. Having the latter phrase in the nominative case shows that it is the subject of an implied sentence. The verb and predicate nom. of the first assertion are implied here: "but new creation [is something, does matter.]" The phrase καινὴ κτίσις occurs only twice in the NT, both in Pauline texts. The essential question is whether the referent of this phrase refers to the individual or to

---

27. In the NA28 text τι has an accent because it is an enclitic preceding an enclitic; see D. A. Carson, *Greek Accents: A Student's Manual* (Grand Rapids: Baker, 1995), 49, for discussion of this phenomenon. The Westcott-Hort text has a different accentuation, τι ἔστιν, which would be the accentuation if ἐστιν were to receive the interpretive emphasis. Westcott and Hort do not state their reasons anywhere for this accentuation, but Robertson, *Grammar*, 234, presumes they regard the verb as receiving the emphasis here. The difference for exegesis is minimal.

28. In English we often use the phrase "That's nothing!" to communicate the same idea, albeit in the other direction.

the new world order brought about in Christ. The latter is favored based upon strong connections to the context: Paul has just spoken in the prior verse about how the world, properly construed as the anti-God world system, has been nullified by the cross (Dunn, 343). In addition, this phrase connotes Jewish apocalypticism that saw God remaking the world (de Boer, 402; Moo, 397–98). But the individual interpretation can be defended based on the other Pauline use and the context within Galatians. The other reference in 2 Cor 5:17 has a bit more context than the one here and can profitably inform what Paul intends in this passage. The paragraph in which that reference is found details Paul's ministry of reconciliation, through which individuals are restored to God through the gospel about Christ. This particular verse speaks of the transformation of the individual as a result of the gospel: ὥστε εἴ τις ἐν Χριστῷ, καινὴ κτίσις· τὰ ἀρχαῖα παρῆλθεν, ἰδοὺ γέγονεν καινά, "Therefore if anyone is in Christ, [he is a] new creation. Old things have passed away; behold, new things have come!" This verse marks the believer as a new entity, remade in Christ, fit and capable of a relationship with God. The same emphasis is found in the Galatians passage. This is confirmed by the parallel this verse has with prior material. The wording here is very similar to the wording in Gal 5:6, as indicated by this table:

5:6	6:15
ἐν γὰρ Χριστῷ Ἰησοῦ	γὰρ
οὔτε περιτομή	οὔτε . . . περιτομή
τι ἰσχύει	τί ἐστιν
οὔτε ἀκροβυστία	οὔτε ἀκροβυστία
ἀλλὰ πίστις δι' ἀγάπης ἐνεργουμένη	ἀλλὰ καινὴ κτίσις

This arrangement shows that the prior mention of πίστις δί ἀγάπης ἐνεργουμένη is parallel to καινὴ κτίσις. The clear meaning of the former should be allowed to influence the uncertain interpretation of the latter. Taking into consideration the reference in 2 Cor 5:17 also, it is reasonable to see καινὴ κτίσις as a reference to the changed life of the individual who is now led by the Spirit, not the Law (so also Witherington, 451).[29] This concept parallels the discussion of co-crucifixion that Paul mentions in 2:19–20. This new creation of the individual certainly signifies a bold movement of God to renew his creation *en toto*, but it must be construed within the framework of already/not yet: The individual in Christ is already made new, but the creation as a whole still awaits its renewal. Thus here "new creation" is an interpretation of Paul's anthropology (Betz, 319), not primarily his eschatology.

---

29. This interpretation is argued exceptionally well by M. V. Hubbard, *New Creation in Paul's Letters and Thought*, SNTSMS 119 (Cambridge: Cambridge University Press, 2002), 188–232.

6:16 *καὶ ὅσοι τῷ κανόνι τούτῳ στοιχήσουσιν*. This verse with its miniature benediction marks the end of the central argument Paul advances in this paragraph. This verse in effect ends the comparison Paul makes between himself and his opponents, and then the following verse introduces new material. As a benediction, this verse serves to pronounce a real and true blessing upon those who follow Paul's gospel, but it also serves to motivate the Galatians to make that choice, as Paul has desired all along. The clause ὅσοι τῷ κανόνι τούτῳ στοιχήσουσιν is another pendant nom., similar to the one that he used in v. 12 but referring to a different class of people. These clauses provide a fitting *inclusio* to this short paragraph: Paul begins by speaking of the opponents, "those who want to make a good show in the flesh," and closes by speaking of those who remain faithful to his gospel, "those who conform to this rule," that is, those who lay aside circumcision and uncircumcision to focus on the new creation in the individual brought about by the cross of Christ and empowered by the Spirit. The verb στοιχέω occurred previously in Gal 5:25 within the context of Paul's discussion about the Spirit. The repetition of the verb here thus alludes to the context of the Spirit's work as the referent of the rule. This main verb is fut. tense, which is somewhat unexpected in the context. This could be a simple predictive fut., but it could also be gnomic, indicating the general nature of Paul's utterance. One might expect a form of πᾶς if Paul intended a gnomic idea, but ὅσοι is general enough in this context to allow for a gnomic force. Paul thus makes a general statement, intending that his readers would see themselves as the referent. The dat. phrase τῷ κανόνι τούτῳ serves to qualify the main verb; the dat. indicates the rule or standard to which one conforms. The demonstrative pronoun points to a rule contained in prior material. Most naturally the prior verse contrasting circumcision/uncircumcision and new creation is the rule in view, but the repetition of the verb from Gal 5:25 and its allusion to the Spirit is another important conceptual connection. This oblique reference to a rule or standard refers in essence to the entirety of Paul's gospel: the new life of the individual brought about through faith in Christ, resulting in the blessing of the Spirit.

εἰρήνη ἐπ' αὐτοὺς καὶ ἔλεος καὶ ἐπὶ τόν Ἰσραὴλ τοῦ θεοῦ. The latter part of v. 16 is a benediction, bringing the paragraph that began in v. 12 to a conclusion. The nouns εἰρήνη and ἔλεος form the compound subject of the clause. The implied verb would likely be an optative, used to indicate a prayer or wish.[30] The prepositional phrase ἐπ' αὐτούς indicates the recipients of the blessing; the acc. pronoun points back to the pendant nom. clause that began the sentence. At issue in this passage is the referent of the benediction. Does Paul intend to refer to one group or two? What is the identity of the group(s)? As a *crux interpretum* this problem is discussed at length by many commentators and scholars (for especially helpful presentations see

30. See. e.g., Jude 2 where the optative is used, but contrast to 2 John 3 where the fut. indic. is used. See MHT, 3:303, who implies the optative should be implied here.

Longenecker, 297; Moo, 400–403). At stake is the relationship between Jews and Gentiles within the church and the broader relationship of Israel and the church. The grammatical issues in play, which obviously affect one another, are the force of the last *καί* in the sentence and the referent of τόν Ἰσραὴλ τοῦ θεοῦ.[31] To put it simply, if this *καί* is treated as a simple connecting conj., *αὐτούς* and *τόν* Ἰσραὴλ τοῦ θεοῦ would naturally be construed as different entities, very likely to be identified as Gentiles on the one hand and Jews on the other. If *καί* is taken adverbially, either as ascensive or adjunctive, one could construe *αὐτούς* and τόν Ἰσραὴλ τοῦ θεοῦ as the same entity, the following phrase clarifying to whom the pronoun refers.[32] Either construal is possible given the grammar of the sentence. The best interpretation sees two groups in view, one a smaller subset of the larger group. This is defended in a number of ways. The argument of the book as a whole points in this direction. Paul has maintained throughout the book that Jews and Gentiles are equally in Abraham's family—indeed, *equal* as well—but their distinctiveness as Jew and Gentile is not overridden. Put another way, Jews and Gentiles remain Jews and Gentiles even within Abraham's unified family. The blessing is that each is included without distinction. Given that broad emphasis, the passage here likely refers both to Jews and Gentiles, and any construal of the grammar should indicate that. Paul begins the verse with a clause that has a generic referent: "As many as live in conformity to this rule." This refers to any who accept Paul's gospel. There is no grammatical or contextual reason that it should be limited only to Gentiles; Paul would certainly intend it to apply to Jews who had accepted his gospel. The latter phrase, τὸν Ἰσραὴλ τοῦ θεοῦ, logically acts as a specification of a subset of this larger generic group. The *καί* would serve adverbially to focus further attention on this subgroup. A rendering that brings out this subtext could read as follows: "And those who act in accordance with this rule [whatever their ethnicity], peace and mercy upon them, [but] especially upon Jews, the Israel of God." This identification is supported by the fact that the name Israel was not used of the church until Justin Martyr in AD 160 (George, 440; Schreiner, 381). Thus the Israel of God would be Jewish Christians who faithfully follow Paul's gospel. This passage in miniature reflects his later arguments in his other epistles. In Rom 9:1–5, Paul acknowledges the important place Jews have in God's plan. In Eph 2:11–13, Paul shows the importance of Jews in salvation history by showing how Gentiles were previously excluded from them. Following this interpretation, Paul at the same time allows for full inclusion of Gentiles in Abraham's family based on faith and recognizes the important place of Jews in God's plan. He maintains complete fidelity to the scriptural witness of the

---

31. The first *καί* connects v. 16 to the prior material, and the second *καί* connects the nouns εἰρήνη and ἔλεος within the compound subject.

32. See, e.g., Zerwick, *Biblical Greek*, 154: "Gal 6:16 «peace upon them (= the new creation) *καί* (= «that is»?) upon God's Israel»."

OT regarding God's election of Israel as well as the new situation, inclusion of the Gentiles, brought about in Christ.

6:17 Τοῦ λοιποῦ κόπους μοι μηδεὶς παρεχέτω. With this sentence Paul issues a closing command to his readers and, by extension, to the opponents who would be present when the letter was read in the churches. The asyndeton at the beginning paired with the content marks this sentence as a solemn pronouncement. The phrase Τοῦ λοιποῦ is an adv. use of the adj. λοιπός. In the gen. case it means "from now on, in the future."[33] Paul's prohibition in this sentence applies from this time forward. The prohibition proper is conveyed by two elements: the pronoun μηδείς as the subject and the verb παρεχέτω as the impv. The pres. tense of the impv. coupled with the negative pronoun in tandem with the adv. use of τοῦ λοιποῦ indicates that this prohibition should be taken as cessation of action in progress.[34] The verb παρέχω in this context means "cause, make happen."[35] The noun κόπος, meaning "trouble" or "difficulty," is acc. pl. and acts as the dir. obj. of the verb. The pl. should be considered emphatic, indicating the great extent or intensity of difficulties Paul has in mind. The dat. pronoun μοι is the indir. obj., indicating the one to whom the action is directed ultimately. All of this fits the broader situation of the letter: The opponents have been creating trouble for Paul in Jerusalem and in Galatia, between him and the Jerusalem apostles on one hand and between him and the Galatians on the other. Here Paul commands that they cease this activity.[36]

ἐγὼ γὰρ τὰ στίγματα τοῦ Ἰησοῦ ἐν τῷ σώματί μου βαστάζω. Paul's command to the opponents to stop causing trouble for him is grounded in what he states here. Taken as a whole, this phrase emphasizes Paul's suffering as an apostle and, by extension, his authority in that role. He places the pronoun ἐγώ at the beginning of the sentence for emphasis. Paul emphasizes himself, specifically the condition of his body, as grounds for his command. The main verb of the sentence, βαστάζω, "I carry/bear," comes all the way at the end of the sentence. This verb occurred previously three times in the epistle (Gal 5:10; 6:2, 5). This passage bears a close affinity to the last of these references. Paul may imply that suffering in his role as an apostle is the load that he must naturally and appropriately bear. In between the subject and the verb of this sentence are two important phrases that modify the main idea. The first is the noun τὰ στίγματα modified by the gen. τοῦ Ἰησοῦ. The noun στίγμα means "mark" or "brand," and the gen. indicates possession. It is possible but not certain that Paul uses this term to allude to the common practice of marking or branding a slave. The key point is that the marks show ownership by the

33. BDAG, 602.

34. Wallace, *Greek Grammar*, 724.

35. BDAG, 776.

36. As Paul's later letters describe, he wrestled with these kind of people again in varied ways and locations. Thus his command was not heeded.

Lord; they testify without doubt that Paul belongs to him. This hearkens back to Paul's statement in the introduction to the book where he identified himself as Christ's slave, Χριστοῦ δοῦλος (1:10). The prepositional phrase *ἐν τῷ σώματί μου* is dat. indicating location. It is *in* or *on* Paul's very own body that his connection to Christ as his slave is marked. Most likely Paul refers to the wounds and scars that he received because of his apostolic ministry (so most commentators).[37] The justification for Paul's prohibition directed toward the opponents is his role as an apostle, as Christ's slave. The scars he bears in his body are the "brand" that marks him as holding that office. They are testimony to his authority as an apostle. The opponents can make no such claim. Indeed, they seek to mitigate any persecution that they might receive because of the cross (6:12). The proof of the authority for each is found in the body. The opponents can point to circumcision, which has mitigated their persecution. Paul can instead point to scars received because of preaching the gospel. They implicitly support his apostolic authority. This forms an effective coda for the book, as it mirrors the attestation of his apostolic authority in the introduction (see 1:1). That attestation was directed toward the Galatians; this is directed toward the opponents.

6:18 *Ἡ χάρις τοῦ κυρίου ἡμῶν Ἰησοῦ Χριστοῦ μετὰ τοῦ πνεύματος ὑμῶν, ἀδελφοί. ἀμήν*. In keeping with epistolary convention, Paul closes the book with a benediction. As such, it is similar to other benedictions in shape and tone (see Phil 4:23; 1 Thess 5:28; 2 Thess 3:18; Phlm 25). The noun *Ἡ χάρις* is the nom. subject of the understood verb, likely an optative form expressing a wish or prayer. The gen. *τοῦ κυρίου ἡμῶν Ἰησοῦ Χριστοῦ* indicates source, showing from whom the grace comes. The prepositional phrase *μετὰ τοῦ πνεύματος ὑμῶν* indicates the recipient of the Lord's grace, but it should be understood as a metonymy for the Galatians as a whole. Paul uses the nom. for voc. *ἀδελφοί* again to express spiritual kinship with the Galatians. It is a final appeal on the basis of their relationship (Dunn, 348). He concludes the letter with the interjection *ἀμήν* as a final expression of faith in the Lord's ability to work in the Galatians to bring them back to his gospel.

In many ways, Paul ends this letter where he began it, focusing on his apostolic authority given through the Lord Jesus Christ. At the beginning of the letter he focused on the source of that authority. Here he focuses on its proof. There is a stark contrast between himself and the opponents who seek to draw the Galatians away from his gospel. They preach their message of circumcision for their own purposes and to their own ends. They wish to

---

37. So also BDAG, 945. From the beginning of Paul's missionary activity, he experienced persecution. Acts 13:50 specifically mentions persecution and forceable removal from Pisidian Antioch. Acts 14:19 refers to Paul being stoned by Jews in Lystra. No matter how early Galatians was written, Paul's physical suffering for the gospel preceded it. See also deSilva, 514, who makes the same point in comparison with Paul's well-known catalog of difficulties in 2 Cor 11:23–25.

exalt themselves and avoid persecution. Paul has an entirely different focus. His ministry is focused not on himself but on the cross of Christ. That is the essence of his gospel. It has brought him persecution. Indeed, he can point to the scars on his body as proof that he has fulfilled his apostolic ministry. But this persecution validates his authority. He closes his letter with this focus not simply as an artistic flourish but as the final argument that he has maintained all along: His preaching of the gospel was rooted in his apostolic ministry and authority. The Galatians would do well to consider this as they decide whether to return to Paul's gospel.

Theological Comments

One of Paul's central themes in the book of Galatians is his apostolic authority. In this paragraph he returns again to that theme. It is especially important that he highlight that again in contrast to the opponents, who inherently have no authority at all. As Paul closes the letter, he uses every last argument in his arsenal to bring the Galatians back to his gospel. There are three things to deduce about Paul's authority. First, the writing of Galatians is an exercise of Paul's apostolic authority over the Church. Second, this authority is centered in his apostolic office received from Christ, not his personality as such. Paul never expects anyone to follow his gospel simply because of the power of his person. His authority is rooted in the commission he received from the Lord Jesus Christ. Third, his authority creates a definitive contrast between him and the opponents. They ultimately are self-serving. Paul is ultimately self-sacrificing. This emphasizes his role as slave to Christ: Paul willingly sacrifices himself as needed for the advancement of the gospel.

Paul addresses directly in this paragraph the difficult topic of persecution. In so doing, he sets up a powerful contrast between himself and the opponents. He has endured persecution, while they have avoided it. Persecution from those who disagree with the gospel is the expected result of Paul's apostolic proclamation. With reference to who truly speaks for the Lord, persecution serves to identify the one who is Christ's slave. Thus persecution serves an important rhetorical function by validating Paul as the right messenger of the Lord.

In this paragraph Paul speaks more vividly of the cross than he has done before. His words show that the cross is the central proclamation of his gospel. The cross is not simply a historical event that the Lord endured. For Paul it is the spiritual, existential fulcrum around which the believer's life pivots. Thus Paul's Christology would not only answer the question "What would Jesus do?" It must go forward to ask the question, "What did Jesus do at the cross? And what is the effect of that upon the believer?" In Paul's thinking the cross of Christ is the central event that demarcates the believer's existence. Negatively it severs the believer's relationship with the world. Paul was co-crucified with Christ, but he was also crucified relative to the world, ending its control over him. Positively it reorders the believer's relationship to God. The cross is the means by which God joins the believer to his new creation. The internal change as a result of believing the gospel reorients the believer to an entirely new mode of existence in which God makes all things new.

Application and Devotional Implications

Paul's focus on his apostolic authority in this paragraph leads naturally to some specific applications for believers who read this epistle. To put it in the form of a question, what is the proper response we should have as we read Paul's defense of his apostleship? The most important analogy to note is that we are not in the position of Paul but rather that of the Galatians. We are confronted with Paul's gospel and his claim to authority in the reading of the epistle just as they were, so our response should be just as theirs should have been. In response to Paul's claims, believers should recommit themselves to his authority as expressed in the biblical text. This will manifest itself in two ways based on the teaching of this paragraph. First, we should turn away from any false teachers and their message and return to Paul and his gospel. Paul presents a stark choice between himself and the opponents. The only proper response when faced with a claim counter to the gospel is to stay faithful to the gospel Paul proclaimed. Second, we should take up his focus on the cross as the central fulcrum point of the gospel, the key of its power and message. We must never forget that the Christian gospel is a gospel about Christ crucified. His earthly life led to the cross, and his resurrection life springs from the cross. The believer's attachment to the world is killed by the cross, and his new life to God begins upon the cross. The cross is central to the gospel we believe and proclaim, and we do well to remind ourselves and reaffirm our devotion to it.

By comparing himself to the opponents, Paul gives believers an important way to identify false leaders in the church: False servants of Christ are identified by their self-serving motives. Paul spends a fair number of words dissecting the intentions of the opponents. They wanted to exalt themselves, and they wanted to avoid persecution. These metrics become an important tool for evaluation of those teaching and leading in the local church. Their focus should not be on themselves, but rather upon the Lord Jesus Christ. They should not shy away from difficulties that come from the true exercise of their ministry in service of the gospel. Leaders can helpfully examine themselves in light of this mandate. As a teacher both in seminary and the local church, I must constantly ask myself where the focus of my ministry resides. If those who sit under my teaching are more enamored with me than with Christ when the lesson is over, something is amiss and needs correction. This is also important for objective, external assessment of leaders by the church body. Too often in ministry leaders are given free rein with limited oversight of their personal motives and intentions. A healthy church will have in place a way to shepherd the shepherd concerning his attitude and approach to ministry. The church I presently attend is led by an elder board, on which our pastor sits and participates regularly. The elders provide spiritual oversight over the pastor certainly with reference to his ministerial duties but also over his personal, spiritual relationship with the Lord. It is not a perfect arrangement, but it is healthy and provides a means by which our pastor is cared for and the church is protected.

Paul's mention of persecution in this paragraph is sobering because it shows a stark reality that believers must acknowledge. The gospel that saved us, that we proclaim, is contrary to this world. Our co-crucifixion with Christ separates us from its power and enables us to live out from under its domain. This results in persecution of those who live in accordance with the gospel. Believers should be willing to suffer for our proclamation of the gospel and for living it out. Paul's proclamation of the gospel led directly to suffering. This persecution came from two places: from those within the church who did not agree with the implications of his gospel, and from those outside the church who were completely opposed to his gospel. We are in the same position as we proclaim and live the gospel. We must proclaim it even if there are those inside the church who do not accept the ramifications and implications. As Paul ably demonstrates here in Galatians and elsewhere (e.g., Eph 2:11–22), a primary implication of the gospel is the removal of race-based divisions in the church. The church must live out an integrated gospel. In this world marred by racism, that message will be opposed and persecuted, often from within the church. But that persecution does not remove our responsibility to live in light of this implication. Similarly, we must proclaim and live the gospel even if it leads to persecution from those outside the church. In our contemporary society it is clear that the Christian message no longer holds any type of cultural relevance. Rather, the gospel is regarded as opposed to everything our culture now holds dear. This means those who proclaim it and live it will be persecuted, sometimes viciously, by those outside the church. This does not remove our responsibility, though, to be salt and light as the Lord gives opportunity. Instead, we should take solace with Paul, and point to our wounds as confirming signs that we are Christ's slaves, serving him in this world for which he went to the cross.

Additional Exegetical Comments

6:11 On the basis of a number of exegetical decisions, the most important of which is that *ἔγραψα* is not an epistolary aor. but rather a reference to the entire letter that Paul himself wrote, Lenski, 312, concludes that "Paul is here referring to this entire epistle and says that all of it came from his own hand, that none of it was dictated, that all of it was written in large script."

Selected Bibliography

Bahr, G. J. "Paul and Letter Writing in the First Century." *CBQ* 28 (1966): 465–77.

———. "Subscriptions in the Pauline Letters." *JBL* 87 (1968): 27–41.

Carson, D. A. *Greek Accents: A Student's Manual.* Grand Rapids: Baker, 1995.

Hengel, M. *Crucifixion in the Ancient World and the Folly of the Message of the Cross.* Trans. J. Bowden. Philadelphia: Fortress, 1977.

Hubbard, M. V. *New Creation in Paul's Letters and Thought.* SNTSMS 119. Cambridge: Cambridge University Press, 2002.

Longenecker, R. N. "Ancient Amanuenses and the Pauline Epistles." In *New Dimensions in New Testament Studies*, ed. R. N. Longenecker and M. C. Tenney, 281–97. Grand Rapids: Zondervan, 1974.

Reece, S. *Paul's Large Letters.* LNTS 561. New York: Bloomsbury T&T Clark, 2016.

Bibliography

Technical Monographs

Arichea, D. C., Jr., and E. A. Nida. *Galatians: A Translator's Handbook on Paul's Letter to the Galatians*. New York: United Bible Societies, 1976.

Barclay, J. M. G. *Obeying the Truth: A Study of Paul's Ethics in Galatians*. SNTW. Edinburg: T&T Clark, 1988.

Barrett, C. K. *Freedom and Obligation: A Study of the Epistle to the Galatians*. Philadelphia: Westminster, 1985.

Ciampa, R. E. *The Presence and Function of Scripture in Galatians 1 and 2*. WUNT 2.102. Tübingen: Mohr Siebeck, 1998.

deSilva, D. A. *Galatians: A Handbook on the Greek Text*. Baylor Handbook on the Greek New Testament. Baylor University Press, 2014.

Elliott, S. *Cutting Too Close for Comfort: Paul's Letter to the Galatians in Its Anatolian Cultic Context*. LNTS 248. London: T&T Clark, 2003.

Grainger, J. D. *The Galatians: Celtic Invaders of Greece and Asia Minor*. Yorkshire: Pen & Sword History, 2020.

McGahey, J. R. " 'No One is Justified By Works of the Law' (Galatians 2:16a): The Nature and Rationale of Paul's Polemic against 'Works of the Law' in the Epistle to the Galatians." Ph.D. dissertation, Dallas Theological Seminary, 1996.

Morland, K. A. *The Rhetoric of Curse in Galatians: Paul Confronts Another Gospel*. Emory Studies in Early Christianity Atlanta: Scholars, 1995.

Russell, W. B., III. "Paul's Use of Σάρξ and Πνεῦμα in Galatians 5–6 in Light of the Argument of Galatians." Ph.D. dissertation, Westminster Theological Seminary, 1991.

Silva, M. *Interpreting Galatians: Explorations in Exegetical Method*. 2nd ed. Grand Rapids: Baker, 2001.

Articles and Essays

Abegg, M. G. "Paul, 'Works of the Law' and MMT." *BAR* 20 (1994): 52–55.

Adams, S. E. "Paul's Letter Opening and Greek Epistolography: A Matter of Relationship." In *Paul and the Ancient Letter Form*, ed. S. E. Porter, and S. A. Adams, 33–55. Leiden: Brill, 2010.

Aletti, J. N. "L'argumentation de Ga 3,10–14, une fois encore: difficultés et propositions." *Bib* 92 (2011): 182–203.

———. "Paul's Exhortations in Gal 5,16–25: From the Apostle's Techniques to His Theology." *Bib* 94 (2013): 395–414.

Amir, Y. "The Term Ιουδαϊσμός (IOUDAISMOS), A Study in Jewish-Hellenistic Self-Identification." *Imm* 14 (1982): 34–41.

Armitage, D. "An Exploration of Conditional Clause Exegesis with Reference to Galatians 1,8-9." *Bib* 88 (2007): 365–92.

Arndt, W. F. "Galatians 3:17 Once More." *CTM* 20 (1949): 374–77.

Arnold, C. E. "Returning to the Domain of the Powers: Stoicheia as Evil Spirits in Galatians 4:3,9." *NovT* 38 (1996): 55–76.

Arzt-Grabner, P. "Paul's Letter Thansgiving." In *Paul and the Ancient Letter Form*, ed. S. E. Porter, and S. A. Adams, 129–158. Leiden: Brill, 2010.

Aus, R. D. "Three Pillars and Three Patriarchs: A Proposal Concerning Gal 2:9." *ZNW* 70 (1979): 252–61.

Baarda, T. "τί ἔτι διώκομαι in Gal 5:11: Apodosis or Parenthesis?" *NovT* 34 (1992): 250–56.

Bacon, B. W. "On Gal. iii.16." *JBL* 16 (1897): 139–42.

———. "The Reading of οἷς οὐδέ in Gal. 2:5." *JBL* 42 (1923): 69–80.

Bahr, G. J. "Paul and Letter Writing in the First Century." *CBQ* 28 (1966): 465–77.

———. "Subscriptions in the Pauline Letters." *JBL* 87 (1968): 27–41.

Baird, W. "Visions, Revelation, and Ministry: Reflections on 2 Cor 12:1–5 and Gal 1:11–17." *JBL* 104 (1985): 651–62.

———. "What is the Kerygma: A Study of 1 Corinthians 15:3–8 and Galatians 1:11–17." *JBL* 76 (1957): 181–91.

Bammel, E. "Gottes DIATHĒKĒ (Gal 3:15–17) und das jüdische Rechtsdenken." *NTS* 6 (1960): 313–19.

Barnett, P. W. "Apostle." In *Dictionary of Paul and His Letters*, ed. G. F. Hawthorne, and R. P. Martin, 45–50. Downers Grove, IL: InterVarsity, 1993.

Barrett, C. K. "Allegory of Abraham, Sarah, and Hagar in the Argument of Galatians." In *Rechtfertigung: Festschrift für Ernst Käsemann z 70 Geburtstag*, 1–16. Tübingen: Mohr Siebeck, 1976.

Barton, G. A. "The Exegesis of ἐνιαυτούς in Galatians 4:10 and its Bearing on the Date of the Epistle." *JBL* 33 (1914): 118–26.

Bauckham, R. "Barnabas in Galatians." *JSNT* 2 (1979): 61–70.

Baugh, S. M. "Galatians 3:20 and the Covenant of Redemption." *WTJ* 66 (2004): 49–70.

Beale, G. K. "Peace and Mercy Upon the Israel of God : The Old Testament Background of Galatians 6,16b." *Bib* 80 (1999): 204–23.

———. "The Old Testament Background of Paul's Reference to 'the Fruit of the Spirit' in Galatians 5:22." *BBR* 15 (2005): 1–38.

Berchman, R. M. "Galatians 1:1-5: Paul and Greco-Roman Rhetoric." In *Judaic and Christian Interpretation of Texts: Contents and Contexts*, ed. J.

Neusner, and E. S. Frerichs, 1–15. Lanham, MD: University Press of America, 1987.

Bercovitz, J. P. "Kalein ('to call') in Gal 1:15: Evidence that Paul Was Already a Believer When Christ Appeared to Him?" *Proceedings* 5 (1985): 28–38.

Best, E. "Paul's Apostolic Authority—?" *JSNT* 27 (1986): 3–25.

Bock, D. L. "Why I am a Dispensationalist with a Small 'd.'" *JETS* 41 (1998): 383–96.

Borchert, G. L. "A Key to Pauline Thinking—Galatians 3:23–29: Faith and the New Humanity." *RevExp* 91 (1994): 145–51.

Bovon, F. "Une formule prépaulinienne dans l'Épître aux Galates (Ga 1:4–5)." In *Mélanges offerts à Marcel Simon: Paganisme, Judaïsme, Christianisme: Influences et affrontements dans le monde antique*, ed. A. Benoit, M. Philonenko, and C. Vogel, 91–107. Paris: Éditions E. de Boccard, 1978.

Boyer, J. L. "The Classification of Infinitives: A Statistical Study." *GTJ* 6 (1985): 3–27.

Brehm, H. A. "Paul's Relationship with the Jerusalem Apostles in Galatians 1 and 2." *SwJT* 37 (1994): 11–16.

Bruce, F. F. " 'Called to Freedom': A Study in Galatians." In *New Testament Age: Essays in Honor of Bo Reicke*, ed. W. C. Weinrich, 61–71. Macon, GA: Mercer University, 1984.

Bundrick, D. R. "Ta stoicheia tou kosmou (Gal 4:3)." *JETS* 34 (1991): 353–64.

Burer, M. H. " 'Sons of Abraham' in Galatians 3:7 as a Spiritual, Qualitative Designation." *BSac* 173 (2016): 337–51.

Callan, T. "Pauline Midrash: The Exegetical Background of Gal 3:19b." *JBL* 99 (1980): 549–67.

Campbell, R. A. " 'Against Such Things There is No Law'? Galatians 5:23*b* Again." *ExpTim* 107 (1996): 271–72.

Carson, D. A. "Mirror-Reading with Paul and against Paul: Galatians 2:11–14 as a Test Case." In *Studies in the Pauline Epistles: Essays in Honor of Douglas J. Moo*, ed. M. S. Harmon, and J. E. Smith, 99–112. Grand Rapids: Zondervan, 2014.

Chabert, A. "βάρη et φορτίον: vocation et limite de la liberté en Christ : Une proposition de lecture de Gal 6,2 et 6,5." *RivB* 60 (2012): 357–70.

Chester, S. "When the Old Was New: Reformation Perspectives on Galatians 2:16." *ST* 119 (2005): 320–29.

Chisholm, R. B. "Evidence From Genesis." In *A Case for Premillennialism: A New Consensus*, ed. D. K. Campbell, and J. L. Townsend, 35–54. Chicago: Moody, 1992.

Choi, H.-S. "Πίστις in Galatians 5:5–6: Neglected Evidence for the Faithfulness of Christ." *JBL* 124 (2005): 467–90.

Cohn-Sherbok, D. "Some Reflections on James Dunn's: 'The Incident at Antioch (Gal 2:11–18).'" *JSNT* 18 (1983): 68–74.

Cole, H. R. "The Christian and Time-Keeping in Colossians 2:16 and Galatians 4:10." *AUSS* 39 (2001): 273–82.

Collins, C. J. "Galatians 3:16: What Kind of Exegete Was Paul." *TynBul* 54 (2003): 75–86.

Collins, J. J. "Introduction: Towards the Morphology of a Genre." In *Semeia 14: Apocalypse: The Morphology of a Genre*, 1–20. Missoula, MT: SBL, 1979.

Colwell, E. C. "A Definite Rule for the Use of the Article in the Greek New Testament." *JBL* 52 (1933): 12–21.

Cook, D. "The Prescript as Programme in Galatians." *JTS* 43 (1992): 511–19.

Cranford, M. "The Possibility of Perfect Obedience: Paul and an Implied Premise in Galatians 3:10 and 5:3." *NovT* 36 (1994): 242–58.

Das, A. A. "Another Look at ἐὰν μή in Galatians 2:16." *JBL* 119 (2000): 529–539.

Davies, J. P. "What to Expect When You're Expecting: Maternity, Salvation History, and the 'Apocalyptic Paul.'" *JSNT* 38 (2016): 301–15.

Davis, B. S. "Severianus of Gabala and Galatians 6:6–10." *CBQ* 69 (2007): 292–301.

———. "The Meaning of Προεγράφη in the Context of Galatians 3.1." *NTS* 45 (1999): 194–212.

Di Mattei, S. "Paul's Allegory of the Two Covenants (Gal 4.21–31) in Light of First-Century Hellenistic Rhetoric and Jewish Hermeneutics." *NTS* 52 (2006): 102–22.

Dodson, J. R. "The Voices of Scripture: Citations and Personifications in Paul." *BBR* 20 (2010): 419–31.

Donfried, K. P. "The Kingdom of God in Paul." In *The Kingdom of God in 20th-Century Interpretation*, ed. W. L. Willis, 175–90. Peabody: Hendrickson, 1987.

Du Toit, A. B. "Galatians 6:13: A Possible Solution to an Old Exegetical Problem." *Neot* 28 (1994): 157–61.

Dunn, J. D. G. "4QMMT and Galatians." *NTS* 43 (1997): 147–53.

———. "The Incident at Antioch (Gal 2:11–18)." *JSNT* 18 (1983): 3–57.

Dunne, J. A. "Suffering in Vain: A Study of the Interpretation of Πάσχω in Galatians 3.4." *JSNT* 36 (2013): 3–16.

Dupont, J. "Pierre et Paul à Antioche et à Jerusalem." *RSR* 45 (1957): 42–60, 225–39.

Eastman, S. G. "The Evil Eye and the Curse of the Law: Galatians 3.1 Revisited." *JSNT* 83 (2001): 69–87.

Edwards, J. R. "Galatians 5:12: Circumcision, the Mother Goddess, and the Scandal of the Cross." *NovT* 53 (2011): 319–37.

Elliott, J. H. "Social-Scientific Criticism: Perspective, Process and Payoff: Evil Eye Accusation at Galatia as Illustration of the Method." *HTS Teologiese Studies/Theological Studies* 67 (2011): 1–10.

Elliott, S. "Choose Your Mother, Choose Your Master: Galatians 4:21–5:1 in the Shadow of the Anatolian Mother of the Gods." *JBL* 118 (1999): 661–83.

Emerson, M. Y. "Arbitrary Allegory, Typical Typology, or Intertextual Interpretation? Paul's Use of the Pentateuch in Galatians 4:21–31." *BTB* 43 (2013): 14–22.

Esler, P. F. "Making and Breaking an Agreement Mediterranean Style: A New Reading of Galatians 2:1–14." *BibInt* 3 (1995): 285–314.

Fee, G. D. "Freedom and the Life of Obedience (Galatians 5:1–6:18)." *RevExp* 91 (1994): 201–17.

Feuillet, A. "Chercher à persuader Dieu (Ga 1:10a): Le début de l'Épitre aux Galates et la scène matthéenne de Césarée de Philippe." *NovT* 12 (1970): 350–60.

Filtvedt, O. J. " 'God's Israel' in Galatians 6.16: An Overview and Assessment." *CurBR* 15 (2016): 123–40.

Fitzmyer, J. A. "Crucifixion in Ancient Palestine, Qumran Literature, and the New Testament." *CBQ* 40 (1978): 493–513.

Fletcher, D. H. "Retrograde Redemptive History: The Law in Galatians 5:2–4." *RestQ* 58 (2016): 23–38.

Fuller, L. K. "The 'Genitive Absolute' in New Testament/Hellenistic Greek: A Proposal for Clearer Understanding." *JGRChJ* 3 (2006): 142–67.

Furnish, V. P. " 'He Gave Himself [Was Given] Up. . . .': Paul's Use of a Christological Assertion." In *The Future of Christology: Essays in Honor of Leander E Keck*, ed. A. J. Malherbe, and W. A. Meeks, 109–21. Minneapolis: Fortress, 1993.

Garlington, D. B. " 'Even We Have Believed': Galatians 2:15–16 Revisited." *CTR* 7 (2009): 3–28.

———. "Paul's 'Partisan ἐκ' and the Question of Justification in Galatians." *JBL* 127 (2008): 567–89.

Gaventa, B. R. "The Maternity of Paul: An Exegetical Study of Galatians 4:19." In *The Conversation Continues: Studies in Paul and John in Honor of J. Louis Martyn*, ed. R. T. Fortna, and B. Gaventa, 189–201. Nashville: Abingdon, 1990.

Gignilliat, M. "Isaiah's Offspring: Paul's Isaiah 54:1 Quotation in Galatians 4:27." *BBR* 25 (2015): 205–223.

Glodo, M. J. "Dispensationalism." In *Covenant Theology : Biblical, Theological, and Historical Perspectives*, ed. G. P. Waters, J. N. Reid, and J. R. Muether, 329–45. Wheaton: Crossway, 2020.

Goddard, A. J., and S. A. Cummins. "Ill or Ill-Treated? Conflict and Persecution as the Context of Paul's Original Ministry in Galatia (Galatians 4.12–20)." *JSNT* 16 (1993): 93–126.

Gombis, T. G. "The 'Transgressor' and the 'Curse of the Law': The Logic of Paul's Argument in Galatians 2–3." *NTS* 53 (2007): 81–93.

Goodrich, J. K. " 'As long as the heir is a child': The Rhetoric of Inheritance in Galatians 4:1–2 and P.Ryl. 2.153." *NovT* 55 (2013): 61–76.

———. "Guardians, Not Taskmasters: The Cultural Resonances of Paul's Metaphor in Galatians 4.1–2." *JSNT* 32 (2010): 251–84.

Gordon, D. T. "A note on παιδαγωγός in Galatians 3:24–25." *NTS* 35 (1989): 150–54.

Grove Eastman, S. "Israel and the Mercy of God: A Re-Reading of Galatians 6.16 and Romans 9–11." *NTS* 56 (2010): 367–95.

Gundry, R. H., and R. W. Howell. "The Sense and Syntax of John 3:14-17 with Special Reference to the Use of οὕτως...ὥστε in John 3:16." *NovT* 41 (1999): 24–39.

Habel, N. C. "Form and Significance of the Call Narratives." *ZAW* 77 (1965): 297–323.

Hahn, S. "Covenant, Oath, and the Aqedah: Διαθήκη in Galatians 3:15–18." *CBQ* 67 (2005): 79–100.

Harner, P. B. "Qualitative Anarthrous Predicate Nouns: Mark 15:39 and John 1:1." *JBL* 92 (1973): 75–87.

Harrison, R. K., and C. J. Hemer. "Antioch (Syrian)." In *New Bible Dictionary*, ed. D. R. W. Wood, 51–52. Downers Grove: InterVarsity, 1996.

Hay, D. M. "Paul's Indifference to Authority." *JBL* 88 (1969): 36–44.

Hays, R. B. "Christology and Ethics in Galatians: The Law of Christ." *CBQ* 49 (1987): 268–90.

Hedrick, C. W. "Paul's Conversion/Call: A Comparative Analysis of the Three Reports in Acts." *JBL* 100 (1981): 415–32.

Hengel, M. "Paul in Arabia." *BBR* 12 (2002): 47–66.

Hoehner, H. W. "Did Paul Write Galatians?" In *History and Exegesis: New Testament Essays in Honor of Dr. E. Earle Ellis for His 80th Birthday*, ed. S.-W. A. Son. London: T&T Clark, 2006. 150–69.

Hoerber, R. G. "Paul's Conversion/call." *Concordia Journal* 22 (1996): 186–88.

Houlden, J. L. "A Response to James D. G. Dunn." *JSNT* 18 (1983): 58–67.

Howard, G. "Was James an Apostle? A Reflection on a New Proposal for Gal. i 19." *NovT* 19 (1977): 63–64.

Hultgren, A. J. "Paul's Pre-Christian Persecutions of the Church: Their Purpose, Locale, and Nature." *JBL* 95 (1976): 97–111.

Hunn, D. "Does the Law Condemn the World? Law, Sin, and Faith in Galatians 3,22–23." *ZNW* 106 (2015): 245–61.

———. "Galatians 3:6–9: Abraham's Fatherhood and Paul's Conclusions." *CBQ* 78 (2016): 500–514.

———. "Galatians 3.10–12: Assumptions and Argumentation." *JSNT* 37 (2015): 253–66.

———. "Pistis Christou in Galatians: The Connection to Habakkuk 2:4." *TynBul* 63 (2012): 75–91.

———. "Pleasing God or Pleasing People? Defending the Gospel in Galatians 1–2." *Bib* 91 (2010): 24–49.

———. "The Baptism of Galatians 3:27: A Contextual Approach." *ExpTim* 115 (2004): 372–75.

———. "The Hagar-Sarah Allegory: Two Covenants, Two Destinies." *Bib* 100 (2019): 117–34.

———. "Why Therefore the Law?: The Role of the Law in Galatians 3:19–20." *Neot* 47 (2013): 355–72.

———. "Ἐὰν μή in Galatians 2:16: A Look at Greek Literature." *NovT* 49 (2007): 281–290.

———. "Πίστις in Galatians 5.5–6: Neglected Evidence for 'Faith in Christ.'" *NTS* 62 (2016): 477–83.

———. "Πίστις Χριστοῦ in Galatians 2:16: Clarification from 3:1–6." *TynBul* 57 (2006): 23–33.

Hurtado, L. W. "Lord." In *Dictionary of Paul and His Letters*, ed. G. F. Hawthorne, R. P. Martin, and D. G. Reid, 560–69. Downers Grove, IL: InterVarsity, 1993.

———. "The Jerusalem Collection and the Book of Galatians." *JSNT* 5 (1979): 46–62.

Hutchinson, R. F. "The Syntax of זֶרַע with Especial Reference to Its Bearing on Gal. 3:16." *JBL* 50 (1931): xxxiii–xxxiv.

Jaquette, J. L. "Paul, Epictetus, and Others on Indifference to Status." *CBQ* 56 (1994): 68–80.

Jeremias, J. "OMŌS: (1 Cor 14:7; Gal 3:15)." *ZNW* 52 (1961): 127–28.

Jewett, R. "The Agitators and the Galatian Congregation." *NTS* 17 (1971): 198–212.

Jobes, K. H. "Jerusalem, Our Mother: Metalepsis and Intertextuality in Galatians 4:21–31." *WTJ* 55 (1993): 299–320.

Johnson, H. W. "The Paradigm of Abraham in Galatians 3:6–9." *TJ* 8 (1987): 179–99.

Johnson, S. L. "Paul and 'the Israel of God' : An Exegetical and Eschatological Case-Study." *MSJ* 20 (2009): 41–55.

Just, A. A., Jr. "The Apostolic Councils of Galatians and Acts: How First-Century Christians Walked Together." *CTQ* 74 (2010): 261–88.

Keith, C. " 'In My Own Hand': Grapho-Literacy and the Apostle Paul." *Bib* 89 (2008): 39–58.

Kerry, S. "An Exegetical Analysis of Galatians 3:1-5, with Particular Reference to Pneumatological Themes That Relate to the Onset and Continuation of Christian Identity, with Respect to Law and Gospel." *Journal of Biblical and Pneumatological Research* 2 (2010): 57–86.

Kilgallen, J. J. "The Strivings of the Flesh. (Galatians 5,17)." *Bib* 80 (1999): 113–14.

Kirchschlaeger, P. G. "The Relation Between Freedom, Love, Spirit and Flesh in Galatians 5:13." *AcT* 33 (2014): 130–42.

Knox, J. "On the Meaning of Galatians 1:15." *JBL* 106 (1987): 301–304.

Köstenberger, A. J. "The Identity of the Ἰσραὴλ Τοῦ Θεοῦ (Israel of God) in Galatians 6:16." *Faith and Mission* 19 (2001): 3–24.

Kreitzer, L. J. "Eschatology." In *Dictionary of Paul and His Letters*, ed. G. F. Hawthorne, R. P. Martin, and D. G. Reid, 253–69. Downers Grove, IL: InterVarsity, 1993.

Kuck, D. W. " 'Each Will Bear His Own Burden': Paul's Creative Use of an Apocalyptic Motif." *NTS* 40 (1994): 289–97.

Lambrecht, J. "Abraham and His Offspring: A Comparison of Galatians 5,1 with 3,13." *Bib* 80 (1999): 525–36.

———. "Critical Reflections on Paul's 'Partisan ἐκ' as Recently Presented by Don Garlington." *ETL* 85 (2009): 135–41.

———. "Is Gal 5:11b a Parenthesis? A Response to T. Baarda." *NovT* 38 (1996): 237–41.

———. "Paul's Coherent Admonition in Galatians 6,1–6: Mutual Help and Individual Attentiveness." *Bib* 78 (1997): 33–56.

———. "The Right Things You Want to Do: A Note on Galatians 5,17d." *Bib* 79 (1998): 515–24.

Lappenga, B. J. "Misdirected Emulation and Paradoxical Zeal: Paul's Redefinition of 'The Good' as Object of ζῆλος in Galatians 4:12–20." *JBL* 131 (2012): 775–96.

Lategan, B. C. "Reconsidering the Origin and Function of Galatians 3:28." *Neot* 46 (2012): 274–86.

López, R. "Views on Paul's Vice Lists and Inheriting the Kingdom." *BSac* 168 (2011): 81–97.

———. "Paul's Vice List in Galatians 5:19–21." *BSac* 169 (2012): 48–67.

Lull, D. J. " 'The Law Was Our Pedagogue' : A Study in Galatians 3:19–25." *JBL* 105 (1986): 481–98.

Lyall, F. "Roman Law in the Writings of Paul: Adoption." *JBL* 88 (1969): 458–66.

Martin, N. "Returning to the *stoicheia tou kosmou*: Enslavement to the Physical Elements in Galatians 4.3 and 9?" *JSNT* 40 (2018): 434–52.

Martin, T. W. "The Brother Body: Addressing and Describing the Galatians and the Agitators as Adelphoi." *BR* 47 (2002): 5–18.

———. "The Syntax of Surprise, Irony, or Shifting of Blame in Gal 1:6–7." *BR* 54 (2009): 79–98.

———. "Whose Flesh? What Temptation? (Galatians 4.13–14)." *JSNT* 21 (1999): 65–91.

Matera, F. J. "The Culmination of Paul's Argument to the Galatians: Gal 5:1–6:17." *JSNT* 10 (1988): 79–91.

Matlock, R. B. "ΠΙΣΤΙΣ in Galatians 3.26: Neglected Evidence for 'Faith in Christ'?" *NTS* 49 (2003): 433–39.

McKnight, S. "Jesus and the Twelve." In *Key Events in the Life of the Historical Jesus*, ed. D. L. Bock, and R. L. Webb, 181–214. Tübingen: Mohr Siebeck, 2009.

Meier, J. P. "Biblical Reflection: The Conflict at Antioch (Gal 2:11–14)." *Mid-Stream* 35 (1996): 471–75.

Miller, E. L. "More Pauline References to Homosexuality?" *EvQ* 77 (2005): 129–34.

Moo, D. J. "Creation and New Creation." *BBR* 20 (2010): 39–60.

Morgado, J., Jr. "Paul in Jerusalem: A Comparison of His Visits in Acts and Galatians." *JETS* 37 (1994): 55–68.

Muir, S. "Vivid Imagery in Galatians 3:1—Roman Rhetoric, Street Announcing, Graffiti, and Crucifixions." *BTB* 44 (2014): 76–86.

Mullins, T. Y. "Formulas in New Testament Epistles." *JBL* 91 (1972): 380–90.

Murphy-O'Connor, J. "Gal 4:13–14 and the Recipients of Galatians." *RB* 105 (1998): 202–7.

———. "Paul in Arabia." *CBQ* 55 (1993): 732–37.

———. "The Unwritten Law of Christ (Gal 6:2)." *RB* 119 (2012): 213–31.

———. "ΙΕΡΟΣΟΛΥΜΑ/ΙΕΡΟΥΣΑΛΗΜ in Galatians." *ZNW* 90 (1999): 280–81.

Na, K.-Y. "The Conversion of Izates and Galatians 2:11–14: The Significance of a Jewish Dispute for the Christian Church." *HBT* 27 (2005): 56–78.

Neyrey, J. H. "Bewitched in Galatia: Paul and Cultural Anthropology." *CBQ* 50 (1988): 72–100.

Olson, S. N. "Pauline Expressions of Confidence in His Addressees." *CBQ* 47 (1985): 282–95.

Orchard, B. "Ellipsis Between Galatians 2:3 and 2:4." *Bib* 54 (1973): 469–81.

———. "Once Again the Ellipsis Between Gal 2:3 and 2:4." *Bib* 57 (1976): 254–55.

———. "The Problem of Acts and Galatians." *CBQ* 7 (1945): 377–97.

Pao, D. W. "Gospel Within the Constraints of an Epistolary Form: Pauline Introductory Thanksgivings and Paul's Theology of Thanksgiving." In *Paul and the Ancient Letter Form*, ed. S. E. Porter, and S. A. Adams, 101–27. Leiden: Brill, 2010.

Pigeon, C. "« La Loi du Christ » en Galates 6, 2." *Studies in Religion* 29 (2000): 425–38.

Popkes, W. "Two Interpretations of 'Justification' in the New Testament: Reflections on Galatians 2:15-21 and James 2:21-25." *ST* 59 (2005): 129–46.

Porter, S. L. "The Gradual Nature of Sanctification: Σάρξ as Habituated, Relational Resistance to the Spirit." *Them* 39 (2014): 470–83.

Pratt, J. R. "The 'Israel of God' in Galatians 6:16." *Detroit Baptist Seminary Journal* 23 (2018): 59–75.

Rastoin, M. "Framing Freedom: Galatians 4:1–7 and Pauline Rhetoric." *RB* 121 (2014): 252–66.

Reicke, B. I. "The Law and This World According to Paul: Some Thoughts Concerning Gal 4:1–11." *JBL* 70 (1951): 259–76.

Roberts, C. H. "A Note on Galatians II 14." *JTS* 40 (1939): 55–56.

Roberts, J. H. "Paul's Expression of Perplexity in Galatians 1:6: The Force of Emotive Argumentation." *Neot* 26 (1992): 329–38.

Roth, D. T. "What ἐν τῷ κόσμῳ are the στοιχεῖα τοῦ κόσμου?" *HTS Teologiese Studies / Theological Studies* 70 (2014): 1–8.

Russell, W. B., III. "Does the Christian Have 'Flesh' in Gal 5:13–26?" *JETS* 36 (1993): 179–87.

———. "The Apostle Paul's Redemptive-Historical Argumentation in Galatians 5:13–26." *WTJ* 57 (1995): 333–57.

Saeger, L. D. " 'Für Unsere Sünden': 1 Kor 15,3b Und Gal 1,4a Im Exegetischen Vergleich." *ETL* 77 (2001): 169–91.

Sampley, J. P. " 'Before God, I Do Not Lie' (Gal. 1:20): Paul's Self-Defence in the Light of Roman Legal Praxis." *NTS* 23 (1977): 477–82.

Sänger, D. " 'Vergeblich bemüht' (Gal 4.11)?: zur paulinischen Argumentationsstrategie im Galaterbrief." *NTS* 48 (2002): 377–99.

Scacewater, T. A. "Galatians 2:11–21 and the Interpretive Context of 'Works of the Law.'" *JETS* 56 (2013): 307–23.

Schliesser, B. " 'Christ-faith' as an Eschatological Event (Galatians 3.23–26): a 'Third View' on Πίστις Χριστοῦ." *JSNT* 38 (2016): 277–300.

Schreiner, T. R. "Is Perfect Obedience to the Law Possible: A Re-Examination of Galatians 3:10." *JETS* 27 (1984): 151–60.

———. "Paul and Perfect Obedience to the Law: An Evaluation of the View of E. P. Sanders." *WTJ* 47 (1985): 245–78.

Schweizer, E. "Slaves of the Elements and Worshipers of Angels: Gal 4:3, 9 and Col 2:8, 18, 20." *JBL* 107 (1988): 455–68.

———. "Zum religionsgeschichtlichen Hintergrund der Sendungsformel." *ZNW* 57 (1966): 199–210.

Shanks, M. A. "Galatians 5:2–4 in Light of the Doctrine of Justification." *BSac* 169 (2012): 188–202.

Silva, M. "Abraham, Faith, and Works: Paul's Use of Scripture in Galatians 3:6–14." *WTJ* 63 (2001): 251–67.

Smit, P.-B. "No Small Difference? Galatians 4.1 and the Translation of Διαφέρει." *BT* 66 (2015): 170–75.

Smith, M. J. "The Role of the Pedagogue in Galatians." *BSac* 163 (2006): 197–214.

Snyman, A. H. "Modes of Persuasion in Galatians 6:7–10." *Neot* 26 (1992): 475–84.

Sprinkle, P. M. "Πίστις Χρίστου as an Eschatological Event." In *The Faith of Jesus Christ: Exegetical, Biblical, and Theological Studies*, ed. M. F. Bird, and P. M. Sprinkle, 165–84. Peabody, MA: Hendrickson, 2009.

Stanley, C. D. " 'Neither Jew Nor Greek': Ethnic Conflict in Graeco-Roman Society." *JSNT* 19 (1997): 101–24.

Stanley, D. M. "Become Imitators of Me: The Pauline Conception of Apostolic Tradition." *Bib* 40 (1959): 859–77.

Staples, J. A. "Altered Because of Transgressions? The 'Law of Deeds' in Gal 3,19a." *ZNW* 106 (2015): 126–35.

Stein, R. H. "Relationship of Galatians 2:1–10 and Acts 15:1–35: Two Neglected Arguments." *JETS* 17 (1974): 239–42.

Stewart, E. C. "I'm Okay, You're Not Okay: Constancy of Character and Paul's Understanding of Change in his Own and Peter's Behaviour." *HvTSt* 67 (2011): 1–8.

Suggit, J. "The Fatherhood of God: Galatians 1:3." *Neot* 37 (2003): 97–103.

Taylor, J. "The Jerusalem Decrees (Acts 15.20, 29 and 21.25) and the Incident at Antioch (Gal 2.11–14)." *NTS* 47 (2001): 372–80.

Taylor, J. W. "The Eschatological Interdependence of Jews and Gentiles in Galatians." *TynBul* 63 (2012): 291–316.

Tite, P. L. "How to Begin, and Why? Diverse Functions of the Pauline Prescript with a Greco-Roman Context." In *Paul and the Ancient Letter Form*, ed. S. E. Porter, and S. A. Adams, 57–99. Leiden: Brill, 2010.

Tolmie, D. F. "Angels as Arguments? The Rhetorical Function of References to Angels in the Main Letters of Paul." *HTS Teologiese Studies/Theological Studies* 67 (2011).

———. "The Interpretation and Translation of Galatians 5:12." *AcT* 29 (2009): 86–102.

Trudinger, L. P. "ΕΤΕΡΟΝ ΔΕ ΤΩΝ ΑΠΟΣΤΟΛΩΝ ΟΥΚ ΕΙΔΟΝ, ΕΙ ΜΗ ΙΑΚΩΒΟΝ: A Note on Galatians 1:19." *NovT* 17 (1975): 200–202.

Van Voorst, R. E. "Why is There No Thanksgiving Period in Galatians? An Assessment of an Exegetical Commonplace." *JBL* 129 (2010): 153–72.

Van Wyk Cronjé, J. "The Stratagem of the Rhetorical Question in Galatians 4:9–10 as a Means towards Persuasion." *Neot* 26 (1992): 417–24.

Vanhoye, A. "Un médiateur des anges en Ga 3:19–20." *Bib* 59 (1978): 403–11.

Walker, W. O., Jr. "Galatians 2:7b-8 as a Non-Pauline Interpolation." *CBQ* 65 (2003): 568–87.

———. "Galatians 2:8 and the Question of Paul's Apostleship." *JBL* 123 (2004): 323–27.

———. "Why Paul Went to Jerusalem: The Interpretation of Galatians 2:1–5." *CBQ* 54 (1992): 503–10.

Wallace, D. B. "Galatians 3:19–20: A *Crux Interpretum* for Paul's View of the Law." *WTJ* 52 (1990): 225–45.

Weima, J. A. D. "Gal 6:11–18: A Hermeneutical Key to the Galatian Letter." *CTJ* 28 (1993): 90–107.

———. "The Pauline Letter Closings : Analysis and Hermeneutical Significance." *BBR* 5 (1995): 177–97.

Wenham, D., and A. D. A. Moses. " 'There Are Some Standing Here.' : Did They Become the 'Reputed Pillars' of the Jerusalem Church? Some Reflections on Mark 9:1, Galatians 2:9 and the Transfiguration." *NovT* 36 (1994): 146–63.

Westerholm, S. "On Fulfilling the Whole Law (Gal 5:14)." *SEÅ* 51–52 (1986): 229–37.

Williams, S. K. "Promise in Galatians: A Reading of Paul's Reading of Scripture." *JBL* 107 (1988): 709–20.

Willits, J. "Isa 54,1 in Gal 4,24b–27: Reading Genesis in Light of Isaiah." *ZNW* 96 (2005): 188–210.

Willson, M. A. "Cursed is Everyone Who is Hanged on a Tree': Paul's Citation of Deut 21:23 in Gal 3:13." *TJ* (2015): 217–40.

Wilson, T. A. " 'Under Law' in Galatians: A Pauline Theological Abbreviation." *JTS* 56 (2005): 362–92.

———. "The Law of Christ and the Law of Moses: Reflections on a Recent Trend in Interpretation." *CurBR* 5 (2006): 123–44.

———. "Wilderness Apostasy and Paul's Portrayal of the Crisis in Galatians." *NTS* 50 (2004): 550–71.

Winger, M. "The Law of Christ." *NTS* 46 (2000): 537–46.

———. "Tradition, Revelation and Gospel: A Study in Galatians." *JSNT* 53 (1994): 65–86.

———. "Unreal Conditions in the Letters of Paul." *JBL* 105 (1986): 110–12.
Winter, J. G. "Another Instance of ὀρθοποδεῖν." *HTR* 34 (1941): 161–62.
Woyke, J. "Nochmals zu den 'schwachen und unfähigen Elementen' (Gal 4.9): Paulus, Philo und die στοιχεία του κόσμου." *NTS* 54 (2008): 221–34.
Wright, N. T. "Justification: Yesterday, Today, and Forever." *JETS* 54 (2011): 49–63.
———. "Paul, Arabia, and Elijah (Galatians 1:17)." *JBL* 115 (1996): 683–92.
Young, N. H. "Paidagogos: The Social Setting of a Pauline Metaphor." *NovT* 29 (1987): 150–76.

General Books

Aland, K., and B. Aland. *The Text of the New Testament: An Introduction to the Critical Editions and to the Theory and Practice of Modern Textual Criticism*. Trans. E. F. Rhodes. 2nd ed. Grand Rapids: Eerdmans, 1989.
Baur, F. C. *Paul the Apostle of Jesus Christ, His Life and Works, His Epistles and Teachings*. A Contribution to a Critical History of Primitive Christianity. 2 vols. Trans. E. Zeller. 2nd ed. London: Williams and Norgate, 1873.
———. *Paulus, der Apostel Jesu Christi. Sein Leben und Wirken, seine Briefe und seine Lehre. Ein Beitrag zu einer kritischen Geschichte des Urchristenthums*. Stuttgart: Becher & Müller, 1845.
Bebbington, D. *Evangelicalism in Modern Britain: A History From the 1730s to the 1980s*. London: Unwin Hyman, 1989.
Bird, M. F., and P. M. Sprinkle. *The Faith of Jesus Christ: The Pistis Christou Debate: Exegetical, Biblical, and Theological Studies*. Peabody, MA: Hendrickson, 2009.
Bock, D. L. *Acts*. BECNT. Grand Rapids: Baker: 2007.
———, and Mitch Glaser, eds. *The Gospel According to Isaiah 53: Encountering the Suffering Servant in Jewish and Christian Theology*. Grand Rapids: Kregel, 2012.
Boring, M. Eugene, Klaus Berger, and Carsten Colpe, eds. *Hellenistic Commentary to the New Testament*. Nashville: Abingdon, 1995.
Brannan, R. *Historic Creeds and Confessions*. Bellingham, WA: Lexham Press, 2001.
Burer, M. H. *Divine Sabbath Work*. BBRSup 5. Winona Lake, IN: Eisenbrauns, 2012.
Burkitt, F. C. *Christian Beginnings: Three Lectures*. London: University of London Press, 1924.
Burton, E. D. W. *Syntax of the Moods and Tenses in New Testament Greek*. 1900; Reprint, Grand Rapids: Kregel, 2000.
Carson, D. A. *Greek Accents: A Student's Manual*. Grand Rapids: Baker, 1995.
———. *The Gospel According to John*. Grand Rapids: Eerdmans, 1991.
———, and D. J. Moo. *An Introduction to the New Testament*. 2nd ed. Grand Rapid: Zondervan, 2005.

Chafer, L. S. *Systematic Theology*. Abridged ed. Wheaton, IL: Victor, 1988.

Ciampa, R. E., and B. S. Rosner. *The First Letter to the Corinthians*. PNTC. Grand Rapids: Eerdmans, 2010.

Cranfield, C. E. B. *The Epistle to the Romans*. 2 vols. ICC. Edinburgh: T&T Clark, 1975–1979.

Davies, W. D. *Torah in the Messianic Age and/or the Age to Come*. JBL Monograph Series 7. Philadelphia: Society of Biblical Literature, 1952.

Deissmann, A. *Light From the Ancient East: The New Testament Illustrated By Recently Discovered Texts of the Graeco-Roman World*. Trans. L. R. M. Strachan. 4th ed. New York: George H. Doran. Reprint. Peabody, MA: Hendrickson, 1927. Reprint 1995.

Dibelius, M. *James*. Trans. M. A. Williams. Rev. by Heinrich Greeven. Hermeneia. Philadelphia: Fortress, 1975.

Dixon, P. S. "The Significance of the Anarthrous Predicate Nominative in John." Th.M. thesis, Dallas Theological Seminary, 1975.

Dunn, J. D. G. *The Theology of Paul the Apostle*. Grand Rapids: Eerdmans, 1998.

Edwards, M. J., ed. *Galatians, Ephesians, Philippians*. ACCSNT 8. Downers Grove, IL: InterVarsity, 2005.

Exler, F. X. J. *The Form of the Ancient Greek Letter of the Epistolary Papyri (3rd c. B.C. - 3rd c. A.D.): A Study in Greek Epistolography*. 1923. Reprint. Chicago: Ares, 1976.

Fanning, B. M. *Verbal Aspect in New Testament Greek*. OTM. New York: Oxford University Press, 1990.

Gaventa, B. R. *Our Mother Saint Paul*. Louisville: Westminster John Knox Press, 2007.

Gentry, P. J., and S. J. Wellum. *Kingdom Through Covenant: A Biblical-Theological Understanding of the Covenants*. Wheaton, IL: Crossway, 2012.

Guthrie, D. *New Testament Introduction*. 4th ed. Downers Grove, IL: InterVarsity, 1990.

Harris, W. H., III. *1, 2, 3 John: Comfort and Counsel for a Church in Crisis*. 2nd ed. Dallas: Biblical Studies Press, 2009.

Harrison, J. R. *Paul's Language of Grace in Its Graeco-Roman Context*. WUNT 2.172. Tübingen: Mohr Siebeck, 2003.

Hays, R. B. *The Faith of Jesus Christ: An Investigation of the Narrative Substructure of Galatians 3:1–4:11*. SBLDS 56. Chico, CA: Scholars, 1983.

Hedges, D. W. "Apollonius' Canon and Anarthrous Constructions in Pauline Literature: An Hypothesis." M.Div. Thesis, Grace Theological Seminary, 1983.

Hengel, M. *Crucifixion in the Ancient World and the Folly of the Message of the Cross*. Trans. J. Bowden. Philadelphia: Fortress, 1977.

———, and A. M. Schwemer. *Paul Between Damascus and Antioch: The Unknown Years*. London: SCM, 1997.

Hoehner, H. W. *Chronological Aspects of the Life of Christ*. Contemporary Evangelical Perspectives. Grand Rapids: Zondervan, 1977.

———. *Ephesians: An Exegetical Commentary*. Grand Rapids: Baker, 2002.

Hubbard, M. V. *New Creation in Paul's Letters and Thought*. SNTSMS 119. Cambridge: Cambridge University Press, 2002.

Johnston, J. W. *The Use of Πᾶς in the New Testament*. SBG 11. Peter Lang, 2004.

Jordan, C. *The Cotton Patch Version of Paul's Epistles*. New York: Association, 1968.

Lapide, C. A. *In Epistolas Divi Pauli*. Commentaria in Scripturam Sacram 18. Paris: L. Vivès, 1876.

Llewelyn, S. R., and R. A. Kearsley. *New Documents Illustrating Early Christianity: A Review of the Greek Inscriptions and Papyri Published in 1980–81*. Macquarie University: Ancient History Documentary Research Centre, 1992.

Marshall, I. H. *Luke: Historian & Theologian*. New Testament Profiles. Downers Grove, IL: InterVarsity, 1988.

Martyn, J. L. *History and Theology in the Fourth Gospel*. NTL. Louisville, KY: Westminster John Knox, 1968.

McCaulley, E. *Sharing in the Son's Inheritance: Davidic Messianism and Paul's Worldwide Interpretation of the Abrahamic Land Promise in Galatians*. LNTS 608. London: T&T Clark, 2019.

Metzger, B. M. *A Textual Commentary on the Greek New Testament*. 2nd ed. Deutsche Bibelgesellschaft: United Bible Societies, 1994.

———. *The Canon of the New Testament: Its Origin, Development, and Significance*. Oxford: Oxford University Press, 1987.

Mitchell, S. *Anatolia: Land, Men, and Gods in Asia Minor*. 2 vols. Trans. Oxford: Oxford University Press, 1993.

Moulton, J. H., and G. Milligan. *Vocabulary of the Greek Testament*. New ed. Peabody, MA: Hendrickson, 1997.

Neusner, J., A. J. Avery-Peck, and W. S. Green, eds. *The Encyclopaedia of Judaism*. 4 vols. Leiden: Brill, 2005.

Oxford Society of Historical Theology. *The New Testament in the Apostolic Fathers*. Oxford: Clarendon, 1905.

Pate, C. M. *The Reverse of the Curse: Paul, Wisdom, and the Law*. WUNT 114. Tübingen: Mohr Siebeck, 2000.

Porter, S. E. *Idioms of the Greek New Testament*. 2nd ed. Sheffield: Sheffield Academic Press, 1995.

Ramsay, W. M. *St. Paul the Traveller and the Roman Citizen*. New York: G. P. Putnam's Sons, 1896.

Reece, S. *Paul's Large Letters*. LNTS 561. New York: Bloomsbury T&T Clark, 2016.

Richards, E. R. *Paul and First-Century Letter Writing: Secretaries, Composition, and Collection*. Downers Grove: InterVarsity, 2004.

———. *The Secretary in the Letters of Paul*. WUNT 2.42. Tübingen: Mohr Siebeck, 1991.

Robbins, V. K. *Exploring the Texture of Texts: A Guide to Socio-Rhetorical Interpretation*. Valley Forge, PA: Trinity Press International, 1996.

———. *The Tapestry of Early Christian Discourse: Rhetoric, Society and Ideology.* New York: Routledge, 1996.

Roberts, C. H. *Manuscript, Society and Belief in Early Christian Egypt.* The Schweich Lectures of the British Academy 1977. London: Oxford University Press, 1979.

Robertson, A. T. *A Grammar of the Greek New Testament in the Light of Historical Research.* 4th ed. Nashville: Broadman, 1934.

Runge, S. E. *Discourse Grammar of the Greek New Testament: A Practical Introduction for Teaching and Exegesis.* Peabody, MA: Hendrickson, 2010.

Sanders, E. P. *Paul and Palestinian Judaism: A Comparison of Patterns of Religion.* London: SCM, 1977.

Schott, H. A. *Epistolae Pauli ad Thessalonicenses et Galatas.* Leipzig: Joannis Ambrosii Barthii, 1834.

Scott, J. M. *Adoption as Sons of God: An Exegetical Investigation into the Background of υἱοθεσία in the Pauline Corpus.* WUNT 2.48. Tübingen: Mohr Siebeck, 1992.

Smyth, H. W. *A Greek Grammar for Schools and Colleges.* rev. by Gordon M. Messing ed. Cambridge: Harvard University Press, 1956.

Son, K. *Zion Symbolism in Hebrews: Hebrews 12:18–24 as a Hermeneutical Key to the Epistle.* Paternoster Biblical Monographs. Milton Keynes: Paternoster, 2005.

Stirewalt, M. L., Jr. *Paul, the Letter Writer.* Grand Rapids: Eerdmans, 2003.

Thiselton, A. C. *The First Epistle to the Corinthians.* NIGTC. Grand Rapids: Eerdmans, 2000.

Wallace, D. B. *Granville Sharp's Canon and Its Kin.* SBG New York: Peter Lang, 2009.

———. *Greek Grammar Beyond the Basics: An Exegetical Syntax of the New Testament.* Grand Rapids: Zondervan, 1996.

Waltke, B. K., and M. O'Connor. *An Introduction to Biblical Hebrew Syntax.* Winona Lake, IN: Eisenbrauns, 1990.

Watson, F. *Paul and the Hermeneutics of Faith.* Edinburgh: T&T Clark, 2004.

Webb, W. J. *Slaves, Women & Homosexuals: Exploring the Hermeneutics of Cultural Analysis.* Downers Grove, IL: InterVarsity, 2001.

Weima, J. A. D. *Neglected Endings: The Significance of the Pauline Letter Closings.* JSNTSup 101. Sheffield: Sheffield Academic Press, 1994.

Westcott, B. F., and F. J. A. Hort. *Introduction to the New Testament in the Original Greek.* Cambridge: Macmillan, 1881.

Winer, G. B. *A Treatise on the Grammar of New Testament Greek, Regarded as a Sure Basis for New Testament Exegesis.* 3rd rev. ed. Edinburgh: Clark, 1882.

Wright, N. T. *Paul and the Faithfulness of God.* Minneapolis: Fortress, 2013.

———. *Pauline Perspectives: Essays on Paul, 1978–2013.* Minneapolis: Fortress, 2013.

———. *The Climax of the Covenant: Christ and the Law in Pauline Theology.* Minneapolis: Fortress, 1993.
Yearbook of American & Canadian Churches 2012. Nashville: Abingdon, 2012.
Zerwick, M. *Biblical Greek: Illustrated By Examples*. Trans. J. Smith. Scripta Pontificii Instituti Biblici 114. Rome: Pontifical Biblical Institute, 1963.

Ancient Sources

Aristotle. *Politics*. Trans. H. Rackham. LCL 264. Cambridge, MA: Harvard University Press, 1932.
Augustine, and Eric Antone Plumer, trans. *Augustine's Commentary on Galatians.* Oxford Early Christian Studies. Oxford: Oxford University Press, 2003.
Brannan, R., K. M. Penner, I. Loken, M. Aubrey, and I. Hoogendyk, eds. *The Lexham English Septuagint*. Bellingham: Logos Bible Software, 2012.
Braude, W. G. *Pesikta Rabbati: Discourses for Feasts, Fasts, and Special Sabbaths.* YJS 18. New Haven: Yale University Press, 1968.
Cain, Jerome and Andrew, trans. *Commentary on Galatians.* The Fathers of the Church: A New Translation 121. Washington, D.C.: Catholic University of America Press, 2010.
Danby, H. *The Mishnah*. London: Oxford University Press, 1933.
Diodorus Siculus. *Library of History, Volume V: Books 12.41–13*. Trans. C. H. Oldfather. LCL 384. Cambridge, MA: Harvard University Press, 1950.
Diogenes Laertius. *Lives of Eminent Philosophers, Volume II: Books 6–10*. Trans. R. D. Hicks. LCL 185. Cambridge, MA: Harvard University Press, 1925.
Duling, D. C. "Testament of Solomon: A New Translation and Introduction." In *The Old Testament Pseudepigrapha*, vol. 1, ed. J. H. Charlesworth, 935–987. New York: Doubleday, 1983.
Heiser, Michael S., and Ken Penner, eds. *Old Testament Greek Pseudepigrapha with Morphology*. Bellingham, WA: Lexham Press, 2008.
Herodotus. *The Persian Wars, Volume I: Books 1–2*. A. D. Godley. Vol. 117 of LCL. Cambridge, MA: Harvard University Press, 1920.
Hippocrates, Heracleitus. *Nature of Man. Regimen in Health. Humours. Aphorisms. Regimen 1-3. Dreams. Heracleitus: On the Universe.* Trans. W. H. S. Jones. LCL 150. Cambridge, MA: Harvard University Press, 1931.
Holmes, Michael W., ed. *The Apostolic Fathers: Greek Texts and English Translations*. Grand Rapids, MI: Baker, 2007.
Josephus. *Jewish Antiquities, Volume I: Books 1–3*. Trans. H. S. J. Thackeray. LCL 242. Cambridge, MA: Harvard University Press, 1930.
———. *Jewish Antiquities, Volume II: Books 4–6*. Trans. H. St. J. Thackeray, and R. Marcus. LCL 490. Cambridge, MA: Harvard University Press, 1930.
———. *Jewish Antiquities, Volume III: Books 7–8*. Trans. R. Marcus. LCL 281. Cambridge, MA: Harvard University Press, 1934.
———. *Jewish Antiquities, Volume V: Books 12–13*. Trans. R. Marcus. LCL 365. Cambridge, MA: Harvard University Press, 1943.

———. *The Life. Against Apion*. Trans. H. S. J. Thackeray. LCL 186. Cambridge, MA: Harvard University Press, 1926.

McCown, C. C. *The Testament of Solomon: Edited From Manuscripts at Mount Athos, Bologna, Holkham Hall, Jerusalem, London, Milan, Paris and Vienna*. Leipzig: J. C. Hinrichs, 1922.

Neusner, J. *The Mishnah: A New Translation*. New Haven: Yale University Press, 1988.

Pauli, C. W. H. *The Chaldee Paraphrase on the Prophet Isaiah*. London: London Society's House, 1871.

Philo. *On Flight and Finding. On the Change of Names. On Dreams*. Trans. F. H. Colson, and G. H. Whitaker. LCL 275. Cambridge, MA: Harvard University Press, 1934.

———. *On the Creation. Allegorical Interpretation of Genesis 2 and 3*. Trans. F. H. Colson, and G. H. Whitaker. LCL 226. Cambridge, MA: Harvard University Press, 1929.

———. *On the Decalogue. On the Special Laws, Books 1–3*. Trans. F. H. Colson. Loeb Classical Library 320. Cambridge, MA: Harvard University Press, 1937.

Plato. *Cratylus. Parmenides. Greater Hippias. Lesser Hippias*. Trans. H. N. Fowler. LCL 167. Cambridge, MA: Harvard University Press, 1926.

———. *Lysis, Symposium, Gorgias*. Trans. W. R. M. Lamb. LCL 166. Cambridge, MA: Harvard University Press, 1925.

Plisch, U.-K. *The Gospel of Thomas: Original Text with Commentary*. Trans. G. S. Robinson. Stuttgart: Deutsche Bibelgesellschaft, 2008.

Plutarch. *Lives, Volume I: Theseus and Romulus. Lycurgus and Numa. Solon and Publicola*. Translated by Bernadotte Perrin. Loeb Classical Library 46. Cambridge, MA: Harvard University Press, 1914.

Polybius. *The Histories, Volume V: Books 16–27*. Trans. W. R. Paton. LCL 160. Cambridge, MA: Harvard University Press, 2012.

Roberts, Alexander, and W. H. Rambaut, eds. *The Writings of Irenaeus*. Ante-Nicene Christian Library. Edinburgh: T&T Clark, 1883.

Schaff, Philip, ed. *Saint Chrysostom: Homilies on Galatians, Ephesians, Philippians, Colossians, Thessalonians, Timothy, Titus, and Philemon*. Vol. 13. A Select Library of the Nicene and Post-Nicene Fathers of the Christian Church, First Series. New York: Christian Literature Company, 1889. Logos Bible Software.

Sophocles. *Ajax. Electra. Oedipus Tyrannus*. Edited and translated by Hugh Lloyd-Jones. Loeb Classical Library 20. Cambridge, MA: Harvard University Press, 1994.

Xenophon. *Anabasis*. Trans. C. L. Brownson. Revised by John Dillery. LCL 90. Cambridge, MA: Harvard University Press, 1998.

Scripture Index

Old Testament

Deuterocanonical Books

4 Kingdoms

1 Maccabees

2 Maccabees

3 Maccabees

4 Maccabees

Sirach

Tobit

Wisdom of Solomon

New Testament

Matthew

Mark

Luke

John

Galatians

COMPREHENSIVE WITHOUT COMPROMISE

THE EVANGELICAL EXEGETICAL COMMENTARY SERIES: TRUSTED SCHOLARSHIP YOU'LL TURN TO AGAIN AND AGAIN

Learn more at lexhampress.com/EEC